ROMAN STATE &
CHRISTIAN CHURCH

ROMAN STATE
&
CHRISTIAN CHURCH

A Collection of Legal Documents
to A.D. 535

P. R. COLEMAN-NORTON

VOLUME THREE

WIPF & STOCK · Eugene, Oregon

Wipf and Stock Publishers
199 W 8th Ave, Suite 3
Eugene, OR 97401

Roman State & Christian Church Volume 3
A Collection of Legal Documents to A.D. 535
By Coleman-Norton, P. R.
Copyright©1966 SPCK
ISBN 13: 978-1-5326-6617-9
Publication date 8/23/2018
Previously published by SPCK, 1966

AD MAIOREM DEI GLORIAM

PER QVEM REGES REGNANT ET LEGVM CONDITORES

IVSTA DECERNVNT

ATQVE

IN MEMORIAM

IMPERATORVM CAESARVM

CONSTANTINI THEODOSII IVSTINIANI

AVGVSTORVM NOMINATORVM MAGNORVM

QVI PROVIDENTIA DEI FIDEI DEFENSORES

ECCLESIAM CHRISTIANAM ENIXISSIME CONFIRMAVERVNT

CONTENTS

VOLUME ONE

Preface	vii
Abbreviations	ix
Table of Documents	xi
Introduction	xxxvii
Names and Dates of Emperors	lxxiii
Documents Nos. 1–177	1

VOLUME TWO

Documents Nos. 178–486	371

VOLUME THREE

Documents Nos. 487–652	845
Appendix on Persecutions	1179
Titles of Address	1197
Glossary	1199

INDEXES

Sources	1249
Persons	1254
Places	1279
Subjects	1288
Biblical Quotations and Allusions	1344
Classical Quotations and Allusions	1348
Legal Quotations and Allusions	1350
Patristic Quotations and Allusions	1355

487. LETTER OF MARCIAN ON LAWLESSNESS OF THEODOSIUS AND ON CONDEMNATION OF HERETICS, 453

(M 7. 513-18)

This letter is apparently the last of a series of imperial epistles treating the Palestinian aftermath of the Fourth Ecumenical Council of Chalcedon in 451. It rehearses much which both Marcian and his consort Pulcheria wrote in earlier letters (nos. 483-6) on the same subject: recounting the cruel conduct of Theodosius, the monk who usurped the see of Jerusalem for twenty months in 452-3, affirming the imperial acceptance of the orthodox faith as delivered at Nicaea and at Chalcedon, anathematizing heretics, and exhorting the Palestinian clergy (to whom it is addressed) to remain loyal to the true religion.

Copy of the sacred letter of the same most pious Emperor Marcian, sent to the holy synod [1] in Palestine.

We think that our Piety's fervour about the faith and how great zeal we daily have employed about the most holy and orthodox faith escape no one's notice, but that above all persons your Devoutnesses and all who are embraced in the God-beloved catalogue of most holy priests [2] know this precisely.

But the envious Devil, warring diligently [3] upon the people of the Christians, ceases not in contriving subtle devices against the holy and orthodox faith and, having despaired of previous heresies, now has invented another by the heretical opinion of the impious Eutyches,[4] who has emulated Photinus'[5] and Apollinaris'[6] and Valentine's[7] and Nestorius'[8] opinion, which has borne for us the impious Theodosius, both the precursor of Antichrist and the imitator of Simon's[9] error. And since he has misperceived[10] the truth (for how could he have agreed to this, when he belongs to the party of Antichrist, rather when he has donned him entirely?) and since he has seen plainly that unless he fashions some things worthy of his villainy and impiety he will not have hearers, he contrives certain things and composes letters, which only the Devil could fashion, and by these he has not ceased to calumniate the holy synod in Chalcedon as having ordained that two Sons and two Christs and two person sought to be worshipped. And thus having deceived the simpler persons' souls and some other persons surrendered to the Devil, he had persons running to him; and truly having collected even monks and hermits and a crowd from these, he overturns [11] cities, accomplishes [11] murders in their midst (not of ordinary persons, but of holy and devout men), dares [11] burnings and seditions and revolutions against the State itself, by accomplishing simultaneously confusion of divine and human matters and by breaking open prisons and by loosing murderers, who have dared things near akin to him, and other persons who are kept for punishment on nefarious crimes,[12] as if giving to all persons a licence for sinning in whatever deeds they can desire. And as if the previous things are trivial, he advances [11] to things more serious than these. For having yielded to his impiety, he springs [11] upon the throne [13] of the thrice-blessed Apostle James,[14] since he thought that he would not possess it safely unless he could kill the most holy Bishop Juvenal, who long ago [15] had been set in it according to the sacred canons. Therefore he dispatches [11] men for the purpose of killing him. But when he missed the aforesaid man because of the constancy of his faith and the Holy Trinity's inclination [16] toward him, he kills [11] Severian, the most holy bishop of the Scythopolitans' city,[17] along with those with him. He becomes [11]—as indeed he thought—in possession of the throne.[13] But not content with this, he expels [11] the devout bishops from the holy churches and from the episcopate [18] in other cities and in their places appoints [11] others who share with him in impiety and in lawless actions.

Accordingly you all know accurately these things boldly done by him, since indeed he practised a great part of his deeds against your Devoutnesses. And when these things had come to our Serenity's hearing,[19] along with the hearing, by a just ordinance (not applying, indeed, a punishment worthy of his wrongs, but chastising him with humane feeling) his wrongs have been ended. When he perceived this, he runs [11] from the Jerusalemites' city and flees [11] all Palestine, which he has treated evilly, as your Holinesses have ascertained with your own eyes. And in Mount Sinai along with some who share with him in his lawless designs he hides [20] himself, at any rate lurking somewhere there against the truth and wishing to bring to completion the things long ago undertaken by him and to reduce to slavery there the simpler persons' souls by his falsehoods, in calumniating the holy synod [21] and in saying against it (rather against his own salvation) certain things which harmonize with only his impious soul and tongue.

Wherefore our Piety, watching over the zeal for the most holy and orthodox faith (for we believe that on it our Empire depends and is supported), to Macarius,[22] the most devout bishop, and the archimandrites and all the monks in the aforesaid mountain has sent a sacred letter,[23] refuting the abominable Theodosius' insanity and impiety and advising them to flee his falsehoods and to reverence the simple and blameless faith, just as we have received it from the 318 holy fathers in Nicaea,[24] and to extrude this man from the aforesaid revered places, lest even these may be polluted from Theodosius' impiety, or to deliver him with his satellites to the province's governor [25] for the purpose of transporting him to the court of the most magnificent and most distinguished master of the soldiers of the East,[26] ex-consul and patrician, since there is fear (for the Devil, whom Theodosius has donned, is of manifold evil) lest he, somehow having fled these places and again having approached the places of Palestine, may sow his impieties in these parts and may mislead simpler persons' souls.[27]

To your Devoutnesses we have sent this our sacred letter, advising your Sanctities to be on guard for the abominable man's arrival and to preoccupy the multitude's ears and minds by proclaiming the orthodox faith's truth and by teaching that we, being of our fathers' holy and orthodox faith, believe according to the 318 holy fathers'[24] creed.

Moreover we hate and detest Photinus'[5] and Apollinaris'[6] and Valentine's[7] and Nestorius'[8] impiety and besides Eutyches'[4] recent heretical opinion. And we believe that our Lord and Saviour Jesus Christ has been born from the Holy Spirit and the Virgin Mary, the Mother of God, confessing one and the same Son Jesus, perfect God and perfect man the same, truly God and truly man the same; we worship the Saviour Christ, in no way divided or separated or converted, praying to continue in this faith unshakenly and anathematizing persons saying or having said or having written or even daring to say that there are two Sons or two Christs. And the ecumenical synod lately convened at Chalcedon[21] has confirmed this holy and orthodox faith, by having made no increase or decrease in the holy creed exhibited by the 318 holy fathers[24] and by having condemned the heretical opinion of Eutyches[4] alone by a verdict agreeable to the holy fathers.[21]

For in this faith our Mightiness has relied and in this desires to continue and prays that our Empire will be guarded by it.

Therefore, by proclaiming our true and august and orthodox faith, which indeed also the holy synod in Chalcedon[21] has confirmed, to all the multitude and especially to the archimandrites, who do not follow the opinion of the abominable Theodosius, who (as far as is in him) has overturned the cities and the churches, do not shrink from rather assiduously making the accustomed prayers both for us and for the Roman State.

1. After Juvenal, patriarch of Jerusalem, had recovered his see from the intruding monk Theodosius in July 453, he summoned a synod to assist in restoring discipline in his patriarchate. While their synodal letter (M 7. 520–1) was not addressed to Marcian, the present letter may have been evoked by imperial notice of the synod's letter to the regular and secular clergy under Juvenal's jurisdiction.

2. The Latin version has "bishops", which is the better reading, if priests

were excluded from the synod, since bishops seem to have been the sole subscribers to the synod's encyclical (M 7. 521). But see no. 16, n. 4.

3. The phrase is ἐξ ἔργου, which probably is equivalent to the Latin *ex* (or *de*) *industria*. If so, it also can mean "purposely", "intentionally".

4. The Constantinopolitan heresiarch, who founded the Christological heresy named after him.

5. Bishop of Sirmium and founder of Photinianism.

6. Bishop of Laodicea in Syria and author of Apollinarianism.

7. One of the chief Gnostics (*fl.* 135–60).

8. Patriarch of Constantinople and inventor of Nestorianism.

9. The reference is to the protoheresiarch, on whom see no. 422, n. 7.

10. The participle ἀπαραισθείς appears to be a ἅπαξ λεγόμενον and is ascribed by the translator to *alpha epitatikon* + παραισθάνεσθαι.

11. The verb is historical present for vividness and lively narration, since at the time of writing Theodosius was in self-imposed hiding.

12. Literally "lawless charges", but the charges are that lawless acts have been committed.

13. The episcopal chair in a bishop's church.

14. Both the first and the second "bishop" of the Christian congregation in Jerusalem were named James: the first perhaps the oldest and the closest relative of Jesus, the second a more distant kinsman. Probably the first, who suffered martyrdom under King Herod Agrippa I in 44, is meant. The second, known as "the Lord's brother" (Gal. 1. 19), was murdered in 62.

Consult W. K. Prentice's essay "James the Brother of the Lord" in P. R. Coleman-Norton, ed., *Studies in Roman Economic and Social History in Honor of Allan Chester Johnson* (Princeton, 1951), 144–51.

15. Juvenal's episcopate began in 421—some thirty years ere the event here recorded.

16. The word (ῥοπή) is literally "turn of the scale" and metaphorically "decision", "outcome", "decisive influence".

17. St Severian (Severinus here) was murdered in 452.

18. See no. 158, n. 1.

19. Literally "ears".

20. No longer historical present tense, for Theodosius still was in hiding when the letter was written.

21. The Fourth Ecumenical Council of Chalcedon in 451.

22. Bishop of Pharan or Mount Sinai.

23. No. 483.

24. At the First General Council in 325.

25. Count Dorotheus, as is written in no. 484.

26. There is a variance in the title with that given on no. 483 at n. 22. Each is possible and which is correct is unknown. Here it is στρατηγὸς τῆς ἕω = *magister militum per Orientem*, on which see no. 106, n. 4 *ad fin*.

27. Whether Macarius expelled Theodosius from Mount Sinai is not

known. However, the monk departed from the mountain eventually and, betrayed near Sidon to the imperial constabulary, died in a monastery in Constantinople in 457.

488. LETTER OF MARCIAN ON RELIGIOUS WOMEN'S LEGACIES, 455

(*LNMarc.* 5)

The principal object of this law, which refers to earlier legislation on the disposal of property by women in the religious life (nos. 150, 225, 227), is to permit such women to bequeath whatever they have wished to the Church and to all classes of the clergy.

Part of this law is preserved by Justinian (*CI* 1. 2. 13).

Emperor Marcian Augustus to Palladius, praetorian prefect.[1]

Often unexpectedly arisen matters supply an occasion for writing and enacting laws and cause either new sanctions to be established or enacted sanctions of rather severe and rather harsh character to be abrogated. For in each category it is an equally equitable procedure either to promulgate what is just or to abolish what is grievous.

Since my Piety in the most honourable Senate's presence was discussing recently concerning the will of Hypatia,[2] a woman of most distinguished memory, who designated among others Anatolius, a religious priest, as heir in a clear share of her property, and it seemed doubtful whether the wishes of widows who by their will leave something to those clergymen, who under religion's pretext enter such women's homes, ought to be valid; since a law of Valentinian and Valens and Gratian [3]—of deified [4] memory—allows those ecclesiastics, who wish to be called by the name of Continents,[5] to acquire nothing either by any generosity whatever of widows or by their last will, but since, contrary to this, was read the constitution of Valentinian, Theodosius, and Arcadius [6]—of deified [4] memory . . .[7] it seemed to us, when investigating and considering, that the legislator's [8] intention had wished by a just and reasonable regret to abolish the force of the earlier constitutions. For since in the first law mention only of widows [3] has been made, but in the second only of deaconesses,[6] it is perceived that this constitution,[9] which bears in mind only widows and deaconesses, has spoken about each of the two laws.[10]

And since this about the legislator's [8] wish and about the law's [9] sanction seemed good to us, we have ordered the entire will to be re-read and to be unrolled;[11] and when it had been found that also other parts of the said will had been ordered so properly and prudently that she has neglected none deserving well of her, that she has given much to the sacrosanct churches, much to paupers, much to monks through respect for religion, much to redemption of captives, because she had been disquieted by their miserable lot, that she has offered much to her freedmen through regard for services given to her, we noticed also that the other part of the disposition, wherein she has left Anatolius, the priest, as her heir, had been arranged orderly. For the movables, which properly and piously she has left to very many persons, she has wished to be executed fully by this man, that he should perform the function not only of heir but also even of dispenser. And therefore by my authority I have confirmed the will of this aforesaid Hypatia, of most distinguished memory, also in that part wherein she has instituted Anatolius, the priest, as heir.

But lest for the future or from the previous constitutions,[12] of which we have made mention above and which I now command to be abrogated utterly, or from doubt of the present matter perchance some ambiguity may be left, in providing for decedents' security or assurance, we [13] ordain by this general law, which shall exist forever, that if a widow or a deaconess or a virgin consecrated to God or a nun (or if a woman is called by any other name or religious honour or dignity) by her will or codicil (which, however, has been supported in other respects by every procedure of law) shall have believed [14] that to a church or to a martyry or to a clergyman or to a monk or to paupers anything ought to be left, either in whole or in part, in any material or kind whatsoever,[15] this in every way should stand valid and firm,[16] whether this shall have been left by institution or by substitution,[17] whether by legacy or by trust, in the aggregate [18] or by particulars,[19] whether by written or by unwritten will—with all ambiguity about a matter [20] of this kind removed for the future.[21]

With equal validity I command, Palladius, dearest and fondest cousin, to be confirmed whatever shall have been bestowed on a church or a martyry or a clergyman or a monk or paupers by donations also or by any generosity whatever of widows as well as deaconesses or virgins, who have been consecrated to God, or nuns.

Therefore your illustrious and magnificent Authority should cause to come to all persons' notice by edicts, posted according to custom, these matters which by this law's general sanction I have decreed.

Given on 22 April at Constantinople, the most distinguished Anthemius being consul.

Interpretation: To nuns, widows, deaconesses, and all religious matrons it is permitted by this law that whether by will or by trust or by nomination of an heir or by codicils or by any other writings

488. RELIGIOUS WOMEN'S LEGACIES, 455

at all they should have the power of leaving what they shall have wished to the Church, bishops, priests, or deacons, and all clerics. And if they shall have wished to substitute for their own heirs any persons whatsoever after the said persons' [22] death, they should have the power.

1. Of the East.
2. Hardly the accomplished Alexandrian of that name, on whom see no. 98, n. 14, and Charles Kingsley's novel of the same name (1853), for she died about forty years before this law's date (see no. 347). While it is true that some estates require many years for settlement, it is unknown whether the historical Hypatia's was still in litigation when this letter was written. Moreover, so far as we know, the Alexandrian Hypatia never was married, although slander attributed to her intimate intercourse with at least one Egyptian magistrate.
3. No. 150.
4. See no. 127, n. 7.
5. See no. 150, n. 2.
6. No. 225.
7. Editors suppose that reference to no. 227 has fallen from the text here and so mark a lacuna.
8. Theodosius I, who in no. 227 abrogated no. 225.
9. No. 227.
10. Nos. 150 and 225.
11. An instance of hysteron proteron, unless for *unrolled* we choose "reflected upon", each of which *replicare* can mean. But a scroll or roll (*volumen*) was read as it was unrolled.
12. Nos. 150, 225, 227.
13. Here begins Justinian's excerpt, which omits among the next ten words *this, which . . . that*.
14. Justinian prefixes here "has believed or".
15. Or possibly "in any situation or pretext whatsoever", "in any shape or form whatsoever", "in any circumstance at all—real or feigned".
16. Two days later Valentinian III and Marcian issued to Palladius a mandate, which Justinian preserves (*CI* 1. 3. 24) among the laws on bishops and clergymen, though it has no direct reference to the Church. Using language taken from the present constitution, it ordains that what has been left to poor persons by will or by codicil should not lose its effect as if left to uncertain persons, but in every way should stand valid and firm.
17. *Institution* is the appointment of one heir, while *substitution* is the appointment of alternative heirs to meet the case where the first heir may be disqualified. On this see *GI* 2. 174–90 and no. 218, n. 6.
18. That is, succession to one's entire property (*per universitatem*), on which see *GI* 2. 97–190.
19. Singular number in Justinian.

20. Plural number in Justinian.
21. Here ends Justinian's excerpt.
22. The heirs.

489. LETTER OF MARCIAN ON PENALTIES FOR EUTYCHIANS AND APOLLINARIANS, 455

(PL 56. 551-4)

This constitution, while it calls for adherence to the Catholic faith (as defined at the Fourth Ecumenical Council held at Chalcedon in 451), lays its greater emphasis on punishments of various kinds for persons who persist in espousing Eutychianism and Apollinarianism as well as aid and abet the adherents of these heresies. It is directed especially against Egyptians, for they seem at that time to have been rather inclined to these innovations of doctrine.

The document, translated from the *Codex Canonum Ecclesiasticorum et Constitutorum Sanctae Sedis Apostolicae*, 28, is preserved partially in *CI* 1. 5. 8, 1. 7. 6, and wholly by St Isidore of Seville in his *Collectio Canonum* (*PL* 84. 176–8), by Isidorus Mercator in his *Collectio Decretalium* (*PL* 130. 317–20), by Mansi, 7. 517–20.

Also another constitution of the same Marcian Augustus about maintaining the Catholic faith and about Eutychians and Apollinarians and their punishments.[1]

The same Augustus to Palladius, praetorian prefect.[2]

Although already by our [3] Gentleness' most sacred constitution [4] has been cautioned and has been designated what [5] severity must be exercised against those who, having followed the heretical perversity of Eutyches [6] or of Apollinaris,[7] have deviated from the Catholic religion and faith, nevertheless the citizens and the inhabitants of the Alexandrian city have been infected by such great poisons from Apollinaris, that it shall be necessary to decree by a law, even now repeated, those things which already [8] previously we have ordained. For it is necessary that the severity of the ordinances should be manifold, when the licence of crimes is frequent. Moreover care for maintaining the orthodox faith ought to be employed by my Serenity so much the more considerably as divine matters are superior to human affairs.[9]

Therefore, whosoever [10] either in this sacred city [11] or in the Alexandrian city or in the entire Egyptian diocese [12] and in different other provinces follow Eutyches' [6] profane perversity and thus do not believe as the 318 holy fathers, establishing the [13] Catholic faith in the Nicene city,[14] propounded, also as the other 150 venerable bishops, who afterward convened in the genial Constantinopolitan city,[15] and as Athanasius and Theophilus and Cyril, holy bishops of the Alexandrian city [16] believed; whom also the Ephesian Synod [17] (over which Cyril of blessed memory presided, in which Nestorius' [18] error was ejected) followed in all points; whom also recently the venerable Chalcedonian Synod [19] followed, agreeing in absolutely every particular with the earlier councils of bishops and taking nothing from or adding nothing to the sacrosanct creed, but [20] condemning Eutyches' [6] deadly dogmas—let them know that they are Apollinarian [8] heretics. For Eutyches [6] and Dioscore [21] followed with sacrilegious mind Apollinaris' [7] most villainous sect and therefore all these who follow Apollinaris' [7] or Eutyches' [6] perversity should know that they must be smitten with those penalties which [22] have been decreed by previous deified [23] emperors' constitutions against Apollinarians [24] or by our Serenity's later ordinance against Eutychians [25] or by this most august law itself against the said persons.

Because the Apollinarians, that is, the Eutychians (to whom, although there is a difference in appellation, yet there is affinity in the depravity of heresy; and indeed the name is different but the sacrilege is the same), whether they are in this genial city [11] and in different provinces or in the Alexandrian city or in [26] the Egyptian diocese, neither so believe, as [27] the aforesaid venerable fathers [8] believed, nor communicate with the most reverend bishop of the Alexandrian city, Proterius, who holds the orthodox faith,[28] pursuant to the previous deified[11] emperors' most sacred[8] constitutions, which have been promulgated concerning Apollinarians, they may not have the power of making a testament and of establishing a last will[29] and may not take that which shall have been left to them from anyone's testament; also they may not acquire anything from any donation; but if anything shall have been conferred on them either by the generosity of a living person or by the wish of a dying person,[30] this should be adjudged forthwith to our fisc. They themselves moreover may not transfer anything from their own property to any persons by the legal title[31] of donation.[32]

Also it may not be lawful for them to create and to have bishops or priests and other clergymen, since they know that these [8] Eutychians or Apollinarians who shall have dared to impose on anyone the name of bishop or of priest or of clergymen as well as those who shall have attempted [33] to retain the sacerdotal name imposed on themselves [8] shall undergo the penalty of exile with [34] the loss of their own property.[35]

Moreover [36] those who hitherto [37] have been [38] clergymen of Catholic churches [39] or monks of the orthodox faith and,[37] after having abandoned Almighty God's true and orthodox cult,[40] have followed or hereafter shall follow [41] Apollinaris'[7] or Eutyches'[6] heresy and abominable dogmas,[42] we order to be repressed by all the penalties which have been established against heretics either by this or [43] by former laws and also to be driven outside the very soil of the Roman Empire,[44] just as statutes of preceding laws have ordained about Manichaeans.[45]

Moreover all Apollinarians or Eutychians should not establish [46] for themselves either churches or monasteries; they should not arrange assemblies and meetings [47] by day nor by night; they should not congregate either at anyone's house or at an estate or at a monastery or at any other [48] place whatsoever for the purpose of celebrating [49] the rites of their most deadly sect. And if they shall have done this and if it shall have been established that this has been done with the owner's willingness, after the fact has been proved in a judge's investigation [50] the house or the estate wherein they shall have met should be joined to the fisc without delay; but we order the monastery to be adjudged to the orthodox church of that city in whose territory it is. But if they shall have convened interdicted assemblies [51] and meetings without the owner's knowledge, but with the knowledge of him who exacts the rents of the house or of the leaseholder or of the manager or of the overseer of the manor, the leaseholder or the manager or the overseer or whosoever he is who [52] shall have received them in the house or the estate or the monastery and shall have allowed illicit assemblies and meetings to be held, if he is of low and abject rank, he should be corrected publicly by cudgels both for his own punishment and for an example to others; but if they are honourable persons, they should be compelled to pay into our fisc ten pounds of gold in the category of a fine.[53]

Moreover we order no Apollinarian or Eutychian to aspire to any governmental service,[54] except cohortaline or on a frontier.[55] But if any shall have been found to perform governmental service [54] outside cohortaline or on a frontier,[56] they, after their belt [57] has been removed, should be deprived of association with honourable persons and with the palace and they should not dwell in any city or village or district other than in that wherein they have been born. But if any have been born in this genial city,[11] they should be expelled both from the most sacred court and from every metropolitan city throughout the provinces.[3]

Moreover on no Eutychian or Apollinarian should be bestowed the ability of publicly or privately summoning gatherings [58] and of assembling meetings and of arguing about heretical error and of asserting a villainous dogma's perversity.

Also to none it should be permitted either to declare or to write or to proclaim [59] or to emit anything contrary to the venerable Chalcedonian Synod [60] or to publish others' writings [61] on the said subject; none should dare to have books of this character [62] and to keep writers' sacrilegious documents. But if any persons shall have been caught in these crimes, they should be condemned by perpetual deportation.

Moreover we order those persons who through zeal of learning shall have heard disputes about unpropitious heresy to undergo the loss of ten pounds of gold, which must be paid into our fisc.[63]

Moreover all papers and books of this kind, which shall have contained the deadly dogma of Eutyches,[6] that is, of Apollinaris,[7] should be burned by fire, that the villainous perversity's very traces, when burned by flames, may perish.[64]

And indeed it is just, Palladius, dearest and fondest cousin, that an equal magnitude of penalty should overthrow most monstrous sacrileges.[65] Therefore your illustrious and magnificent [66] Authority by edicts posted according to custom should cause to bring what we have decreed by this most sacred constitution to the notice of all persons in this genial city [11] and the different provinces and especially in the Alexandrian city and throughout the entire Egyptian diocese, that all the severity, which we ordain,[67] straightway should be exercised on those who shall have been arrested as criminals—the governors of provinces and their apparitors [68] and also the defenders of cities [69] knowing that if they either shall have neglected those matters which we have decreed by this law's most religious sanction must be maintained or shall have permitted these to be violated with any temerity, they should be compelled to pay into our [70] fisc a fine of [71] ten pounds of gold; and besides they shall sustain peril to their own reputation.

Also the matters which by our Perpetuity's law we have decreed as equally valid concerning pagans throughout the entire Roman Empire should be employed most urgently against those persons who, it shall have been known, celebrate profane rites and impious worship of images and forbidden sacrileges.[72]

Given on 1 August at Constantinople, the deified[23] Valentinian Augustus and the most distinguished Anthemius being consuls.[73]

1. St Isidore reads "Another of Marcian Augustus against the above-named heretics" and the other Isidore has "Also another of Emperor Marcian against the said heretics". *CI* has no caption.

2. *CI* reads each time "Emperor Valentinian and Marcian Augusti to Palladius, praetorian prefect"; St Isidore has "Emperor Marcian Augustus to Palladius, praetorian prefect"; the other Isidore gives "Emperor Marcian Augustus to Palladius, praetor". Palladius' office was in the Orient.

3. Singular in the Isidores.

4. Probably the allusion is to no. 476.
5. Isidorus Mercator reads "because" (*quia* for *quae*) erroneously.
6. The Constantinopolitan archimandrite, who founded the heresy named after him.
7. Bishop of Laodicea in Syria and author of the heresy named for him.
8. Isidorus Mercator omits this word.
9. St Isidore unites this sentence with the preceding sentence, each of which the other Isidore omits, by reading ". . . the manifold severity . . . should be maintained . . .; moreover, care for the orthodox faith . . ."
10. Here begins *CI* 1. 5. 8.
11. Constantinople.
12. The civil diocese of Egypt was created as an entity distinct from the diocese of the East in the prefecture of the East *c*. 381. Its governor, who had been known as *praefectus Aegypti*, then, instead of being called *vicarius* (as other diocesan administrators ordinarily were named), received the title of *praefectus Augustalis*.
13. Isidorus Mercator inserts "holy".
14. In 325 at the First General Council.
15. In 381 at the Second General Council.
16. *CI* and the Isidores read ". . . Cyril of holy remembrance, bishops of the Alexandrian city".
17. In 431 at the Third General Council.
18. Patriarch of Constantinople and founder of Nestorianism.
19. In 451 at the Fourth General Council. The Isidores convert the proper adjective into a proper noun in the locative case.
20. Isidorus Mercator reads "whether" (*seu* for *sed*) erroneously.
21. This patriarch of Alexandria presided at the Robber Council of Ephesus (*Latrocinium*) in 449 and secured there the rehabilitation of Eutyches, but was deposed by the Council of Chalcedon in 451 and died in Asia Minor as an exile in 454.
22. Isidorus Mercator ends the sentence thus: "previous deified emperors against Apollinarians or our Serenity later against Eutychians has ordained".
23. See no. 127, n. 7.
24. Such as nos. 194, 196, 213, 264, 395.
25. Of nos. 477, 480-4, 487 emitted by Marcian and mentioning Eutychians probably no. 487 is the law meant.
26. All the other versions have "within" and Isidorus Mercator reads "within Egypt".
27. St Isidore substitutes "what" and the other Isidore prefixes "just".
28. *CI* omits the rest of the paragraph.
29. Isidorus Mercator omits *and . . . will*.
30. For the conditional clause Isidorus Mercator reads "but if anything shall have befallen them either by generosity or shall have been conferred by the wish of a living person or of a dying person".

31. Literally "by title and by legal right"; a hendiadys.
32. For the sentence Isidorus Mercator gives "They themselves moreover may not be able to give anything from their own property to any persons".
33. *CI* has "been allowed".
34. Isidorus Mercator for *shall undergo . . . with* reads "must be smitten by exile and by".
35. *CI*, which resumes with this paragraph, reads "We forbid them to create . . . clergymen, since these Eutychians or Apollinarians who . . . themselves know that they shall undergo . . .". Both Isidores follow Justinian's interpretation.
36. This paragraph is not in *CI* 1. 5. 8, but appears as *CI* 1. 7. 6.
37. *CI* and Isidorus Mercator omit the word.
38. *CI* omits the verb, which St Isidore has in the future perfect and the other Isidore puts in the pluperfect.
39. St Isidore reads "of Catholic Rome's churches" and the other Isidore gives "of churches from this Catholic Rome"—thus testifying to textual tampering in Roman interests.
40. *CI* reads "the orthodox religion's true cult" and Isidore Mercator has "God's true cult".
41. *CI* omits *or . . . follow*.
42. Isidore Mercator omits *and . . . dogmas*.
43. All the other versions omit *either . . or*, the Isidores reading "even".
44. Isidorus Mercator omits the rest of the sentence, at the end of which *CI* 1. 5. 8 resumes.
45. Such as nos. 219, 382, 387, 395, 440, 480.
46. *CI* and Isidorus Mercator read "build".
47. The words are *parasynaxes* and *conventicula*, both denoting illicit secrecy. The first is transliterated from Greek and for it Isidorus Mercator has the simple Greek-transliterated form *synaxes*.
48. St Isidore omits the word.
49. The Isidores for *for . . . celebrating* read "as celebrators of".
50. Isidorus Mercator for the clause has "finally noted judicially", where he takes *after the fact* (*post rem*) as "finally" (*postremo*). Previously his editor capitalizes *domino* to signify "the Lord's" (i.e. "God's"), which, of course, is senseless. Later he omits the phrase "without delay".
51. Here Isidorus Mercator has the compounded form, however, in the wrong case, for he omits the connective and makes this noun depend upon the next. Later his editor lower-cases *domino* correctly, but omits *or of the overseer*.
52. The other versions omit *he is who* and pluralize the pronouns.
53. For *in . . . fine*, which Isidorus Mercator omits, St Isidore reads "of fined category".
54. See no. 186, n. 4.
55. *CI* omits *except . . . frontier*. On *cohortaline* see no. 320, n. 5.
56. For *outside . . . frontier CI* reads "in any governmental service whatever"

and Isidorus Mercator reduces the clause to "But if any shall have done otherwise". On *cohortaline* see no. 320, n. 5.

57. On this thought see no. 476, n. 39.

58. Isidorus Mercator omits *and . . . error* and St Isidore omits *of assembling.*

59. The Isidores substitute "read".

60. Isidorus Mercator omits *or . . . subject.* Cf. *supra* n. 19.

61. That this is the true reading both Justinian and St Isidore show, for they read *super eadem re scripta*, whereas the *Codex* joins the last two words to produce "rescripts", which here is meaningless.

62. Isidorus Mercator omits the rest of the sentence.

63. Isidorus Mercator reads for this sentence "Moreover these persons . . . heresy should undergo . . . which shall be applied . . ."

CI adds "Also they who shall have attempted to teach illicit things should be restrained by the last punishment". The "last punishment", of course, is death.

64. Isidorus Mercator omits *of . . . kind* and then *that . . . Apollinaris'* and finally *by fire . . . perish.*

65. *CI* omits *Palladius . . . cousin* and all of the following sentence to *criminals.* Isidorus Mercator from the sentence saves only *dearest cousin*, with which he starts the next sentence.

66. Isidorus Mercator omits *and magnificent.*

67. St Isidore reads "which is ordained".

68. *CI* has the abstract word.

69. Isidorus Mercator omits *and . . . cities.*

70. *CI* and St Isidore omit the word.

71. St Isidore for *a fine of* reads "when fined".

72. Isidorus Mercator for *by . . . decreed* reads "we have chosen" and then omits after *rites* the rest of the sentence. *CI* omits the entire sentence.

73. *CI* omits *deified* and *most distinguished*; St Isidore omits *Augustus* and takes *most distinguished* with both men; each adds "for the eighth time" to Valentinian; both read correctly "Anthemius". The other Isidore after *Constantinople* reads incorrectly "Divus for the eighth time and Antemius for the fourth time being consuls. Granted."

490. MANDATE OF MARCIAN ON PATRIARCHAL JURISDICTION IN ECCLESIASTICAL INTERESTS, 456

(*CI* 1. 4. 13)

The emperor orders that anyone instituting a lawsuit against a steward or a cleric of any of the churches under the jurisdiction of the Constantinopolitan patriarch must plead his case in the patriarchal court.

Pitra prints (2. 537) a late Greek paraphrase of this law.

Emperor Marcian Augustus to Constantine, praetorian prefect.[1]

We decree that whoever shall have wished to arraign by some lawsuit a most reverend steward of the Catholic churches, which are under the most religious archbishop of this genial city,[2] or any other clergyman of the said churches (whether on ecclesiastical cases or on cases of his own interests and pertaining to himself alone) should state his case before the said most blessed archbishop, who in hearing the matters will exhibit the twin trustworthiness and sincerity of both a priest[3] and a judge.

However, an episcopal trial should be open to plaintiffs wishing it; and none who aims an action of this sort against the sacrosanct churches or the aforesaid clergymen should be brought unwillingly before the most religious archbishop as his judge.[4]

Given . . .[5] Varanes and John being consuls.

1. Of the East.
2. Constantinople.
3. See no. 16, n. 4.
4. An *episcopal trial* could be before a bishop or an archbishop—in this case before the Constantinopolitan patriarch, who sometimes was called an archbishop or a bishop and who was in holy orders a bishop.
5. On the date see no. 491, n. 10.

491. MANDATE OF MARCIAN ON CLERICAL DEFENDANTS IN LAWSUITS, (?)456

(*CI* 1. 3. 25)

This statute directs plaintiffs refusing to prosecute clergymen in episcopal courts to plead before the praetorian prefect only, sets sureties for convicted clergymen to guarantee compliance with verdicts, and lowers for clergymen the costs of litigation owed for services by judicial apparitors.

Emperor Marcian Augustus to Constantine, praetorian prefect.[1]

Since an episcopal hearing—when the plaintiffs, however, are willing—is allowed to clergymen called into court, if a plaintiff shall not have wished to experience a most holy archbishop's judgement, he should know that your most eminent office's[2] examination must be sought against the Catholic clergymen stationed under this city's[3] most reverend archbishop or against the most reverend steward concerning his own as well as ecclesiastical affairs and in any other forum [4] or before any other judge he should not attempt to ensnare the said clergymen in lawsuits and to implicate them in civil or criminal cases.[5]

Moreover the said most reverend clergymen of the orthodox churches, which are under this renowned city's [3] religious bishop, in a case wherein either they themselves or the attorneys (whom they shall have provided for themselves) are defeated by the authority of the verdicts should furnish to the plaintiffs (by whom they shall have been summoned) as a surety [6] the steward or the defender of this city's [3] most sacred Church, who appears as surety up to fifty pounds of gold. Moreover the most reverend steward himself of this genial city's [3] Church, when defeated in a lawsuit, should not furnish a surety for himself, inasmuch as he himself also will be a surety of other clergymen, but should be liable to his own good faith. But if a lawsuit of different clergymen (the most reverend steward excepted), which must be prosecuted, seems to exceed the said sum, a clergyman defeated in the lawsuit should give to the plaintiff for the residual amount his own bond, in which, however, no oath is inserted because by ecclesiastical rules and by the canon instituted by most blessed bishops in ancient times clergymen are forbidden to take an oath.[7]

Moreover we have decided that to the plaintiffs the said most reverend steward or the other different clergymen under this most splendid city's [3] most blessed archbishop, when admonished by the authority of your verdicts, should pay only two solidi [8] for their compulsory fee [9] and for the appointment of an attorney, if they shall have wished to litigate through him. And this concerning also your Eminence's other different apparitors in the services, which according to custom are offered by the office staff, we order to be observed in the aforesaid clergymen's cases, that the costs or the expenses of the lawsuit by clergymen may be shown to be fewer and more humane.[10]

1. Of the East.
2. See no. 311, n. 5.
3. Constantinople.
4. On the use of this word as a synonym for court see no. 334, n. 5.
5. Pitra prints (2. 533) a late Greek paraphrase for this paragraph: "For clergymen of Constantinople called into court the competent judge should be the archbishop, if the plaintiff is satisfied with this. But if the plaintiff declines his judgement for clergymen, only before the praetorian prefects should be prosecuted both the clergymen of the royal city and the steward, whether the case is ecclesiastical or private to them, and in no other forum before any other judge they should be prosecuted in either civil or criminal cases."
6. This type of surety (*fideiussor*) seems to have been the most binding as

well as the most inclusive known to Roman law and to have been the latest form developed.

7. Probably based on *CA* 5. 12, 8. 47. 20. Justinian cancelled this concession for the clergy, when in 531 he required all defendants and their advocates to take an oath on the Gospels (no. 619; cf. *II* 4. 16. 1).

Pitra prints (2. 560) a late Greek paraphrase for this paragraph: "Clergymen of Constantinople, when plaintiffs are unwilling to prosecute them before the patriarch, are judged, when plaintiffs and defendants, only before the prefects on private and ecclesiastical and criminal matters. And the clergymen furnish the steward or the defender of the church as surety and not another up to fifty pounds and if the matter should be in excess they should make an unsworn acknowledgement for the amount in excess; for the laws and the canons forbid a clergyman to take an oath. But the steward, when defendant, does not give surety."

8. On the solidus see no. 434, n. 7.

9. *Commonitio* (ordinarily "admonition") is supposed to be equivalent here to *exactio* (impost).

10. From no. 490 editors suggest the subscription "Given . . . Varanes and John being consuls". For the date we have there only *VIII . . . April*, which, since either *Kal.* or *Id.* is missing, may represent either 25 March or 6 April.

492. EDICT OF LEO I ON BURIAL OF HERETICS, 457

(*CI* 1. 5. 9)

The emperor[1] permits heretics to be buried according to orthodox and ordinary practice.

Emperor Leo Augustus.
Since we have considered it to be humane and holy, we order heretics to be buried with the customary burial rites.

Given at Constantinople on 13 August, Constantine and Rufus being consuls.

1. When Emperor Marcian died, Leo the Thracian was an obscure military officer (*tribunus militum*) and a steward of the patrician Aspar, who, as an Arian and an Alan, could not acquire the sovereignty, but whose authority in the army was such that he could sway the Senate to accept Leo, on whose devotion Aspar had decided that he could count, as the new sovereign. To compensate for Leo's subordinate station the Senate arranged for Anatolius, patriarch of

Constantinople, to perform the ceremony of coronation. Thus on 7 February 457 a Christian sovereign first was crowned by a Christian prelate. Later Christian princes copied this precedent, whereof the future would find formidable consequences fashioned by the clergy—notably in Pope St Leo III's cunning coronation of Charlemagne on 25 December 800 in Rome as the Augustan emperor of the revived Roman Empire in the West.

Such is the tradition, though Anatolius may have acted similarly at Marcian's accession (see Bury, 1. 236, n. 4).

493. EDICT OF LEO I ON EPISCOPAL INTEREST IN MANUMISSION AND IN RESTRAINT OF ACTRESSES, 457–67
(*CI* 1. 4. 14)

By this law bishops are authorized to grant freedom to slaves rescued from prostitution and to prevent unwilling women from becoming actresses.

Emperor Leo Augustus to the people.
None shall dare to lead into unchastity or to prostitute either a slave or a free person, not even if he should be a musician or at other times an actor.

If a slave should have been prostituted, he shall be claimed for freedom by anyone going without any expense to the magistrates in the several places or to the most God-beloved bishops.

And it shall be their concern not to permit an unwilling woman— slave or free—to participate in mimes or dances or to be compelled to perform another spectacle in the theatres.

494. EDICT OF LEO I ON CLERICAL MANUMISSION OF PROSTITUTES, 457–67
(*CI* 11. 41. 7)

The only part of this defective statute [1] affecting the Church [2] provides that a cleric or a monk should save a slave from prostitution by claiming such a person for manumission.

Emperor Leo Augustus to the people.
. . . But if a slave should be prostituted, he [3] shall be claimed [4]

freely [5] by anyone—whether a man or a woman or a clergyman or a monk claims him . . .

1. The initial section and the subscription are lost.
2. The edict's other paragraphs, containing prohibitions against prostitution and penalties for disobedience, are not translated, though they are not without interest.
3. Since the construction is neuter, either a male or a female may be meant.
4. For the purpose, that is, of setting the slave free.
5. At no judicial expense to his rescuer.

495. LETTER OF LEO I ON AN ALEXANDRIAN DISPUTE, 458
(Evagrius, *HE* 2. 9)

This constitution in epistolary form orders Anatolius, patriarch of Constantinople, to convene bishops and clerics [1] for an investigation of and a report on the appended petitions *pro* and *con* [2] the affair of Timothy II,[3] the Monophysite patriarch of Alexandria, who refused to respect the canons of the Council of Chalcedon (451) and who was creating disturbances in Alexandria.[4]

While the emperor was quite exculpable in referring the ecclesiastical aspects of the controversy to the Constantinopolitan patriarch's and the latter's domestic synod's [1] decision, because they could be considered experts, whereas he was not, yet such a reference was resented by Timothy's Alexandrian adherents, who naturally regarded it as another evidence of the encroaching power of a rival patriarchate.[5] Not only the Constantinopolitan Synod declared against Timothy, but also 61 bishops and three monks, consulted by letter, from other Christian centres decided against the Alexandrian.[6] So Leo banished Timothy in 458 to Gangra in Paphlagonia and then in 460, since he continued his agitation, to the Tauric Chersonese (Crimea), where he dwelt until the emperor's death in 475.

Nicephorus quotes the entire document (*HE* 15. 18), while Zacharias Rhetor *sive* Mytilenaeus in Syriac (*Chron.* 4. 5) preserves its conclusion.

Copy of the sacred epistle of the most pious Emperor Leo, sent to Anatolius, bishop of Constantinople, and to all the metropolitans throughout the world and to the other bishops.[7]

Emperor Caesar Leo, Pious, Victor, Triumpher, Greatest, Ever-August, Augustus to Bishop Anatolius.

Through prayer it repeatedly pertained to my Piety that all the orthodox and most holy churches—and still more also the cities under the Romans' government—should enjoy the greatest tranquillity and that nothing should befall to throw into confusion their serene state.[8] But what sort of things lately have happened in the Alexandrians' city we believe that your Sanctity already knows. But that you may be instructed more completely about all the events as to what has been the cause of so much tumult and confusion, we have sent to your Godliness copies of the petitions which the most reverend bishops and clergymen, who have come from the aforesaid city and the Egyptian diocese to the royal city of Constantine, have brought to my Piety against Timothy, and—what is more—copies of the petitions which persons, who have come to our sacred court from the Alexandrians' city in behalf of Timothy, have delivered to our Serenity, so that your Sanctity can learn clearly what has been done by the aforesaid Timothy, whom the people of the Alexandrians' city and the dignitaries [9] and the officials [10] and the shipowners [11] request as a bishop for themselves, and concerning the other matters which are embraced by the text of the petitions, and, besides these, concerning the synod in Chalcedon,[12] with which they not at all agree, according as their subjoined petitions signify.

Therefore your Devoutness should cause immediately to assemble before your own presence all the orthodox holy bishops residing at present in this royal city and in addition also the most devout clergymen. And after all matters carefully have been investigated and have been examined, since now is in confusion Alexander's city, for whose quiet state [13] we have the greatest anxiety, declare your opinion concerning the aforesaid Timothy and the synod in Chalcedon,[12] without any fear of man and apart from favour and enmity, placing before your eyes only the fear of the Almighty God, since you know that concerning this matter you will give an account to his pure Godhead, in order that we, having been instructed perfectly by your letters, may be able to give the proper formulary on all points.[14]

1. These would include not only those normally resident in Constantinople, as the text testifies, but also visiting clergy, for at all times the eastern capital entertained on ecclesiastical business numerous clerics of various grades. These constituted the so-called domestic synod, which met on the patriarch's call. The authority of such a synod was recognized by the Fourth General Council at Chalcedon in 451 (canon 9). Similar synods existed in the western capitals of Rome, Milan, Ravenna during the western emperors' residence there.

2. Evagrius gives only parts of the petition against Timothy (op. cit., 2. 8), but Mansi has both petitions (7. 523–30, 536–7).

3. Nicknamed "the Cat" (Αἴλουρος; *Aelurus*), he was consecrated by only two consecrators, who had been deposed from the episcopate, and by his enemies was called a bloody bandit, a gladiator, a heretic, a parricide, a usurper —not to extend the list.

495. AN ALEXANDRIAN DISPUTE, 458

4. It was charged *inter alia* that his partisans had murdered Proterius, the orthodox patriarch of Alexandria, and, after having dragged his corpse around the city and having feasted on it like cannibals, burnt it and scattered its ashes to the winds.

5. Perhaps Anatolius also was not averse from asserting his patriarchal prerogatives by forging another link in the chain of his patriarchate's eastern primacy, which had been constructed by canon 3 of the Second General Council at Constantinople in 381 and had been rewelded by canon 28 of the Fourth General Council at Chalcedon in 451. But from the Alexandrian view a Constantinopolitan domestic synod (cf. *supra* n. 1) could have had only an advisory action in Alexandrian affairs. See also nos. 284, n. 4, and 527, n. 76, for Alexandrian interference in Constantinople.

6. Mansi gives their names and sees (7. 523-4) and many of their answers sent to the sovereign (7. 537-627). Leo's letters to them have not survived, but they doubtless paralleled the present document, as the caption suggests.

7. The caption in Nicephorus is "Leo's encyclical epistle, sent to Bishop Anatolius and to the rest, about the synod in Chalcedon and against Timothy Aelurus".

8. Or "settled serenity", taking the literal "both settled condition and serenity" as a hendiadys.

9. These are the ἀξιωματικοί (*honorati*), who hold or have held high office in civil, court, military, municipal, or provincial service. Sometimes the title without the post was bestowed on a favoured person.

10. Probably decurions; in Greek οἱ πολιτευόμενοι.

11. The ναύκληροι (*naucleri* or *navicularii*), who were members of a corporation charged with shipment of public provisions by sea. They seem to have transported these provisions at their own expense in ships constructed at their own cost for the labour (though the materials were supplied to them) and to have discharged this duty of shipment in rotation. As their responsibilities were great, so were their privileges. At their death their sons and/or heirs were liable for recruitment into the vacancies.

12. This is the Fourth Ecumenical Council of the Church, convened in 451 principally to combat the Monophysite heresy by redefinition of the orthodox position.

13. Or "settled quietude". Cf. *supra* n. 8 for a similar hendiadys.

14. For the last sentence Zacharias has "Do ye, without fear of man or partiality, and unbiased by influence or by favour, setting the fear of God alone before your eyes, and considering that to Him alone ye must make your defence and give your account, tell me briefly the common opinion held by you the priests of our dominion, what ye think right, after having carefully investigated the transactions of Chalcedon and concerning the consecration of Timothy of Alexandria" (F. T. Hamilton and E. W. Brooks, *The Syriac Chronicle Known as that of Zachariah of Mitylene* [London, 1899], 69).

496. LETTER OF LEO I AND MAJORIAN ON REGULATIONS FOR NUNS, 458

(*LNMaior.* 6)

Of this long law only so much is translated as pertains to Christian maidens dedicated ecclesiastically to virginity, about whom various regulations (particularly in respect to their heirship) are established by the emperors. Less than one half of the law concerns this topic; the rest treats secular widows and their successions. Five years later Emperors Leo I and Severus abrogated all this law's provisions except that concerning secular widows' usufruct of their betrothal gifts (*LNS* 1; dated 20 February 463).

Emperors Leo and Majorian Augusti to Basil, praetorian prefect.[1]

By having accepted the rudder of guiding the Empire we are bound to consider how our State may be preserved and may progress both by arms and by laws and by complete reverence for religion, on which very much is conferred by this correction,[2] if the cherishable noble quality of noble women, when multiplied by procreation of children, should increase, if pious relations between parents and children should not be altered by any vices of plots and if a not unwilling spirit should accept God's true worship. For our ancestors effected this first of all: that they should stablish the State by arms and by religion, whose holy veneration we should forbid to be harmed by mortals' fabrications and figments.

For who can endure that parents by such plans not so much should dedicate as damn daughters, whom they hate, that they deliver them, while still fixed in their minor years, to the necessity of continuous virginity and they place the sacred veil on the heads of unwilling women, lest it should be allowable for adolescent minds to desire anything else, although an observance of this sort, accepting a spiritual system [3] with a religious intention, should be adopted not at the compeller's command but by spontaneous and mature deliberation? For with great applications must be avoided and by-passed the allurements of human desire, to which the ardour of adolescence especially impels them, that, after youth's passion has been abated, God-dedicated virginity apart from any sin of repentance [4] may deserve to come to the years of old age and to the palm of celestial service.[5] For what does it profit, if maidenly desire, when suppressed by paternal power,[6] should conceive deeply a furtive desire for marriage and, when repressed from legitimate association, should be drawn into illicit allurements?

Wherefore, lest poverty and shame by such impiety of parents should be imposed upon nubile persons and lest—what particularly must be abolished—offence against Almighty God should be occasioned by execrable mockeries, by an edictal law we ordain that daughters who a father or a mother shall have decided, after they have been taken from secular intercourse, should serve the Christian faith's precepts by continuous virginity, when remaining in the resolution of the blessed life, should not be consecrated by acceptance of the veil of the honoured head before they, after they have completed forty years of life, shall have deserved to be adorned with such fillets because of guiltless observance, so that the sequence of much time and the custom of celestial service [5] may not leave an approach for a perfidious wish on account of new desires.

But if before the established space of time anyone of the aforesaid parents shall have caused or shall have allowed a pious maid to be veiled, while inflamed with other longings of her adult sex, he should be fined by a third part of his goods.

Also the same penalty shall constrain her who, destitute of parents, shall have wished to be consecrated within the aforesaid age's years.

Also deacons who contrary to prohibitions shall have supplied service for this affair should be punished by proscription.

And because there has begun to be considered the case of these women, whom we wish to pass willingly and not compulsorily to the divine religion's cult, if anyone, dismissed [7] by her parents' hatreds, shall have assumed the resolution of preserving her virginity and if she is removed from the association of her brothers in a certain manner by parricidal artifice, lest she, who ought to be given to a marital bond, should not acquire either a father's or a mother's suitable largess [8] or from these, when dying, an equal succession with the remaining children, when now freed by the death of her dying parents and not yet passed the forty years of life during which she has not been able to be veiled, she should obtain the liberty of marrying from the time when she now shall have begun to be legally independent.[9] For she must not be judged sacrilegious who shall have shown that she has not wished this [10] previously or at least has not been able to fulfil this,[10] because the honourable estate of wedlock had been sought, since the Christian religion's instruction and doctrine have decreed that it is better that virgins should marry than that through natural ardour of impatience they should not preserve the virtue of the chastity which they have professed.[11]

Accordingly, when she, having acceded to the nuptials, shall have come into matrimony, the disherison coming to her from her parents [12] because of this or the amount of the Falcidian fourth [13] alone left to her should not harm her, but pursuant to the norm of the old law [14] she, as though not named, should enter by accrual [15] into either an equal or a half share, if the heirs have been written either as statutory or as extraneous,[16] respectively. Therefore deserving of such reward and succession must be deemed she who, having proposed voluntarily procreation of children, strives to vindicate her own family's noble quality from extinction.

Moreover we favour so much these women who with spontaneous and praiseworthy resolution have accepted the observance of holiness by the love of virginity,[17] that if perchance wicked persons' profane desire shall have tried by the crime of rape to violate a God-dedicated spirit, he who shall have committed this not only should be subject to the divine constitutions' vengeance,[18] but also should be rendered liable to anyone's accusation—so that whoever shall have assailed with proved facts a person polluted by so great a crime, after these rules have been ordained, should obtain the sentenced person's property and resources. And this crime we command to be so far removed from religious women that if anyone shall have tried anything similar in the case of any woman at all, he also should know that he must be smitten with an equal punishment . . .[19]

And we command all these things established for the future to be valid from the day of the issue of the law, Basil, dearest and fondest cousin. Therefore your illustrious and exalted Magnificence by posted edicts shall publish the most salutary sanction, that all persons may know that when irreligious minds' frauds and impious fabrications have been removed there has been established this constitution, which shall benefit the correction of morals and the public welfare, since our ancestors' vigour has been restored to earth by all persons' combined piety.[20]

Given on 26 October at Ravenna, our Lord [21] Leo Augustus and Majorian Augustus being consuls.

1. Of Italy.

2. That is, this corrective law.

3. The word is *philosophia*, which here denotes more than mere "philosophy" and connotes a way of life in pursuit of holy wisdom: the monastic life.

4. He means that after assumption of monastic vows a change of intention is sinful.

5. The metaphor is military and the word translated *service* is *militia*. The branch or wreath of palm as a symbol of victory, borrowed from the Greeks, was introduced into Rome in 292 B.C., according to Livy (*Ab Urbe Cond.* 10. 47. 3).

6. This phrase is the famous and familiar *patria potestas*, the Roman father's customarily recognized and legally exercised authority over his legitimate children (and their legitimate children) so long as they continued in his control. The rights adherent to this authority allowed a father to withhold his consent to the marriage of anyone under his power, irrespective of age. It was not until

the Principate that in 9 the *Lex Iulia et Papia Poppaea* first provided a remedy against fathers who refused their consent with the object of preventing their children from marrying.

7. To a nunnery.

8. As a dowry.

9. The phrase is *suae potestatis* (of her own power) for the commoner *sui iuris* (of her [his] own right).

10. Service as a nun.

11. Such is St Paul's notable teaching in 1 Cor. 7. 9, but see verses 1, 2, 7, 8, 34, 38 in this chapter.

12. Praeterition of statutory heirs (*sui heredes*), who were all such persons as were under the *potestas* or in the *manus* of the deceased and became *sui iuris* at his death, invalidated a will by the civil law (*ius civile*), for the Roman will, based on universal succession, had to disinherit expressly either as individuals or in a class those *sui heredes* whom the testator did not want so to act. But a testator's failure to do so cast the probate of his will by praetorian law (*ius honorarium*) into the rules of intestate succession, whereby, exactly as outlined later in this sentence, an omitted *suus heres* shared in the estate. See also no. 218, n. 9.

13. See no. 392, n. 4.

14. Given in *GI* 2. 124 as follows and of republican origin.

15. Statutory heirs not named in a will were said to enter by accrual (*accrescere*—the word here) into an inheritance. This right was the *ius accrescendi*.

16. Any testator's heir not legally subject to his power was called an outsider (*extraneus*). Such a nominated heir was given time (never less than a hundred days) to decide whether he would take the inheritance. See no. 218, n. 9.

17. If "the observance of virginity by the love of holiness" is meant—and this order seems more sensible in view of 1 Cor. 7. 34, then we have here a violent case of hyperbaton in Latin.

18. See nos. 92, 126, 372.

19. The rest (§§ 5-11) of the law is omitted as irrelevant until the enabling paragraph.

20. Both text and translation of the causal clause are uncertain.

21. Since Majorian had been Augustus for almost eighteen months, it seems strange that he too was not given the title of "our Lord" in this subscription.

497. LETTER OF LEO I AND MAJORIAN ON ADMISSION OF CURIALS TO THE CLERICATE, 458

(*LNMaior.* 7)

Since only one section of this law and of its interpretation pertains to the Church, only that much along with the preamble and the conclusion is translated.

In it the emperors establish regulations regarding those members of the senatorial class who withdraw from their communities to avoid public duties for a financially easier life among the clergy.

Emperors Leo and Majorian Augusti to Basil, praetorian prefect.[1]

None is ignorant that curials are the sinews of the State and the vitals of the municipalities; and their assembly antiquity rightly has called "the lesser senate".[2]

But the governors' iniquity and the tax collectors' punishable venality have caused this: that many, deserting their native places, with disregard for the splendour of their lineage chose secret retreats and residence on another's rural estate, bringing also on themselves the following disgrace: that while they wish to enjoy the patronages of powerful persons, they polluted themselves by union with female tenant farmers [3] and with female slaves.[3] And so it has happened that both the orders [4] were lost to the cities and some men almost forfeited the status of their own freedom by the contagion of a baser association . . .[5]

And since always there must be hindrance to the tricks of those persons who are unwilling to be what they have been born to be,[6] whatsoever curial or guildsman perhaps shall have withdrawn himself from his municipality under the name of the clericate by any pretext of religion, pursuant to the previous laws' statutes,[7] if he should be proved to be placed below the rank of the diaconate, without delay he should be recalled to his origin.[8]

But if he is found at the time of this law's issuance already a deacon or a priest or a bishop, whether he still is obligated for performances or his public duties have been completed, he should learn that he should alienate nothing from his patrimony.

And if it shall have befallen that he has progeny or relatives of the masculine sex who certainly can satisfy a municipal senate's needs, forthwith he should not desist from delivering to them a half of all his resources, retaining for himself the residuary six-twelfths for usufruct. If the male sex shall have been lacking, without doubt he should observe the said rules in the case of his daughters, if, however, they are united in wedlock with curials.[9] And if by chance they shall have been

497. ADMISSION OF CURIALS TO THE CLERICATE, 458

lacking completely, the aforesaid person's patrimony shall belong to his city's order.[4]

Of course, if any such person, bound by his origin's [8] bonds, from these persons whom we order to be returned to the orders,[4] shall have believed that he should be hidden within the Church under the pretence of divine service, the archdeacon should be constrained to restore him . . .

Of course your illustrious and exalted Magnificence by its powers shall admonish the governors of all provinces that they should compel each and every city's chief magistrates and elders to produce the lists (which antiquity has compiled) of the municipal senates as well as of all other guilds, disclosing under peril of their capital punishment the families of persons obligated under execution of public records, so that what rules have been established may be brought by posted edicts to all persons' notice.

Given on 6 November at Ravenna, Leo and Majorian Augusti being consuls.

Interpretation: . . . Moreover, if a curial or a guildsman, unwilling to be what they have been born to be, shall have wished to be clergymen and shall have been established in any office whatever before [10] the diaconate, without any delay they should be recalled to the office of their origin.[8]

But if he already shall have been ordained a deacon or a priest or at any rate a bishop, whether he shall have discharged or shall not have discharged his public services, he should presume to alienate nothing from his patrimony.

And if anyone shall have had sons or relatives of the masculine sex, upon which persons only a municipal senate's need is imposed that it can be observed, to those persons he should not delay to give immediately a half from his resources, but should retain for himself a half for usufruct. But if he shall not have had either sons or at least relatives of the male sex, but shall have daughters, whom the law makes alien from the public need, then to them he should deliver six-twelfths of his goods, if, however, they shall have accepted curials as husbands, both through whom the public need can be fulfilled and from whom sons justly may be called curials. But if they shall not have been united with curials, the aforesaid curial's patrimony shall belong to his municipality's order.[4]

Moreover, if anyone of these persons, who—we have said above—ought to be recalled to his own order [4] or origin [8] without excuse of official rank, shall have fled for refuge to a church's precincts, the archdeacon should be obligated that he must produce him . . .

1. Of Italy.

B

2. In contrast, of course, to that in Rome (rather than to that in Constantinople, for this constitution emanated from Ravenna).

3. While *colona* can mean a woman who cultivates rented land, probably not so much independent "farmerettes" are meant as daughters of *coloni*, on whom see no. 528, n. 5.

An *ancilla* may be a hired woman in domestic service, but commonly is used to mean a female slave—thus St Jerome translates δούλη (properly a homeborn slave as opposed to one bought or made)—by which the Blessed Virgin Mary is made to characterize herself in the Magnificat (Luke 1. 48).

4. That is, the members of the senatorial order. See no. 325, n. 6.

5. Omitted portions (§§ 1-6, 8-17) treat municipal senators' flight from their communities to rural districts, their marriage with lower-class women, their alienation of property, gubernatorial requisitions of various kinds, collection of taxes.

6. So in *CT* 7. 21. 3, 12. 1. 170; *LNT* 6.

7. Nos. 439 and 478.

8. That is, his original status as senator or guildsman.

9. A case of antiptosis: to avoid a dative and an ablative the Latin has a genitive and an ablative—"united by wedlock of curials".

10. That is, before in time, which is below in rank.

498. MANDATE OF LEO I ON RESPECT FOR THE CROSS AND RELICS, 459

(*CI* 1. 3. 26)

This statute calls for the deposit of crosses and of martyrs' relics in religious edifices and forbids their introduction into secular buildings, particularly those built for public utility or entertainment.

Emperor Leo Augustus to Vivian, praetorian prefect.[1]

We decree that hereafter monks or any other person at all of any status whatever or condition should not attempt illegally to bring the venerable Cross or the holy martyrs' relics into public buildings or into any places whatever fabricated for the people's pleasures or should not dare to occupy those places which have been constructed either for public reasons or for the people's amusements.[2] For since religious buildings are not lacking, there they can place, after previously (as is proper) the most religious bishops have been consulted, the martyrs' relics—not by certain persons' usurpations, but by the most reverend bishops' judgement.

Therefore each and every individual—both monk and one of any other profession at all—should maintain zealously and should take care to preserve perpetually his own patience and self-restraint, which our laws and the public discipline and the name of the monks themselves demand.

Given on 17 September, Patrick being consul.

1. Of the East.
2. But it is reported earlier of Emperor Alexander Severus that when Christians had occupied a certain place which previously had been public property and when cooks claimed that it belonged to them, by rescript he replied that it was better that a god should be worshipped there in any way whatsoever than that it should be surrendered to cooks (see no. 4, n. 2 *ad init.*).

499. LAW OF MAJORIAN ON ECCLESIASTICAL PRIVILEGE, (?)459–60

(*LNMaior.* 10)

Of this law, which comes between *LNMaior.* 9 (dated 17 April 459) and 11 (no. 500; dated 28 March 460) and therefore presumably was issued in that interval, nothing except the title is extant. In full the rubric reads: "Neither a senator of the city of Rome nor a church to be compelled to deliver to the fisc anything left to them in accordance with a will by certain persons and on urban peoples".

From the title it appears that the law treated two topics: legacies and city-dwellers. It is unknown under what circumstances the fisc could have claimed property bequeathed to a Roman senator or to a church and of course it also is unknown what the law ordained about persons living in cities.

500. MANDATE OF LEO I AND MAJORIAN ON FORCED ORDINATION TO THE CLERICATE, 460

(*LNMaior.* 11)

While the full title of this law includes mention of episcopal courts and of various matters, nothing on these has descended to us and we do not know even what "various matters" were treated in it.

Monetary and personal relief is provided for those who have been compelled to enter the clerical state. If bishops have been privy to such practice, they are cited to appear before the pope. Parents who force their children into the clerical life are fined.

Emperors Leo and Majorian Augusti to the illustrious Ricimer, count and master of each soldiery [1] and patrician.

Concerning material necessary to the place.[2]

For undertaking the duty of the clericate we have given [3] to each and every person an option, not a law,[4] because, as we allow any holy burden whatever to be imposed on willing persons, so we order it to be removed from unwilling persons. For some bishops' [5] persuasion imposes that burden upon resistant persons, so that the offence of interposing violence trains unforeseeing minds to hatred of pious religion.

For this reason, therefore, we remove the freedom of this presumption, so that if anyone shall have been proved, when compelled by force, under public disgrace to have undertaken the clericate's duties, on voluntary accusers or on him, if he himself shall have wished to allege what wrongs he has suffered, we bestow the freedom to seek condemnation of crimes of this character before competent judges: so that, if charges in a suit [6] shall have been established according to the laws, an archdeacon should be compelled to pay to him who endured the wrong ten pounds of gold, which must be paid hereafter, if he desists from the suit,[7] for the purpose of profit to the accuser's resources or [8] to the community's order [9]—that person, who, because he had been compelled, could not have been consecrated, having been restored to his own desire.

And because from an attempt of this kind . . .[10] nor it is proper for a bishop to be alien from a sense of shame, he should be summoned to the apostolic see's bishop,[11] that he may incur the brand of illegal presumption in that most reverend see.[12]

Because, to be sure, a not unjust suspicion exists that very often trickeries of parents are involved in this business, while they favour with excessive love some children and persecute other children with unjust decision, we order fathers and mothers alike, if they shall have been proved to have subjected their unwilling sons to the aforesaid burden, to be afflicted by the loss of a third of their goods, which shall profit the resources of the son himself.

To be sure, if anyone shall have been ordained bishop unwillingly, we permit this consecration to be violated by no accusation.[13]

Given on 28 March at Arles, the most distinguished Magnus and the most distinguished Apollonius being consuls.

Interpretation: This law has not been written in its entirety [14] for this reason: because what things it says "on various matters" are considered already expressed in other laws with an evident interpretation. But it has this additional matter, which we have caused to be written at this place, "on those who are ordained clergymen unwillingly", which by itself without interpretation can be understood.

1. See no. 106, n. 4.
2. This rubric (found also in *CT* 2. 10. 6; dated 422), reveals that we have only an excerpt of a larger law and it is equivalent to the commoner phrase "and after other matters". Each is a notation by the ancient compilers, who followed the instructions of *CT* 1. 1. 5–6 (dated 429 and 435).
3. In Latin this verb is in the infinitive mode and depends upon a verb in a finite mode which may have been in the omitted part.
4. The word is *lex* and is understood in the sense of a regulation.
5. See no. 16, n. 4.
6. This phrase is an editorial emendation.
7. This phrase is inserted by the translator. The idea seems to be that the plaintiff profits either way: the archdeacon must pay him and/or the municipal senate, whether the accuser continues or discontinues his legal action.
8. Editors suggest "or" for *and*.
9. See no. 325, n. 6.
10. The lacuna may be filled by some such words as "bishops do not abstain".
11. Since the constitution was published at Arles, the bishop of Rome is meant, for he had ecclesiastical jurisdiction over the West.
12. That is, the papal court, where he would be tried.
13. The idea may be that in time even an unwillingly consecrated bishop because of his rank becomes reconciled to his office and therefore that he shall not be entitled to release.

Editors depress into the *apparatus criticus* a passage found here in some manuscripts and considered to be spurious. It concerns violation of the right of sanctuary and it threatens capital punishment for violators of the law. This, however, may have been one of the clauses on "various matters" forecast in the law's title.

14. That is, not copied either by the compilers or by the interpreter, for it is unknown to whom the excerpting process is due.

501. MANDATE OF LEO I ON SANCTUARY, 466
(*CI* 1. 12. 6)

While generally safeguarding the right of sanctuary in that no fugitive may be snatched from a church without due process, the emperor places on the Church's stewards and defenders the responsibility to see that judges' sentences are executed in respect to delivery both of person and of property, to search for what movables have been carried by the fugitives into the church, to surrender defaulting fugitives of an inferior status, and to inform the competent authority about the result of their search for refugees.

Emperor Leo Augustus to Erythrius, praetorian prefect.[1]

By the present law to be valid throughout all places—this royal city [2] excepted, wherein we, dwelling by Propitious Divinity, as often as need shall have demanded, when invoked by individual cases and persons, provide immediate constitutions—we decree that no persons of absolutely any status should be expelled or surrendered or dragged as fugitives from the orthodox faith's sacrosanct churches and that on these persons' behalf from the venerable bishops and the religious stewards should not be exacted what may be owed by these persons; but persons who shall have dared to undertake this or to do it or to attempt it at least by bare thought and consideration must be smitten with capital and last chastisement of punishment.[3] Therefore from these places and their precincts, which the rules of previous laws have ordained, we permit no persons at any time to be expelled or to be ejected and none to be detained and to be confined in the reverend churches themselves in such a way that anything either of things pertaining to nourishment or of clothing or repose should be denied to him.

But if the fugitives themselves indeed appear publicly and in sacred places offer themselves to be met by seekers, they themselves (with reverence for the places observed) should be warned by the judges' sentences, to which they are subject, for the purpose of giving such a reply as each one shall have perceived meets his own case.

But if they hide in the ecclesiastical precincts, the religious steward or the defender of the Church or at least the person whom episcopal authority shall have chosen as more suitable for these affairs, when warned, should present the secreted and hiding person without any trouble, if he is found within the church's precincts.

But when he shall have been summoned [4] by a civil action on a public or a private contract, it should be in his decision to reply—either by himself or, if he shall have preferred, when a representative procurator has been furnished in the usual way—in the inquiry of that judge by whose sentences he is smitten. But if he should decline to do this or should delay, the usual arrangement of judgements and of laws should be observed.

Accordingly, if he possesses immovable property, after the usual formalities of the edicts by the judge's sentence either delivery or sale of his property is held up to the amount of the debt. But if he has movable property and if he hides this outside the church's limits, this,

501. ON SANCTUARY, 466

when sought by the judge's sentence and by the prosecutor's care, wheresoever it is hidden, after it has been extracted, should profit public and private accounts on behalf of the course of equity and the amount of the debt. Of course, if it is held within the church's precincts or is proved to have been concealed or deposited with anyone of the clergymen, after it has been sought by the zeal and the foresight of the most reverend steward or by the diligence of the defender of the Church, it should be brought, coming in any way whatever, to the sacrosanct church, that with equal arrangement of equity regard for the fisc or the State or the creditors and for any proper claimers should be had from the said property to the amount of the debt. If it is said to have been deposited or entrusted anywhere, we wish there to be so much caution [5] in searching that, if it is asserted by supposition alone to have been concealed with anyone, by the venerable bishop's authority he [6] should be ordered to make satisfaction also from his own conscience.[7]

We add [8] that the things which we have decreed about principal persons [9] we command also to be observed in the persons of sureties or of mandators or of property belonging to them or of servants and of associates or of partners or of persons at all obligated in the said cases, obviously (if the fugitives shall have wished to have these very persons also with themselves within the churches' limits) that public and private debts may be paid also by these persons' property and that search for property wherever it has been deposited by them may proceed. And these things indeed concerning free-born and free persons.

Of course, if a slave or a tenant farmer or a serf or a servant or a freedman and any other such person of a household or subjected to a stipulation,[10] after specified property has been disturbed and has been removed, shall have betaken himself (by having withdrawn himself secretly) to sacrosanct places, immediately by the religious stewards or defenders, as soon as they shall have been able to know this, through persons, obviously to whom they [11] belong, they [12] themselves being present on behalf of ecclesiastical discipline and the character of the deed done, when either appropriate punishment or most humane intercession proceeds, they,[11] made secure by forgiveness of pardon and by interposition of an oath, should be returned to their own place and condition—the property which they shall have had with them being restored. For it is not fitting for them to linger longer within the church, lest to their patrons or owners the just services should be denied by their absence and lest they themselves at the church's loss should be nourished by disbursements for the needy and the poor.

Moreover amid these matters, which look sedulously to the solicitude and the care of the religious steward or of the defender of the

Church, the following also shall be observed: that incessantly they should search within the churches for the persons and the cases of those fleeing for refuge, then they should inform rather pressingly the judges or the persons to whom the cases and the persons pertain, that rather diligently they may execute the fitness of equity.

Given on 28 February at Constantinople, Leo Augustus for the third time being consul.

1. Of the East.
2. Constantinople.
3. Here is a case of enallage, more particularly that of antiptosis, for either *capital* or *last* and even both adjectives belong in thought with *punishment* rather than with *chastisement*, where the Latin puts these.
4. The verb twice translated "warned" above (*monere*) here seems to be used in the sense of being warned to appear in court: hence *summoned*.
5. Or "so great a pledge" to be forfeited in the event that the search will be fruitless.
6. The person who has asserted that it is secreted somewhere.
7. Pitra prints (2. 560) a late Greek version of this sentence.
8. This main verb in English is in Latin a participle in an independent sentence.
9. That is, debtors who have fled from creditors and have taken refuge in churches.
10. Or possibly "slavery". The idea is that the person definitely is bound to another by some sort of legally recognized status.
11. The fugitives.
12. The steward or the defender.

502. MANDATE OF LEO I ON EX-OFFICIALS IN THE CLERICATE, 466

(*CI* 1. 3. 27)

To all legitimately retired functionaries, save commissaries charged with superintendence of military supplies, the emperor grants an unmolested service in the Church, if they desire to enter the ecclesiastical establishment.

The same Augustus to Erythrius, praetorian prefect.[1]
Whoever, after the periods of his governmental service [2] have been completed and the duties or services which he owed either by custom or by law to any status whatever have been completed, shall have betaken himself to the society of clergymen and shall have

preferred and shall have chosen to be numbered among the true orthodox faith's ministers should not be recalled by the harshness of any verdict whatsoever and should not be withdrawn by inopportune charges from God's temples, to which he has consecrated himself, but should continue securely and quietly in the said most blessed ministries, toward which after the lassitude of long labour he has been drawn by a better plan because of the peacefulness of the rest of his life, replying with due process of law to whatever actions against him and his patrimony are appropriate by lawful accusation—with the exception of commissaries,[3] whom the statutes of a most sacred constitution [3] have ordained to be subjected forever to your Eminence's orders and to the public services.

Given on 6 March at Constantinople, Leo Augustus for the third time being consul.

1. Of the East.
2. See no. 186, n. 4.
3. See nos. 110, n. 5, and 383, n. 6.

503. MANDATE OF LEO I ON ALIENATION OF ECCLESIASTICAL PROPERTY TO HERETICS, (?)466–72

(*CI* 1. 5. 10)

To heretics the emperor prohibits the sale of real property on which churches or oratories have been erected. Violation of the ordinance entails confiscation of property by the imperial treasury.

The same Augustus to Erythrius, praetorian prefect.[1]

If any persons of the orthodox religion by a true or a sham purchase or by any other legal right or title whatever shall have wished to transfer manors and estates and immovable properties in which the orthodox faith's churches or oratories have been established to any person whatever of a heretical sect and thinking things contrary to the orthodox faith, we wish that no wish of this sort, applied between living persons or arranged by a secret decision, should be valid, even if it shall have been assigned by a seller of the orthodox faith or with a fictitious alienee under any situation at all; but we judge all documents of this sort to be invalid as if absolutely not written. For we decree that these manors and estates, which to heretical persons by any way whatever shall have been transferred or granted, should be claimed for our fisc's resources.

For whether these manors should remain with orthodox owners or possessors or should have come to our fisc's legal controls, it is necessary for the churches and the oratories established in these to be restored rather diligently and rather carefully. For our Serenity's foresight leads everywhere to this end: that Almighty God's temples, in which our faith's institutions endure, renewed by assiduous care throughout all ages, should be preserved. For it cannot be doubted that if estates in which the true faith's churches and oratories have been established and integrity is revered should come to heretics, by these persons they would be deserted and abandoned altogether, would be free from all care, would be bereft of all rites and accustomed mysteries,[2] would be deprived of all splendour, would be attended by no peoples' meetings and by no clergymen's observances, and as a result of this without doubt the churches would perish, would go to ruin, would be razed. For heretics have not been able to plan at any time about the restoration of those things which they absolutely did not want.

By removing all these matters we have come to the present law.[3]

1. Of the East.
2. See no. 75, n. 42.
3. The compiler of the *Syro-Roman Lawbook* (on which see no. 32, n. 9) probably refers to this law when he writes (§ 118) that "the blessed [*beatus* for *divus*, on which see nos. 32, n. 9, and 127, n. 7] Leo, the faithful king, himself also in his days honoured Christ's Church and overwhelmed heretics" (*FIRA* 2.794).

504. LAW OF UNKNOWN EMPEROR ON DISTURBANCE OF CHURCHES, 466–534

(*CI* 1. 12. 7)

This defective statute, issued sometime in or after 466, prohibits persons from disturbing churches by introduction of lawsuits (apparently in the presence of congregations) and provides the proper channels for their reception.

He who has an action or a lawsuit against anyone shall not throw the churches into an uproar by himself or by another, but shall go to the magistrates.

If there is need for the emperor in the case of sinful acts, he shall inform him through the archbishop.

He who does contrary to these things is punished.

505. LAW OF UNKNOWN EMPEROR ON DECORUM IN CHURCH, 466-534
(CI 1. 12. 8)

Some emperor between 466 and 534 directs the procedure for acceptance of petitions when he attends church and prohibits demonstrative accompaniment of such presentation on pain of punishment.

As often as according to custom on the great feasts we enter into the most holy Great Church [1] or also into other churches, we leave to our most glorious quaestor [2] both to accept and to bring to us the petitions of persons in need.

He who employs tumults or outcries during the period of feasts in the Great Church [1] or also in other churches shall fail immediately in his case, even if he should have seemed to have something reasonable, and he shall be ejected by the prefect [3] and he shall be subjected to punishments.

He who fears a powerful person [4] shall approach us through the archbishop or the defenders of the Church.

1. Probably Hagia Sophia in Constantinople, though there is no subscription. Rebuilt after the fire of 404 (no. 285, n. 2) and dedicated by Theodosius II in 415, it was burned during the Nika riot in 532. The present cathedral, the last great gift of Greek genius to us, consecrated in 537 by Justinian I (who—like Nero in 64—had the chance to reconstruct his capital) and converted into a mosque by the Turks in 1453, has been a national museum since 1934.

Procopius provides a detailed description of its building and beauty (*De Aed.* 1. 1. 22–78). The latest work on it in English seems to be E. H. Swift's *Hagia Sophia* (New York, 1940). But the brief sketch of Hagia Sophia by Gibbon, who felt that this magnificent monument of the Roman Solomon's fame excited only the "rational curiosity" of European tourists, is still a classic (4. 244–8).

2. His full title is quaestor of the sacred palace (*quaestor sacri palatii*). As the emperor's chief legal minister, the quaestor composed imperial rescripts to petitions: hence he was the appropriate official to receive petitions. Such was Tribonian, who directed the commission which drafted the *Corpus Iuris Civilis* (528–34).

3. Probably the urban prefect (*praefectus urbi* or *urbis*), who was the principal civic magistrate in Constantinople (and in Rome) in the Empire.

4. See no. 127, n. 6.

506. MANDATE OF LEO I AND ANTHEMIUS ON RESTRICTION OF THE LEGAL PROFESSION TO CHRISTIANS, 468

(*CI* 1. 4. 15)

This ordinance, repeated by Justinian (*CI* 2. 6. 8), permits only Christians to become lawyers and penalizes both those who violate the statute and those who condone such violation.

Emperors Leo and Anthemius Augusti to Nicostratus, praetorian prefect.[1]

None either in your Grandeur's tribunal or in a provincial court or in any judge's court [2] should enter into the lawyers' guild,[3] unless he shall have been imbued with the Catholic religion's sacrosanct mysteries.[4]

But if anything shall have been done or tried by any method or by some device, your Sublimity's office staff should sustain the loss of a hundred pounds of gold on account of condemnation.

Moreover, whoever contrary to our Serenity's prudent decree shall have dared to seize the office of advocate by surreption and shall have offered prohibited patronage,[5] the said person, after he has been removed from the office of advocate, shall sustain specifically the sentence of proscription and of perpetual exile—the governors of provinces knowing that he under whose administration anything of this kind shall have been tried shall sustain proscription of a half of his property and the penalty of exile for five years.

Given on 31 March at Constantinople, Anthemius Augustus for the second time being consul.

1. Of the East.
2. Literally "in any judge's presence".
3. The phrase is *togatorum consortium*, whence *togati* furnishes our generic term "men of the robe" as applied to lawyers collectively.
4. See no. 75, n. 42.
5. To other meanings of *patronage* already noticed in this sylloge (e.g. nos. 241, n. 2, and 345, introd.) now must be added another example: legal assistance given by a lawyer to a litigant in the latter's trial. Here such aid is forbidden, because the lawyer who offers it has assumed surreptitiously the office of an advocate.

507. MANDATE OF LEO I ON EPISCOPAL INTEREST IN LEGACIES FOR RANSOM OF CAPTIVES, 468

(*CI* 1. 3. 28)

When a testator has bequeathed a legacy or a trust for redemption of prisoners of war, but has failed to name the person to fulfil his wish in this matter, then by this statute the bishop of the deceased's birthplace or deathplace—as the case may be—administers the money left for this purpose.

Pitra prints (2. 492) a late Greek version.

The same Augustus to Nicostratus, praetorian prefect.[1]

We decree that it is permitted to none, if he has been instituted heir by will or succeeds by intestacy or is found to be a fideicommissary or a legatee, to break or to violate with wicked intention a pious testator's disposition by asserting that a legacy or a trust which is left for ransom of captives is not firm, but we decree[2] that by all means it[3] is demanded to benefit the business of a pious object in view of the testator's wish.

And if indeed a testator shall have signified by whom he desires the ransom of captives to be made, he who specially has been designated should have permission of demanding the legacy or the trust and should fill the testator's desire in accord with his own conscience.

But if, when a person has not been designated, a testator shall have determined distinctly only the total of the legacy or of the trust which is due to benefit the said cause, the most reverend bishop of that city whereof the testator is born should have the opportunity of demanding what shall have been bequeathed for this object, for the purpose of fulfilling without any delay—as is fitting—the deceased's pious design. Moreover, when the most religious bishop shall have obtained monies of this sort left by a pious decision, immediately, when the transactions occur, he shall be obligated to reveal in the presence of the province's governor the amount of these monies and the time when he has received these. But we command him after the space of one year to disclose both the number of the captives and the prices given for them, that by all means may be fulfilled such pious wishes of decedents: in such manner, however, that the most religious bishops freely and without any expenses should execute the aforesaid transactions, lest through regard for humanity the bequeathed monies should be disbursed by expenses of lawsuits.

But if the testator who has left a legacy or a trust of this sort without having designated a person should be of a barbaric nation and if some doubt about his fatherland shall have emerged, the most reverend bishop of that city wherein the said testator has died also should have the right of claim for the legacy or for the trust, for the purpose of fulfilling in all ways the deceased's design.

But if the testator shall have met his death in a village or in a district, the most reverend bishop of that city under which the village or the district is known to be shall have the right of demand.

And lest the deceased persons' pious design should be concealed by defrauders' wicked cunning, all persons who in any way whatever shall have known whatever shall have been left by a testator for a cause of this sort should have the free opportunity of bringing it to the notice of either the most distinguished governor of the province or the most reverend bishop and they should not shudder at the name and the suspicion of an informer, since their fidelity and industry lack not praise as well as honour and likewise piety, when they shall have brought truth into the public hearing [4] and light.

Given on 18 August at Constantinople, Anthemius for the second time being consul.

1. Of the East.
2. The last two words are supplied in the translation.
3. The legacy or the trust.
4. Literally "ears".

508. MANDATE OF LEO I AND ANTHEMIUS ON EPISCOPAL ELECTION, 469

(*CI* 1. 3. 30)

This statute assails the simoniacal selection of bishops by assigning penalties for such practice.

Pitra prints (2. 464) for the first time a late Greek version of this statute which shows some important variations.[1]

The same Augusti to Armasius, praetorian prefect.[2]

If it shall have happened that anyone either in this royal city [3] or in all the other provinces which are scattered throughout the whole world should be advanced by God's sponsorship to the rank of bishop, he should be promoted by the pure minds of men, by the simple conscience of election, by the sincere judgement of all persons.

None should purchase the episcopate's [4] rank by the venality of money: how much anyone should merit it, not how much it suffices him to give, should be estimated. For surely what place can be safe and what circumstance can be excused, if God's venerable temples are captured by money? What wall for integrity or what rampart for faith shall we provide, if a cursed hunger for gold [5] creeps into the venerable sanctuaries? [6] What, finally, can be protected or secure, if uncorrupted sanctity is corrupted? The profane ardour of avarice should cease to menace the altars and from the sacred shrines should be repelled the sinful shame. So virtuous and humble a bishop should be chosen in our times that, whithersoever he shall have come, he should purify all places by the integrity of his own life.

Not by money, but by prayers a bishop should be ordained. He ought to be separated so far from canvassing that he should be sought as worthy of being compelled;[7] when asked, he should withdraw; when invited, he should flee. Only the need for excuse should be a vote in his favour,[8] for clearly he is unworthy of the episcopate,[4] unless he shall have been ordained unwillingly,[9] since whoever is detected to have slunk into this holy and venerable seat of the bishop by the intervention of money or if anyone is detected to have accepted anything that he should ordain or should choose another person, he should be removed from the episcopate's [4] rank by an accusation proposed after the fashion of a public accusation and of injured majesty.[10]

For we decree that he not only should be deprived henceforth of this honour, but also should be condemned to perpetual infamy, and that a similar punishment should attend all those whom a like wickedness contaminates and equalizes.[11]

Given on 8 March at Constantinople, Zeno and Marcian being consuls.

1. Pitra prefixes to his text (translated below) an ancient jurisconsult's preface, wherein the author apparently accepts *CI*'s Latin version as an abbreviated form of the statute and then turns that version into Greek.

"The constitution's concise sense: that none for money should ordain or should be ordained a bishop; that he who does this should be expelled from his seat and should be dishonoured forever. Since the pronouncement has been stated at a great interval of time and is difficult, it has been necessary even in the edict at its [the constitution's] foot to say that it is as follows:

"If anyone in the royal city or in any other whatsoever is ordained bishop by God's will, he should be ordained by pure mind and by bare conscience of selection. And none should purchase the episcopate by buying it with payment, for it should be considered if he who takes it is also worthy of it—not how much gold he can furnish. For what kind of place would be safe or what kind of circumstance must be avoided, if God's venerable temples should be sold for money? For whom should we find either of purity of character or steadfast in faith, if a cursed hunger for gold has entered into the venerable sanctuaries?

For, finally, what can be steadfast or secure, if the uncorrupted episcopate should be corrupted by money? The profane tower of cupidity should yield to these; the unholy offence should be repelled from the sacred shrines. So temperate and meek in character a bishop should be selected in our times that he should purify every place to which he comes by the integrity of his own life.

"Not by payment, but by prayer should he be chosen. A bishop ought to stand aloof so far from flattery that he should be sought as worthy of being compelled; when asked, he should withdraw; when invited, he should flee; only the need for excuse should be a vote in his favour. For clearly he is unworthy of the episcopate, unless he has been ordained unwillingly.

"Whoever has slunk into the holy and venerable seat of the bishop by interposition of money or has taken it for ordaining or selecting another, we declare that this person, accused after the fashion of a public accusation, as if of injured majesty, should be expelled from the episcopate's rank and not only should be deprived of this honour, but also should be condemned to perpetual dishonour.

"Behold! [Pitra conjectures "Not"] an unusual kind of dishonour: for whenever the offence makes persons similar to those whom it contaminates, a similar punishment also should attend them."

2. Of the East.

3. Constantinople.

4. See no. 158, n. 1.

5. The expression *cursed hunger for gold* (*auri sacra fames*) appears in Vergil, *Aen.* 3. 57.

6. The thought of the conditional clause comes from Persius, *Sat.* 2. 69, on which see no. 598, n. 13.

7. It is said that Emperor Alexander Severus, who often quoted Persius' line (n. 6 *supra*), appointed as praetorian prefect a man who even had attempted to evade the appointment, for the emperor expressed the opinion that the unwilling and not the office-seeking persons ought to hold positions in the State (Scriptores Historiae Augustae: *Sev. Alex.* 19. 1).

8. That is, the fact that a person sought for the episcopate should feel compelled to excuse himself from consideration should favour his candidacy.

9. Cf. the phrase *nolo episcopari* (I do not wish to be a bishop), which traditionally for centuries, with a semblance of modesty, was used as a matter of form by persons elevated to episcopal rank.

10. The term is *laesa maiestas*, whence the English expression "lese majesty" through the French phrase *lèse-majesté*. In the Greek paraphrase (n. 1 *supra*) it is βλαβεῖσα ἡ καθοσίωσις.

11. That is, debases to the simoniacal prelate's level.

509. MANDATE OF LEO I AND ANTHEMIUS ON OBSERVANCE OF SUNDAY, 469

(*CI* 3. 12. 9)

The emperors particularly mark Sunday as a day to be free from all judicial and legal activities, besides banning attendance at the theatre and at the circus. Penalties are prescribed for violation of the statute.[1]

Emperors Leo and Anthemius Augusti to Armasius, praetorian prefect.[2]

We wish festal days, days dedicated to the Highest Majesty,[3] to be occupied by no pleasures and not to be profaned by any vexations of collections.[4]

Accordingly we decree that the ever-honourable Lord's day [5] must be venerated in such a way that one should be excused from all indictments, no correction should press anyone, no collection of surety should be demanded, service of legal documents should be at rest, advocacy in court should lie hid, the said day should be free from trials in court, the court crier's rude voice should be silent, litigants should recover breath from controversies, they should have an interval of truce, opponents should come to each other without fear, reciprocal repentance should enter minds, they should make joint covenants, they should talk about agreements.

And, however, while relaxing these activities of a religious day, we do not allow anyone to be engaged in obscene pleasures. On the said day the theatrical stage or the contest of the circus or the tearful spectacles of wild beasts [6] should claim nought for themselves; even if a festival to be celebrated for our origin or birthday shall have befallen, it should be postponed.

He shall sustain loss of governmental service [7] and proscription of patrimony, if anyone shall have believed that he should be present at spectacles on this festal day or an apparitor of any judge whomsoever shall have believed on the pretext of public or private business [8] that these matters which have been established by this law ought to be violated.

Given on 9 December at Constantinople, Zeno and Marcian being consuls.

1. The author of the *Syro-Roman Lawbook* (on which see no. 32, n. 9) attributes this constitution to Leo, who—he says (§ 118)—"increased the honour of the day of our Lord's Resurrection, which is the Lord's day [see no. 34, n. 5], and caused lawsuits to cease and that magistrates and powerful persons [the compiler has abstract for concrete nouns] should not use their

powers, but that everyone in humility should be joined together in Christ's Church. And he ordered that none on the Lord's day should arraign his partner and should seek a suit of any cause whatsoever—neither of an obligation nor of a delict, which he should have committed, nor of another matter" (*FIRA* 2. 794). He does not mention prohibition of pleasures and imposition of penalties, which later paragraphs of the constitution contain.

2. Of the East.

3. Mommsen suggests *dei* for *dies*, thus giving the reading of this explanatory phrase as "dedicated to God's Highest Majesty".

4. Either of debts (more probably) or of taxes.

5. See no. 34, n. 5.

6. In a letter "remarkable for showing a refinement very rare" in republican Rome, Cicero declares (*Ad Fam.* 7. 1. 3) that the spectators showed no pleasure in such *tearful spectacles* (*lacrimosa spectacula*) as apparently were the wild-beast hunts (*venationes*) provided by Pompey in 55 B.C. twice daily for five days, on the last of which were exterminated elephants. Though Cicero considers that there is a certain compassion and a sort of sentiment that that huge animal has an association with the human race, Pliny is more precise in telling that the twenty elephants' wailing and piteous bearing, when they saw no escape from their slaughter, so affected the audience that it rose in tears and *en masse* cursed Pompey (*Nat. Hist.* 8. 7. 21).

On wild-beast hunts see L. Friedländer, *Roman Life and Manners in the Early Empire* (London, 1913), 2. 62–74 and his notes thereon in 4. 521–9.

7. See no. 186, n. 4.

8. Of a legal nature.

510. MANDATE OF LEO I AND ANTHEMIUS ON ALIENATION OF ECCLESIASTICAL PROPERTY, 470

(*CI* 1. 2. 14)

This constitution, pertaining only to property owned by or given or sold or bequeathed to the Constantinopolitan Church, prohibits both the patriarch and the steward from any kind of permanent alienation of such property. Penalties are pronounced against violators of the statute. However, the steward is authorized to contract for usufructuary enjoyment of ecclesiastical property, if he considers such possession useful to the Church.

It seems surprising that almost 150 years elapsed between the State's authorization for the Church to accept legacies (no. 36)[1] and this imperial regulation of the administration of ecclesiastically owned property received through such bequests.[2]

510. ALIENATION OF ECCLESIASTICAL PROPERTY, 470

Emperors Leo and Anthemius Augusti to Armasius, praetorian prefect.[3]

We order that hereafter to no archbishop presiding over the sacrosanct Church in this royal city,[4] to no steward to whom is committed the management of ecclesiastical property, should be the power under the semblance of any alienation whatever to transfer to any person whatever manors, whether urban or rural estates, finally, fixed properties or tenant farmers or slaves established on these estates or civil provisions,[5] which have been assigned to the religious Church by the last will of anyone whatever or by that of his survivor, but that indeed he should divide,[6] should cultivate, should extend, and should enlarge these estates, and should not dare to make a surrender to anyone in respect to the said estates.

But whether by any testament whatever made lawfully or by codicil or by mere declaration or by legacy or by trust or in view of death or by any other last decision whatever or certainly by gift made while alive or by contract of sale or of donation or by any other title whatever anyone shall have wished his patrimony or a certain part of his patrimony in manors or estates or houses or provisions [5] or slaves and tenant farmers and their peculia [7] to belong to the aforesaid venerable Church, they should preserve all these undisturbed and absolutely without any diminution, knowing that on no occasion or time for repayment of plausible favour or of giving thanks has been permitted to the many power of donating or certainly of alienating to persons wishing to purchase, not even if all the clergymen with the religious bishop and the steward should consent in alienation of these properties. For it is proper that these things, which belong to or hereafter shall have come to the legal rights of the most blessed Church, should be guarded respectfully intact (just as the sacrosanct and religious Church herself); that as she herself is the perpetual mother of religion and of faith, so her patrimony should be preserved perpetually unimpaired.

To be sure, if by bold spirit and by sacrilegious mind any of the stewards or men shall have believed that these our Perpetuity's statutes ought to be violated, he himself, indeed, who by wanton attempt in the category of donation or of purchase or of exchange or of any other contract whatever shall have tried to acquire or to have ecclesiastical estates, except in that category wherein we now ordain, should lose every product of his own temerity of this sort; and rewards and gifts, which for the sake of this transaction shall have been given to stewards or to any other persons whatever, should be acquired for the Church's gains and advantages.

Moreover the estates and all things established on these with the proceeds or the incomes and the accessions of the entire intervening time [8] should be claimed by the clergymen themselves and by the secular [9] stewards, that they should be considered absolutely as if bought or sold by none, because these things, which are done contrary to the laws, must be held as unperformed.

Moreover the steward who shall have done this, rather shall have permitted it to be done, or shall have consented in absolutely any sale of this sort whatever or donation or exchange, except that which we concede by the present law, finally, in any alienation whatever, should be deprived of the administration of the stewardship committed to him and from his goods should be restored whatever has befallen the Church as a loss therefrom and his heirs and successors and descendants should be expelled by competent action from the ecclesiastics in respect to this deed or consent—the drafters who shall have dared to compose the instruments of prohibited contracts of this kind to be smitten by the punishment of irrevocable exile; also the judges or persons having the legal right of records [10] who shall have completed the records of donations or of contracts of this kind to be condemned by deprivation of their rank and of all their goods.

To be sure, lest every avenue of advantageous foresight for the religious stewards and every occasion of profit for the venerable churches should seem to be excluded, we grant that that which generally is judged profitable should occur with the necessary maintenance of caution. Therefore, if ever a religious steward of this royal city's [4] Church shall have seen clearly it to be expedient that the temporary possession of usufruct of certain properties and estates, whether—obviously—urban or rural, belonging to the ecclesiastical legal right, should be offered to anyone so desiring on his own petition, then the steward, for the time which shall have suited both or for a day of his life,[11] if he should be asked by him who desires it, with him who shall have chosen this property should enter into and should write pacts by which should be determined the time within which it shall have been agreeable for it to be offered, and by which it should be clear what he shall have accepted by way of any thanks whatever in return for this favour in offering the temporary usufruct of the ecclesiastical estate, but after the determined time and the satisfaction of the times [12] the proprietorship of the returns steadfastly recurring to the ecclesiastical legal right and ownership: in such a way, obviously, that whether in the completed period, which shall have been established between them, or at the time of his death, if this also shall have been decided, he who shall have received by intervening pact the ecclesiastical property for the sake of having the usufruct of certain returns should relinquish to the Church along with his own ownership of the estates and the fixed properties and their tenant farmers and slaves no less returns than of another such quantity as he had accepted. For, unless

510. ALIENATION OF ECCLESIASTICAL PROPERTY, 470

pacts shall have been entered on this condition, we also decree that these should not be valid, but that an ecclesiastical property, as if transferred by no legal right, should remain in its own legal right and ownership, and we decree that it should be claimed by ecclesiastics or by stewards.

Given [13] at Constantinople, Jordanes and Severus being consuls.

1. For interim evidence on legacies left to churches or to ecclesiastics see nos. 150, 225, 227, 488.

2. An exception appears to be no. 507, whereby a bishop becomes the executor of a trust or of a legacy created for redemption of captives—but only when a testator has not designated a trustee or a legatee—and is instructed how to administer the money. But no. 507's date is between seventeen and twenty-nine months prior to the present document and the Church (in the person of a bishop) only secondarily can be said to be trustee or legatee. That Christians earlier were involved officially in ransoming prisoners of war is learned from no. 308. See introd. to no. 515.

3. Of the East.

4. Constantinople.

5. See no. 301, n. 7. But in the present document is meant the Church's annual income from its agricultural land donated or sold or bequeathed to it by individuals.

6. Either for easier and more efficient administration or for leasing. The word (*dividere*) in mercantile language also means to sell in parcels, but, since all alienation is prohibited, this cannot be the meaning.

7. On this see no. 337, n. 6.

8. From the transaction to its detection.

9. Or "temporary", if the guilty steward has been discharged and an interim appointment has been made.

10. That is, the official duty of recording or registering documents.

11. That is, his last day alive—as appears below. Our idiom is "for the term of his life".

12. Or possibly "after the determined and agreed period of the time". While the Latin seems awkward, the meaning appears to be "at the mutually agreed end of the usufruct".

13. Month and day are missing from the subscription.

511. MANDATE OF LEO I ON ORTHODOXY FOR CIVIL OFFICIALS, (?)470

(*CI* 12. 59. 9)

In this law the emperor ordains that certain and mostly minor officials in the imperial civil service must profess orthodox Christianity as a condition of admission to office.

The same Augustus to Hilarian, master of the offices.

We decree that commissions [1] of chancery officials [2] and of secret-service agents,[3] nonetheless of apparitors of the most honourable praetorian prefecture throughout the East, also of those who are reckoned in different judges' offices, should carry the oaths of governmental service [4] in the usual manner, in accordance with the sacred commissions,[1] not everywhere nor at pleasure by authorizations only or by copies of sacred letters, but in accordance with only authentic sacred commissions,[1] subscribed by our hand and manifested by our decision, so that no trickery or fraud can be attached to these; also we order that admittance should be from persons who are of the true and the Catholic faith.

But those performing governmental service [4] otherwise, unless they should be from these, whom ancient custom has taught thoroughly should be added to the apparitorship by authorizations only, after the fraud has been detected by the zeal of anyone accusing them, we decree not only should lose their counterfeit governmental service,[4] but also should undergo the stigma [5] of proscription and we fine them by the loss of all their goods.

1. The word is *probatoria*, a document appointing an imperial official in the Dominate.

2. The word is *memorialis* and is applied to a member of the secretariat. Some lexicographers believe that he was a historiographer. Doubtless the term descended from the Principate, when one of the imperial bureaux of the burgeoning civil service was called in the second century *a memoria*, on which see no. 256, n. 2.

3. On these see no. 256, n. 3.

4. See no. 186, n. 4.

5. The word is *stilus*, a word of varied meanings, ranging from the stylus used in writing to the style of writing or of speaking, but generally retaining the connotation of pointedness.

512. MANDATE OF LEO I AND ANTHEMIUS ON RESTRICTION OF MONKS TO MONASTERIES, 471

(*CI* 1. 3. 29)

To prevent disputative monks from causing disturbances in eastern cities the emperors forbid them to leave their monasteries and to live in cities, especially Antioch, excepting such monks as are apocrisiarians.

Emperors Leo and Anthemius Augusti to Zeno, master of the soldiers.[1]

Persons dwelling in monasteries should not have authority to depart from monasteries and to live either in the Antiochenes' city or in other cities—only those called apocrisiarians being excepted, on whom we confer permission, if they wish, to enter because of only necessary commissions.

And these themselves who enter should take care not to discuss about worship or dogma or to deceive the populace's rather simple minds by counsels looking toward sedition or tumult, since they know that, if they disregard the things ordained by our Piety, they shall be subject to the laws' austerity.

Given on 1 June at Constantinople, Leo Augustus for the fourth time and Probian being consuls.

1. The Greek for this expression is simply στρατηγός, but it seems that it should be στρατηγὸς τῆς ἕω (as in no. 487, n. 26), for Zeno, Leo's son-in-law, was *magister militum per Orientem* (on which see no. 106, n. 4 *ad fin.*) ere his accession to the throne.

513. MANDATE OF LEO I ON BIBLICAL OATHS IN SALES, 472

(*CI* 11. 32. 3)

By this ordinance (abbreviated in *CI* 6. 24. 12) the emperor orders chief officials and senators and proprietors in provincial cities to swear on the Bible that they will render a proper decision in contracts for sale of municipally owned property, for the income from such sales is allocated by this law for the reparation of civic fortifications.

Emperor Leo Augustus to Erythrius, praetorian prefect.[1]

If by title of inheritance or legacy or trust or donation any house or civil provisions [2] or any buildings whatever or slaves have come or shall have come to the legal right of the renowned [3] or any other city whatever,[4] concerning this it shall be permitted to the cities to enter a contract of sale for their own advantage, that the sum of the money collected therefrom may be spent usefully for renewing or restoring the public walls.[5]

But, anticipating with unwearied care, lest anyone should be able to attempt anything disadvantageous against the cities' advantages, but that sales of this sort should proceed without any cheating or chicanery [6] or collusion or connivance, we decree that this must be observed for the future: that if indeed it shall have happened that a house or civil provisions [2] or any other buildings whatever or slaves belonging to this renowned city [3] should be sold, they should be sold not otherwise except by imperial authority.

But in the provinces, when all or the most part of curials as well as of dignitaries [7] and of rentiers of the city to which the aforesaid properties belong are present, we order that, after the Sacrosanct Scriptures have been introduced, each and every one of these who shall have assembled should indicate one by one the opinion which they think beneficial for their native city, in order that the buyer thus at length may be able to have a competent security by the recital of their decision intervening in the provincial court.

Moreover we decree that these contracts of sales—whether they already have been completed or shall have been entered later—should be steadfast.

Given on 26 February, Marcian being consul.[8]

1. Of the East.
2. See no. 301, n. 7.
3. By *renowned city* is meant probably Constantinople. Since, though the subscription is silent on the site of the enactment's emission, the document is addressed to the praetorian prefect of the East, whose headquarters was there.
4. Thus far the shorter version, which has only two alterations: it casts the conditional clause into a declarative sentence by omitting *if any* and it alters its double into a single predicate "can come".
5. The word is *moenia*, which more than *muri* connotes walls as a means of protection and security.

It must be remembered that the perils of barbarian invasion increased in the East as the Empire progressed in age. Leo's reign was marked also by "the struggle for ascendancy between the foreign and native powers in the State" (Bury, 1. 316). To counteract both internal and external danger, then, the placing of cities' bulwarks in a better posture of defence by extracting for their repair as much revenue as possible from sales well could concern the sovereign.

6. From its inclusion in this series *nundinatio*, which literally is "holding of

market on the ninth day" and then ordinarily means "trafficking", here acquires the coloration of crooked dealing.

7. See no. 495, n. 9.

8. The editorial correction is translated for the received reading of "Given on 26 February, Marcian and Zeno being consuls".

514. MANDATE OF LEO I AND ANTHEMIUS ON CLERICAL WILLS, 472

(*CI* 1. 3. 33)

This law allows clergymen of any rank, even if subject to paternal power (*patria potestas*), both to own property and to will it to their children and to extraneous heirs.[1]

The same Augusti to Erythrius, praetorian prefect.[2]

The sacrosanct orthodox faith's bishops and priests, also deacons, who, when their characters once have been approved and they are of most spotless integrity, shall have deserved to come to this rank, should claim, as if their own goods, whatever things they shall have been able to acquire and to have, when living in the said rank and station of the clericate, even if they have been placed in a father's or a grandfather's or a great-grandfather's power and are considered still their survivors.[3]

Concerning these persons: if ever it shall have been agreeable to them, when the free ability of testation or of donation or of alienation by any other title at all has been conceded, that never at any time these goods should be bestowed upon brothers or sisters or persons born from these, but that they should come to their later children [4] and any extraneous heirs [1] whatever and should not be claimed by their fathers or grandfathers or great-grandfathers, but by their own children [4] as principal inheritances, certainly the properties should proceed to these persons to whom they themselves shall have granted it as peculium [5] or by alienation made amid the living [6] or by a last and truly recognized will at the time of death.

Given on 4 April, Marcian being consul.

1. See no. 496, n. 16.
2. Of the East.
3. That is, their heirs (*sui heredes*), or whom see no. 496, n. 12.
4. See no. 570, n. 1.
5. On this word see no. 624, n. 3.
6. That is, probably as a gift *inter vivos*, on which see no. 595, n. 5.

515. MANDATE OF LEO I AND ANTHEMIUS ON CLERICAL DEFENDANTS IN LAWSUITS, 472
(CI 1. 3. 32)

This constitution establishes various rules about venue, sureties, fees, unjust accusations in cases where the clergy are cited as defendants.

Apparently out of place in this statute is a section releasing clergymen of all grades, monks, inmates of almshouses, superintendents of hostels—provided that all these are orthodox—from public services of an extraordinary character.

This constitution is of more than ephemeral interest, for it appears to be the earliest extant statute [1] recognizing that the Church as a corporation is concerned with what one may call pious foundations, though doubtless money and property donated or sold or devised to the Church were devoted lawfully to such service soon after Christianity had been declared a lawful religion in 313 (no. 12).[2] While, of course, corporate Christian charity ascends into the earliest apostolic days,: charitable foundations, apart from such pagan guilds and corporations[4] as had charitable objectives (which sometimes were secondary), appear first in the Christianized Empire, after donations to local churches and usually for specific purposes have been made, and assume the character of corporations.

About the operation of such eleemosynary establishments (almshouses, asylums, gerontocomiums, hospitals, hostels, nurseries, orphanages) little is learned from imperial legislation before the reign of Justinian I,[5] whose statutes[6] show that bishops and (particularly) stewards with precisely defined powers controlled in the Church's name the money and the property of such foundations and were administrators (ordinarily through deputies as heads of houses) rather than owners *stricto sensu*.[7]

Pitra prints (2. 534-5) a late Greek paraphrase of this law, to which the anonymous author of the *Syro-Roman Lawbook* (see no. 32, n. 9) also attracts (§ 118) attention (*FIRA* 2. 794-5).

The same Augusti to Erythrius, praetorian prefect.[8]

All of the orthodox faith (wheresoever they are and hereafter shall be) who are bishops [9] and clergymen (of whatever rank they are), also monks, in civil lawsuits from the verdict of a major or a minor judge absolutely neither should be haled to external courts nor should be compelled to leave the province or the district or the region which they inhabit.[10] None of them should be ordered through pitiable necessity to leave their churches or monasteries, which they inhabit through regard for religion, but before their own ordinary judges, that is, the governors of provinces, in the places where they dwell and submit to the churches' services, they should defend the prosecutions

515. CLERICAL DEFENDANTS IN LAWSUITS, 472

of all persons prosecuting against themselves, that at least in these hours and times, wherein it shall have happened that religious men are free from the turbulent service of the praetorium [11] and when the calumniating industry of plaintiffs shall have relaxed them temporarily,[12] they, betaking themselves with wise mind to their monasteries and venerable churches, with solicitous prayer and rather easily from nearby may serve the sacrosanct altars, because they have been settled in their own homes and households.

Moreover in this royal city,[13] whenever by reason of whatsoever circumstances it shall have happened that bishops or priests or all other clergymen, who serve the sacrosanct churches, or monks from any other provinces at all are found, whom, however, anyone shall have wished to call into litigation, it should be permitted to none to accuse the said persons in any other court unless only in your Sublimity's tribunal, where for them the due honour of beatitude is preserved and a copious supply of orators for defensive actions is provided abundantly.

Besides, when in the provinces they shall have been summoned as a result of the decision or the interlocutory sentence of him who rules the province, whether these persons are considered bishops [9] or clergymen of any rank or monks (provided they are proved to be orthodox), those who in their own lawsuits or contracts are accused should furnish no other persons as sureties than defenders of their own church or those whom they call stewards, lest, while a prosecutor's stubborn and greedy impudence demands extraneous sureties, a manifold discomfiture should be inflicted upon innocent poverty.

Moreover in this royal city,[13] when persons found coming from any province whatsoever in litigation shall have been accused in your Honour's court (which to them alone we have assigned), the orthodox faith's most reverend bishops [9] and certainly the stewards or the defenders of the Church or clergymen in their own civil or ecclesiastical lawsuits should not be molested by any insult of furnishing a surety, but either should be delivered wholly to substituted suretyships (which, however, the customary security of stipulations shall have fortified)[14] or should be entrusted to warranties [15] and their own declaration and the obligations of their own properties—with this being observed, nevertheless, that in ecclesiastical lawsuits it is right for no other person to be summoned except him whom the bishop's prudence shall have selected as superintendent of the poor, that is, the steward of the Church (for without doubt it is proper for this person to be appointed by the bishops [9]): and, however, we command him, when summoned, to be entrusted to the good faith of the defender of the Church.[16]

Collectors in all minor trials indeed [17] should not either hope or even dare to accept in the very summons of bishops [9] or of clergymen more than one half-aureus.[18]

But if an apparitor of your Grandeur pursuant to the decision of your most glorious office [19] shall have advised persons living in the province, we order him not to take more than two solidi [20] in the category of fees.[21] But in this magnificent city [13] the said apparitor of your Grandeur should be content with one aureus for the sake of fees [21] from provincial clergymen, no matter to what sum he who shall have been summoned should be exposed as liable.

Besides no collector should attempt to annoy any clergymen with contumelies, to molest them with incitements, to reproach them with insults, or to harass them with corporeal outrages—those persons who shall have undertaken anything of this kind, after the loss of their belt [22] and of their patrimony, deserving to be smitten straightway with the last punishment.[23]

With each and every privilege whatsoever generally as well as specifically assigned to the orthodox faith's sacrosanct churches, hostels, or almshouses perpetually to be reserved by all means, we command that these and their bishops [9] or clergymen of whatever rank or monks or beggars or hostel-wardens (considered as of the orthodox faith) should not be oppressed by any extraordinary public services.[24] For we judge it unsuitable to our age that upon most blessed men should be imposed these burdens of weight, which to rather many persons for a different reason we remit.

Besides, lest to anyone may be conceded his lucrative temerity and that calumniators' shameless audacity may be curbed, we order that as often as those who by a proposed action shall have summoned bishops [9] or clergymen or monks and all others above described either in your Grandeur's tribunal or in a provincial court, if, when the case has been heard, they shall have been convicted of having accused them without just and lawful claim, they should be compelled to repay to them all lawful costs and expenses, which, it shall have been established, they have endured from the outset of the controversy begun by the wickedness of these very persons;[25] that they, when recalled at least by this dread of justest censure and when assailed by continually persistent harassments, should assent that, after the clamours of disputes now have been quieted, they should restrain themselves, because necessity henceforth is their teacher.

Given at Constantinople on 4 April,[26] Marcian being consul.

1. No. 506 excepted, but see no. 510, n. 2, for an estimate of such exception.
2. See nos. 36 and 510, nn. 1 and 2.
3. E.g. 1 Cor. 16. 1–3; Acts 4. 32–5, 6. 1–6; Gal. 6. 10; *CA* 4. 9. See no. 127, n. 5.

515. CLERICAL DEFENDANTS IN LAWSUITS, 472   899

In the ecclesiastical establishment the depressed, the oppressed, the repressed, the suppressed long had had their haven. Such wealth as the Church had and was to have was the so-called patrimony of the poor (cf. St Ambrose, *Ep.* 18. 16 in *PL* 16. 1018), whom bishops, such as St Augustine in the West (Possidius, *Aug. Vita*, 23 *ad init.* = *PL* 32. 52–3) and St Chrysostom in the East (Palladius, *Dialogus de Vita Chrys.*, 5 *ad fin.* = *PG* 47. 20), supported from revenues received from the Church's possessions or even from the oblations of the faithful.

St Ambrose's phrase is *sumptus egenorum* (cf. the expressions in nos. 519, n. 8, and 520, n. 8) and his thought here is paralleled in his *De Officiis*, 2. 15, where he draws from Cicero's earlier treatise *De Officiis*, 2. 18. 62–3 (cf. 1. 14. 42— 17. 58 for Cicero's fuller presentation).

4. See no. 133, n. 1.

5. The earliest evidence (nos. 515, 518, 522, 537), which ranges in date from 472 to 518, increases in interest as it nears Justinian's accession. Since the same institution originally and often ministered to various needs and received foundlings, orphans, paupers, wayfarers (particularly poor pilgrims), the sick, and the aged, the strict differentiation implied by the names of these establishments arose gradually. That such institutions were founded first in the East accounts for the West's use of their names transliterated into Latin from Greek to designate the principal purpose of each establishment. On the subject of such "pious causes" consult P. W. Duff, "The Charitable Foundations of Byzantium" in P. H. Winfield and A. D. McNair, eds., *Cambridge Legal Essays . . . Bond . . . Buckland . . . Kenny* (Cambridge, 1926), 83–99.

6. Starting with no. 579 (q.v.).

7. See W. W. Buckland and A. D. McNair, *Roman Law and Common Law* [2] (Cambridge, 1952), 57–9.

8. Of the East.

9. See no. 16, n. 4.

10. The *Syro-Roman Lawbook* says that Leo "honoured in this also clerics, lest anyone could surrender any one of them because of debt—whether he should wish to surrender [a cleric] for a large [debt] or for a small [debt]" (*FIRA* 2. 794). But this restriction is rather narrow in view of the original ordinance.

11. A provincial governor's official residence, wherein a hall (*auditorium*) served as the courtroom for hearing cases pleaded in the provincial capital.

12. Pitra omits *and . . . temporarily*, which he considers some jurisconsult's comment.

13. Constantinople.

14. The editors suggest that this parenthesis perhaps should be appended to *declaration*, which in Greek versions it qualifies.

15. Provided by themselves.

16. Before the next paragraph the editors suggest that the following sentences (which the Greek versions contain) have been omitted from this Latin

law: "Non-orthodox collectors should not summon a bishop or a clergyman. And not even in the beginning heretics should be collectors. But if a heretic shall have had governmental service [see no. 186, n. 4] and shall have summoned a bishop or a clergyman of any rank whatever, he should be punished capitally. Orthodox".

This conjecture is confirmed by Pitra's late paraphrase, which has the first appearance of "collectors" as a singular noun, has "heretic" in the third sentence unexpressed but implied, and inserts "orthodox" before "bishop". The only difficulty with Pitra's text is the three forms of a verb derived apparently from κομπεύεσθαι, which is unreported anywhere and which the editors seem to equate with *convenire*. In the second sentence the verb appears as κομπευέσθωσαν and therefore should be translated "should summon", which is not the same as the editors' *exsecutores fiant* (should be collectors).

17. In Latin this sentence is a participial construction containing no finite verb.

18. The aureus, which was the standard Roman gold coin of the late Republic and throughout the Principate, was stabilized by Diocletian in 296 at sixty to the pound. See no. 433, n. 7.

The *Syro-Roman Lawbook* states that Leo "ordered that they [clerics] should pay as a fee [see no. 606, n. 20] a half-denarius; but if the collectors shall have exacted more, it should be recovered from them [collectors] double" (*FIRA* 2. 794–5).

19. See no. 311, n. 5.
20. See no. 433, n. 7.
21. See no. 606, n. 20.
22. See no. 476, n. 39.
23. That is, death.
24. See no. 226, n. 3.
25. The accusers, whose cases have been concocted illicitly.
26. Such is the rare reversed order.

516. MANDATE OF LEO I AND ANTHEMIUS ON FOSTER-FATHERS' MANAGEMENT OF WARDS' PROPERTY, 472

(*CI* 1. 3. 31)

In Justinian's Code this statute is set in the title "On Bishops and Clergymen", probably because the Church from apostolic days traditionally evinced an interest in orphans.[1] The only specific references to Christianity in this law regulating administration of orphans' property are that the care of orphans is a pious and religious duty and that some persons rear orphans through a God-fearing motive.

The same Augusti to Dioscore, praetorian prefect.[2]
With no subtlety of the law opposing, we order this renowned city's[3] foster-fathers of orphans, who indeed are their wards, just as if guardians, but of youths, just as if curators, without any inconvenience of a suretyship, in cases arising in court as well as outside court, as need shall have demanded, to defend and to protect, after the analogy of a guardian and of a curator, their persons and properties, if they can have any; in such a way, obviously, that in the presence of public persons, that is, recorders, or, when the transactions occur in this indeed renowned city,[3] before the most perfect master of the census, but in the provinces before their governors or the defenders of the places, their properties should be delivered to those persons by whom these must be guarded; that if they shall have perceived that any parts of the said properties ought to be alienated perhaps because of interest or another urgent cause or for the reason that they cannot be maintained, after an estimate has been made previously, it shall be permitted to them to enter a contract of alienation, that the monies for these properties, which are collected therefrom, may be guarded by the said persons.

Moreover it is proper for foster-fathers of orphans temporarily so to execute this sort of pious and religious duty that they should not at all be subjected to guardians' or curators' obligations to render account. For it is burdensome and unfair for them, who because of fear of God hasten to support and—as it were—with paternal affection to rear minors destitute of parents and of property, to be annoyed by certain persons' cunning machinations, if so it shall have happened.

Given on 1 June at Constantinople, Marcian being consul.

1. The part about visiting the fatherless in the famous definition of religion in Jas. 1. 27 is the positive aspect of the analogous prohibition in the Mosaic law (Ex. 22. 22), which the primitive Christians inherited first and then transmitted.

2. Of the East and, if the date is correct, an interrupter of Erythrius' tenure (see nos. 513–15 and 517).

3. Constantinople.

517. MANDATE OF LEO I AND ANTHEMIUS ON PRENUPTIAL GIFTS IN MIXED BETROTHALS, 472
(CI 1. 4. 16)

From a longer statute (CI 5. 1. 5) on the subject of disposition of premarital presents to bind a future marriage Justinian's compilers of his Code set amid the specifically Christian laws the following section concerning the disposal of such donations in the case of a fiancée's refusal to wed because of a difference in religion between her and her fiancé, the implication being that only one of the pair professes invincibly Christianity and that such tenacity is an impediment to successful wedlock.

The same Augusti to Erythrius, praetorian prefect.[1]
If intended nuptials have not been prohibited by laws and if after betrothal earnests [2] a fiancée [3] shall have refused marriage to a fiancé [4] because of difference of religion, if indeed it shall have been proved that, before the said betrothal earnests had been given, the woman or her parents have known this said situation, they are bound to impute this to themselves.[5]

But if, being ignorant of these matters, they shall have accepted betrothal earnests or, after earnests had been given, such a [6] reason for repentance shall have intervened, after only the said gifts have been returned they should be kept free in respect to a penalty of other than simple value.

And in like manner we decide also that this should be kept concerning promises in respect to earnests to be received and not presented.

Given on 1 July at Constantinople, Marcian being consul.

1. Of the East.
2. These prenuptial presents usually were unilateral (whether by fiancé to fiancée or *vice versa*) and were subject to return, if the marriage did not occur for a good reason, but remained with the innocent party when no good reason existed. When a fiancée dissolved the betrothal through her fault, the penalty was restoration of the gift and quadruple its value (CT 3. 5. 11; dated 380), but the present law lowered the penalty to the value of the gift. The larger law (see introd.) authorizes a quadruple penalty only if so specified at the betrothal; otherwise it makes no distinction in penalty, which is assessed at the simple value of he betrothal earnests, for dissolution of the betrothal by the fiancee with or without good reason. No penalty, is put on a fiancé who refuses to marry his fiancée. The gift ordinarily was mentioned in the betrothal contract and consequently was called *donatio ante* (later *propter*) *nuptias*.

3. In *CT* 3. 5. 6 (dated 335) it is said that a fiancée rarely gives a betrothal gift.

4. Here the larger law reads: "because of base or unchaste manner of life or difference of religion or of sect or for this reason, because the putative husband shall not have been able to perform coitus, whence hope of progeny arises, or on account of another just reason for excuse".

5. That is, their loss lies in the return of the gift.

6. The longer version for *such a* substitutes "any just".

518. MANDATE OF LEO I AND ANTHEMIUS ON PRIVILEGES FOR ECCLESIASTICAL INSTITUTIONS, 472

(*CI* 1. 3. 34)

By this directive are confirmed all privileges hitherto enjoyed by churches as well as by eleemosynary establishments managed by a certain Nico,[1] who, a priest, is concerned particularly with the oversight of orphans.

The same Augusti to Dioscore, praetorian prefect.[2]

By this pragmatic sanction we decree that in perpetuity should be guarded as firm and unimpaired all privileges, which by previous emperors or by your Serenity or by judicial directions or by gifts in regard to each and every circumstance whatsoever or by custom—whether concerning the right of providing quarters for guests or in any other matters whatsoever—have been presented to an orphanage or hermitages or churches or almshouses or hostels or monasteries and to all other persons also and properties of their legal control belonging to the administration of Nico, the most religious priest and fosterfather,[3] or to those persons who after him shall have succeeded to his post—according to the analogy of Zoticus [1] of most blessed memory, who is said to have devised previously the duty of this sort of piety. And indeed this seems to be exceedingly necessary, since truly support or training should be provided for orphans and needy persons and ecclesiastical uses and almshouses and hermitages.

With regard for piety we decree that also buildings and the other abovenamed properties belonging to the aforesaid man's administration or afterward in any way whatever about to come to his responsibility or that of those who after him shall have been called to the administration of the said orphanage should possess perpetually—after the fashion of this renowned city's venerable Great Church [4]—all the

c

privileges which the said holy Church either now obtains or later shall acquire.

Given on 23 December at Constantinople, Marcian being consul.

1. Not identifiable.
2. Of the East. See no. 516, n. 2.
3. Not so much a foster-father as a public guardian of orphans, as appears from the context (the word ὀρφανοτρόφος seems to contain both meanings), for such duty was performed usually by priests, because such establishments as here listed ordinarily were supervised by the clergy.
4. Hagia Sophia in Constantinople.

519. EDICT OF GLYCERIUS ON SIMONIACAL ORDINATION, 473

(PL 56. 896–8)

While Glycerius, one of the Burgundian-sponsored puppet-emperors of the West, in his brief reign of fifteen months was occupied chiefly with diverting from Italy into Gaul a Pannonian-originated Ostrogothic invasion, yet he found time to legislate against persons who procured ecclesiastical preferment to the episcopate through simony.[1]

Copy of the sacred edict of Emperor Glycerius given to the most distinguished Himelco, praetorian prefect of Italy.

At the beginning of our Sovereignty [2] nothing ought to be ordained by our Supernal Majesty's admonition sooner than that the Christian religion's sacrosanct mysteries [3] should be revered with rather great reverence, because it ought not to be doubted that God, the author of the universe, assists mortal affairs by so much the more as a purer worship has esteemed divine matters through the innocence of priests.

Hitherto living in the intercourse of private life, we indeed have had proof for a long time that by clergymen's increasing vices bishoprics for the most part are not acquired by merit but are procured by price—and this unbecoming cupidity has been made into a custom, as if it had been allowed now to appear as such. Zeal for a good conscience has been discarded and this has caused one to invoke by payment of money that for which one has been bound to hope from God.[4] Hence it has arisen that the power of secularism rather than respect for bishops is considered and that they, who used to be called bishops, prefer to be tyrant-ridden citizens [5] and that they by neglect of religion, since they are appointed under the patronage of men, care more for public than divine affairs, because they rejoice in impunity for their own delicts by this very privilege of perpetuity,[6] and that they, as if with the zeal of a certain management,[7] steal the churches' resources, which they, by covering the disgraceful deeds of their dastardly design, say are the riches of the poor,[8] by giving rewards to some at court,[9] by obligating themselves to others by financial bonds,[10] and by selling for the gain of the debtor what ought to be preserved for needy persons.[11]

Wherefore we believe that it has happened that the Divinity, offended because we show that we are experienced in so many evils, averted his Majesty's favour and vexed the Roman race with such great misfortunes as have come to pass. For with what effrontery or with what impudence is prayer addressed to the author of the whole world by him, who for the offering of sacrifice is not selected by the judgement of the Sacrosanct Trinity, but is elevated by men's favour? Or what can bishops of such a character, who have subjected the holy mysteries [3] to traffickings, not think is purchasable?

And quite moved by reason of these matters, we ordain by this law, which shall continue forever, that whoever shall have attained to the episcopate by the soliciting aid of persons, let him possess in worldly fashion what in wordly fashion he will have gotten—that is, that he should know that after the period of one year has ended he must be deprived of the episcopate. By all means the count of our patrimony [12] should control the disbursements of his ecclesiastical estate of the said year wherein he is called a bishop.[13]

Also whoever shall have consecrated such a person or shall have known that any money had been given or promised to anyone by him who is to be consecrated or shall have believed that there must have been tricky dissimulation in him who, he perceives, has wished to attain to this rank not by clean conscience but by base bribe, let him, having been demoted in equal manner [14] from his episcopate,[15] pay a similar penalty for indiscreet consecration—an opportunity for declaring this secret crime having been granted not only to those who have been appointed in the Church,[16] but also to any persons whatsoever of our religion, and all, who shall have been able to prove their accusations, knowing that they shall receive a reward for their holy accusation according to our will.[17]

Also citizens of any city whatsoever, whom not a person's worthiness, which ought to be sought, but venality, which ought to be punished, tempts to acclamations of candidates, should know that they must be expelled from residence in their native community, for which they have so bad regard, and that a large amount must be taken from their property and that it has been allocated to our fisc.[18]

Therefore from the churches let foul as well as profane auctioneering depart; let go-betweens of shameful bribery cease. It is a sin for heavenly matters to be settled in an auction. Let the great function of the episcopate [15]—as has been said—be solicited not by monies but by merits and, pursuant to the regulation of ancient bishops,[19] let the greatness and the character of the candidates be weighed and let the life of the selected one be examined. For it is too detestable that anyone at all, about to come to the honour of the episcopate by illicit corruption, should exhaust the Church's wealth, of which he ought to be the manager rather than the master, ere he obtains control of it.

And by this our Serenity's letter we think that the plans of perverse persons can be checked and that good consciences can be incited to greater enthusiasms for virtues. This also we cannot doubt about Almighty God's justice and righteousness, Himelco, dearest and fondest cousin: that more easily we ought to be protected by divine aids, from whose omnipotence we ask assistance through innocent and approved bishops.

Wherefore your illustrious and lofty Magnificence shall spread throughout the entire community of our Empire by the proclamation of an edict posted by you this our Serenity's law, which corrects both bishops and ministers [20] of the sacrosanct religion.

And by the divine hand: Farewell, Himelco, dearest and fondest cousin.

Given on 11 March at Ravenna, the Lord Leo Perpetual-Augustus being consul [21] for the fifth time.

---

1. Spiritual trade is termed simony, which is the desire both to sell and to buy spiritual things, that is, those which appertain to the sanctuary of God and to the cure of the soul. It owes its name to Simon Magus, the traditional founder of heresy, on whom see no. 422, n. 7, and who would have bought the gift which God had given by the Holy Ghost to St Peter and St John (Acts 8. 18–21).

2. Glycerius was proclaimed emperor on 5 March 473 and this edict was emitted on 11 March.

3. See no. 75, n. 42.

4. The Latin is rather compressed, but it is believed that the translation in the text preserves the sense.

5. This word (*tyrannopolita*) is reported only in St Sidonius (*Ep.* 5. 8. 3), for lexicographers ignore its presence in this *locus*. The idea seems to be that worldliness is the tyrant which bosses the bishops.

6. It is not clear what is meant by this phrase. Perhaps the notion is that they always can purchase immunity as they have bought their bishoprics.

7. This may be an oblique shaft against zealous peculation of civil officials, whose tactics bishops have copied.

8. The phrase is *pauperum divitiae* in a paradox. See nos. 515, n. 3 *ad fin.*, and 520, n. 8.

9. To gain advancement to the episcopate.

10. To get the money with which to offer bribes.

11. That is, they use the Church's wealth to discharge their personal obligations, a practice which results in their own gain.

12. If this constitution is correct, the *comes sacri patrimonii* as a finance minister was established in the West ere Anastasius I appointed him in the East at least eighteen years later, if the emperor made this innovation in the first year of his reign. Bury, 1. 442, knows only the Anastasian action, on which the law in *CI* 1. 34. 1 is undated and may be any time between 491 and 518.

13. See no. 16, n. 4.

14. That is, the consecrator(s) may not remain in office beyond the year of him who has been consecrated.

15. See no. 158, n. 1.

16. That is, the clergy as opposed to the laity, for whom provision is made next.

17. If the order of Latin words should be changed slightly, it would be possible to read what perhaps is meant: "for their accusation which according to our decision is holy".

18. It is hoped that the last two clauses represent the sense of what is meant, but it seems strange that no definite monetary penalty is set instead of the vague *large amount (tantum)*. Possibly the text is defective here as well as in the next sentence, which the editor certainly stigmatizes as such (*locus depravatus*).

19. The oldest qualifications for the episcopate were concocted by St Paul in 1 Tim. 3. 1–7, but council after council legislated on this matter.

20. In both classical and ecclesiastical Latin the fundamental idea of the word *minister* (here used) is an assistant to a higher personage. In Latin of this period it is applied to any ecclesiastical official below the rank of presbyter (priest) and it especially is associated with deacon; but in this document, since there is no point in opposing deacon to bishop, it should be taken to mean any cleric inferior to the episcopate. See no. 15, n. 3.

21. This word is supplied editorially.

520. EDICT OF HIMELCO, DIOSCORE, AURELIAN, AND PROTADIUS ON SIMONIACAL ORDINATION, 473

(*PL* 56. 898)

This edict implements the preceding imperial edict (no. 519).

Felix Himelco, praetorian prefect, Dioscore, Aurelian, Protadius the most distinguished praetorian prefects,[1] said·

520. SIMONIACAL ORDINATION, 473

As our lord, the most invincible [2] emperor, Glycerius, on behalf of the happiness of a better world and for the correction of his subjects,[3] has believed that by edictal ordinances it should be prevented lest anything resulting from episcopal [4] ordination should be essayed to the Supernal Majesty's harm and lest the merit of a good conscience should become the pretext for venal suffrage, it clearly shines in a previously produced response [5] of the royal speech, to wit, that divine matters may not be supported by worldly suffrages, in order that, after auctioneering has been abolished and crimes of wicked deeds have been abrogated, the criterion of an excellent conscience should confer possession of episcopal [4] lappets,[6] lest what ought to have been useful, obviously, to conciliate the Divine Clemency's Majesty by pious distributions [7] should be expended, like secular aids, in acquisitions of patronage, which money surely a heart devoted to the Supernal Majesty—and not an avaricious one—had collected for the support of the poor.[8]

Nor anyone of profane plan of life should exist, who as a bishop [9] should be obliged to differ from such religious regulations with sacrilegious mind, unless anyone shall have wished to make admission about the guilty conscience of his own promising. For, as we trust that these decrees will please men of praiseworthy morals, so we do not doubt that men of baser minds will be offended at these salutary statutes.

Accordingly we have believed that the whole world ought to be reminded by this edictal proclamation that henceforth they should withdraw themselves from unlawful canvassings and suffrages, lest it should be necessary, in connection with the entanglement of their own guilty conscience, which always in the Divine Majesty's concern is considered punishable, to undergo pursuant to the most sacred statutes the punishment for their own sin.

Given on 29 April at Rome.

1. Though from the previous edict (no. 519) it is obvious that Himelco, praetorian prefect of Italy, is to arrange for its implementation, yet according to custom he associates with himself in its superscription his three colleagues in the other prefectures of the Empire.

While Dioscore seems to have been praetorian prefect of the Orient (see n. 2 to nos. 516 and 518), yet scholars are not agreed about the offices held by Aurelian and Protadius. Haenel assigns to Aurelian the praetorian prefecture of Illyricum and to Protadius that of the Gauls; Ziradini reverses this assignment; Mommsen makes Aurelian Protadius one person and is uncertain about his post; Seeck supposes that Dioscore Aurelian Protadius is one person and a praetor. Consult B. Borghesi, *Les préfets du prétoire* (Paris, 1897), 480, 747.

2. The hollowness, if not the absurdity, of some of the imperial titles (see no.

124, n. 9) is illustrated by this superlative adjective. No exploit of Glycerius on a battlefield is known by the time of this edict's emission, for his removal of the threat of an Ostrogothic invasion was due only to his diplomacy, and no information about any other important public act of his has been transmitted to us. Even if he had been *most invincible* during the 55 days between his accession and the publication of his prefect's edict, his end belied his epithet, because, when Leo I's nominee, Julius Nepos, landed in Italy, probably escorted by eastern soldiers, Glycerius seems not to have staged any resistance to his rival and appears to have accepted deposition without defiance.

3. Literally "mortals".
4. See no. 526, n. 11.
5. See no. 218, n. 5.
6. The two lappets attached with fringed ends to the back of a mitre still are called *infulae* (the word used here symbolically for the office of the mitre's wearer), though *fasciae* and *vittae* also occur. Under the pagan dispensation they seem to have been a white and red band of woollen stuff, worn upon a priest's forehead as a sign of religious consecration and of personal inviolability. In early Christian usage the mitre was held more firmly upon the head by tying the lappets under the chin (so A. A. King, *Liturgy of the Roman Church* [London, 1957], 142). Lappets later were assumed as a badge of public office and as such were affected by the emperors (see no. 630, n. 9).
7. The idea is that money given to charitable projects wins God's blessing upon the giver. That almsgiving anoints the soul is an age-old supposition and finds its Biblical sanction in such passages as Ps. 41. 1, Prov. 19. 17, Tobit 4. 7-9, Matt. 5. 16, Luke 19. 8, Acts 20. 35, 2 Cor. 9. 6-7, Gal. 6. 10, 1 Tim. 6. 17-19, Heb. 13. 16, 1 John 3. 17. See no. 515, n. 3.
8. See nos. 515, n. 3, and 519, n. 8. The phrase here is *alimonia pauperum*.
9. See no. 16, n. 4.

521. MANDATE OF LEO I AND ZENO ON TREASURE-TROVE, 474

(*CI* 10. 15. 1)

Only the beginning of this constitution is translated, for only it has religious significance, in that the sovereigns regard discovery and use of treasure-trove as a divine benefit bestowed on mankind.

Emperors Leo and Zeno Augusti to Epinicus, consular.[1]
None for the future should dare to disturb our Piety's benign ears by effusive prayers about treasure to be sought on his own or another's

ground or about it when found by another or by himself. For we grant to each and everyone free power, lest invidious calumny should attend God's further benefit,[2] to seek on his own grounds, indeed, provided without wicked and punishable sacrifices [3] or any other art odious to the laws, and to use, when found, treasure (that is, movable things hidden by unknown owners in an older time), that it may be superfluous to demand by prayers this which already by law has been allowed [4] and that the liberality of the imperial magnanimity may seem to anticipate demands . . .

Given on 10 October, Leo Junior [5] Augustus being consul.

1. Mommsen suggests that for *consular* should be written "count of the sacred largesses". At this time in Latin *consularis* meant not necessarily an ex-consul, but was applied to governors of certain provinces.

2. Discovery of treasure traditionally appears to be a stroke of luck, a windfall, a gift from the gods (see no. 223, n. 2 *ad init.*), and under the Christian dispensation a divine benefaction. The notion seems to be that a person falsely and enviously laying legal claim to the finder's find impairs the discoverer's enjoyment of his discovery, since God's first benefit would be the discovery and his further benefit would be the use of what has been found. For divine assistance in finding treasure-trove see no. 223, n. 2 *ad med.*

3. In the rest of the constitution nothing is said about what penalty will be assessed against persons utilizing sacrifices and (magical) arts to assist their search.

4. See no. 223 and the laws therein cited in n. 3.

5. The four-year-old grandson of Leo I. He succeeded his grandfather in 474 and also died within that year of his grandsire's death.

522. LAW OF ZENO ON PROMISES ABOUT SHRINES AND CHARITABLE INSTITUTIONS, 474-7

(CI 1. 2. 15)

By this defective [1] and ungrammatical statute Zeno rules that a promise to erect Christian oratories and charitable institutions should be binding on the promissor and his heirs, who are liable to lawsuits on failure to perform the promise.

Since a promise without consideration, unless it had been made by stipulation, seems to have been invalid hitherto, this introduction of an action to support an informal promise of a donation marks an innovation in Roman law.[2]

522. SHRINES AND CHARITABLE INSTITUTIONS, 474-7

Emperor Zeno Augustus.

... If anyone should make a donation of movable or immovable or self-moving properties [3] or of any legal status whatever to the legal personality of any martyr or apostle or prophet or the holy angels at all,[4] as being about to build a house of prayer [5] to the memory of the one for whose name he arranges the pious donation, the said donation, if only he has exhibited the transaction of the records according to the divine ordinances [6] (and in these cases it is necessary to know this), is valid and in every way is in exaction,[7] if the holy building has been begun or if it has not been begun, but has been promised only by donation, the donor has shown [8] his own intention, so that both he and his heirs should be liable to an action for what has been professed piously and they should build the sacred oratory,[9] which is promised—as has been said—by the donation, and should furnish unfailingly to it, when built or while being built, the enjoyment coming from the said liberality.

In every way let the same things be valid also in the so-called hostels or hospitals or almshouses, professed to be built by donations according to the way as has been aforesaid.

To the most God-beloved bishops in every place or to the most devout stewards is given licence to instigate appropriate action in accordance with this our divine ordinance against persons in need of judicial compulsion—which indeed it is unseemly even to mention—in matters wherein they have professed piously.[10]

However, in reference to this regulation, that when the matters which are agreeable to this law have been fulfilled and when the pious profession of the donors has been transmitted into deed, it should be granted that the administration of the donations should proceed according to what has seemed best to the givers and according to the regulations imposed upon them.[11]

1. The superscription is restored and the subscription is missing. From its position in the Code it may be dated 474-7, for Zeno's reign began in 474 and the subsequent statute by him is dated 477. Editors indicate that the opening words are lost.
2. See no. 601, n. 3.
3. Usually, but not necessarily, livestock.
4. From as early as Constantine I's reign (see no. 36), Roman law recognized and regulated gifts of real and personal property to ecclesiastical establishments. Doubtless some of such donations were welcomed by the clergy, who encouraged gifts as a means of averting God's wrath or of thwarting Satan's malice in times of natural calamities and of epidemics, especially the latter, for as later was remarked by a noted French Jesuit explorer and historian, Pierre François Xavier de Charlevoix (1682-1761), "pestilences are the harvests of the

ministers of God" (quoted by A. D. White, *A History of the Warfare of Science with Theology in Christendom* [New York, 1932], 2. 71, n.).

5. That is, an oratory, which εὐκτήριος (of prayer) without οἶκος (house) can mean, when used substantively in the neuter gender as at n. 9 *infra* in text.

6. By *CT* 8. 12. 1 and 3 (dated 316 or 323 and ?316; cf. *CT* 8. 12. 5 and 6 [dated 333 and 341]) Constantine I enacted that gifts must be registered in writing. Constantine's further requirement, that delivery of the property should occur (*CT* 8. 12. 1; cf. *CT* 8. 12. 7 [dated 355]), is abrogated by this law. See nos. 581, n. 4, and 596, n. 5.

7. That is, demand for fulfilment can be made.

8. The Greek verb is subjunctive and depends on some expression now lost at the beginning of the law.

9. Cf. *supra* n. 5.

10. This sentence lacks a principal verb in both Greek and Latin, being construed as a genitive absolute in the former and as an ablative absolute in the latter.

11. This sentence also has no principal verb in either the Greek original or the Latin translation. Some phrase such as "we decree" after *regulation* should be supplied to complete the sense.

523. EDICT OF ZENO ON RETENTION OF THE URBAN EPISCOPATE, (?)474–84

(*CI* 1. 3. 35)

This defective statute, which has an editorially supplied superscription and lacks a subscription, from its position in the Code cannot be dated after the first decade of Zeno's reign. With two exceptions (explained in the law), the emperor authorizes each city to have its own bishop [1] (in opposition to the ecclesiastical encroachment of larger cities upon smaller cities, especially when the latters' sees fall vacant) and assigns a penalty for contraveners of his constitution.

Emperor Zeno Augustus.

... We ordain that every city, whether renewed in preceding times or not extant previously but through imperial munificence created,[2] by all means should have its inseparable and own bishop, who will have the management of ecclesiastical matters in it—to none being permission absolutely through any means whatsoever or indeed through a sacred imperial order to take from any city whatsoever its proper episcopate or also the territory demarcated for it or any particular legal right and to make it tributary to other cities in this particular or otherwise in any way whatsoever.

Not only shall be invalid the attempt of a person acting contrary to these things and trying to take from cities already renewed or places built into cities or hereafter perhaps to be renewed or to be built into cities the legal right of its proper episcopate or to take any other thing of the privileges conferred or even about to be conferred upon them, but also he himself who opposes the common and each individual advantage, when dishonoured, shall be stripped of his property—the same punishments being valid also against him who (as has been said previously) attempts to do any such thing also through an imperial rescript.

Having ordered these regulations generally and having taken into consideration the condition of the most holy churches disposed in dependence upon Tomi of the Scythians' province and because it is not possible for the said most holy churches, which are damaged by barbarians' incessant inroads[3] or even otherwise somehow live together in poverty, to be preserved otherwise, unless it should happen through the forethought of the God-beloved bishop of Tomi (which is also the nation's metropolis), we ordain that these should be exempted from the present sacred legislation and nowise should be subjected to its compulsion, but should remain in their own status.[4]

And in the same manner we wish the city built recently into a city in the Isaurians'[5] nation to the honour and the worship of the gloriously triumphant martyr Conon,[6] that is, the city of the Leontopolitans, to be exempted from the rules presently legislated, so that it should remain in its status (just as it now is), because—for many persons dispute exceedingly eagerly whether it is proper for it to have a bishop separately or to be counted under the care and the foresight of the most God-beloved bishop of Isauropolis—it has seemed to be a city and to enjoy political rights unceasingly and to the full, but that it should remain always under the care of the said bishop.

1. Evagrius (*HE* 3. 12) reports that Emperor Zeno sanctioned by law that he whom both the clergy and the people should have chosen after the death of Timothy III (d. 482), patriarch of Alexandria, would be the bishop of that see. This action, of course, was not the first instance of imperial intervention in episcopal selection (see e.g. no. 61), but it testifies to the late continuance of clerical and laic election in the East, where generally the choice of bishops was confined to provincial bishops after 325, when the First General Council of Nicaea recommended (canon 4) that a bishop should be constituted by all the bishops of the province wherein his see was situated.

The history of episcopal appointment ascends, of course, to the apostolic age, when the apostles apparently selected their successors. Thus St Paul left St Titus, traditionally the first bishop of the Cretans, in Crete with authority to ordain presbyters (Titus 1. 4-5; Eusebius, *HE* 3. 4. 5) and consecrated St Timothy, traditionally the first bishop of the Ephesians, at Ephesus with directions to defend the faith (1 Tim. 1. 3, 2 Tim. 1. 6; Eusebius, loc. cit.). But by the mid-third century St Cyprian, bishop of Carthage, writes that Pope St Cornelius (251-3) was made bishop of Rome by the judgement of God and of his Christ, by the testimony of almost all the clergy, by the suffrage of the populace which then was there, by the college of ancient priests (*sacerdotes*) and of good men, when none had been made so before him (*Ep.* 55. 8 = CSEL 3. 629-30; cf. *Ep.* 68. 2 = CSEL 3. 745). This kind of choice continued in the West (see e.g. introd. to no. 137, no. 352, n. 2), for the Latin canonists interpreted the Nicene canon as simply requiring the provincial bishops' presence at the consecration. Popular election persisted among Roman Catholics until the eleventh century, when the bishop began to be elected by the clergy of the cathedral church.

Participation by the people in episcopal election perhaps emanated from the practice in pagan Rome. There the pontifex maximus (on whom see Introd., n. 26 *ad med.*) was elected by vote of seventeen of the thirty-five tribes (chosen by sortition) of the Tribal Assembly as early as 212 B.C. and by 104 B.C. the priests (*sacerdotes*) of the three great political priesthoods (pontiffs, augurs, quindecimvirs), who previously had been chosen by their colleagues, were selected by the people (Paterculus, *Hist. Rom.* 2. 12. 3; Suetonius, *Nero*, 2. 1).

2. The most obvious examples are the four eastern patriarchal cities: Alexandria, founded by Alexander the Great in 332 B.C.; Antioch, constructed by Seleucus I Nicator in 300 B.C.; Jerusalem, refounded by Hadrian as Aelia Capitolina in 130; Constantinople, rebuilt from Byzantium by Constantine I in 330.

3. Barbarian forays into the territory of Tomi (later Constantiana, now Constanta) along the Black Sea were recorded during 8-16, when the poet Ovid, then in exile there, in his *Tristia* (e.g. 3. 10. 51-76, 4. 1. 75-84, 5. 10. 15-34) and *Epistulae ex Ponto* (e.g. 1. 2. 13-22) reported in vivid verse what troubles the townsfolk suffered from the savage tribesmen. It is of melancholy interest to mark that after more than four centuries conditions had not improved, despite the temporary annexation of Dacia (Rumania) across the Danube as a buffer province (106-271).

4. That is, the statute waives the theory and accepts the fact that the bishop of Tomi, who, as metropolitan of the province of Scythia Minor, alone appeared competent, though compelled by circumstances external to his and the emperor's control, to administer what measures he could enforce, even though such action meant a decrease of civic rights in that region.

5. From the district of Isauria in Asia Minor came the imperial author of this statute. So far as recorded history ascends, it reports that the Isaurians, ever impatient of imposed control, proved a sharp thorn in the side of their con-

querors and a predatory menace to their neighbours (see no. 302). Although subdued by Publius Servilius Vatia in 75 B.C. to such a degree that he acquired the *agnomen* Isauricus and celebrated a brilliant triumph in Rome for his conquest, Isauria seems never to have been a district of proper provincial status until sometime in the Dominate, but for about four centuries after its Servilian subjugation (which was little more than nominal, as the event showed) remained a semi-autonomous enclave, admitting perfunctory allegiance to Rome, when it suited its predators or after occasional punishment, and was gerrymandered from time to time among adjacent provinces for administrative purposes. Upon acquisition of provincial rank the insubordinate nature of its montane inhabitants achieved added notoriety in that it was one of the few provinces wherein the civil powers were invested in the military governor, for the *comes* (count) there was likewise the *praeses* (governor). Under Anastasius I, who succeeded Zeno, Isaurian interference with circumjacent citizens was reduced so much by his measures, that by Justinian I's accession their banditry ceased to be conspicuously bothersome.

6. Probably the martyr of this name under Decius (249–51) in Pamphylia, a province adjacent to Isauria.

524. LETTER AND EDICT OF BASILISCUS AND MARK ON THE CHRISTIAN FAITH, 475

(Evagrius, *HE* 3. 4 and 7)

These encyclicals are imperial enactments of Basiliscus (who usurped the sovereignty of the Eastern Roman Empire from Zeno, his nephew by marriage, for about twenty months in 475–6) and of his son Mark first to anathematize the *Tome* of Leo[1] and the canons of the Council of Chalcedon[2] and then to repudiate this condemnation by rescission of the anathema.[3]

Zacharias Rhetor *sive* Mytilenaeus quotes portions of the letter in his Syriac chronicle (*Chron.* 5. 2),[4] but Nicephorus has in Greek both letter and edict (*HE* 16. 3 and 7).

I. Encyclical of Basiliscus.[5]

Emperor Caesar Basiliscus, Pious, Victor, Triumpher, Greatest, Ever-August, Augustus and Mark, Noblest Caesar[6] to Timothy, the most reverend and most God-beloved archbishop of the Alexandrians' megalopolis.[7]

As many laws in behalf of the correct and apostolic faith as the most pious emperors before us—all who have persevered correctly in worshipping the Blessed,[8] Ageless, and Life-giving Trinity—have ordained, these we wish to be invalid for no time at all, by reason of having been always in the past salutary for the whole world, but rather we promulgate them as our own personal laws.[9]

We, preferring before every effort concerned with human affairs piety and zeal in behalf of our God and Saviour Jesus Christ, who has created and has glorified us, believing also that the unifying bond of Christ's flocks is the salvation of us and of every subject, both an unbroken foundation and an unshattered wall of our Empire, consequently incited reasonably by godly zeal of intention and bringing to our God and Saviour Jesus Christ the unity of the holy Church as the first-fruits of our reign, ordain that the basis and the security of human well-being, that is, the creed of the 318 holy fathers, who long ago in Nicaea with the Holy Spirit had been assembled,[10] into which both we and all believers before us have been baptized,[11] only should govern and should prevail over the orthodox people in all God's holiest churches as the only definition of the precisely fixed faith and sufficient for the destruction of every heresy entirely and for the utmost unity of God's holy churches—the acts in this royal city[12] by the 150 holy fathers for the confirmation of the sacred symbol itself against those who blaspheme against the Holy Spirit[13] and, besides, all the acts in the Ephesians' metropolis[14] against the impious Nestorius[15] and those who afterward were of that one's mind, of course, having their own validity.[16]

But the things which have divided the unity and the good order of God's holy churches and all the world's peace, manifestly Leo's so-called *Tome*[1] and all the things which in Chalcedon[17] have been said and have been transacted[8] for an innovation against the mentioned holy creed of the 318 holy fathers[10] in definition of the faith or in exposition of the creed or of interpretation or of instruction or of discourse, we ordain that they should be anathematized both here and everywhere in every church by the most holy bishops everywhere and that they should be committed to fire, wherever they may be found, because concerning[18] all heretical dogmas Constantine and Theodosius the Younger[19] (the emperors who were of pious and blessed lot before us) so have ordained; and that, since they thus have become invalid, they should be discarded from the one and only Catholic and Apostolic Orthodox Church as repealing the everlasting and saving definitions of the 318 holy fathers[10] and those of the blessed fathers who in the Holy Spirit declared decrees at Ephesus;[20] and that, in short, it never should be permitted to anyone either of priests or of laymen to devise for himself any deviation from that most sacred statute of the holy creed; and that with all the innovations made in Chalcedon[17] against the sacred creed there should be anathematized also the heresy of those not confessing that the Only-Begotten

Son of God in truth was made into flesh and assumed man's nature from the Holy Spirit and from Mary, the Holy and Ever-Virgin and Mother of God, but talking marvels—that he was either from heaven or according to fantasy and appearance; in short, every heresy, and whatever other thing at whatever time and in whatever manner and at whatever place of the whole world had been devised as an innovation in respect to thought and word toward the transgression of the sacred creed.[21]

But since it is the property of royal providence from its predictive inspection to lavish upon its subjects security, not only for the present but also for the future time, we ordain that the most holy bishops everywhere should subscribe to this our sacred encyclical epistle, when shown to them, distinctly declaring that they submit to only the sacred creed of the 318 holy fathers,[10] which the 150 fathers confirmed,[13] as it seemed best by definition also to the most holy fathers who subsequently convened in the Ephesians' metropolis [14] that it is necessary to agree to only the holy creed of the 318 holy fathers [10] for a definition of faith, while they anathematize every obstacle for the orthodox people produced in Chalcedon [17] and entirely eject these from the churches as being obstructive to the world's and our welfare.

The persons who, after these our sacred letters—which we believe have been promulgated according to God, since they treat the unity desired by all for God's holy churches—attempt ever to advance or actually to name the innovation against the faith produced in Chalcedon,[17] whether [22] in instruction or in discourse or in writing at whatever time or in whatever manner or at whatever place, such persons, as sharing the blame for disturbance and confusion in respect to God's holy churches and every subject and as hostile to both God and our salvation, we command—according to the laws, suppended to this our sacred encyclical,[23] already ordained before us by Emperor Theodosius (who is in blessed and sacred lot) against such malice— that, if they should be bishops or clergymen, they should be deposed, if monks or laics, they should be subjected to exile and to every kind of confiscation and to extreme penalties. For thus the Holy and Homoousian Trinity, both creator and vivifier of all things, ever in the past worshipped by our Piety and now being served by us through the destruction of the mentioned tares [24] and the confirmation of the correct and apostolic traditions of the holy creed, thereby becoming propitious and well-disposed to both our souls and every subject, shall administer [25] with us continually and shall bring peace to human affairs.

II. Counter-encyclical [26] of Basiliscus.

Emperors Caesars Basiliscus and Mark.

We ordain that the apostolic and orthodox faith, which from the beginning and from the first in the Catholic churches has prevailed, which until our reign has prevailed and during our reign prevails and in perpetuity ought to prevail, into which also we have been baptized and in which we believe, itself alone should prevail unimpaired and unmoved and, so prevailing, continually should be in authority in all the Catholic and apostolic churches of the orthodox and that nothing else should be sought. On this account also we command that the acts produced in our reign—whether encyclicals or [27] also others or anything at all as regards faith or ecclesiastical constitution—should be invalid and should be brought to an end, while Nestorius [15] and Eutyches [28] and every other heresy and all who are likeminded are anathematized; and that concerning this subject there should not be a synod or other investigation, but that these matters should remain unbroken and unmoved; and that to Acacius,[3] the most reverend and most holy patriarch and archbishop, should be restored the provinces, the ordination to which this royal and glorious city's [12] see [29] used to have—the present most God-beloved bishops, of course, remaining in their own sees,[29] no prejudice arising from this [30] after their death to the legal right of ordination belonging to this royal and glorious city's [12] holy [31] see.[32]

That this our sacred statute imposes the force of a sacred ordinance is ambiguous to none.

1. In 449 Pope St Leo I the Great sent this celebrated dogmatic epistle, defending the orthodox doctrine on Christ's incarnation, to St Flavian, patriarch of Constantinople.

2. Timothy the Cat (Timotheus II Aelurus), Monophysite patriarch of Alexandria, whom Basiliscus had recalled from an exile enduring for almost eighteen years, persuaded the usurper to declare for heresy by issuing this encyclical.

3. Acacius, patriarch of Constantinople, so skilfully excited the Constantinopolitan monks (always avid for action) and citizens that their demonstration (see no. 411, n. 3 *ad fin.*) induced Basiliscus to rescind his circular letter and to issue a counter-encyclical.

It appears that Acacius, from whom is named the Acacian schism (on which see introd. to no. 527), was nothing profounder than a politician endeavouring to achieve his personal ends. It seems also that he had no thorough perception of theological principles.

4. Zacharias' version is so loose that to compare it word by word with Evagrius' Greek, which Nicephorus rather carefully copies, will serve no useful purpose. After giving (in n. 9 *infra*) a sample of how the first paragraph of the text appears in F. J. Hamilton's and E. W. Brooks' translation of Zacharias' Syriac (London, 1899), only major discrepancies in idea will be noted.

5. Zacharias' caption is "The second chapter tells about the encyclical letter of Basiliscus and Marcus, which is to the following effect" and Nicephorus reads "The encyclical letters against the holy fourth synod, written by Basiliscus, from the procurement of Timothy and Peter".

6. See no. 28, n. 7.

7. Zacharias' superscription is "The king Basiliscus, the believing, victorious, all-virtuous ruler, Augustus, along with Marcus the most illustrious Caesar, to Timothy the reverend and God-loving archbishop of the great city Alexandria".

8. Nicephorus inserts "and".

9. In pursuance of the decision made in n. 4 *supra* Zacharias for this paragraph reads: "Concerning all the laws justly and righteously enacted by the believing and memorable kings who have gone before us, for the salvation and good guidance of all the world and in defence of the true faith as taught by the apostles and holy fathers, it is our will that all these laws should be ratified and not lightly annulled. Rather do we agree to them and hold them to be of equal validity with our own."

10. In 325 at the First Ecumenical Council, when the Nicene Creed was formulated.

11. Nicephorus inserts "this".

12. Constantinople.

13. The Second Ecumenical Council in 381 is meant. The 150 prelates are said both to have confirmed and to have supplemented the Nicene Creed at Constantinople.

14. The Third Ecumenical Council in 431. About two hundred prelates there condemned Nestorianism and defended the divine maternity of the Blessed Virgin Mary.

Zacharias speaks of "the faith which was also confirmed by the transactions of the two Councils of Ephesus, along with the chief priests of Rome and Alexandria, Celestine and Cyril and Dioscorus, in condemnation of the heretic Nestorius".

If he couples the Third General Council of 431 with the Robber Council of 449 (both held at Ephesus)—and no other important synod of Ephesus is known between 431 and the date of Basiliscus' encyclical—Zacharias has made a sorry union, for, so far from confirming the faith, the Robber Council under the direction of Dioscore, patriarch of Alexandria, rehabilitated Eutyches, archimandrite of Constantinople, who founded Eutychianism, and deposed the saintly Flavian, patriarch of Constantinople, who died from maltreatment in prison.

15. Patriarch of Constantinople and founder of Nestorianism.

16. That is, the emperor's choice of the creed composed at Nicaea was without prejudice of the canons decreed at the two later general councils of 381 and 431.

17. The Fourth Ecumenical Council in 451 is meant. The prelates, who numbered between 150 and 665 (if the larger number is correct, it was the

largest of the general councils held till 1123 and it has been exceeded since then only four times—1139, 1215, 1869–70, 1962–5—so far as accredited prelates assisting, exclusive of visitors, are concerned), condemned Eutychianism (Monophysitism) and declared that in Christ are two natures: human and divine.

18. Nicephorus erroneously reads "from" (παρά for περί).
19. That is, Constantine I and Theodosius II. See e.g. *CT* 16. 5. 1, 2, 38–66 for legislation of the one or the other against heretics.
20. Again (cf. n. 14 *supra*) Zacharias mentions two synods at Ephesus.
21. About here Zacharias' excerpt ends.
22. Nicephorus omits this word.
23. Neither Evagrius nor Nicephorus adds these laws.
24. See Matt. 13. 24–30, 36–40.
25. Nicephorus substitutes "live".
26. Plural in Nicephorus.
27. Nicephorus omits *encyclicals or*.
28. Since Constantinopolitan heresiarchs and their doctrines, which taught unorthodox views on the person of Christ, were condemned at the Council of Chalcedon, this anti-circular now reverses Basiliscus' previous position.
29. See no. 311, n. 5.
30. Nicephorus omits the phrase.
31. Or "illustrious". It is impossible to distinguish between these Greek adjectives except in poetry, for the only difference is the quantity of the penult.
32. The emperor's earlier encyclical in annulling the conciliar canons of Chalcedon apparently abrogated the Constantinopolitan patriarchate's jurisdiction over the Levantine churches, which the Synod of Chalcedon had subjected to the see of Constantinople (canon 28). This counter-circular restores this authority.
Cf. *supra* n. 29.

525. MANDATE OF ZENO ON CONCUBINES' MARRIAGES AND ON LEGITIMATION OF CHILDREN, 477

(*CI* 5. 27. 5)

The chief Christian interest in this law, which authorizes men to marry their free-born concubines and which legitimates children born from such women before their marriages and previous to the law's publication, is the testimony in the preamble to the Christianization of the Empire inaugurated by Constantine I,[1] whose constitution on concubinage [2] the present law partially re-enacts. Zeno, however, refuses legitimation to bastards born to concubines

525. MARRIAGES AND CHILDREN, 477

after the law's promulgation, since henceforth men may marry their concubines and may have from them legitimate children.[3]

Since Constantine's law on natural children and their mothers has not survived,[4] it is impossible to say whether or not his conversion to Christianity influenced his legislation on this topic, for it could have been promulgated before his interest in the Christian conception of marriage had been excited and, moreover, such an enactment could have been effected equally under a non-Christian régime.

Emperor Zeno Augustus to Sebastian, praetorian prefect.[5]

Renewing the most sacred constitution of the deified [6] Constantine, who with the Christians' venerable faith protected the Roman Empire, concerning taking free-born concubines as wives, rather also concerning considering children born from the said women either before marriage or afterward as their own and legitimate, we order that they who before this law have procreated children of any sex whatever by a chosen concubinage of free-born women (marriage not intervening) and who, of course, have no wife and no legitimate offspring acknowledged from a lawful marriage, if they shall have wished to take as wives them who previously had been concubines, should be able to contract a legitimate wedlock with free-born women of this kind—as has been said—as well as that children of each sex, procreated from a previous concubinage of the said women, as soon as marriage with their mothers shall have been celebrated, should be his own, so far as the father is concerned, and in his power also with those who afterward shall have been acknowledged from the said marriage or only those, if no other then should be born; the children[7] should succeed also anew their fathers so wishing in accord with a will[8] as well as should seek a paternal inheritance by intestacy—the pacts which at the time of marriage shall have ensued concerning dotal property or property of a donation before marriage also pertaining to their persons,[9] that the children[7] along with their brothers[10] perchance born afterward from the said parents or they only, if no other has been procreated, should receive the dowry and the donation before marriage in view of the laws' tenor and also the pacts' emoluments.[9].

But those persons who at the time of this most sacred law not yet have acquired any offspring from association of free-born concubines should not at all enjoy this law's benefit, since it is permitted to them, when legitimate children or wives do not exist, to bind the said women by the legal right of marriage to themselves previously and to procreate legitimate children, namely by preceding marriage, nor they whom they shall have wished to be born from a free-born concubine, when after this law marriage has been postponed, ought to demand especially that they should appear afterward lawful and legitimate.

Given on 20 February after the consulate of Armatus.

1. It is of interest, perhaps, to note that the first Christian emperor's mother, St Helena, a Bithynian barmaid, is said by some ancient historians (e.g. Zosimus and Orosius) to have been first the concubine and then the wife of Constantius I Chlorus (305-6), who afterward was compelled, when he was chosen Caesar in 292, to repudiate her for remarriage with Theodora, Maximian I's (286-305, 306-10) stepdaughter.

2. Though the relation of the sexes in concubinage (*concubinatus*) was not unlike marriage (*matrimonium*) in many respects, the chief difference was that in the former a father could not claim legally paternal power (*patria potestas*) over children born from his concubine, although he probably exercised ordinary paternal rights over their education in all its phases.

Concubinage, though recognized in Roman law, was discouraged by Christian emperors, who disapproved it. For legislation on concubinage and on natural children and on their mothers, who usually were concubines, see *CT* 4. 6; *LNT* 22; *LNMarc*. 4; *CI* 5. 26-7; see also *D* 25. 7.

3. By *CI* 5. 27. 10 in 529, however, Justinian revived Constantine's statute and cancelled Zeno's harsh constitution on this point.

4. It apparently stood as *CT* 4. 6. 1 and reference to it is in *LNMarc*. 4. 1. 4.

5. Of the East.

6. See no. 127, n. 7.

7. The last two words are supplied in the translation for clarity and to serve as the subject of the later *should succeed* and *should receive*.

8. Then, as now, parents could disinherit children by so stating in their testaments (see no. 496, n. 12).

9. See no. 517, n. 2.

10. The word (*fratres*) must be understood to include sisters.

526. MANDATE OF ZENO ON RESCISSION OF BASILISCUS' ECCLESIASTICAL LEGISLATION, 477

(*CI* 1. 2. 16)

During the twenty months of Basiliscus' usurpation of the Eastern Empire the tyrant's Monophysitic predilections produced ordinances against orthodoxy (see no. 524). After his recovery of the sovereignty Zeno abrogates in this constitution whatever Basiliscus legislated against the ecclesiastical establishment and he restores particularly in this statute the Constantinopolitan patriarchate's privileged position, which Basiliscus impaired under the influence of Timothy II Aelurus, patriarch of Alexandria.

The same Augustus to Sebastian, praetorian prefect.[1]

We decree that, after the things which in a certain manner have been done against the very God of the orthodox religion have been abrogated and have been annulled totally, there should be restored to their full right and should be recalled to their regularity all things which before our Gentleness' departure [2] prevailed firmly concerning the orthodox religion's faith and the status of the most holy churches and martyries: the things to be abrogated utterly which in the time of the tyranny [3] have been renewed against these:[4] both against the venerable churches, whose episcopal supervision [5] our Piety's father, Acacius, the most blessed and most religious bishop and patriarch [6] administers, and against all other churches, which are situated throughout the different provinces, and also against their most reverent bishops, whether about the right of episcopal elections [7] or about the expulsion of any bishop whatever in those times caused by anyone at all or about the prerogative of seating before others [8] in a council of bishops or outside a council or about metropolitical or patriarchal privilege during the said impious times, in order that, after there have been abolished and have been rescinded the things which have ensued through wicked commands of this kind or pragmatic sanctions or impious constitutions or formularies, there should be preserved inviolate the things which by previous emperors of divine [9] remembrance before our sovereignty and then by our Gentleness have been granted or have been established concerning the holy churches and martyries and religious bishops, clergymen, or monks.

Through respect for the royal city [10] we also judge and ordain that the sacrosanct Church of this most religious community,[10] the mother of our Piety and of all Christians of the orthodox religion and the most holy see of the said royal city,[10] should have steadfastly in perpetuity all privileges and honours concerning elections of bishops [11] and the right of seating before others [8] and all other things, which it is recognized to have had before our sovereignty or while we were reigning.

Given on 17 December, after the consulate of the most distinguished Armatus.

1. Of the East.
2. Zeno fled from his mother-in-law's intrigues on 9 January 475 and was succeeded by his uncle-in-law Basiliscus, whose adherence to Monophysitism inspired legislation unfavourable to the orthodox. Revolution against Basiliscus, who was unpopular also on account of his ministers' avidity for money, restored Zeno in August 476.

3. So is characterized the brief usurpation of Basiliscus.

4. Basiliscus' edicts are regarded as reintroducing Monophysitism.

Zeno simply follows imperial precedent in revoking a tyrant's or a usurper's constitutions, for *CT* 15. 14 contains thirteen laws (dated from 324 to 413), which, distinguishing between such intruders' illegal and legal enactments, annul the former and accept the latter and stabilize generally matters of private law.

5. The word is *sacerdotium*, which here means somewhat more than "episcopate" or "priesthood" (on which meanings see no. 158, n. 1).

6. Of Constantinople.

7. The phrase is *de iure sacerdotalium creationum* (cf. *infra* n. 11).

8. This right was derived from canon 3 of the Second Ecumenical Council at Constantinople in 381.

9. See no. 127, n. 7.

10. Constantinople.

11. The phrase now is *super episcoporum creationibus*, which shows that the adjective *sacerdotalis* (*supra* n. 7) must be equivalent to *episcopalis* (see nos. 16, n. 4, and 158, n. 1).

527. LETTER OF ZENO ON ECCLESIASTICAL UNITY, 482

(Evagrius, *HE* 3. 14)

This celebrated constitution or instrument of union, commonly called Zeno's *Henoticon*, an unhappy and an unsuccessful law to conciliate both orthodox and Monophysites, induced instead the first great schism between Rome and Constantinople, when this imperial fiat, accepted half-heartedly in the East and rejected whole-heartedly in the West, ignored the decisions of the Fourth General Council of Chalcedon (451).

Most Egyptians and Syrians opposed the Chalcedonian canons and in Monophysitism (condemned at Chalcedon as teaching unsound doctrines on Christ's person) found an outlet for their national and anti-imperial sentiments (see Introd. to no. 476). Of the five great patriarchates Alexandria and Antioch and Jerusalem were in schism from Rome and Constantinople; above five hundred bishops in these three jurisdictions at the time of this document's issue were avowed supporters of Monophysitism. To heal this rent in the Church Zeno addressed himself, applying his law first to Egypt and Syria and then to the entire Empire.[1]

While the *Henoticon* was ostensibly orthodox, yet it offended Christians in the West more by its omissions than by its assertions. Pope St Felix III (II) wrote to Zeno and to Acacius, patriarch of Constantinople, of whom the latter had inspired the former to seek some *modus vivendi* for the dissentient factions, in exhortation to continue in defence of the faith without compromise. When orthodox bishops had been deposed in favour of Monophysite intruders and when the papal legates to New Rome (Constantinople) had met with short shrift and had been compelled to receive what the pope considered an uncanonical Holy Communion, Felix excommunicated Acacius and thus inaugurated the Acacian schism, which endured until 519, since during that interval Constantinople preferred communion with the eastern patriarchates to union with orthodox Rome.

So far as the East was concerned, the *Henoticon*, since in undertone it was heretical, satisfied most of the Monophysites, save for their extremists, who sought a denunciation of the Chalcedonian definition of faith, and few of the Dyophysites, who desired a confirmation of the Council of Chalcedon. Those who rejected the *Henoticon* eventually received the epithet of *acephali* (headless) as being bereft of either emperor or patriarch.

But this constitution has also a political significance. The gradual loss of the Empire's western provinces, which were being converted into kingdoms governed by barbarian chieftains temporarily giving only nominal obedience to the eastern emperor, who was too impotent to insist on more than constitutional pretensions, while he was forced to accept the *fait accompli*, must have attracted Zeno's attention to the circumstance that the centre of gravity eventually and at long last had moved eastward. So it is a tribute to his political genius that he sensed the changed situation and thought by this constitution to compose the theological differences among his disaffected and riotous subjects as the initial step in reconciliation to the imperial rule—only to discover instead that the fanatics on both sides found such flaws in the document that, as the theological terms could not be compromised, so the political concord which he craved could not be procured. Zeno's attempt to achieve political unity not only ended disastrously, but also perpetuated ecclesiastical discord.

Nicephorus preserves the *Henoticon* in Greek (*HE* 16. 12), while Liberatus (*Breviarium*, 17 = *PL* 68. 1023–4) and Facundus (*Defensio Trium Capitulorum*, 12. 4 = *PL* 67. 845–8) have it in Latin, the last, however, quoting selected sections of it. Zacharias Rhetor *sive* Mytilenaeus has it in Syriac (*Chron.* 5. 8) and there is an anonymous and partial version in Armenian, translated by F. C. Conybeare in *AJT* 9 (1905) 735–7.

Zeno's Henoticon.[2]

Emperor Caesar[3] Zeno,[4] Pious, Victor, Triumpher,[5] Greatest, Ever-August, Augustus[6] to the most devout[7] bishops and clergymen and monks and laics[8] throughout Alexandria and Egypt and Libya and Pentapolis.[9]

Considering the source and the constitution and the power and the invincible shield of our Empire as the only right and true faith,[10] which through divine intervention[11] the 318 holy fathers, assembled in Nicaea,[12] expounded and the 150 holy fathers, convened similarly in Constantinople,[13] confirmed, by night [14] and by day [14] we have employed [15] every prayer and effort and the laws, that through it God's [16] Holy Catholic and Apostolic Church, the incorruptible and immortal mother of our imperial sceptres,[17] may be increased [18] everywhere [19] and that the pious laymen [20] with most God-beloved bishops [21] and most [22] God-fearing clergymen [23] and archimandrites and solitaries,[24] continuing in [25] peace and concord with respect to God, may offer acceptable supplications in our Empire's behalf.[26] For, while [27] the Great God and [28] our Saviour Jesus Christ, who was incarnate and was born [29] from Mary, the Holy Virgin and Mother of God, approves [30] and receives [30] readily our laudation [31] from harmony and worship,[32] the enemies' races will be erased and will be obliterated,[33] all will bend their own necks to our power after God,[34] peace and its [35] blessings and kindly temperature of the air [36] and abundance of fruits and the other benefits will be lavished on human beings.[37]

Since then the faultless faith preserves both us and the Roman affairs, to us have been brought petitions [38] from God-fearing [39] archimandrites and hermits and other venerable men,[40] beseeching [41] with tears that there should be unity for the holiest [42] churches and that [43] members should be knit to members,[44] which the hater [45] of good from most distant times [46] has bustled [47] to sever,[48] knowing that, when warring against the Church's complete [49] body, he [50] will be [51] conquered.[52] For it happens [53] from this that there are uncounted generations,[54] as many as time in so many years has withdrawn from life,[55] that some, deprived of the washing of regeneration,[56] have departed,[57] that others, not having partaken of the Divine [58] Communion, have been transported to the inexorable departure of mankind,[59] that myriad murders have been undertaken and by the amount of blood-sheddings not only the earth but also as well the very air have been polluted.[60] Who would not pray that these things should be transformed into good?[61]

Therefore we have been eager for you to know that both we and the churches everywhere [62] neither have held nor hold nor shall hold nor know persons who hold [63] another creed or teaching or definition of faith or faith save the aforesaid holy creed [64] of the 318 holy fathers,[12] which the said 150 holy fathers [65] have confirmed.[13] But if anyone should hold such, we consider him an alien.[66] For we have confidence that this alone (as we said) preserves our Empire and all the peoples, when they obtain this alone, are baptized,[67] after they are deemed worthy of salutary enlightenment.[68] And this all the holy fathers who were convened in the Ephesians' city [69] followed, who also deposed the impious Nestorius [70] and those who later were of that one's mind.⁷¹ And this Nestorius with Eutyches ⁷² and the persons ⁷³ who have thoughts opposed to what has been said we also anathematize,⁷⁴ receiving also the said *Twelve Chapters* ⁷⁵ from Cyril,⁷⁶ who is of saintly memory, the archbishop of the Alexandrians' holy Catholic Church.

We also confess that the Only-Begotten Son of God, also God,⁷⁷ who according to truth was made man, our Lord Jesus Christ, consubstantial with the Father in respect to Godhood and himself consubstantial with us in respect to manhood, having descended and having been incarnate from ⁷⁸ the Holy Spirit and Mary, the Virgin and Mother of God, is one ⁷⁹ and not two, for we say that both his miracles ⁸⁰ and his sufferings, which he willingly underwent in the flesh, are of one person.⁸¹ For we not at all accept the persons who divide ⁸² or combine ⁸³ or introduce an apparition,⁸⁴ inasmuch as according to truth ⁸⁵ the sinless incarnation from the Mother of God has not made an addition of a Son,⁸⁶ for the Trinity has remained a Trinity,⁸⁷ even after one of the Trinity, God the Word, became incarnate.

Knowing, then, that neither God's ²² holy ⁸⁸ orthodox churches everywhere nor the most God-beloved ⁸⁹ priests presiding ¹⁹ over these nor our Majesty have been content with nor are content ⁹⁰ with a creed or a definition of faith other than the said holy teaching,⁹¹ let us,⁹² not at all hesitating, unite ⁹³ ourselves.⁹²

These things we have written,⁹⁴ not devising a new faith, but fully assuring you. But every person who has thought or thinks anything else,⁹⁵ either now or any time, either in Chalcedon or in any synod whatever, we anathematize, especially the said Nestorius ⁷⁰ and Eutyches ⁹⁶ and the persons who are of their mind.

Be you joined, therefore, to the spiritual mother, the Church, by enjoying in her the same holy communion with us ⁹⁷ according to the said one and only definition of the faith of the 318 ⁹⁸ holy fathers.¹² For our ⁹⁹ all-holy ¹⁰⁰ mother, the Church, awaits to embrace you as genuine sons ¹⁰¹ and yearns to hear your long-delayed and dear voice.¹⁰²

Therefore urge ¹⁰³ yourselves, for by doing these things you will draw to yourselves the good will of our Lord and Saviour and God, Jesus Christ,¹⁰⁴ and by our Majesty you will be praised.

1. The political aspect of Monophysitism in Egypt and in Syria is portrayed ably by E. L. Woodward, *Christianity and Nationalism in the Later Roman Empire* (London, 1916), 41–66. See also Introd., n. 43. Add now Vasiliev, 88–90, 105–6, 115, 196, 208–10.

The case of Egypt is especially interesting, for Egypt ever stood apart from the life of the Empire. This separatism was seen in the fact that not a few puissant patriarchs of Alexandria, its megalopolis, exercised greater control over the Egyptians than the civil government's officials could make effective.

On Egypt see also A. C. Headlam, *The Doctrine of the Church and Christian Reunion* (New York, 1920), 177–9, and add now E. R. Hardy, *Christian Egypt: Church and People—Christianity and Nationalism in the Patriarchate of Alexandria* (New York, 1952), 3–143.

2. Nicephorus' caption is "Concerning Emperor Zeno's so-called *Henoticon*, neither rejecting nor receiving the holy Synod in Chalcedon".

Zacharias' caption reads "The eighth chapter [of his *Chronicle*] comes next, containing the Henotikon of Zeno".

The caption of the Armenian version is "The document of union, which was sent by the hand of the blessed Pregmius [*al*. Pergamius], the Augustal [Augustal prefect of Egypt, on whom see no. 489, n. 12], from the sovereign, Zeno, of good will and from Acacius, chief of the bishops that are in Constantinople, to the blessed Peter, chief of the bishops and true patriarch and faithful of the city of Alexandria".

3. Facundus substitutes "Flavius" for the first two titles.

4. Zacharias inserts "the king" and substitutes "believing" for the next epithet.

5. The Armenian version has "renowned, great and ever good" for this epithet and the next two adjectives.

6. Liberatus and Facundus omit the word, while after it the Armenian version supplies "ruler of the world".

7. For the superlative Facundus supplies "orthodox", Liberatus substitutes "all the holy", the Armenian translator has "God-fearing", Zacharias omits the adjective.

8. Of these four categories Zacharias and Liberatus omit the clergymen and the monks, while Facundus, also omitting the clergymen, substitutes "archimandrites" for *monks* and the Armenian version has "all the others" for the last group.

9. The Armenian version adds "hail in the Lord!"

10. The Armenian copyist has "As to our authority and championship, our might and the arms impregnable of our sovereignty and kingdom, ye shall know that these consist in the true and orthodox faith"; Zacharias reads "Since we know that the origin and stability and invincible might of our empire is in the only right and true faith".

11. Zacharias substitutes "inspiration" and the Armenian version has "advent".

12. In 325.

13. In 381.

14. Plural in Liberatus. The Armenian version reverses the phrases.

15. Present tense in Zacharias, while the Armenian version substitutes "we seek" and turns the three verbal objects into prepositional objects of accompaniment and means.

16. The Syriac and the Armenian copies omit the word.

17. Zacharias has "of the sceptre of our kingdom".

18. The Armenian version has "to increase and foster by means of this faith everywhere the holy and Catholic apostolic Church, which is the incorruptible and immortal mother of our scepre" for *Holy . . . increased.*

19. Liberatus omits the word.

20. Zacharias has "the believing people" and the Armenian scribe has "all the pious congregations may abide and remain".

21. Liberatus reads "most holy archbishops", Zacharias has "pious and holy bishops", the Armenian version gives "the true chief bishops".

22. Zacharias omits the word.

23. The Armenian version reads "and with devout men who have taken vows".

24. Liberatus omits *and solitaries,* while the Armenian version for this and the preceding group reads "with the monks and anchorites".

25. Zacharias inserts "godly", apparently from the phrase *with respect to God,* which he omits.

26. The Armenian copy for *may . . . behalf* reads "accepting from our royal selves steadfast prayers, which we offer".

27. Zacharias has "if" and the Armenian version has "when".

28. The Armenian version omits *the . . . and.*

29. Zacharias omits *and was born.*

30. Future tense in Zacharias.

31. Liberatus has "equally glorification" for *readily our laudation.*

32. Zacharias reads "our unanimous praise and service" and the Armenian translator gives "our praises offered as with one voice and our worship" for *our . . . worship.*

33. Liberatus omits *and . . . obliterated.*

34. Zacharias reads "sway, which is next to God" and the Armenian version has "under God to the yoke of our authority" for *to . . . God.*

35. Zacharias inserts "consequent", which reinforces the Armenian reading here of "and the prosperity resulting therefrom".

36. The Armenian scribe expands this third expression into "fair winds and fine seasons".

37. Zacharias associates this phrase with *benefits.*

38. The Armenian version has "supplications and prayers".

39. Liberatus has "most loved by God", Zacharias has "God-loving", the Armenian version has "pious".

40. Zacharias names only archimandrites and hermits, whom the Armenian copy calls monks and anchorites.

41. The Syriac and the Armenian versions insert "us".

42. The positive degree is used by the Armenian translator.

43. Liberatus reads "beseeching unity for the holiest Church, that".

44. Zacharias reads "that the limbs may be joined together" and the Armenian version has "to gather into one body the scattered limbs".

45. Satan is meant. Since Zacharias pluralizes the word, he means devils or perhaps heretics or schismatics.

46. Zacharias has "for a long time", while the Armenian translator reads "on many occasions".

47. Zacharias has "striven", Liberatus has "tried", the Armenian version has "been intent".

48. The Armenian copy adds "and cut off from one another".

49. Liberatus omits the adjective, which Zacharias expands into "whole and perfect".

50. Facundus inserts "easily".

51. Zacharias has present tense.

52. The Armenian version for *knowing . . . conquered* (which the Greek applies to Satan) begins a new sentence (which it applies to human beings): "Let them therefore know this, that if anyone conflict with and oppose the concordant and whole-membered body of holy church, he shall be delivered over to discomfiture."

Facundus converts the participial construction into a finite verb "for he knows", Zacharias into "because he knows", Nicephorus into "if he knows".

53. Perfect tense in Zacharias, who omits the next phrase.

54. Thus far in this sentence the Armenian translation reads "For from such a condition of things there has resulted unto races innumerable the very greatest hurt and damage".

At this point a new sentence starts: "How many times, in the past years of our own life, have some" etc.

55. Zacharias reads "of life" and joins it to *years*.

56. That is, without having been baptized, as the Armenian translator takes it, when he writes "salutary baptism of regeneration". The expression in the text occurs first in Titus 3. 5.

57. Thus far in this sentence Facundus reads as follows and then concludes this excerpt: "For it has happened from this division through so many generations of so many years that some indeed, cheated of the washing of regeneration, departed from this life and the rest [*et caetera*]".

Liberatus, joining this sentence to the preceding one and making it depend upon *knowing* therein, reads to this point: "and that it has happened from this that uncounted generations, in so many years deprived of life, have departed— some indeed cheated of the washing of regeneration".

58. Liberatus reads "sacred"; the Armenian version inserts "sacrament and the".

59. The Armenian scribe substitutes "death" for this word.

60. Both Syriac and Armenian versions make a sentence of this last clause: the one reads "And they have been wasted by myriads of murders; and through the profuse blood-shedding, not the earth alone, but even the very air itself has

been defiled"; the other reads "And many a time have some dared to commit murder and to pollute the earth with bloodshed, and not the earth alone, but the air of heaven as well".

61. The Armenian version adds "and that we may behold union?" and begins the next paragraph thus "For these reasons we have hastened to acquaint you that everywhere there shall be a union and unity of orthodox and holy church".

62. Zacharias reads "and the holy churches of the orthodox everywhere and and the God-loving priests who rule them", all of which the Armenian copy omits, but Liberatus follows Zacharias to "everywhere", substituting "most holy" for the adjectival form.

63. The Armenian translator omits *nor know . . . hold*.

64. The Armenian version for *or faith . . . creed* has "than that which was pronounced to be aforetime the holy faith, namely, that".

65. Zacharias adds "who met in council here" and the Armenian copyist adds "when assembled in Constantinople".

66. For this sentence the Armenian version has "We know not if anyone doth entertain another form, but, if anyone do, we reckon him to be an outcast from us".

67. Zacharias reads "are baptized upon the simple reception of this creed alone".

68. Liberatus substitutes "baptism" for this word.

The Armenian copy paraphrases the sentence thus "In this faith alone do we find our comfort, as we said before, and through this we reckon that we will maintain alive our realm and sovereignty as well as all the concordant congregations that have been made worthy of saving baptism and have received it in its oneness and sameness".

69. In 431. Liberatus says simply "at Ephesus" and Zacharias has "in council at Ephesus".

70. Patriarch of Constantinople and founder of Nestorianism.

71. This sentence in the Armenian version appears as "By it especially were those who met together in Ephesus illuminated, who were followed and imitated by all the holy fathers who deposed and expelled the lawless Nestor [sic], as also those who after his time held and still hold his opinions".

72. The Constantinopolitan archimandrite and originator of Eutychianism.

73. Zacharias omits *and . . . persons.*

74. Liberatus shows haplography in omitting all between *Nestorius* at n. 70 and the phrase *with Eutyches* at n. 72. For *and . . . anathematize* he has "Persons thinking otherwise we anathematize".

For the sentence thus far, which both Oriental versions end at *anathematize*, the Armenian scribe writes "This same Nestorius we anathematized along with Eutyches, though they hold opinions contrary to one another, and also those who entertain their opinions or shall entertain them—all these we anathematize".

75. From this point three variations appear: Liberatus has "which are said to have been constructed by Cyril, of memory lovable to God, who was the archbishop of the Alexandrians' Catholic Church"; Zacharias reads "delivered by the ever-memorable, God-loving Cyril, formerly archbishop of the Catholic Church of Alexandria"; the Armenian copy gives "known as those of the devout and pious Cyril, who was chief of the bishops of the holy Church of Alexandria".

76. This sainted prelate composed a letter containing a dozen propositions (the *Twelve Chapters*) for Nestorius to anathematize. Nestorius' refusal led soon to the convocation of the Third General Council of Ephesus (431). Some suspect, however, that Cyril also was playing politics in—so to speak—putting Nestorius on the spot and was only imitating his lithomaniac uncle and predecessor in the patriarchate, Theophilus, whose intervention in what he considered orthodox interests led to the exile of St John Chrysostom from the Constantinopolitan patriarchate earlier in this century, for the Alexandrian patriarchs' jealous rivalry and rancorous intrigues against the patriarchs of Constantinople constitute an abominable chapter in the ecclesiastical annals of the East. See nos. 284, n. 4, and 495, n. 5.

77. Zacharias has "himself God" and the Armenian version reads "is God in very truth", the latter advancing *according to truth* to this place.

78. Zacharias has "through" and the Armenian copy has "by". Before *Mary* the former inserts "from" and the latter puts "of" and also reverses the order of the procession.

79. "Son" is inserted by Liberatus, Zacharias, and the Armenian.

80. Zacharias adds "which he wrought" and before *miracles* the Armenian version inserts "the works of power".

81. Liberatus and the Armenian version add "the Only-Begotten Son of God", of which Zacharias retains "Son of God".

82. Nestorians.

83. Eutychians. The Armenian translator substitutes "say that he was changeable or alterable".

84. Eutyches asserted that Christ's flesh was merely imaginary and not homoousian with our flesh. The Armenian version omits this third alternative.

85. Zacharias and the Armenian version read "true" for the phrase and the latter adds "incorruptible".

86. The Armenian copy reads "an additional Sonship".

87. Liberatus and Zacharias omit the word. The Armenian version concludes the sentence and its copy with "until it willed and became man, the Word God one through the Trinity".

88. Liberatus uses the superlative degree.

89. Zacharias has "God-loving" in the positive degree and with the others has for the next word "priests", on which see no. 16, n. 4.

90. Liberatus and Zacharias read "have received or do receive".

91. Another excerpt of Facundus reproduces this much of the paragraph

thus "Because the holy Catholic churches, which are everywhere, and the God-lovable priests [with Liberatus *sacerdotes*, on which see no. 16, n. 4], who preside over these, believe not otherwise".

92. Liberatus, Facundus, Zacharias turn the pronoun into the second person.

93. Nicephorus substitutes "we have united".

94. Facundus inserts "to you".

95. Facundus reduces the relative clause to "who thinks otherwise" and concludes this excerpt with *we anathematize*.

96. Nicephorus by error reads "Eutychius". On Eutyches cf. *supra* n. 72.

97. Liberatus reads "by being of the same mind with us, placed in the same communion" and Facundus, who starts another excerpt with this paragraph only to end it at this point, substitutes "that you may enjoy one divine communication".

98. Liberatus substitutes "same" for the numeral, which Zacharias also omits.

99. Nicephorus has the second person.

100. Liberatus substitutes "holiest".

101. Zacharias after *Church* reads "longs for you, that she may embrace you as beloved children" and Liberatus has "awaits to embrace sons, as if she has borne you", associating with the notion of welcome the later expression *long-delayed* as the phrase "after a long time".

102. For this sentence Facundus in his last excerpt gives three sentences, of which the first is ungrammatical: "For our holy mother, the Church, just as she has acknowledged you as her own sons, embrace her. For she yearns after a long time to hear your sweet voice. Join yourselves, therefore, to her."

103. Liberatus mistakenly reads *cogitate* (consider), when he should have *cogite* (urge).

104. Zacharias reads "God and Saviour Christ" for *Lord . . . Christ*; Liberatus omits *and God, Jesus Christ*.

528. MANDATE OF ZENO ON ADMISSION OF TENANT FARMERS TO ASCETIC LIFE AND OF SLAVES TO THE CLERICATE, 484

(*CI* 1. 3. 36)

Zeno legislates against the practice of farmers deserting their landlords to enter the monastic life and against masters allowing their slaves to become clergymen without having manumitted them.

The emperor also warns all provincial clergymen that they are under the provincial governors' jurisdiction.

Pitra has two late Greek paraphrases of the first three paragraphs (2. 480 and 595).

528. TENANT FARMERS AND SLAVES, 484

The same Augustus to Sebastian, praetorian prefect.[1]

We order that creations of serfs,[2] according to an old constitution,[3] should be absolutely of no importance, unless the obvious agreement of owners of landed estates, whence they must originate,[4] shall have concurred, but that to the said owners of farms, who obviously shall have agreed in making the creation not in accordance with what has been said, should be awarded the ability of exercising their own legal right over their own serfs according to the analogy of all other tenant farmers,[5] as if no creation had intervened.

And this same thing we decree should be observed also about farmers who, since they had been conscripted by the bonds of a serf-like status, obviously seeking a solitary life, shall have thought that they ought to offer themselves to any monasteries whatever contrary to the will of owners of farms.

By all means we forbid, even with their master's wish and knowledge,[6] slaves to be joined to associations of clergymen, since it is legitimate for their masters, after freedom first has been given to slaves, to open, if they shall have wished this, a lawful road for them to undertake clergymen's duties.

Moreover we decree that with the decisions of the most distinguished men who govern the provinces should comply likewise all persons, without any distinction of privilege [7] (since they, nevertheless, are subject to gubernatorial jurisdiction, whether they are bishops or any kind of clergymen or monks or of any status whatsoever)—on the most distinguished governors of provinces being imposed absolutely no necessity of journeying to the places wherein the accused persons dwell, since it befits not only the laws, but also even the natural law, for persons, whom the situation shall have compelled, to be called to court for judicial decisions, not for the governors themselves—and this also it is unjust to be said—to be brought to the governed, but through judges assigned by them to advance the investigation of the case in places where the accused persons live.

Given on 28 March at Constantinople, Theodoric [8] being consul.

1. Of the East.
2. These are the *adscripticii*, registered tenants bound to the soil and transferred with it from one owner or possessor (as the case might be) to another. Though free politically, yet their economic and social status was only slightly superior to that of a slave. In *CI* 11. 48. 21 (dated 530) they are opposed both to freemen and to slaves. Cf. *infra* n. 5.
3. It is uncertain what law is meant, but perhaps *CI* 11. 48. 13 (dated 400) is indicated.
4. A person could become a serf in one of four ways: (1) birth, (2) prescription, (3) agreement, (4) governmental compulsion. On these modes see

R. Clausing, *The Roman Colonate* (New York, 1925), 26–9, and the references to the legal documents there cited.

The ordinary source of supply, however, seems to have been birth, which appears to be that indicated here.

5. These are the *coloni*, the commonest designation in *CT* and *CI* for the cultivating class of agricultural tenants bound to the soil. Their position, not unlike that of the *adscripticii* (cf. supra n. 2) or of the *originarii* and the *inquilini* (see no. 478, n. 19), with whom—in some scholars' opinion—they seem identical, was intermediate between freemen and slaves and yet had certain characteristics of each class. While they were free-born in personal status, yet they were slaves of the land itself (*servi terrae ipsius* [*CI* 11. 52. 1; dated 392–5]), whereon they were a landowner's or a leaseholder's perpetual tenants, who, if they should have deserted the land, could be recovered by their landlords. Besides their status being hereditary by the Dominate, their position also could arise by voluntary undertaking, by failure to assert their independence within a certain time (the time varied in various periods and places), and by denunciation (landowners denouncing vagrants to the authorities could have them assigned to their estates). It was Constantine I, the elaborator of many details of Diocletian's administrative reforms, who bound *coloni* and their progeny to the land which they worked and who in effect established serfdom (*CT* 5. 17. 1; dated 332). Much legislation on *coloni* exists (see Clausing, op. et loc. cit.), but their obligations differed in different provinces and periods.

The almost annual succession of statutes against farm hands fleeing from farms—either to find a kindlier proprietor's protection or to join the urban unemployables and unemployed, who depended on doles, or to become a brigand or to seek shelter in the hills or amid the woods or to wander with vagrant barbarian bands—testifies both to these laws' inefficacy and to the plantations' reduced productivity.

6. A hysteron proteron.

7. A *privilegium* was an ordinance excepting a person (or case) from ordinary regulations. Although outlawed as early as 449 B.C., because unfavourable treatment usually resulted to the individual involved (*FIRA* 1. 64; *TT* 9. 1–2), the meaning of *privilegium* evolved into the notion of an exceptional favour conferred upon a person (see no. 62, n. 11).

This statute waives the presentation of such a prerogative in this situation.

8. King of the Ostrogoths (474–526), surnamed the Great, and ally of Zeno, whose previous honours heaped on the barbarian master of Italy culminated in the conferment of the consulship for this year. Theodoric's double position of a Gothic king and a Roman official is significant of the situation whereby the Goths, who profoundly reverenced the Roman Empire, established their realms on Roman soil as federates of the Roman emperors.

529. MANDATE OF ZENO ON ADMISSION OF SLAVES TO ASCETIC LIFE, 484

(CI 1. 3. 37)

This statute allows slaves to become monks with the permission of their masters, whose rights of ownership must be suspended for the duration of such religious life, but orders slaves who have left the monastic life to resume their servile status.

Pitra (2. 595) prints a late Greek paraphrase of this statute.

The same Augustus to Sebastian, praetorian prefect.[1]

To slaves, if they shall have been supported by their master's will, should not be denied permission for participating in the solitary life, provided, however, that their masters should not be unaware that, if they shall have granted to their slaves the opportunity of departing to the monasteries' manner of life, they must be deprived of the ownership of the said slaves, so long as the said slaves shall have continued in the said condition of monks: otherwise, if, when perchance the solitary life has been abandoned, they shall have transferred themselves to another situation, it is decided that they should return to the yoke of slavery, which they had escaped by the manner of life of the monastic profession.[2]

Given on 13 April, Theodoric [3] being consul.

1. Of the East.
2. Pitra prints (2. 549) an excerpt from the late Greek version of a law and prefers to let others see whether it, though it does not concern slaves, should be added to this statute: "We generally legislate that it is permitted to none established in any ecclesiastical grade whatsoever to depart from it and to become a layman—persons knowing (and so doing) that they shall be deprived —as is equitable—of the belt [see no. 476, n. 39] imposed upon them or of rank or of governmental service [see no. 186, n. 4] and they shall be delivered to their own city's order" [see no. 325, n. 6].

Upon re-entry into lay life ex-clerics presumably would regain their civilian posts in the government, if they had held any, but this statute strips them of these and confines them to their municipal senates, whence, perhaps in due time, they might emerge for service in superior echelons of government.

3. See no. 528, n. 8.

530. LAW OF UNKNOWN EMPEROR ON ECCLESIASTICAL EXACTION OF OFFERINGS, 484–524
(CI 1. 3. 38)

From its position in the Code this law may be assigned to either Zeno or Anastasius I or Justin I, for, if the compilers have set it in chronological sequence, it belongs to the period 484–524.

In this document two regulations are promulgated: (1) persons abandoning the monastic life must leave their property in or to the monasteries; (2) clergymen subject to the patriarch of Constantinople must not exact payment of offerings from unwilling laymen (especially farmers) by threatening them with ecclesiastical censure.

Those who leave their monasteries do not take what movables—of whatever quantity these are—they brought into them, even if the transaction of the records about these has not been completed. But in donations of immovables it is necessary for the legal regulations to be maintained, since eviction is not withdrawn from him who has made the donation.[1]

And this also we ordain: that none of the most God-beloved bishops or suffragan bishops or itinerant bishops or clergymen should constrain laymen unwillingly to payment of offerings (which in the provinces [2] are called first-fruits or oblations), by exacting these as if a kind of tax, or also should impose on farmers, received in the clergy and especially on those who are not under the absolute control of the most God-beloved bishops or of the most holy churches concerning them, the so-called transport animals [3] or other such-like charges or services, or should lay on these persons excommunications or anathematizations on account of these causes and, as a result (which is even a godless thing to mention), should deprive them of participation in the sacred mysteries [4] and of venerable and salutary baptism itself (for we have learned that this has been suffered by certain persons and that truly entire villages and districts and clergymen [5] as well as those situated outside the clergy have been under such excommunications or anathematizations)—such action, most monstrous and full of every impiety and looking toward the reproach of the orthodox faith itself, being debarred in every way and no custom which introduces so irrational an exaction being able to be valid.

For it is obvious that it is particularly proper for each person to contribute willingly from his own labours to God and to those who serve him whatever he himself should think right and not to be forced and compelled to this, when perhaps he is poor and not in enjoyment of the fruits from agriculture because of certain fortuitous dearths, as is likely. For on this account we forbid compulsion; we, however, not only do not debar, but even approve the voluntary intention of persons making offerings.

Wherefore, confirming by very great penalties the ordinances made by us, we command that he who dares to transgress any of the aforementioned matters should be expelled both from the most holy church itself, to which he has been committed, and from its affairs and that everyone who attempts to do some such act should be removed from the affairs which pertain to the homes,[6] with whose management he has been entrusted, and from their administration, since indeed he shows himself unworthy of this and of the priesthood [7] itself. Moreover he shall be punished by a penalty of ten pounds of gold.

What things have been formulated by us through this sacred pragmatic law we ordain are to be valid and to be maintained throughout only this royal city,[8] however, and its territory and the remaining places and regions under the ordination [9] of the see of this glorious city [8] and of the most God-beloved metropolitan bishops ordained by it, so that also those bishops, under their metropolitans obtaining the episcopate or the priesthood or the remaining aforementioned presidencies and administrations, should be subjected to the said formularies and should maintain these.

1. This ruling agrees with the previous provision: anyone leaving a monastery voluntarily or by compulsion must leave with it whatever property he has brought or has given to it.
2. Literally "places", "districts", "regions".
3. This term (ἀγγαρεία; *angaria*), on which see no. 434, n. 2, survives in international law as "angary": a belligerent's right, when necessary, to take or to use or to destroy properties of neutrals.
4. See no. 75, n. 42.
5. Apparently some clerics made such demands of other clerics.
6. The ecclesiastically administered charitable institutions are meant.
7. See no. 158, n. 1.
8. Probably Constantinople, since the document is in Greek.
9. That is, places wherein ecclesiastical officials were subject to the Constantinopolitan patriarch's power of ordination.

531. LAW OF UNKNOWN EMPEROR ON MONASTIC DISCIPLINE, 484-524

(CI 1. 3. 39)

To either Zeno or Anastasius I or Justin I belongs this law, which the Code's compilers have set between statutes dated in 484 and in 524.

Besides declaring that no person should preside over more than one monastery at a time, this directive places on the local bishop responsibility for the abbot's conduct and on the abbot the accountability for the monks' behaviour—all in the interest of good order.

We ordain that none should be abbot over two monasteries, but that these indeed should be under the most God-beloved bishop of the territory wherein they exist, but that each should have one abbot and that the bishop should be responsible for the abbot's condition [1] and for his acts and the abbot for that [2] of the monks; and in this way all discipline should be maintained and henceforth nothing in accord with confusion or insult should be done by the persons who have embraced this holy character.[3]

And it is necessary that these matters should be maintained both now and perpetually for the future time.

1. Or "appointment", but probably "settled life" or "peaceful attitude" is meant.
2. The Greek is so concise that it literally avoids mention of abbatial control over the monks' acts, but not to extend the meaning is absurd in view of the history of monachism.
3. The word (σχῆμα) sometimes stands for the monastic garb itself.

532. LAW OF UNKNOWN EMPEROR ON THE BIBLE'S USE IN AN OFFICIAL INVESTIGATION, 485-534

(CI 12. 60. 7)

This defective ordinance, which seems to be an interpretation, orders the introduction of the Scriptures—presumably for use in taking an oath that right decision will be rendered—into a gubernatorial inquiry about the integrity of any law carried from the capital into a province. Since only this section is of Christian interest, only this much is translated. The rest of the law describes a governor's duty after his acceptance or rejection of the law's validity and prescribes penalties for neglect.

There is a possibility that the phrases here construed to indicate the Bible are merely extravagant epithets conferred on the actual constitution under examination, for to almost everything associated with the emperor in the Dominate were applied such adjectives as appear here.

Every person executing either a divine order or a magisterial order first ought to exhibit it to the governor, that the governor may inquire if in these should be no cause for falsity according to either deception or contrariety to the laws.

The execution occurs both by writing and without writing, the divine words,[1] of course, lying before him and all the rentiers present making the inquiry with him . . .

But if governors, having yielded to a bribe, should not make an inquiry, the holy words [2] lying before them, or also should disregard it, they are penalized in respect to money and are expelled from the govenorship and are in peril for their safety . . .

1. The phrase is τὰ θεῖα λόγια, which the editor turns into *divina scriptura*.
2. Here the phrase is τὰ ἅγια λόγια, which the editor represents by *sacrosancta scriptura*.

533. LAW OF ZENO OR OF ANASTASIUS I ON RIGHT OF RESIDENCE FOR MANICHAEANS, 487 or 510

(*CI* 1. 5. 11)

This statute without superscription, assigned to either 487 (Zeno) or 510 (Anastasius I), forbids to Manichaeans the right to reside anywhere in the Empire.

We ordain that persons who prefer the Manichaeans' deadly error should have no freedom or leave to dwell in any place whatever of our State; but that, if ever they should have appeared or should have been found, they should be subject to capital punishment.

Given on 9 August, the most distinguished Boethius being consul.[1]

1. The date of this document would be 510, if it could be determined that Boethius the consul is Anicius Manlius Severinus Boethius, who was consul in that year, who was the first of the scholastics, and who in prison, while awaiting

his execution, wrote the famous dialogue *De Consolatione Philosophiae*. On him see E. K. Rand, *Founders of the Middle Ages* (Cambridge, Mass., 1928), 135–80. Rand suggests that Boethius, because his death was due partly to his defence of the Catholic faith against the Arian Theodoric (on whom see no. 528, n. 8), deserves canonization.

His Father, Flavius (?) Nar ... Manlius Boethius, was consul in 487.

534. LAW OF ANASTASIUS I ON EPISCOPAL INTEREST IN PURCHASE OF GRAIN, 491–505
(*CI* 1. 4. 17)

From *CI* 10. 27. 3 is extracted all but one section (§ 1)—and this is alien from ecclesiastical argument [1]—of a defective statute on selection of a public purchaser of grain. When grain is needed, the needy city's bishop and principal senators choose this temporary official from local magistrates' aides or ex-aides (see no. 539).

> Emperor Anastasius Augustus.
> ... We ordain that a public purchaser of grain ...
> Whenever in any city should be need for public purchase of grain, the appointment for him [2] shall be according to the scrutiny and the selection of the bishop in each city and of the chief men among the rentiers: not according to what appears to the appointers nor as to what persons they should wish—but only the officials who in that district are in governmental service [3] or [4] have relinquished their order [5] being appointed through the said persons for the public purchase of grain, since more easily these men, having been familiar with public affairs from long periods, accomplish the burden of the public purchase of grain.
> He who transgresses or permits the law to be transgressed shall pay a penalty of thirty pounds of gold.

1. It treats the duties of the public purchase of grain.
2. Apparently the public purchaser of grain is meant.
3. See no. 186, n. 4.
4. The Greek has "and", but the Latin translation has *or*, which is wanted.
5. See no. 325, n. 6.

535. LAW OF ANASTASIUS I ON EPISCOPAL INTEREST IN MILITARY PAYMENT, 491–505
(CI 1. 4. 18)

This defective statute seems to have been adapted from another and longer ordinance of Anastasius on the subject of payment of provisions to soldiers [1] (CI 12. 37. 19).[2] It authorizes the bishop of a town to participate with the town's chief magistrate and defender in supervising payment to the soldiers stationed there.

> The same emperor.
> ... We ordain ...
> The soldiers posted and attending in garrison duty shall receive in their quarters payment in kind (contributed from the farmers in the city or its territory) for their provisions [3] at the determination of the bishop and of the chief magistrate or of the defender in the event of default of the chief magistrate. And the member of the landowners' guild responsible for collection and payment of its taxes [4] is not compelled to give appraisal in cash.[5]

1. This is the *annona*, on which see no. 301, n. 7.
2. The pertinent part (§ 1 *ad fin.*) is "If he takes payment in kind, he shall take what is supplied in the district according to the determination of the most God-beloved bishop of the places and of the most distinguished defender of the city".
3. Here *annona* is transliterated into Greek, for the law is in Greek.
4. From *the* to *taxes* is all one word in Greek: συντελεστής.
5. This is in accord with the practice in the Dominate, when military wages were commuted into payments in kind for subsistence.

536. MANDATE OF ANASTASIUS I ON SOLDIERS AS GUARDS FOR CHURCHES, 491–518
(CI 12. 37. 17)

This ordinance, undated but ascribed to Anastasius I, orders soldiers assigned to guard churches (and secular institutions and persons) to be paid not by the State but by those who benefit from such protection. The emperor also requires a written order from himself for authorization of such service and sets penalties for official negligence toward and violation of the directive.

436. SOLDIERS AS GUARDS FOR CHURCHES, 491-518

The same Augustus to Arcadius, praetorian prefect.[1]

When it often happens on account of certain very great and inescapable reasons that soldiers are assigned or even have been assigned to certain persons for guard or for another cause of this kind and when it is not proper by this means to sustain some public loss or expense, we order that if any very brave soldiers from any unit [2] whatever have been or shall have been assigned by our Divinity to municipal senates or certain corporations or sacrosanct churches or other persons for guard (as has been said) or for another such cause, through their transfers not any impairment should be thrown upon the public revenues in regard to payment of provisions [3] or of rations,[4] which must be furnished to them, and that the person or persons [5] to whom they have been or shall have been assigned should acknowledge the said expenses by all means from their own property—only this being furnished from and being charged upon the public revenue for the said provisions [3] and rations [4] which is charged in those places from which the aforesaid soldiers have come or shall have come—or that, if the abovementioned persons shall have refused the aforementioned payment, the said soldiers should not leave their own places or those who shall have left for these places should return without any delay.

This in every way must be guarded:[6] that none of the most devoted soldiers should be assigned to any person or corporation without our Serenity's special order produced in writing.

If it shall not at all have cared to insert into the records this our Gentleness' formulary, as often as anything shall have been established concerning certain soldiers to be assigned, and likewise to publicize what those persons to whom they have been given ought to acknowledge (according as it has pleased us), your Highness' office staff must be compelled [6] to pay whatever expense the public treasury shall have sustained from this cause and to refill it from their own property as well as a fine of thirty pounds of gold because of their sloth, nay rather connivance.

Governors of provinces and their apparitors,[7] nevertheless, if they shall have violated our statutes or shall have permitted these to be violated, must be smitten [6] with the payment of the same condemnation.

1. Of the East.
2. The *numerus*, on which see no. 584, n. 8.
3. The *annona*, on which see no. 301, n. 7.
4. The *capitus* or *capitum*, a word sometimes used for fodder for the animals attached to a military unit.
5. The Church, of course, is a juristic person.

6. This principal verb is in a gerundival construction in Latin. A main verb of command should be understood.

7. The Latin has the abstract for the concrete.

537. LAW OF ANASTASIUS I ON ALIENATION OF ECCLESIASTICAL PROPERTY, 491–518
(CI 1. 2. 17)

This defective and dateless constitution of Anastasius I is reminiscent of another constitution at least a score of years earlier (no. 510). It forbids alienation of property belonging to churches and to charitable institutions operated by the Church (whether in Constantinople or elsewhere) except for certain specified reasons, provides for protocolization of authorized transactions, and sets a monetary penalty for violation of the procedure.

Editors assign no date to this ordinance in Anastasius' reign and also indicate that its opening section has been lost.

Emperor Anastasius Augustus.

... We ordain that the things concerning this royal city's [1] most holy Great Church [2] (under which it is proper to be included the most holy houses,[3] whose properties and expenditure of the so-called daily allowances and remaining expenses it itself has taken upon itself), as determined and prevailing, should remain for themselves unshaken and invulnerable and guarded in every way; and that all the privileges which through any time or way belonged to and are still due to the said Great Church [2] and to this royal city's [1] see also should be firm.

We ordain that all alienation of immovable properties or of civil provisions [4] belonging to or about to belong to the venerable houses, which has been done in any way or is practised or is able to be conceived, should cease, unless perchance because of some necessary and useful need arising for the said venerable houses would be profitable for these the sale of such a property or its hypothec [5] or its exchange or its continuous emphyteusis,[6] that is, whenever the price of the property sold is about to be allocated to payment of debts (not when existing simply or as it happens, but when lying upon one of the aforesaid [3] venerable houses from certain successions or inheritances or from necessary and needful causes) or also to acquisition and to purchase of some other property more needful and more necessary to them or also to be expended for the said house's renewal or care, which is urgent and does not allow long delay—the same reasons excepted in reference to the prohibition concerning loans and hypothecs [5] for these; but exchange, whenever it is sought in the same way for something more needful and more necessary and capable of acquiring for one of the said venerable houses a revenue worthwhile and not less than that of the property thus given;[7] but emphyteusis,[6] whenever the amount of the revenue is not at all diminished or also what is given is absolutely unproductive;[7] for in the case of such properties, which produce no gain because of unproductivity but inflict loss, we do not forbid to the said houses donations or alienations.

But what has been done is valid not otherwise, unless one of the said reasons should be evident in the records; in Byzantium,[8] in the office of the master of the census; in the provinces, in the offices of the defenders; the Sacred Scriptures being set before them; in the case of churches, the stewards and the clergymen dwelling there being present; in the case of monasteries, it is necessary for the hegumens and the other monks to be present; in the case of almshouses, the director and the assistants and the alms-folk; in the case of hostels, the director and all the assistants of the direction found therein; and similarly in the case of orphanages; so that what pleases the majority should prevail —the bishop of the places in which this is customary to happen also consenting; the master of the census or the defender not being able to refuse to go to the venerable house in which such a transaction is being arranged and defending it [9] honestly.[10] For they are subject to a penalty of twenty pounds of gold as a result of transgression.

And afterward are made contracts which mention the reasons and the transaction of the records [11] and the names of the persons present [12] and of him in whose presence it was arranged.[13]

But if any of the said matters should have been overlooked, the creditor and the purchaser lose the property and the debt and the price;[14] he who receives for exchange loses both what he has given and what he has received; he who receives for emphyteusis [6] for his own life or for gift or for alienation returns what he has received and again as much as what has been given.[15]

The said matters also have a place in reference to properties which are about to become ecclesiastical and which will be holy.

When movables, apart from sacred utensils, are available and suffice for the said reasons, the alienation and the hypothec [5] of necessary immovables and of breads [16] are invalid.

1. Constantinople.
2. Hagia Sophia.
3. Probably eleemosynary institutions such as those mentioned in text after n. 8 *infra* are meant, although οἶκος (the noun here) in Christian Greek often means "church". See introd. to no. 515.

The editor believes that an enumeration of the holy houses is lacking, for later in the subsequent sentence the appearance of *aforesaid* suggests an earlier explanation, and thus supplies in Latin (here translated) the following words from a collection of ecclesiastical constitutions published in Paris in 1661: "But the other churches and monasteries and hostels and orphanages of the said city and of its vicinity and the institutions under the ordination of its archbishop or of the metropolitans ordained by him or of the persons ordained by them."

4. See nos. 301, n. 7, and 510, n. 5.

5. Greek ὑποθήκη (transliterated into Latin *hypotheca* and Anglicized as "hypothec"). The Romans borrowed the word from the Greeks to mark the third and final stage of their theory of mortgage, wherein by *hypotheca* A who borrowed from B pledged by mere agreement (without formality) and without delivery of either ownership or possession a certain property to B as security for A's debt to B. This last step—to eliminate such transfers—in the development of the Roman doctrine of mortgage was taken in the Principate, for it seems doubtful that it was known under the Republic.

6. Greek ἐμφύτευσις (transliterated into Latin *emphyteusis* and Anglicized as "emphyteusis"). It is the long-term lease in Roman law. This form of tenure, less than ownership and more than hire, ascended to the State's grant of longer or perpetual leases on land acquired by conquest. Such leases were popular with corporations (most corporations are notoriously inefficient landlords), especially ecclesiastical in the East (where were vast tracts of waste land owned by the State and leased to the churches), for their tenure generally freed them from management of the property and yet secured to them an annual income from their sub-lessees, on whom fell the administration, the reclamation, the cultivation of such estates. The holder of such a lease is in Greek ἐμφυτευτής, in Latin *emphyteuta*, in English "emphyteute".

The practice of letting State-owned lands to private persons on a long-term or almost permanent basis, for such a lease could be alienated as well as bequeathed, on the conditions that they paid a small rent and cultivated as well as improved such estates, began in the Empire, particularly in the East (whence is accounted its Greek name) but by Constantine I's reign was extended to privately owned land and houses on the same basis.

It was not until the reign of Zeno that the final definition of emphyteusis was enunciated (*II* 3. 24. 3).

7. Neither the Greek original nor its Latin version has a verb for this clause. A predicate like "is allowed" seems necessary.

8. The old name for Constantinople (see no. 62, n. 2).

9. That is, representing the institution's interest.

10. In all but the second clause after *defenders supra* a principal verb is lacking, the construction in Greek being participial, but the translators into Latin occasionally insert a finite verb.

11. The *records* (ὑπομνήματα) are either the notes entered in the ledgers of the parties or the public records where the deeds are registered.

12. Probably as witnesses.

13. That is, either the master of the census or the defender of the community. The notes (ὑπομνήματα), of course, would contain already the names of the parties to the transaction.

14. Two individuals are considered here: the creditor loses the property as security for the loan and the money lent; the purchaser loses the property and the money paid. Other cases are considered next.

15. The emphyteute returns the ecclesiastically owned property, loses what he already has paid for it, and pays again the same amount—all as a penalty.

16. Probably are meant the loaves offered to the churches for the clergy's daily sustenance—a practice traceable through Christian antiquity to St Paul's admonition (I Cor. 9. 7–14) and beyond that to the Mosaic ordinances (Num. 5. 9–10, 18. 8–19; Deut. 18. 1–8).

538. LAW OF ANASTASIUS I ON CHRISTIAN FUNERALS IN CONSTANTINOPLE, 491–518

(*CI* 1. 2. 18)

This statute, which seems to be an interpretation of a law, endows the Constantinopolitan Church with money for free funerals.

The same emperor.

The ordinance assigns to Constantinople's Great Church [1] seventy pounds of gold as revenue for funerals to be held without cost in Constantinople and as far as the new walls [2] and Blachernae,[3] for Sycae [4] is a part of the city.

It assesses against transgressors a penalty of fifty pounds of gold each.

1. Hagia Sophia.

2. Probably the sea walls extended in 439 by Cyrus, urban prefect, along the Golden Horn in the north and in the south along the Sea of Marmara, to meet the land wall built in 413 by Anthemius, praetorian prefect of the East. But some medieval historians credit Cyrus also with restoration of the Anthemian wall in 447, when an earthquake had damaged it extensively.

3. A suburb north-west of the city, into which it was incorporated under

948 540. SELECTION OF CIVIC DEFENDERS, 503 OR 504

Heraclius (610-41), containing then an imperial palace which much later became the regular residence of the imperial family.

4. This suburb (now Galata), forming region 13 of the city, abounded in fig trees (whence the name) and, though formally a part of Constantinople (as this document declares), was unfortified. Communication with Sycae across the Golden Horn was by ferry, though farther to the north-west one could cross by wooden (later stone) bridge to Blachernae. Justinian embellished Sycae greatly.

539. LAW OF UNKNOWN EMPEROR ON EPISCOPAL INTEREST IN PURCHASE OF GRAIN, 491–534

(*CI* 10. 27. 4)

This brief and defective statute's position in Justinian's Code indicates that it belongs to a year after 491. From its tenor local officials through episcopal forethought must arrange for public purchase of grain (see no. 534).

... One [1] has come ...
By the bishop's provision the officials in the district attend to the public purchase of grain.

1. The subject is unexpressed and may be of any gender.

540. MANDATE OF ANASTASIUS I ON SELECTION OF CIVIC DEFENDERS, 503 or 504

(*MAMA* 3, no. 197)

This inscription, broken into fourteen fragments, of which the principal remnant, found at Corycus (now Korghoz) in Cilicia, was published as early as 1846, belongs from internal evidence apparently to either 503 or 504. Only enough of the chief fragment survives to warrant with editorial suggestions a translation.

Its subject, resembling that of nos. 311 and 541, treats the selection of municipal defenders, in whose election the local bishop and his clergy must have a voice.

Indiction¹ . . .

Emperor Caesar . . . Pious, Victor, Triumpher, Ever-August, Augustus to Leontius . . .²

Indacus, the most holy bishop of the Coryciotes' city, and the pure clergy assigned under him and the rentiers and the inhabitants of the said city³ have been suppliants of our Serenity about various topics, which successively—and these we know appertain to your Excellency—we have comprehended by a divine formulary.

Wherefore we ordain that he who from time to time is a defender, who ought to protect the aforesaid city from harm, and its ephor⁴ should not at all be appointed by the patronage of persons having authority or power for this,⁵ but for the future should be the proposal by vote and by scrutiny⁶ of the present and the from-time-to-time most God-beloved bishop of it⁷ and of the pure clergy assigned under him and of the aforesaid chosen men among all rentiers and inhabitants—none of the chief men of the office staff in the several places or of the so-called ordinaries⁸ daring by invocations or by petitions or by intercessions . . . or the defender of the written city or its ephor⁴ . . .

1. See no. 435, n. 9 *ad fin.*
2. Praetorian prefect of the East.
3. To the rentiers also this phrase perhaps belongs.
4. Probably the *curator civitatis*. The best-known ephors were the powerful Spartan magistrates a millennium ere this document's date.
5. That is, by civil officials.
6. A hysteron proteron.
7. Corycus.
8. A provincial governor's apparitors.

541. MANDATE OF ANASTASIUS I ON SELECTION OF CHRISTIANS AS CIVIC DEFENDERS, 505

(*CI* 1. 4. 19)

This directive, repeated in *CI* 1. 55. 11, permits only Christians to be chosen for the office of defender of a city and prescribes episcopal and sacerdotal sanction for selection to such position.

The same Augustus to Eustathius, praetorian prefect.¹

We order that for performing the administration of defenders should be appointed only those who, imbued with the orthodox religion's sacrosanct mysteries,[2] shall have disclosed this particularly under attestation of records—the orthodox religion's most religious bishop also being present—by depositions solemnized with the obligation of an oath. For we command them to be appointed thus, that they should be created by decree of the most reverend bishops and clergymen and distinguished men and rentiers and curials.[3]

Given on 19 April, Sabinian and Theodore being consuls.

1. Of the East.
2. See no. 75, n. 42.
3. This sentence with the phrase about the defenders' Christian indoctrination is taken from no. 311.

542. LETTER OF ANASTASIUS I ON ANATHEMATIZATION OF HERETICS, 505

(*AJT* 9 [1905] 739-40)

F. C. Conybeare, whose translation of this letter from Armenian is adapted stylistically, dates the document in 505 from a marginal note at its end. In this letter the emperor adheres to his predecessor Zeno's *Henoticon* (no. 527), but goes beyond it in anathematizing the Fourth General Council of Chalcedon (451) and Pope St Leo I's *Tome*, including also not a few heresiarchs of varying shades of opinion, in a futile effort to solve the religious confusion in the Empire without sacrificing eastern to western interests.[1]

Politically Anastasius seems to have had the same aim as had Zeno (on whom see introd. to no. 527 *ad fin.*), but here he openly sides with the Monophysites to wean them from their separatist tendency.

The letter which was composed by Anastasius, the emperor, against all heretics.

Whereas there is one definition of the faith which we hold due to the 318 holy fathers, who assembled in Nicaea,[2] which teaches us that of the Holy Trinity one was our Lord Jesus Christ, the Word of God, who was made incarnate of the Holy and God-bearing Virgin Mary and was made man.[3] This definition was also received by the holy 150 fathers, who assembled in Constantinople [4] to discuss the Holy Spirit. And withal by the blessed council which met in Ephesus [5] and anathematized Nestorius,[6] the heretic, and all who think and believe with him, as also in the letter which is called the *Henoticon* [7] of Zeno, the orthodox emperor; likewise also in the letter of the blessed John, the archbishop of Alexandria; which have the following purport, namely, he [8] anathematizes the *Tome* of Leo and the Council of Chalcedon, which contravened the said definition and defined them to be two natures after their union in Christ.

But we, as we have received from the holy and true fathers, deny that there are two natures and confess that there is only one nature out of two, which was made incarnate God the Word; and we anathematize [9] the Council of Chalcedon and along with it also Leo and his *Tome* and all those who assert that there are two Christs and two Sons, the one before all eternity and the other in these last times. And those who say that there are two natures, after admitting their union, and two persons and two modes and two properties and two diversities or two several operations of the several natures—these we reject and anathemize,[9] because they are found to be contrary to the *Twelve Chapters* of the blessed Cyril.[10]

We anathemize [9] Paul of Samosata [11] and Diodore [12] and Theodore [13] and Nestorius [6] and Theodoret [14] and Lutharis [15] and Andrew [16] and Hibas [17] and Kure [18] and John of Egea [19] and Bardsuma [20] and Acacius the Persian [21] and Apollinaris [22] and Eutyches [23] and Sabellius [24] and Arius [25] and Eunomius [26] and Macedonius [27] and Mani [28] and Marcion [29] and Bardesanes [30] together with their filthy teachings. And we anathematize [9] all who believe as they believe, unless they repent, and all heresies, which conflict or will conflict with the right faith of the Catholic Apostolic Church, and all who do not avow that Mary is the Mother of God,[31] the Holy Virgin, and that from her was made flesh and became man unchangeable and inseparable he who is equal and is the Son of the substance of God the Father and was also the Son of our nature in virtue of his Incarnation. And one is that existed before the Incarnation; likewise was he [one] [32] that existed after the Incarnation; as we said above, one nature of the incarnate God the Word we acknowledge. He suffered as a man and by his sufferings took away our sufferings; and he died and by his death slew death and remained impassible and immortal as God.

To him and to the Father, who sent him,[33] and to the Holy Spirit be glory to eternity of eternities. Amen.

1. Since Anastasius I's religious policy has received little attention from English-writing scholars, it may be helpful to attract attention to what seems to be the most recent study of it in English: P. Charanis, *Church and State in the Later Roman Empire: The Religious Policy of Anastasius the First, 491–518* (Madison, Wis., 1939). Add now Vasiliev, III, 115.
2. The First General Council in 325.
3. Even in English this sentence wants a conclusion.
4. The Second General Council in 381.

5. The Third General Council in 431.

6. Patriarch of Constantinople and founder of Nestorianism.

7. No. 527.

8. The obscurity of the Armenian may account for the obscurity of the English. If by *he* is meant Zeno in his *Henoticon*, the Armenian copyist errs, for it was Emperor Basiliscus who anathematized both Leo's *Tome* and Chalcedon's canons (no. 524). On the other hand, probably *he* refers to John II, patriarch of Alexandria, and a condemner of the *Tome* and of the canons. Only Monophysites, it may be said, interpreted the doctrinal definition of Chalcedon as opposed to the faith as confirmed at the three earlier ecumenical councils, on which cf. *supra* nn. 2, 4, 5.

9. Four occurrences of the first person plural number of either *anathematize* or *anathemize* occur in this letter. If the Armenian verb is the same, perhaps *anathematize* (the more usual form) should be read.

10. On these see no. 527, n. 76.

11. Bishop of Antioch, an able exponent of ante-Nicene Monarchianism.

12. Probably the bishop of Tarsus, in whose writing were the seeds of Nestorianism.

13. Probably the bishop of Mopsuestia, Pelagian in doctrine.

14. Probably the ecclesiastical historian, who was bishop of Cyrus and whose theology was not unexceptionable.

15. Apparently not identifiable.

16. Probably the pro-Nestorian bishop of Samosata.

17. Otherwise Ibas, bishop of Edessa, a Nestorian leader.

18. Perhaps the Nestorianizing bishop of Aphrodisias.

19. A Nestorian priest, who wrote a work against the Council of Chalcedon

20. Probably Barsumas, a follower of Ibas, sometime bishop of Nisibis and chief propagandist of Nestorianism in Persia.

21. The Nestorian-sympathizing bishop of Seleucia-on-the-Tigris.

22. Bishop of Laodicea in Syria and founder of Apollinarianism.

23. Heretical monk of Constantinople, the propagator of the heresy named after him.

24. The heresiarch, whose exposition of Modalism generated the heresy named after him.

25. The Alexandrian heresiarch, after whom is called Arianism.

26. Bishop of Cyzicus and founder of Eunomianism.

27. Arian bishop of Constantinople and founder of Macedonianism.

28. Otherwise Manes, the founder of Manichaeism.

29. The Pontic Gnostic.

30. The last of the Gnostic leaders.

31. "Theotokos" in Conybeare's translation.

32. Bracketed by Conybeare.

33. On the Father sending the Son see e.g. John 5. 23, 36, 37; 6. 44, 57; 8. 16, 18; 10. 36; 11. 41, 42; 12. 49; 14. 24; 17. 21, 23, 25; 20. 21.

543. LETTERS OF ANASTASIUS I ON SUMMONING SEVERUS TO COURT, 507 or 508
(PO 4. 618, 622-3)

In E. J. Goodspeed's English translation of Athanasius' Ethiopic account of *The Conflict of Severus, Patriarch of Antioch* (which account appears to ascend through an Arabic version to a Greek original) occur two letters from Anastasius: the one addressed to Romanus and John (the chief monks in a Syrian monastery, where Severus, then a monk, was in residence) and the other sent to Severus himself.[1] The object of these epistles was to secure the presence of Severus, whose fame as a defender of Monophysitism had spread to Constantinople, at the imperial court to assist Anastasius in his pro-Monophysite policy, which was obstructed by Macedonius II, patriarch of Constantinople, whose opposition to the emperor's religious programme led to his deposition and deportation in 511.[2]

I

Let the fathers [3] know that we purpose well in our heart and we desire of your Holiness [4] the lamp that is to be placed upon the lamp-stand, that it may give light therefrom;[5] we desire that it illumine the provinces of the king (which is Severus). And we ask of the Lord that you may not hide in a measure him who abides with you and may not quench him, but it is meet to put him upon the lamp-stand, that he may illumine all the field of Christ our Lord, which is the Church of the Lord. And now we ask of your Holiness [4] that you reveal him, that he may enlighten us, even as we before have made our prayer unto our Lord and unto your Holiness.[4]

Fare ye well in the Lord.

II

Do you ask of me a strong assurance?[6] For we indeed know that he who cares for you is ever with those whom he leads. And you know that a host shall surround me, but as for you, angels shall encompass you on every side and upon their hands they shall bear you up, lest you dash your foot against a stone.[7] For the blasphemy of the schismatics is as a stone of stumbling.[8]

As the Lord, the Lord God of Constantine,[9] lives,[10] there shall be no plague nor peril come nigh you nor approach your dwelling.[11] Behold, now, I have sent to you *as* [12] a solemn pledge—because of my fear [13] of your friends—my messengers, who shall abide with you. And hasten, therefore, and join us, who are thirsting for you, that we may satisfy our hope and our desire before you, even as the children of the Hebrews in the day wherein Jesus entered into Jerusalem.[14]

Wherefore, beloved Severus, be not anxious or distressed, *saying* [12] that, when you come to us, we will not hearken to you and that we will not reject Bishop Macedonius, the blasphemous heretic;[15] and let not this thought be in your perfect heart. And if we have edification from your Holiness, we will cast out Judas and receive Matthias.[16]

In the peace of the Lord may we rejoice with you.

1. Slight alterations are made in the translation to accommodate it to the style of this sylloge.
2. For a fuller account of the situation in the capital and of Anastasius' religious policy consult P. Charanis, *Church and State in the Later Roman Empire: The Religious Policy of Anastasius the First, 491–518* (Madison, Wis., 1939), 31–43.
3. The fellow-monks of Severus.
4. Probably singular for plural, for Romanus and John are the letter's recipients.
5. Adapted from Matt. 5. 15.
6. Between these letters Athanasius records that Severus, whose writings had excoriated by name the orthodox defenders of the Fourth General Council of Chalcedon (451), sought from the emperor a written pledge that no harm would come to him in Constantinople from his opponents. Anastasius' answer is the second letter.
7. Based upon Ps. 91. 11–12; Matt. 4. 6; Luke 4. 10–11.
8. 1 Pet. 2. 8.
9. The reference to Constantine is apposite, for he convoked the First General Council of Nicaea (325), from whose doctrine Severus and other Monophysites believed that the Chalcedonian fathers had departed.
10. "As the Lord liveth", of course, is a common phrase in the Old Testament: Judges 8. 19; Ruth 3. 13; 1 Sam. 14. 39; *et al.*
11. Ps. 91. 10.
12. Goodspeed's italics.
13. Probably *fear* in the Biblical sense.
14. Matt. 21. 1–11; Mark 11. 1–11; Luke 19. 28–40; John 12. 12–19.
15. From the Monophysitic viewpoint, of course.
16. Acts 1. 23–6.

544. LETTER OF ANASTASIUS I ON CONVOCATION OF THE HERACLEAN COUNCIL, 514

(CSEL 35. 501-2)

The adherence of Anastasius to his Monophysite predecessor Zeno's *Henoticon* (no. 527) and his persecution of such eastern bishops as refused subscription to it were contributing causes in 513 to Vitalian's rebellion, which was composed by the emperor's promise to convoke a general council of the Church in 514 at Heraclea on the Propontis to take measures for healing the Acacian schism, which had separated Old Rome from New Rome since 484, and thus to reconcile the recalcitrant orthodox element of the Empire (see introd. to no. 527).

This letter, the first of a series of six from Anastasius to Pope St Hormisdas, of which only four have legal significance (nos. 544-7), calls the promised council. Papal delegates arrived too late to attend the synod, which had met and had disbanded without accomplishing anything, but conveyed the pontiff's uncompromising attitude in confirmation of Pope St Felix III's condemnation of the memory of Acacius, sometime patriarch of Constantinople, while the emperor persisted in his position that living adherents of the deceased Acacius should not be banned from the Church.

Contemporary evidence that Anastasius was averse from Hormisdas' presence at the council is supported by the fact that the second letter summoning the synod (no. 545) was received in Rome before the first letter, which (the formal summons) arrived too late to allow the pope to make the necessary preparations to attend so important an assemblage.

It was not until after Justin I's accession in 518 that reconciliation was reached through submission to papal requirements and formally was recognized on 28 March 519 in Constantinople (no. 554).

While this and later documents from *CSEL* are not *stricto sensu* legal instruments in that their authors (Anastasius I, Justin I, Justinian I) could impose their will on the pope, who no longer (after 476, when the West was lost) looked legally as a subject to a Roman sovereign, yet room should be reserved for these, because the emperors evidently considered that their commands could be enforced through pressure exerted by their nominal viceroy in the person of the Ostrogothic master of Italy and since such documents demonstrate the State's attitude toward the Church—an attitude accepted and acknowledged at least in the East.

Anastasius Augustus to Pope Hormisdas.

Divine matters must be set above all affairs and indeed we are confident that when Almighty God is propitious the State should be both preserved and improved.

Therefore, because certain doubts about the orthodox religion appear to have been aroused in parts of Scythia,[1] it has pleased particularly our Clemency that a venerable synod should be held in the Heraclean city [2] of the province of Europe, that with harmonious spirits and by all truth investigated our true faith may become known more clearly to all the world, that thereafter there can be no doubt or discord.

Wherefore may your Sanctity deign to come to the aforesaid Heraclean city by 1 July with what most reverend bishops it shall have pleased you and whom you shall have approved to be worthy of the churches established under the supervision of your episcopate and versed in respect to the orthodox religion.

Given on 28 December at Constantinople, the most distinguished Senator being consul. Accepted on 14 May, the most distinguished Florentius being consul.

1. Monophysitism, which had led to the rupture between Rome and Constantinople, was especially rife in Scythia (and Syria and Egypt) and was not unconnected with certain national aspirations and anti-imperial sentiments there.

2. Known as Perinthus throughout most of antiquity, this city on the Thracian side of the Propontis assumed the name of Heraclea about 300. Sometimes it appears as Heraclea Thraciae and as Heraclea Perinthus.

545. LETTER OF ANASTASIUS I ON ECCLESIASTICAL UNITY, 515

(CSEL 35. 499–500)

This second letter in this series (nos. 544–7) arrived in Rome before the first letter (no. 544) had been received. It is more conciliatory in tone than the previous letter and it reinforces the imperial desire for a council to compose the theological differences dividing the East and the West.

Victor Anastasius, Pious, Fortunate, Renowned, Triumpher, Ever-August to Hormisdas, the most holy and religious archbishop and patriarch.

We think it not unknown to your Beatitude that in view of the nature of time even by the provident admonition of Divine Scripture has been arranged a time for speech and a time for silence.[1] Accordingly the past time of silence has given to us incentives for speech and, therefore, we have observed that it is suitable to commit to your hearing the matters which are aroused among us under the appearance of religion. Hitherto, if indeed there was austerity on the part of those to whom had been committed the care of the episcopate,[2] which you now occupy, it used to make us refrain from sending letters; but now the current pleasant opinion about you has brought to our memory the goodness of paternal affection, so that we require those things which God and our Saviour taught by divine discourse to the holy apostles and particularly to the blessed Peter, in whom he established the strength of his Church.[3]

Therefore by these prefatory beginnings we urge that your Apostolicity make itself the mediator for those matters which have been excited from the districts of Scythia,[4] as a result of which also we have perceived that a council should be made to convene, that by the removal of contentions unity may be restored to the holy Church. Moreover all desires will be fulfilled for us, if by your prayers and by frequent comfort of letters you shall have been mindful of us.

Given on 12 January at Constantinople and accepted on 28 March, the most distinguished Anthemius and the most distinguished Florentius being consuls. By Patrick.[5]

1. An allusion to Eccles. 3. 7.
2. Anastasius refers to Hormisdas' predecessors, of whom there were four (and an anti-pope), since the schism started. His reign coincided also with their pontificates, although the separation occurred under Zeno, whom he succeeded.
3. An obvious reference to the Roman interpretation of Matt. 16. 18, on which see no. 442, n. 7 *ad med.*
4. Vitalian's revolt (see introd. to no. 544) began and his general headquarters were in Lower Moesia below the Danube River, but a millennium before Anastasius the Scythians had roamed in Europe as far west and south as the north-eastern Balkans.
5. Patrick, as master of the soldiers in the emperor's presence, earlier had treated with Vitalian on behalf of Anastasius.

546. LETTER OF ANASTASIUS I ON ECCLESIASTICAL UNITY, 515-16

(CSEL 35. 537-40)

The third letter of this series (nos. 544-7) exhorts Pope St Hormisdas to take steps toward reunion of the Eastern and the Western Churches. Its chief interest, however, is an imperial confession of faith, in which also Anastasius anathematizes the Monophysite heresiarchs.

Copy of the letter of Anastasius Augustus to Pope Hormisdas.

By Ennodius and Fortunatus, bishops, Venantius, priest, Vitalius, deacon, and Hilary, notary.[1]

To Almighty God we return thanks, because your Sanctity, trained by heavenly teachings, has appointed (as we have asked) as legates of the faith Ennodius and Fortunatus, the venerable bishops, and also the religious men Venantius, the priest, Vitalius, the deacon, and Hilary, the notary, such men as the loftiness of the case demanded, who should be able to satisfy the importance of the negotiation by the light of ecclesiastical discourse and who, God effecting it, searching subtly all things which pertain to the Christians' right and true faith, both themselves have showed (as was fitting) and from us have understood (as was proper) that one is God's Church, founded everywhere on apostolic doctrines.

Wherefore who should dare to think otherwise than the truth itself has it about our Lord Jesus Christ's Incarnation,[2] unless that he should confess that the Son, equal and consubstantial with the Father, for our salvation according to the archangel's announcement[3] was made man in the Virgin's womb by assuming flesh from the same Virgin[4] and, just as the apostle says, in a servant's form, that he might assume by the flesh the Cross on our behalf?[5]

Concerning whom the blessed Apostle Peter says to the Jews: "You desired a murderer to be released to you, but you killed the author of life";[6] concerning whom it also is read in the Apostle Paul: "Having become obedient even unto death, even the death of the Cross".[7] For we confess that the Mother of God, the Blessed Virgin Mary, in true flesh and with rational and intelligible soul[8] bore for us God as a Saviour, whom we believe and we prove to have been begotten of the same being[9] with God the Father and with the Holy Spirit before the ages and likewise also of the same being[9] with us, except for our sins, in the end of the times,[10] just as the Prophet David says: "Thou art my God from my mother's belly."[11] And, nevertheless, our substance so was assumed without defect or disorder of our body, that in the same flesh God's Son, about to judge the world, may come, exhibiting to the eyes of all the evidences of the wounds and of the nails, just as it is written: "And they shall see him whom they have pierced."[12]

Also with all the orthodox we shun the most impious Nestorius[13] and Eutyches[14] and likewise we loathe, condemning and anathematizing, both the persons and the teachings—worthy to be likened to detestable sacrileges—of those who similarly have wished either not to know the divine dispensation and the remedies for human infirmity or to blaspheme these when known. Therefore Almighty God from the beginning of life has inserted in our thoughts such a purpose in regard to our Clemency's faith that we also believe that our Empire is protected.

Moreover we wonder why you have wished to write to us anything about the most blessed fathers who convened at Chalcedon,[15] as long as the matters which had been established by them are shown to have been confirmed by our predecessors' many decrees and since neither has been held another synod by which what matters have been determined by that council were made weak, nor from us has issued a law by whose novelty the aforesaid episcopal council's statutes were cancelled, especially since the synod itself has said that whosoever shall have wished to teach a faith other than what at Nicaea[16] the 318 venerable fathers have established or to alter it ought to be anathema. Moreover also them whom we have included above, that is, Nestorius[13] and Eutyches,[14] they condemned and we also condemn them. For in this case for us testify also the divine letters, sent not once but often to Alexandria, by which we have reproved them,[17] because they, departing from the anathema of the Chalcedonian Council[15] or of Bishop Leo[18] of venerable memory, thought that the indicated doctrine of the faith could not suffice for themselves. Whence not a little zeal on our part and the aim at present also continue, that we can withdraw these same persons from an unnecessary[19] anathema and unite them to the universal holy Church.

But concerning the point which alone seems to be remaining: our will would have agreed with your request perhaps so far as the churches' unity is concerned, except that we believed that other scandals for the venerable churches are aroused from this. Now consider everything which ought to be done, because our Clemency judges it to be grievous that living persons should be expelled from the venerable Church because of dead persons and we know that the measures which you write on this matter cannot be arranged without much effusion of human blood.[20] Nevertheless you should be able to accomplish all things by hoping for better counsel from God than from these men, who, running through the provinces, by their own errors desire discord inimical to the Holy Gospels and the churches. Therefore provide that the churches' unity may be pleasing to the Supernal Majesty, because who opposes us in these matters, which we have mentioned, we do not recognize that he blames us on good grounds. However, in all matters you should be able to realize the purity of our will by the recital of your legates.

Moreover we ask that your Apostolicity should deign to pray for us: and that you do this with willing mind we shall be able to know by this reason particularly, if God shall have deigned to grant to us by your arrangements the perfect unity of the churches. For that voice of God has committed and has conferred upon those who love him the great benediction, whereby he has declared: "My peace I give to you, my peace I send to you." [21]

1. These papal envoys took to Rome this reply to the pope's requirements for repairing the ecclesiastical rupture.
2. The Monophysitical view on the person of Christ was at the bottom of the Acacian schism, which Anastasius appears anxious to heal.
3. Gabriel was the (arch)angel who appeared to the Virgin Mary in the scene of the Annunciation, so celebrated in art (Luke 1. 26-38).
4. This teaching is taken partly from the Nicene, partly from the Athanasian, Creed.
5. A paraphrase of Phil. 2. 7-8.
6. Acts 3. 14-15.
7. Phil. 2. 8.
8. *Rational soul* is taken directly from the Athanasian creed.
9. *Homousion* (= ὁμοούσιον) is the Latin word, a definition which many heretics denied.
10. He means "in time since the creation of the world" or perhaps "in our time" with the accessory notion of living in "the last days"—a concept as old as the New Testament (Heb. 1. 2; cf. Gal. 4. 4.)

The identity of substance and the difference in times are adapted from the Athanasian Creed.

11. Ps. 22. 10.
12. John 19. 37.
13. Heretical patriarch of Constantinople.
14. Constantinopolitan archimandrite and founder of Eutychianism.
15. The Fourth General Council held in 451.
16. The First General Council held in 325.
17. Cf. *supra* n. 2.
18. Pope St Leo I is remembered *inter alia* for his chief aim to maintain ecclesiastical unity, toward which his celebrated *Tome*, accepted at Chalcedon, contributed so greatly.
19. Unnecessary in the sense that Alexandria, for generations the most celebrated centre of Christian learning, should have known the true faith sufficiently well so as not to have fallen from its standards.
20. Religious riots in Eastern Christendom need no documentation.
21. John 14. 27.

547. LETTER OF ANASTASIUS I ON ECCLESIASTICAL UNITY, 516

(CSEL 35. 503-4)

Two envoys of high position at the imperial court carried from Emperor Anastasius to Pope Hormisdas the following letter, which was an additional move on the emperor's part to end the Acacian schism (see nos. 544-6). The only important item in it, however, is the introduction of the imperial ambassadors, who, we are told in it, are to inform the pope about the results of the emperor's lengthy deliberation with eastern bishops [1] and are to press the pope to settle the schism.

Anastasius Augustus to Pope Hormisdas.

By the most distinguished Theopompus and the most distinguished Severian.[2]

All things which kindness has conceived are propagated by the pleasant application and the praiseworthy haste of men's minds nor do they think that rest can be given to themselves, until they shall have brought desired matters to a most salutary conclusion, and then a certain rest from haste itself results, provided that hope of its prayers shall have come to pass. And at present this we have endured with definite reason, until heavenly favour should give both an admittance to our request and a serene conclusion to your promise.

Therefore, because either the very great length of the journey or the hibernal severity beyond the usual nature has made uncertain for us what we were wishing,[3] meanwhile within our hearts we have restrained our desires, though striving for the divine benefits which decide the results of a good cause by their own intervention. Therefore knowing that dutiful conduct in this cause has conferred upon us a first favour, in that the embassy sent fortunately returned to your Beatitude,[4] we have advanced to a second favour, in that there is sent and directed by us an embassy,[5] by which both may be made mention of those things, which with very holy men we have considered with long deliberation, and also under God's direction the serene light of our request as well as of your favour may shine brilliantly anew and to the whole world awaited joys may be given.

Accordingly for the recital and for paying the honour of greeting we have sent to your Sanctity the illustrious Theopompus, count of the domestics, who conducts the school of our sacred palace,[6] loyal to us both because of his own character and because of his love for our paternal province,[7] and also the most distinguished Severian, count of our sacred consistory, who, explaining by their own voice the exposition of the letter, should stimulate to speed the decided [8] matters, which we believe have been pleasing also to the celestial mercy.

Given on 16 July at Constantinople, the most distinguished Peter being consul.

1. What was the nature of the results of the discussion is not mentioned in the letter.
2. These functionaries, who were laymen, when the pope expected an ecclesiastical embassy (*CSEL* 35. 561–2), are described later in the letter.
3. More than six months had elapsed since Anastasius last wrote to Hormisdas, who had made no reply. So by this letter the emperor prods the pope to make some move in the matter.
4. Since Anastasius had not heard directly from Hormisdas, he must have been informed by others about the papal legation's safe return to Rome.
5. The envoys are the bearers of this letter.
6. In the Dominate officials of the imperial palace, secret-service agents (on whom see no. 256, n. 3), palatines (on whom see no. 186, n. 3), and the imperial bodyguards (*domestici;* δομέστικοι) were organized in groups (σχολαί; *scholae*) and were called generically scholars or scholarians (σχολάριοι; *scholares*). This was a derisive nickname denoting their leisurely life (σχολή; *schola*) rather than their learning (the later meaning of the noun). Each school, of which about this document's time there were five in the West and seven in the East, was commanded by a count (earlier titles: tribune or provost). Since Theopompus was count of the domestics, his command then was over one school (nominally five hundred strong) of the court's garrison.
7. Epirus Nova. The emperor was born at Dyrrhachium (modern Durrës or Durazzo in Albania).
8. Or possibly "when read"; in any event the emperor means that his envoys are to expedite in Rome the papal part in the settlement of the schism.

548. LETTER OF ANASTASIUS I ON ECCLESIASTICAL UNITY, 516

(*CSEL* 35. 506–7)

These imperial instructions to the Roman Senate were designed to secure the Roman senators' support in the settlement of the Acacian schism (see introd. to no. 527), toward which, the emperor intimates, the pope is making slow progress. The Senate's answer to the emperor's communication, which their reply describes as a sacred order as well as a mandate, indicates that the senators addressed the pope on the emperor's behalf and received the same general reply as those which the pope had sent to the emperor, who regarded these as unsatisfactory.[1]

Anastasius Augustus to the Senate of the city of Rome.
By the most distinguished Theopompus and the most distinguished Severian.[2]

Emperor Caesar Flavius Anastasius, Renowned Pontiff, Renowned Germanicus, Renowned Alamannicus, Renowned Francicus, Renowned Sarmaticus, with the Tribunician Power for the twenty-fifth time, Consul for the third time, Pious, Fortunate, Victor and Triumpher, Ever-August, Father of the Fatherland sends greeting to the proconsuls, the consuls, the praetors, the plebeian tribunes, his Senate.

If you and your children are well, it is well; I and my army are well.[3]

As often as there is consultation with propitious good will for each part of the State,[4] not only exhortation but also demand is believed to be suitable, that the mind, stimulated by two motives coalescing into one, may be able to attain what is favourable and good for the details. For if Christ, our God and Lord, both by kindliest good will and by a certain request of divine dispensation [5] has recalled us to himself and has restored us, redeemed by his own blood, to freedom,[6] that he might offer salvation to mortality,[7] it does not appear absurd both in the eyes of the most glorious king[8] and in the eyes of the most blessed pope [9] of the kindly city of Rome for the conscript fathers, having agreed to the imperial request, to hope for those things which, God favouring, may advantage both us and them in common; that is, let them not hear runaways' reports, invented and composed with falsehood alone, but, having taken satisfaction from what both the truth and the interrogation of envoys, who have been sent, has made clear, let them unite for a desired peace with good will acceptable to God.

It is indubitable, therefore, from a long series of years that a large portion of public affairs lays claim to your steadfastness. Accordingly your most holy assembly ought to contend with skilled interest and provident effort both in the interest of the noble king,[8] to whom has been committed the power and the care of ruling you, and in the interest of the venerable pope, to whom has been given the faculty of intercession with God, that they may deign to bestow the goodness of their minds in that respect wherein the members of each part of the State [10] may be healed with hoped-for healing. For you will satisfy your old custom and one exceedingly well known to your deliberation, if you, God being propitious, shall have made an effort to achieve a result by considering, by expecting, by demanding those things which are suitable for the public interest.

Given on 28 July at Chalcedon, Peter being consul.

1. In the next year Anastasius relinquished his efforts to settle the schism, when he wrote rather angrily his last extant letter to Hormisdas (11 July 517) and at the end of it said (*CSEL* 35. 565): "We can tolerate being insulted and being made insignificant, but we cannot tolerate being ordered."

2. Theopompus was count of the domestics and Severian was count of the sacred consistory.

3. This stereotyped salutation, save for the addition of *your children*, is as old as the Ciceronian age and is characteristic of official letters (cf. Cicero, *Ad Fam.* 15. 2. 1); variations, of course, are found.

4. That is, the spiritual and the temporal powers, for the Latin word for *each* means properly "each of two"; cf. *infra* n. 6.

5. The idea seems to be that the Son has entreated the Father to let him be a mediator between God and Man.

6. From the bondage of eternal death, probably, in view of the subsequent clause.

7. A case of antimeria (abstract for concrete): mortal men are meant.

8. Anastasius apparently accepted Theodoric the Great, on whom see no. 528, n. 8, as his viceroy in Italy.

9. Hormisdas.

10. The thought perhaps looks to a reconciliation more between emperor and pope than between Christendom's divided parts, but probably Anastasius hoped that the latter reunion would result, after the temporal and the spiritual powers had come to terms. Hence his appeal to the Senate to put pressure on the pope.

549. LETTER OF JUSTIN I ON ECCLESIASTICAL UNITY, 518

(CSEL 35. 587-8)

Not two months elapsed after Justin I had succeeded Anastasius I on the throne at Constantinople before he opened negotiations with Pope St Hormisdas in Rome to end the Acacian schism, which had divided East and West ecclesiastically since 484 (see introd. to no. 527).

It is interesting to note that Justin and his successor Justinian, "whose influence was felt from the first year of his uncle's reign",[1] reversed the religious policy of Anastasius and his predecessor Zeno, who had favoured the Monophysites (nos. 527 and 542), although this *volte-face* toward orthodoxy again arrayed their Egyptian and Syrian subjects in opposition to the Empire and accelerated their future alienation.[2]

549. ECCLESIASTICAL UNITY, 518

This document, the first of several written by the emperor to the pope, asks for papal envoys to be sent to Constantinople to discuss ways and means to close the breach, which, as the event proved, was composed in the spring of 519. See introd. *ad fin.* to no. 544.

Justin Augustus to Pope Hormisdas.

The most blessed John, bishop of this royal city,[3] and all the other religious bishops who are found here from sundry districts and communities have informed our Serenity that they have composed a letter to be presented to your Sanctity[4] in the interest of the concord of those who cherish the true and orthodox faith and in the interest of its venerable churches' unity and they have asked earnestly that also our epistolary letter on this matter should proceed to you. And having embraced willingly their petitions, inasmuch as we ever have been disposed to be lovers of unity, we have decided that this divine letter ought to be forwarded to your Beatitude, that you may deign to aid these received desires[5] of the aforesaid most reverend bishops and to placate the Supernal Majesty by your prayers on behalf of us and the State, whose direction has been entrusted from heaven to our Piety.

Moreover, that the rights of peace and of unity and of concord may be made more fully clear to your Sanctity, arrange to send to our most sacred court some most religious bishops[6] who embrace and desire peace. For on account of this reason we have sent the noble Gratus,[7] count of our sacred consistory and master of the secretarial bureau of the records,[8] of whom we have an outstanding opinion, hitherto noted on many occasions.

Given on 7 September at Constantinople, the most distinguished Magnus being consul.

1. So Vasiliev, 131, and see no. 550, nn. 1 and 2.
2. See Introd., n. 43, and introd. to nos. 476, 527, 542. Add now Vasiliev, 88–90, 105–6, 115, 196, 208–10.
3. Constantinople.
4. The patriarch's letter is in *CSEL* 35. 591–2.
5. Or "that you may deign, when this has been received, to aid the desires".
6. See no. 16, n. 4.
7. The carrier of the letter.
8. See no. 256, n. 2.

550. LETTER OF JUSTINIAN I ON ECCLESIASTICAL UNITY, 518

(*CSEL* 35. 592-3)

In implementation of his uncle Justin I's letter (no. 549) on healing the ecclesiastical division of East and West (see introd. to no. 527) Justinian, the future first emperor of that name, wrote also to Pope St Hormisdas the following letter, which, since Justinian was the directing power behind the throne during his uncle's brief reign,[1] is included as representing the imperial will,[2] for it seems clear that Justin's ecclesiastical policy had Justinian as its real author.

While Justin's letter asks Hormisdas to send legates to conclude the reunion, Justinian categorically summons the pope to come to Constantinople personally and without delay. The papal reply to Justinian has not been preserved, but in any event Hormisdas sent an embassy with minute and definite instructions [3] about reunion.[4]

See introd. *ad fin.* to no. 544.

Copy of Justinian's epistle.

Divine Clemency, having regard for the human race's sufferings, has deigned to grant the desirable time, for which with highest prayers we have wished, that all Catholics and those perfectly loyal to God may be able to commend themselves to its Majesty. Therefore to your Apostolicity I have sent this letter, with free licence now granted to me by celestial benefit.[5]

For our lord, the most unconquered emperor,[6] ever embracing the orthodox religion and with most ardent faith desiring to recall the sacrosanct churches to concord, presently has gained the imperial insignia through celestial judgement [7] and has offered officially the bishops [8] stationed here to be united to the Church according to the apostolic regulations. And indeed a great part of the faith has been settled under God's leadership; only about the name of Acacius is it appropriate for your Beatitude to undertake agreement.[9]

Wherefore our lord, the most serene prince, has sent the noble Gratus,[10] a friend of one accord with me, with an august letter to your Sanctity, that by all means you may deign to come to Constantinople to arrange the remaining matters of the concord. But apart from any delay we expect your arrival, but if any slowness—which ought not to occur—perhaps should have restrained you, hurry meanwhile also to send bishops,[11] because the whole world in our territories, converted to unity,[12] does not permit delays.

Therefore hasten, most holy lord, lest in your absence should be ordained what ought to be ordained in your presence. For we know what your Beatitude's and your predecessors' letters, sent to the East, contain about this same case.

But that nothing may be overlooked, because the case has been mentioned rather often to the most unconquered king,[13] the negotiation in the matter of religion also has been entrusted to your son, the noble Gratus, under the favour of our Lord Jesus Christ.[14]

1. Bury remarks that "In the *Secret History* [*Historia Arcana* or *Anecdota*] Procopius treats the reign of Justin as virtually part of that of Justinian. That this view of Justinian's influence was generally accepted is shown by passages in the *Public History* [*Historiae* or *De Bellis*] and the *De aedificiis*" (2. 21, n. 4).

A. A. Vasiliev confirms this view in his *Justin the First* (Cambridge, Mass., 1950), where he holds (v) that Justinian's "rule behind the throne, of course, started, in my opinion, from the moment of Justin's elevation", though the formal co-option occurred on 4 April 527, when the ailing Justin had less than four months of life left to him, and (6) that "the reign of Justin I is to be regarded as the unofficial reign of Justinian". Add now Vasiliev, 131.

Justinian, like Augustus and Constantine, was simultaneously of the past and of the future, which was the basic reason why for so long he was able to dominate the present.

2. Vasiliev believes (op. cit., 4) that Justin, who was "without theological education and without interest in the complicated subtleties of the religious problems of his time ... naturally left the religious policy of his administration ... to his nephew, who at that time was already an accomplished theologian". Not only was Justinian "an accomplished theologian", but F. Gavin thinks that he also was "the most conspicuous theologian of the sixth century and the formulator of the ideal which to this day flourishes as normative for the whole of Eastern Christendom" (*Seven Centuries of the Problem of Church and State* [Princeton, 1938], 7).

On Justinian's ecclesiastical policy consult Bury, 2. 360–80; Gavin, op. cit., 14–23; Vasiliev, 148–51.

3. The instructions are in *CSEL* 35. 605–7.

4. Vasiliev, op. cit., 135.

5. He means by this that the emperor has allowed him to write to the pope.

6. Justin.

7. Justin in an earlier letter to the pope (*CSEL* 35. 586) wrote that he had come to the throne through the favour of the Inseparable Trinity.

8. See no. 16, n. 4.

9. Acacius, patriarch of Constantinople, was excommunicated by Pope St Felix III (II) in 484 for his sponsorship of the Monophysite party of Alexandria, his vague and loose grasp of theological principles, his attempt to exalt the authority of his see over the entire East. One of the insistent demands made by successive pontiffs, when approached on settlement of the ensuing schism, was the erasure of Acacius' name from the diptychs (on which see no. 554, n. 1) at Constantinople. To this problem Justinian refers.

10. Identified in no. 549 at n. 7 in text.

11. To represent the pope and to present the papal terms. For the Latin term used here cf. *supra* n. 8.

12. A gross exaggeration, else there would not have been need to persecute Monophysites later—as was done.

13. Apparently Theodoric the Great, on whom see nos. 528, n. 8, and 548, n. 8.

14. The editor notes that the letter was given on 7 September and was accepted on 20 December.

551. LETTER OF JUSTINIAN I ON EXPULSION OF MONKS FROM ROME, 519
(CSEL 35. 644-5)

Early in 519, before the reunion of Christendom after the Acacian schism dating from 484 (see introd. to no. 527), several monks from the province of Scythia Minor appeared in Constantinople with a formula known as Theopaschism (that one of the Trinity had suffered in the flesh) to reconcile orthodox and Monophysites. Rebuffed by papal legates present in the capital to compose the disunion and denounced as heretical by Constantinopolitan monks, the Scythians departed for Rome to lay their opinion before Pope St Hormisdas.

In this letter to the pope Justinian warns him that four of these monastic meddlers are en route to Rome and asks Hormisdas not only not to receive them but also to return them to him after proper correction.

Copy of Justinian's letter.

Justinian to the holy, most blessed because of his merits, and apostolic lord, lord father, Pope Hormisdas.

By the Gracious Divinity, which ever instructs the Catholic Church through augmentations of faith, the unity of the holy churches has come to pass by virtue of your Apostolicity's teaching and authority.

But since we have learned that certain persons, monks by name, for whom discord more than love and God's peace is an intention, desiring to disturb certain matters and departing from here, have taken the road to your Angel,[1] may your Beatitude, recognizing from the present writing the reason of their malice, deign to receive them so as they deserve and to drive them far from yourself, because the foolish talk of these very persons, who hasten to introduce in the Church novelties which neither the four venerable synods [2] nor the holy Pope Leo's [3] letters are known to contain, seems to excite disturbances in every district.

551. EXPULSION OF MONKS FROM ROME, 519

Wherefore also from the most reverend men, bishops and deacons, guided by your Apostolicity . . .[4] may your Angel [1] deign to send to us and may order to expel these very persons, smitten by deserving correction (as has been written above). Therefore we ask this, that (as has been written above) your Beatitude [5] should order particularly to direct a letter of this character [6] by the same bearer to us. Moreover their names are Achilles, John, Leontius, and Maurice.[7]

This is our chiefest cause of worry, lest the unity which your labour and prayer have accomplished [8] should be destroyed by restless men, for we hope in God that, if there is anything which still differs from the peace of the whole world, this also by your prayers may be united to the apostolic see's communion.[9]

Moreover, presuming upon paternal love in respect to your Beatitude's benevolence, we ask too much, namely that you should deign liberally to make illustrious and to make conspicuous by relics of the holy apostles both us and their basilica, built here in our home under the title of the aforesaid venerable ones,[10] realizing that you can bestow on us nothing, neither gift nor favour, most blessed lord father, greater than if you shall have fulfilled our request.

Moreover by the aforesaid [11] secret-service agent,[12] who quickly has taken the road, we also have sent for the adornment of the altar of the holy apostles [13] two all-silk altar cloths;[14] and, receiving these, order immediately with your most efficacious prayers that mention of us should be made.

1. The "angel of the church" is an expression as old as the first Christian century, wherein the author of the Apocalypse wrote to the angels of the seven churches in Asia (Rev. 2. 1, 8, 12, 18, 3. 1, 7, 14).

As late as 30 March 1952 Pope Pius XII, the then successor of Pope St Hormisdas, was described similarly by "a noted Jesuit speaker, the Rev. Riccardo Lombardi, . . . speaking . . . from the steps of St. Peter's Basilica . . . as 'the angel of our city [Rome]' " (*The New York Times*, vol. 101, no. 34,400, p. 6, col. 3; 31 March 1952).

2. These probably are the four general councils thus far recognized by both East and West: Nicaea (325), Constantinople (381), Ephesus (431), Chalcedon (451).

3. Pope St Leo I.

4. The poor syntax of this document has achieved such a climax here that editors here mark a lacuna, which defies acceptable conjecture to fill. Probably the name of the letter-carrier belongs here. From a later letter of this year it appears that the messenger is a certain Eulogius (no. 553).

5. This is probably the understood subject, for none is expressed.

6. This is the first of several unsuccessful attempts by Justinian to elicit from Hormisdas a definite answer on the problem described in the next note.

7. These four seem to have been Scythian monks, who maintained the Theopaschite doctrine. While Justinian appears averse from this thesis at this time, later he emitted an edict (no. 636) in favour of it and procured a confirmation of it from Pope John II.

The Theopaschite controversy is significant in that it is one of the first signs of the victory of Aristotle over Plato in Christian philosophy, according to F. Loofs, *Leontius von Byzanz* (Leipzig, 1887), 255.

8. Justinian refers to the recent settlement of the Acacian schism, which was ended about three months before this letter's date.

9. While the Latin here has *anything, which, this* in the neuter gender, Justinian probably has personal objects in mind and means "anyone", "who", "he".

10. Apparently a church in or attached to the so-called House of Hormisdas (named after and assigned to a Persian prince of that name who had taken refuge with Constantine the Great), later known as the House of Justinian, who dwelt there until his accession in 527. Its façade still stood as late as 1923.

If this identification is rejected, the other possibility is the Church of the Holy Twelve Apostles, on which see no. 463, n. 5.

11. Apparently mentioned in the lacuna (cf. *supra* n. 4).

12. See no. 256, n. 3.

13. Perhaps one for each basilica where St Peter and St Paul were buried: San Pietro in Vaticano and San Paolo fuori le Mura.

14. The word is *pallius*, a variant of *pallium* (whence our English "pall"), not to be confused with the woollen pallium sent by the pope ordinarily only to archbishops on their petition.

552. LETTER OF JUSTINIAN I ON THEOPASCHISM, 519

(*CSEL* 35. 648–9)

It seems that Justinian, soon after the dispatch of his first letter on this subject (no. 551), altered his attitude toward the Scythian doctrine of Theopaschism and, before Pope St Hormisdas could reply to his first letter, sent this second letter in the belief that the Theopaschite formula might reconcile orthodox and Monophysites and might be the foundation of ecclesiastical peace. Justinian urges Hormisdas to decide quickly about the doctrine that one of the Trinity suffered in the flesh, for the raising of this novel theological teaching was threatening the peace of the Constantinopolitan Church, whence the controversy was likely to emanate throughout the East—as the event proved.

Copy of Justinian's letter.
By Proemptor's [1] brother.[1]

We wish that whatever is more circumspect, whatever is more constant, should be performed on behalf of the holy faith and the sacred churches' concord.

Accordingly to your Beatitude both our brother, the most renowned Vitalian,[2] through the noble Paulinus, the defender of your church,[3] has written in answer and we ourselves have taken care by the same person to indicate that your Beatitude ought to perform those things which confer peace and concord on the holy churches. Forthwith, however, with our most pious emperor's [4] letters we have sent him to carry a rather definite reply to your Sanctity, for the aforesaid religious man, the defender, can inform your Sanctity as to how important a question [5] has arisen in our territories.

Accordingly we ask that, if it is possible, after a very speedy reply has been given and the religious monks have been satisfied, you return John [6] and Leontius [6] to us, for, unless by your prayers and diligence that question shall have been solved, we fear that the holy churches' peace cannot prosper. Therefore, knowing that both the benefit and the peril of this situation is observed by you, diligently investigate and return to us a very firm reply by the aforesaid religious monks, if it is possible, before our envoy [7] comes to your Beatitude, for on this alone depends the entire matter.

1. Unidentified.
2. Vitalian in the preceding reign of Anastasius I (see introd. to no. 544) had begun in 513 a rebellion against that emperor partially and ostensibly to heal the Acacian schism, but, though honoured by the new emperor, Justin I, with the consulate for 520, was murdered ere its expiration at the alleged instigation of Justinian, who, it is said, wanted to remove any rival between him and his uncle the emperor.
3. One of the papal representatives travelling between Rome and Constantinople. A *defensor ecclesiae* (later called *advocatus ecclesiae*) was a layman, ordinarily a nobleman, who was charged with defending its rights against force. But in the present case this Paulinus would have had small success in such a defence and, as a matter of fact, the application of force was not considered, for the East and the West were at peace ecclesiastically with each other at this time and Constantinople in the reign of Justin was more than meeting every Roman demand. So Paulinus best may be regarded as a lay representative of Hormisdas in Constantinople on a temporary mission, whence he was returning to Rome.
4. Justin I.
5. This was the controversy over Theopaschism, newly raised in the East (see no. 551, n. 7).

6. One of the four Scythian monks named in Justinian's earlier letter (no. 551) as en route to Rome for papal decision about Theopaschism.

7. Paulinus.

553. LETTER OF JUSTINIAN I ON THEOPASCHISM, 519

(*CSEL* 35. 645-6)

A third letter from Justinian to Pope St Hormisdas on the Theopaschite teaching that one of the Trinity suffered in the flesh seeks to elicit from Rome a definite reply, which, as the event showed, never came, for the pope hesitated to sanction such an interpretation which could and perhaps was designed to aid the Monophysites, though it could be construed in an orthodox manner.

Eventually the Scythian monks, who had preached this formula both in Constantinople and in Rome, were expelled—so they said—from Rome, although the pope, who had been annoyed at their importunity and was inclined to remit their case to the patriarch of Constantinople for decision, failed to commit himself to a definite opinion concerning their doctrine.

Also a copy of Justinian's letter.

In order that the fullest perfection of the faith may come to us through your Beatitude's teaching, again we have sent the active Eulogius, the secret-service agent,[1] for various reasons but also for this, through whom we earnestly ask that in all matters by your Apostolicity's carefully examined and most careful reply it [2] may be confirmed in the confession of the Catholic faith. For after by the Divine Mercy unity once has been granted to the Catholic Church,[3] certain persons assert that Christ, God's Son, our Lord, ought to be preached as one of the Trinity having suffered in the flesh for our salvation.[4]

If this ought to be received, let your Reverence with paternal foresight deign to inform us by your own most careful rescript what we ought to follow or what we ought to avoid on this subject, since the words seem to make dissension, for among all Catholics one meaning is shown to exist.[5]

Therefore, holy and venerable father, once for all impose this undertaken labour on yourself, following in this matter also your predecessors, whose memory you embrace and adorn by association in the pontificate, and hasten to make us free and secure from this dispute. For we believe to be Catholic that which by your religious reply shall have been announced to us. But because it has been said that Scythian monks [6] have approached your see on this subject, after a reply has been furnished to them pursuant to the tradition of the fathers and the order of the rules, command them, fearing nothing, to return with your letter, of which do you direct that certified copies also be given to the aforesaid active Eulogius. For on that account we ask that all these matters you arrange rather carefully, that an opportunity for falsehood and artifice should not be given, since, embracing the Catholic faith with the highest desire, we seek that unity by your teaching should be granted to the whole world.

1. On this official see no. 256, n. 3.
2. The subject seems to be either the perfection of the faith or its transmission from Rome to Constantinople.
3. Reference is to the recent settlement of the Acacian schism, which had persisted for a generation.
4. This Christological formula, while susceptible of orthodox interpretation, appears to have been devised in the interest of heterodoxy. Pope St Hormisdas' refusal to accept this formula, which for a time appeared in the *Trisagion* (the Armenian Church retained it for more than a millennium), eventually led Justinian to enact it into law (no. 636), which Pope St John II confirmed.
5. Justinian means that the essence of Catholicism is to be united in one interpretation of any doctrine, but particularly, perhaps, of this teaching.
6. Named in a previous letter (no. 551 at n. 7 in text).

554. LETTER OF JUSTIN I ON ECCLESIASTICAL UNITY, 519

(*CSEL* 35. 610–12)

This letter to Pope St Hormisdas announces the final imperial step to end the ecclesiastical breach between East and West, which had existed since 484 (see introd. to no. 527). This event was effected on 28 March 519 at the imperial palace in the presence of the emperor and the senators, when John II, patriarch of Constantinople, subscribed to the papal terms of reunion and when the names of Acacius and his four heretical successors in the patriarchate as well as the names of Emperors Zeno and Anastasius I were deleted from the diptychs.[1]

Justin Augustus to Hormisdas.
Victor Justin, Pious, Fortunate, Renowned, Triumpher, Ever-August to Hormisdas, the most holy and most blessed archbishop and patriarch.

You should know, most religious father, the end which for a long time was being sought by the highest efforts; you should know clearly—even before those who have been sent to you should have arrived—that the most blessed John, bishop of our New Rome,[2] along with his clergy agrees with you, varying by no ambiguities, divided by no discords; you should know that that by him has been subscribed a certificate,[3] which you had decided must be submitted, conforming with the council of the holiest fathers.[4] All whom truth's gleaming brightness illuminates concur with keen action to undertake vows for your as well as the Constantinopolitan see; all whom the clear way delights hasten most willingly, follow the father's holiest ordinances, most excellent laws; and, by having supported the counsels of certain ones who were keeping the right path and by having corrected the counsels of other ones who were wandering uncertainly, in this way the situation is produced that the unity of the Undivided Trinity they themselves also revere with the unity of their minds. In accordance with the tenor of the certificate, which we have mentioned, it has been affirmed that amid the divine mysteries[5] for the future will not be made mention of the transgressor Acacius,[6] sometime bishop of this royal city,[2] and also of the other bishops,[7] who either first went against the apostolic ordinances or were the followers of his error, corrected by no repentance even to their last day.

And since all our territories have been admonished that they should imitate the example of the royal city,[2] we have considered that the imperial orders ought to be dispatched everywhere; with such great duty for religion we are inflamed, with such great zeal we strive for the peace of the Catholic faith, on behalf of re-bestowing celestial-sent peace for our State, on behalf of winning for my subjects heavenly protection. For what can be found more pleasing, what more just, what more illustrious than for those whom the same kingdom contains and worship of the same faith illumines not to dispute about different matters, but, with thoughts collected in the same course, to revere ordinances published not by human mind but by the providence of the Divine Spirit?

Therefore let the Sanctity of your religion pray that the assistance of the divine gift may grant to be preserved by continual perpetuity what by very vigilant zeal is provided for the peace of the churches of the Catholic faith.

Given on 22 April at Constantinople.

1. In the early Church it was customary to inscribe on diptychs (a kind of notebook constructed by the union of two tablets, joined by hinges or by rings, made of various materials, often elaborately decorated) the names of those, whether living or dead, who were considered members of the Church. Their

liturgical use can be dated from our mid-third century and lingered longer in the East than in the West, but varied at different periods and in different churches: sometimes the names in the diptychs were read during Mass from either altar or ambo by either priest or deacon; at other times diptychs simply were deposited on the altar during Mass. Exclusion from such registers was regarded as a severe ecclesiastical penalty.

2. Constantinople.

3. This document (*CSEL* 35. 607-10) was signed on 28 March 519, was sent to Rome on 22 April, and on 19 June was received there.

4. An allusion to the First General Council of Nicaea in 325.

5. That is, during divine worship or the celebration of Mass. See no. 75, n. 42.

6. As patriarch of Constantinople he caused in 484 the first great schism (named after him) between East and West (see introd. to no. 527).

7. See no. 16, n. 4.

555. EDICT OF JUSTIN I ON ORTHODOXY FOR SOLDIERS, 519 or 520

(*CI* 1. 4. 20)

It recently has been suggested that this document, generally assigned to Justinian I, emanates from Justin I, his uncle and predecessor, and is the edict ascribed in Syriac sources to the latter.[1]

The directive commands that anyone enlisting in the army must invoke witnesses to testify on oath that he is an orthodox Christian. Violation of the edict entails fines. According to Syriac sources an additional punishment for non-adherence to orthodoxy was deprivation of rations and of other privileges pertaining to military service.

Most of the soldiers seem to have obeyed the imperial order,[2] which, it is supposed, applied only to the regular Roman soldiers as distinct from other military personnel.

Emperor Justin Augustus.[3]

None serves in the army, unless in the rosters he has been attested on the Holy Gospels in the presence of three persons to be an orthodox Christian[4]—the act being performed before the commander where[5] he is about to serve in the army and two coins[6] being given for this.[7]

But if this has been disregarded, the commander gives fifty pounds and his staff[8] twenty and he[9] who has served in the army ten.[10] And he[9] is discharged and the persons who falsely testified are punished corporally and the penalties are paid into the private estates [11] at the peril of the count.[12]

1. So A. A. Vasiliev, *Justin the First* (Cambridge, Mass., 1950), 233, 242–4. Cf. *infra* n. 3.

2. See Vasiliev, op. cit., 233, 242, n. 193.

3. Since editors bracket the Greek superscription, which gives "Justinian" for *Justin*, the superscription seems suspect.

4. This reversal of the early Church's rebuke against any Christian—let alone an orthodox one—serving in the State's armed forces is only one of the Roman Army's legacies to the Christian Church, on which see Toynbee, 7. 338–44. For Christians in the Roman Army consult A. D. Nock's article "The Roman Army and the Roman Religious Year" in *HTR* 45 (1952) 223–9.

At least four generations (c. 385) ere this edict's emission recruits swore "by God and Christ and the Holy Spirit and the emperor's majesty, which next to God must be loved and cherished by the human race" (Vegetius, *Epit. Rei Mil.* 2. 5).

5. The Latin translation renders ἔνθα by *sub quo* (under whom).

6. Greek νομίσματα; Latin *solidi*, on which see no. 433, n. 7.

7. In this offer and in its acceptance may be perhaps the origin of the king's (queen's) shilling, tendered by a recruiter and taken by a recruit, in the British Army, wherein such acceptance until 1879 betokened a binding enlistment.

8. Here τάξις, usually equivalent to *ordo* (on which see no. 325, n. 6), is translated by *officium* (as in nos. 567 at n. 15 and 651 at n. 26) and, instead of "office staff", must mean "military staff" in this situation.

9. The recruit.

10. All these amounts ordinarily would be in gold, but for a common soldier to be fined ten pounds in gold seems fairly severe.

11. Of the emperor.

12. The count of the private estates is held responsible for collection.

556. LETTER OF JUSTIN I ON ECCLESIASTICAL UNITY, 520

(*CSEL* 35. 636–7)

After the ecclesiastical reunion of East and West in 519 certain eastern prelates were reluctant to accept the imperial submission to the papal requirements for reunion and continued to maintain unorthodox opinions about the Trinity. In this letter Justin asks Pope St Hormisdas for an authoritative answer, after the pope shall have been informed about the details of the dispute by an imperial message.

Justin Augustus to Pope Hormisdas.
With what great zeal we burn for the most sacred churches to be brought together in concord we are known to have made clear for a long time, since even from the beginning of our Sovereignty we have thought that your Sanctitude should be reminded how you might direct certain persons [1] that by their intervention some remedy could be found for these matters and since, before those who have been sent [1] should have arrived, we have prepared all things whereby more easily might be transacted the matters which had to be arranged in this most flourishing city.[2]

But since to our Divinity have been presented prayers from various eastern provinces discussing certain matters about the Catholic faith and declaring the secrets of their own thought, which they testify have been decided among themselves about the Undivided Trinity and which they show that they will retain firmly, and since Dioscore,[3] after these had been read, has asserted that some matters had been inserted in a not consistent order, we deservedly have thought that to you should be revealed those matters which we have been shown.

Accordingly not much later by us will be sent a certain person to inform your Beatitude about all matters and to make known to you the supplications which have been presented to us and to bring back your Piety's reply, that the incongruous doubts can be removed at last.

Therefore, untroubled about our intention, deign to placate for us with solicitous prayers the Highest Divinity.

Given on 19 January at Constantinople, Vitalian and Rusticius being consuls.

1. The papal legates with instructions about the requirements for reunion of Christendom separated since the Acacian schism in 484.
2. Constantinople.
3. A deacon and one of the papal commissioners, who remained in Constantinople as observers of the application of the union (effected on 28 March 519) in the various regions of the Empire.

557. LETTER OF JUSTIN I ON EPISCOPAL APPOINTMENTS, 520

(*CSEL* 35. 650–1)

Soon after Justin I had been elected emperor in 518, Pope St Hormisdas began an epistolary campaign by writing both to Justin and to others to enlist support in Constantinople for the restoration of three eastern bishops to their sees, whence Anastasius I had extruded them *c.* 512 and where with imperial sanction others had succeeded them. Since the three prelates, Helias (Elias) of Caesarea in Cappadocia, Thomas and Nicostratus of unidentified sees, were among the first to participate in the reunion with Rome in 519, the pope was anxious for their rehabilitation. But the emperor in this letter to the pope announces his decision, which, so far as is known, prevailed, that Helias' successor was so popular that it was unwise to degrade him and that Helias must wait for reinstatement after the incumbent's death; as for Thomas and Nicostratus, action in their cases called for postponement until the final settlement of the reunion.

Justin Augustus to Pope Hormisdas.

Since it is in our mind, most religious father, that in every matter our plans should be consistent, then also in the case of Helias, the most reverend bishop, we believe that, with your legates advising, there ought to be established this which has been seen clearly to be the more expedient between two different methods.

For both at present the favour of all defends the pontiff of the Caesareans' city, whom because of his very excellent practices not only the inhabitants think most strongly ought to be retained, but also almost the entire East without doubt venerates, and he who has been previously in that same episcopate [1] complains that he has been removed unjustly. Accordingly it has seemed to be proper that neither we should make an attack against the prayers of uncounted multitudes and that a man renowned in integrity should be deposed from his see, of which he shows himself worthy, nor we should permit to be taken entirely from his predecessor the hope of re-seeking again his place, of which he asserts that he has been deprived without cause, but we should act rather temperately in a doubtful situation, in such a way that this same Helias, the most reverend bishop, should remain in retirement, but, after his successor should have died, then at length he should return to the see, whence he left,[2] after there have been observed previously all matters which the statutes of the most sacred regulations demand for gaining permission for return and also after there has been interposed the consent of your apostolic see as well as of this most flourishing city [3] and of other cities,[4] to which this matter is an interest.

Also concerning Thomas and Nicostratus, the most religious

bishops, after the rest of the venerable churches also shall have been joined to you in unity, there shall be subjected to accomplishment all the things which we shall have considered worthy to be established, under the guidance of heavenly protection, pursuant likewise to the arrangement of the most sacred regulations.

Accordingly, since our resolution ought to be revealed also to your Holiness, that from it also may be manifested the desire in which we direct every effort to settle and to moderate controversies and to preserve desired peace among all persons, we have decided also that there ought to be sent the present letter, admonishing especially that by your prayers the Heavenly Divinity should be entreated for the safe condition of the State.

Given on 7 June at Constantinople in the consulate of Vitalian and Rusticius.

1. See no. 158, n. 1.
2. Since Helias' successor, Soterichus, was still alive sixteen years after this letter's date, some suppose that Helias did not survive the intruder's death.
3. Probably Constantinople, as being the New Rome, and claiming a primacy of honour in the East, at least when it could not exercise jurisdiction (see no. 375, n. 7); but perhaps Caesarea, as the interested see.
4. Either the eastern patriarchates or Caesarea's suffragan sees.

558. LETTER OF JUSTIN I ON DIPTYCHS OF EASTERN CHURCHES, 520

(CSEL 35. 649–50)

To implement the solution of the Acacian schism (484–519) Justin I congratulates Pope St Hormisdas on the reconciliatory work of the papal legates in Constantinople and concurs with Hormisdas on what bishops' names are to be deleted from the diptychs. At the same time, however, the emperor warns the pope of the difficulty of papal insistence on erasure of the names of such prelates as are beloved by the people of their dioceses and he informs Hormisdas that he soon will send to the pontiff an envoy to discuss in more detail this matter.

Justin Augustus to Pope Hormisdas.
By our legates, that is, Germanus, John, bishops, Felix, Dioscore, deacons, and Blandus, priest.[1]
Highest thanks indeed ought to be paid to you, because you do not hesitate to expend keen attention to joining and uniting the venerable churches. Moreover in this matter especially shines brightly perfect

skill, because you select men who with sincere and honest mind can serve your Sanctitude's benevolent prayer. Therefore Germanus, the most reverend bishop, and also Felix and Dioscore and Blandus, the most religious men, have shown themselves attentive with so much industry and have engaged in so much wisdom, that, as far as pertains to their duty, when all matters had been transacted in full and had been elaborated, no altercation further remained.

But since mortal frailty is of such condition that it desires to be treated rather indulgently in respect to itself and a plain reply to be made to its questions, especially when some cause has descended upon an immense multitude of men, it has happened that in this indeed very flourishing city [2] whatever has been ordained about the case of religion and about celebrating the unity with the apostolic see in the time of John of most religious memory,[3] when he was in the episcopate [4] of this royal city,[2] was preserved—God favouring it—steadfast and also in several other cities your command has been approved and has been received, but other cities need a certain milder regulation in respect to the names of their bishops—not of those who specifically have been enumerated in the epistle which your Sanctitude is known to have sent to us, but of others whose memory those cities in which they, surviving, are known to have flourished love especially.

Wherefore indeed your Sanctitude's legates have no freedom to exceed the tenor of the mandate with which they have been sent;[5] but the whole limit of the business depends now only on your decision, so that he alone who has set in motion the first beginnings of the matter is obligated to conclude the peace.

But these and also certain matters will be mentioned more explicitly by our legate, who a little later will be sent.

But at present we have believed that your Reverence ought to be entreated as well as ought to be advised by the returning most religious men,[1] that you may employ your prayers for our Sovereignty and for the State's unimpaired condition.

Given on 9 July at Constantinople, Vitalian and Rusticius being consuls.

---

1. These were the papal legates sent to Constantinople in 519, who at long last were returning to Rome after completion of their mission.

2. Constantinople.

3. The second patriarch of that name, recently deceased after less than two years at the head of the Constantinopolitan Church. In his patriarchate the Acacian schism was healed.

4. See no. 158, n. 1.

5. Hormisdas had given his envoys most precise instructions about their mission (*CSEL* 35. 605–7).

559. MANDATE OF JUSTIN I ON A RELIGIOUS CELEBRATION AT CYRUS, 520

(M 9. 364-5)

This directive, which lacks a superscription, orders Hypatius, master of the soldiers in the East, to investigate the report that Sergius I, bishop of Cyrus, authorized a special celebration to honour Theodoret, his illustrious predecessor in that see and the renowned ecclesiastical historian, whose theology was not without suspicion. Sergius, who recently had been appointed to Cyrus, sanctioned the celebration to show his sympathy with his people, who were such warm admirers of Theodoret that lately they, under the leadership of two clerics, had placed Theodoret's image in a chariot and had escorted it through the town with a psalm-singing procession. After the investigation Sergius was deposed.

To us have been read the records compiled by the defender of the Antiochene city, wherein were inserted the testimonies of soldiers making known—that we may speak briefly—that before the most reverend Sergius came to the Cyrestene city certain persons, that is, Andronicus, a priest and a defender, and George, a deacon, taking the image of Theodoret, who everywhere is accused because of error of faith, placed it in a chariot and brought it into the Cyrestene city, singing and showing that they are of the same sect. Moreover Sergius, after he had accepted the city,[1] also celebrated an assembly for Theodoret himself and Diodore[2] and Theodore[3] and also a certain Nestorius,[4] who, he said, was a martyr, although the province[5] has no martyry fitting this name.[6]

We therefore obviously wonder, first, indeed, if such records compiled in the city have escaped your Eminence's notice; then, if, when you had known what has happened, you not without[7] delay have made an investigation of the matter, especially since Sergius was said to be living there[8] and to be with the most reverend Paul.[9]

But also to us a little later were read the records compiled by the defender of the Cyrestene city, what the most reverend secretaries[10] of the most reverend Sergius have said—these records containing the words of many persons: that neither anything ever has been preached nor an assembly has been made in the name of a certain Nestorius. Moreover besides these we have heard the records and the petition both of Sergius himself and of the remaining bishops of the province Euphratensis, who everywhere reject Nestorius' name and indeed avow that they avoid his sect, but that they concur with the four holy councils.[11]

Therefore we sanction that your Eminence should abandon no acuity or zeal, but indeed without delay should summon the bishop of the Cyrestene city living there—as we have heard—but also should draw to yourself the soldiers, who are found to have offered testimonies in the records compiled at Antioch, from the third troop of the Stabilisians,[12] and also Andronicus and George, who are said to have done the things which have been said about the image, and should inquire with acuity about each and every point, that is, if what is said about the image has happened, and if singing a psalm—of which mention has been inserted in the records compiled at Antioch—in honour of the image they went in procession, and if the most reverend Sergius . . .[13] had known that they were singing these things to the image's honour, and has received the clergymen [14] and communicated with them in the divine mysteries,[15] and if he has proclaimed an assembly for Theodoret and Theodore and Diodore or has granted that it should be held, and if this same thing has been done also in Nestorius' name: your Grandeur should hasten to encompass every way, that no subtlety can escape notice.

Moreover your Eminence should fear not only our indignation, but also God's wrath. It does not irk us also for you to impose an oath in the name of the Lord and Saviour Christ our God, to whom such things pertain, that you should seek the truth itself everywhere. And if indeed the soldiers should be found to have spoken falsely in all matters and to have spoken the truth neither in respect to the image nor to the assembly, not only these things which against Nestorius, but also those things which against Theodoret and Theodore and Diodore are reported, they should be ejected at once from the very brave troop wherein they are known to do military service and their bodies should be racked by all tortures. But if they shall have spoken the truth in their dispositions, whether in respect to the image or in respect to the assembly either for Nestorius or for the other three men,[16] report to us concerning them all, that we can know those who have sinned against the true and immaculate faith, which we also cherish.

Lest any of these matters which have been read to us escape your Grandeur's attention, we have ordered the said records which have been compiled at Cyrus and have been reported to us and also the copies of those records which have been compiled at Antioch to be transmitted to you, that, after all things which we have ordered have been compiled, the very records which have been compiled at Cyrus should be remitted again to us.

And for this case we have sent Thomas, the most devoted secret-service agent [17] and assistant.

I have read.[18]

Given on 7 August at Constantinople, the most distinguished Rusticius [19] being consul.

1. That is, after he had become bishop of the city and had been enthroned in the city's cathedral.
2. Probably bishop of Tarsus.
3. Probably bishop of Mopsuestia.
4. Probably patriarch of Constantinople.
5. Euphratensis.
6. We should say "with this name belonging to it".
7. The litotes is in the Latin.
8. In Antioch temporarily when the report was made. Antioch and Cyrus were about 65 miles apart by direct line.
Hypatius as master of the soldiers of the East had his headquarters at Antioch.
9. Patriarch of Antioch.
10. The word is *responsalis*, which Souter equates with ἀποκρισιάριος. But, while primary meaning of each noun seems to be the same and signifies a person who replies, the duty of the former was more secretarial and the latter's was rather representatorial.
11. These are the first four ecumenical councils: Nicaea (325), Constantinople (381), Ephesus (431), Chalcedon (451).
12. These were cavalrymen in the late Empire.
13. The dots indicate the present absence of words repeated by the compositor of the first edition and not detected by its editor. The omitted words are wanting in the codices.
14. Andronicus and George.
15. That is, admitted them to the sacrament of communion. See no. 75, n. 42.
16. Theodoret, Theodore, Diodore.
17. One of the *agentes in rebus*, on whom see no. 256, n. 3.
18. Notation of a member of the imperial secretariat or possibly, but not probably, of the emperor.
19. The text has Rusticus incorrectly.

560. LETTER OF JUSTIN I ON DIPTYCHS OF EASTERN CHURCHES, 520

(CSEL 35. 701–3)

While the emperor was able to heal the Acacian schism in 519 by compelling the removal of certain names from the diptychs of the Constantinopolitan Church (no. 554), he was unable to enforce this requirement for reunion with the Roman Church upon some other churches in the Empire and, therefore, in this letter to Pope St Hormisdas requests the pope to waive this demand in the interest of peace. But Hormisdas remained adamant in his refusal to modify his attitude on this point, although he appeared satisfied with the several professions of faith presented by the recalcitrant churches, which were chiefly in the patriarchates of Jerusalem and Antioch.

Justin Augustus to Pope Hormisdas.

With what zeal we ever have been and are for conciliating the sentiments of persons practising the Catholic faith, that with the same mind all should worship the undivided light of the Trinity, we are understood to have made known that at length may be found a remedy for the discords of persons contending over different viewpoints, at one time by sending voluntarily to your Beatitude as envoy Gratus, the noble master of the secretarial bureau,[1] for this very purpose, at another time by receiving with favourable and willing mood the most religious men, whom the apostolic see has believed ought to be sent as mediators of unity. For surely, so to speak, we have looked at peace itself and at them [2] with pleasant eyes and with outstretched hands we have thought them [2] worthy to be embraced; indeed also with all attention we have ordained that the venerable Constantinopolitan Church and many others should support your wishes, not only in all other matters but also in withdrawing from the sacred diptychs the names which you particularly have demanded ought to be removed.[3]

But there have been several cities and churches, both Pontic and Asian and especially eastern, whose clergy and laity, though thoroughly assailed by all threats and persuasions, nevertheless to no avail have been influenced that they should abrogate and should remove the names of bishops whose repute has flourished among them, but they count life harsher than death, if they shall have condemned the dead, in whose life, when alive, they used to glory. What therefore are we to make of this kind of stubbornness, which, in not heeding the word, exists and despises tortures to such a degree that it judges it glorious and gladsome for itself, if it should desist from the body sooner than from religious opinion? Indeed there seems to us the need of acting rather mildly and rather leniently. And if these qualities of mildness and leniency are not in your Sanctitude, then these have not been able to be found in another person. For, not desirous for blood and punishments—and this is even unpleasant to mention—we have accepted a petition,[4] not that by a trifling distinction may remain uncompleted the desires for concord, but to promote by what arrangement we can the union of the members of the Church.

Accordingly will it be more preferable that for the sake of minor

560. DIPTYCHS OF EASTERN CHURCHES, 520

matters so many multitudes should be separated entirely from us or that, after insignificant points have been conceded and remitted, greater matters and those which by all means must be investigated should be corrected, that at least in view of their necessary aspects may be selected for amendment those matters on which it has not been permitted to achieve entire acceptance?[5] Accordingly we demand remission for the names, not of Acacius,[6] not of each Peter,[7] not of Dioscore[8] or of Timothy,[9] whose names your Sanctity's letters sent to us contained, but for the persons whom reverence for bishops has celebrated in other communities,[10] with the exception also of the cities where your Beatitude's memorandum[11] already has been accepted in its entirety, unless your Benevolence shall have decided that this part also should be emended more gently.[12] But the situation does not stand in want of the apostolic see's judgement, so that remission rather than an already considered and explored ruling ought to be pronounced: if indeed Anastasius[13] of most religious memory, the Eminence of your Church, openly and obviously has decreed, when he was writing about this same matter to our predecessor,[14] that it was sufficient for persons desiring peace, if only the name of Acacius[6] should be unmentioned.[15] Therefore he follows the earlier ordinances of your see who judges that not all the memorials of the dead are to be contemned, on the ground that it would be considered unworthy and unsuitable, if your leniency should be broadcast in every part of the earth as not rather mild to all—not only to the dead but also to the living.[16] And this indeed we should not have doubted would be so pleasing to you, that the world would be made more joyful by an immediate pacific reply.

Moreover your Sanctity remembers that a little while ago we have written[17] that from the East to us have been sent petitions embodying the wish and the opinion of these very persons, in which they show that they will persevere firmly and from which they reckon that there can be no retreat for any reason. Accordingly we have believed that in the present offence ought to be sent to you this document,[18] according to our promise, by John,[19] the most reverend bishop, that its contents, acknowledged also by your see, may avail for collecting and uniting everywhere the venerable churches and particularly that of Jerusalem, to which all pay so much favour, as if to the mother of the Christian name, that none dares to separate himself from it. Accordingly it is fitting for your Sanctitude to declare also by an epistolary letter the proper consensus, that, when known and revealed to all that the content of this same document is praised also by you and tenaciously is observed, the world may be more joyful.

Given on 9 September at Chalcedon, Rusticius being consul. Accepted on 30 November, the abovewritten being consul.

1. See no. 549, nn. 7 and 8.

2. The papal envoys sent to conduct negotiations on ending the rift between Rome and Constantinople.

3. This act was one of the chief causes for the settlement of the Acacian schism in 519, which began in 484, when Pope St Felix III (II) excommunicated Acacius, patriarch of Constantinople, for his sponsorship of the Monophysite party of Alexandria, for his vague and loose grasp of theological principles, for his attempt to exalt the authority of his see over the entire East. One of the insistent demands made by successive popes, when approached on healing the ensuing breach, was the erasure of the names of Acacius and his supporting successors in the patriarchate, Fravitta, Euphemius, Macedonius II, Timothy, and of their contemporary emperors, Zeno and Anastasius I, from the diptychs (on these see no. 554, n. 1) at Constantinople.

4. Cf. *infra* n. 18.

5. The drift of this Latin-compressed and English-expanded clause of purpose is that, since Justin's experience has shown that he cannot secure from *all* the eastern churches complete concurrence with the papal demands in the excision of names of all Monophysite prelates from these churches' diptychs, it is best to compromise this point and to be content with correction of the most necessary points of doctrine, which, after all, is the more important goal.

6. Patriarch of Constantinople.

7. Peter Balbus (or Mongus), patriarch of Alexandria, and Peter Fullo, patriarch of Antioch, are meant.

8. Dioscore II, patriarch of Alexandria.

9. Timothy II, patriarch of Alexandria, on whom see no. 495, n. 3.

10. That is, not in Alexandria and in Antioch, where measures of correction remained to be taken, as the pope admonished the emperor in 519 (*CSEL* 35. 624. 2–7). Egypt and Syria were strongholds of Monophysitism.

11. This was a *libellus* (literally "little book") containing papal requirements for restoration of communion with Rome.

12. That is, there should be no privilege of not complying with the papal demand about purgation of diptychs on the part of such cities as have accepted the entire papal requirement, unless, the emperor hopes, the pope would waive that part of his demand.

13. Pope Anastasius II.

14. Emperor Anastasius I. Cf. *infra* n. 16.

15. That is, when the diptychs were read, the name of Acacius should not be read among the others listed therein.

16. The epistle, which is in M 8. 188–92, does not confirm entirely the emperor's claim. Although Anastasius says that only Acacius' name must be suppressed, yet he mentions nothing about the non-suppression of the names of the others in communion with Acacius. However, the pope suggests that he will receive persons whom the patriarch has baptized or has ordained. That he could decree this dispensation by apostolic authority Anastasius II was well

aware, because he knew that Pope St Gelasius I, his immediate predecessor, had promised to perform the same act.

17. No. 556.
18. Their petition to the emperor (*CSEL* 35. 703-7), accompanied by supporting letters from Epiphanius, patriarch of Constantinople (*CSEL* 35. 707-10), and from Justinian, Justin's nephew and successor (no. 561), was sent to the pope at the same time. This petition contained a profession of faith from Syrian clergy, who in not a few details concurred with the Theopaschite formula of the Scythian monks.
19. One of the papal legates sent to Constantinople in 519 to heal the Acacian schism.

561. LETTER OF JUSTINIAN I ON DIPTYCHS OF EASTERN CHURCHES, 520

(*CSEL* 35. 715-16)

This letter to Pope St Hormisdas contains Justinian's request, modelled on that of his uncle [1] (no. 560) written on the same day, for a milder papal policy toward such eastern regions as were insistent upon retention of certain episcopal names in their diptychs. At the end of the letter Justinian lays definitely upon Hormisdas the responsibility for effecting ecclesiastical peace.

Copy of Justinian's letter.

Justinian to the lord, the most blessed man and holy father, Hormisdas, pontiff of the city of Rome.

Your Beatitude also is a witness to how much respect for religion we have and to how solicitous we ever have been for uniting the holy churches.

For after our lord, the renowned emperor,[1] became ruler, through all persons going to Italy we sent letters,[2] requesting your Apostolicity, as was proper.[3] Now indeed, lest any of these things which is suitable to be done should be overlooked, John, the most reverend bishop,[4] Heraclian, the priest, and Constantine, the deacon of the sacrosanct Church of this city,[5] have been sent to the city [6] happily, that they may receive a fresh answer on all matters on which your son,[1] the most serene emperor, has written.

Therefore your Sanctity should deign to receive willingly the aforesaid most religious men and, when prayers have been made and when the Divinity has been placated, should ordain reverently all matters in such wise that nothing further should remain for ambiguity.

For it seems to us that the Son of the Living God, our Lord Jesus Christ, born of the Virgin Mary, whom the greatest of the apostles preaches as having suffered in the flesh,[7] is said rightly to reign as one in the Trinity with the Father and the Holy Spirit and we believe not unfaithfully in the person of his Majesty in the Trinity and from the Trinity.

Moreover concerning the deceased bishops' names make arrangements mildly and as becomes a pacific father, because also your predecessor [8] of blessed remembrance wrote to Anastasius [9] of imperial memory that, if only the name of Acacius [10] would be removed,[11] we should have one communion.[12] Therefore it is not a serious matter which your see has urged us to perform. For you ought to imitate the most holy Leo, the Roman pontiff, and, as he wrote to Leo,[13] so you also, after all doubts have been excised, ought to write in reply a perfect and pacific letter [14] to the most unconquered prince, your son,[1] for the Church's sake,[15] that you may be before the tribunal of the future Judge [16] an associate of those whose see you occupy by sacerdotal [17] law.

Your Apostolicity therefore should show that it deservedly has succeeded to the Apostle Peter, since the Lord will be demanding from you—namely, the chief shepherd [18]—the salvation of all persons who have been able to be saved by strengthened concord.[19] For we, after the topics about which you have received written information have been concluded, shall not permit a further controversy of religion to be agitated in our State nor is it fitting for your Sanctity to hear persons disputing about superfluous matters.

1. Justin I.

2. Nos. 550–53, if Justinian refers only to himself; otherwise nos. 549–54, 556–8, 560, if Justin and Justinian are meant.

3. The sense is incomplete, unless it be understood that the letters asked the pope to propose a formula for reuniting the churches of the East with those of the West.

4. Otherwise unidentified.

5. Constantinople.

6. Rome.

7. 1 Pet. 4. 1, a Theopaschite text.

8. Anastasius II.

9. Anastasius I, who preceded Justin I.

10. Patriarch of Constantinople, under whom began the schism called after him.

11. From the diptychs.

12. See no. 560, n. 16.

13. The first emperor of that name. The letter is in PL 54. 1155–90.

14. Literally "pages".
15. An editorial conjecture to fill a lacuna is translated.
16. God.
17. See no. 526, n. 11.
18. The thought that Hormisdas is in succession to St Peter suggests an obvious allusion to his shepherdhood, based on the divine commission in John 21. 15–17.
19. That is, God will expect Hormisdas to exercise his pontificate in such a way that the lost (schismatic) sheep will be restored to the ecclesiastical fold by the pope's pastoral concern in confirming peace among the churches.

562. LETTER OF JUSTINIAN I ON THEOPASCHISM, 520

(*CSEL* 35. 655–6)

In this imperious letter—an omen of his future attitude toward the Papacy—Justinian again presses Pope St Hormisdas to decide about the definition that one of the Trinity suffered in the flesh—the essence of Theopaschism.

Copy of the illustrious Justinian's letter.

With the favour of our Lord Jesus Christ, in the present world may he reign who bases his sovereignty on the sacred religion, since he who first has appeased divine affairs governs well human affairs.[1] And we rejoice that this has happened at the present time.

For your son, the most clement emperor,[2] when he had received the rule [3] by the Eternity's benefaction, seized upon the necessity for explaining the causes of faith and by a delegation sent to your Sanctity we earned the apostolic see's bishops,[4] by whose arrival the sacrosanct churches' concord has increased not moderately at our insistence, as was proper.[5] For after the name of Acacius, which created the division, had been removed utterly in accord with the tenor of the memorials which you have sent,[6] in this royal city [7] and in many communities has advanced the desired unity, which, since it has been discovered by the greatest labours, it is fitting to venerate forever and which is necessary to be guarded and which none shall permit to be retracted by any arguments at all, which the Eternal Majesty [8] duly has laid to rest. But because the enemy [9] of the human race frequently hastens to hinder prosperous courses, some of the Easterners cannot be compelled either by exile or by sword and by fire to condemn the names of bishops who died after Acacius;[10] and this difficulty contrives delays to the general concord.

Accordingly your heavenly inspired Sanctity should consider the quality of the times and, after this error's authors have been condemned (that is, Acacius the Constantinopolitan, Peter and Timothy Aelurus and Dioscore the Alexandrians, and Peter the Antiochene),[11] should deign to end this long-standing conflict concerning all the others' names by having settled the question, that you may deliver the people, whom our God has entrusted [12] to be ruled, from bloodshed and that for our Lord you may gain the people not by persecution and by blood but by sacerdotal [13] patience, lest, while we wish to win souls, we should lose both the bodies and the souls of many persons. For it is suitable for long-standing errors to be emended by leniency and clemency, especially because your Beatitude's predecessors [14] very often wished to recall the bishops of our State to their communion, if only Acacius and all the other aforesaid persons could be pretermitted in silence. It is not, therefore, a weighty matter which your see has advised to perform.

We also ask more and more the following: that your Sanctity, with celestial grace received, should deign to consider the things which the eastern bishops assert and to offer a fitting consent to their faith. For it seems to us that the Son of the Living God, our Lord Jesus Christ, born of the Virgin Mary, whom the chief of apostles [15] proclaims as "having suffered in the flesh",[16] is said rightly to reign as one in the Trinity with the Father and the Holy Spirit. For just as it seems ambiguous to say simply "one of the Trinity" without the preceding name of our Lord Jesus Christ, so we do not doubt that his Person is in the Trinity with the Persons of the Father and the Holy Spirit. For without Christ's Person the Trinity can be neither believed religiously nor adored believingly, as the holy Augustine says "Or any Person from the Trinity" and in another place "He alone in the Trinity received a body" and again "One of three".[17]

Therefore we, most reverently paying our respects, ask that you, mindful of the future judgement, dispose the case in such wise, lest any doubt should be left for the future, that by the removal of every scruple of discord the bonds of desired peace throughout the whole world should be renewed and the concord of the venerable churches should flourish and the members of one body [18] should be regathered into their proper state. For justly is praised that physician who so hastens to heal old illnesses in such a way that from these new wounds are not born.

Therefore your Apostolicity should know especially that, since the said two points have been settled, all the bishops [4] of this State willingly embrace our communion.

Accepted on 17 September, the most distinguished Rusticius being consul.

1. This exordium appears to be complimentary to Justin the emperor.
2. Justin I.
3. Literally "sceptres", used in the plural tropically as a symbol of authority.
4. See no. 16, n. 4.
5. The reference is to the legation sent by Justin to Hormisdas and to the legates sent by the latter to the former in an effort to extinguish the Acacian schism (see no. 558, n. 5).
6. See no. 558, n. 5.
7. Constantinople.
8. It is uncertain whether God or Justin is meant.
9. Satan.
10. Some of these are listed in the next sentence. Condemnation would be shown by erasure of the names of such heretical prelates from the diptychs in the several churches.
11. All these were patriarchs of their respective cities. Egypt and Syria were strongholds of Monophysitism.
12. Whether to pope or to emperor or to both is unclear. But perhaps this refers to Justinian himself, whose attainment of great power early in his uncle's reign seems undisputed (see no. 549, n. 1).
13. See no. 526, n. 11.
14. These were St Felix III (II), St Gelasius I, Anastasius II, St Symmachus.
15. St Peter.
16. 1 Pet. 4. 1.
17. Of these quotations the first is from his *De Trinitate*, 2. 9. 16, the second is dubious, the third is from his *Enchiridion de Fide*, 12. 38.
18. For the thought cf. 1 Cor. 12. 12, 20; Eph. 5. 30.

563. LETTER OF JUSTINIAN I ON DIPTYCHS OF EASTERN CHURCHES, 520

(CSEL 35. 659–60)

Justinian informs Pope St Hormisdas on the departure of the papal legation for Rome, after it had solved the Acacian schism (484–519), that the imperial government wishes the pope to reach a speedy conclusion about the names of bishops in the diptychs of eastern churches, because the sooner that this delicate problem will be resolved the sooner peace will be established in the East.

Copy of Justinian's letter.
Justinian to the lord, the most blessed and apostolic father, Hormisdas, pope of the city of Rome.
With what great reverence we respect your Beatitude you know

from many letters, from the time when the most serene emperor,[1] your son, became ruler.

At present, also saluting with due modesty your Sanctity, we ask rather earnestly that by assiduous prayers and by very frequent entreaties you should labour for the venerable churches' concord and that to us—just as we also have written after all things [2] by your legates [3]—your Apostolicity should deign to send a firm and undoubted reply by Eulogius, the admirable tribune and notary, both about the language [4] on which the controversy hinges and about the names of the bishops [5] deceased after Acacius [6]—all matters which have been ordained by your present legates enduring firmly in perpetuity.

And truly John, the religious bishop,[7] who is about to go to Rome, is detained by bodily illness.

But before his arrival also—and we, however, are dismissing him soon (the Divinity favouring), because now he is better—nothing prohibits peace from emerging, after doubt about religion has been removed, since neither those matters which have fallen into ambiguity are difficult nor is it expedient that the cause of eternal life should be protracted any longer, lest by postponement of the time something more uncertain should be created.

Therefore your Sanctity, not unmindful of the Supernal Eternity and of the fearful judgement, should hasten that what matters have been entrusted to you should be consigned to an efficacious remedy, that all may perceive rightly that you have been allotted the primacy of the apostolic see.

These things, therefore, which are written to you by your sons,[8] order with paternal affection to be performed the sooner the better. For you know how admirable is the glory to abolish root and branch the errors of so many years in the period of your pontificate.

1. Justin I.
2. That is, after the act of reunion in 519.
3. They carried with them to the pope at least six letters, among which were nos. 558 and 562.
4. A possible allusion to the Theopaschite formula, on which Justinian long awaited an answer.
5. Their names are in no. 560, n. 3.
6. Patriarch of Constantinople, whose name has been given to the schism.
7. One of the papal legates and ordinary of an unknown see (see no. 561, n. 4). In *CSEL* 35. 658-9 Justin I also explains to Hormisdas John's detention in Constantinople because of sickness and promises to send him to Rome as soon as his health will allow.
8. Justin and Justinian, perhaps also Empress Euphemia, whose letter to Hormisdas is preserved in *CSEL* 35. 652.

564. LETTER OF JUSTINIAN I ON ECCLESIASTICAL UNITY, 520

(*CSEL* 35. 743)

In this brief letter to Pope St Hormisdas urging the pope to consider milder terms for bringing the eastern churches into communion with Western Christendom by accommodating papal requirements to the flexible religious policy of Justin I's government, Justinian reveals his impatience with Hormisdas' long silence on the acceptability of the Theopaschite formula as a means of reconciling orthodoxy and Monophysites.¹

Copy of the illustrious Justinian's letter.
Your Apostolicity diligently knows with what great fervour for the faith your son,² the most serene emperor, and we have been from the beginning. Never have we ceased to do the things which pertain to the establishment of the divine religion, on behalf of which recently we also have sent to Rome most reverend bishops,³ that there may be an unimpaired settlement about topics on which doubt was directed toward these matters.

But we are ignorant of what difficulty has emerged that hitherto not at all are settled those matters which seem to be very simple.

Saluting, therefore, your Reverence, we ask that no occasion should be presented whereby anyone can be in doubt about you, but do you, having before your eyes the Supernal Majesty's judgement, deign to expedite these matters by all means.

1. More than six months had elapsed before the pope replied to the letters sent by Justin and Justinian on 9 September 520. And then the papal reply evaded the imperial suggestions and reaffirmed the pontiff's inflexibility in religious matters (*CSEL* 35. 716–22).
2. Justin I.
3. See no. 16, n. 4.

565. MANDATE OF JUSTIN I ON CLERICAL INTERVENTION IN PROBATE, 524

(*CI* 1. 3. 40)

This statute, extracted from *CI* 6. 23. 23 with slight changes, forbids magistrates and defenders of the Constantinopolitan churches who have had the habit of intervening in the probate of wills from continuing this practice, directs that only the master of the census is competent for probate, and assesses a large fine against contemners of this constitution.

Emperor Justin Augustus to Archelaus, praetorian prefect.[1]

By a renewed promulgation we think that not only the judges of any tribunal whatsoever, but also the defenders of the churches of this genial city,[2] into whom a very shameless kind of penetration into deceased persons' last wills [3] had crept, must be forewarned that they should not touch the matter, which belongs, according to the commands of the constitutions, absolutely to none at all except to the master of the census.

For it is absurd,[4] rather even opprobrious, for clergymen,[5] if they should consider that they are skilled in judicial discussions—violators of this sanction being smitten with a penalty of fifty pounds of gold.

Given on 19 November at Constantinople, Justin Augustus for the second time and Opilio being consuls.

1. Of the East.
2. The later version omits this phrase, by which is meant Constantinople.
3. For *penetration* ... *wills* the later law reads "announcement".
4. Justinian inserts in the later version "if office staffs are disturbed by promiscuous activities and someone withdraws trustworthiness from another".
5. The defenders of the church are included here among the clergy.

566. LAW OF UNKNOWN EMPEROR ON MONASTIC RIGHTS, (?)525

(*ILCV* 1. 1642 a and b)

It is not certain what type of constitution or from which emperor this much-mutilated inscription is, but it is assigned to the sixth century because of the style of its incision and it may be dated between 500 and 535 because of contemporary evidence collected by its editors. Discovered at Kairwan in Tunisia [1] and first edited in 1893, the constitution appears to command that a certain monastery dedicated to St Stephen, the protomartyr,[2] should be protected from certain invasion of its rights,[3] among which is that of the monks to elect their abbot.

... and not to permit ... the monastery; the abbot or the priest ... the monks, when present, should choose for themselves the abbot without partiality or by the proposed offering of monies.[4]

We ordain [5] ... to be free from unreasonable demands ... are wont to be done in the case of ministers of churches. We order, therefore . . . in the said Monastery of St Stephen the Martyr . . . they shall have been pleased; moreover, indeed, from its own . . . monastery constituted or for themselves . . .

. . . of the edict [6] . . . We declare [5] . . . only in . . .

1. Kairwan (*al.* Kairuân) is some eighty miles south-east of Tunis and, founded *c.* 670, is one of the sacred cities of Islam. The district formed part of the province of Byzacium, a later subdivision of the old Roman province of Africa.
2. See Acts 6. 5—7. 60.
3. Perhaps against episcopal encroachment, as the editorially assembled evidence testifies in the case of the monastery at Hadrumetum (situated in the same province), which in 525 was troubled similarly.
4. That is, bribery.
5. The Latin for these words is expressed in cursive capitals imitating the notation of the imperial hand. Perhaps the monks had the stonecutter use this style to impress the reader.
6. The appearance of this word here need not brand this constitution as an edict, for we know not what edict is meant.

567. LAW OF JUSTIN I AND JUSTINIAN I ON PENALTIES FOR HERETICS, 527

(*CI* 1. 5. 12)

This important law, which lacks both superscription and subscription and is preserved in Greek, perhaps resulted from Pope St John I's visit to Constantinople in 526. Part of its interest arises from the evidence in its preamble that hitherto Justin had tried to pursue a lenient policy toward heretics, but that in the last year of his reign he resorted to severe strictures upon religious dissidents and issued this law as "a manifestation of the imperial anger inspired by ruined hopes".[1] A lengthy list of restrictions and of punishments is embodied in the edict, which embraces (besides heretics) Manichaeans, Samaritans, Jews, Greeks (i.e. pagans), but excludes specifically Goths (probably as a compliment to Theodoric the Great, king of the Ostrogoths [474–526], an Arian—as were most of the Goths), who had constituted a distinct branch of the military establishment for more than a century.

Emperors Justin and Justinian Augusti.[2]

. . . Therefore we have permitted heretics to assemble and to have their own denomination, that they, having felt shame for our patience, willingly may come to their senses and may turn to the better.³ But a certain intolerable recklessness has entered into them and they have infiltrated themselves, having disregarded the laws' command, into governmental services,⁴ in which the very words ⁵ of the royal formularies show that such persons should no longer participate.⁶

We call heretics other persons, just as the accursed Manichaeans and those about like these; indeed it is unnecessary that they even should be named or should appear anywhere at all or should defile what they have touched. But the Manichaeans—as we have said—thus ought to be expelled and none ought either to tolerate or to overlook their denomination, if indeed a person diseased with this atheism should dwell in the same place with others, but also a Manichaean, wherever on earth appearing, ought to be subjected to punishments to the extreme degree.

As for other heretics, of whatever error or denomination they may be (for we call everyone a heretic who is not of the Catholic Church and of our orthodox and holy faith), but even also for pagans,⁷ who try to introduce polytheism, and also for Jews and Samaritans: we resolve not only to reinstate and to make firmer by this present law the provisions of already established laws, but also to ordain more, through which greater security and honour and consideration for partakers of our pure faith will ensue.

It will be possible for all persons to perceive—as we have said—that from persons not worshipping God correctly even their secular properties are withheld.

We command therefore that none of the aforesaid persons either should partake of any position at all or should wear either a civil or a military belt ⁸ or should belong to any order,⁹ except that of the so-called cohortalines,¹⁰ for we wish them as a result of their origin to be held subject to it and not to have dismissal as a result of their evil belief,¹¹ so that they, remaining in it and fulfilling all duties necessarily and bearing every burden (whatever it is of the said governmental service),⁴ should be prevented both from promotion and from execution against orthodox Christians in the category of public and private debts—their progeny, of course, being subject to such a status and they themselves certainly being brought to it, if meanwhile they have been able to escape notice.

We do not permit the said heretics to participate in the office of either defender or father of a municipality, so that by the pretext of security therein they may not maltreat both the other Christians and especially the most God-beloved bishops and may not acquire for themselves any authority to judge or to condemn (as also has been legislated by those before us).

Assuredly we do not allow them to be enrolled among the wisest ¹²

567. PENALTIES FOR HERETICS, 527

advocates of lawsuits, since for such persons more than for many persons it is proper to perceive correctly the divine dogmas, in so far as they also spend their life in speeches.

But also we order persons who are heretics and (still more before these) pagans [7] or Jews or Samaritans and persons like these, who have partaken of any of these functions which we have mentioned or have attained a position or the register of persons pleading lawsuits or have embraced [13] governmental service [4] or have worn [13] any kind of belt, [8] immediately to be ejected from participation in these functions. For we wish both now and always all the said functions to be clear from such persons' association, not in this glorious city [14] only, but entirely in every province and every place. And this is not altogether new: surely the divine formularies of the belt [8] given to most of the governmental services [4] have the addition that the person who has taken this [8] must be orthodox—unless, however, even this would seem to be ours, since we have revived and have not overlooked it as previously, when it both was disregarded by some and was observed as far as the letters only: for affairs should be considered the personal interest not so much of those who have devised their origin as of those who use best what have been devised.

But if anything should have been done wrongly contrary to what has been ordained by us, we show him who has applied himself to forbidden functions as a person not only useless for the undertaking and we forbid him absolutely to participate in it, but also we fine him with a penalty of thirty pounds of gold. And on those to whom it is their duty to enrol and to register such persons in the public record, if, having learned about the error of one's belief, they still have accepted him and have not spoken against him and have not excluded him, we impose a penalty of eight pounds of gold. Indeed we do not let the magistrates go unpunished, if indeed they allow those, who they know are of the persons forbidden by us, to be numbered in their own office staffs [15] (the governmental service [4] of the cohortalines, [10] obviously, having been excepted), but also from them we exact a penalty of fifty pounds of gold. From as many of the said groups as it should happen that the penalty fits, the most magnificent count of the most sacred treasury shall make demand for it and shall bring it into the sacred private estates.

Taking consideration, however, that frequently we enrol the Goths among the most devoted federates, [16] on whom neither their character nor their past life has imposed such accounts, we have decided to remit for them some of the severity [17] and to permit them to be among the federates [16] and to be honoured, in so far as it has commended itself to us.

But knowing that non-orthodox parents often have differing

opinions (the father or the mother wishing to bring their common children to the orthodox persons' faith, but one of two sides resisting), we ordain that the opinion of the one leading the children to the orthodox faith should be stronger and in all respects superior, for the procedure partly will share the parents' opinion and it will be that the better side has won. But aiding those children whom the fathers, not sharing our pure faith, hate, although they are not able to accuse them of sin, since they have been forbidden in the laws, because, though perceiving their parents' error, they share our pure faith, by this divine pragmatic law we decree that the father should provide for such children in proportion to his property a share of both sustenance and things necessary for other manner of life, but, demanding—as it were—a punishment, because they have restored a soul, he should not neglect them when famishing and when wanting the things for life and when compelled somehow through lack—of which it is not proper to speak—to return to their former error.

Moreover a dowry for daughters distressed on this account and gifts before marriage for males, against whom they can charge nothing else of the things prohibited in the laws, by all means they should give freely, according as the reckoning of their property allows, and they should give in marriage their daughters to men and their sons to women according to law—to orthodox persons, however, and to ones worthy of the affair. For it is terrible and absolutely wicked that persons, honoured by their children in all other respects, should show harshness toward them as a result of such a reason, on account of which they would become better by emulating them, not by punishing them.

The persons having glorious magistracies in this greatest city,[14] even as it pertains to each, the governors (whether greater or lesser) throughout the provinces, even as is fitting for each, shall take thought for these things ordained by us. And also to the most blessed archbishop and patriarch of this greatest city [14] and to the most holy bishops of other cities as well as to those having patriarchal and metropolitical sees and to the lesser prelates it shall be an object of care to co-operate in careful observation and to join in examination whether these things are maintained firmly and to reveal it to us, that also with greater vehemence, if necessary, we may prosecute the neglecters of the matters ordained concerning the orthodox faith.

1. So A. A. Vasiliev, *Justin the First* (Cambridge, Mass., 1950), 225.
2. The superscription has been restored by editors.
3. It is unfortunate that the beginning of the edict has been lost, for in it—as *therefore* (διὰ τοῦτο) testifies—were the reasons for the imperial concessions to heretics.

4. See no. 186, n. 4.
5. Literally "letters".
6. See no. 555 for Justin's similar restriction upon recruits.
7. See no. 121, n. 3.
8. See no. 476, n. 39.
9. See no. 325, n. 6, and cf. *infra* n. 15.
10. See no. 320, n. 5.
11. The words *and . . . belief* are out of place in the Greek text, where they stand as the next independent sentence, and should be inserted in the translation here according to an editorial note.
12. Merely a complimentary epithet here, for the following idea does not appear to allow an exception that the presence of heretics would be tolerated among second-rate lawyers.
13. A good case of zeugma, where one verb (περιβάλλειν) in the perfect middle participle must be accommodated to the meanings of two different objects.
14. Constantinople probably, for there is no subscription.
15. Here the Latin version has *officia* for τάξεις, whereas at n. 9 *supra* it has *ordo* for τάξις; but each meaning is possible, as appears in nos. 325, n. 6, and 555, n. 8.
16. In this century these were recruited mostly from barbarians within the Empire, partly from Roman subjects. They seem to have been cavalrymen and to have been an important part of the field army.
17. Of the statute.

568. RESCRIPT OF JUSTIN I AND JUSTINIAN I ON AN ORATORY'S ESTATES, 527

(*ILCV* 1. 23; *FIRA* 1. 466–7)

The priests of a certain oratory of St John,[1] which owned considerable land in Pamphylia, appealed to the emperors against depredations which their estates and tenants had suffered from imperial troops and from others endowed with authority or exercising force. This rescript replies to the priestly petition and promises redress upon the governor's certification of their complaints.

The beginning of Justinian's joint reign with his uncle found the Orient in a deplorable condition. Governors pillaged their subjects, great seigneurs ravaged farms, impressed farmers, and forced sales from reluctant churchmen, while the imperial soldiery was perhaps the greatest burden of all on the populace. Both brigands and the special police, established to combat them, equally plundered the citizenry. This document and the complaints which elicited it are, therefore, not unique.[2]

568. AN ORATORY'S ESTATES, 527

The original rescript was in Latin, to which was appended a literal Greek translation. The latter has been preserved in better condition and in cases of doubt, therefore, has been translated in preference to restorations in the Latin text. The bilingual stone containing the inscription was found (1889) near the village of Ali-Faradin-Yaïla in Asia Minor.

Emperors Justin and Justinian Augusti to Archelaus, praetorian prefect of the East.[3]

Since it is proper that our taxpayers should be preserved at all events unmolested, it is especially necessary that the properties belonging to the venerable Oratory of St John the Apostle [1] should enjoy this provision.

Wherefore by a competent response's [4] sacred sanction we decree that, if their entreaties are true, the properties mentioned in their petitions and their tenant farmers or serfs and managers or leaseholders should remain safe from all outrage, as much from soldiers in transit or suppressors of violence [5] as from those troops who are known to have their stations near the said properties, none of these daring to oppress them with any damage whatsoever under any pretext whatever.

And this our Divinity's formulary the most illustrious governor of the province with his office staff shall provide in every way to be enforced strictly, since the severest penalty shall not at all be lacking against those who act rashly against our royal statutes and since all plundering, already perpetrated or about to be done, shall cease on the part of those opponents who provide themselves with a sacred statute or with another petition or in any other way whatsoever.[6]

Given on 1 June at Constantinople, the most distinguished Mavortius being consul.

In the emperor's hand: I have replied in writing.

I have certified.[7]

1. H. Grégoire, *Recueil des inscriptions grecques chrétiennes d'Asie Mineure* (Paris, 1922), 1. 314, thinks that perhaps this church may be that of St John in Ephesus, in whose favour Justinian I emitted an edict (535–6; given by Grégoire, 107) and which during his reign he replaced, because it was small and dilapidated on account of its age, with a larger and beautiful edifice, rivalling—so Procopius says (*De Aed.* 5. 1. 4–6)—that of the Holy Twelve Apostles in Constantinople (on which see no. 463, n. 5). Concurring with Grégoire is J. N. Bakhuizen van den Brink, *De oud-christelijke Monumenten van Ephesus* (Den Haag, 1923), 119–26, esp. 120.

If Grégoire's proposal is sound, the situation of a church possessing property in distant districts is not unparalleled (see no. 630, n. 3).

2. Perhaps may be mentioned in this connection the short Greek inscription

published in *Revue des études grecques*, 15 (1902) 321, and dated early in Justinian's reign. It sets boundaries for the Martyry of St Dius (a Cappadocian saint) in Pontus. Although its editor thinks that the purpose of the inscription was to implement Justinian's law of 535 (*N* 7) prohibiting alienation of ecclesiastical property, it is not necessary, if he is correct, to refer it to such a late date, because already in 470 (no. 510; see also nos. 503 [dated 466–72] and 537 [dated 491–518]) that practice was prohibited. Rather it may well have been posted to define against predators the limits of the martyry's lands.

The emended inscription reads: "Boundaries of the holy and glorious martyr Dius, granted by our most pious King Flavius Justinian". While I accept the correction of ΟΡΟΙ ΤΟΥ [ὅροι τοῦ: "boundaries of the"] for Ο ΤΟΠΟΣ [ὁ τόπος: "the place"], because the transition is easy and the participle ΠΑΡΑΣΧ-ΕΘΕΝΤΕΣ [παρασχεθέντες: "granted"], being plural, demands a plural antecedent and ΟΡΟΙ ΠΑΡΑΣΧΕΘΕΝΤΕΣ occurs elsewhere, yet to turn ΒΑΣ [βασιλέως: "king"] into ΦΛΣ [Φλαβίου: "Flavius"] seems unnecessary, especially since the inscription reads ΒΑΣΙΛΕΩΝ [βασιλέων: "kings"] before the abbreviated form ΒΑΣ. So I should read "King of Kings Justinian".

3. This superscription has been supplied by an early editor, but it is reported that the space available for it seems scarcely sufficient. However, A. A. Vasiliev, *Justin the First* (Cambridge, Mass., 1950), 408, accepts it.

4. See no. 218, n. 5.

5. G. βιοκωλύτης; L. *violentiae prohibitor*: a member of the local constabulary.

6. The idea in the last causal clause seems to be that some of the depredators may rely on a previously issued ordinance—about which nothing is known—authorizing encroachment on ecclesiastical property or on their own pending petition to permit such depredation.

The Greek version ends here.

7. This note shows that the document was recorded in an imperial bureau after examination.

569. EDICT OF JUSTINIAN I ON PENALTIES FOR HERETICS, (?)527

(*CI* 1. 1. 5)

This document contains another of Justinian's professions of his theological belief and also condemns the fautors of Nestorianism, Eutychianism, Apollinarianism, who must expect fitting correction as a result of their heretical opinions.

569. PENALTIES FOR HERETICS, (?)527

Emperor Justinian Augustus.

Since the correct and unblemished faith, which God's Holy Catholic and Apostolic Church preaches, has received in no way an innovation,[1] we, following the teachings of the holy apostles and of those who after them have been distinguished in God's holy churches, have believed it right to make manifest to all persons how we think about the hope in us, following the tradition and the confession of God's Holy Catholic and Apostolic Church.

For, believing in the Father and the Son and the Holy Spirit, we worship one substance[2] in three hypostases,[2] one divinity, one power, a Consubstantial Trinity. We confess that in the last days[3] God's Only-Begotten Son, God of God, before the ages[4] and without time[4] born from the Father, co-eternal with the Father, he from whom are all things and through whom are all things, having descended from the skies, became incarnate from the Holy Spirit and Mary, the Holy, Glorious Ever-Virgin and Mother of God, and assumed man's nature and endured the Cross and was buried[5] and arose on the third day, recognizing one and the same person's miracles and sufferings, which voluntarily he endured in the flesh. For we know not God the Word to be one and Christ to be another, but one and the same person consubstantial with the Father according to his divinity and the same one consubstantial with us according to his humanity. For the Trinity has remained the Trinity, even though one of the Trinity was made incarnate as God the Word; for the Holy Trinity admits not the addition of a fourth person.

Therefore, since these things are thus, we anathematize every heresy, especially Nestorius,[6] the man-worshipper, who divides our one Lord Jesus Christ, God's Son and our God, and does not confess properly and according to truth Mary, the Holy, Glorious Ever-Virgin and Mother of God, but says that one is God the Word from the Father and another from Mary, the Holy Ever-Virgin, has been made God by grace and by affinity toward God the Word: and, notwithstanding, also the crazy Eutyches,[7] who introduces a representation and denies the true Incarnation from Mary, the Holy Ever-Virgin and Mother of God, that is, our salvation, and does not confess that he is in all respects consubstantial with the Father according to his divinity and the same is consubstantial with us according to his humanity: and likewise the soul-destroying Apollinaris,[8] who says that our Lord Jesus Christ, God's Son and our God, is without understanding and introduces a mixture or a disorder into the Incarnation of God's Only-Begotten Son, and all persons who have been or are likeminded with him.

For after this our proclamation and after the assurance given by our most God-beloved bishops in each and every place, if any persons should be found henceforth to be of an opposite opinion, they should not expect to be worthy of pardon, for we command such persons to be subjected to appropriate correction as confessed heretics.

1. This point is a commonplace in patristic doctrine. Early testimony comes from Tertullian, who in his *De Praescriptione Haereticorum* takes to task heretics for importing novel interpretations into "the faith which was once delivered unto the saints" (Jude 3). See e.g. chapters 20-2, 25-8, 31, 32, 35-7.
2. Here again are οὐσία and ὑπόστασις, on which see no. 67, n. 17. See 1 John 5. 7.
3. Reminiscent of Heb. 1. 2; cf. Gal. 4. 4 and 2 Thess. 2. 2.
4. Reminiscent of Eph. 1. 4, Col. 1. 17, 1 Pet. 1. 20.
5. Since Justinian seems to take his language from Christian creeds, it is noteworthy that he here omits the article asserting that Jesus "descended into hell" (*descendit ad inferos*). This article doubtless is derived from early patristic exegesis of 1 Pet. 3. 18-20. So far as the three chief creeds in common use during the twentieth century are concerned, it should be stated (1) that this article is a later addition to the so-called Apostles' Creed and appears in some symbols by the mid-fourth century; (2) that it never secured a place in the Nicene Creed (325) or the Niceno-Constantinopolitan Creed (381) as authorized by the Fourth Ecumenical Council at Chalcedon in 451, when the fathers assembled there attributed it to the Second General Council at Constantinople in 381; (3) that it also is in the so-called Athanasian Creed (*Quicunque vult*), whose composition may be set between, say, 380 and 600. But neither the Apostles' Creed was framed by the apostles nor the Nicene Creed came from the First General Council at Nicaea nor the Athanasian Creed was the composition of St Athanasius of Alexandria (293?-373)—see E. J. Bicknell, *A Theological Introduction to the Thirty-nine Articles of the Church of England*[3] (London, 1955), 147-70, esp. 161.
6. Patriarch of Constantinople and founder of Nestorianism.
7. Constantinopolitan archimandrite and inventor of Eutychianism.
8. Bishop of Laodicea in Syria and author of Apollinarianism.

570. LAW OF JUSTINIAN I ON ORTHODOX CHILDREN AS HEIRS OF HERETICAL PARENTS, 527-9

(*CI* 1. 5. 13)

This statute without superscription and subscription permits orthodox children of heretical parents to inherit their parents' property, whether the decedents were testate or intestate.

Heretics' orthodox children who have not done wrong against them take undiminished what is appropriate for them by intestacy. And a last will made contrary to these provisions is invalid—liberal persons being protected, unless they are prohibited according to some law.[1]

But if they shall commit any offence against their parents, they are accused and are punished. And those who have done wrong have a fourth of their property according to the testaments.[2]

The same provisions also concerning Jews and Samaritans.

1. According to *II* 2. 18. 6–7 a testator must leave to his children at least a quarter of what they would have received if he should have died intestate.

A parent who is over-generous and leaves to his children more than that which they can claim under rules of intestacy if their parent has died without a will is protected in his or her generosity by law, unless some statute to limit parental generosity is applicable. See also no. 187.

2. The fact that the children may have offended the parents is immaterial, provided that the former are orthodox and the latter are heretical. See also no. 187.

571. LAW OF JUSTINIAN I ON DISABILITIES FOR HERETICS, 527–9

(*CI* 1. 5. 14)

This ordinance without superscription and subscription threatens death for heretics who organize meetings, perform certain ecclesiastical rites, act as certain civic officials, administer real estate, and, in general, do anything which has been interdicted for them.

Heretics cannot hold assemblies or meetings or synods or ordinations or baptisms or have exarchs or be entrusted with or be concerned with the office of father of a municipality or the office of defender of a municipality or manage estates by themselves or by interposed persons or do any of the things which have been prohibited.

The transgressor is imperilled to the uttermost.[1]

1. Probably capital punishment is connoted.

572. MANDATE OF JUSTINIAN I ON MANICHAEANS' WILLS, 527-9

(*CI* 1. 5. 15)

This defective statute, addressed to an unknown official, debars Manichaeans from free disposition of their property by will and compels them to leave it only to their children, if they are orthodox; otherwise their property is confiscated entirely.

... Since persons who have been unfortunate in respect to the Manichaeans' impious error are worthy not only of punishment while they live, but also of the circumstance that after their death they may not give their property to whom they wish or to whom the law gives it by intestacy, we use the present divine pragmatic law to your Magnificence,[1] by which we command that the property of persons possessed by this disease should be examined;[2] and that if their children or any of their descending relatives [3] should be free of such sort of madness, these should be allowed to share the property given to them by law, but that if any other cognates of the deceased persons either are called to their inheritance according to those persons' last will (which indeed has been forbidden) or have accepted a donation from such a person while living or even have been honoured with a legacy from, of course, the same person, their property or the things donated or bequeathed should be taken from them absolutely and should be attached to the public treasury.

1. A magistrate of high rank, probably a praetorian prefect.
2. That is, inventoried.
3. While the degrees of relation are indefinite, the Romans had no special names for descendants in a degree (each generation counting one degree) lower than the sixth (*II* 3. 6. 6): *trinepos* (great-great-great-great-grandson) and *trineptis* (great-great-great-great-granddaughter). Few Roman testators could have survived to see a descendant at such a distance, even if each generation had legitimate children at the earliest possible legal age.

573. LAW OF JUSTINIAN I ON DISABILITIES FOR MANICHAEANS, 527-9

(*CI* 1. 5. 16)

By this defective ordinance persons who had turned from Manichaeanism to Christianity and then have relapsed into their heresy are threatened with capital punishment. The statute also orders the burning of Manichaean books and directs search for Manichaeans in official posts.

... If anyone of the Manichaeans' impious cult should have crossed to the right and true faith and after our so great benevolence and many admonitions and periods conceded for repentance should have been found henceforth passing to or living with his former error and having some association with anyone of those of their deadly error and, immediately having detained this person, should not have delivered him or should not have reported him to the most magnificent or the admirable or the most distinguished magistrates,[1] he shall be liable to extreme punishments,[2] not retreating to any excuse nor being able to postpone by any subterfuges the punishments imposed on him.

But the persons enrolled in any positions or governmental services [3] or guilds shall employ every eagerness to investigate whether anyone among them is of this forbidden madness and to reveal him when found, knowing that if ever any such person should have been found among them and should have been charged as subject to penalties, because that person was known to be such, they themselves will not escape fitting punishment, although they have not happened to be of the same error with him. For who, when knowing the wrongdoer, do not make this one known, they appear to do the same wrongs. Therefore all shall know that they who after repentance made in any way whatever are caught again in the Manichaeans' loathsome blasphemies will obtain no benevolence and they shall be eager with pure and unchangeable intention to attract by choice of better things both God's benevolence and our good will.

And we ordain the following: that if anyone having books concerning in all ways the Manichaeans' impious error should not have made these known, that they might be burned and might disappear entirely from men, or even if such books should have been found with him for any pretext at all, likewise he also should submit to the proper penalty.

But we judge especially to be worthy of extreme punishments [2] those persons who, having pretended to abandon this impious error and to pursue the orthodox Christians' salutary dogma, later are seen to delight in rascally men's association and to cherish those persons' interests and in every way to conceal with them their impieties. For they who formerly have passed their time in impious assemblies and later have been deemed worthy of the Christians' august dogma would continue thus in security, if they should have appeared to have communed with none of those impious men of such association or, if they have associated with any of them, to have reported this person immediately and to have delivered him to a lawful judge (for by this only they shall show to all that they have supported the holy and venerable dogma not through any impious pretence but by correct intention): so that if, when they have neglected these things, they should have been caught in converse with such impious men and in eagerness to hide them and not to deliver them to the laws (thus showing themselves unworthy of all pardon), they shall undergo penalties which are suitable and have been imposed justly on persons originally impious.

1. There is perhaps confusion here. One hardly expects that a Manichaean, later turned Christian and still later lapsed into Manichaeanism, would report to the authorities a fellow-Manichaean, unless it be true that "every man has his price". Probably another subject for *should have delivered* and *should have reported* should be substituted.
2. Pluralized but meaning death.
3. See no. 186, n. 4.

574. LAW OF JUSTINIAN I ON DISABILITIES FOR SAMARITANS, 527-9

(CI 1. 5. 17)

By this incomplete law, which probably interprets a statute, Samaritans may bequeath or may donate or may alienate property to only orthodox persons. Bishops are directed to report violations of the ordinance and such violations lead to confiscation of the property so misdirected.

... of the holy ...
Samaritans' synagogues are destroyed and, if they shall try to build others, they are punished.
They are not able to have successors by testament or by intestacy, except orthodox persons, and do not give donations or otherwise alienate to persons not orthodox.

But the fisc claims these things [1] through bishops' and magistrates' [2] provision.

1. That is, property willed or donated or sold to non-orthodox persons.
2. Or possibly "provincial governors'".

575. LAW OF JUSTINIAN I ON DISABILITIES FOR HERETICS, 527–9
(*CI* 1. 5. 18)

By this law, whose beginning is missing, the emperor legislates against several heretical sects by forbidding their adherents to alienate property, by excluding them from governmental service, by restating that generally those serving the State must be orthodox, by ruling on cases of inheritance where testators and heirs may or may not be orthodox, by banning heretics from the legal profession, by forbidding pagans to become teachers, by establishing penalties for violation both of the law and of its administration, and by charging bishops to bring such cases to the attention of the provincial governors as well as to inform the emperor about gubernatorial laxity in enforcement of the ordinance.

This constitution is excellent evidence for Justinian's determination to eradicate heterodoxy and to ensure that only the orthodox should be favoured in the Empire. Regarding himself as responsible for his subject's welfare, the sovereign wishes to secure the salvation of their souls. This aim appears in the passion for uniformity perceived in this ukase.

The same emperor.
... Making provision for all things advantageous for our subjects, we have provided for this above all as first and most necessary before other things: that we may save their souls through all persons revering the orthodox faith with pure thought and, on the one hand, worshipping and glorifying the Holy and Consubstantial Trinity and, on the other hand, confessing and venerating the Holy, Glorious and Ever-Virgin Mary, the Mother of God.

And therefore, since we have found very many persons errant in divers heresies, with zeal we have caused them to change to a better opinion both by exhortations paying court to God and by divine edicts, but also to correct by laws the preference which has fallen not correctly into their thoughts and to prepare them both to recognize and to revere the Christians' true and only salutary faith.[1]

And these things have occurred both in the case of other heresies and especially in the case of the unholy Manichaeans, of whom the Borborians are a part, concerning whom stated terms have been constituted by us.[2] And the things which we already have legislated concerning Samaritans [3] we ordain should prevail in the case of Montanists and Tascodrogitans and Ophitans, that is, so that they neither should dare to have any synagogue, wherein they, having assembled, shall participate in impious and ridiculous words and actions, nor should be able to transmit their property to anyone by legal right of either inheritance or of trust [4] in testaments or by intestacy, whether that one should be a cognate or a stranger, only unless the person called to their succession or written by them as heir or honoured by some trust [4] should embrace the orthodox faith.

In the case of all other heresies—we call heresies those which think and worship contrary to the Catholic and Apostolic Church and the orthodox faith—we wish the law already established by both us [5] and our father [5] of divine lot to prevail, in which not only about them, but also about Samaritans and pagans [6] suitable things have been constituted, so that persons diseased with such things neither should be in governmental service [7] nor should enjoy any rank nor also in the guise of any teacher whatever of education should drag contrarily the simpler persons' souls to their own error and in this way should make them lazier toward the orthodox persons' true and pure faith; but we let only those persons who are of the orthodox faith teach and obtain public subsistence.

But if anyone should embrace the true and orthodox faith by having pretended so for the sake of having governmental service [7] or advocacy or rank or public administration and, having been advanced by this hypocrisy, should have been seen to have a wife or children seeking after the despised heresy and should not have brought these to recognition of true things, we order that he absolutely should be expelled from his advocacy or governmental service [7] or rank or public administration; but, if he should have continued to escape notice, he should not be able to alienate to a heretical person anything of the things belonging to him by donation or by any other contract at all or by last will; and the things bequeathed to heretical persons and the inheritance descending from him to a heretic should be claimed by the treasury [8]—persons who are truly orthodox Christians being able either to take [9] anything from him while living or to inherit anything from him when dead. For generally we order that persons who are in positions or governmental services [7] or advocacies or are filling these and all persons who generally participate in any public distinction or favour whatever should be succeeded in inheritance by only orthodox Christians—whether children or cognates or strangers called by them.

For we also absolutely forbid that persons should participate in these things—we mean the things descending by inheritance or donation or other source to a heretical person; but if anyone should have appeared to do some such thing, what things have been given or bequeathed in this way should be claimed by the treasury.

But if a heretical man should live in wedlock with an orthodox woman or conversely a heretical woman should have an orthodox man, we command that the children of these by all means should be orthodox; and that if it should have happened that some of their children are orthodox, but some for any cause whatever remain in the same or even another heresy, only the orthodox ones should be heirs of the father and of the mother—the ones remaining heterodox having no entrance in regard to the paternal or maternal inheritance; but also that if all the children of persons so living in mutual wedlock should have remained in the same error, then these also should be expelled from both parents' inheritance; but that if a cognate in any degree whatever of persons so living in wedlock should have appeared of the orthodox faith, this one should be called to the inheritance of both; but that when no orthodox Christian cognate appears, our most sacred treasury should take those persons' property—the most magnificent count of our sacred private estates at the time and the section serving him examining with all care the matters ordained by us and claiming these persons' property, which will be appropriate for them to do as a result of the fact that any of the aforesaid matters has been transgressed.

But if any one of the persons banned by us, that is, pagans [6] or Manichaeans or Samaritans, or heretics about equal to these, generally should have canvassed for governmental service [7] perhaps or rank or advocacy or any public administration whatsoever or should have dared to teach or to acquire public subsistence or generally to do any of the prohibited things, but should not have been discovered by every office staff (both military and civil), to which these matters belong, both here [10] and in the several countries,[11] the delinquent himself, as soon as he has been detected, shall fall under the penalties previously mentioned by us; but persons who have not denounced these things—whether they should be in office staffs or should serve in other magistracies, to which these matters refer—shall deposit a penalty of twenty pounds of gold for each person and similarly a fine of thirty pounds of gold pursues [12] every magistracy (both military and civil) both here [10] and in the several countries.[11]

But also, if it [13] should have prosecuted and should have exacted the penalty and should have shown itself not neglectful of the things legislated (the penalty being suitable for such and such a person or case), we ordain that the most magnificent count of the most sacred treasury both should exact this and should receive it and should bring it to the sacred private estates, knowing that, unless he himself through the school [14] of the most devoted palatines [15] serving him and the school [14] itself in every way should have searched such things and should have made exactions from the guilty persons, he himself shall deposit a penalty of fifty pounds of gold and the school [14] obedient to him, looking toward its own peril, besides the corporal [16] penalty suitable against the school,[14] shall deposit [17] the imposed penalty, unless it should have laid hold of the things legislated by us.

The most God-beloved bishops of each city, who always examine the affairs in each city attempted contrary to this our divine legislation by anyone at all, shall have [18] the same charge and shall make [18] these things clear to the most distinguished governor of the province, that that one may transmit into act the things piously commanded by us: that if the most God-beloved bishops should have seen that the province's governor is administering carelessly the affair, it is proper for them to make this clear to us ourselves, in order that we may lay the careless ones under the said penalties, under which we have ordained that persons committing wrongly any of the said things should be brought—the most God-beloved bishops in the several places knowing also that, if they should have neglected any of these things, they shall come to the Lord God and his eternal judgement, but, when their carelessness is exposed, they also shall be in peril concerning the episcopate itself.[19]

1. The infinitives *to correct* and *to prepare* depend upon the preceding finite verb *have caused*.
Procopius provides corroboration for this concern, when he writes that Justinian, "having found that the belief concerning God was wandering into error and was forced to go in many directions during earlier times, completely destroyed all the roads leading to errors and caused it to stand in the firmness of faith on one foundation" (*De Aed.* 1. 1. 9).

2. See nos. 572 and 573.

3. See no. 574.

4. See no. 218, n. 7.

5. See no. 567. His *father* is his uncle Justin I.

6. See no. 121, n. 3.

7. See no. 186, n. 4.

8. An editorial suggestion would set the next paragraph, which seems dislocated, after this word.

9. By donation or by contract.

10. Probably Constantinople, although there is no subscription to confirm the suggestion.

11. That is, "provinces", doubtless.

12. The Greek construction shifts from the future indicative (*shall deposit*) to the present infinitive.

13. Any competent magistrate or his office staff is meant. Then the count of the treasury transmits to the private estates the penalty imposed by the magistrate or by his office staff.

14. See no. 547, n. 6.

15. See no. 186, n. 3.

16. Literally "to the body".

17. The verb is supplied by the translator.

18. In this independently printed sentence the principal verb is in the infinitive mode and depends upon the previous sentence's main verb.

19. That is, the emperor on earth will expel them from the episcopate, on which rank see no. 158, n. 1.

576. MANDATE OF JUSTINIAN I ON SANCTUARY, 527-34

(*N*, App. 1, Ed. 10)

This constitution[1] denies ecclesiastical sanctuary to cohortalines[2] who embezzle public funds and directs exile of such peculators, whom bishops must expel from the churches upon receipt of verbal good faith that the offenders will be escorted without molestation beyond the frontier. Such clerics as refuse to release the criminals must reimburse the fisc and run the risk of expulsion from ecclesiastical status.

Concerning cohortalines.[2]

Preamble: From the frequent circumstances themselves we have perceived the cohortalines'[2] trickery, which they have with regard to the treasury.

Therefore, since we have been taught that also this is one piece of their audacity: to take into their hands the public funds[3] and to conceal themselves within the holy places and thus to appear to escape the penalties with which they deserve to be punished, we ordain[4] ... your Excellency[5] (and this also we have written to the provinces' most God-beloved bishops),[6] that if any of them should have fled into the divine precinct, to your Excellency should be the power to order these to be outside that province and to be in whatever place you should have wished—this having been ordered: that the most God-beloved bishops should hold it necessary to set them outside the holy places, after accepting the so-called word that in those places, into

576. SANCTUARY, 527-34 1013

which ... to depart,[7] and that the public officials [8] should take them to the said places without any difficulty whatever.

Therefore in this way your Excellency shall employ the ordinances against the cohortalines.[2]

For this also has been threatened against the most God-beloved bishops and their clergymen: that if they should not have wished to eject them from the province with the so-called word and to take them to the places into which they have been sent, with the faith of the word (that they should dwell there equally as in the holy places), they at their own expense, but not from ecclesiastical payments, shall preserve the treasury free from loss, not having been exempted even from peril regarding the priesthood.[9]

Conclusion: Therefore your Excellency shall hasten to give to action and to conclusion the things which have occurred to us and are exhibited through this divine pragmatic law.

1. This law is the tenth among the thirteen so-called Edicts of Justinian, printed by R. Schöll and W. Kroll in the first appendix to their third stereotyped edition of Justinian's Novels.
2. See no. 320, n. 5.
3. The word (δημόσια) may mean either taxes or public debts paid to the State or even the public archives. Here the first meaning is probably intended.
4. The lacuna is manuscriptal.
5. It is unknown to whom the law was addressed.
6. The directive to the bishops is not extant.
7. The editors fill the Greek gap with Latin words, which, translated, mean "they have been ordered" and they add "they will be safe".

The addition, if correct, preserves for both bishops and fugitives the right of sanctuary, in that the former surrender the latter to the secular authorities who have given their word that the delinquents will be unmolested in their place of exile. Presumably, however, some attempt to make the rascals disgorge their peculation is made somewhere in the process.

8. These (οἱ δημοσιεύοντες, translated as *ministri publici*) are not defined further, but they are presumed to be persons in the State's service, whose duty here is to remove fugitives from justice.
9. That is, in addition to reimbursing the fisc *de suo*, they will be deprived of their clerical status, on which word (ἱερωσύνη or *sacerdotium*) see no. 158, n. 1.

577. CONSTITUTION OF JUSTINIAN I ON STATUS OF THE SMYRNAN CHURCH, 527–65

(SEG 4. 517)

Two fragmentary inscriptions on marble, found at Ephesus in 1911, present a new episode in the history of the long conflict for pre-eminence between Ephesus and Smyrna.[1] The document apparently rejects either the petition or the claim of the archbishop of Smyrna to be the metropolitan of Asia (Minor), which rank the head of the Church in Ephesus had enjoyed since the First General Council of Nicaea (325),[2] but it confirms the Church in Smyrna as autocephalous and its head as archbishop, rights which appear to have been won soon after the Fourth General Council of Chalcedon (451).[3]

... that he[4] was worthy of such honour from this one[5] and he was called the beloved disciple of God[6] by all and was the first to lean on the bosom of God.[7] Thence he obtained those ineffable words, through which, having manifested to us his divine inspiration and ineffability,[8] justly he has been called "theologian"[9] and "son of thunder",[10] seeing that he speaks not humanwise, but from heaven proclaims and reveals to us the most secret matters of dogmas. The magnitude of his honour is so great that God declares authoritatively both to his Holy Mother and from his Holy Spirit that the most holy apostle is the son[11] by adoption[12] of the same mother, who, though being the Mother of God,[11] was the mother[12] of the most holy apostle according to the words of God ...

... when the most holy Martyr Polycarp[13] held the privilege of the episcopate, no other one could contend with this one in holiness or priesthood.[14] But he himself would not have accepted the exceptional glory both of the apostles and of the disciples and, if any should attempt to invest your apostolic Timothy[15] with it, the Smyrnans never would have assented to the proposition. Wherefore the Smyrnans' see has been deemed worthy both to be autocephalous and to be counted among the archbishops ...[16]

1. It recalls an earlier inscription (C. T. Newton and E. L. Hicks, eds., *The Collection of Ancient Greek Inscriptions in the British Museum* [Oxford, 1890], 3. 2. 489), wherein Antoninus Pius (between 140 and 144) excuses the Smyrnans for having forgotten through inadvertence—he charitably says—the titles of Ephesus in an official letter and promises the Ephesians that for the future the Smyrnans will be more courteous on the condition that the former also shall use the prescribed formulas in documents addressed to the latter. Dio Chrysostom declares that already in Nerva's and Trajan's times (96–117) these cities' feud over precedence was of long standing (*Orat.* 34, *Tars. Alt.* 48).

Under the Christian emperors Ephesus enjoyed the title of "First and Greatest Metropolis of Asia" (ἡ πρώτη καὶ μεγίστη μητρόπολις τῆς 'Ασίας), reported epigraphically in *Hermes*, 4 (1870) 187.

2. Implied in canon 6, which was recognized in canon 2 of the Second General Council of Constantinople in 381.

3. So H. Grégoire in *Byzantion*, 1 (1924) 715, where he dates the conversion from bishopric to archbishopric between 451 and 457 and to the same period assigns Smyrna's advancement to autocephality after long subordination to the Ephesian metropolitanate.

4. Cf. *infra* n. 6.

5. Perhaps God or Jesus Christ.

6. A traditional characterization of St John, the youngest disciple, who died (tradition tells) at Ephesus. Founded on John 13. 23, 19. 26, 20. 2, 21. 7, 21. 20.

7. John 13. 23, 21. 20.

8. The idea seems to be that St John the Disciple, traditionally the author of the Gospel according to John (the most "spiritual" of the four canonical Evangels) reveals to men the spark of divinity in him.

9. So the title of the Apocalypse calls him, though the translators of the King James version of the Bible have preferred their contemporary usage of "divine" for *theologian*—a connotation not yet obsolete. Traditionally, of course, St John the Evangelist and St John the Revelator are one and the same.

10. Mark 3. 17.

11. John 19. 26.

12. Conjectural: various proposals to begin this line have been made.

13. Bishop of Smyrna and martyred in 156 at the age of 86. Tradition tells that St Polycarp was a disciple of St John, but it is not certain which John is meant.

Since according to the account of his martyrdom the pagans and the Jews resident in Smyrna accused St Polycarp of being the teacher of Asia (= Asia Minor) and the father of the Christians (*Martyrium Polycarpi*, 12. 2), it is no wonder that the Church of Smyrna considered that in its glorious martyr, to whose pre-eminence even non-Christians had witnessed, it had a strong support in its contest with the Church of Ephesus.

That veneration of executed Christians' relics was practised as early as St Polycarp's martyrdom is quite clear (op. cit., 18. 2–3)—a practice which may have ascended as high as the apostolic age, if the case of St Stephen the Protomartyr (Acts 8. 2) can be considered—as some scholars suppose—conclusive. See also no. 206, n. 7.

14. See no. 158, n. 1.

15. This disciple of St Paul was both a native of and the first bishop of Ephesus (1 Tim. 1. 3; cf. 2 Tim. 1. 18, 4. 12).

16. Concrete for abstract: by antimeria "archbishoprics" is meant.

578. EDICT OF JUSTINIAN I ON COMPOSITION OF THE CODE, 528

(CI, Constitution *Haec*)

This document, usually prefixed to editions of Justinian's *Codex*,[1] announces to the Constantinopolitan Senate the emperor's plan to collect previous sovereigns' constitutions into one code, which was destined to bear his name [2] and to constitute a part of the *Corpus Iuris Civilis*.[3] Justinian, the most theologically minded of Roman rulers, professes in its opening sentence, of which only part is translated, that he has conceived this project in reliance upon divine assistance.

Emperor Justinian Augustus to the Senate.

These things,[4] which to many previous emperors seemed to need necessary correction, yet in the interim none of them dared to bring this to a result, at the present time we have decided with Almighty God's aid to give to the common interests and to amputate the prolixity of lawsuits, by curtailing, indeed, the multitude of constitutions . . . by composing, moreover, one code under the fortunate designation of our name,[2] into which ought to be collected the constitutions of the three aforesaid codes [5] as well as the new constitutions established after these [6] . . .[7]

Given on 13 February at Constantinople, our Lord Justinian Perpetual-Augustus being consul for the second time.

1. See Introd., n. 3 *ad init*.
2. *Codex Iustinianus*, the title given to it by Justinian himself in his Constitution *Cordi* (dated 534), usually prefixed to editions of the Code.
3. See Introd., n. 3 *ad fin*. for the origin of this phrase.
4. *Haec*, the edict's opening word, whence the constitution takes its name. See also no. 617, n. 6.

By giving *these things . . . to the common interests,* as the author later asserts, is meant his presentation of his Code to the public for its information, guidance, and adherence.

5. The *Codex Gregorianus* (c. 294), compiled by a now unknown Gregory, and the *Codex Hermogenianus* (c. 365), its continuation by an unidentified Hermogenian, are unofficial collections of imperial laws from Hadrian's reign (117–38) onward and remain either in fragments or as incorporated into subsequent sylloges of Roman or barbarian laws. The *Codex Theodosianus* (effective 439), the first official compilation of imperial constitutions, starts with those emitted by Constantine I (306–37) and is described in the text of Introd. after n. 6. These three codes Justinian used as the basis of his own *Codex*.

6. Such are the so-called *Leges Novellae*, promulgated by Theodosius II after 438 and by succeeding sovereigns.

7. Justinian then names the ten commissioners who will compile the Code, outlines their wide powers of condensation, excision, addition, revision, clarification, and notifies the Senate of the expected result.

579. MANDATE OF JUSTINIAN I ON SELECTION OF BISHOPS, ON MANAGEMENT OF ECCLESIASTICAL PROPERTY, ON CLERICAL DUTIES, 528

(*CI* 1. 3. 41)

In this statute are regulated several subjects, of which the first and chiefest is qualifications of candidates for the episcopate. Next are discussed the estates of bishops. Then the management of ecclesiastical property by stewards and by superintendents of the Church's various charitable institutions is canvassed. Unworthy means used to obtain ordination to any clerical rank then are mentioned for condemnation. The last topic treats the liturgical functions of clerics, some of whom appear to be lax in their duties and to employ substitutes for their services.

Emperor Justinian Augustus to Atarbius, praetorian prefect.[1]

Taking ever every forethought for the most holy churches and for both honour and glory of the Holy Immaculate and Consubstantial Trinity, through which we have believed that both we ourselves and the common polity will be saved, and also following the holy apostles' teaching [2] concerning the obligation of ordaining blameless bishops,[3] who particularly have been ordered through their prayers [4] to procure the Benevolent God's favour for public affairs, by the present law we ordain that, as often as in any city whatever it should happen that the sacerdotal [5] see is vacant, a vote by the persons inhabiting the said city should be taken concerning three persons who have borne a character for correct faith and holiness of life and the other virtues,[2] so that from these the most [6] suitable should be selected for the episcopate.[7] For if the holy and glorious apostles, who accepted the episcopate [8] from the Lord Christ our God [9] and filled the earth with all virtues and transmitted his teaching to all persons, have not spared even their life in this world for our salvation, how is it not just for them who succeed to their rank and are instituted as bishops [3] of the most holy churches to have possessed [10] a pure character [11] and to despise money [12] and to extend their entire life to the Benevolent God?

And therefore it is proper for such persons to be chosen and to be ordained bishops [3] who have neither children nor grandchildren,[13] since it cannot be that he, when occupied with life's cares (which children particularly provide for parents),[14] should have his entire interest and good intention about the divine liturgy and ecclesiastical affairs. For when certain persons because of hope toward God and because of their souls' salvation run toward the most holy churches and bring and bequeath their property to these very places for expenditure on beggars and paupers and these other pious uses, it is absurd for bishops to take these things for their own profit or to spend these on their own children and kinsfolk.[15] For it is necessary for a bishop, not impeded by passionate attachment to fleshly children, to be a spiritual father of all the faithful. On this account, therefore, we forbid him who has children or grandchildren to be ordained bishop.[13]

Moreover we ordain that those who are or shall be bishops should have not at all permission to will or to donate or by other device whatever to alienate anything of their resources, which, after they have become bishops, they have acquired either from wills or from donations or in other manner whatever, except only what before their episcopate they had from whatever cause or after their episcopate has come or shall come to them from parents and uncles and brothers and sisters.[16] But we order to belong to the most holy church of which they are bishop and to be claimed by it all things which after ordination have come to them from whatever cause (as has been said) apart from the said persons—no other person being able to take from this for his own profit. For who can doubt that those who have bequeathed or bequeath or in any other manner have transmitted or transmit their own substance to these have had regard for the episcopate [8] itself and do this, believing that not only they will spend piously the things bequeathed by them, but also they will add their own substance to these things?

But from this our general legislation we except only whatsoever properties have been controlled by Epiphanius, the most holy archbishop and patriarch of this fortunate city,[17] until the present day; for we ordain that in respect to the things about to come to him after the present the ordinances made by us should prevail and that these things should belong to the most holy Great Church.[18]

But after the death of the most God-beloved bishops the stewards at the time should be asked for accounts of the properties bequeathed by them due to belong to the most holy Church in accord with this our legislation.[19]

579. SELECTION OF BISHOPS, 528

And we order the stewards themselves to be created according to judgement and scrutiny, since they should know that by all means in each year they shall submit to the most holy bishop accounts of their administration and that they shall restore to the ecclesiastical properties all that in respect to ecclesiastical properties they may appear to have damaged or to have made as their own profit—so that if they, surviving, should submit such accounts, the said procedure should occur; but if they should die before they should submit the said accounts, then their heirs should be subjected to such an inquiry and should be constrained to restitution of all things to which they may appear to be obligated as a result.

We also have believed that we ought to make regulations in respect to the persons who have accepted or shall accept the management of the holy hostels and hospitals and almshouses and orphanages and nurseries.

And in the case of these persons we annul all authority to transfer to other persons the possessions acquired by them, after they have received the said functions, either by wills or by other manner whatever or device, except whatever they happened to have previously or afterward came to them from parents or uncles and brothers and sisters. But we order that all things, as much as belong to the said holy houses or have come or shall come to their superintendents, after they have accepted such management, should belong to the said holy houses and should be administered piously for the persons who are in them or are treated there. For it is obvious that he who bequeaths or donates in writing or without writing to hostel or hospital or almshouse or orphanage gives for this reason: that it should be administered piously by the superintendent, because he has much occasion for piety through the persons placed under his care. And is it not just that this person should not spend on them or for them what he receives for the purpose of persons placed under his care and should take the said things for his own person and should make it his own profit by disdaining the fear of God. For who cannot consider that the person having such management has accepted this for this reason: that on it he should spend not only as much as results from external sources for him, but also as much as he happened to have?

And also we order this: that as much as may happen to remain after the expenditure necessarily made by such persons for the persons placed under their care and after the attention to both the properties and the houses should be applied to purchase of revenues.[20] For everywhere our object is that properties marked for pious uses should be brought to growth or increase, for thus everyone wishing to do something for his own soul will give more readily, if he should believe that the things offered by him will be administered piously. But if it should happen that anyone of these persons should be removed from the management which he had, we ordain that accounts of all the administration performed by him should be asked with the fear of the Lord God by him who is appointed in his place (according as it is encompassed by this our divine legislation)—the person appointed after him knowing that he shall submit an account on this matter to the Lord God.

We also ordain (according as it has been determined by the divine canons) that neither a bishop nor a rural bishop nor an itinerant bishop nor a priest nor another clergyman of whatever rank should be ordained because of a gift;[21] and that a person by offering anything should not be created either a steward or a defender of the Church or a manager of a hostel or a superintendent of a hospital or a director of an almshouse or a director of an orphanage or a director of a nursery or a person in charge of poor relief, but according to the judgement and the scrutiny of the most God-beloved bishops in the several places these persons should be proposed. But if anyone should have been found giving or taking anything for the purpose of the said ordinations and managements, whether he should be a bishop or a clergyman, we order both the offerer and the taker to be outside the episcopate [8] and the clericate, in addition to the fact that they are under the Lord God's condemnation. But if anyone should have been created through patronage [22] and should have been found giving anything, we order the person so created to be outside the clericate. But if a steward or a defender of the Church or a rural bishop or an itinerant bishop or a manager of a hostel or a superintendent of a hospital or a director of an almshouse or a director of an orphanage or a director of a nursery or a person called in charge of poor relief should have appeared to be offering anything for securing such management for himself, we also ordain that this person should be removed from such management.

We also ordain that all clergymen in each church by themselves [23] should chant both nocturnal and matutinal and vespertinal services, lest only in consuming ecclesiastical properties they should appear to be clergymen, bearing indeed the name of clergymen, but not fulfilling the function of a clergyman in respect to the Lord God's liturgy. For it is absurd that when necessity is imposed upon them, persons enrolled [24] instead of them should chant, for, if many of the laymen for the sake of benefiting their own soul, when attending the most holy churches, should show themselves eager about psalmody, how is it not absurd that clergymen, appointed for this purpose, should not perform their own profession? Wherefore we order that clergymen by all means should chant and that they should be investigated by the most God-beloved bishops at the time and two archpriests of each church and the so-called provost [25] or exarch and the defender of each most holy church and that persons not found devoting themselves faultlessly to the liturgies should be placed outside the clergy. For the persons who have established or have founded the most holy churches for their own salvation and the common polity have bequeathed to them their substance, through which the divine liturgies were bound to be performed, on the condition that through the most devout clergymen performing the liturgies in the most holy churches the Lord God may be worshipped.

We offer to every person knowing any transgression of these things permission to report [26] and to reveal this.

We order that these ordinances made by us should be followed to the limit and should be carried into action with God's favour—persons daring to transgress these looking first for peril from the Lord God's judgement, then penalties inserted in this very legislation.

Given on 1 March at Constantinople, our Lord Justinian Perpetual-Augustus being consul for the second time.

1. Of the East.
2. 1 Tim. 3. 1-7; Titus 1. 6-9; *CA* 2 *passim*, 3. 20, 8. 3-5, 47 *passim*.
3. See no. 16, n. 4.
4. Cf. Acts 6. 4, where the apostles devote themselves to prayer.
5. See no. 526, n. 11.
6. The Greek prefers the comparative degree, though more than two candidates must be considered.
7. In Roman law this seems to be the earliest reference to a popular choice of three candidates for elevation to the episcopate. While popular participation in such selection later ceased, yet the custom of three candidates, though at times and in places suspended, has persisted in various parts of the Church into our own day, whenever nomination of a bishop is permitted. Nothing about the appointing authority is said here, but the practice during the sixth century in the Eastern Empire was that the archbishop (metropolitan) of a civil province made his choice from the three nominees named by the populace. See no. 523, n. 1 *ad init.*

On the other hand, when the apostles acted to select a substitute for the suicide Judas Iscariot, they appointed only two candidates and from these they chose one (Acts 1.15-26). But traditionally three is a preferred number in sacred matters (so Vergil, *Ecl.* 8. 73-5) as well as in Roman Law (see no. 324, n. 7).

8. See no. 158, n. 1.
9. In view of the two following present infinitives, perhaps this perfect infinitive should be interpreted gnomically and should be given a present sense.
10. Or "course of life", "purpose or plan of action".
11. So St Paul in 1 Tim. 3. 3 and Titus 1. 7.
12. But St Paul permitted bishops not only to marry, but also to procreate in wedlock: 1 Tim. 3. 2, 4, 5; Titus 1. 6. But see no. 372, n. 4.

13. So St Paul wishes persons to be "without carefulness" by remaining single (1 Cor. 7. 32–3).
14. So *CA* 8. 47. 39.
15. *CA* 8. 47. 39–40.
16. Constantinople.
17. Hagia Sophia in Constantinople.
18. This sentence lacks a principal verb in Greek and depends upon that of the preceding sentence.
19. That is, properties which will produce income for the institutions.
20. So *CA* 8. 47. 30.
21. Or in its bad sense "collusion".
22. That is, without substitutes.
23. The Latin version, while it translates γραπτούς properly as *scriptos*, yet supplies in a questionized parenthesis *vicarios* to overcome the obscurity. Obviously some sort of registered substitute is meant.
24. G. ἄρχων, L. *praepositus*. What was such an official's ordinary function is uncertain, especially in view of the attributive participle, which points to fluidity of nomenclature.
25. Apparently this word (προσαναγγέλλειν) occurs in Greek only here.

580. LETTER OF JUSTINIAN I ON EPISCOPAL JOURNEYS TO CONSTANTINOPLE, 528

(*CI* 1. 3. 42)

The emperor orders the Constantinopolitan patriarch to circularize the bishops subject to him that they should not leave their sees to promote ecclesiastical business in the capital without imperial instruction, but that they should send several priests to tend to such transactions.

The same emperor to Epiphanius, archbishop of Constantinople and patriarch.

Taking ever every forethought for the most holy churches, through which we have believed that our Sovereignty is strengthened and public affairs are fortified by the Benevolent God's grace, yet truly eager to save our and all others' souls and for the sake of this caring continually, lest the advantages for the most holy churches situated in whatever city should be neglected utterly and lest in these the divine liturgies should be impeded as a result of the most God-beloved bishops'[1] absence or should be performed improperly and lest the most holy churches' properties should be exhausted through expenditures in respect to bishops[1] and clergymen and servants going with

580. EPISCOPAL JOURNEYS TO CONSTANTINOPLE, 528

them both on journeys and while here, so that frequently there is need for loans and the resulting burden comes upon the most holy churches themselves, in addition to the fact that the administration of ecclesiastical properties does not proceed properly during the period of the most God-beloved bishops'[1] absence, we have considered that we ought to use this divine letter to your Beatitude.

We command that you through this letter should make clear to all most pious bishops[1] assigned under you throughout each province's metropolises that it is not proper for anyone of these or of the most God-beloved bishops assigned under a metropolitan in a province's other cities, at his own initiative apart from our divine special command, to leave the most holy church administered by him and to go to this fortunate city,[2] whatever business arises, but to send hither one or two of the holy clergy under him and to make clear to our Piety[3] about what matters they wish, coming to us either through themselves directly or through your Beatitude's intervention, and thus to obtain our just and prompt aid.

For if anything of the matters brought to us should appear to us to be such that it needs the presence of the most God-beloved bishops[1] themselves, in this case we shall order them to be present. But apart from such our divine order we permit none to be present—the person transgressing these rules and overstepping the observance (introduced rightly and piously by us for the most holy churches' honour) knowing that he will experience no little indignation, but also will be removed,[4] if he should be a metropolitan, by your Beatitude, but, if of cities under a metropolitan, by the metropolitan himself. For we have not considered it necessary to determine a monetary penalty against persons overpassing this our divine disposition, lest the resulting damage should devolve upon the most holy churches, whose properties we are eager to remain free from every diminution.

Therefore your Sanctity shall be eager to bring these matters to the knowledge of each of the most God-beloved metropolitan bishops assigned under you and to forward to our Piety the replies (that they have understood about these matters) sent by each both through the metropolitans and through the most God-beloved bishops themselves of the province's remaining cities.

Given on 1 March at Constantinople, our Lord Justinian Perpetual-Augustus being consul for the second time.

1. See no. 16, n. 4.
2. Constantinople.
3. Doubtless by means of commendatory letters, on which see no. 270, n. 3 *ad fin*.
4. Literally "will be under separation".

581. MANDATE OF JUSTINIAN I ON DONATIONS FOR PIOUS PURPOSES, 528

(*CI* 1. 2. 19)

While Justinian confirms older statutes authorizing the validity of donations made to the Church and to its charitable institutions without requiring public registration to perfect such gifts, yet the emperor here raises the maximum worth of such donations falling in the unregistered category.

Emperor Justinian Augustus to Menas, praetorian prefect.[1]

What in accord with old laws,[2] though obscurely stated, was attacked by certain persons—that donations made concerning pious causes, though not published in the records, yet should be valid—this by definite and distinct law we judge: that in other cases, indeed, the old laws [2] concerning publication of donations should remain intact.

But if anyone shall have made donations up to five hundred solidi [3] in any properties whatever either for a holy church or for a hostel or for a hospital or for an orphanage or for an almshouse or for any community whatever, these donations also without transaction of the records should be valid;[4] but if the donations should be of larger amount (an imperial donation obviously excepted), it should not be valid otherwise unless it has been published in the records [4]—permission to be given to none for any other cause whatever (as if there has been reliance upon the law of piety), except for those cases which we specifically have explained, to alter completely the ancients' statutes introduced concerning publication of donations.

Given . . . , our Lord Justinian Perpetual-Augustus being consul for the second time.[5]

1. Of the East.
2. See no. 522, n. 6.
3. See no. 433, n. 7 for the value of a solidus.
4. From *II* 2. 7. 2 we learn that the previous minimum for public registration of gifts was two hundred solidi. This limit, supposed to have been set by Constantius I, was confirmed by *CT* 3. 5. 13 (dated 428). See no. 522, n. 6.
5. Editorial conjecture translated, for the subscription is defective.

582. MANDATE OF JUSTINIAN I ON EPISCOPAL INTEREST IN DISPUTED LOANS, 528

(*CI* 1. 4. 21)

This ordinance, adapted from the last two sections of a larger law (preserved in *CI* 4. 30. 14), on non-payment of money by a creditor to a debtor, who has contracted with the creditor to borrow money from him, authorizes a bishop to receive the debtor's complaint that the money—or other things (as the case may be), for Justinian enlarges the law beyond mere money—has not been paid by the creditor (who may have withheld physical delivery of the loan for various reasons, some of which may have been fraudulent). But a bishop only so acts when another administrator is not available to accept the debtor's accusation.

The same Augustus to Menas, praetorian prefect.[1]

If the person[2] who has been written as having paid the money or as having given other things[3] should be present indeed, or if, however, he should perform some administration[4] in the provinces, so that it may seem difficult to send to the said person a declaration of money paid,[5] we give to him[6] who may wish to use the said exception[7] permission to approach other judges [8] and through them to show to him [2] against whom he casts an exception of this kind that by him [6] has been made a complaint concerning money not paid.

But if [9] there should not be another administrator, civil or military, or through some cause it should be difficult for him [6] who opposes [10] the said complaint to go to him [2] and to do the things which have been said, we give permission both to declare his [6] said exception to the creditor [2] through a most reverend bishop and to interrupt thus the statutory time.[11]

And that this also has a place in the exception of a dowry not paid has been received.[12]

1. Of the East.
2. The B of n. 3 *infra*.
3. Sometimes oral contracts were attested by written instruments. In the case under consideration here A (the borrower) has given to B (the lender) a chirograph that B has paid the money or has given other things by way of a loan to A. At this point, whether B has paid or has given is immaterial. If B pays or gives, good; but if B has not paid or has not given and later sues A on the chirograph, then A's defence is the *exceptio doli seu non numeratae pecuniae* (exception of fraud or of money not paid), which in Justinian's time must be pleaded within a biennium (*CI* 4. 30. 14. pr.). See also *II* 4. 13. 2.
4. *CI* 4. 30. 14. 5 inserts "either in this genial city [Constantinople] or".

5. Ordinarily a defendant could be sued only in the place of his domicile, i.e. a plaintiff could demand performance only within the jurisdiction to which his defendant was subject—but exceptions occurred (*II* 4. 6. 33). In the present case A (the injured borrower) happens to find B (the fraudulent lender) out of A's town and so—as later appears—presents his plea before other judges, viz. judges not in A's place of residence. See no. 478, n. 16.

6. The A of n. 3 *supra*.

7. Cf. *supra* n. 3 *ad fin*.

8. The longer version inserts "either in this genial city [Constantinople] or in the provinces".

9. The longer version inserts "in the provinces either".

10. In the sense of "introduces"; that is A of n. 3 opposes B of n. 3 by opposing B's attempt to collect money never lent by B.

11. Since only two years were allowed for pleading such an exception (cf. *supra* n. 2 *ad fin*.), by registering with an official (here a bishop in the absence of a magistrate) one's complaint and by showing the present impossibility of serving it one prevents time from running against oneself.

12. The longer version for *received* has "certain".

583. LAW OF JUSTINIAN I ON EPISCOPAL INFORMATION ABOUT PAGANS, (?)528

(*CI* 1. 11. 9)

In an effort to eradicate pagan worship this defective statute (which from its position in Justinian's Code may have emanated from any emperor between 472 and 534, but which usually is ascribed to Justinian)[1] bids bishops to attract the attention of the secular authorities to pagan practices. The ordinance particularly debars pagans from disposing their property for purposes of worship and orders the proscription of such property for municipal use as well as confirms earlier emperors' constitutions against paganism.

... We order our magistrates both in this royal city[2] and in the provinces to advance with all zeal, both by their own resources and when by the most God-beloved bishops they have been instructed in such matters, to investigate legally all the impieties of pagan[3] worship, so that these may not occur and, when occurring, may be punished; but, if the correction of these exceeds the provincial authorities, to announce these to us, so that the responsibility for wrongful acts and a punitive action should not come upon themselves.

But to none it shall be possible either to bequeath in a testament or by a donation to give anything to persons or to places for introduction of the impiety of paganism,³ although this should not be contained specifically in the words of the will or testament or donation, but otherwise can be comprehended with truth by the judges.

But things so bequeathed or donated shall be taken from those persons or places to which they have been given or have been bequeathed, but shall belong to the cities in which such persons dwell or also under which such places are situated, so that they should be consumed according to the likeness of public revenues.

All penalties, as many as have been threatened against pagan ³ error by previous emperors or have been introduced on behalf of the orthodox faith, shall be ⁴ valid and perpetually firm and shall be maintained ⁴ by the present pious legislation.

1. Bury (2. 367-70) follows earlier scholars in attributing to this statute and to no. 600 the closing of the philosophical schools in Athens, where a continuous pagan tradition (later inimical to Christianity) had been maintained since the days of Plato (427?-347 B.C.) and Aristotle (384-322 B.C.).
2. Probably Constantinople, for the subscription is lost.
3. See no. 121, n. 3.
4. The principal verb in English is a participle in Greek in the construction of the genitive absolute.

584. LAW OF JUSTINIAN I ON ECCLESIASTICAL EXCLUSION FROM MILITARY PROVISIONING, c. 528

(*CI* 1. 2. 20)

While it is not clear how the Church came to share in the supplies levied annually for the armed forces (στρατιωτικὴ σίτησις or *militaris annona*), unless this had occurred in a time of surplus or of a reduction in the military establishment, at any rate by this statute Justinian outlaws the conveyance of military provisions to oratories or churches or monasteries on the ground that the guilds concerned with such service are under normal strength and that consequently these are occupied fully with supplying the soldiers and the sailors.[1]

The same emperor.

As a result of a divine formulary [2] or a magisterial [3] ordinance or any governor's [4] order whatever, military provision should not be transferred to houses of prayer [5] or clergymen [6] or monasteries, since corporations,[7] forsooth, are deficient for the units.[8]

1. Though it is known that the Church shared in the *civilian* provisions earlier (nos. 301, 510, 537) and in this year of 528 (see the grant to the Monastery of Metanoia near Alexandria in Egypt: *Catalogue général des antiquités égyptiennes du musée du Caire* [Cairo, 1916], 3. 25-8) and later in 535 (*N* 7. 8), yet no other evidence exists that the Church shared in the *military* provisions or that there had been a surplus or that the armed forces had declined in number or that the guilds were undermanned and therefore had difficulty in servicing military and naval needs.

On the *annona* see no. 301, n. 7.

2. Usually an imperial rescript in reply to a written question.
3. Perhaps praetorian prefects are meant.
4. Abstract in the original Greek for what should be (as here) concrete. The Latin version supplies the next word, which is necessary even in Greek to complete the sense.
5. That is, oratories; see no. 522, nn. 5. and 9.
6. Probably concrete for abstract: one expects "churches" to complete the series.
7. Such guilds as those of dealers in grain, dealers in oil, shipowners, who performed service for the *annona*.
8. The independent military unit of the Dominate was called ἀριθμός (as here) or *numerus*. Its strength is estimated variously between two and four hundred, though smaller and larger numbers are recorded occasionally. These companies served communities as garrisons.

585. LAW OF JUSTINIAN I ON LEGACIES TO CLERGYMEN OR CHURCHES OR CHARITIES, 528-9

(*CI* 6. 48. 1)

In this defective constitution which collects miscellaneous rules on bequests to unidentified persons considered as classes (such as relatives, guilds, military units, freedmen) only those ecclesiastically interesting sections (on the clergy [§ 10] and on churches and charitable institutions [§ 26]) are translated.

Pitra prints (2. 496) a late Greek version.

Emperor Justinian Augustus.
... If anyone should have bequeathed anything either to the sacred

Senate[1] or to a city's senate or to an office staff serving great magistrates[1] or those in provinces or to a guild of physicians or of teachers or of lawyers or to soldiers or to fellow-workmen[2] or to clergymen or—simply—to any unprohibited guild whatever, the bequest is valid ...

... And concerning bequests, demanded in perpetuity, to churches, to hostels or to almshouses or to holy houses or to the community of all the clergy or for redemption of captives or to paupers themselves or to captives[3] ...

1. In Constantinople.
2. Pitra's late Greek version omits reference to the workers.
3. Since this section is a simple rubric, the editors implement it in the *apparatus criticus* by the subsequent extract from the *Nomocanon*, 2. 1: "And in the end of the same constitution: If a bequest should have been made piously for once or for a year either to churches or to hostels or to almshouses or to holy houses or to the community of the clergy or for redemption of captives or to the paupers themselves or to captives, the deceased's will prevails."

586. MANDATE OF JUSTINIAN I ON EPISCOPAL INTEREST IN PRISONERS, 529

(*CI* 1. 4. 22)

This directive, partly duplicated in *CI* 9. 4. 6, extends episcopal interest in justice by commanding bishops on Wednesdays or Fridays to visit prisoners, to investigate the causes of their incarceration, to report any remissness or carelessness in the conduct of the prisons.

The same emperor to Menas, praetorian prefect.[1]

We desire that none should be cast into prison without an order of the glorious or the admirable or the most distinguished magistrates[2] in this fortunate city[3] or in a province or of the defenders in the cities.

In the case of those imprisoned or to be imprisoned the most God-beloved bishops of the places on one day (the fourth or the sixth[4]) of each week should examine[5] persons in prisons and with precision should investigate[5] the reasons for their detention and whether they happen to be slaves or freemen, whether they have been imprisoned for money matters or for other accusations or for murders.

The most glorious and the admirable and the most distinguished magistrates both of this fortunate city [3] and of the provinces should prepare [5] to do in these places those things which our sacred constitution, sent on this matter to the most glorious prefects,[6] states explicitly [7]—authority being given to the most God-beloved bishops at the time,[8] if they should see any carelessness existing on the part of the most glorious and the most magnificent and the most distinguished magistrates at the time [8] or on the part of the office staffs which obey them, to denounce this, that appropriate punitive action may be brought against the careless persons.

Given on 18 January at Constantinople, Decius being consul.

1. Of the East.
2. During the fourth century all the important magistracies and imperial offices entitled their incumbents to be called by certain honorific epithets. Thus the director of one of the central ministries was *illustris* (ἰλλούστριος), a diocesan vicar was *spectabilis* (περίβλεπτος), a provincial governor was *clarissimus* (λαμπρότατος). From about the mid-fifth century an *illustris* could be called also *magnificus* or *magnificissimus* (μεγαλοπρεπής or μεγαλοπρεπέστατος), as later in this order. Before the mid-sixth century—as shown in this document—a new rank, superior to the illustriate, was instituted: *gloriosus* or *gloriosissimus* (ἔνδοξος or ἐνδοξότατος, as in this directive). See no. 495, n. 9.

On the system's success see W. Durant, *The Age of Faith* (New York, 1950), 7—a rhetorical résumé.

3. Constantinople.
4. Literally "the day of preparation" (παρασκευή); i.e. that before the Jewish Sabbath. The day of preparation then is the Christian Friday.
5. The verb is an infinitive dependent upon an understood verb of command.
6. The praetorian prefects are meant.
7. For this much of this paragraph *CI* 9. 4. 6 inserts the following and then resumes as precisely as it precedes:

"And if they are slaves, within twenty days they should be ejected, after they either have been chastened or have been surrendered to their masters, or, if their masters should not appear, they should be released.

"A freeman cast into jail because of money matters shall be released on providing sureties; but if he is in want of sureties, the suit against him shall be decided within thirty days and he shall be released. But if the case should need more time, then until the end of the lawsuit it shall be trusted to his denial on oath that he knows anything about the matter; but if after denial on oath that he knows anything about the matter he should have deserted before the completion of the investigation, he shall be deprived of his own property.

"If a freeman, held on an accusation, should have been cast into prison, he shall give sureties and shall be released. But if he is in want of sureties, he shall remain in prison as long as only six months, within which the suit against him shall be decided, unless indeed he is summoned on a capital charge. For such a person is not trusted for a surety, if he should have been accused of course by public persons [i.e. officials]; but again within six months the suit against him ought to take its end. But if he should have been summoned not by public persons, but by a private accuser, then a surety is confirmed. But if he should not be able to give sureties, he is guarded for only one year, within which the suit against him must be decided by all means.

"But when presumption about them as guilty exists, they should be in ward, till when the lawsuit should have been completed.

"But if sentence already has occurred against them when incarcerated, it should be executed, whether it is corporal or monetary, for they [the guilty] have permission in a monetary sentence to surrender their property.

"The bishops should caution the magistrates, who know that both they themselves and their office staffs shall furnish ten pounds [of gold, if negligent]".

The translator has supplied bracketed words to complete the sense. Several of the main verbs in the passage are either infinitives or participles in a genitive absolute construction (for the text is Greek) and are dependent upon a verb of command.

8. This phrase seems to be inserted to make the mandate of general application.

587. MANDATE OF JUSTINIAN I ON EPISCOPAL INTEREST IN EXILES, 529

(CI 9. 47. 26)

After announcing sundry rules regulating the sentence of exile the emperor concludes by commanding bishops to see that the imperial commands are observed by exiles. Only the concluding section (9), which is of ecclesiastical interest, is translated.

The order seems to be an interpretation of an ordinance.

Emperor Justinian Augustus to Menas, praetorian prefect.[1]

... Bishops in the several places shall provide that in persons exiled perpetually or for a certain stated time the things commanded by the constitution should be observed carefully.

Given on 18 January at Constantinople, Decius being consul.

1. Of the East.

588. MANDATE OF JUSTINIAN I ON SEGREGATION OF MONKS AND NUNS, 529
(CI 1. 3. 43)

The emperor here legislates against the association of monks with nuns in a communal life and ordains their segregation into separate communities. Bishops and governors are directed to apply the law after expiration of a year's grace granted to effect the authorized alteration in the monastic mode of life.

The same emperor to Menas, praetorian prefect.[1]

Providing for the most holy churches' and the pure monasteries' decorum, we forbid all men dwelling in monasteries to live with women who are nuns or to contrive any pretext for having any association with them (for this introduces a just suspicion of meeting with them continually and whenever they wish), but so to be segregated that they shall have no participation with one another for any reason whatever and that no pretext of a course of life with one another should be sought either by the latter or by the former. But men alone by themselves should live in each monastery, segregated from the nuns who are nearby for any reason whatever, and the women alone by themselves, not mingled with men, for the purpose that all supposition of indecorous social intercourse should be destroyed absolutely.[2]

But if the men should be more in number, it is fitting that by provision of the most God-beloved bishops in each city the women should be transferred into another suitable place and that to them should be given a convent, wherein it shall be proper that they by themselves should live decorously for the future. But if the women should have been found to be more in number or even equal in number, the men should be transferred, but the women should stay in the convent, so that, however, the ones leaving should divide with the ones staying in proportion the said monastery's[3] movable and immovable and self-moved[4] properties.[2]

For the necessary answers[5] of the women living alone by themselves one old man should be appointed by the city's most God-beloved bishop, but for fulfilling the divine liturgies and distributing to them the Holy Communion[6] should be given one priest and one deacon of glorious life, who are obligated to perform only the aforesaid services, not indeed to live and to dwell with them.[2] For if these matters are observed, both for them who choose to live alone will life be happy and the affairs of our common polity will be fashioned by the Benevolent God's very ready aid. These things, then, are what we

588. SEGREGATION OF MONKS AND NUNS, 529

have approved and also have believed to be well even so in respect to common affairs, because the aid of this our divine constitution, when added to these, will be seen to be not slight as a result.

Moreover for these things in no way to be transgressed there is need of very exact watchfulness, which cannot occur otherwise than when each city's most God-beloved bishops oversee carefully the ways of life of the monks living in the monasteries assigned under their care and, if they should perceive any such lapse, when by all means they prevent what is attempted by them [7] and when they induce by penalties the persons who after our prohibition still hold to these things and when they compel their ways of life to be pure and segregated from female social intercourse. For to the most God-beloved bishops, if they rightly should intend to consider this matter, it is known that as a result of guarding this decorous course of life of the most devout monks and not adding to it impropriety or indecorum the common affairs of our polity will have the Benevolent God as propitious.

But lest the most God-beloved bishops themselves should suppose that this our divine command is incidental, we wish them to know that if any one of them should seem not to be examining closely with all exactness these matters or not through the aforesaid ways correcting an obvious lapse, he will be liable to the Lord God's judgement and now will come on him our royal punitive action and he will be in peril with regard to his priesthood [8]—and no other greater indignation being lacking.

Therefore your Excellency shall cause this our divine legislation to be manifest to the most God-beloved bishops in each metropolis and to the provinces' most splendid governors, by adding this: that they, if there should be need, should give all aid to the cities' most devout bishops, on the condition that they prevent these things which we have commanded to be abolished, and, if they should have found them employing any laxity, they should make this manifest to us through their own information, in order that all should know that the things incumbent on them and the punishment determined as a result of negligence should be observed.

Moreover the most God-beloved metropolitans should give heed both to make this our divine law manifest also to the other most devout bishops of the same province and to exhort all persons, fearing the determined penalty, to observe these matters with sleepless earnestness.

Concerning the fact that the fulfilment of this our divine legislation should not be delayed, but that the most devout monks themselves who at present are living with nuns should think that little time has been given them for the due separation to occur, we determine this to last for a year, computed from when this our divine law should be made manifest, so that after a year's passage, if it should have appeared that the common life continues in the same pattern, the punishments inserted in this our divine law should be applied in every way.

Given on 18 January, Decius being consul.

1. Of the East.
2. This sentence, printed independently in Greek and so translated into English, lacks a verb and appears to depend on that of the preceding sentence.
3. Or "convent" as the case may be. One word (μοναστήριον) does duty for both.
4. Such as livestock.
5. That is, as we should say, "for answering the needs", such as what manual services beyond female strength a man can perform.
6. Plural in Greek.
7. The solitaries.
8. See no. 158, n. 1.

589. MANDATE OF JUSTINIAN I ON EPISCOPAL INTEREST IN PRIVATE PRISONERS, 529

(CI 1. 4. 23)

This statute, partly repeated in *CI* 9. 5. 2, where it has an added interpretation (which is translated here), prohibits private prisons and bids bishops to liberate persons imprisoned in such places.

The same Augustus to Menas, praetorian prefect.[1]

By all means we forbid private prisons to be established in cities or in villages [2]—obviously the persons detained being released from detention by the providence of the most God-beloved bishops in the several places.

Given on 21 January [3] at Constantinople, Decius being consul.

The ordinance commands that private prisons should not exist and that the persons doing this both should be subject to a fine and should live in a public jail as many days as any person may have been confined in the prison created by them—of whatever station or dignity they should be—and that also by the providence of the bishop [4] and of the magistrate [4] they should lose the lawsuit competent to them against the persons who have been confined.

But if the magistrate shall be negligent, he places himself under peril both in respect to his property and in respect to his safety.

1. Of the East.
2. *CI* 9. 5. 2 omits the rest of this sentence and adds without warning a captionless interpretation.
3. The day in *CI* 9. 5. 2 is the 18th.
4. Of the city or of the village concerned.

590. MANDATE OF JUSTINIAN I ON CONFIRMATION OF THE CODE, 529

(*CI*, Constitution *Summa*)

This document, usually prefixed to editions of Justinian's *Codex*,[1] confirms the completion as well as the reception of this collection of imperial constitutions from Hadrian's reign (117–38) onward and directs the use of this part of the *Corpus Iuris Civilis*[2] throughout the Empire. In this mandate the emperor acknowledges thrice the divine aid shown both to the Empire and to him.

Emperor Justinian Pious, Fortunate, Renowned, Victor and Triumpher, Ever-August to the illustrious Menas, praetorian prefect[3] for the second time, ex-prefect of this genial city,[4] and patrician.

The highest[5] protection of the State, coming from the source of two circumstances, arms and laws, and thence strengthening its own vigour, as well in past times has made as for eternity, with God's favour, will make the fortunate race of Romans to be placed before all nations and to dominate all . . .

But since it is necessary to extirpate utterly the multitude of constitutions, both recorded in the three old codes[6] and added in later times after their[6] completion,[7] by reducing to brevity their[6] mist, which entraps the right decisions of judges, we have dedicated ourselves, with ready mind, to provide this common benefit under God's direction . . .

And Almighty God granted his own assistance to our zeal undertaken on behalf of the State . . .

Given on 7 April at Constantinople, the most distinguished Decius being consul.[8]

1. See Introd., n. 3 *ad init*.
2. See Introd., n. 3 *ad fin*. for the origin of this phrase.
3. Of the East.
4. Constantinople.

5. *Summa*, the mandate's initial word, whence the constitution takes its name. See also no. 617, n. 6.

6. These codes are those of Gregory, Hermogenian, Theodosius II and are described in no. 578, n. 5.

7. For constitutions promulgated after the *Codex Theodosianus* had been completed in 438 see no. 578, n. 6.

8. The third prefatory constitution to the *Codex Justinianus*, that called *Cordi*, issued 16 November 534, to confirm the revised edition of the *Codex* (on which see Introd., n. 3 *ad init.*), contains nothing of religious interest.

591. MANDATE OF JUSTINIAN I ON EPISCOPAL INTEREST IN FOUNDLINGS' RIGHTS, 529

(*CI* 8. 51. 3)

This constitution, appearing abbreviatedly earlier in Justinian's Code (1. 4. 24), includes bishops among the officials charged with maintenance of regulations on the legal status of foundlings. Since only the last section (3) is of ecclesiastical interest, only it is translated.

Emperor Justinian Augustus to Demosthenes, praetorian prefect.[1]

. . . The most distinguished governors of provinces as well as the most religious bishops and also the gubernatorial office staffs and the fathers [2] and the defenders of municipalities and all civil aid [3] shall maintain these regulations.[4]

Given on 17 September at Chalcedon, the most distinguished Decius being consul.

1. Of the East.

2. That is, of municipalities, for the context shows that the foundlings' fathers are not meant.

3. Probably all apparitors are included.

4. For this section the shorter statute reads simply: "Not only governors of provinces but also the most religious bishops shall observe these regulations."

In each version a participle serves as the verb of this independent sentence.

592. MANDATE OF JUSTINIAN I ON BIBLICAL OATHS BEFORE JUDICIAL TORTURE OF SLAVES, 529

(CI 2. 58. 1)

The emperor requires that prior to torturing slaves to elicit the truth about an inheritance the examiner must swear on the Scriptures that he is free from hatred toward the slaves and that he is not trying to uncover their offences against the co-heirs of the estate.

Emperor Justinian Augustus to Demosthenes, praetorian prefect.[1]

In all lawsuits, whether it shall have been contested on account of letters [2] or on account of records or on account of anything else, in which the necessity of proof presses, we ordain that not otherwise the offering of the said proofs should be compelled unless previously he who demands these shall have offered an oath about calumny,[3] which oath he has not proposed that he may spread allegations of this sort, for through fear of the solemn obligation[4] the litigants' contentious perseverance is curbed.

Moreover, lest certain persons coming to the inquisition of slaves [5] should exercise wrongly their mind's cruelty, to those who demand inquisition of slaves [5] it should not be granted [6] otherwise to come to this or to be heard by judges unless previously, after the Sacrosanct Scriptures have been touched, they should depose that they have come to this not through hatred of the slaves or on account of offences to the co-heirs, but because otherwise they cannot ascertain or show the truth about the inherited property.

Given on 20 September at Constantinople,[7] the most distinguished Decius being consul.

1. Of the East.
2. That is, "written signs or marks" or "words" or "writing" probably rather than "correspondence". The word is *littera*.
3. See no. 334, n. 3.
4. The *sacramentum*: originally a litigant's oath that his cause was just—loss of the lawsuit was held to prove that the litigant was a perjurer, who then became *sacer* (accursed) and was outlawed—but by the time of the *Twelve Tables* (449 B.C.) a litigant's solemn deposit of money had the same effect: the sum varied according to the disputed object's value and the loser forfeited his stake to the State's treasury (*FIRA* 1. 30; *TT* 2. 1a). Parallel with this procedural institution, which disappeared during the Principate, and doubtless developed from its original significance as an oath, the *sacramentum* became a soldier's oath to the standards in the Republic and in the Empire to the emperor.

From the military sphere the *sacramentum* evolved into an oath sworn by magistrates and officials to observe the laws. Meanwhile the original meaning of the word revived and it is in that sense that it is used in this constitution.

5. In such cases torture ordinarily was employed on the theory that without it no slave would speak the truth, despite the fact that experience of this supplementary means of ascertaining the truth not seldom had been shown to be worthless. A slave charged with participation in a crime was subject to torture either by his master, when the offence touched him, or under official authority, when the offence affected either another than his owner or the State. In a case, however, where a master was murdered all the household's slaves could be tortured. See no. 204, n. 3.

6. The finite verb is in Latin an infinitive dependent upon the preceding sentence's main verb.

7. An editorial conjecture proposes 17 September for the date and Chalcedon for the place.

593. MANDATE OF JUSTINIAN I ON EPISCOPAL INTEREST IN GAMBLING, 529

(*CI* 1. 4. 25)

This directive imposes on bishops the duty to inquire into and to stop the practice of gambling and to reform gamblers through the instrumentality of civil officials.

A Latin interpretation of an epitome of a larger general law on the subject exists in *CI* 3. 43. 1, where two Greek interpretations from later collections also are printed.[1]

The same emperor to Demosthenes, praetorian prefect.[2]

As many matters as have been legislated by us concerning the so-called cubes or dice and their prohibition,[3] in these matters also to the most God-beloved bishops we give power both to investigate and to stop the occurrences and to restore to discretion the offenders through the most distinguished governors of provinces and the fathers [4] and the defenders of municipalities.

Given on 22 September at Constantinople, Decius being consul.

1. In all three interpretations bishops are empowered to investigate gambling:
(1) Latin Interpretation: ". . . Bishops of places investigating this and using the governors' aid . . . by giving to bishops power of investigating this and of checking it by the governors' aid."
(2) Greek Interpretation I: "The constitution . . . entrusting . . . to bishops

to investigate and to prohibit and to annul all contracts made in these matters..."

(3) Greek Interpretation II: "... Bishops having power to investigate these matters—governors and fathers and defenders aiding them..."

2. Of the East.

3. Gambling with dice was prohibited by Roman law probably as early as 204 B.C., in which year probably was passed a *lex alearia* (see G. Rotondi, *Leges Publicae Populi Romani* [Milano, 1912], 261). Perhaps under it (or a later law) was convicted Licinius Denticulus, whom Mark Antony, his fellow-gambler—so Cicero charges (*Phil.* 2. 23. 56)—reinstated to civic rights. From the Digest's title on dicers (*De Aleatoribus*) it appears that at a banquet it was lawful to gamble with dice for the food (11. 5. 4. pr.), that an unidentified senatusconsult prohibited gambling for money, with certain exceptions (11. 5. 2. 1), and that the praetorian edict refused legal redress to a householder, if, when a game of dice was in progress in his house, the host was beaten or his property was damaged or was stolen (11. 5. 1. pr.), but allowed an action for robbery to the players, if one player had robbed another player (11. 5. 1. 1), and punished a person using violence for the purpose of a game of dice (11. 5. 1. 4).

Cicero classes dicers with adulterers (*In Cat.* 2. 10. 23) and mimes and procurers (*Phil.* 8. 9. 26; cf. 3. 14. 35).

4. Of municipalities.

594. MANDATE OF JUSTINIAN I ON OATHS IN LAWSUITS, 529

(*CI* 4. 1. 12)

Only so much of this lengthy law defining all oaths which are offered in lawsuits whether by the judge or by the parties is translated as pertains to Christian aspects. This section (5) directs the judge's attention to whether the oath should be sworn on the Bible or in oratories.

The same Augustus to Demosthenes, praetorian prefect.[1]

... Moreover in all cases in which solemn obligations [2] are offered we decide that the judicial observations should continue pursuant to the quality of the persons: whether the oath ought to be offered under the judge himself [3] or in homes [4] or when the Sacred Scriptures have been touched or in sacrosanct oratories...

Read at the seventh milestone [5] in the new consistory of Justinian's palace.[6]

Given on 30 October, the most distinguished Decius being consul.

1. Of the East.
2. On *sacramentum* (the word for this phrase) see no. 592, n. 4.
3. Since a judge sat on a raised tribunal, an oath taken before him there appropriately was accomplished *under* him.
4. Persons who legitimately could not appear in court were sworn at their homes.
5. This word is supplied by the translator from no. 595.
6. See no. 595, n. 7.

595. MANDATE OF JUSTINIAN I ON DONATIONS AND LEGACIES TO ECCLESIASTICAL INSTITUTIONS, 529

(CI 1. 2. 22)

In this directive the emperor grants to ecclesiastical institutions relief from taxation on gifts and legacies bestowed on these, inasmuch as he considers that the distinction drawn between things divine and human should be preserved.

The same Augustus to Demosthenes, praetorian prefect.[1]

We ordain that properties falling to venerable churches or hostels or monasteries or almshouses or nurseries [2] or orphanages or homes for the aged [3] or if there is any other such association, as a result of any senatorial [4] liberality exhibited either in life [5] or in anticipation of death or in last wills, should be free and immune from designations of articles acquired as pure gain [6]—the law, obviously, which has been established about designations of this sort, keeping its own strength, indeed, in the case of other persons, but on the part of the churches or of the other houses, which have been allotted to pious associations, mitigating its vigour in respect for piety. For why should we not make a distinction between things divine and human and wherefore should not be preserved an appropriate prerogative for celestial favour?

And these matters ought to prevail not only in cases which future time shall have created, but also in cases still pending and not yet settled by judicial termination or by friendly arrangement.

Read at this renowned city's seventh milestone in the new consistory of Justinian's palace.[7]

Given on 30 October, the most distinguished Decius being consul.[8]

1. Of the East.

2. The Greek original (βρεφοτροφεῖον) of the Latin word (*brephotrophium*) indicates that such institutions specialized in foundlings as distinct from orphans.

3. Though nothing is in the Greek original (γεροντοκομεῖον) of the Latin word (*gerontocomium*) to indicate that the inmates of such houses were poor, the dictionaries give such a connotation. At any rate this seems to have been a characteristic of homes for elderly persons throughout most of history.

4. That is, on the part of municipal senators endowing or contributing to such institutions.

5. The phrase is *inter vivos*, applied to donations made while the donor is alive and not in view of his approaching death, in which case the expression is *mortis causa*, the next phrase translated in the text.

In Roman law donations were of two kinds: (1) *donatio mortis causa*, where A gave property to B (or C on B's behalf) on condition that it should belong to B (or C), if A died, but that if A should survive the anticipated death, which had induced A to give the gift, B (or C) must return the given property to A; (2) *donatio inter vivos*, where A conveyed gratuitously to B property, usually not revocable.

For betrothal gifts, which came in this class, see no. 517, n. 2.

6. Among such articles was property conveyed by inheritance, legacy, trust, gifts, dowry.

By this ordinance it seems that in the case of ecclesiastico-eleemosynary institutions the doctrine that two grounds of ownership both gainful (*duae lucrativae causae*) cannot coincide in the same person for the same article (*II* 2. 20. 6) is upset.

7. This was the Hebdomon (on the shore of the Sea of Marmara and near the Golden Gate), enlarged or rebuilt by Justinian. The site is identified with Makri Keui, exactly seven (Roman) miles distant from the Forum Augusteum (the centre of old Byzantium), where was set the monument of the Μίλιον (milestone), whence was measured the mileage over the roads radiating from the capital.

8. Editors supply the subscription and query the date.

596. MANDATE OF JUSTINIAN I ON DONATIONS FOR PIOUS PURPOSES, 529

(*CI* 8. 53. 34)

While in the Dominate and even in Justinian's reign gifts were given to charitable institutions not operated by the Church, yet it seems reasonable to include so much of this law as may concern ecclesiastically controlled foundations (§§ pr.—1a), for we cannot be certain that such were not in the legislator's thought when he drafted the subsequent sections of this constitution on donations.

The same Augustus to Demosthenes, praetorian prefect.[1]

We ordain that every donation, whether common [2] or made before marriage,[3] amounting up to three hundred solidi [4] should not need records,[5] but should have a common form,[6] that up to the sum of two hundred solidi [4] it should not reach,[7] but donations both common and before marriage should be similar in such observance.

But if anything shall have been donated above the lawful limitation, this which is in excess only should be [8] not valid, but the remaining amount, which has been established within the law's limits, should endure [8] in its own strength, as if this, when absolutely nothing else has been added, should be believed to be in the place of what has not been written or understood.

Excepted are donations [9] both imperial and those which issue for most pious purposes: of which it has been ordained both by previous emperors and by us [10] that imperial donations indeed deservedly should be unworthy to be made under observance of records, but should have their own firm majesty, but we decree that the others, which have regard for piety, up to the sum of five hundred solidi [4] should be valid and without records [10] . . .

Read at the seventh milestone [11] in the new consistory of Justinian's palace.[12]

Given on 30 October, the most distinguished Decius being consul

1. Of the East.
2. Probably donations between husband and wife (*inter virum et uxorem*), on which see no. 31, n. 4; certainly between living persons (*inter vivos*), on which see no. 595, n. 5, and which include, of course, juristic persons (the pious foundations later mentioned).
3. See no. 517, n. 2.
4. On the value of the solidus see no. 433, n. 7.
5. See nos. 522, n. 4, and 581, n. 4.
6. A variant reading (*formam*) for "fortune" or "lot" (*fortunam*) is translated.
7. That is, the previous amount of two hundred solidi is cancelled and is replaced by the aforesaid amount of three hundred solidi not requiring registration. See no. 581, n. 4.
8. This principal verb is an infinitive in Latin and depends upon the main verb of the previous sentence.
9. This construction is an ablative absolute in Latin, where the sentence is printed independently.

10. No. 581.
11. The Latin word for *milestone* (*miliarium*) is omitted.
12. See no. 595, n. 7.

597. MANDATE OF JUSTINIAN I ON THE CHURCH AS DEPOSITORY OF DISPUTED REVENUE, 529

(*CI* 11. 48. 20)

When title of ownership has been disputed by tenant farmers, they must continue to pay their rents in the absence of a surety, who will guarantee eventual payment, annually to the local or metropolitan church (as the case may be), which shall hold this revenue against settlement of the lawsuit as to who is the rightful receiver of the returns from the land.

The rest of this law dealing with payment of taxes is of no ecclesiastical interest and is not translated.

Emperor Justinian Augustus to Demosthenes, praetorian prefect.[1]

In imposing speed upon lawsuits we ordain that, if ever tenant farmers of whatever status shall have spoken [2] against the owners of the land, when they doubt concerning this very matter whether or not he is the owner of the land (however, we mean those persons who do not have sufficient security as a result of long and extended time or lengthy and long-standing acceptance of returns,[3] in which cases permission of not even contradiction [1] is left to the tenant farmers, for prescription of long time [4] or most constant succession of returns [3] debars tenant farmers' attacks), we decree [5] that there should be the following formulary concerning the payment of returns [3] or of public taxes: that, if such tenant farmers (as we have mentioned above) shall have offered a suitable surety for the total sum, which is being paid by them, they will restore all returns [3] without any delay to them,[6] if the owners' case should be judged better, and such a surety should be accepted for a triennium and, when it has been completed, should be renewed again; in the meantime the tenant farmers in no way by the owners should be disturbed concerning the returns.[3]

But if the tenant farmers shall not have wished or shall not have been able to do this, then the said returns [3] should be exacted annually by the governor's office staff throughout the usual times, for which they also were being paid to the owners, and should be deposited in a sacred building, that is, in the treasury of the city under which the landed estate has been situated, or, if the local church should not be suitable for reception of the monies, in the metropolitan church, that they may remain with all security and after the fullest determination either may be given to the owners or may be restored to the tenant farmers.

But if the returns [3] are brought not in gold but in kind, either in whole or in part, in the interim through the governor's office staff the fruits should be sold and their prices should be deposited according to the aforesaid manner . . .

Read at the seventh milestone [7] in the new consistory of Justinian's palace.[8]

Given on 30 October,[9] the most distinguished Decius being consul.

1. Of the East.
2. That is, probably raised the issue in court to combat payment to an uncertain owner.
3. Returns or rents (*reditus*) could be in cash or in kind; from the sequel provision is made for each case.
4. See no. 65, n. 6 *ad med.*
5. After the long parenthesis the emperor either forgets that he already has a principal verb (*sancimus*) or inserts another (*censemus*) for emphasis.
6. The owners.
7. See no. 596, n. 11.
8. See no. 595, n. 7.
9. The date is supplied editorially.

598. MANDATE OF JUSTINIAN I ON ALIENATION OF ECCLESIASTICAL PROPERTY, 529

(*CI* 1. 2. 21)

The emperor allows ecclesiastical properties, such as sacred utensils, robes, votive offerings, to be sold or to be mortgaged or to be pledged only for raising money to redeem prisoners. Otherwise such as have been sold or have been pledged must be restored by lawsuits, if necessary, no matter in what condition these articles may be after alienation.

Pitra prints (2. 498) a late Greek version.

The same Augustus to Demosthenes, praetorian prefect.[1]
We ordain that none is permitted to withdraw the most sacred and

598. ALIENATION OF ECCLESIASTICAL PROPERTY, 529   1045

secret [2] vessels or vestments and all other votive offerings, which are necessary for the divine religion (when even the old laws have ordained that these articles, which belong to divine right, should not be encumbered by human legal obligations [3]), either for sale or for hypothec [4] or for pledge, but that from those persons who shall have dared to undertake these they by all means should be claimed both by the most religious bishops and by the stewards and also even by the custodians of the sacred vessels: to them must be left no action either for recovering the price [5] or for exacting the interest, for which the articles have been pledged, but by rejecting all actions of this sort they by all means should be compelled to restitution of these articles.

But if these articles either have been or shall have been melted or in another way altered or scattered,[6] nevertheless demand either for the very physical elements or for their price should be due,[7] whether by an action *in rem* [8] or *per condictionem* [9] or *in factum* [10] (whose tenor in many and various points of law often has been admitted)—the case of captivity, of course, excepted in places wherein this (which we abominate) shall have befallen. For if there shall have been necessity in the ransom of captives, then we concede that both the sale and the hypothec [4] and the pledge of the aforesaid divine articles should occur, since it is not absurd for persons' lives [11] to be preferred to any vessels [12] or vestments whatever—this obtaining not only in future lawsuits, but also in trials pending.[13]

1. Of the East.
2. Secret because associated with the divine mysteries (the Mass). Since no Latin transliteration of the Greek adjective μυττηρικός (of *or* belonging to the mysteries) exists, Justinian uses the Latin adjective *areanus* (secret *or* especially sacredly secret). On the other hand, the Latin noun *mysterium*, transliterated from the Greek noun μυττήριον, is commoner than the Latin noun *arcanum* in denoting the sacred mysteries in ecclesiastical Latin. See no. 75, n. 42.
3. Gaius in the second century had defined for the jurisconsults what belonged to divine right and had shown what was exempt from private ownership (*GI* 2. 3, 9). In this doctrine Justinian followed Gaius (*II* 2. 1. 7). See no. 641, n. 2.
4. See no. 537, n. 5.
5. When sold. The next phrase Justinian explains.
6. That is, divided by separation, as one might remove jewels from a chalice or embroidery from a vestment.
7. The Latin lacks a finite verb here.
8. An *actio in rem* takes its rise from real rights as opposed to obligatory rights arising either from contracts or from delicts, which latter rights are enforced by an *actio in personam* (on which see no. 604, n. 6): the *actio in rem* is the assertion of one's claim against or over or for a thing, whether corporeal

(as in this case of ecclesiastical property) or incorporeal (as an easement), which claim can be enforced against anyone at all without specification of personality (GI 4. 3: II 4. 6. 1–2).

9. An *actio per condictionem*, perhaps the latest of the republican *legis actiones* (proceedings according to statute), is employed where the plaintiff serves notice on the defendant, after the former has claimed and the latter has denied either a certain sum of money or a certain thing, to appear in court within thirty days for acquittal or for conviction. In other words, A and B agree to litigate: such an agreement is called *condictio* (GI 4. 18–19). But by Justinian's time *condictio* was synonymous with *actio in personam*, wherein A contends that some property should be conveyed to him by B (II 4. 6. 15).

10. An *actio in factum* may be either *concepta* (GI 4. 46, 183; II 4. 6. 12, 16. 3) or *civilis* (D 19. 5). In the former case the question is merely one of facts, whereof their truth or falsity determines the result of the suit, and the action may be pursued either *in rem* or *in personam*. In the latter case the question of facts falls outside the category of cases for which a specific formula is found. These lead to a formula *in ius concepta*, where the question becomes one of law (*ius*), i.e. whether the article possessed by the defendant belongs to the plaintiff (as the plaintiff alleges).

11. Or possibly "souls".

12. An editorial emendation is translated.

13. Patristic testimony before this law's date testifies to the practice (widespread both in the East and in the West) of converting the Church's property to ransom prisoners of war. Of the several notices may be noticed in the East that of Socrates (*HE* 7. 21), who says that in 422 Acacius, bishop of Amida in Mesopotamia, after telling his clergy that God needs neither patens nor chalices, for he neither eats nor drinks, since he needs nothing—a statement reminiscent of Persius' question to the pontiffs as to what influence has gold in religious service (*Sat.* 2. 69)—melted the sacred treasures and with the result ransomed and fed about 7,000 prisoners of war, whom Persians had captured, and in the West that of Victor Vitensis (*Hist. Pers. Afr. Prov.* 1. 8. 25 = *CSEL* 7. 12), who tells that in 455 Deogratias, bishop of Carthage, busied himself to sell in parcels all the ministry's gold and silver utensils to free the multitude of captives carried to Africa from the sack of Rome in that year by Vandals and Moors. These prelates merely practised what earlier St Ambrose had approved (*De Off.* 2. 28. 136–7 = *PL* 16. 148–9) and St Augustine had authorized (Possidius, *Aug. Vita*, 24 *ad fin.* = *PL* 32. 54).

599. MANDATE OF JUSTINIAN I ON ORTHODOX CHILDREN'S RIGHTS IN HERETICAL PROPERTY, 529

(CI 1. 5. 19)

Besides ordaining that orthodox children must not be disinherited for religious reasons by their heretical parents, Justinian adds the duty for the latter to support the former with the necessities of daily life as well as to provide both dowries and prenuptial donations (as the case may be) for them.

The same Augustus to Demosthenes, praetorian prefect.[1]

We know that many are orthodox children of whom neither father nor mother is of the orthodox religion.

And therefore we ordain that not only in the case where one of the two is of the orthodox religion, but also in these cases in which each parent, that is, the father and the mother, is of an alien [2] sect, only those children who have been adorned with the venerable name of the orthodox should be called to their succession—whether by testament or by intestacy—and should be able to accept donations or other gifts from these—all their other children who have followed not the love of Almighty God, but their paternal or maternal impious disposition,[3] being repelled from every benefit.

However, when orthodox children are not living, the said properties or successions should come [4] to their agnates or cognates,[5] but still orthodox. But if neither agnates nor cognates [5] should be found right,[6] then the said properties should be claimed [4] for our fisc's resources.

But lest, however, we should seem to provide for children when their parents die, but to introduce no provision while they live (which also has been known to us from the fact), we impose upon such parents the necessity to support orthodox children according to their patrimony's amount and to furnish for them all things which suffice for life's daily conduct, but both to give dowries for daughters or granddaughters and to assign antenuptial donations for sons or grandsons—in every case gifts of this kind being estimated according to the patrimony's resources, lest on account of their preference for divine love the children should have been defrauded of paternal or maternal provision.

All matters, of course, which our constitutions have constituted [7] about penalties on account of pagans and Manichaeans and Borborians and Samaritans and Montanists and Tascodrogitans and Ophitans and all other heretics must be confirmed [8] by this our law and shall be valid [8] in perpetuity.

1. Of the East.
2. Literally "another's", also "strange", "inimical".
3. Perhaps "affection" should be used for *affectio* to balance *love* (*amor*) already used.
4. The principal verb in this independently printed sentence is an infinitive dependent upon the main verb of the previous sentence.
5. For these concrete nouns the Latin by antimeria has abstract nouns meaning relation by blood or by adoption on male side only ("agnation": *agnatio*) and relation by blood on either male or female side ("cognation": *cognatio*).

The family of the civil law (*ius civile*) is the agnatic family; the family of the law of nations (*ius gentium*) is the cognatic family. By Justinian's time the latter had superseded the former in Roman law.

6. Probably in the sense of having right (orthodox) belief.
7. The etymological figure in Latin is expressed in English.
8. This principal verb is a participle in the construction of the ablative absolute.

600. LAW OF JUSTINIAN I ON CONVERSION OF PAGANS TO CHRISTIANITY, (?)529
(*CI* 1. 11. 10)

This defective statute (usually ascribed to Justinian, though from its place in his Code any emperor in the period 472–534 may have emitted it), while it emphasizes conversion of pagans to Christianity, penalizes Manichaeans and Christian apostates and pagans who do not seek instruction in Christianity, debars pagans from the teaching profession,[1] and punishes pagans who pretend to be Christians for the sake of civic preferments and at the same time permit their families to foster pagan practices.

. . . Since certain persons have been found possessed by the error of unholy and abominable pagans [2] and doing those things which move the Benevolent God to just wrath, we have not consented to leave uncorrected matters concerning them, but, because we have known that they, having abandoned the true and only God's worship, brought sacrifices by irrational error to idols and celebrated feasts full of unholiness, we have subjected those who have sinned, after they had been thought worthy of holy baptism, to vengeance proper to their convicted sins—and this rather humanely.

But for the future through the present law we proclaim publicly

600. CONVERSION OF PAGANS TO CHRISTIANITY, (?)529

to all persons that they who have become Christians and are thought worthy of holy and salutary baptism at any time, if they should have appeared still remaining in the error of the pagans,[2] shall be subjected to extreme punishments.[3]

But it concerns these—as many as have been thought not yet worthy of venerable baptism—to make themselves known, when living either in this royal city [4] or in the provinces, and to approach the most holy churches along with their wives and children and all the household belonging to them and to be taught the Christians' true faith and, after they thus have been taught thoroughly and have discarded clearly their former error, to be thought worthy of salutary baptism or to know that, if they esteem little these matters, they neither shall share in any of the affairs of our State nor shall be permitted to be owners of movable or immovable property, but that, when deprived of every resource, they shall be abandoned in poverty besides being subjected also to appropriate penalties.

Moreover we prohibit all knowledge being taught by persons diseased with the insanity of the unholy pagans,[2] so that by this way they should not pretend to instruct persons who wretchedly resort to themselves, but in reality, of course, destroy the instructed persons' souls, but also that they should not enjoy subsistence from the treasury, since they do not have permission from divine letters or pragmatic formularies to claim for themselves licence for any such thing. For if anyone either here [4] or in the several provinces [5] should have appeared to be such and not as having run to our most holy churches with his own—as has been said—children and wife,[6] he shall succumb to the aforeshown penalties and the treasury shall claim their [6] properties, but they themselves shall be delivered into exile.

But if anyone in our State should have been caught concealing sacrifices or also sinning in respect to idolatry, this person shall be brought under extreme punishments,[3] to which Manichaeans and—that is to say the same—Borborians justly submit, for we judge that these also are like those.

And we legislate also the following: that their children of young [7] age immediately and without any delay should obtain salutary baptism, but that they, when they who have exceeded already that age are in need of it, should attend the most holy churches according to the divine canons and should be taught thoroughly the Divine Scriptures and thus should grasp instead genuine repentance and, having rid themselves of old error, should obtain venerable baptism, for in this way they should receive firmly and carefully should guard the true faith of orthodox persons and not again should change their course to old error.

Moreover we command that as many as fraudulently indeed have come or should have come to salutary baptism by a motive of having governmental service [8] or rank or property, but should have abandoned their wives or children or others belonging to their household in the pagan [2] error, these should have their property confiscated and absolutely should not share in our State, but also should be subjected to punishments worthy of them, since they clearly have not obtained holy baptism by pure faith of their own accord.

These things, therefore, we legislate in the case of sinning pagans [2] and Manichaeans, of which Manichaeans it has been shown that Borborians are also a part.

1. See no. 583, n. 1.
2. See no. 121, n. 3.
3. Death is, of course, the last of all punishments.
4. Probably Constantinople, for there is no subscription.
5. Literally "throughout the country", but the preposition (κατά) has often a distributive use.
6. The Greek has the poetic plural or else conceives of a plural subject by this time, after it has started with a singular subject.
7. Literally "small".
8. See no. 186, n. 4.

601. MANDATE OF JUSTINIAN I ON DONATIONS FOR PIOUS PURPOSES OR TO RELIGIOUS PERSONS, 530

(CI 8. 53. 35)

In the translated part of this law (§ 5c–e) touching upon donations to charitable institutions (presumably controlled by the Church,[1] though not necessarily even in Justinian's age) and to ecclesiastics Justinian supports an earlier enactment of Zeno, who introduced an action to support an informal promise for donation,[2] although hitherto a promise without consideration and without stipulation seems to have been invalid.[3]

The emperor concludes his directive on donations by warmly declaring that refusal to fulfil a promise to give a gift for pious purposes or to religious persons on the pretext that there has been no legal formality observed will bring upon the defaulting promissor both lawful and divine punishments.

The same Augustus to Julian, praetorian prefect.[4]

602. MANUMISSION IN CHURCH, 530

... For since it is in anyone's judgement to do this which he determines, he ought either at least to leap to it zealously or, when he has hastened to come to it, not to defraud his purpose by certain invented artifices and to cover so great irreligion by certain quasi-lawful screens.

And so much the more these matters should be [5] firm, if a donation should have been destined for pious acts or for religious persons—the observance of records being observed [6] in these ways according to what has been aforesaid specially by us in such cases [7]—lest in the aforesaid cases as a result of certain machinations not only an irreligious but also an impious donor should be perceived and should expect not only lawful but also celestial punishments.

And in all the abovementioned cases not only those persons, while they live, but also their successors are compelled [7] to render the donated properties not only to those persons to whom the donation has been made but also to their heirs.

Given on 18 March at Constantinople, the most distinguished Lampadius and the most distinguished Orestes being consuls.

1. The inference here is strong, since pious foundations and religious persons are connected in this constitution.
2. No. 522.
3. See the so-called *Vatican Fragments* on the *Lex Cincia de donis et muneribus* in *FIRA* 2. 519–34, esp. §§ 263, 264a, 310. See also no. 31, n. 4.
4. Of the East.
5. The principal verb is an infinitive in Latin dependent upon an understood verb of command.
6. The etymological figure exists in the Latin text.
7. No. 581.

602. MANDATE OF JUSTINIAN I ON MANUMISSION IN CHURCH, 530

(CI 7. 15. 1)

While two-thirds of this constitution concerns the liberation of slaves held as usufruct,[1] only the last third (§ 3 here translated) touches manumission of slaves in general, wherein one method is that of bestowing freedom on them in the presence of a Christian congregation,[2] and obviously is appended as a separate clause to the law. The interest of this legislation is twofold: (1) the emperor in an effort to effect equity allows the ascendants of either sex to permit their descendants of either sex to free slaves on their behalf; (2) no evidence of this extension appears in the Digest, although it was promulgated more than three and a half years later.

    Emperor Justinian Augustus to Julian, praetorian prefect.[3]
    ... To this law we add also the following: that, since the ancient difference of persons has been exploded,[4] it should be permissible for parents, both male and female, to impose upon sons and daughters—whether established at home [5] or emancipated—of any degree a mandate that they may bring into freedom slaves—whether before a judge or in the sacred churches [6] or according to another lawful method which the mandator shall have wished.[2] For when also in successions [7] and in almost all other matters there is no distinction between free persons, this ought to be observed also in the present case, particularly on behalf of freedom, which it is proper to the Roman laws and especially to our Divinity both to cherish and to protect.

Given on 18 March, the most distinguished Lampadius and the most distinguished Orestes being consuls.

    1. A usufruct or the right to use and to take the fruits of anything which is not consumed by use for the recipient's lifetime, unless a shorter term is agreed by the owner and the usufructuary, extends to the services of slaves. In such cases A (usufructuary) has a right to the labour of B (slave), who belongs to C (owner). But while A can inflict moderate castigation upon B to compel him to work, he cannot so maltreat him that his value to C will be impaired upon the usufruct's expiration. Whatever B acquires through B's own toil or by B's dealing with A's property becomes A's; but whatever B acquires by other means becomes C's (*GI* 2. 91, 94, 3. 164–5; *II* 3. 28. 1–2).
    2. For the various modes of manumission see no. 26, n. 1.
    3. Of the East.
    4. Such a difference e.g. existed in the incapacity of a mother to emancipate her children (Paul, *Sent.* 1. 13a. 2 = *FIRA* 2. 331).
    5. Literally "in the private religious rites of a family" (*in sacris*), that is, under the paternal power (*patria potestas*) of the head of the family (*paterfamilias*), who conducted his household's religious rites. See no. 214, n. 6 *ad med.*
    6. See no. 26.
    7. That is, inheritances to estates.

603. MANDATE OF JUSTINIAN I ON THE BIBLE'S SIGNIFICANCE IN LAWSUITS, 530

(*CI* 3. 1. 13)

Only so much of this long law on expedition of civil trials is translated as concerns the Scriptures' use in an undefended action (§ 4). The introduction of the Bible (presumably for an oath to be sworn on it that a litigant's cause is just) is interpreted to represent God's presence as sufficient for a litigant's absence; thus the trial by this fiction can be completed, for both parties are conceived as present.

Emperor Justinian Augustus to Julian, praetorian prefect.[1]
... Moreover, when an undefended action is set in motion (whether for a plaintiff or for a defendant), the examination should be conducted without any obstacle. For when the Terrible [2] Scriptures are introduced in the midst, a litigant's absence is completed by God's presence and a judge should not dread the obstacle of appeal, when for him who is known to be absent contumaciously is no permission of challenge—a circumstance which has been established also in old laws as of plainest legal right [3] ...
Given on 27 March at Constantinople, the most distinguished Lampadius and the most distinguished Orestes being consuls.

1. Of the East.
2. The adjective appears to be causative and connotes the fear which violation of an oath sworn on the Scriptures should instil into the violator. Perhaps it is borrowed from Joel 2. 11 (cf. 2. 31 and Heb. 10. 31).
3. The oldest imperial statute denying an appeal in such circumstances appears to date from 213 (*CI* 7. 65. 1).

604. MANDATE OF JUSTINIAN I ON PRESCRIPTION AFFECTING THE CHURCH, 530

(*CI* 1. 2. 23)

Treating the topic of prescription (the extinction of rights through lapse of time), which starts to run from the moment when the right of action exists and yet is not exercised, Justinian by this ordinance fixes the term at a hundred years, after which an ecclesiastical or charitable foundation cannot institute a suit in the fields of succession, legacies, donations, contracts of sale. The emperor allows also the same period in the case of money left to ransom captives.

Eleven years later Justinian reduced the time to forty years (*N* 111).

The same Augustus to Julian, praetorian prefect.[1]

That between divine and public law and private interests should be an appropriate distinction, we ordain that, if anyone shall have left any inheritance or legacy or trust or shall have given anything under the title of donation or shall have sold anything either to sacrosanct churches or venerable hostels or almshouses or monasteries of males or of virgins or orphanages or nurseries or homes for the aged or also to the legal control of communities, for properties bequeathed or donated or sold to these should be a very long claim, which must not be compressed by any usual prescription of time.[2]

Moreover, if in the case of redemption of captives also any monies or properties have been bequeathed or have been donated by legitimate manner, we decree also that there should be a very long claim for these.

And indeed it lies in our heart that an action of this sort should not be confined by any limits of time. But lest we appear to extend this to infinity, we choose the longest time of men's life and we grant that not otherwise this action should be ended, unless the circuits of a hundred years should have been exceeded:[3] for then only we allow a claim of this sort to disappear.

Accordingly, if to the said most religious places or to communities shall have been bequeathed either an inheritance or a legacy or a trust, or if a donation or a sale shall have occurred in any movable or immovable or self-movable [4] properties whatever, or if certain things shall have been bequeathed or donated for redemption of captives, there should be almost perpetual claim and, according to what has been said, it should be extended to a hundred years—no other exception of time to be used, whether it is promoted against first persons [5] or against their heirs or successors.

Moreover in all these cases we allow not only personal actions,[6] but also actions *in rem* [7] and the hypothecary action [8] according to the tenor of our constitution,[9] which has granted hypothecary actions also to legatees, and on all the aforesaid we impose only the one terminus of life itself, that is, the limits of a hundred years.[3]

Moreover we ordain that all these things should be observed in those cases which either shall have been created afterward or already have been brought to trial.

Given on 28 March [10] at Constantinople, the most distinguished Lampadius and the most distinguished Orestes being consuls.

1. Of the East.

2. See no. 65, n. 6 ad med.

3. Two pagan professions as to why a hundred years constitute the longest span of human life are of interest: Varro (*De Ling. Lat.* 6. 11) says that a century (*seclum*, more properly *saeculum*) was what the Romans called the space of a hundred years, named from "old man" (*senex*), because they thought this the longest stretch of life for "ageing" (*senescendi*) men. Pliny (*Nat. Hist.* 11. 70. 184) preserves the Egyptian explanation that the human heart increases by two drachms in weight annually until the fiftieth year and thereafter decreases at the same rate, so that man does not live beyond his hundredth year because of cardiac failure.

4. Such as livestock.

5. That is, those first involved.

6. More usually called not *personalis actio* (as here), but *actio in personam*. The *actio in personam* concerns obligatory rights rising from contracts or quasi-contracts or delicts or quasi-delicts—in this case from the first two. That is, it is the assertion of one's claim against or over a specified person, whether natural or juristical, to compel him either to act or to abstain from acting in accordance with an already existent obligation (*GI* 4. 2; *II* 4. 6. 1).

7. See no. 598, n. 8.

8. This action (*actio hypothecaria*) pertains to cases wherein the lender and the borrower have agreed that any article should be a pledge when the lender did not receive possession of it from the borrower. It is an *actio in rem* for the recovery of what has been hypothecated from the debtor or from any third person in possession of it (*CI* 4. 10. 14). Justin I limited its use to forty years (*CI* 7. 39. 7. 1; dated 525). See no. 537, n. 5.

9. *CI* 6. 43. 1 (dated 529).

10. Editors note an alternative date: 18 March.

605. MANDATE OF JUSTINIAN I ON BIBLICAL OATHS IN LAWSUITS, 530

(*CI* 3. 1. 14)

Since everywhere secular forces fail to furnish a sufficient warrant for law and order, it is no matter for marvel that a religious-minded monarch like Justinian resorts to religion as an aid in a programme to preserve the public peace. Into the solemn sessions of tribunals is introduced the Bible to remind both judges and litigants of the celestial court and to be employed by lawyers for either party in swearing an oath to support honest cases.

The same Augustus to Julian, praetorian prefect.[1]

We approach no new and unwonted matter, but one indeed

acceptable to ancient legislators,[2] but bringing to lawsuits, when indeed it has been contemned, no light loss. For to whom has it not been known that the ancient jurors accepted a judicial ballot [3] not otherwise unless they had offered a solemn obligation [4] that in every way with truth and observance of the laws they would determine the trial?

Therefore, when we have found that we must travel a not unusual road and our previous laws which have been posted about oaths [5] have furnished to litigants not the least experience of their usefulness and accordingly are lauded deservedly by all persons, we have come to this law (which shall be valid in perpetuity), by which we ordain that all judges, whether major or minor, whether those who have been placed in administrations either in this royal city [6] or in the world, which is ruled by our controllers,[7] or those to whom we commit audience [8] or who are granted by major judges or who from their own jurisdiction have the faculty of judging or who undertake cases to be settled from guaranty (that is, mutual promise to abide by an arbiter's award,[9] which imitates a trial) or who accomplish an arbitrator's judgement or have been chosen on the authority of verdicts and by the parties' consent and generally all judges of all kinds whatever, umpires of Roman law, should accept the beginning of litigations not otherwise unless the Sacrosanct Scriptures are deposited before the judicial seat: [10] and this should remain not only in the beginning of the litigation, but also in all proceedings until the very termination and the reading of the definitive sentence. For thus they, while directing their attention to the Sacrosanct Scriptures and consecrated by God's presence, shall settle litigations as a result of greater aid, for they will know that they judge others not more than they themselves are judged,[11] when even more terrible to themselves than to the parties is judgement, if the litigants indeed present cases to be weighed under men, but they themselves present cases to be weighed [12] with God associated as a searcher.[13]

And indeed this judicial oath should be known to all and to Roman laws should come from us the best augmentation and it must be observed by all judges; and, if it should be overlooked, it should be perilous for the contemners.

Moreover pleaders of lawsuits who, offering their support, enter for each party, when the issue shall have been joined, after the narration [14] has been propounded and the contradiction has been presented in any court of any sort, major or minor, or before arbitrators, whether from mutual promise to abide by an arbiter's award [9] or otherwise given or chosen, should offer an oath, when the Sacrosanct Gospels have been touched, that they with all their ability and with all assistance take care to present for their clients what they shall have thought to be

605. BIBLICAL OATHS IN LAWSUITS, 530

just and true, abandoning no zeal which is possible for them; moreover that they themselves, after the case entrusted to them has been investigated, knowingly and wittingly do not support the litigation with bad conscience, because it is dishonest and utterly hopeless and composed from mendacious allegations, but that, if any such thing, as the contest proceeds, shall have become known to them, they would retire from the case by separating themselves utterly from association of this sort; and that, when this has ensued, no permission to fly to another advocate's support should be granted to a spurned litigant, lest a dishonest advocacy should be substituted after better ones have been contemned.

But if, however, after very many pleaders have been employed and an oath has been offered by all, some of these, as the lawsuit proceeds, shall have believed that it ought to be supported, but some shall have refused, the ones refusing indeed should depart, but the ones wishing should remain, for the termination of the lawsuit can appear—some rather timidly have abandoned the trial and some rather boldly have advanced the trial [15]—no permission to substitute others for the refusers being given to litigants in this part.[16]

Given on 29 March [17] at Constantinople, the most distinguished Lampadius and the most distinguished Orestes being consuls.

1. Of the East.

2. The classic collection of opinions on oaths is in *D* 12. 2 ("On Swearing an Oath whether Voluntary or Compulsory or Judicial"), wherein most of the evidence comes from early in the third century of our era. See also *GI* 4. 171 and *II* 4. 16. pr.

3. The word is *calculus*, which in the most ancient period was a stone (white for assent or acquittal, black for denial or condemnation) used in voting and deposited into an urn or a basket.

In criminal juries during the late Republic jurors were sworn (Cicero, *Pro Sex. Rosc. Amer.* 3. 8; *In Verr.* 1. 10. 32, 2. 1. 4. 9, 2. 5. 8. 19; *Pro Clu.* 10. 29).

4. On this word (*sacramentum*) see no. 592, n. 4.

5. If Justinian refers to his own legislation, he may have in mind *CI* 4. 1. 11 and 12 (both dated 529), 2. 58. 1 (dated 529).

6. Constantinople.

7. Literally "rudders" (*gubernacula*) but in the plural (as here) usually by transfer to mean persons in governmental control and sometimes the abstract notion of the State itself.

8. In the judicial sense of a hearing conducted by a judge.

9. From *mutual* to *award* is one word in Latin (*compromissum*).

10. The word translated "judgement seat" in the Authorized Version is in the Vulgate *tribunal* in all but one *locus* (Jas. 2. 6, where it is *iudicium*). Here it is *iudicialis sedes*.

11. For the thought, which is a commonplace, see Matt. 7. 1-2; Mark 4. 24; Luke 6. 37-8; Rom. 2. 1-3.

12. The last five words are repeated in the translation for clarity.

13. On God as searcher in judgements cf. 2 Chron. 19. 5-7.

14. That is, the prosecution's exposition of the facts (*narratio*).

15. The Latin is awkward. The idea in *termination . . . appear* seems to be that the end of the suit is in sight, since not all the advocates have abandoned the suit.

16. That is, at this point of the proceedings.

17. An alternative day is the 27th, editorially suggested.

606. MANDATE OF JUSTINIAN I ON EPISCOPAL INTEREST IN MUNICIPAL MATTERS, 530

(*CI* 1. 4. 26)

This constitution (of which parts appear in *CI* 3. 2. 4, 10. 30. 4, 12. 63. 2) enjoins upon bishops various duties in connection with municipal administration, such as supervision of public works, inspection of financial accounts, reception of legislation, judication in claims emerging from suretyships, prevention of illegal exaction by officials, and imposes penalties on the prelates for disobedience to the law's demands.

The same emperor to Julian, praetorian prefect.[1]

Concerning civic incomes or revenues [2] coming to cities in each year from public or private funds, either bequeathed to these by certain persons or donated or otherwise devised or acquired, whether allocated for works [3] or for purchase of grain or for a public aqueduct or for heatings of baths or for harbours or for constructions of walls or of towers or for repair of bridges or for paving of roads or, simply, for the citizens' uses, whether from public or private causes (as has been said): we ordain that the most God-beloved bishop and three men of good repute and of the chief men in all respects in the several cities, assembling together, in each year should inspect the works performed and should provide that these should be surveyed and that the persons who administer or who have administered these should render accounts; and that in the constructing of the records it should be evident that the works have been completed or the funds for purchase of grain and for baths or concerning paving of roads or concerning an aqueduct or for any other such projects have been administered.

606. INTEREST IN MUNICIPAL MATTERS, 530

And we wish that all these matters should continue undiminished for all time and that in the constructing of the records it should be manifest that he who has administered these or indeed has appeared to be under liability but has paid his obligation is free from liability and that he who has undertaken this constructing thus should have security. For [4] we shall send, whenever we should have wished, a person pleasing to us who shall inspect the accounts made by them and, if he should have found these in right condition, he shall make a decision procuring completely security for them and their heirs and successors, on condition that occasions for second accounts or investigations no longer should remain—all matters being done thus with strictness in the presence of the Holy Gospels, since our scrutiny, whenever we should have wished, shall be imposed on them.

However, it is necessary that the most God-beloved bishop and the persons making the accounts with him should strive that, if any works have been designated for unlimitedness of expense, in each year they should be renewed carefully from civic revenues and incomes.

But if, however, he who has administered these should not have wished to submit accounts and should not allow the most God-beloved bishop of the places and the rentiers designated for this to call him for accounts, then he should be compelled [5] to do this by the most distinguished governor of the province and by the office staff obedient to him, being forced without any penalty, on condition that by all means he submits accounts to the most God-beloved bishop of the city and to the chief men of the cities and pays to the city that which appears to be owed by him.

We take from our governors all power to send into the districts auditors [6] or accountants or tax equalizers for scrutinies of public accounts; but if they should have done any such thing contrary to our judgement, then, if a divine formulary should have been procured for any persons by surreptitiousness, to the most God-beloved bishop of the city should be power to receive the divine formulary, but to inform about it to us, that we may know whether it has been written to the governor [7] himself by our divine command or has been produced by surreptitiousness, so that, if it should have appeared to be produced by some surreptitiousness, then what has been performed should be invalid and the person who has procured this should submit to peril.

But if a decision or a memorial or any ordinance of any of our magistrates should have been sent and if an audit of accounts concerning the aforesaid chief points should have been entrusted, by all means we wish the most God-beloved bishop of the city and the chief men in the city not to accept these, but for the governor of the province and for the rentiers themselves and for the citizens to have power to reject such orders and not to provide one obol [8] for the purpose of this case. But if the most God-beloved bishop should have been remiss in this respect, he shall have the Lord God hostile and he shall await royal indignation, because he has kept a silence servile and unworthy of sacerdotal [9] freedom of speech.

But also, if in the several districts anyone exhibits promotions of any magistrates whatever or of consuls or general formularies of the most glorious prefects or of any other of our magistrates or should produce exhibitions of constitutions or of divine memorials or of general letters or even foundations [10] of royal statues, for this person should not be [5] licence to claim beyond six coins [11] for each information or for each formulary or each constitution or divine memorial or general letter or foundation [10] of statues in each province to which he takes these, so that—as many cities as the province may have—it should make no difference to him, but he should claim only six gold coins.[11] But if he should have claimed anything more, this he should pay [5] fourfold [12] —the bishop of the city having also power to prevent this and the same penalties impending in this case, that is, ten pounds of gold apiece both for the governor of the province and for the office staff obedient to him and for the most God-beloved bishop, if they should yield to them who wish to demand excess payment and by all means should not prevent this.

To [13] none of our magistrates we absolutely allow to dispatch into the provinces any such formularies concerning purgation of watercourses or of sewers or concerning demolition of buildings near walls or dissolution of things made in stoas or overthrow of so-called servitudes [14] and of ruinous places or of intercolumnar spaces or concerning images or absolutely suchlike inventions or, simply, civic controversies, but it shall be possible for the most God-beloved bishop of the city and the chief men in the city and the governors of the provinces and the rentiers and the citizens not to accept this, when any such formulary has been exhibited, but to prevent and to reject all execution and all exaction introduced thence—the same penalty being imminent also against the most God-beloved bishops, unless they should have prevented this.

Moreover the most God-beloved bishop and the father [15] and the remaining rentiers with good reputation ought to provide that none should permit a civic or public place situated near the wall or in public stoas or streets or anywhere else to be possessed causelessly by anyone or to let any civic place to any persons without our divine formulary.

The same persons also should investigate [5] the matters concerning the so-called apportionments of water belonging to certain persons, obviously in accord with the divine formulary, and some should not have more and others less than what is proper.

But we do not allow our subjects [16] to be subjected to penalties by

606. INTEREST IN MUNICIPAL MATTERS, 530

pretext of suretyships or by reason of an agent's position; but if those who have been served notice should have sufficient immovable property, they should offer only a bond of an oath; but if they should not have any, then they should furnish surety up to the amount already settled, however, without any penalty; but if the claimants should dispute about the trustworthiness of the sureties or about the oath, the most God-beloved bishop and the father [15] and the defender of the municipality, assembling together jointly, should judge whether the surety appears trustworthy for the amount of the claim and whether it should be necessary for the claimant, claiming nothing for the suretyship or for the oath, to accept this surety, except unless,[17] in accord with our special command or any of the highest magistrates, he should have been ordered to take the person, because he had not trusted the surety; for then to the claimant shall be power not to claim the surety and to do this, however, without any penalty [18]—in this case the same penalties prevailing against both the most God-beloved bishop and the most distinguished governor of the province, if they should have allowed any of these matters to be transgressed or should not have informed immediately about these doings of any transgressor.

Obviously they should not allow [19] anything more than the limit determined by our constitution to be claimed on the pretext of fees [20] or an assessment from whatever reason to be made in the cities because of necessity, unless only from those reasons in reference to exhibitions of promotions and of constitutions and of divine or general memorials or of formularies or of letters or of all such documents, about which we previously have legislated in these [21] and which for their own advantage and welfare citizens should have wished perhaps to be made for civic works or for purchase of grain or for another cause satisfactory to all persons in accord with munificence and from which the city's common weal will be advantaged—the threats already made by us being maintained against persons trying to transgress these and against the most God-beloved bishops not bringing it [22] to us.[23]

Each city's most God-beloved bishop, when he knows all the things constituted by us in these matters and indeed also about appraisal of lodgings and prevention of disarmaments and as many matters as are contained in our divine constitution [24] written concerning these matters for the common weal, ought to apply himself to its fitting execution.

Given on 24 June at Chalcedon, the most distinguished Lampadius and the most distinguished Orestes being consuls.

1. Of the East.

2. The phrase *incomes and revenues* appears in reverse as the title of an extant treatise by Xenophon on the resources of Athens: Πόροι ἢ περὶ προσόδων.

3. That is, public works in general (ἔργα; *opera*), though the word is applied to various occupations, such as farming, fishing, weaving, seafaring, mining.

4. The rest of this paragraph and most of the next four paragraphs are adapted from *CI* 10. 30. 4, which is a long law on auditors' duties, but which contains no reference to episcopal action.

In the next line the persons making the accounts (*accounts made by them*) are apparently the administrators and the contractors; but in the next paragraph *the persons making the accounts* are the bishop and the leading men, who either render accounts of their supervision or endorse the administrators' or the contractors' account—perhaps both.

5. This principal verb is an infinitive in Greek and depends upon the preceding sentence's principal verb.

6. The Latin word *discussores* is used amid the Greek, but it is declined here as if it is a noun of the first declension, thus showing *as* in the accusative plural, doubtless due to influence of the next two Greek nouns, which belong to the first declension in Greek and end in ας.

7. The Greek has the abstract for the concrete of the English.

8. This was the smallest Greek coin in value and in time became a symbol for worthlessness.

9. See no. 526, n. 11.

10. On such might be inscribed laws.

11. The Latin translation equates these (νομίσματα) with solidi, on which see no. 433, n. 7.

12. Up to this point the paragraph is taken verbatim from *CI* 12. 63. 2. pr.–1 with the exception that there it begins with the words "We ordain", thus eliminating the need for the first n. 5 in the paragraph, but for the rest of the paragraph after n. 12 it reads thus: "both the governor and the bishop and the chief men of the city and all civic and public aid preventing. For the bishop shall be under royal indignation, but the governor shall be expelled from his governorship and his property shall be confiscated and he shall be exiled, and his office staff is in danger."

13. This and the next two paragraphs are adapted from *CI* 10. 30. 4, but again (cf. *supra* n. 4) without mention therein of episcopal responsibility.

14. The word is προδουλεῖαι, found apparently (and in the plural) only in *CI*, where it represents *servitus* (easement). Probably only urban praedial servitudes (*iura urbanorum praediorum*) are meant, for these affect chiefly buildings, such as the insertion of beams into A's house-wall to support covering for a walk for B alongside the wall.

The easements of this type current in Justinian's time are listed in *II* 2. 3. 1.

15. Of the municipality.

16. The word means strictly "subject to taxes" (ὑποτελής).

The following words *subjected . . . position* seem to indicate that from con-

606. INTEREST IN MUNICIPAL MATTERS, 530

tractors and their agents no penalties for failure to perform their part on the public works (hitherto mentioned) should be exacted ordinarily. But, as appears later in the paragraph, exceptions are expected to occur, when a public-minded citizen is dissatisfied.

17. An excellent example of pleonasm (πλὴν εἰ μή).

18. This paragraph to this point occurs also in *CI* 3. 2. 4. 3–5, after which is substituted—so far as the bishop and the governor are concerned—the following sections (6–7): "The God-beloved bishop of the places, if he should have allowed the law to be transgressed or should not have informed against the transgressor, both offends God and shall make trial of royal action. Likewise also the province's governor, if he shall be negligent of the law, both is deposed from his governorship and, after his property has been confiscated, is exiled perpetually."

19. This verb in this independently printed sentence is a participle in the Greek construction of the genitive absolute.

20. Transliterated into Greek from Latin *sportula* and neuterized. A *sportula* originally was a little basket containing either food or money or both, given in the Republic by patrons to clients in recompense for their services. By the Dominate the word came to mean any gift given to win favour, especially gratuities presented by litigants to apparitors and even to higher officials. Legislation regulating the scale of such fees dates at least from Julian II's reign (*FIRA* 1. 331–2).

21. By *in these* is meant the various kinds of documents just listed.

22. The information.

23. This paragraph is adapted from *CI* 12. 63. 2. 3–4, where is read: "[We ordain that] neither an assessment should be made by him on the pretext of these reasons beyond the six gold coins [cf. *supra* n. 11] nor even from willing persons should be accepted anything, but the taker should pay fourfold.

"And when the citizens wish perhaps that they should be assessed either for public work or for purchase of grain or ask from the emperor that this should be entrusted to them, they ought not to suffer any loss in regard to this, lest the priests [i.e. bishops; see no. 16, n. 4] should incur indignation, but the governors should be deprived of their governorships and should be exiled and their property should be confiscated. The office staff is punished corporally, unless it has informed the emperor about what has been done contrary to the constitution."

24. *CI* 12. 40. 12 prohibits a governor on tour in his province from demanding money in exchange for either refusing local billeting or disarming his retinue in towns where billeted.

607. MANDATE OF JUSTINIAN I ON MANUMISSION IN CHURCH, 530

(*CI* 7. 15. 2)

This document's importance is seen in that from the directive we learn that slaves freed in the presence of a Christian congregation are not required to be above thirty years of age.[1] Justinian here extends this exemption to all liberated slaves, no matter by what method their masters have manumitted them.

The same Augustus to Julian, praetorian prefect.[2]

If anyone should give freedom to his own slave, whether in church or before any tribunal whatever or in the presence of him who has permission by the laws to give freedom, whether in a testament or another last will directly or resulting from a feoffment in trust,[3] he should be compelled in no way to demand the age of the persons who come to freedom.[4]

For we wish not only the person who is older than thirty years to acquire Roman citizenship,[1] but, as in freedoms conferred in church [5] there is no such difference in age, so in all freedoms which are given by masters, whether in last dispositions [6] or by judges or in another lawful way, we ordain this to be observed: that they all should be constituted Roman citizens, for we decree that our citizenship must be enlarged rather than must be lessened.

Given on 1 August, the most distinguished Lampadius and the most distinguished Orestes being consuls.

1. The legal doctrine of a minimum age-limit at thirty years seems to have been that not until that term slaves were supposed to be suited for the responsibilities of Roman citizenship. But there is no hint that manumission of a slave under thirty years old was void. The requirement is recorded in the Aelio-Sentian Law of 4 (*GI* 1. 18).
2. Of the East.
3. See no. 26, n. 1 for various methods of manumission.
4. Infants (*D* 40. 1. 25) as well as unborn babes (*D* 40. 5. 13) could be manumitted.
5. Literally "ecclesiastical freedoms". See no. 26.
6. That is, wills.

608. MANDATE OF JUSTINIAN I ON EPISCOPAL INTEREST IN GUARDIANSHIP, 530

(*CI* 1. 4. 27)

This directive, adapted apparently from *CI* 5. 70. 7. 5-6c, empowers provincial bishops to assist in the ratification of a curator named in a parent's will for an insane person as well as in the selection of a curator for such a person in the absence of any testamentary nomination.

The same Augustus to Julian, praetorian prefect.[1]
Concerning creation of curators who are given to the insane [2] of each sex it has seemed necessary to us to ordain how these ought to be made.
If [3] indeed a father shall have given in his last will a curator [4] for an insane man or for an insane woman, who have been appointed his heirs [5] or have been disinherited [5] (when also it is necessary for suretyship to be unused, because the paternal testimony suffices for giving security),[6] he himself who has been given should enter upon the curatorship, in such a way, however, that [7] in the provinces [8] before their [8] governors [8]—the most religious bishop of the places being present as well as three chief men, the records being interposed, the Sacrosanct Scriptures having been touched—he should promise [9] that he would manage all things rightly to the advantage of the insane and would not neglect what things he should have thought would be advantageous to the insane and would not do what things he should have believed would be not advantageous;[10] and, after an inventory has been written publicly with all exactitude, he should accept the property and should arrange it according to his opinion under hypothec [11] of the property belonging to him after the analogy of tutors and curators of an adult.
But if, however, a parent shall not have accomplished a testament, but the law shall have called a curator inasmuch as he is an agnate or, when that one is wanting or not suitable though perhaps living, it shall have been necessary to give him a curator from judicial selection,[12] then,[13] of course, also in the province before the governor of any province whatever and the most religious bishop of the city and also three chief men the creation should proceed, in such a way that,[13] if indeed a curator possesses property suitable and sufficient for trust in his governance, even without any security his nomination should proceed. But if, however, his registered property should not be found such, then also a suretyship for as much as is possible should be sought from him.
By all means [14] the creation shall be made [15] in every case, when

the Sacrosanct [16] Scriptures have been introduced, but when the curator himself, of whatever property or dignity he is, furnishes the aforesaid oath for managing the property advantageously and writes publicly an inventory and when a hypothec [11] of the curator's property must be applied in all respects, that the property of the insane can be governed advantageously from all sides.[17]

Given on 1 September at Constantinople, the most distinguished Lampadius and the most distinguished Orestes being consuls.

1. Of the East.
2. The adjective is *furiosus*, whose meaning is sufficiently wide to be extended from the legal concept of insanity to any type of mental instability. See no. 621, n. 3 *ad init*.
3. Here begins *CI* 5. 70. 7. 5.
4. In *II* 1. 23. 1 it is stated that, though a curator is not given by will, yet, if given, the praetor or the provincial governor—depending on decedent's domicile—confirms such an appointment. This privilege apparently ascends as early as Marcus Aurelius (*D* 27. 10. 16. pr.), although Dio Cassius (*Hist. Rom.* 44. 35. 2) reports that in Julius Caesar's will guardians for Octavius (later Augustus), his grand-nephew and his heir, were named. If so, probably they were confirmed magisterially.
5. See no. 496, n. 12.
6. On the analogy of guardians (*tutores*) appointed by will for normal persons, guardians (*curatores*) testamentarily named for abnormal persons were not required to give security for proper performance of duty, because the doctrine was that the testator himself had approved their honour and diligence by the mere nomination of them (*GI* 1. 199–200; *II* 1. 24. pr.). See also no. 628, n. 2.
7. The other version inserts "in this most flourishing city [Constantinople] he should be brought before the urban prefecture, but".
8. The other version has the singular.
9. Literally "draw forth" (*depromat*): the other version has "declare" (*edicat*).
10. The other version ends the sentence here and converts the rest of it into a new sentence.
11. See no. 537, n. 5.
12. Here are the two other methods of appointing curators: the intervention of the nearest agnate ascended to the *Twelve Tables* of 449 B.C. (*FIRA* 1. 39–40; *TT* 5. 6); in default of such relatives magistrates made the appointments under the *Lex Plaetoria* (*c*. 192 B.C.). See no. 628, n. 2.
13. For the material between this repeated number the other version has: "according to the aforesaid division in this indeed most flourishing city before the most glorious urban prefecture the creation should proceed; but if indeed the person of the insane should be noble, when also the most flourishing Senate

has been convoked, that from inquiry a curator of the best and spotless reputation should be named; but if he [the insane] should not be such a person [i.e. noble], also with the most glorious urban prefect alone presiding, this should proceed."

14. The other version inserts "indeed".

15. In both versions there is no finite verb as predicate, the structure of the sentence being cast into the ablative absolute.

16. The other version reads simply "sacred".

17. The other version adds: "But in the provinces all these matters being observed, that before the governor of any province whatever and the most religious bishop of the city and also three chief men the said creation should proceed—with the same observation being applied for the oath and for the inventory and security and mortgage of the curator's property in all respects."

609. MANDATE OF JUSTINIAN I ON FOSTER-DAUGHTERS' MARRIAGES, 530

(CI 5. 4. 26)

Justinian decides that a foster-father can contract a legal marriage with a foster-daughter, provided both that she has been baptized and that nought in her rearing should result in the marriage being considered as a continuance of the father-and-daughter relation.

The same Augustus to Julian, praetorian prefect.[1]

If anyone should have presented his foster-daughter with freedom [2] and should have given her in marriage to himself, it used to be doubted among the ancients whether or not a marriage of this sort seems to be legitimate.

We, therefore, deciding the ancient ambiguity, decree that marriage is not prohibited. For if every marriage is introduced from affection and in such union we see nothing impious and contrary to laws, wherefore shall we think that the aforesaid marriage must be inhibited? For also no man should be found so impious that he would have given in marriage to himself her whom from the beginning he has had in a daughter's place, but it must be believed in his case that from the beginning not as a daughter he has reared her and has presented her with freedom [2] and has thought her afterward to be worthy of marriage with him—of course, by all means that person being prohibited from coming to marriage whom (whether or not she should be a foster-daughter) anyone has received from sacrosanct baptism,[3] when nothing else can so induce paternal affection and just prohibition of marriage than a joining of this sort, through which by God's mediation their souls are united.

Given on 1 October at Constantinople, the most distinguished Lampadius and the most distinguished Orestes being consuls.

1. Of the East.
2. That is, by emancipation from his paternal power.
3. The idea seems to be that baptism created a quasi-paternity upon the foster-father.

610. MANDATE OF JUSTINIAN I ON EPISCOPAL INTEREST IN PRENUPTIAL SETTLEMENTS BY LUNATICS' CHILDREN, 530

(*CI* 1. 4. 28)

Provincial bishops are directed to co-operate with provincial governors in determining the amount of a prenuptial settlement given by a curator in the name of a lunatic's child about to marry.

This constitution reappears in *CI* 5. 4. 25. 3-5, a longer law on the marriage of insane persons' offspring.

The same Augustus to Julian, praetorian prefect.[1]

Children [2] of a demented person as well as of an insane person of whatever sex can contract a legitimate marriage—a dowry as well as a donation before marriage [3] being furnished by their curator:[4] the opinion of the person as well as the arrangement of the dowry and of the donation before marriage, however, being determined [5] by the appraisal of the most excellent urban prefect in this indeed royal city,[6] but in the provinces by that of the most distinguished governors of these and of the bishops of the places, the curators of the demented person as well as of the insane person and also those of their category who are noblemen being present, so that, however, from this situation [7] no loss to the property of an insane person or of a person stricken in his mind [8] should arise either in this royal city [6] or in the provinces, but that all matters should proceed gratuitously, lest such misfortune of persons should be pressed heavily also by the detriment [9] of expenses.

611. JURISDICTION IN CLERICAL LAWSUITS, 530   1069

Given on 1 October at Constantinople, the most distinguished Lampadius and the most distinguished Orestes being consuls.

1. Of the East.
2. The longer law discusses first the ancient doubt whether mentally diseased persons' children can contract valid marriages—not, of course, on biological grounds, but on the legal difference between a demented person (*demens*) and a person (apparently violently) insane (*furiosus*). Justinian in this law extends the privilege of marriage from children of *dementes* to children of *furiosi*, beginning after his historical preamble thus: "Accordingly, since these matters have been doubted, we, deciding such ambiguities, ordain . . . that children not only of a demented person but also of an insane person" etc., as follows in the translated text.
3. This comes from the fiancé's side and corresponds to the dowry given for the fiancée. See no. 517, n. 2.
4. Both the afflicted person and his or her minor children would have a guardian.
5. This possibly means that the fiancé's and the fiancée's opinion as to the size of the premarital donation and of the dowry respectively is considered as a matter, at least, of courtesy, but that the entire matter is decided finally by the persons next named.
6. Constantinople.
7. That is, the higher personages' service as a check on the curators' and the contracting parties' opinions on what of the lunatic's property should be assigned for prenuptial settlements.
8. Instead of *demens* (out of one's mind) used hitherto now is found *mente captus* (seized in one's mind). Each seems opposed to *furiosus* (insane).
9. The other version reads "increment".

611. MANDATE OF JUSTINIAN I ON EPISCOPAL JURISDICTION IN CLERICAL LAWSUITS, 530

(CI 1. 4. 29)

This constitution concerns chiefly the venues and the appeals of suits in which clerics are involved, but sets fees to be paid for service of summons and allows civil and criminal cases to be heard in secular courts at the clerical litigants' choice.

The same emperor to Julian, praetorian prefect.[1]
We ordain that none of the most devout clergymen—whether by

any fellow-clergyman or by any of the so-called laymen—should be accused at once and from the first before the most blessed patriarchs of each diocese, but first according to the sacred laws before the bishop of the city wherein the clergyman dwells; but that, if he has suspicion in regard to him, he should do this before the bishop of the metropolis; but if—as it may be—not even in regard to him he should be satisfied, then he should take the person to be judged to the holy synod of the district—three most God-beloved bishops who are first according to order of ordination assembling with the metropolitan and deciding the suit in the orderly array of the whole synod.

And if he should have liked the judgement,[2] he should abandon [3] the matter.[2] But if he should have thought that he has been injured, then he should appeal [3] to that diocese's most blessed patriarch and by all means should abide [3] by his judgement,[2] just as if he had happened to be chosen judge from the beginning. For it has been legislated by those before us that against such episcopal sentences is no place for appeal.

The same procedure should be observed [4] also, even if a bishop should have been the one accused—whether by any of the so-called laymen or by any of the most God-beloved clergymen or by any other God-beloved bishop.

For we absolutely forbid the immediate laying of accusations before the most holy patriarchs and that persons accused should be taken into another district, unless someone should have made the accusation for this purpose, on condition that the case should be transferred to the district's most God-beloved bishop; for then there shall be permission to lay the accusation even before the most God-beloved patriarchs and to compose a letter to any of the most God-beloved bishops in the several places, so that he should hear the case according to the way previously indicated by us.

And surely should not be allowed [3] to him [5] permission to go to the most devout clergymen and to excite the aforementioned with excess of so-called fees [6]—a kind of offence which we have learned is being committed hitherto.

For we allow to be given for each person of those summoned not beyond the sixth part of a coin [7] concerning the pretext of fees [6] to those [8] sent by the most God-beloved patriarchs and metropolitans or, if a bishop should be the one accused, to be offered up to six coins [7] only and no more than this for whatever amount [9] and whatever case.

The same procedure should prevail [4] also in the case of metropolitans, whenever before them should have been laid any accusation against any of the bishops under them or of that province's clergymen.

For if in the case of civilian suits we have striven eagerly to contract

611. JURISDICTION IN CLERICAL LAWSUITS, 530

the limit of fees [6] and of costs and have resolved to transmit this to legislation,[10] we legislate that much more in the case of ecclesiastical accusations due proportion should be observed.

However, if, when a case has been sent by the most God-beloved patriarch to any of the most God-beloved metropolitans or to another of the most God-beloved bishops, a verdict should have been given and should not have been liked by one party and an appeal should have been made, then to the archiepiscopal see should be carried [3] the appeal and there according to what hitherto prevails the decision should be made.[3] But if anyone should have dared to do anything against this, he shall pay to him from whom too much has been extorted [11] double all as much as he has taken [12] and he shall be under ecclesiastical punishment by the most holy patriarch at the time or the most God-beloved metropolitan, after he is removed from the ecclesiastical lists.

We order the accusations necessarily to be made only before the most God-beloved bishops or metropolitans or before the holy synods or the most God-beloved patriarchs, if the matter should look to ecclesiastical status; but if the matters of the disputes should be civil, we allow the persons, when willing, to institute such inquiries before the said most God-beloved bishops, but we do not compel the unwilling persons, since for them are civil courts, if those should be more liked, before which it is possible also to litigate on criminal charges.[13]

But since some of the most God-beloved patriarchs in the provinces wherein they are also have metropolitical position and some throughout the whole diocese make ordinations of the most God-beloved bishops—whether metropolitans or others—under them, in their cases we ordain those matters which already we have decreed concerning the most God-beloved metropolitans. For he should be called justly a metropolitan who in consequence of the holy canons has authority over the bishops under a metropolis.

Given on 18 October at Constantinople, Lampadius and Orestes being consuls.

1. Of the East.
2. Pluralized in Greek, but singular in the Latin version.
3. The predicate of this sentence is an infinitive in Greek, dependent on the main verb of the preceding sentence.
4. This predicate is a participle in Greek and in the construction of the genitive absolute.
5. The complainant.
6. See no. 606, n. 20.
7. The Latin translation equates this (νόμισμα) with solidus, for whose value see no. 433, n. 7. Since one gold solidus was equivalent after Anastasius I's

reign to twelve silver miliaresia, one-sixth of a solidus consisted of two miliaresia.

8. The summoners (*viatores*) attached to ecclesiastical (and other) courts.

9. Since nearly every legal penalty in Roman law could be converted into a monetary equivalent, it was possible to calculate some apparitorial fees in proportion to the amount for which the plaintiff had sued the defendant. Therefore, ordinarily, as the greater were the damages, so the fees for legal services of various kinds were higher.

10. As in *CI* 3. 2. 4, of which the ecclesiastical parts appear in no. 606.

11. The preceding seven words are represented in Greek by one participle (ὑπερπραχθείς) apparently reported only here.

12. By this is not meant necessarily that the person has been a thief or a robber.

13. The word is ἔγκλημα, which generally seems to pertain to written complaints leading to private suits, but the Latin translator, if he uses *crimen* (his word) in its late Latin sense, perhaps relies upon its adjectival form ἐγκληματικός in *CI* 4. 20. 16. pr., where it is reported to mean "criminal" and where he turns it by *criminalis*.

612. MANDATE OF JUSTINIAN I ON LEGACIES TO THE CHURCH, 530

(*CI* 1. 3. 45)

This constitution contains various regulations relating to property willed to the Church for its charitable foundations. Much of it concerns efforts of heirs to procrastinate or to compromise or to avoid execution of testators' wishes; in such cases either episcopal or gubernatorial action is authorized. Among the several injunctions may be noted episcopal supervision of the institutions and penalties assessed on delinquent heirs.

The same emperor to Julian, praetorian prefect.[1]

We ordain that, if anyone dying should make a pious disposition [2] or by way of institution [3] either through legacy or through trust [4] or through donation in anticipation of death [5] or through other lawful way whatever (whether he should have enjoined on a bishop at the time [6] that care should be arranged to fulfil what wishes have been made by him or should have been silent about this or even should have forbidden the contrary), it is necessary for the heirs to do and to fulfil in every way what has been ordered; but if they should not have done this voluntarily, then the most God-beloved

612. LEGACIES TO THE CHURCH, 530

bishops in the several places should investigate thoroughly these matters and should demand that they fulfil all things according to the deceased's wish.

But if the testator should have ordered the building of a church, within three years they should prepare by all means that this should be fulfilled, but if the construction of a hostel, within one year only they should be compelled to do this, since this time has been set as sufficient to fulfil what wishes have been made by deceased persons— it being possible both for a building to be rented and to bed sick persons therein,[7] until the matters of the building of the hostel have been completed.[8] But if they should have been ordered to give anything once for pious causes they should be compelled immediately to do this, that is, after the opening of the will and they who have been honoured by these things have accepted the inheritance or the bequest.[8] But if the said time should have passed and neither the church nor the hostel should have been built nor the person placed in charge of this should have entertained guests, then the most God-beloved bishops themselves should demand what things have been bequeathed for this and are required properly for this and should effect the buildings of the most holy churches and the construction of hostels or of homes for the aged or of orphanages or the making of almshouses or of hospitals or the purchase of captives or whatever other pious action which pleased the deceased and should propose as administrators of these either managers of hostels or directors of orphanages or directors of nurseries or superintendents of homes for the aged or, in a word, administrators and curators of pious actions—the persons who have not done this no longer being able (after the said time's passage and the said inconsideration) to inject themselves into the administration of the said matters or to repel the most God-beloved bishops from the administration of them; the most distinguished governors of provinces having imposed compulsion on the heirs in every way to fulfil these matters.[8] For indeed it also has been declared explicitly by the ancient laws that compulsion to fulfil the decedents' wishes should be placed upon the persons permitted to have what things they have bequeathed.

If the decedents should have appointed specifically over the properties any persons, such as managers of hostels or directors of almshouses or superintendents of hospitals or directors of nurseries or directors of orphanages or superintendents of homes for the aged or custodians or stewards, or, in short, administrators of pious actions, the most God-beloved bishops should let those persons have the administration, but they themselves should not administer, but should inspect their administration and should praise it, if it goes correctly, but should correct it, if it is erroneous in any respect, and, when the administration is very bad, they should expel them and should install others who have in mind fear of the Great God and the terrible day of the great and endless judgement, in looking steadfastly toward which it is proper for them to do all things with their thought directed toward God.[8]

But if the decedents should not have appointed specifically over the administrations any persons, but should have bestowed it all in the authority of the heirs, but they should have been negligent, then the most God-beloved bishops themselves should administer it and should propose directors of almshouses or superintendents of hospitals or managers of hostels or directors of orphanages or directors of nurseries or superintendents of homes for the aged or stewards or custodians or administrators, who also herein have in their mind reverential awe toward the Great God, so that by every means and by every way and by every device the things piously ordered should be brought into effect.[8]

We ordain that for the entire period through which the written heirs should have deferred to perform the dispositions made the fruits and the returns and all lawful increase from the time of the testator's death should be demanded from them, the delay [9] not being considered from the lawsuit's commencement or from the accusation, but the so-called delay [9] (when the addition of the fruits and the like takes place) appearing to occur by the law itself. The same condition prevails, if even not by an heir, but by a trustee [10] or by a legatee a pious legacy of this kind should have been bequeathed and the person honoured by the legacy should have accepted it; and then to the most God-beloved bishops should be opportunity to demand that such persons so honoured should perform the things ordered.[8] But if the most God-beloved bishops, influenced perhaps by the written heirs or by legatees [11] or by trustees,[12] in the several places should have neglected to perform this, to the metropolitan of a province or to the archbishop of a diocese therein, learning these things, as well as to everyone of the citizens wishing to do this, shall be opportunity to investigate and to compel the pious work or the pious present to be fulfilled by all means; for, since the thought of piety is common, it is proper also that the efforts for its fulfilment should be established as common—everyone having from this our law an opportunity to institute the statutory condiction [13] and to demand that the bequests should be fulfilled; the most God-beloved bishop who neglects these matters knowing that he himself should experience in addition to celestial punishments also royal punitive action for such heedlessness.

Moreover, that the decedents' heirs, seized by still greater fear, or the persons burdened by such quite good actions may not delay the doing of these, we also ordain this: that if persons honoured by these, when importuned by the most God-beloved bishops, thereupon should

612. LEGACIES TO THE CHURCH, 530

delay so that even exaction by the governors should be needed, then should be exacted from them not only the simple bequest, but also absolutely double. For if among the ancients there were certain cases in which as a result of denial the sentence's penalties were weighted double,[14] why in this case is it not fitting to chastise by demand for double the persons who have not acted voluntarily, but both have postponed the time and later have been importuned by the most Godbeloved bishops and then have not yielded immediately to these and even have needed gubernatorial importunity?

But if decedents should have wished that their heirs should fulfil some pious action whenever they [15] would die, but not in their lifetime, and that this should be observed and that meanwhile the heirs should not be compelled to do anything, it is necessary that they,[15] when dying, by all means should fulfil these things which the testator has wished to be done after their death.[8] But when a certain delay has been made by that person's heirs, it is necessary that these things, which previously we have formulated, should be done.

But if certain things of the legacies called annual [16] should have been bequeathed or should have been donated to the clergy perhaps or monasteries or female ascetics or deaconesses or almshouses or hostels or hospitals or nurseries or the most holy churches' poor persons or, in short, some corporations, which are lawful [17] and not at all are prohibited, of those collected from a great number, but if the persons then found at a certain time should have wished it to be discharged by accepting money [18] in place of such an action,[19] it shall not be permitted to do this or, if done, to be valid, but he who has purchased and he who has discharged these things shall suffer the loss of the money. For truly since it is necessary that to persons living at a certain period of time should be an abundance of money, but that to persons living later should be a total lack of bequests, neither the very name of annual legacies [16] nor the deceased's perpetual memory will be preserved, on account of which he has bequeathed this annual legacy,[16] but straightway will be obliterated, when destroyed along with the alienation of the bequests. Therefore we ordain that these persons should remain perpetually obligated by such donations, so that, even if there should be any alienation, both this should be invalid and the persons at any time in control of the holy houses [20] should have the opportunity to sue and to demand the said things—no time of prescription [21] lying against them, because in every year such suit is engendered.

But the bequeather's properties should be a pledge for such legacies, so that from the very properties should be the opportunity for satisfaction to result for the holy actions, not only in the case of bequests but also in the case of their fruits and returns and all lawful increase—

1076   612. LEGACIES TO THE CHURCH, 530

no long-time prescription [21] (as has been said) being able to apply to the possessors, however much time anyone should have counted.[8] Except unless between him who has been burdened by an annual legacy [16] and him who has been charged with such a demand in accord with sacerdotal canons and our laws there should be made an arrangement, intending that instead of the annual legacy [16] should be given by this person so burdened a prolific return and one not subjected to many public burdens, but also having an additional payment absolutely not less than the fourth part of a clear return or [22] indeed however much more should have seemed best between them.[8] For if any such agreement should have been written and such return should have been given and should have been undertaken by written pacts and settlement and this has become manifest by transaction of the records, we ordain that the demand of an annual legacy [16] against him who has been burdened by it should be fruitless, but that the return itself instead of the legacy should become perpetually destined for this and cannot be alienated by anyone according to any form of alienation whatever. But if nothing such ensues, we ordain that (according to what has been said previously by us) the persons who have been burdened by such things should be subject perpetually to the donation of the annual legacies,[16] so that the name and the memory both of the deceased and of the annual legacy [16] should be preserved perpetually in the deeds themselves.

Given on 18 October at Constantinople, Lampadius and Orestes being consuls.

1. Of the East.
2. By a will.
3. Of an heir to one's estate.
4. The Latin word *fideicommissum* is reproduced as *fideicommisson* in the Greek context. See no. 218, n. 7.
5. The Latin phrase *mortis causa* appears thus within the Greek phrase.
6. That is, whoever happened to be bishop *pro tempore* was named in his episcopal capacity without necessarily being mentioned by personal name.

In the rest of the parenthesis are three possibilities: (1) positive statement about wishes, that is, definite conditions to be followed in their execution; (2) silence about wishes, that is, no precise instruction about their implementation, which is left to the heirs' discretion as executors; (3) negative statement about wishes, that is, certain things about their fulfilment must not be done.

7. Mention of the ill suggests that the hostel (ξενών) is rather a hospital (νοσοκομεῖον, a late synonym for the former).
8. The Greek has no finite form acting as the principal verb of this sentence, which depends upon such a form in the preceding sentence.
9. The Latin word *mora* (technically "laches") is used amid the Greek. The

juristic doctrine is that a person is in *mora* generally when he does not act until after the time that he is obligated to act; that time is generally after performance has been demanded and has been declined (*D* 22. 1. 32. pr.). But here Justinian calculates the *mora* longer: from the testator's death. But ordinarily there is no *mora*, if in good faith the existence of the obligation has been disputed (*D* 22. 1. 24. pr., 50. 17. 63). In legacies and in trusts—the situation here—a debtor's *mora* subjects him to payment of interest. Whether *mora* exists seems to be a question of fact rather than of law.

10. The Latin word *fideicommissarius* is reproduced as *fideicommissariu* (genitive singular) in the Greek context. See no. 218, n. 7.

11. Here the word is a mixture of Greek and Latin: *legatarion* (genitive plural).

12. The word combines Greek and Latin: *fideicommissarion* (genitive plural). See no. 218, n. 7.

13. In the Greek context appears the Latin phrase *ex lege condicticion*: more correctly *ex lege condicticia*, more fully *actio ex lege condicticia*, more usually *condictio ex lege*. According to *GI* 4. 5 and *II* 4. 6. 15 a real action (*actio in rem*) is termed a vindication (*vindicatio*) and a personal action (*actio in personam*) is called a condiction (*condictio*). Although originally and in strict form a condiction according to law (*ex lege*) denoted the claimed property's certainty and individuality (such as a certain sum of money or plot of ground or slave) quite apart from the reason for which was made the claim, yet later it could be brought to enforce any statutory order or prohibition (as here). Justinian also used the *condictio ex lege* (his term for the post-classical *condictio*) to prosecute any claim acknowledged as actionable, when a specifically named action was not available.

14. The doctrine of double damage levied against a defendant who denies liability and cannot win acquittal is as ancient as the *Twelve Tables* in 449 B.C. (*FIRA* 1. 43; *TT* 6. 2) and appears almost a millennium later in Justinian's Institutes (*II* 4. 6. 19, 4. 16. 1).

15. The heirs.

16. These are the *annua* (called here *annalia*, transliterated into Greek) *legata*, in effect, annuities, which in reality are successive legacies, whose payment is unconditional, although each succeeding payment is subject to the condition "if the annuitant lives" (*D* 36. 2. 10, 33. 1. 4).

17. Or "pious" perhaps.

In the next line the words *of . . . number* indicate that the pious causes and the corporations mentioned are only some of a larger number which could be considered as beneficiaries of a decedent's will. On governmental authorization of "approved" corporations see no. 133, n. 1.

18. Literally "gold".

19. That is, to effect a settlement by taking a lump sum perhaps according to such a table of life-expectancy as appears in *D* 35. 2. 68. pr.

20. The Church's charitable institutions previously listed.

21. See no. 65, n. 6 *ad fin.*

22. The conjunction is translated from the Latin version, for the Greek conjunction (ἐπείτοιγε: "for truly since") seems senseless here.

613. MANDATE OF JUSTINIAN I ON CLERICAL CELIBACY, 530
(*CI* 1. 3. 44)

In an effort to enforce the ecclesiastical enactments concerning the celibacy of clergymen in major orders Justinian confers on such canons the validity of civil laws, deposes violators from the priesthood, debars clerical progeny from succession to patrimony and from capacity to accept donations from their fathers, and invalidates contracts which such clergymen make.

This enactment is an excellent specimen of how seriously Justinian at almost the start of his reign regarded his responsibilities as lay head of the Church and of how in its internal affairs he asserted his authority. Herein appears his aim to identify Church and State more intimately and to organize these institutions into one organism by ordaining that ecclesiastical canons should carry the same sanction as imperial constitutions. Several years later the same emperor specifically set the canons of the first four ecumenical councils [1] on an equal level with secular law.[2]

The same emperor to Julian, praetorian prefect.[3]

Though the sacred canons allow neither the most God-beloved priests nor the most devout deacons or subdeacons to marry after such ordination, but concede this to only the most devout cantors and lectors,[4] we see certain ones despising the sacred canons and procreating children from certain women, with whom according to the sacerdotal ordinance they cannot be married.

Therefore, since the penalty for the deed was in only expulsion from the priesthood, but since our laws also wish the divine canons to have no less force than the laws, we ordain that in regard to them should prevail the matters which seem best to the sacred canons, just as if these had been written in the civil laws, and that they all should be stripped of both the priesthood and the divine service and the dignity which they have. For even as such things have been forbidden by the holy canons, so also according to our laws the deed has been prohibited and in addition to the said penalty of expulsion the ones born or to be born from such an absurd mutual corruption are not legitimate, but partake of the ignominy of such descents.[5] For we deter-

613. CLERICAL CELIBACY, 530

mine them to be such as the laws define as born from incestuous [6] or nefarious [6] marriages, so that they should not be considered natural or base-born, but, in all ways interdicted and unworthy of succession to parents, neither they nor their mothers nor through intermediate persons being able to accept a donation from them—but all gifts coming to them from their fathers going to the most holy church, of which those who commit this sin are members. For what the sacred canons forbid, this also we prohibit through our laws.

But if any simulated obligation, forsooth, should befall in pretension of loans or other contracts by making, forsooth, the partaker of such sexual corruption liable, we wish this both to be invalid and the present of such things to go not to the person for whom the details of the covenant have been fixed, but to the most holy church.

Given on 18 October at Constantinople, the most distinguished Lampadius and the most distinguished Orestes being consuls.

1. Nicaea I, 325; Constantinople I, 381; Ephesus, 431; Chalcedon, 451.
2. *N* 131. 1 (dated 545).
3. Of the East.
4. Despite the apostolic practice of marriage (see no. 372, n. 1), to which—that one may cite only one of several ante-Nicene references—St Clement of Alexandria testifies in his *Stromata* (3. 6. 52–3; cf. Eusebius, *HE* 3. 30. 1, for his reproduction of this testimony), the *Constitutiones Apostolorum*, which may be ante-Nicene in date, specifically prohibit all unmarried clergy, save only readers and singers, from marrying after their ordination (8. 47. 27). See no. 372, n. 4.

While in 325 Nicaea's canon 3 forbids any cleric to maintain in his house any woman other than his mother or sister or aunt or such persons only as are above all suspicion, yet it cannot be construed into a law against clerics' wives, according to H. C. Lea, *An Historical Sketch of Sacerdotal Celibacy in the Christian Church* [2] (Boston, 1884), 53–6.

In 451 Chalcedon's canon 14 allows readers and singers to wed, provided that their brides are orthodox; canon 15 prohibits deaconesses from marrying; canon 16 enjoins celibacy on monks and on nuns.

See Lea, op. cit., 31–88 for a discussion of clerical celibacy during this sylloge's period.

5. This sentence has no finite verb in Greek for its predicate and depends upon that of the preceding sentence.
6. Transliterated into Greek from the Latin adjective, whence comes our English adjective.

614. MANDATE OF JUSTINIAN I ON ABBATIAL ELECTION, 530

(CI 1. 3. 46)

The emperor establishes the rule that excellence of character and not seniority of service should be the controlling factor in selection of superiors for monasteries and for convents and that episcopal sanction must validate the election.

The same emperor to Julian, praetorian prefect.[1]

We believe that to our sacred laws we ought to add also this, which provides holy leaderships [2] from excellence, but not from seniority,[3] so that in the holy monasteries or hermitages, when the abbot or the abbess [4] dies, by no means the man next in line or the woman second in dignity should succeed (for we know that by nature's operation neither all are similarly good nor all are equally bad), but whom both good life and august character and application to asceticism commend [5] and the common aggregate of the rest of the monks [6] or their largest part [7] should have considered suitable for this and, when the Holy Gospels [8] are introduced, should have chosen to be called to the leadership.[2] So that, if the first after the deceased should be the best and worthy to rule the monks, that one should be preferred above the others; but if there is one after that one, similarly the vote for the abbot [4] should be cast for him.[9] But if none of these should have appeared worthy, then the one suitable from all—of whatever rank he may be—should be selected abbot,[4] being of august life and of august living and able to save the persons entrusted to him; for it is proper that all rule and all authority over human beings should be neither from seniority [3] nor from lots [10] nor from fortuitous circumstances, but from selection and from finer quality, and for the group [11] the post [11] should be filled [12] by all persons' witness.[9]

These things should be made known to the most God-beloved bishop in the several places, so that he, knowing about the person elected and approving that this is rightly done, should be in agreement with the electors and should induct him into the abbot's [4] post.[9]

And it is necessary that the patriarch at the time and the most God-beloved bishops in the several places should approve their election, for they themselves also have [13] the judgement [14] of the Lord God and fear the future judgement,[14] if they shall make their proposal by having paid attention not to election but to some human emotion, since they themselves also have in this life and in the future life punishment from God, because their heedlessness furnishes causes for sins to many souls.

And all these matters should prevail in the case of the most devout women and virgins, who are abbesses [4] ruling the holy hermitages or monasteries.[9]

The rest of every sacerdotal [15] order [16] of God's ministry should be advanced according to its own ranks and no innovation should be made as a result of our present law.[9]

Given on 17 November at Constantinople, Lampadius and Orestes being consuls.

1. Of the East.
2. The word is ἡγεμονία, with which is collated the participle ἡγούμενος (leader [whether abbot or prior] of a monastery), whence comes the English transliteration "hegumen", still applied to the head of a small religious community in the Eastern Church, whereas "archimandrite" is reserved for the head of a large monastery or of several monasteries.
3. Literally "from [long] times": that is, mere length of time in the monastic life should not lead automatically to the abbacy.
4. The masculine and the feminine of the participle in n. 2 *supra*.
5. Editors note the absence of a finite verb in Greek to act as predicate and supply in Latin a substitute, which here is translated.
   For the thought compare Horace (*Ep.* 1. 1. 59–60): "You will be king (*rex*), if you will do rightly (*recte*)"—part of a paronomastic verse in trochaic tetrameter sung by boys in some game of skill. St Isidore has the entire line, which ends "if you will not do, you will not be" (*Orig.* 9. 3. 4).
6. Or nuns, as the case may be. The grammatical case used is common to all genders and, *mutatis mutandis*, wherever *monks* occurs, "nuns" also should be understood, although Justinian uses masculine forms of various nouns and pronouns.
7. Since monks can be considered a conspicuous corps in the Church's militia—indeed, the most militant order of the Jesuits originally was called the Company of Jesus and its head has still the title "General"—and since the Church saw a moral equivalent for war in monasticism, which represented the Church militant against worldliness within its membership, and since a fourth-century monk could say to Palladius, author of the *Historia Lausiaca* (on which see no. 284, n. 2), "For Christ's sake I am guarding the walls" (op. cit., 18), then perhaps it is not too far-fetched to see in the majority vote for abbatial election an application of that principle inherited from pagan soldiers, who applied it occasionally in a crisis to choose a commander (e.g. after Alexander the Great's death in 323 B.C., according to Curtius, *Hist. Alex. Mag. Maced.* 10. 6. 1–18). But what democratic soldiers did they simply copied from their custom when civilians, since both in Greek city-states and in Rome the citizens, convoked in assemblies (whether for legislative or electoral or judicial functions), made most of their decisions by either open or secret majority vote.
8. On these each member of the community would swear to attest his vote for his candidate.

9. This independent sentence in Greek lacks a finite verb, which should be supplied from the preceding sentence.

10. Cleromancy, of course, is ancient. Laocoon, whom with his sons the two serpents from the sea slew in the Trojan War's last year (traditionally 1184 B.C.), was selected by sortilege as Poseidon's priest (Vergil, *Aen.* 2. 201). And the apostles practised it in filling Judas' place among them after his suicide (Acts 1. 26), but Justinian here outlaws its use in ecclesiastical elections.

11. It seems impossible in English to reproduce the juxtaposed *figura etymologica* of τάγματι ("order" in the sense of "group") τάξιν ("order" in the sense of "post"), each derived from τάσσειν (to order, to group, to post). Not even the Latin version attempts it. See no. 325, n. 6.

12. The Greek construction of the dative of reference permits the juxtaposition noted in the preceding note, but requires the insertion of a more significant verbal form in this case than "be": hence *filled*.

13. That is, are subject to God's judgements rather than in a subtler sense represent God as judges on earth—as Constantine I once claimed for them (no. 49, I) and as subsequent history so sorrowfully has shown, when prelates fraught with pride have forgotten the prohibition in Matt. 7. 1–5 (but see 1 Cor. 6. 2–3).

14. Paronomasia of κρῖμα and κρίσις.

15. See no. 526, n. 11.

16. Cf. *supra* n. 11.

615. MANDATE OF JUSTINIAN I ON LEGACIES TO THE CHURCH, 530

(*CI* 1. 2. 25)

Justinian uses this statute to clarify ambiguous situations arising from wills not precisely drawn in respect to bequests to the Church.

Already in Ulpian's (*ob.* 228) age deities (or rather their temples) could not be instituted heirs except in such cases as senatusconsults or imperial constitutions authorized.[1] But with the Christianization of the Empire ensued a difference in the application of the law, for Justinian here recognizes Jesus Christ or an archangel or a martyr as heir. If the saints, as some scholars suppose, were the successors of pagan divinities and whereas Diana (Artemis) of the Ephesians, e.g., earlier had owned property both secular and sacred, whether movable or immovable, so now Christian saints could be considered the proprietors of what pertained to the churches consecrated to them.

The same emperor to Julian, praetorian prefect.[2]

Since in many previous wills we have found such institutions of

615. LEGACIES TO THE CHURCH, 530

heirs, in accordance with which anyone has written either our Lord Christ as sole heir, by not having added any house of prayer,[3] or our said Lord Jesus Christ as heir to one-half or to other unequal shares, but some other person as heir to one-half or to another portion (for already we have met with several wills made in this way and we see much uncertainty existing therefrom according to the ancient laws), in correcting also this situation we ordain that, if anyone should write our Lord Jesus Christ as heir either solely or partly, the most holy church in the same city or village or place in which the deceased has dwelt seems unreservedly to be instituted heir and the inheritance is claimed by its most God-beloved stewards solely or partly according as it is written heir—this same condition being valid, if a legacy or a trust[4] has been left—and that these belong to the most holy churches on the condition that the said things should proceed for the support of paupers.

But[5] if remembrance of one of the holy archangels or of the worshipful martyrs has been made, though he has not made mention of the church[6] (and this we know has been so disposed by a certain person and one indeed born of distinguished parents and distinguished in education concerning laws and words),[7] if there is in that city or its territory a house of prayer[3] in honour of that most venerable archangel or of a most holy martyr, this seems to have been written as heir; but if such a church[8] does not exist in the said city or its territory, in this case the venerable churches[8] in the metropolis.[9] And[5] if any such church[8] indeed should be found in it,[10] to it[10] should seem to be left the inheritance or the bequest or the trust;[4] but if any such church[8] should not appear to be even there,[10] in turn the most holy churches in the place[11] should take also this.

Obviously all remaining churches[12] rightly yield to the most holy churches, unless the deceased clearly, however, had intended to impose one name but had mentioned another (and therefore we, knowing that some such circumstance happened according to a certain will in Pontus, there again provided[5] that the truth should prevail instead of what had been written).[13]

If,[5] however, the deviser should not have assigned a specified place, but in that city or the neighbouring district should have been found many oratories[14] of the same name established, if in someone of these the deceased often used to attend and used to have some greater attachment for it, the bequest should seem to have been left to that. But[5] if none such should be found, to the needier church[8] of the same name and the one needing aid such a bequest of the inheritance should seem rather to have been left.

Given on 20 November[15] at Constantinople, the most distinguished Lampadius and the most distinguished Orestes being consuls.

1. In one of Ulpian's fragments (22. 6) are listed nine pagan deities capable of such inheritance. Of these three were in Europe, five were in Asia, one was in Africa (*FIRA* 2. 285).
2. Of the East.
3. An oratory: see no. 522, n. 5.

The idea seems to be that no qualification about the use of the inheritance—as e.g. to or for an oratory—has been specified in the will, but that its application is unrestricted and in the discretion of ecclesiastical officials.

4. This word appears in Latin as *fideicommisson* amid the Greek.
5. The principal verb in this sentence, which is edited (and translated) independently, is an infinitive in Greek (as well as in the Latin version), depending apparently on the main finite verb (*we ordain*) of the first sentence.
6. That is, not having identified the particular church (οἶκος) in the will.
7. A homely aside.
8. As in n. 6 *supra*, church is οἶκος (Latin *domus*).
9. The completed sense is that then the churches in the metropolis of the deceased's district shall qualify as heir.
10. The metropolis.
11. Where the deceased dwelt.
12. The distinction between the ordinary churches (οἶκοι) and the most holy churches (ἐκκλησίαι) may be drawn in the difference in dedication.
13. This principle had been proclaimed in *CI* 6. 23. 4 (dated 239).
14. Here the word is εὐκτήριον without οἶκος (cf. *supra* n. 3).
15. Editors suggest the 18th as the true date.

616. MANDATE OF JUSTINIAN I ON DISABILITIES FOR HERETICS, 530

(*CI* 1. 5. 20)

Besides prohibiting heretics from using ecclesiastical enclosures for commercial purposes this ordinance bans Montanist clergy from Constantinople, condemns their rites, forbids Montanists to traffick in slaves, and bars charity to poor Montanists.

The same emperor [1] . . . to the count of the private estates.

We have known that unholy heretics even after our laws [2] and the movement made against them still dare both to assemble and to appoint certain leaders of their madness and to call these exarchs and to effect baptisms and to wish to use certain privileges, when within

616. DISABILITIES FOR HERETICS, 530

holy precincts have been set their shops, which it is proper for only those honouring the right faith to use.

On this account, therefore, we ordain that your Excellency also should forbid them now, that especially in any other place, but particularly in this fortunate city,[3] they should not effect any gatherings or baptisms or should not dare to fasten upon the name or the property of the venerable communion, which are proper only to persons revering the right opinion and properly honouring the Christians' venerable name. But we do not permit persons having shops within holy precincts to use certain privileges through a motive for shops, knowing that, if after this our divine proclamation they also should have appeared to fasten upon any such of the prohibited things or in this royal city [3] or in other places to dare to effect secret assemblies or baptisms or to give unspeakable communion to themselves or to do any of the forbidden things, they shall be brought under proper penalties to which it is necessary that persons opposing the laws and not observing their power should submit—persons who furnish to them their houses for effecting secret assemblies knowing that they shall undergo this penalty of which preceding divine ordinances speak.

And these things generally concerning all heretics. But specially in regard to the unholy Montanists we ordain: that none of their so-called patriarchs and associates or bishops or priests or deacons or other clergymen—if indeed it is quite proper to call them by these names—should be permitted to reside in this fortunate city,[3] but all should be expelled, lest some of the rather simple-minded persons, having heard their absurd myths and following their impious teachings, should destroy their own souls.

But we do not permit them generally to transact business within the pure bounds, so that the orthodox faith's pure mysteries [4] may not be heard by persons who are both polluted and unworthy of every clean and pure sound heard.

And we ordain that their wanton common meals and impious and condemned drinking-parties, in which, assembling, they try to prey upon the rather simple-minded persons' souls, should be forbidden. For it is necessary that it should have been forbidden that these persons who have turned from them to the right faith should live anew impiously with persons diseased in the same ways and perhaps from this association and life again should return to their previous possession by evil spirits.

We also forbid them to trade in slaves,[5] lest they, having sold these to their fellow-worshippers, should have caused them to be of their own heretical belief.

Similarly we forbid that to persons of the Montanists' superstition should be given any alleviation by way of plea on the part of the so-called dignitaries [6] (to whom from the greatest judges and most holy Great Church [7] it has been accustomed for something to be supplied on the plea of poverty distressing them), which alleviation should not be proper to be supplied to persons of the said superstition, since it has nothing at all sound or temperate, but by all persons justly is hated and condemned, so that also, if anyone dispenses irrational protection to them, we ordain that this person also should be chastened by a penalty of ten pounds of gold.

Therefore all these matters we wish to be observed carefully by both your Excellency and those having magistracies over the peoples [8]— the office staff obedient to you and the provincial office staffs being suspect in respect to the same penalty, unless they should have observed these matters, and indignation no less being imposed on persons who at all times have a magistracy (to which now your Excellency is superior), if they should have permitted any of the ordained matters to be transgressed or if they themselves should have transgressed these, and the governors of the peoples,[8] if they should have neglected this, similarly being chastened by a penalty of ten pounds of gold.

Given at Constantinople on 22 November, the most distinguished Lampadius and the most distinguished Orestes being consuls.

1. The lacuna apparently contained a personal name.
2. Nos. 571 and 575.
3. Constantinople.
4. See no. 75, n. 42.
5. This word's (ἀνδράποδον) original significance—"one captured in war and sold into slavery"—seems to have disappeared by Justinian's time.
6. See no. 495, n. 9.
7. Hagia Sophia in Constantinople.
8. The provincials are meant.

617. LETTER OF JUSTINIAN I ON COMPOSITION OF THE DIGEST, 530

(D, Constitution *Deo Auctore*)

This document, usually prefixed to editions of Justinian's *Digesta* or *Pandectae*,[1] is noteworthy for the Christian cast of its contents, which instruct the quaestor Tribonian [2] about the emperor's plan for the collection of jurisconsults' [3] opinions into a tome of fifty books,[4] the Digest or the Pandects,[1] which forms a part of the *Corpus Iuris Civilis*.[5]

617. COMPOSITION OF THE DIGEST, 530

The parts lacking religious interest are not translated.

Emperor Caesar Flavius Justinian Pious, Fortunate, Renowned, Victor and Triumpher, Ever-August to Tribonian, his quaestor, greeting.

Governing under God's authority [6] our Empire, which to us by his Celestial Majesty has been delivered, we both complete wars fortunately and adorn peace and sustain the State's government; and we so raise our minds to Almighty God's aid, that we trust in neither arms nor our soldiers nor leaders of wars nor our skill, but we refer all hope to the Supreme Trinity's sole providence, whence both have proceeded the elements of the entire universe and has been derived their disposition throughout the world . . .

But with hands lifted to heaven and with eternal aid invoked, we replaced [7] this care also in our minds, having relied on God, who in the magnitude of his excellence can both grant and complete quite desperate achievements . . .

And since his material [8] has been collected by the Deity's supreme liberality, one ought to erect it in a very beautiful work and to consecrate, so to speak, a proper and most holy temple of justice and to distribute the whole law into fifty books and distinct titles . . .

All cities are bound to follow the usage of Rome, which is the capital of the world, not it to follow other cities. Moreover it must be understood that Rome is not only the old city, but also our royal city,[9] which, with God's favour, has been founded with better auguries [10] . . .

Moreover our consummation,[11] which will be composed by you, God approving, we command to have the names of Digests or Pandects [1] . . .

All these things, therefore, your Prudence, with God being placid, together with other most learned men,[12] should strive to accomplish and to bring to an exact as well as a very swift end, that the codex, consummated and digested into fifty books, may be presented to us for the very great and eternal memory of the matter and for the proof of Almighty God's providence and for the glory of our rule and of your service.

Given on 15 December at Constantinople, the most distinguished Lampadius and the most distinguished Orestes being consuls.

1. *Pandectae* is the Latin transliteration of the Greek title.
2. On him see no. 640, n. 1.
3. On them see no. 308, n. 15.
4. The labour of collecting into fifty books some 9,000 opinions from more than 2,000 treatises written within a period of over six hundred years

was the work of a commission of seventeen professors and lawyers headed by Tribonian (on whom see no. 640, n. 1). The Digest was published on 16 December 533 with statutory force from 30 December of that year (Constitution *Tanta*, 23 [no. 642]).

5. See Introd., n. 3 *ad fin*. for the origin of this phrase.

6. *Deo auctore* (literally "God [being] the author"), the epistle's initial phrase, whence the constitution takes its name. The same system of citation, i.e. the first word or words, is still used for papal pronouncements, e.g. Benedict XV's apostolic constitution, which on 27 May 1917 ratified the completion of the thirteen-year-old revision of the *Codex Iuris Canonici* and decreed that this code's prescriptions should be effective from 19 May 1918, is cited as *Providentissima Mater Ecclesia* (The most provident Mother Church), the first three words of this promulgatory document.

7. Justinian just has commented on the very difficult, if not impossible, task of collecting and correcting the entire Roman jurisprudence and of presenting in one work the scattered treatises of so many jurists.

8. Excerpts from the jurisconsults' treatises are meant.

9. Constantinople, on which see no. 62, n. 2.

10. In *CT* 13. 5. 7 (dated 334) Constantine I claimed that he had endowed the city called after him with the epithet "Eternal" (on which see no. 140, n. 1) in conformity with God's command. Sozomen (*HE* 2. 3 *ad init.*) reports that Constantine had planned his capital at Troy (see no. 62, n. 2 *ad med.*), but in obedience to a nocturnal vision, wherein God appeared to him, was led by God to Byzantium.

Such a Christian sanction for Constantinople could be considered superior to the pagan auspices attendant upon the foundation of Rome, of which exist some 25 distinct legends. For a well-documented account of these legends, many of which are simply variations of the same story, consult G. C. Lewis, *An Inquiry into the Credibility of the Early Roman History* (London, 1855), 1. 376–410, esp. 395–401.

11. That is, the completed work.

12. The sixteen other collaborators with Tribonian (see n. 4 *supra*) are named in the Constitution *Tanta*, 9 (no. 642).

618. EDICT OF JUSTINIAN I ON CONTRACTUAL USAGE OF ECCLESIASTICAL PROPERTY, 530

(*CI* 1. 2. 24)

This defective statute concerns the Constantinopolitan Church in establishing rules for leasing ecclesiastical realty and in regulating the appointment of recorders who maintain the records of such transactions. Penalties are provided for maladministration.

The same emperor.
... Making provision for all ecclesiastical properties and particularly for those pertaining to this fortunate city's [1] most holy Great Church,[2] our and all persons' mother, which is the head of all other churches,[3] we ordain that for the future no leasing of ecclesiastical properties should occur by colonary legal right,[4] but that the name, recognized by no law, should be abolished. However, all other contracts, as many as it has been permitted to the said most holy Great Church's [2] most God-beloved bishops to make, it is allowed to them to execute in relation to those whom they should approve, apart from this royal city's [1] most glorious or most magnificent office-holding magistrates; for in regard to these in no way we allow them to make such a kind of leasing of immovable properties, since no other person is interposed for circumvention of our sacred regulation, whether this person has any connection with the magistrate functioning with authority or without former connection has been received recently by him for this purpose.

The most God-beloved stewards should know [5] that, if anything should occur contrary to these regulations, they shall be constricted from their own resources to pay to the most holy Great Church [2] the valuation of the leased property. The most glorious and most magnificent office-holding magistrates who advance to such letting should know [5] that, although they should have striven to escape detection by well-considered methods and should have interposed such persons, who (they suppose) will escape detection always, because they do this deed for themselves, still afterward, when the truth is proved, the contract absolutely shall be invalidated and for penalty they shall pay to the most holy Great Church [2] the valuation of the property.

But if through another method one shall persuade or shall compel that an ecclesiastical property should come to oneself, what has been done is invalid and what has been granted on this score to a person of the Church is restored to it and, in addition to the said matters, both he who has granted the property is subject to a penalty of twenty pounds of gold and he who has accepted it for contriving that the contract should occur pays double the worth of what has been granted —and all the properties belong to the Church.

Beyond twenty years realty is not let on contract by the Church.

It is proper to grant only to rich persons ecclesiastical properties on emphyteusis [6] because of return of status, and not beyond the person to whom an emphyteusis [6] is granted and two successive heirs,[7] and not to remit more than a sixth part of the assessment maintained at the time of the leasing.

But if one shall damage the property, within the appointed time [8] one is expelled and repairs the loss.

But if the steward should be careless or should lease to poor persons, he acknowledges the damage.[9]

The registrars of the Great Church [2] cannot receive its realty through an interposed person in respect to rent or emphyteusis [6] or any other way. The registrars are created by petition advanced and bearing the patriarch's and the steward's subscription. And if any of these persons should appear to be a thief or a traitor or otherwise unfit, it is permitted to the patriarch and the stewards to remove him from the catalogue. For the secretarial bureau of the East [10] are created fifteen registrars, for that of Asia [10] sixteen, for that of Pontus [10] fifteen, for the habitation [11] fifteen, for that of Thrace [10] eight, for that of Antiochus [12] six, for that of Calopodius [13] six, for that of expenditure [14] ten, for that of legacies nine.[15] And they receive by reason of customary practices a tax of two per cent for bonds of emphyteuses [6] and a tax of one per cent rental and the remaining contracts.[16] But if there should be created a registrar above the said number,[17] he is ejected and to the Church pays fifteen pounds and he who appointed him pays twenty pounds.

After strict investigation the stewards should calculate at the patriarch's decision the expense produced by emphyteutes [6] and leaseholders and administrators—each steward investigating the affairs pertinent to his own administration, but the rest subscribing to the accounts pursuant to the patriarch's written command "I have acknowledged"; and what is calculated apart from such observance the stewards pay from their own resources.

Moreover the registrars receive a tax of one per cent on the calculated expense and the monies paid; but he who takes more is ejected immediately both from the registrar's service and from the sacerdotal rank.[16]

And we ordain the following: that the most God-beloved stewards, themselves who now are and in due season shall be, every month or at longest every two months should render accounts to the most holy Great Church's [2] treasurers, since they know that, if they should have neglected this, they shall experience peril.

1. Constantinople.
2. Hagia Sophia in Constantinople.
3. At least in the Byzantine Empire, where the patriarchate of Constantinople was accorded primacy next after the Church of Rome since the Second Ecumenical Council at Constantinople in 381. For Roman Catholic Christendom see nos. 375, n. 7, 442, n. 7, 645, n. 3.

618. USAGE OF ECCLESIASTICAL PROPERTY, 530

4. G. παροικικὸν δίκαιον; L. *colonarium ius*. On the *colonus* (tenant farmer) see no. 528, n. 5.

The idea here seems to be that the Church should not lease its farmland to entrepreneurs whose concessions would be operated by peasants.

5. Instead of a principal verb the Greek has a participial construction in the genitive absolute.

6. See no. 537, n. 6.

7. Assuming a generation to be 33 years, here is seen perhaps the origin of our 99-year lease.

In the previous line the words *because . . . status* refer to the termination of emphyteusis, whereby the lease is ended at either the death of or the voluntary relinquishment by the emptyteute's second successive heir. Then the property regains its original status, though it may be leased again to another emphyteute. Only wealthy persons are designated as emphyteutes because the emperor probably believes that less harm will come to the ecclesiastical property from their management, though the law provides remedies against anyone's maladministration.

8. That is, before expiration of tenure.

9. As due to be repaired by himself.

10. An imperial diocese containing several provinces.

11. Presumably an office (perhaps the garrison) relating to the imperial palace.

12. He later (558) may have been provost of the sacred bedchamber. What his administrative duty was at this time (530) is not known.

13. Unidentifiable, unless later praetorian prefect of Italy (554). What his function was when the edict was published (530) is not known. The name, which is unusual, appears in a funeral inscription (*ILCV* 1. 709B), discovered and preserved in the Basilica of San Paolo fuori le Mura (on which see no. 211, n. 1). Therein Calopodius is described as a *notar(ius)*, which may correspond to the χαρτουλάριος (*chartularius*) of this constitution. But the coalescence of these two Calopodii into one person is conjecturable.

14. Perhaps that of the privy purse or of largesses, in which latter sense the Latin translation seems to take it.

15. Professor Clyde Pharr in a private communication suggests that the registrars, who are enumerated here and are mentioned elsewhere in this law, evidently were employed in the administration of ecclesiastical property, but apparently were attached to various imperial bureaux (on which see no. 256, n. 2) for administrative co-ordination. The emperor established the quota of registrars for each bureau and here indicated three types: geographical, functional, personal. Why two of these bureaux were denoted apparently by their directors' name (cf. *supra* nn. 12 and 13) is unknown, but Pharr proposes conjecturally that these two were of recent creation, perhaps supplementary to the other and older bureaux, and not yet had received either functional or geographical designation.

16. Perhaps such fees due to the registrars made these bureaucrats so rich that a century earlier (*c.* 414) the anonymous author of the comedy *Aulularia sive Querolus* could say "Give to me the wealth which those who manage records (*chartae*) attain" (p. 18, vv. 2-3; ed. R. Peiper [Leipzig, 1875]). An inscription (dated 361-3) giving a tariff of fees for judicial services rendered by apparitors to litigants is in *FIRA* I. 331-2; the amount of paper (*carta*) to be provided in various circunstances is prescribed, lest litigants should be overcharged, for apparently registrars and recorders purchased paper from governmental stocks—a State monopoly after Aurelian's reign (270-5)—at their own expense and then charged litigants not only its cost but also as much more as they could extract from them.

17. In *CI* 12. 49. 10 (dated 485-6) Zeno already had regulated the number of registrars in civil administration.

619. MANDATE OF JUSTINIAN I ON BIBLICAL OATHS IN LAWSUITS, 531

(*CI* 2. 58. 2)

Justinian requires from all parties—whether principals, if possible, or their attorneys or their guardians or their agents in any event—to lawsuits a solemn oath sworn on the Scriptures that their litigation is just and rules that recalcitrant plaintiffs and defendants should lose their cases.

The same Augustus to Julian, praetorian prefect.[1]

Since we have permitted that judges should settle lawsuits not otherwise unless when the Sacrosanct Gospels have been introduced and since we have arranged that pleaders of lawsuits in all the world which has been placed beneath the Roman sovereignty should swear first and thus should conduct their lawsuits,[2] we have considered it necessary to establish also the present law, by which we ordain that in all litigations, which shall have been started after the present law, neither the plaintiff nor the defendant in the beginning of the litigation should engage in the contests otherwise unless after the narration and the response, before each party's advocates should offer the lawful solemn obligation,[3] the principal persons themselves should submit an oath: the plaintiff indeed should swear that he has begun the litigation, not with the intention of calumniating,[4] but by thinking that he has a good case, but the defendant should not employ his allegations otherwise unless previously he himself also shall have sworn that he, thinking that he employs good perseverance, has come to resist, and afterward each party's very fluent advocates should offer an oath—a matter which

619. BIBLICAL OATHS IN LAWSUITS, 531

already has been arranged by us—obviously on the Sacrosanct Gospels placed before the judge.

But if, however, either a person's position or sex [5] shall not have permitted this person to come to the judge, in the home of the litigant the solemn obligation [3] should occur [6]—the other party or his procurator obviously being present.

And this ought to be observed also, if they are tutors or curators or any other persons who by lawful authority manage the administration of others' property. For it is suitable that they themselves also should be affected by an oath to the effect that "they themselves, knowing the case, thus come to it".[7] For neither the ward nor the adult nor other persons of this sort, but they themselves, who for them manage the tutorship or the curatorship or another lawful administration, can know the case and thus can come to court in this way—that they should swear "after the opinion of their own mind".[8]

And although the true nature of the lawsuit is perhaps different, yet that which anyone believes and thinks, this must be sworn [9]—all other oaths, which either descend from past laws or have been arranged by us, enduring in their own firmness.

But if, however, either party shall have been absent and the lawsuit is pleaded by a procurator, the plaintiff should not have permission to entrust to his procurator the litigation to be engaged unless previously by intervening proceedings in the province where he dwells he should submit a solemn obligation [3] against calumny;[4] and in the same manner, if the defendant shall have been absent and perhaps either shall have appointed the obligation to be paid by a procurator, whom he has determined, or a defender shall have intervened for him, he himself either with the plaintiff present by himself or by the chosen procurator or even in his absence, if the judge shall have perceived this, should offer amid the proceedings the oath which previously has been arranged for the defendant to give.

But because we fear that perhaps certain ones, using some collusion, may seem to remit for themselves a solemn obligation [3] of this kind and as a result of the aforesaid dissimulation may mock our ordinance, we ordain that all judges, although as a result from what has been agreed mutually they know, exercising their own power, that we have established the present law not for the advantage of private persons, but for the common interest, not at all should permit such a solemn obligation [3] to be remitted, but in every way this should be exacted both from the plaintiff and from the defendant, lest gradually it may seem that things of this kind should be subject to fraud and that the solemn obligation [3] either of the principal persons or of the advocates should be curtailed in any part whatsoever.

And we also ordain that this must be added to this law: that if anyone shall have wished to begin litigation for another, when no mandate has been proffered, but by surety shall have secured that the certain property will have his own person as its owner, lest even as a result of this machination the law may seem to be circumscribed, we ordain that if any such thing shall have emerged for the future, whether anyone shall have wished to begin litigation on behalf of one person or on behalf of any corporation or village or any community, he indeed should offer the usual surety, but the litigation should not proceed at all further, unless within a time set by the judge he should cause the principal persons to submit a solemn obligation [3] or, with his opponent present, if he shall have preferred this, or with another acting for him or when the other party amid the proceedings in the presence of the defender of the places entirely yields, a solemn obligation [3] of this kind should proceed from either the very one for whom the action is made or the party which is greatest in number or worthy of the community.

But if the plaintiff shall have been unwilling to submit a solemn obligation [3] against calumny [4] and this shall have been approved lawfully, it should not be permitted for him to come to litigation, but he should lose his instituted action, as if a dishonest litigant, and the judges' harshness should befall him with just threatening and should expel him as far as possible from the court.

But if, however, the defendant shall have refused to submit this solemn obligation,[3] in those points which have been comprehended in the narration he should be considered as one who has confessed and it should be permitted for the judge to proffer sentence as the very character of the situation shall have suggested. For thus not only litigations, but also calumniators [4] will be lessened; thus all will think that they appear in sanctuaries instead of courts.[10] For if the very principal parties of litigants should engage in litigations by an oath and the pleaders of lawsuits should provide a solemn obligation [3] and the judges themselves, when the Holy Scriptures have been introduced, should make an examination of the whole lawsuit as well as should proffer their own decision, what else is it unless God instead of men must be believed to be the judge in all lawsuits?

Accordingly, with long-standing calumny [4] and its evasions ceasing, our plain and advantageous constitution should be clear in all lands and should be the greatest remedy for settling lawsuits.

But we wish the aforesaid solemn obligation [3] in litigations which indeed not yet have been started to be offered in the very beginning of litigation.

But if, however, lawsuits should be found still pending both after the litigation has been introduced and after the usual judicial securities have been offered, if indeed each person shall have been present and stays in the same city or in its territory, both in these lawsuits the solemn obligation [3] should have [9] a place and the offering of an oath should be compelled [9] in the first commencement after this law.

But if, however, one party shall have been absent, lest because of a person's absence the litigation may seem to be delayed and something contrary to our design may happen and what has been introduced for the advantage of litigations may be transformed into an opposing character, we order that indeed the person present by all means should give a solemn obligation,[3] but to the absent one in litigations still pending this should be permitted according to what has been aforesaid.[11]

But if, however, each principal party shall have been absent, lest the litigations may be protracted longer, even without the giving of a solemn obligation [3] the pending litigations should run through their own course.

Posted [12] on 20 February at Constantinople after the consulate of the most distinguished Lampadius and the most distinguished Orestes.

1. Of the East.
2. No. 605.
3. The phrase is *sacramentum*, on which see no. 592, n. 4.
4. See no. 334, n. 3, where *calumnia* is discussed.
5. E.g. no magistrate invested with the *imperium* (the community's supreme authority in its dealings with the individual citizen or subject), no priest while officiating, no judge while judging could be summoned into court (*D* 2. 4. 2) and generally women were forbidden to conduct cases in court (*CT* 2. 12. 5, 9. 1. 3, 9. 24. 1); though matrons could be summoned, they were not subject to force to compel their appearance (*CI* 1. 38. 1).
6. The finite verb in English is in Latin an infinitive dependent upon the main verb in the preceding sentence.
7. Earlier another emperor had commanded an addition to oaths: Caligula caused himself and his sisters to be added thus: "And I shall not hold myself and my children dearer than I hold Gaius and his sisters" according to Suetonius (*Gaius*, 15. 3).
8. This was part of the formula of the oath: *ex sui [mei, tui] animi sententia* in many writers' witness, e.g. Cicero, *Acad.* 2. 47. 146, *De Or.* 2. 64. 260, *De Off.* 3. 29. 108; Livy, *Ab Urbe Cond.* 22. 53. 10, 43. 15. 8; Quintilian, *Inst. Orat.* 8. 5. 1; Gellius, *Noct. Att.* 4. 20. 3–5; *D* 22. 5. 3. 2 *ad fin.* Cicero also has a long discussion on fidelity to oaths (*De Off.* 3. 26. 97—32. 115; cf. 1. 13. 39–40).
9. This verb in Latin is in the infinitive mode and depends upon an understood verb of ordering.
10. Ammianus Marcellinus (*Res Gestae*, 30. 4. 13) remarks that when courts continue rightly, they are temples of equity; when they are corrupted, they are deceptive and hidden pits.

11. *This* is the solemn obligation which must be sworn before the absent litigant's lawyer can plead for his principal (see *supra* sixth paragraph).

12. The editor suggests "Given" by analogy with other laws of the same date.

620. MANDATE OF JUSTINIAN I ON EPISCOPAL CELIBACY, 531
(*CI* 1. 3. 47)

Justinian threatens expulsion from the episcopate for such bishops as have wives or children, since apparently his previous prohibition against such persons being consecrated bishops (no. 579) had little effect.

The same emperor to John, praetorian prefect.[1]

We ordain that none should be selected for the episcopate, unless he should be suitable in other respects and good and neither should live with a wife nor should be a father of children, but instead of a wife should devote himself to the most holy Church and instead of children should have the entire Christian and orthodox people,[2] since he knows thus that from the beginning [3] we have made regulations about the succession of the most God-beloved bishops [4] and that with this intention a law has been published [4] and that persons who do or have done anything contrary to these regulations are unworthy of the episcopate entirely.[5]

For after this our constitution persons who have ventured to make any bishops or to become bishops contrary to its meaning neither shall be among the bishops nor shall remain in the churches, but, having been ejected from them, they shall give place to others of an ordination both genuine and pleasing to God in all respects.

Given on 29 July at Constantinople after the consulate of Lampadius and Orestes.

1. On John the Cappadocian, praetorian prefect of the East, whose enemies considered him a coarse monster, consult Bury, 2. 36–9, 55–9.
2. Perhaps this thought comes from the celibate St Paul, who calls the Corinthians his "beloved children" (1 Cor. 4. 14).
3. No. 579 was promulgated in 528, hence early in the emperor's reign.
4. No. 579.
5. Literally the "entire episcopate".

621. MANDATE OF JUSTINIAN I ON EPISCOPAL INTEREST IN GUARDIANSHIP, 531

(*CI* 1. 4. 30)

This constitution, partly adapted in *II* 1. 20. 5 (effective two years later), authorizes the co-operation of provincial bishops in the nomination of guardians for wards and directs that the records of such appointments should be filed in the local church's archives.

The same emperor to John, praetorian prefect.[1]

We ordain that in guardianships of minors—whether they should be of the first or of the second age of life [2] or even certain others,[3] to whom the law gives guardians—if the items of the property of minors should be only up to five hundred gold coins,[4] the appointment should not await the provinces' governors [5] or should not be encompassed with great costs, since perchance the governors are not resident in those cities wherein it happens that the guardianship proceeds, but that the appointments of the guardians should be before that city's defender or prefect (but in Alexandria before its judge),[6] along with its most God-beloved bishop or also public persons,[7] if the city should abound in these—a surety being given for the amount of the property according to the said persons' judgement and all other matters proceeding as have been usual in the case of the guardians and of the surety, since only the change of persons, before whom these things are done, is introduced from the present legislation because of the minors' advantage.[8]

Of course all matters should be done [9] according to the giving of two coins,[10] on account of which particularly this constitution has been instituted—a penalty being imposed, if anyone should have dared to take more or should have delayed to establish the guardianship through hope of greater gain, not only repaying thrice all which he should have taken, but also being removed from the administration itself.

Moreover, since the proposals of the guardians are made before the defender, the city's most God-beloved bishop also being present, we ordain that the transactions should be stored in the most holy church's very archives, so that there should be a perpetual record of the transaction and that the security from this for those who obtain the guardianship should not be lost.

In this great city [11] guardianships should be transacted [9] before only the most distinguished praetor, just as already it has been legislated.[12]

Given on 29 July at Constantinople after the consulate of Lampadius and Orestes.

1. Of the East.

2. Gaius (*ob. c.* 180) finds many forms of guardianship among Romans and quotes varying numbers reached by various jurists (*GI* 1. 188), but it is simpler to set the broad division between tutorship (*tutela*) and curatorship (*cura* or *curatio*). In general, for minors modern scholars distinguish two types: tutorship of children below the age of puberty (*tutela impuberum*), which was fourteen for boys and twelve for girls and corresponds with the text's *first age of life*, and curatorship of males and of females from the age of puberty till completion of their twenty-fifth year (*curatio minorum*), which is the text's *second age of life*.

3. Curatorship was established also for persons who were handicapped mentally (insane: *furiosi*; feeble-minded: *mente capti* or *non compotes mentis*) and physically (deaf: *surdi*; dumb: *muti*; incurably diseased: *morbo perpetuo laborantes*) and who were spendthrifts (*prodigi*).

While tutorship of women (*tutela mulierum*) ascended at least as far as the Twelve Tables (449 B.C.) except for Vestal virgins (*FIRA* 1. 37; *TT* 5. 1) and for women not under a father's power (*patria potestas*) or in a husband's control (*manus mariti*), with the result that during most of Roman history no Roman woman ever was legally her own mistress, for she had either a father or a husband or a guardian (as the case might be), yet by Justinian's time tutorship of females declined to the guardianship—under normal circumstances—of girls below the age of puberty.

Curatorship of women followed in all respects the analogy of curatorship of men.

4. The Latin version equates these (χρυσά) with solidi, on which see no. 433, n. 7.

5. This innovation runs counter to a constitution of the previous year (no. 608), where provincial governors both appoint curators in the absence of testamentary directions and ratify such nominations, as well as to *II* 1. 20. pr. and 1. 23. 3, where they appoint both tutors and curators, but appears to accord with *II* 1. 20. 5 in cases where up to five hundred solidi are involved and where almost the same language (in Latin) is used as is employed here (in Greek) later.

6. The Latin word *iuridicus* is introduced here amid the Greek. This same official received as early as the reign of Aurelius the power to appoint tutors (*D* 1. 20). This Alexandrian magistracy can be traced to the principate of Tiberius (14–37).

7. *II* 1. 20. 5 explains that these (δημόσια πρόσωπα in Greek text; *publicae personae* in Latin translation and in *II*) are magistrates (*magistratus*).

8. *II* 1. 20. 5 reads thus (after an explanation of how guardians are appointed [§ 4]): "However, curtailing by our constitution [probably this document] difficulties of this sort relating to [the appointing] persons, since the governors' order has not been awaited, we have arranged that, if the ward's or the adult's property is worth up to five hundred solidi, defenders of cities along with the

most religious bishop of the same city or before other public persons, that is, the magistrates, or the Alexandrian city's judge [cf. *supra* n. 6: *iuridicus*] should appoint tutors or curators—statutory security being furnished according to the said constitution's standard: of course, at the risk of those who receive it."

9. This predicate is a participle in the Greek construction of the genitive absolute, for the sentence has no principal finite verb.

10. The Latin version equates these (νομίσματα) with solidi, on which see no. 433, n. 7.

11. Constantinople.

12. According to *CT* 6. 4. 16 (dated 359 and repeated in *CI* 1. 39. 1) the praetor appointed both tutors and curators. By *CT* 3. 17. 3 (dated 389 and repeated in *CI* 5. 33. 1) the urban prefect, assisted by ten senators and by the praetor presiding over suits pertaining to tutorship, selected tutors as well as curators. Pursuant to *CT* 3. 17. 4 (dated 390 and repeated in *CI* 5. 35. 2) the urban prefect, aided by the praetor who presided over appointment of tutors, chose guardians for minors whose mothers refused tutorship and preferred (second) marriage and when no statutory tutors were available (*CI* omits last clause).

Presumably the most recent law governed the case and, pursuant to the then almost 1,000-year-old principle—which tradition ascribes to the *Twelve Tables* (*FIRA* 1. 73; *TT* 12. 5)—that the latest law invalidates earlier enactments inconsistent with it, Justinian refers here to *CI* 5. 35. 2 (= *CT* 3. 17. 4), which gives the praetor some power in selecting guardians for minors, although the urban prefect appears to be his superior in this situation.

622. MANDATE OF JUSTINIAN I ON HERETICS' EVIDENCE IN COURT, 531

(*CI* 1. 5. 21)

This statute prevents a heretic from witnessing in a lawsuit wherein an orthodox person is a litigant, while it allows heretics (with a few classes of these debarred) and Jews to give evidence in cases to which such fellow-believers are parties. It excepts, however, testimony from heretics required in contests over wills and contracts.

The same Augustus to John, praetorian prefect.[1]

Since many judges in settling litigations have bothered us, because they are in need of our response,[2] that it should be related to them what must be determined about heretical witnesses, as to whether their testimonies should be accepted or should be rejected, we ordain that against the orthodox litigants to no heretic or also to persons who cherish the Jewish superstition should be mutual participation in testimonies, whether the one or the other party is orthodox.

Among themselves, however, to heretics or to Jews, when they shall have decided that there must be litigation, we grant an intermingled compact and that witnesses suitable to litigants also should be introduced—these, of course, having been excepted: whom either Manichaean madness (of which it is very manifest that Borborians also are a part) or pagan superstition engages, no less Samaritans and whoso are not unlike those, that is, Montanists and Tascodrogitans and Ophitans, to whom every legal action has been forbidden in view of the similarity of their guilt. But also indeed for these, that is, Manichaeans and Borborians and pagans [3] and Samaritans and Montanists and Tascodrogitans and Ophitans, we ordain that all testimony, just as also other lawful intercourses, should be forbidden; but we wish that for other heretics only judicial testimonies against the orthodox, according to what has been established, should be inhibited.

But their testamentary testimonies and what they adopt in last wills or in contracts we permit because of the usefulness of necessary use without any distinction, lest the means of proofs should be straitened.

Given on 29 July at Constantinople after the consulate of the most distinguished Lampadius and the most distinguished Orestes.

1. Of the East.
2. See no. 218, n. 5.
3. See no. 148, n. 4.

623. MANDATE OF JUSTINIAN I ON CLERICAL INTEREST IN PROPERTY LEFT TO PRISONERS AND PAUPERS AS HEIRS, 531

(CI 1. 3. 48)

By this law, when captives or poor persons are made heirs to an estate, the bishop and the ecclesiastical steward or the warden of a hostel—as the case may be—of the decedent's city must qualify as heirs in the interest of the testator's unspecified heirs and must not derive any personal profit from their administration of the property. The statute also directs that the portion to which the heir-executor legally is entitled as an inducement to enter as heir must not be claimed, for the entire estate must be devoted to the testator's pious intention.

Pitra prints (2. 494) a late Greek version of this law.

The same Augustus to John, praetorian prefect.[1]

If anyone for the purpose of shunning the Falcidian Law,[2] when he desires to leave his entire substance for redemption of prisoners, shall have written these very prisoners as heirs, lest his decision to have left it to—as it were—indefinite persons as instituted heirs should seem to be oppugned, we order that such an institution by him for the respect to piety should be valid and should not be rejected.[3]

But if anyone shall have written the poor as heirs and if a definite almshouse or definite churches should not be found to be the poor, concerning whom the testator had thought, but by an indefinite term the poor shall have been instituted heirs, in like manner we also decree that an institution of this sort should be valid.

And if indeed he shall have written prisoners as heirs, the bishop and the steward [4] of the city wherein the testator is known to cherish his home [5] and to dwell should undertake the inheritance and by all means the inheritance should result in favour of redemption of prisoners, whether through annual returns or through sale of movables or of self-movable [6] properties—absolutely no profit from this being left either to the steward or to the bishop or to the sacrosanct church. For if on this account retirement has been made by a specified heir, so that the Falcidian proportion [2] is not introduced, in what way is it tolerable for this property which comes in a sacred category to be lessened by the Falcidian [2] or another pretext? [7]

Moreover, where indiscriminately the poor have been written as heirs, there the hostel of the city by all means should acquire [8] the inheritance and the distribution of the patrimony to the sick [9] should be made [8] by the manager of the hostel, according to what we have established in the case of prisoners:[10] either through division of annual returns or through sale of movables or self-movables,[6] in order that immovable properties may be bought from these and an annual living may accrue to the sick.[9] For who is poorer than persons who have been straitened by lack and, having been removed into a hostel and working with their own bodies, cannot effect for themselves a necessary living?

By all means permission must be given both in the first and in the second case to bring an action and to exact debts, that these may be expended for the prisoners or for the sick.[9] For if we have given to them the legal right and the name [11] of heirs, without, however, the emolument of the Falcidian Law,[2] it is necessary for them both to exact debts and to reply to creditors.

But if, moreover, in a city there should be richer hostels or almshouses, lest the giving of the monies should seem uncertain, then to that hostel or almshouse which is discerned to be poorer should be assigned [8] the said properties or monies—this obviously being judged by the most reverend bishop of the places and by the clergymen stationed under him.

But if no hostel should be found in the city, then according to the ordinance concerning prisoners the sacrosanct church's steward at the time or bishop should accept the inheritance and without the Falcidian proportion [2] the said monies should be distributed to the poor who in the city are either utterly mendicant or lacking other sustenance.

Nevertheless we ordain that all these matters have a place,[12] when the nomination of a definite hostel or of a definite almshouse or of a definite church has not ensued from the testator, but his meaning is indefinite. But if he has had regard toward a definite venerable house, we ordain that the inheritance or the legacy should belong only to it— no Falcidian proportion [2] intervening even in this case.

Moreover in all situations of this sort the administrators of sacrosanct properties should expect celestial anger, if they shall have acquired for themselves any profit whatsoever from managements of this sort or if they shall have perceived that this is committed by another person and are not eager to correct by gravest penalty and threat what has been done wrongly.

Given on 23 August at Constantinople after the consulate of the most distinguished Lampadius and the most distinguished Orestes.

1. Of the East.
2. See no. 392, n. 4.
3. The point is that a Roman will could name as heir only a citizen and that a Roman's citizenship was in abeyance, though without prejudice, during his captivity. If a testator then named Roman prisoners of war as his heirs, his entire estate would be considered a legacy and, this being a violation of the Falcidian Law, his will would be invalid—save for Justinian's intervention here. See no. 218, n. 6.
4. That is, the steward of the episcopal church.
5. See no. 242, n. 6.
6. Such as livestock.
7. That is, the ecclesiastics (bishop and/or steward) must serve as heirs in such cases and may not retire from such service on the ground that denial of personal profit from such estates is tantamount to not receiving the Falcidian fourth, on which see no. 392, n. 4.

Sacerdotal intervention in disposition of estates ascends into Roman antiquity, for the pagan pontiffs interested themselves in instituting rules for performance of rites imposed upon those to whom property passed by will (Cicero, *De Leg.* 2. 19. 47—21. 53).

8. This is an infinitive in Latin, for the sentence lacks a principal verb in a finite mode.

9. Or perhaps figuratively "the unfortunate", for a hostel (*xenon* or *xenodochium*) is not necessarily a hospital (*nosocomium*), though doubtless sick persons are discoverable in a lodging for strangers. Sometimes little distinction between the two institutions was made in late legal Latin, though (as indicated) separate words (transliterated from Greek) for each were used.

10. That is, as the bishop (or the steward) acts in the case of a will leaving all the estate to prisoners, so the guest-master of a hostel acts as executor in the interest of the poor who are named heirs.

11. Perhaps a hendiadys: "the legal name".

12. That is, have pertinence or apply.

624. MANDATE OF JUSTINIAN I ON CLERICAL WILLS, 531

(*CI* 1. 3. 49)

To clarify the question whether clergy in major orders can dispose of their personal property by will, while their fathers are living and ordinarily must be mentioned in their wills (when their children own property outright), Justinian legislates that such clergy may devise their own property with full freedom as to whom they wish to bequeath it.

The same Augustus to John, praetorian prefect.[1]

When by the Leonine Law [2] it has been conceded to the most reverend bishops and priests and deacons to have a peculium as if obtained by military service,[3] with this added, that they can dispose of it by will, there was doubt if wills of this sort ought to be attacked on the complaint of contrariety to one's duty,[4] when the same question had arisen concerning all persons who have gained peculia [3] of this sort.

Accordingly we ordain that to the most reverend bishops and priests and deacons, who possess such a peculium (that is, as if obtained by military service),[3] concerning only the properties which belong to a peculium as if obtained by military service [3] not only should be permission to compose last wills according, however, to the laws, because it descends from the Leonine Constitution,[2] but also their last wills, made concerning only these properties, should not be subject at all to anything [5] on the complaint of contrariety to one's duty.[4]

Given on 1 September at Constantinople after the consulate of Lampadius and Orestes.[4]

1. Of the East.
2. No. 514.
3. The phrase *peculium . . . service* is *peculium quasi castrense*. A son under his father's legal control (*filiusfamilias*) gradually secured some proprietary rights in the long history of Roman law. Either in the last years of the moribund Republic and possibly *c.* 45 B.C., when Gaius Julius Caesar was dictator, or under Emperor Titus (79–81) a soldier *filiusfamilias* was permitted to be absolute owner of what was called *peculium castrense*—what property he got by gift from his kin for his outfit or would not have obtained save on military service. As absolute owner, he could will such property whithersoever he wished (*II* 2. 12. pr.).

By successive statutes, starting apparently with Constantine I in 326 (*CT* 6. 35. 15 or 6. 36. 1 = *CI* 12. 30. 1), this military privilege was extended to civilians, chiefly to officials and finally to clergy in major orders (no. 514). Since property acquired by civilians could not be considered as obtained by military service, the adverb *quasi* was prefixed to the adjective *castrense*—a linguistic point which solved a legal problem.

As the second paragraph of this document shows, Justinian allows bishops and priests and deacons to will their *peculia quasi castrensia*, which they first obtained under Leo I's law in 472 (no. 514). See also *II* 2. 11. 6 and for other types of peculia see no. 337, n. 6.

4. A will could be impugned on the ground that it was contrary to the testator's pious (in the Latin sense) duty, if he disinherited his parents or his children or in certain cases his brothers and his sisters. It then was called a *testamentum inofficiosum* and the attack on it was termed *querella testamenti inofficiosi* or (as here) *querella inofficiosi* [sc. *testamenti*].

While Justinian, following earlier legislative enactments, confirmed the doctrine that ascendants could attack a descendant's will on the accusation that it was undutiful, he revoked the agnatic connection and extended the complaint to include germane (but not uterine) brothers and sisters (*II* 2. 18. 1).

In the present document's second paragraph the emperor excludes the superior clergy's wills from the charge of invalidity, if they have failed to mention parents and brothers and sisters (no account is taken of children, for such clergy were supposed to be childless).

5. The text is corrupt, but this seems to be the sense.

625. MANDATE OF JUSTINIAN I ON CLERICAL LAWSUITS, 531

(CI 2. 3. 29)

This statute compels a clergyman to stand on his own decision (apparently freely made by him when entering into a contract) to plead in a secular court, the point being that, if his agent had made such an agreement, the clergyman could renounce his agent's act and could plead in an ecclesiastical court.

Justinian repeats this law (CI 1. 3. 50) in much abbreviated form and pertaining only to clergymen.

Emperor Justinian Augustus to John, praetorian prefect.[1]

If anyone in composing a written compact shall have confessed that he will not use the prescription [2] of the forum [3] because of the belt [4] of his governmental service [5] or rank or even [6] the priesthood's [7] prerogative, although previously it was doubted whether the said writing ought to hold and he who has made this pact ought not to go against his own agreement or permission ought to be afforded to him to depart indeed from the writing and to employ his own legal right,[8] we ordain that it should be permitted to none to go against his own pacts and to deceive the contractors.

For if by the praetor's edict itself agreed pacts, which have been entered neither contrary to laws nor by malicious deception, must be observed by all means,[9] why also in this case are pacts not valid,[10] when another [11] rule of ancient law is that all persons have permission to renounce those things which have been introduced on their behalf? [12]

Accordingly all our judges should observe this in lawsuits and such observation should pertain to petty judges and to chosen[13] referees and arbiters, who should know that, if they shall have been negligent, they also should be understood to make the cause their own.[14]

Given on 1 September at Constantinople after the consulate of the most distinguished Lampadius and the most distinguished Orestes.

1. Of the East.

2. CI 1. 3. 50 reads *prescription* for "proscription" here and this reading is preferred.

3. That is, a secular court in the public plaza of a community, where lawsuits commonly were conducted. See no. 334, n. 5.

4. See no. 476, n. 39.

5. See no. 186, n. 4.

6. CI 1. 3. 50 omits the words between *of* and *the*, thus restricting the reason to priestly prerogative.

7. See no. 158, n. 1.

8. *CI* 1. 3. 50 omits the concessive clause.

9. *FIRA* 1. 339 gives this reconstructed part of the urban praetor's *edictum perpetuum*. According to it the praetor took cognizance of agreed pacts which were not only not contrary to laws but also not contrary to plebiscites, senatus-consults, imperial edicts and decrees and in which no evasion was evident.

All arrangements and covenants recognized and enforced by actions at law the Romans called *contractus* (contracts); agreements not directly enforceable by law but recognizable only as a valid ground for defence they called *pacta* (pacts). Sometimes ere the Ciceronian era (106–44 B.C.) the praetor incorporated into his annual edict the statement that a pact could be pleaded as a good defence against an action on any obligation, whether contractual or delictual.

10. All of this paragraph to this point *CI* 1. 3. 50 omits, joining what follows with the preceding paragraph and, of course, reading it as declarative and not as interrogative.

11. Omitted in the short version.

12. Professor Clyde Pharr suggests in a private letter that Justinian probably was thinking of the equivalent phrase in *D* 4. 4. 41, where Julian, the final editor of the praetorian edict, says that "to everyone it is permitted to disregard those things which have been introduced on his behalf", and that Cicero (106–43 B.C.) evidently was acquainted with this legal principle, since he asks "Will it not be permitted to me not to use that which the law has conferred on me for my own benefit?" (*In Verr.* 2. 1. 9. 25).

CI 1. 3. 50 substitutes for the next paragraph the following: "And we ordain that this general law should obtain in all cases which not yet have been settled by judicial sentence or by amicable agreement."

For the two preceding paragraphs Pitra prints (2. 537) a late Greek paraphrase: "If anyone in composing written contracts shall confess that he has not used the prescription on account of the priesthood's prerogative, we ordain that it should not be possible for him, going against his own pacts, also to deceive the contractor, according to the ancient law's rule, which says that all persons have permission to disregard those things which have been introduced on their behalf. And we ordain that this general law should obtain in all cases not settled either by judicial sentence or by amicable agreement."

13. By litigants.

14. For a judge "to make a cause his own" (*litem suam facere*) was a serious matter, which in the republican period could be punished capitally (*FIRA* 1. 64; *TT* 9. 3) and in the imperial era could lead to an action for damages at the suit of the injured litigant. Such a situation arose usually from bribery or from partiality, occasionally from non-appearance on the day appointed for trial, here from negligence.

626. MANDATE OF JUSTINIAN I ON HERETICS AS SOLDIERS' HEIRS, 531

(*CI* 1. 5. 22)

Justinian extends to heretics the inability to participate in wills made by soldiers.

The same Augustus to John, praetorian prefect.[1]
We command that our divine sanction by which we have ordered none who is fettered by heretics' error to accept an inheritance or a legacy or a trust [2] should have a place also in soldiers' last wills, whether these are witnessed by common or by military law.[3]

Given on 1 September after the consulate of the most distinguished Lampadius and the most distinguished Orestes.

1. Of the East.
2. Probably no. 575.
3. According to the law commonly in use (*commune ius*) seven witnesses were required for a will (whether written or oral) executed privately, i.e. not before a magistrate. But this and other rules regarding wills were relaxed for soldiers on active duty (*GI* 2. 109; *II* 2. 11. pr.). Such exemptions began under Augustus.

627. MANDATE OF JUSTINIAN I ON EPISCOPAL INTEREST IN DETENTION AND IN DEBT, 531

(*CI* 7. 40. 2)

In a provincial governor's absence a provincial bishop is authorized by this constitution, which appears abbreviatedly in *CI* 1. 4. 31, to accept an owner's or a creditor's petition for action on the plea that under certain circumstances a person detains the former's property or owes the latter's loan.

The same Augustus to John, praetorian prefect.[1]
That we may take counsel more perfectly for all persons and that his opponent's absence or power or infancy [2] may harm none absolutely, but that there may be some distinction between slothful and vigilant persons, we [3] ordain that, if ever shall have been absent he who detains [4] another person's property or what is obligated to a creditor and if the property's owner or the creditor desires to propose an accusation and if there should not be permission for him, because his

opponent who detains the property is absent or is afflicted because of infancy or insanity and has no tutor or curator or is established in great [5] power, to him should be given permission to approach the governor or to present to him a petition and to bring this matter into his complaint within the appointed times [6] and to make an interruption of time [7]—and that this should suffice for the fullest interruption.[8]

However, if in no way he shall have been able to approach the governor, at least he should go to the bishop of the places or to the defender of the municipality [9] and should hasten to manifest his wish in writing.[10] However, if either the governor or the bishop or the defender shall have been absent, it should be permitted for him also to declare it publicly where the possessor has his domicile—whether by subscription of recorders or, if the municipality should not have recorders, with subscription of three witnesses—and this should suffice for all temporal interruption—whether it should be for a triennium or for long time or for thirty or forty years.[11]

All other rules which have been established concerning prescription of long time or periods of thirty or forty years [11]—whether by ancient framers of laws or by our Majesty—shall endure [12] in their own strength.

Given on 18 October [13] at Constantinople after the consulate of the most distinguished Lampadius and the most distinguished Orestes.

1. Of the East.
2. In Roman law *infantia* ends at the completion of a child's seventh year. As the meaning of the word shows, a child was considered not to have the ability to speak for himself (in a legal sense); therefore, he could not act for himself legally and whatever could be done for him must be done by his guardian (*tutor*).
3. Here begins the shorter version.
4. While in Roman law possession is occupation of an object with intention to hold it as its owner, detention is mere occupation without the overtone of holding the object to become its owner. Mere occupation generally has no legal remedy to protect the detainer, the great exception being a tenant of land, who cannot possess, since his intention is not to become an owner, but who, if evicted from his farm, can claim the magisterial interdict *quod vi aut clam* (because by force or secretly) to regain his crops (*D* 43. 24. 12).
5. The shorter version substitutes "greatest".
6. That is, within the statute of limitations for starting an action at law. See no. 65, n. 6 *ad fin.*
7. For the divestitive aspects of prescription see no. 65, n. 6 *ad fin.*
8. The shorter version omits the last nine words.
9. The shorter version omits *or . . . municipality*.

10. Here ends the shorter version.
11. On the various limits for prescription see no. 65, n. 6 *ad fin*.
12. This principal verb is in the Latin construction of the ablative absolute, although the sentence (as in English) is printed independently.
13. The shorter version gives 1 October, which date the Latin editor believes to be incorrect.

628. MANDATE OF JUSTINIAN I ON CLERICAL EXEMPTION FROM GUARDIANSHIP, 531

(*CI* 1. 3. 51)

The emperor exempts from the service of tutorship and of curatorship the higher clergy as well as monks, provided that they continue diligent in their conduct of divine services.

Pitra prints (2. 529) a late Greek version of this law.

The same Augustus to John, praetorian prefect.[1]

We ordain generally that all most reverend bishops and also priests or deacons and subdeacons and particularly monks, although they are not clerics, by their own right should have immunity from tutorship—whether testamentary or statutory or appointive [2]—and that these persons should be free not only from tutorship, but also from curatorship, not only of wards and of adults, but also of the insane and of the dumb and of the deaf and of other persons, to whom by the old laws tutors or curators are given.[3]

However, we ordain that those clergymen and monks who continue in the sacrosanct churches or monasteries, not wandering nor indolent concerning the divine services,[4] should have a benefit of this kind, when we grant to them the benefit because of this very reason: when all other services have been abandoned, they should adhere to Almighty God's services.

And we ordain that this should obtain not only in Old Rome or in this royal city,[5] but also in the entire earth, wherever the Christians' name is cherished.

Given on 1 November after the consulate of the most distinguished Lampadius and the most distinguished Orestes.

1. Of the East.
2. Testamentary guardians were named by a testator's will (so *GI* 1. 144

and *II* 1. 13. 3, though in *GI* 1. 154 they are appointive); statutory guardians performed their office by virtue of the provisions of some statute, particularly one of the *Twelve Tables* (FIRA 1. 39–40; *TT* 5. 6–7), and served only when there were no testamentary guardians (*GI* 1. 155; *II* 1. 15. pr.); appointive or dative guardians were chosen by magistrates in cases where neither a will nominated a guardian nor agnates could act as guardians (*GI* 1. 185; *II* 1. 20. pr.).

It is interesting to note that only the second type of guardians was required to post bond for proper performance, the theory being that one named by the testator was approved by him as honourable and diligent (see no. 608, n. 6), that one selected by the magistrate satisfied the selector on the score of suitability, that one compelled by statute to serve might not necessarily be of great responsibility, since he could be simply the nearest kinsman available.

3. Especially in the *Twelve Tables* (FIRA 1. 37–40; *TT* 5. 1, 6, 7). See no. 621, nn. 2 and 3.

Though Justinian here frees the clergy from actual guardianship and though the *Constitutiones Apostolorum* (8. 47. 7) penalize all higher clergymen undertaking secular cares, especially bishops who enter public administration (8. 47. 81), yet many exceptions occurred even under Justinian, who permitted episcopal interest in e.g. disputed loans (no. 582), municipal matters (no. 606), even guardianship (nos. 608, 621, 635), prenuptial settlements by lunatics' children (no. 610), payment of rent (no. 632).

4. A variant reading is "mysteries", on which see no. 75, n. 42.

5. Constantinople, which is missing from the subscription.

629. MANDATE OF JUSTINIAN I ON CLERICAL CANDIDATES, ON EX-CLERGYMEN, AND ON ADMISSION TO ASCETIC LIFE, 531

(CI 1. 3. 52)

This directive touches four chief topics: (1) municipal senators and cohortalines [1] must not enter the sacred ministry; (2) clergymen and monks who leave the Church for secular vocations must become municipal senators and must perform public services; (3) parents must not disinherit their children who embrace the ascetical life; (4) how marriage settlements must be disposed, when either spouse selects the religiously solitary life.

The same emperor to John, praetorian prefect.[2]

We ordain that absolutely hereafter neither a municipal senator nor a cohortaline[1] should become a bishop or a priest—this law not touching persons who previously have been worthy of such priesthood[3]—but absolutely hereafter none of the said station should ascend to the said priesthoods,[4] and especially if already he has happened to perform public services or to submit to orders pertaining to cohortalines.[1]

For it would not be just that he who has been bred in violent exactions and in faults which on this account—as is likely—supervene should lately be a cohortaline[1] or a municipal senator and should do the bitterest things of all,[5] but now should be ordained a priest who admonishes and teaches instructions about benevolence and poverty,[6] unless from infancy and not yet emerged from adolescence he has happened to be reckoned among the most devout monks and to remain in this rank; for then we permit him both to become a priest and to advance to the episcopate—it being obvious that, whenever such a thing should happen and he should appear worthy of the priesthood,[4] he then shall have permission to persevere in the priesthood[3] and to be free from public service, furnishing the fourth part of all his property either to the municipal senate[7] and to the public treasury (according to the law lately established by us on fourth parts[8]) or to the public treasury alone, if indeed he happened to be of cohortalinian[1] station. But if he should have been ranked among the most devout archimandrites and should have remained among them, thus also to him we give the immunity of his station, provided that he furnishes then the fourth part of his property (exactly as we have said), but otherwise we neither allow him to be ordained nor permit an ordainer to do any such thing.

Your Excellency should know[9] that these matters must be observed by all the most God-beloved bishops, who keep in view a penalty concerning the priesthood[3] itself, if they should have done any such thing, in addition to the fact that the person ordained should not enjoy the priesthood,[3] even if formerly he held any rank of the priesthood[4] whatever, but should be reckoned among private persons and should perform public services, to which previously he was subjected.

And all these matters we wish to prevail for the future time, because, moreover, these have been devised first by us—this law not touching absolutely (exactly as we have said) persons who once have deserved such priesthood,[3] but who have permission through substitutes to perform public services according to the ordinance of Theodosius and Valentinian of pious lot, which had been written in reply to Thomas.[10]

Besides these things, we ordain that this also should be just and should prevail and should be customary, which, established from of old and customary, we know not how has been disregarded. For we have remembered reading an ordinance of Arcadius and Honorius of pious lot, which desires clergymen, if they should have happened to neglect their own order [11] and should have entered into any armed military service whatsoever or, when deposed by the most God-beloved bishops, should have dared to serve in the army, to be expelled from the military service which they have taken and to be surrendered to the cities' municipal senates, rendering service to the State hereafter, since they have renounced the Lord God's divine service in answer to the military service's way of life.[12]

And by this our law we ordain that these matters should prevail, ordering them straightway and immediately to become municipal senators of that city whence they are, unless the city should have an excessive abundance of municipal senators, in that case then of a neighbouring or even a remoter city as far as the next province, where most particularly a lack of municipal senators exists. But if they—as is likely—should be hidden, to the municipal senators we give permission to enter immediately upon the properties belonging to them and to possess these and to satisfy themselves thence according to law.

Therefore we ordain that in the case of the most devout clergymen of whatever rank these matters should prevail in perpetuity, wishing even that the law in the case of persons who already have offended should prevail, since it also existed earlier.

But also since we have found a certain ordinance which speaks about monks and desires them not to abandon their own monasteries nor to throw cities into confusion (and which some persons suspect had been ordained for a certain time),[13] we, having taken thence the occasion, have believed that this ought both to be more authoritative and to be revised for all time: so that hereafter to none of the most devout monks should be permission to do any such thing and to abandon the monastic role [14] and to engage in some kind of governmental service [15] or belt [16] or dignity or to pursue a life in the law-courts and to prefer and to recognize human occupations to God's ministry. And whoever does any such thing shall be surrendered to the municipal senate of that city whence he is or of another (just as we previously have said), so that, if he should abound in money, he should sustain monetary public services, especially the ones relating to a corporation—and therein permission exists for the municipal senates (exactly as we have said), if they should be hidden, to seize their properties and to satisfy themselves according to law.

But in all the cases, in which from such causes we order the municipal senates to take something, we wish the municipal senators to acquire a half part not in gold, but in immovable property, whether already existent or to be bought (according to the law previously made current by us), and to pay a half part to your Excellency's common fund,[17] so that also your office [18] may provide vigilantly that such a matter should not escape notice, but, as soon as it occurs, that the appropriate remedy should be made about this matter, unless now indeed such persons voluntarily should have discarded their governmental service [15] or, in short, whatever role they have and should have returned again and actively and really to the monastic life and should have striven to be registered among the most devout clergymen. For if they should have done this within one year from which our present divine law has been decreed, we waive the penalty for them, because we consider that the correction from their asceticism suffices for them.

And these matters we wish to prevail for the future time, since we do not leave outside the said penalty those persons who, having become monks, have done any such thing even since our reign. For, blushing partly because of benevolence and partly because of the time, we waive what previously occurred, since previously it had not been established clearly by law.

Moreover we ordain this: that, whether a father or a mother or any other person as a result of childlessness should have enjoined restoration or substitution upon any persons, whether male or female, but if the latter should not have chosen to enter into a marriage because of the ascetic life, such restorations or substitutions should be voided and they should have licence to devote to whatever way of life (a pious one, however) they wish the property which comes to them and either to spend it while living or to bequeath it when dying, just as if something should have been bequeathed to them under the condition of their procreation of children, and they ought to have this property without compulsion to procreate children.

And we extend the said legislation both to women who live a life of virginity and to the most devout clergymen who have been forbidden absolutely to marry and we give to God this grant, which is worthy of our times.

Moreover we ordain that, whether a man should have wished to enter into a solitary life or a woman, after she has left her husband, should have entered into asceticism, this should not furnish a cause of penalty for them, but that they should receive by all means their own property, so that there should be permission for a wife to take her dowry and for a husband to take his donation before marriage,[19] but that one should claim profit from this not according to separation as a result of repudiation [20] or it should remain with him who has not renounced his wife, but according to an agreement as a result of death, just as departure of one withdrawing from mutual living seems death in relation to marriage, since one is utterly useless to one's spouse; and there should be permission [21] for the one who has chosen asceticism to withdraw for the future after having taken that very amount which the import of the dotal covenants should have shown to be due as a result of the agreements after death, so that, however, the wife should not dare to look toward another marriage on account of the uncertainty of parturition, before a year has passed; but if some such event should occur, then the notice of divorce according to the so-called mutual consent [22] should be sent by the person who has not chosen asceticism and one should do thus whatever one wishes (the profits coming to one according to the aforesaid manner)—obviously what is profit as a result of such a cause being conserved by all means for the common children (if there should be some) of this marriage, if either the wife or the husband should have persevered in the previous marriage.

Given on 27 November at Constantinople after the consulate of Lampadius and Orestes.

1. See no. 320, n. 5.
2. Of the East.
3. See no. 158, n. 1.
4. Here the word is ἱερατεία, which is synonymous with ἱερωσύνη, on which see no. 158, n. 1.
5. While this may be an exaggerated description of the "unrighteousness" of civil officials' acts in performance of their duty, yet Justinian apparently allows no opportunity for conversion and prohibits any "reformed" official from entering the priesthood.
6. With this thought compare St Jerome's complaint about those who have come from paganism to Christianity: "Yesterday in the amphitheatre, today in the Church; in the evening at the circus, in the morning at the altar; formerly a supporter of stage-players, now a consecrator of virgins" (*Ep.* 69. 9 = *PL* 22. 663). But St Jerome was noted for his command of language rather than for his love of charity (see Introd., n. 54 *ad med.*).
7. The Greek has "senators": concrete for abstract.
8. Perhaps this law is that assigned to *CI* 10. 35. 4 (dated 528–31), as editors conjecture.
9. This is a participle in Greek, for the sentence lacks a principal predicate in a finite mode.
10. No. 436.
11. See no. 325, n. 6.
12. Perhaps no. 307, though it contains nothing about clergy serving in the army.
13. Perhaps no. 512.
14. Or "habit [of dress]".
15. See no. 186, n. 4.
16. As the badge of office, on which see no. 476, n. 39. The infinitive is

zeugmatic and must be altered to "to wear", unless there is a hendiadys and for *belt or dignity* we should translate "office with a belt".

17. Literally "table", from the ancient practice of bankers and money-changers sitting at tables (especially in eastern countries).

18. See no. 311, n. 5.

19. On the antenuptial gift see no. 517, n. 2.

20. The type of divorce (*repudium*, here transliterated into Greek) wherein no mutual consent appeared.

21. Repeated in translation to unite the thought in this overlong sentence, such as lawyers love.

22. Literally "with good grace" (*bona gratia*), inserted in Latin amid the Greek words.

Such a divorce never encountered interference from the State until Justinian's reign, when it was permitted on only three grounds: (1) impotency of husband, (2) desire of either spouse to embrace the ascetical life (as here), (3) capitivity of either spouse (*N* 117. 12; dated 542). As a penalty for such divorce not based on the above reasons Justinian later set forfeiture of all property and lifelong confinement in a cenobitic community—of the forfeited fortunes the monastery and the convent receiving one-third, if descendants survive, or two-thirds, if only ascendants exist, or all, if neither ascendants nor descendants are living (*N* 134. 11; dated 556).

630. MANDATE OF JUSTINIAN I ON IMPERIAL PROPERTY FOR ECCLESIASTICAL PURPOSES, 531

(*CI* 7. 37. 3)

Of this lengthy law touching rights of persons who accept or purchase property from the imperial treasury only the concluding sections (3–5), which treat title to properties donated or sold or assigned to ecclesiastical institutions, are translated. Justinian rules that no action to dispute the title after the lapse of a four-year period should be valid. The emperor applies the law especially to donations made by Theodora, his empress, and exempts her from rendering any account for the disposition of vast resources at her disposal.

Emperor Justinian Augustus to Florus, count of the private estates and curator of the imperial household,[1] and to the illustrious Peter, curator of the most serene Augusta's[2] imperial household,[1] and also to the illustrious Macedonius himself, curator of the imperial household.[1]

... Therefore, because we know that we ourselves as well as the most serene Augusta,[2] our consort, already to various persons have donated and have sold and by other titles have assigned many things—and especially to sacrosanct churches and to hostels and to almshouses and to bishops and to monks [3] and to other innumerable persons—and that the same liberality has been accomplished from our or our most serene consort's [2] substance, we ordain also that these persons should have by firm legal right what they have gotten, so that no action indeed should be started against them, but that within a quadrennium to be calculated from the present day should lie open to all persons an approach to start their actions on the said properties against our divine households—they knowing that, when the aforesaid quadrennium has ended, not any return against our households should be reserved for them.

For when the Augustan fortune [4] has obtained many privileges both in donations having every firmness without publication of records [5] and concerning properties which for the occasion the most serene emperor should have donated at the steadfast marriage to the divine Augusta [6] or he himself should get through title of donation from the most serene Augusta,[7] that directly the donation should remain full—with no other time of affirmation to be expected—so that also this should seem to be an imperial privilege. For why should not they have a prerogative worthy of their own fortune, when they labour day and night by their own counsels and by their own labours for the whole world? [8]

And therefore these things, which for the Augustan honour [4] and the security of persons accepting properties our Eternity has established, your Sublimity as well as all our other judges should hasten to observe as about to be valid from that time from which by divine command we have assumed the imperial lappets.[9]

Given on 27 November at Constantinople after the consulate of the most distinguished Lampadius and the most distinguished Orestes.

1. The curators of the imperial household (*curatores dominicae [divinae] domus*) apparently were instituted by Justinian to replace the count of the sacred patrimony (*comes sacri patrimonii*), an official established by Anastasius I. Their function, similar to that of the count of the private estates (*comes rerum privatarum*), was to administer domains acquired by the crown either recently or in the future, most of which had come from the confiscation of the property of Zeno (492) and from that of Isaurian rebels (492–8).

2. Theodora, on whom see no. 650, n. 4 *ad fin*.

3. The wide range of ecclesiastical persons and institutions recipient of the imperial bounty testifies to the tendency at this time both to safeguard and to increase property held by all types of pious institutions. Vasiliev (574) sees in

Justinian's epoch "the most important step in the process of the formation in the Empire of the large church and monastery landownership", which, in the case of monasteries at least, created monastic fiefs and principalities.

4. A reference to Theodora.

5. That is, without having been protocolized documentarily.

6. Justinian married Theodora sometime before Justin's death in 527, but after that of Justin's consort Euphemia, whose opposition to her nephew's marriage (see no. 650, n. 4), persisting till her death (the year is unknown) before Justin's, failed to prevent her nephew from lavishing large sums of money upon his mistress (Procopius, *Hist. Arc.* 9. 31).

7. The sentence lacks a principal verb. Probably "we ordain" should be inserted here. The reference is to Theodora, who is exempted from the old rule forbidding inter-marital donations (see no. 31, n. 4).

8. Theodora's intervention in public affairs was notorious, if we can believe Procopius, who is our principal authority for her political activity (*Hist. Arc.* 10. 13-14, 11. 40, 15. 9-10, 17. 27).

Vasiliev (150-1) vouches for the fact that John of Ephesus, a contemporary Monophysitic historian, calls Theodora "a Christ-loving woman filled with zeal" and "the most Christian empress, sent by God in difficult times to protect the persecuted", for she favoured the Monophysites. However, his reference to *PO* 18. 634, 677, 679, does not confirm this claim—so far as the English version of the Syriac original is concerned. It is possible, of course, that E. W. Brooks, the English translator, has failed to find there these characterizations, which Vasiliev's knowledge of Syriac has compelled him to cite.

9. See no. 520, n. 6.

631. MANDATE OF JUSTINIAN I ON RESCISSION OF THE CLAUDIAN SENATUSCONSULT, 531-4

(CI 7. 24. 1)

Justinian relies upon what he calls "the religion of my times" (by which doubtless Christianity is meant) to repeal the *Senatus Consultum Claudianum*, an enactment of the Senate in 52 during Claudius' reign (41-54) and hence so known. Among its provisions [1] Justinian abrogates (here and in *II* 3. 12. 1) [2] the last surviving clause, which by judicial sentence deprived a freewoman of her freedom and of her property, if she had persisted in cohabitation with a slave whose master had withheld his consent to such intercourse and had warned her thrice.[3] From another of Justinian's statutes (*CI* 11. 48. 24), part of which parallels the present law, it appears that serfs as well as slaves had taken advantage of such liaisons.

Emperor Justinian Augustus to Hermogenes, master of the offices.

When in our times, in which we have sustained many labours for our subjects' freedom, we have believed it to be quite impious that certain women should be cheated of their freedom and that that which has been induced by enemies' ferocity against natural freedom [4] also should be inflicted by the vilest men's lust, we wish that the Claudian Senatusconsult and all its observance in regard to warnings and judges' sentences should cease for the future, lest she, who has been established as free, either when once deceived or when caught by unfortunate passion or by any other way at all, should be reduced into slavery contrary to her birthright's free condition [4] and should be a very bad disgrace to her relationship's splendour, that she who perhaps has relatives honoured with dignities should fall into another's ownership and should dread an owner inferior perhaps to her relatives.[5]

And this ought to be observed also in the case of freedwomen: for the religion of my times in no way allows a woman who once has gained her freedom to be reduced by such disgrace into slavery.

But [6] lest slaves or serfs should think that for them would be unpunished such an effort, which particularly must be feared in regard to serfs,[7] lest gradually the status of such persons should decrease by marriages with freewomen devised by these persons, [8] we ordain that, if any such thing shall have been perpetrated either by a slave or by a serf, his owner—whether by himself or by the province's governor —should have free power to correct by competent [9] castigation and to snatch from such a woman the slave or the serf.[10]

And if he shall have neglected this, he should know that such inactivity will redound to his own hurt.

1. Regard for the law of nations (*ius gentium*) led Vespasian and Hadrian to repeal two of its rules, which reflected the ancient rigour of Roman law: (1) a freeman's children by a slave, whom he believed to be free, should be free, if males, but should be enslaved, if females (*GI* 1. 85); (2) a freewoman and a slave's children should belong to the latter's master, if he would countenance such a connection (*GI* 1. 84).

While Gaius attributes to Vespasian an alteration in this senatusconsult, Suetonius is incorrect in postponing to his principate its passage (*Vesp.* 11), which occurred under Claudius on Tacitus' testimony (*Ann.* 12. 53. 1).

2. In the latter *locus* the emperor characterizes the clause as "unworthy of our times" without any regard for religion as such.

3. The reason anciently assigned for the rule appears to have been that such cohabitation interfered with the slave's work and therefore the master should have some compensatory consolation. The clause is reported in *GI* 1. 86, 91, 161.

Such acquisition of the woman's property was a mode of universal succession (*per universitatem*) and thus made the slave's master her universal successor by the process of the so-called *adquisitio miserabilis*, whereby property passed to private persons.

4. In *D* 1. 5. 4. 1 it is said that slavery is contrary to nature.

5. The fact that a relative is a slave casts no little ignominy upon that slave's relatives according to *D* 40. 12. 1–3.

6. This paragraph reappears as *CI* 11. 48. 24. 1 without mention of slaves.

7. The later law omits *in regard to serfs*, since it treats only those.

8. Neither slave's nor a serf's status was affected by marriage. But in each case his children by a freewoman were free and could not be reduced to either slavery or serfdom. Thus decrease of status would occur in the sense that in the next generation under such conditions there would be fewer slaves and serfs.

9. The later version substitutes "moderate".

10. For *the slave or the serf* the later statute reads "such a man".

632. LAW OF JUSTINIAN I ON EPISCOPAL INTEREST IN PAYMENT OF RENT, 531–4

(*CI* 1. 4. 32)

This dateless constitution, repeated in *CI* 4. 66. 4, permits a provincial bishop in a provincial governor's absence to accept evidence from a long-term lease-holder (emphyteute)[1] of a quasi-perpetual lease of land (emphyteusis)[1] that he is able and willing to pay his fixed rent to his absentee landlord, who on account of his absence has delayed acceptance of the rent. By such action the lessee protects himself from eviction.

The same emperor.[2]

If during three years the emphyteute[1] offers to the owner the rent[3] for emphyteusis,[1] but the owner delays to accept it, because he dwells either in the royal city[4] or in the provinces, it is allowed[5] for the emphyteute[1] to present to him the quitrent[6] and, when a triennium is about to end, if he should not have appeared to take it, to certify it by his seal and to testify about this before either the most glorious prefect of the city or the most glorious prefects of the sacred praetorians or the competent magistrate, to whom the estate's owner is subject, or the patriarch, if the owner is a powerful person;[7] but in the provinces either before the governor or in the governor's absence before the defender of the places or before the bishop of the city wherein the owner of the landed property dwells it is allowed for him [8] to act about this, so that the testimony of one of the said persons may be applied to the act.

And if not even thus the owner should have chosen to take the presented quitrent,[6] the emphyteute [1] shall gain this—the owner having no action for demand of it.

Neither the emphyteusis [1] shall be dissolved by the triennium running past nor the owner shall demand the customary rent of the succeeding years, until he himself, having pressed from above [9] the emphyteute [1] and having sent him a protest, should have started to demand the rent for emphyteusis;[1] for then surely the owner shall not demand the rent for the entire lapsed time, since he himself has been the reason for not taking it, but he shall demand the quitrent [6] for the time running after his protest.

But if the emphyteute [1] should not have deposited considerably the rent for a triennium after the owner's protest, the owner consequently shall eject him from the emphyteusis [1] pursuant to a second constitution of this title.[10]

1. See no. 537, n. 6.
2. This superscription is restored editorially.
3. Among the many meanings of κανών (*canon*), of which the most familiar to the average American are perhaps those pertaining to ecclesiastical matters, one of the latest is the annual payment of tax or tribute from the provinces or of rent to landlords (as here).
4. Constantinople.
5. This verb is in Greek an infinitive, dependent upon some principal predicate in a now-lost previous sentence of the law.
6. In Greek ἐμφύτευμα and in Latin *emphyteuma*.
7. An editorial conjecture in Greek for the last ten English words is translated, for it is supposed that some such words were in the law. See no. 127, n. 6.

The persons mentioned would be resident in Constantinople.

8. The last five words are supplied by the translator to connect the thought with what precedes.
9. By the use of legal machinery.
10. This is *CI* 4. 66. 2; dated 529.

633. RESCRIPT OF JUSTINIAN I ON GOVERNORS' GRANT OF SANCTUARY AND ON EXTORTION FROM HERETICS, 531-5

(N, App. 1, Ed. 2)[1]

This constitution has a double objective in ecclesiastical matters: (1) the limitation of the gubernatorial grant of right of sanctuary, of which advantage has been taken by receivers of taxes, who often abscond with most of their receipts to the shelter of churches; (2) the prohibition of acceptance of bribes from heretics, who offer money to imperial inquisitors for immunity from report and from subsequent prosecution.

Concerning the governors not granting a right [2] of sanctuary in fiscal cases.

The same emperor to John, praetorian prefect.[3]

Preamble: From the things carried to us not in writing by your Distinction we have perceived that the provinces' governors, who grant the right of sanctuary to whom they wish, have applied no little difficulty to the ingathering of public payments. For as a result the persons who receive the public payments, since they advance this security for themselves, do not dispatch [4] the gold laid before them, but themselves retain [4] the greatest part and, when they have owed the gold, misuse [4] the right of sanctuary wrongly granted to them.

Therefore we, using this divine pragmatic formulary to your Excellency, ordain that through your own ordinances you should forbid all the most distinguished governors of provinces to grant a right of sanctuary in fiscal causes, but in only private cases it should be permitted to them to grant to persons seeking it the right of sanctuary and for a stated time, not being able, when the period is completed, to renew it again perpetually—all knowing that, if they accept such a right from them, they shall not be advantaged, but to everyone ordered to pay the public payments owed by them shall be power to constrain them, the right given to them in the several places [5] being of no profit to them, but those alone having security who pursuant to our divine command or pursuant to your Excellency's ordinance accept a right of sanctuary.

Since by your Distinction we have been taught that certain persons, having gone into various provinces in search of persons who have given themselves to the heretics' error and having constrained many of the persons subject to payments because of such cause, have taken very much gold from them on the pretext of presents,[6] we ordain that persons who have dared any such thing both should be constrained and should be brought to the provinces' most distinguished governors

1122   634. INTEREST IN DEBTORS' PROPERTY, 532

and after proofs should pay threefold [7] what has been taken: they should give the simple sum [8] to the very persons mulcted, but the double sum [9] should be brought into the treasury [10] . . .

Conclusion: Therefore your Excellency shall hasten to bring to action the things which have occurred to us and are exhibited through this divine pragmatic law.

1. This law is the second among the thirteen so-called Edicts of Justinian, printed by R. Schöll and W. Kroll in the first appendix to their third stereotyped edition of Justinian's Novels. It is a rescript rather than an edict, as is clear from the first two paragraphs.

2. The word is λόγος, here used in the sense of a rule or a principle or a law embodying the result of λογισμός or reasoning power. From the reasoning that churches were under divine protection as the places wherein God was worshipped officially evolved the rule that persons seeking refuge therein were protected by God's ministers from their pursuers.

3. Of the East.

4. This principal verb in English is in Greek an infinitive, dependent upon the notion of perception in the previous sentence.

5. That is, the provinces.

6. Transliterated into Greek from Latin *sportula*, on which see no. 606, n. 20. Here the word's meaning approximates a bribe not to report the heretic.

7. An editorial emendation is translated.

8. Amid the Greek appears the Latin word *simplum*.

9. Amid the Greek appears the Latin word *duplum*.

10. The remaining two sections of the body of the law are omitted from the translation, as, dealing with collection of taxes, these are not of ecclesiastical interest.

634. MANDATE OF JUSTINIAN I ON ECCLESIASTICAL INTEREST IN CREDITORS' POSSESSION OF DEBTORS' PROPERTY, 532

(CI 7. 72. 10)

When delinquent debtors' properties, unsecured by mortgages (hypothecs),[1] have been alienated by their admitted creditors to satisfy their claims and any surplus above the claims has been received, Justinian rules that such money must be deposited in the treasury of the local church and from such money must be paid the claims of tardy creditors and that early creditors, who have sold or have transferred the properties, must swear on the Gospels that they have been honest in such transactions. Nothing is decreed about the disposition of an unclaimed surplus, which presumably remains in the ecclesiastical treasury.

Only so much of the law is translated as is of ecclesiastical interest (§§ 2 and 3).

Emperor Justinian Augustus to John, praetorian prefect.[2]

. . . Moreover, if those persons who detain possessions or in accordance with a judge's sentence shall have sold the properties or by any other lawful way whatever shall have transferred, after the time determined by us,[3] to other persons all legal right, which they are known to have in the said properties, and shall have accepted specified monies, whatever shall have been found in excess or more than is owed to them, this it is necessary by all means for them to seal in the presence of recorders and to deposit in the treasury of the holy church of that city in which a contract of this kind is made known— the attestation, of course, being written first by the mentioned recorders in the presence also of him who shall have sold or shall have transferred the properties to other persons, that by it may be manifested the amount not only of the monies which have been offered for the sale or the transfer of the properties, but also of those monies which should be found in excess after the debt has been paid; that, if any creditor afterward shall have appeared and shall have shown security for the debt, he may be able to get satisfaction for himself from these monies— the province's governor, obviously, making an examination of the case without any loss [4] and not allowing either the most reverend stewards or the treasurer of the holy church, in which the monies are deposited, to sustain any damage or expense, but by his own questioning commanding that the creditor should accept according to the debt's amount his own debt from the deposited monies.

Moreover, that it should not be permitted to the creditor to make in the sale or the transfer of the properties a deception or any machination or cheating, we order that, when the attestation on this matter has been made known, it should be inserted into the intervening records in the presence of the defender of the places—whether as much as is owed or more or less is collected from the money—and in the presence of not only—as has been said—the recorders, but also the most reverend treasurer, in whose presence, if it shall have happened thus, the monies in excess, when sealed, must be deposited; and the seller or the transferrer of the properties should offer an oath on the Sacrosanct Gospels, when they have been introduced, that neither through favour toward the purchaser or toward him to whom the properties are transferred by the legal right of surrender [5] nor by any intervening deception he has accepted an amount less than the just worth of the properties, but that amount which really with all zeal he could have found.

Given on 18 October at Constantinople in the second year after the consulate of the most distinguished Lampadius and the most distinguished Orestes.

1. See no. 537, n. 5.
2. Of the East.
3. In the omitted section a biennium for persons living in the same province and a quadrennium for persons living in different provinces are allowed for tardy creditors to take their claims to court.
4. To the creditor.
5. The phrase is *ius cessionis*, usually *cessio in iure*, the transfer of title by a fictitious surrender in court.

635. RESCRIPT OF JUSTINIAN I ON EPISCOPAL INTEREST IN GUARDIANSHIP, 533

(N 155)

The only ecclesiastical interest in this reply to a petition by a female minor, who complains about maternal guardianship, is that Ephraim, patriarch of Antioch,[1] where probably the petitioner lived, is associated with Belisarius, Justinian's great general, then master of the soldiers in the East, in the execution of the imperial ordinance granting the petitioner's request. Since only the prelate's nomination is of Christian concern, a summary of the situation [2] is substituted for the complete translation of the document, which is another link in the evidential chain of how the emperor increasingly invoked the hierarchy to help secular authorities in administration of the Empire.

Concerning the necessity that mothers should be subject to accountings pertaining to guardianship.

Emperor Justinian Augustus to General [3] Belisarius.

. . . Conclusion: Therefore your Distinction [4] along with the most blessed archbishop of the Theopolitans' city [1] shall hasten to give to action and to conclusion the things which have occurred to us and are exhibited through this divine pragmatic formulary.

Given on 1 February at Constantinople, our Lord Justinian Perpetual-Augustus being consul for the third time.

1. Antioch was renamed Theoupolis (Lat. Theopolis) after its destructive

earthquake on 29 November 528 (see W. Wroth, *Catalogue of the Imperial Byzantine Coins in the British Museum* [London, 1908], 1. xvi, 53, n. 1). Its archbishop or patriarch both then and at this rescript's date was Ephraim. (I owe this reference to Dr Glanville Downey.)

2. A girl, not quite thirteen years old, entreats the emperor that her mother should be held accountable for the latter's administration of the former's part of her deceased father's estate. The child claims that her mother, who has been her guardian—since 390 by *CT* 3. 17 = *CI* 5. 35. 2 widows who had sworn not to remarry could act as guardians for their children in the absence of testamentary and statutory guardians—and has remarried in violation of her oath, is more devoted to the children of her second marriage, proposes to substitute a man as her guardian, and puts pressure upon the petitioner to write a settlement in her mother's favour and by such settlement to waive any request for an accounting of her father's property at the time of transfer of guardians.

Justinian replies that he had found nothing in his legislation to assist the mother's attitude and promulgates the principle that mothers serving as their children's guardian must render, like other guardians, accounts of their guardianship and especially must not neglect their children from any earlier union to the financial enrichment of themselves or of their second spouses or of the children born from such cohabitation.

3. The Greek calls Belisarius simply *general* (στρατηγός), which the Latin version extends to "master of the soldiers" (*magister militum*), which office he held in the East after 529 and on which see no. 415, n. 10.

4. Belisarius is meant.

636. EDICT OF JUSTINIAN I ON THEOPASCHISM, 533

(*CI* 1. 1. 6)

In this edict, proclaimed not only to Constantinopolitans but also to residents of a dozen other cities, Justinian implicitly reasserts the Theopaschite doctrine that one of the Trinity suffered in the flesh—a formula conciliatorily advanced by Scythian monks in 519 and long awaiting a papal decision, which, it seems, was given favourably by Pope John II, who confirmed this edict and condemned the Akoimetoi (sleepless monks),[1] who controverted it.

The same emperor to the Constantinopolitans.

Worshipping the Saviour and the Lord of all things, Jesus Christ, our true God, above all we desire—as far as it is possible for human understanding to comprehend—to imitate his condescension. And having found that certain persons are mastered by the disease and by the insanity of the impious Nestorius [2] and Eutyches,[3] who, enemies of God and of the Holy Catholic and Apostolic Church, refuse to say properly and according to truth that Mary, the Holy, Glorious Ever-Virgin, is the Mother of God, we have desired that these persons should be taught the Christians' correct faith. But they, being incurable and proclaiming their own error, circumvent—as we have learned— the souls of rather simple persons by confusing them and by offending them and by saying things contrary to the Holy Catholic and Apostolic Church.

Therefore we have believed it necessary to dissolve the heretics' mendacities and to explain to all persons how God's Holy Catholic and Apostolic Church thinks and its most holy priests [4] proclaim, since we also, following them, should establish as clear the matters concerning the hope in us, not by innovating the faith [5] (may it not be so!), but by confuting the insanity of persons who are likeminded with impious heretics. Wherefore, even already having done this in the beginning of our reign, we have made it manifest to all persons.

For [6] we believe in one God, the Father Almighty, and in one Lord Jesus Christ, God's Son, and in the Holy Spirit, worshipping one substance [7] in three hypostases,[7] one divinity, one power, a Consubstantial Trinity. And we confess that in the last days [8] our Lord Jesus Christ, God's Only-Begotten Son, true God of true God, before the ages [9] and without time [9] born from the Father, co-eternal with the Father, he from whom are all things and through whom are all things, having descended from the skies, became incarnate from the Holy Spirit and Mary, the Holy, Glorious Ever-Virgin and Mother of God, and assumed man's nature and endured the Cross for us in the time of Pontius Pilate [10] and was buried [11] and arose on the third day, recognizing one and the same person's sufferings, which voluntarily he endured in the flesh. For we know not God the Word to be one and Christ to be another, but one and the same person consubstantial with the Father according to his divinity and the same one consubstantial with us according to his humanity. For as he is perfect in divinity, so the same one also in humanity is perfect. For the Trinity has remained the Trinity, even after one of the Trinity was made incarnate as God the Word; for the Holy Trinity admits not the addition of a fourth person.

Therefore, since these things are thus, we anathematize every heresy, especially Nestorius,[2] the man-worshipper, and those who have been or are likeminded with him, who divide our one Lord Jesus Christ, God's Son and our God, and do not confess properly and according to truth Mary, the Holy, Glorious Ever-Virgin, God's

Mother, that is, the Mother of God, but say that there are two Sons, that one is God the Word from the Father and another from Mary, the Holy Ever-Virgin, has been made God by grace and by affinity toward God the Word, and deny and do not confess that our Lord Jesus Christ, God's Son and our God, having become incarnate and having assumed man's nature and having been crucified, is one of the Holy and Consubstantial Trinity. For he alone is the one who is worshipped with and glorified with the Father and the Holy Spirit. We anathematize also the crazy Eutyches [3] and those who have been or are likeminded with him, who introduce a representation and deny the true Incarnation of our Lord and Saviour Jesus Christ, from Mary, the Holy Ever-Virgin and Mother of God, that is, our salvation, and do not confess that he is consubstantial with the Father according to his divinity and consubstantial with us according to his humanity; and likewise the soul-destroying Apollinaris [12] and those who have been or are likeminded with him and say that our Lord Jesus Christ, God's Son and our God, is without understanding and introduce a mixture or a disorder into the Incarnation of God's Only-Begotten Son, and all persons who have been or are likeminded with them.

Given on 15 March, our Lord Justinian Perpetual-Augustus being consul for the third time.

The same to Ephesians, the same to Caesareans, the same to Cyzicenes, the same to Amidenes, to Trapezuntians, to Jerusalemites, to Apameans, to Justinianopolitans, to Theopolitans, to Sebastenes, to Tarsians, to Ancyrans.

1. On these see no. 645, n. 35.
2. Patriarch of Constantinople and inventor of Nestorianism.
3. Constantinopolitan archimandrite and founder of Eutychianism.
4. See no. 16, n. 4.
5. See no. 569, n. 1.
6. From here to the end most of what follows is taken verbatim from no. 569.
7. Here again are οὐσία and ὑπόστασις, on which see no. 67, n. 17. See 1 John 5. 7.
8. See no. 569, n. 3.
9. See no. 569, n. 4.
10. See no. 159, n. 27.
11. See no. 569, n. 5.
12. Bishop of Laodicea in Syria and propagator of Apollinarianism.

637. LETTER OF JUSTINIAN I ON CONDEMNATION OF HERETICS, 533

(*CI* 1. 1. 7)

In addressing this letter to Epiphanius, patriarch of Constantinople, Justinian again publishes his theological position, which implicitly supports Theopaschism, condemns Nestorians and Eutychianists, and supports the four ecumenical councils hitherto held.

The same emperor to Epiphanius, the most holy and most blessed archbishop of this royal city [1] and ecumenical patriarch.

Wishing your Holiness to know all things pertaining to ecclesiastical status, we have considered it necessary to employ this sacred letter to you and through it to make manifest to you whatever matters set in motion we have been persuaded you also should know.

For having found that certain persons, alien from the Holy Catholic and Apostolic Church, are following the error of the impious Nestorius [2] and Eutyches [3] and have employed these persons' blasphemies, we have proposed a sacred edict [4] (which also your Holiness knows), whereby we have refuted the heretics' insanity, having altered or altering or transgressing absolutely nothing of ecclesiastical status until now prevailing with God (as also your Beatitude knows), but guarding by all means the status of the unity of the most holy churches in relation to Elder Rome's most holy pope and patriarch, to whom also we have written things similar to these.[5] For we do not permit that any of the things pertaining to ecclesiastical status should not be referred also to his Beatitude, as being the head of all God's most holy priests [6] and since, as often as heretics have existed in these regions, they have been hindered by the opinion and the correct decision of that one's venerable see.[7] For from our present sacred letter your Holiness will learn the things proposed by us, that the persons who try wickedly to understand or to interpret the things pronounced by us correctly in the edict [4] may be refuted by our present sacred letter.

Certain [8] few persons, unbelieving and alien from God's Holy Catholic and Apostolic Church, have dared in Jewish fashion to speak against those matters which by all priests [6] correctly are held and praised and proclaimed, by denying that our Lord Jesus Christ, God's Only-Begotten Son and our God, incarnate from the Holy Spirit and Mary, the Holy, Glorious Ever-Virgin and Mother of God, having assumed man's nature and having been crucified, is one of the Holy and Consubstantial Trinity, to be worshipped with and to be glorified with the Father and the Holy Spirit, consubstantial with the Father according to his divinity and the same one consubstantial with us according to his humanity, having suffered in his flesh and the same one not having suffered in his divinity. By refusing to confess that our Lord Jesus Christ, God's Only-Begotten Son and our God, is one of the Holy and Consubstantial Trinity, they are seen and are proved to be following the impious Nestorius'[2] evil doctrine, saying that according to grace he is God's Son and saying that God the Word is one and Christ is another. And these persons and their dogmas and the persons who have been or are likeminded we anathematize as being alien from God's Holy Catholic and Apostolic Church. For all the priests[6] of the Holy Catholic and Apostolic Church and the most pious archimandrites of the sacred monasteries, following the holy fathers' tradition and having altered or altering absolutely nothing of ecclesiastical status until now prevailing (as has been said), harmoniously confess and praise, proclaiming that our Lord Jesus Christ, God's Only-Begotten Son and our God, before the ages[9] and without time[9] having been born from the Father and in the last days[10] having descended from the skies and having been incarnate from the Holy Spirit and Mary, the Holy, Glorious Ever-Virgin and Mother of God, and having assumed man's nature and having been crucified, is one of the Holy and Consubstantial Trinity. For we know him as consubstantial with the Father according to his divinity and the same one as consubstantial with us according to his humanity, having suffered in his flesh and the same one not having suffered in his divinity, to be worshipped with the Father and the Holy Spirit. For we know not God the Word to be one and Christ to be another, but one and the same consubstantial with the Father according to his divinity and consubstantial with us according to his humanity, having suffered in his flesh and the same one not having suffered in his divinity. For as he is perfect in his divinity, so the same one is perfect in his humanity; for we receive and confess unity according to hypostasis.[11] Therefore, since the Only-Begotten Son and Word of God, before the ages[9] and without time[9] born from the Father, the same also in the last days[10] having descended from the skies and having been incarnate from the Holy Spirit and Mary, the Holy, Glorious Ever-Virgin[12] and Mother of God, and having assumed man's nature, that is, our Lord Jesus Christ is properly and according to truth God, therefore we say that Mary, the Holy, Glorious Ever-Virgin, is properly and according to truth the Mother of God: not because God the Word took a beginning from her, but because in the last days he descended from the skies and from her was incarnate and was born and assumed man's nature. And him we confess (as has been said) to be consubstantial with the Father according to his divinity and the same consubstantial with us according to his humanity, recognizing the same one's miracles and sufferings, which voluntarily he endured in the flesh.

Therefore these are the things in respect to which we, having said these through our sacred edict,[4] have refuted the heretics, to which sacred edict[4] both all the most holy bishops found here and the most pious archimandrites together with your Holiness have subscribed, following by all means the four holy synods and the things formulated by each of them, that is, of the 318 in Nicaea[13] and the 150 in this royal city[14] and of the former in Ephesus[15] and of that in Chalcedon,[16] since it has been made manifest to all persons that we hold and guard the definition of faith, transmitted to all together with us faithful persons of the Holy Catholic and Apostolic Church, that is, the holy creed or symbol, which has been exhibited by the 318 holy fathers,[13] which also in this royal city[1] the 150 holy fathers[14] by having explained it clarified, not because it is deficient, but, since indeed some enemies of the truth attempted to disprove the Holy Spirit's Divinity and others denied the true Incarnation of God the Word from Mary, the Holy Ever-Virgin and Mother of God, therefore the said 150 holy fathers[14] by having explained it through written testimonies clarified the same holy creed. And this the remaining holy synods, that is, the former in Ephesus[15] and that in Chalcedon,[16] having followed the same faith, received and guarded it and proclaimed Mary, the Holy, Glorious Ever-Virgin, as Mother of God and anathematized the persons not confessing her as Mother of God.

Likewise they anathematized persons transmitting another symbol than the holy creed exhibited by the 318 holy fathers[13] and explained and clarified by the 150 holy fathers in this royal city.[14]

And the former synod[17] in Ephesus[15] both condemned and anathematized the impious Nestorius[2] and his dogmas and anathematized both the persons who have been or are likeminded with him and the persons who have agreed with or agree with him.

And the holy synod in Chalcedon[16] both condemned and ejected from God's holy churches and anathematized also the impious Eutyches[3] and his dogmas and the persons who have been or are likeminded with him and the persons who have agreed with or agree with him. And it anathematized all heretics and their dogmas and the persons who have been or are likeminded with them. Likewise it anathematized both Nestorius[2] and his dogmas and the persons who have been or are likeminded with him and the persons who have agreed with or agree with him.

The same holy synod in Chalcedon[16] through its own report both received and confirmed the letter of the great Proclus[18] written to the Armenians about the necessity to say that our Lord Jesus Christ, God's Son and our God, is one of the Holy Trinity.

For if we transgress the said four holy synods or the formulas made by them, we give to the heretics condemned by them and to their dogmas licence to spread again their corruption into God's holy churches. And it is not possible that this ever should be done (may it not be so!), since the said four holy synods through their own dogmas have ejected the heretics and these persons' dogmas. And if anyone doubts about one of the said holy synods, he obviously thinks those dogmas which by it both have been ejected and have been anathematized.

Therefore none should disturb us in vain by holding to the vain hope that we have done or shall do or shall permit to be done by anyone anything contrary to the said holy synods or shall allow to be removed from the Church's sacred diptychs [19] the same holy synod's record. For we anathematize all persons condemned and anathematized by them and the condemned persons' dogmas and the persons who have been or are likeminded with them.

Wherefore your Beatitude should pray both for us and for our Empire, both teaching and assuring all persons about our object and zeal for the faultless faith.

Given on 26 March at Constantinople, our Lord Justinian Perpetual-Augustus being consul for the third time.

1. Constantinople.
2. Patriarch of Constantinople and inventor of Nestorianism.
3. The Constantinopolitan archimandrite and founder of Eutychianism.
4. No. 636.
5. Probably the letter quoted in no. 645 and sent to Pope John II.
6. See no. 16, n. 4.
7. Justinian's reference to Rome is reminiscent of similar deference by Constantius II after St Athanasius had been deposed from the Alexandrian patriarchate for the third time (356). Ammianus (*Res Gestae*, 15. 7. 10) reports that Constantius, always hostile to Athanasius, attempted with ardent desire to have the bishop of Rome sanction with his superior authority the sentence against Athanasius (see no. 94). After Pope Liberius had refused, for this refusal and for additional reasons the emperor also exiled him (see no. 95).
8. Most of what follows in this paragraph appears also in the emperor's letter to the pope (no. 645).
9. See no. 569, n. 4.
10. See no. 569, n. 3.
11. See no. 67, n. 17.
12. This word, wanting in the text, is supplied by editors, for the adjectives *holy, glorious* need a noun before the connective.
13. In 325.
14. In 381 at Constantinople.
15. In 431, as opposed to the Ephesian *Latrocinium* of 449.
16. In 451.

17. The translator has supplied the noun missing from the Greek text.

18. This sainted patriarch of Constantinople at the request of an Armenian synod *c.* 435 sent to Armenia a celebrated doctrinal letter, sometimes called the *Tome of St Proclus*, which seems to have saved the Armenian Church from Nestorian taint. It is in *PG* 65. 855–74.

19. See no. 554, n. 1.

638. MANDATE OF JUSTINIAN I ON RAPISTS OF RELIGIOUS WOMEN, 533

(*CI* 1. 3. 53)

Parts of this constitution, which treats only nuns (whether virgins or widows) and deaconesses, who have been raped, and assigns penalties for rapists and their accomplices and accords compensation for their victims, appear also in *CI* 9. 13. 1 (dated also 533), where Justinian includes rapists of ordinary virgins, matrons, fiancées, freedwomen, and slaves, whose compensation differs from that due to religious women. Since most of the other law, especially in the case of compensation, has no connection with the Church, the shorter version is translated.

The same Augustus to Hermogenes, master of the offices.

We decree that rapists of virgins or of widows or of deaconesses, who shall have been dedicated to God, should be smitten, since they sinfully perform the worst of crimes, with capital punishment, because a wrong is committed not only to the outrage of human beings, but to the irreverence for Almighty God himself.[1]

Accordingly those who shall have committed a crime of this kind and who shall have offered aid to them at the time of assault, when they shall have been found in the very rape and, while the crime is still flaming,[2] shall have been caught by parents of religious virgins or widows or deaconesses or by their kindred [3] or guardians or curators, on conviction should be killed.

Moreover, if, after so detestable a crime has been committed, the rapist shall have been able to defend himself with strength or to escape by flight, in this royal city [4] the exalted praetorian prefects as well as the most glorious urban prefect, in the provinces the most eminent praetorian prefects of Illyricum [5] as well as the masters of the soldiers [6] throughout the different regions of our world and also the admirable prefect of Egypt [7] and the admirable vicars and the admirable proconsuls and no less the admirable dukes [8] and the most distinguished

638. RAPISTS OF RELIGIOUS WOMEN, 533

governors of provinces and also other judges of whatever rank, who shall have been found in places, should apply similar zeal with great solicitude, that they can catch these persons and may afflict them with sternest punishments, when caught in such a crime, after legitimate proofs and those known to the law, without prescription of forum,[9] and may condemn them to the punishment of death.[10]

Moreover, if this shall have been committed against a sanctimonial virgin who lives in a hermitage or a nunnery,[11] whether or not the said virgin has been appointed a deaconess, to the said nunnery or hermitage, where she has been consecrated, the goods of these persons shall be adjudged, that from this property both she herself may have sufficient compensation, while she lives, and the sacrosanct hermitage or nunnery may have all the property with full ownership. But if a deaconess should belong to any church at all, but has not been established in any nunnery or hermitage, but lives by herself, her rapist's substance should be assigned to the church of which she is a deaconess, that from these resources she herself may secure the usufruct, while she survives, from the said church, but the church should have by our favour complete proprietorship and full possession of the said property—none, either judge or another person, daring to despise this.

Moreover the punishments (which we previously have mentioned), that is, of death and of loss of goods, we establish not only against rapists, but also against those persons who shall have accompanied these persons in the assault itself and the rape. But all others who shall have been found as accomplices and abettors of a crime of this kind and shall have been convicted or shall have supported them or shall have brought any aid whatever to them, whether they are males or females, of whatever status or rank or dignity, we subject only to capital punishment,[12] that they should submit to this punishment,[13] whether such a villainy shall have been perpetrated on sanctimonial virgins or on other abovementioned women who are willing or unwilling.[14]

Given on 17 November at Constantinople, our Lord Justinian Perpetual-Augustus being consul for the third time.

1. In the longer version is added as another reason "especially when virginity or chastity, once corrupted, cannot be restored".

2. The adjective is *flagrans*, preserved in the technical phrase *in flagrante delicto*, but here simply *flagrante crimine*.

3. The word is *consanguinei*, originally restricted to brothers and/or sisters, but later extended to any relative, whether or not related by blood (*sanguis*).

4. Constantinople.

5. The longer law adds Africa.

6. See no. 415, n. 10.

7. The count of the East is also named in the longer version.

8. Generals (*duces*) of the armed forces in the provinces.

9. That is, it matters not before which court a rapist wants to plead, for no immunity from prosecution is indulged. See no. 62, n. 11.

10. At this point the longer law adds: "And to them, if they shall have wished to appeal, we give no permission according to the definition of the ancient Constantinian Law", which is preserved in *CT* 9. 24. 1 (dated 326).

11. The word is *monasterium*, as often, but while "monastery" still properly may be used to indicate a cenobitical community of women, "convent" or "nunnery" is preferred in popular usage and has the added merit of averting scandalous misinterpretation.

12. In view of the death penalty earlier in the text (at n. 10), this penalty must mean at least loss of civic rights (*caput*).

13. In the longer version it is ruled in the case of slaves who aid a rapist: "And if anyone shall have been found of servile status among these assistants, we order that one—without discrimination of sex—to be cremated, when also this rightly had been provided by the Constantinian Law" (*CT* 9. 24. 1).

14. In the longer law the last two sentences are: "All chapters of the Julian Law which about rape of virgins or widows or nuns have been placed either in ancient books of laws or in sacred constitutions having been abolished [there is no finite verb] for the future, that only this law in this chapter may suffice for all [laws]. And we ordain that these matters should have place [pertinence] concerning nuns and virgins and widows."

By *the Julian Law* is meant probably one of Augustus' laws on marital relations, likely the *Lex Iulia de adulteriis coercendis* (18 B.C.), which included other sexual offences besides adultery. Fragments of this law are found in juristic writings (*D* 48. 5).

639. EDICT OF JUSTINIAN I ON USE OF HIS INSTITUTES, 533

(*II*, Constitution *Imperatoriam Maiestatem*)

This document, prefixed to Justinian's *Institutiones* [1] and addressed to young men aspiring to be lawyers, contains several indications of the emperor's acknowledgement of divine favour manifested not only in his military victories, but also in his codification of the law into the *Corpus Iuris Civilis*,[2] of which the Institutes are a part.

The parts devoid of religious interest are not translated.

In the name of our Lord Jesus Christ.

639. USE OF JUSTINIAN'S INSTITUTES, 533

Emperor Caesar Flavius Justinian Alamannicus, Gothicus, Francicus, Germanicus, Anticus, Alanicus, Vandalicus, Africanus, Pious, Fortunate, Renowned, Victor and Triumpher, Ever-August to young men desirous of studying law.[3]

The imperial majesty[4] ought to be not only adorned with arms, but also armed with laws . . .

And each end of these[5] with the highest vigilance and the highest forethought we, God favouring, have achieved . . .

Africa[6] as well as other innumerable provinces,[7] after so great intervals of time, through our victories vouchsafed by celestial will, are witnesses by having been added again to the Roman sway and to our Empire . . .

As if going through mid-ocean, by celestial favour we now have completed a work[8] whereof we had despaired. And when this[8] with God's favour had been finished[9] . . .

Given on 21 November at Constantinople, our Lord Justinian Perpetual-Augustus being consul for the third time.

1. See no. 640, n. 1.
2. See Introd., n. 3 *ad fin.* for the origin of this phrase.
3. Literally "to the youth desirous of the laws". The period of *iuventus* (youth), the word here used, was conceived to run from the twentieth to the fortieth year, but doubtless some students started their study of law before they had attained the age of twenty.
4. The words are *Imperatoriam maiestatem*, whence is called this constitution. See no. 617, n. 6.
5. Justinian refers to his ideal of good government both in war and in peace, exemplified, respectively, by his overseas victories and his regard for justice at home.
6. In 533. See also no. 646, n. 1 *ad med.*
7. See no. 646, nn. 16–19.
8. The condensation of emperors' constitutions into the *Codex* and of jurisconsults' responses (on which see no. 308, n. 15) into the *Digesta* or *Pandectae* (on which see no. 617, n. 4), both earlier parts of the *Corpus Iuris Civilis* (on which see Introd., n. 3 *ad fin.*).
9. Justinian concludes by announcing that he entrusted the composition of the Institutes to Tribonian, Theophilus, Dorotheus (on whom see no. 640, n. 1), by giving his reasons for such composition, by sanctioning their validity as part of the law, and by commending their study to students.

640. STATUTES OF JUSTINIAN I ON LEGACIES TO THE CHURCH, 533

(II 3. 27. 7; 4. 6. 19; 4. 6. 23; 4. 6. 26; 4. 16. 1)

From Justinian's *Institutiones* (a brief manual of this sovereign's law as it stood near the beginning of his long reign)[1] are translated the following five excerpts, which concern legacies left to churches.

Excerpt I comes from the title "On Quasi-Contractual Obligations", excerpts II–IV are in the title "On Actions", excerpt V belongs to the title "On Punishment of Persons Recklessly Litigating".

I (3. 27. 7)

In certain cases, however, an amount which, when not owed, has been paid by mistake cannot be recovered.[2] For thus the ancients[3] have determined: in cases where the amount being claimed increases by denial of liability, in those cases the amount paid, when not owed, cannot be recovered—as under the Aquilian Law[4] and also in the case of a legacy. And this rule, indeed, the ancients[3] wished to apply only to those legacies which, definite in amount, were bequeathed to anyone by condemnation.[5] But our constitution, since it has allowed to all legacies and trusts a single nature,[6] has wished this kind of increase to be extended in all legacies and trusts; but not to all legatees it has offered this, but only in legacies and trusts which have been left to sacrosanct churches and all other venerable places, which are honoured in view of religion or of piety. If such legacies, when not owed, are paid, they are not recoverable.

II (4. 6. 19)

... Likewise a mixed action[7] lies against those persons who have delayed to give things, in the category of a legacy or a trust, left to sacrosanct churches or to other venerable places, until they even were summoned into court. Then, indeed, they are compelled to give both the actual thing or the money, which has been left, and as much more as penalty; and therefore the condemnation becomes twice the amount of the original claim.

III (4. 6. 23)

We sue for double damages, for example, in cases of simple theft, of unlawful damage under the Aquilian Law,[4] of deposit in certain cases, also of corrupting a slave . . .[8] Likewise such an action applies in the case of a legacy which has been left to venerable places—according to what we have said above.[9]

640. LEGACIES TO THE CHURCH, 533   1137

IV (4. 6. 26)

... But that action, which is available for those things which have been left to venerable places,[9] is doubled [10] not only by denial of liability,[11] but also if he has delayed payment of the bequest until he is summoned by our magistrates' order; but against a person acknowledging his liability and paying it before he is summoned by our magistrates' order the action is for the simple amount.[12]

V (4. 16. 1)

For instance, under our constitution an oath [13] is administered to all persons who are sued, for a defendant not otherwise can make use of his allegations,[14] unless he first has sworn that, thinking that he has a good defence,[15] he comes to deny the accusation.

But against those persons denying liability in certain cases [11] an action for twice or thrice the original amount is established, as when an action is brought in the category of unlawful damage [4] or of legacies left to venerable places.[16]

1. The textbook was composed by Tribonian, quaestor of the sacred palace and master of the offices under Justinian, assisted by two professors of law, Dorotheus and Theophilus, the former at Beirut (but called to the capital for this task) and the latter at Constantinople. It was based on earlier institutional treatises, especially on the *Institutiones* of Gaius (*ob. c.* 180), and its contents are in character partly theoretical and in part historical. The Institutes was published on 21 November 533 with statutory force from 30 December of that year.

2. When payment for a non-existent debt had been made, there lay an action for its recovery (*condictio indebiti*); but it was essential that (1) what is paid must not really be owed, (2) the payer pays in error, (3) the payee receives in good faith, believing that the debt is due to him. On *condictio indebiti* the doctrine is in *D* 12. 6 and the constitutions are in *CI* 4. 5.

3. The word is *veteres* and refers usually to lawyers of the late Republic and of the early Empire.

4. The *Lex Aquilia*, enacted perhaps in 287 B.C., doubled damages payable by a convicted defendant who had denied his liability in a lawsuit concerning damage done to the plaintiff's property.

5. A legacy *per damnationem* was a legacy which an heir was "condemned" to pay: e.g. "Let my heir be condemned to give my slave Stichus to Lucius Titius" (*GI* 2. 201).

6. That is, assimilated to one type, as he ordained in 529 (*CI* 6. 43. 1. 1).

7. An *actio mixta* is both *in rem* and *in personam*. The usual examples are: (1) when co-heirs divide an inheritance, (2) when joint-owners divide a property held in common, (3) when owners of adjoining properties settle boundary lines (*II* 4. 6. 20).

8. The omission elaborates the last case.
9. See the preceding excerpts.
10. In respect to damages to be paid to the claimant.
11. As provided in the first excerpt.
12. That is, the heir who neither denies nor delays his payment of the deceased's legacy need pay no more than the legacy.
13. This was taken on the Bible, as frequently was the case in Justinian's reign (e.g. no. 619, to which constitution the emperor here doubtless refers).
14. By his *allegationes* must be meant his evidence and his arguments to buttress his contradiction of the plaintiff's charge.
15. Literally "keenness", "earnestness"; the adjective *good* shows that honest perseverance implies belief in the righteousness of his defence.
16. See the preceding excerpts.
Some of these words come from *GI* 4. 171.

641. STATUTES OF JUSTINIAN I ON SACRED AND RELIGIOUS THINGS, 533

(*II* 2. 1. 7–9; 2. 6. 1; 3. 19. 1–2; 3. 23. 5; 4. 15. 1)

Justinian's *Institutiones*[1] illustrate the alteration in the Roman concept of sacred and religious things[2] caused by the State's recognition of Christianity as the established religion of the Empire (no. 167).

Pagans professed that some divinities controlled the upper world and that property, such as temples and offerings, dedicated to their worship was sacred (*res sacrae*)[3] and that other deities ruled the lower world and that property, such as cemeteries and tombs, devoted to their care was religious (*res religiosae*).[3] After Christians had replaced polytheism's supernal and infernal divinities with their trinitarian monotheism,[4] the terms *res sacrae* and *res religiosae* not only preserved their pagan connotation of objects dedicated to divine worship and devoted to divine care as well as the investitive and divestitive and transvestitive facts associated with such property, but also increasingly were converted to Christian institutions and by Justinian's age achieved, as here, authoritative application.

The five excerpts come respectively from the titles "On Division of Things", "On Usucapions and Possessions of Long Time", "On Void Stipulations", "On Buying and Selling", "On Interdicts".

Omissions of immaterial subject matter are indicated by a series of dots.

I (2. 1. 7–9)

Moreover things sacred and religious and sanctioned belong to no one; for that which belongs to divine law is among no one's property.[4]

Sacred things are those which have been consecrated duly [5] and by pontiffs [6] to God, such as sacred buildings [7] and gifts,[8] which have been dedicated duly to God's service [9] and which also by our constitution we have forbidden to be alienated and pledged—the cases of redemption of captives being excepted.[10]

But if anyone shall have attempted to consecrate a thing by his own authority as if for himself, it is not sacred, but profane.[11]

Moreover the place wherein sacred buildings [7] have been built, even after the building has been destroyed, remains sacred, as Papinian also has written.[12]

Each and everyone by his own will makes a place religious, provided he buries a dead person in his own place,[13] but it is not permitted to bury in a common [14] unreligious place,[15] when a partner is unwilling; but it is permitted to bury in a common [15] sepulchre,[16] even when the rest have been unwilling.[17]

Likewise, if the usufruct [18] is another's, it is accepted that the proprietor does not make the place religious unless the usufructuary [18] consents.[19] It is permitted to bury in another's place, if the owner allows;[20] and, though he has ratified it after the dead person has been buried, yet the place becomes religious.[21]

II (2. 6. 1)

But even if sometimes someone shall have possessed a thing with the utmost good faith, yet usucapion by any period of time [22] does not proceed for him, as, for instance, if anyone should possess . . . a thing sacred or religious.[23]

III (3. 19. 1–2)

. . . A stipulation [24] shall be void, . . . if anyone should stipulate for a sacred or religious thing which he believed to belong to human law . . . to be delivered . . .

IV (3. 23. 5)

Places sacred or religious . . . it is vain for anyone to buy knowingly;[25] but if, however, deceived by the seller, he shall have bought these as private or profane places, he shall have an action on purchase,[26] because it may not be permitted to him to have these, that he may get what it is worth to him not to have been deceived . . .[27]

V (4. 15. 1)

. . . Prohibitive interdicts [28] are those by which he [29] forbids something to be done, as, for instance, . . . building in a sacred place . . .[30]

1. See no. 640, n. 1.

2. Both types of these things (*res sacrae* and *res religiosae*) were considered as either outside private ownership (*extra patrimonium*) or beyond a private person's acquisition (*extra commercium*) and therefore as objects of divine law (*res iuris divini*).

Also subject to the above restrictions were some other things, such as municipal walls and civic gates, which in a sense belonged to divine law and were believed to be sanctioned (*res sanctae*), because any offence against these entailed capital punishment. Justinian etymologizes the term thus: "Therefore those parts of the laws, wherein we constitute penalties against those who have acted contrary to the laws, we call sanctions" (*II* 2. 1. 10). But what seems to have been the situation is that things originally were made sanctioned by a religious ceremony (as in I *infra*) with the result that such things could not be violated without a severe penalty (Isidore, *Orig.* 15. 4. 2). Thus, after the retention of the penalty and the discontinuance of the consecration (*D* 1. 8. 9. 3), *res sanctae* still were regarded as subject in a sense to divine law (*GI* 2. 8; *II* 2. 1. 10).

3. *GI* 2. 4.

4. Most of this sentence, except for the inclusion of sanctioned things, comes from *GI* 2. 3 and 9. But this doctrine, which also is in various forms in *D* 1. 8. 1. pr., 1. 8. 6. 2, 18. 1. 4, 18. 1. 6. pr., 30. 39. 9, 41. 2. 30. 1, 41. 3. 9, 48. 13. 1, must be restricted to things which, capable of appropriation, can become objects of private property, for otherwise no longer would be true the Roman legal maxim that what is owned by none becomes the first possessor's property (*D* 41. 1. 3).

5. Cf. *infra* n. 12.

6. The word is *pontifices*, among pagan Romans meaning *pontiffs*, but "bishops" among Christian Romans. So today in the several divisions of Catholic Christianity bishops, but not minor clerics, ordinarily and by custom perform the major ceremonies of consecration, such as hallowing God's house (cf. *infra* n. 8).

7. The phrase is *aedes sacrae*. In classical Latin *aedes* means either a house for human habitation (usually in plural) or a temple of a god (usually in singular), though the distinction between *templum* (an elaborate edifice) and *aedes* (a simple structure) disappears after the Augustan age: thus Suetonius calls the sanctuary of Venus Genetrix in Rome both *aedes* (*Iul.* 78. 1) and *templum* (*Iul.* 84. 1). In later Latin *aedes* sometimes stands for church: thus *Aedes Christi* is the Latin title of Christ Church in the University of Oxford, the college projected by Thomas Cardinal Wolsey in 1525 and established by King Henry VIII in 1546 and traditionally called "The House".

8. E.g. in *D* 24. 1. 5. 12, where a husband for an offering to a god has given to his wife a place wherein she could dedicate a public work, like a public building, which she had promised to make, the place becomes sacred. And also if he should give anything to her, that a gift should be given to a

god or should be consecrated, it is valid, as for instance if he has placed oil for her in a sacred building. While these examples are exceptions to the prohibition against intramarital gifts (*CI* 5. 16. 4), since the donation eventually was dedicated to a deity, yet there is not specific mention of pontifical consecration of these gifts.

9. But a thing about which there is litigious controversy cannot be dedicated to sacred use (*D* 44. 6. 3).

10. See no. 598, later modified in 544, when Justinian enacted that surplus movable *res sacrae* could be sold to pay the Church's debts (*N* 120. 10).

11. That is, its previous character remains unchanged.

While at least as late as the latter part of the second century sacred things ordinarily had been consecrated under public authority (statute of Assembly or resolution of Senate) by a sacerdotal ceremony (*GI* 2. 5) and probably publicly (*D* 1. 8. 6. 3, 1. 8. 9. pr.), yet from early in the third century only emperors could authorize such consecration (*D* 1. 8. 9. 1).

Moreover whatever in the provinces had not been consecrated in accord with the Roman People's authority was not properly sacred, but still was held as if sacred (*GI* 2. 7a). But a provincial governor was bound to tour sacred buildings, after inspection to provide for their repair, to finish the completion of such as had been started, so far as his province's resources permitted, by appointing overseers and diligent artisans, and, if there should have been need, to furnish the aid of the armed forces (*D* 1. 16. 7. 1), on which last point see *CT* 15. 1. 13 (dated ?364).

12. The reference to Papinian (*ob.* 212), praetorian prefect under Lucius Septimius Severus (193–211) and by posterity regarded as the leading luminary of Roman law (*CT* 1. 4. 3; dated 426), is to *D* 18. 1. 73. pr., where the jurisconsult qualifies his statement by attributing the destruction to earthquake and adds that the place cannot be sold. Marcian, his contemporary (*ob. post* 222), maintains a similar doctrine (*D* 1. 8. 6. 3).

13. So also *GI* 2. 6; *D* 1. 8. 6. 4, 11. 7. 2. 9, 11. 7. 3, 11. 7. 4, 11. 7. 41, 24. 1. 5. 10–11. But already in the *Twelve Tables* (449 B.C.) burial within a city, even on one's own land, was banned (*FIRA* 1. 66; *TT* 10. 1). Almost six centuries afterward Hadrian ordained against both violators and consenting magistrates for such burial a fine of forty aurei (on the aureus see no. 515, n. 18) to be paid to the fisc, declared such a site public, and ordered the transfer of such corpses (*D* 47. 12. 3. 5). The jurisconsult Paul (*flor.* 200) pronounced against it also (*Sent.* 1. 21. 2 = *FIRA* 2. 334). And Diocletian and Maximian in their constitution confirmed the old prohibition against intramural interment (*CI* 3. 44. 12; dated 290). See no. 181.

Apropos the Hadrianic authorization of transfer of buried bodies: ordinarily corpses consigned to perpetual sepulture could not be transferred—so later emperors ruled (*D* 11. 7. 39, 47. 12. 3. 4). But burial in another person's property, destruction of a sepulchre by flood or by collapse, and any just and necessary cause were exceptions allowed by judicial action (*D* 11. 7. 7) or by provincial governor's appraisement (*CI* 3. 44. 1) or by pontifical decree (*D* 11. 7. 8. pr.) or by imperial order (*D* 11. 7. 8. pr.; *CT* 9. 17. 7 = *CI* 3. 44. 14). Such removal removed the religiosity of the former site (*D* 11. 7. 40 and 44), was attended with religious rites, and was effected during the night (Paul, *Sent.* 1. 21. 1 = *FIRA* 2. 334).

14. That is, owned in common by several owners.

15. A *locus purus* is a plot which is neither sacred nor sanctioned nor religious (*D* 11. 7. 2. 4) and wherein no interment yet has been made and which, therefore, is free from religion's claims.

16. Religious places include sepulchres, about whose construction, use, accessibility, and violation there is much in the Digest (8. 1. 14. 1, 11. 7. 2. 2 and 5, 11. 7. 10, 11. 7. 12. pr.–1, 11. 7. 37. 1, 11. 7. 42, 11. 8. 1. 5–10, 11. 8. 3–5; 47. 12) and in the Codes (*CT* 9. 17; *CI* 3. 44. 2, 4, 6–8, 13; 9. 19).

While it was held that enemies' sepulchres were not religious for Romans, who with impunity—for the action of violated sepulchre (*actio sepulchri violati*, on which see *D* 47. 12; *CT* 9. 17; *CI* 9. 19) was not competent—could convert stones from these to any use whatsoever (*D* 47. 12. 4), yet this churlish maxim of the law cut both ways, because it also was held that sacred or religious places captured by enemies lost entirely their pristine character, to which, however, they were restored by a kind of postliminium (on which see no. 308, n. 14) upon recapture (*D* 11. 7. 36).

Monuments and cenotaphs are distinguished (*D* 11. 7. 42; cf. 11. 7. 2. 6, 11. 7. 37. 1). Although the jurisconsult Marcian (*ob. post* 222) on the poet Vergil's witness (*Aen.* 3. 303–5) thought that a cenotaph should be a religious place (*D* 1. 8. 6. 5), yet Aurelius and Verus earlier (at least by 169, when their joint rule ended) had denied this by rescript (*D* 1. 8. 7, 11. 7. 6. 1).

17. So also *D* 1. 8. 6. 4, 11. 7. 41, 11. 7. 43.

But in *D* 11. 7. 2. 1 it is said that it is debatable whether such a partner should be held liable and that in any event he can be prosecuted in an action for division of family estate (*actio familiae erciscundae*, on which see *GI* 4. 42; *II* 3. 27. 4, 4. 6. 20, 4. 17. 4; *D* 10. 2) or in an action for division of common property (*actio communi dividundo*, on which see *GI* 4. 42; *II* 3. 37. 3, 4. 6. 20, 4. 17. 5; *D* 10. 3).

18. See no. 602, n. 1.

19. So also *D* 11. 7. 2. 7, 11. 7. 43, 11. 7. 46. pr.

20. Otherwise the place cannot become religious (*CI* 3. 44. 2; dated 216) and such a burier is liable to an action *in factum* (on which see no. 598, n. 10) and is subject to a pecuniary penalty (*D* 11. 7. 2. 1–3, 11. 7. 7).

21. So also *D* 1. 8. 6. 4 and *CI* 3. 44. 2 (dated 216).

22. *Usucapio* is acquisition of ownership through continuous possession by condition of a definite period of time (*D* 41. 3. 3). It ascends as high as 449 B.C. in the *Twelve Tables*, where it is described (*FIRA* 1. 44; *TT* 6. 5) as prescriptive right or use (*usus*). To usucapt property the prospective owner must lay claim to property which is subject to commercial transaction—hence

are excluded sacred and sanctioned things (*D* 41. 3. 9) and things sacred or religious (as here)—and must possess, not merely detain, it by just cause or just title and in good faith for an uninterrupted period of time, which was one year for movables and two years for immovables. Justinian reformed the concept by extending it to include provincial land, by increasing the period for acquisition of movables to three years and of immovables to ten years, if both parties (owner and possessor) lived in the same province, and to twenty years, if both parties lived in different provinces (*II* 2. 6. pr.).

On usucapion see *GI* 2. 40–61; *II* 2. 6; *D* 41. 3–10; see also *CI* 7. 26–40 for imperial constitutions thereon.

23. So also in *D* 41. 2. 30. 1, where it is said that we lose possession, if we have brought a dead person into that place which we were in process of possessing, for we cannot possess a religious or sacred place, although we may despise religion and may consider the place as private. And in *D* 11. 8. 4 it is stated that right to a sepulchre is not granted by long possession to one to whom that right does not belong legally (cf. *CI* 3. 44. 13 [dated 294]).

24. *Stipulatio* is a verbal contract by formal question and formal answer. It is unilateral, for it imposes a duty only on the promisor, and of strict law, for its non-performance induces a strict procedure, wherein the judge must judge strictly according to the law without resort to such freedom as considerations of equity confer. A stipulation was employed for very varied kinds of obligation. By Justinian's time stipulations could be written, without formal requirements, and in languages other than Latin.

For the doctrine on stipulation see *GI* 3. 92–127; *II* 3. 15–20; *D* 45—46. 5; for imperial constitutions thereon see *CI* 8. 37–43.

According to *D* 45. 1. 38. 25 one can stipulate for construction of a sacred building (on which cf. *supra* n. 8) or of a religious place; but generally otherwise stipulations concerning religious or sacred things are to no avail (*D* 45. 1. 83. 5, 45. 1. 91. 1, 45. 1. 137. 6).

25. So also *D* 18. 1. 4, 18. 1. 6 pr.; cf. *CI* 3. 44. 2 (dated 216), 3. 44. 9 (dated 245). And those who knowingly buy and sell things designed for religion, although the sale legally does not stand, yet fall into the crime of lese-religion (*laesa religio*) according to *CI* 9. 19. 1 (dated 240).

26. The *actio ex empto* or *actio empti*, whereby the seller can be compelled either to perform his obligation—which in this case cannot be allowed, for a sacred thing is outside commercial transaction (cf. *supra* n. 2 *ad init.*) and moreover does not receive a valuation (*D* 1. 8. 9. 5)—or to pay compensation. It seems to have been necessary, however, for the purchaser to have paid the price before application for the action (*D* 19. 1. 13. 8).

27. On the other hand, whoever unknowingly purchases sacred or religious places as private places, though the purchase does not hold, yet can prosecute the vendor by the action on purchase (cf. *supra* n. 27), that he may get what it has been worth to him that he should not be deceived (*D* 18. 1. 62. 1).

28. An *interdictum* is an order issued by a magistrate vested with *imperium*,

on application, to avert an anticipated wrong, to prevent a breach of peace, to protect possession as distinct from ownership. Disobedience to an interdict was punishable by incarceration or by fine or by other ordinary means at the issuing magistrate's disposal.

The jurisprudents divided interdicts into four species: (1) prohibitive (*prohibitorium*), (2) restitutive (*restitutorium*), (3) productive (*exhibitorium*), (4) mixed (*mixtum*), where one was required to abstain and to produce. Some interdicts concerned the present, others looked to the past; some lasted for one year, others were perpetual. Although all interdicts were *in personam* in their effect, yet they were conceived as *in rem*.

The doctrine of interdicts is discussed in *GI* 4. 138–70, *II* 4. 15; *D* 43; see also *CI* 8. 1 for imperial constitutions thereon. The part on interdicts in the urban praetor's perpetual edict is in *FIRA* 1. 375–86.

29. Ordinarily a praetor or a proconsul (*GI* 4. 139), but in Justinian's time only the former (*II* 4. 15. pr.).

30. This interdict is cited usually as *ne quid in loco sacro fiat* (lest anything in a sacred place should be made).

Since interdicts are competent concerning sacred or religious places (*D* 43. 1. 1. pr., 43. 1. 2. 1–2), it is not surprising to see this interdict quoted in *D* 39. 1. 1. 1, where "or religious" is inserted, in *D* 43. 1. 2. 1, and in 43. 6. 1. 2 (cf. pr.). In the first *locus* the interdict is associated with announcement of new work (*operis novi nuntiatio*), which is an owner's protest against anyone beginning on the latter's estate a new construction likely to interfere with the former's use of his own estate. Such announcement, moreover, is available to anyone thinking that the integrity of various public places, including those sacred or religious, will be threatened by such an act (*D* 39. 1. 1. 17). In the second *locus* is also the interdict ordering removal of what has been made in a sacred place (*quod <in loco sacro> factum est restituatur*); so also *D* 43. 8. 2. 19 combines both interdicts. In the third *locus* is also the interdict against introducing anything into a sacred place (*ne quid in locum <sacrum> immittatur*), which perhaps pertains to the passage of a sewer. In his comment thereon Ulpian (*ob.* 228) says (§§ 2–3) that the interdict pertains to what is done not for ornament, but for ugliness or for detriment [which must have been a matter of taste, about which there ought not to be dispute—so the proverb *de gustibus non est disputandum*], and that the care of sacred places has been entrusted to those who care for sacred buildings [on which cf. *supra* n. 8].

It may be mentioned that there are available interdicts (1) "concerning force" (*de vi*) for one prohibited from burying a dead person or a dead person's bones (*D* 11. 7. 9); (2) "concerning burying a dead person" (*de mortuo inferendo*) for an owner who desires to bury a dead person in an estate on which the usufruct (on which see no. 602, n. 1) is another's (*D* 11. 7. 43) or for anyone who has a right to bury a dead person without another's permission (*D* 11. 8. 1. pr.–4); (3) "concerning an owner's right" (*de iure domini*) for the above owner whom the above usufructuary (on whom see no. 602, n. 1) prevents

(*D* 11. 7. 43); (4) "concerning building a sepulchre" (*de sepulchro aedificando*) for him who has a right to construct such a tomb or monument and against him who prevents workmen and materials from being assembled for construction or for repair of it as well as against him who attempts its collapse (*D* 8. 1. 5–10); (5) "what by force or secretly" (*quod vi aut clam*) against a monument's wrecker (*D* 47. 12. 2).

642. EDICT OF JUSTINIAN I ON CONFIRMATION OF THE DIGEST, 533

(*D*, Constitution *Tanta*)

After the Digest or the Pandects [1] had been completed in 533, Justinian issued the Constitution *Tanta* [2] to command its use throughout the Empire.

The constitution was issued apparently in Greek, from which are translated the sentences acknowledging divine assistance in its composition and celestial favour shown to the Empire, although two Latin versions (one ancient and rather free, one modern and more literal) exist.

In the name of our Lord and God Jesus Christ.

Emperor Caesar Flavius Justinian Alamannicus, Gothicus, Francicus, Germanicus, Anticus, Alanicus, Vandalicus, Africanus, Pious, Fortunate, Renowned, Victor, Triumpher, Ever-August, Augustus to the great Senate and to all the cities of our world.

God has given to us, after the peace with the Persians,[3] after the defeat of the Vandals [4] and the entire acquisition of Libya [4] and the recovery of most famous Carthage,[5] to bring to conclusion the work of the renewal of the ancient laws—a thing which none of the emperors who had ruled before us even hoped to project for their mind and even was considered wholly impossible for human nature ...

This was proper for supernal influence and celestial philanthropy, but not for any human thought or endeavour or ability at all. Therefore we (this, indeed, has become customary to us), having uplifted our hands to God and having called on him to assist us, undertook and accomplished all this, having used Tribonian,[6] the most glorious master [7] and ex-quaestor of our sacred palace and ex-consul, and certain other glorious and wise men,[8] for the entire service,[9] asking always what was happening and learning what was debatable,[10] putting a proper end to all points as a result of both the knowledge and the benignity placed in us by our Lord God and Saviour Jesus Christ ...[11]

And in these matters nothing about the old escheats [12] has been said by us, since also these things, which prevailed because of a certain unfortunate need in the Romans' polity and which constituted a terrible memorial of the civil wars, ought not to be customary in the times wherein God has granted to us both to pursue peace both at home and abroad and, when there is need to wage war, to conquer very easily with his decisive influence the adversaries . . .[13]

And having offered this struggle [14] to the Lord God, who has granted to us both to pursue peace and to accomplish wars successfully and to establish laws for a universal age both for the past [15] and for the present and for the future . . .

And if in the future there should be anything doubtful and should appear not to have been written in these laws (for Nature, indeed, naturally produces many novelties), God has established the imperial power over men, that it, always arranging anything in necessary matters, both may fulfil the indecision of human nature and may limit it by stated laws and rules . . .

Therefore all (we say, both you, great Senate, and every remaining person of our polity), knowing these things, confess thanks to God, who has kept such great good for your times, and use our laws . . .[16]

Indeed this third most famous consulate God has granted to us, if really in it both the peace with the Persians [3] has held steadfast and this so great volume of laws has been dedicated, which by none of those before us has been devised, and, besides, the third part of the world—we mean all Libya [17]—has been added to our sceptres:[18] all these gifts of the third consulate having been granted to us from our Great God and Saviour Jesus Christ . . .

Given on 16 December, our Lord Justinian Perpetual-Augustus being consul for the third time.

1. See no. 617, nn. 1 and 4.
2. See no. 617, n. 6.
3. In 532.
4. In 533. See also no. 646, n. 1 *ad med*.
5. In 533. See also no. 646, n. 14.
6. On him see no. 640, n. 1.
7. Of the offices (*magister officiorum*).
8. Named in section 9 of this constitution.
9. Of codification.
10. Or "doubtful", as most points were referred to the emperor.
11. The older version soon inserts *de suo*: "And this [that nearly 2,000 jurisconsults' books had to be read and excerpted] was accomplished, by celestial splendour and by the Supreme Trinity's favour, according to our mandates."

643. INVALIDITY OF HERETICS' OATHS, 533   1147

12. G. καδοῦκα, L. *caduca*. Justinian in *CI* 6. 51. 1 (dated 534) six months earlier had abolished testamentary dispositions favouring such persons as could not acquire property under a will and had enacted new regulations about such dispositions as became vacant for any reason.

13. The older version next inserts without regard to the Greek text: "The work, with God's favour, has been consummated into the aforesaid fifty books".

14. G. ἄθλος, L. *labor*; i.e. the work of completing the codification in less than one-third of the time anticipated (three as against ten years), says Justinian).

15. The older version does not translate this phrase, which is senseless and is marked in the critical apparatus for deletion.

16. After this the older version interpolates without warrant "God favouring" into the sentence beginning "Moreover this, which even from the beginning seemed best to us, when we were commissioning [God favouring] this work to be done".

17. The ancient version explains that, after Europe and Asia, Libya (on which see n. 4 *supra*)—Africa in the modern version—has been added to the Empire.

18. See no. 527, n. 17.

643. STATUTE OF JUSTINIAN I ON INVALIDITY OF HERETICS' OATHS, 533

(*D* 12. 2. 5. 3)

From Justinian's *Digesta* or *Pandectae*[1] is translated the following opinion of Ulpian. While it is true that Ulpian's decision dealt with any State-disapproved religion and therefore must have comprehended Christianity, yet, since orthodox Christianity had been established as the Empire's official religion in 380 (no. 167) and because Justinian accepted this jurist's decision as valid some three hundred years after its author's death (228), it must be regarded as applicable to heretical and schismatical associations at least in Justinian's reign.

The opinion belongs to the title "On an Oath, whether Voluntary or Compulsory or Judicial".

But if anyone shall have offered an illicit oath, that is to say, of a publicly disapproved religion, let us see whether it should not be considered as if there had not been an oath:—and this I rather judge must be said.

1. See no. 617, nn. 1 and 4.

644. STATUTE OF JUSTINIAN I ON VOWS, 533
(D 50. 12. 2)

From Justinian's Digest[1] is translated the following opinion of Ulpian. Though Ulpian's dictum dealt with pagan conditions before Christianity had been acknowledged as the Empire's official religion in 380 (no. 167), yet, since Justinian conferred validity upon this jurist's decision over three hundred years after its author's death in 228, it must be regarded as applicable in Justinian's reign.

The opinion belongs to the title "On Promises".

If anyone shall have vowed anything,[2] he is obligated by the vow.[3] And the thing obligates the person of the vower, not the thing which is vowed. For the thing which is vowed, when paid, frees the vows; but the thing itself is not made sacred.

Moreover by the vow are obligated patresfamilias and males of their own status,[4] for a minor son[5] or a slave is not obligated by a vow without a father's or a master's authority.

If anyone vows a tenth[6] of his goods, the tenth[6] ceases not to be among his goods before it shall have been separated. And if by chance he who vows a tenth[6] shall have died before the separation, his heir on account of the inheritance is bound for the tenth,[6] for it is agreed that a vow's obligation passes to an heir.

1. See no. 617, nn. 1 and 4.
2. See Introd. to nos. 522 and 601.
3. Since the institution doubtless belongs to sacred law (*ius sacrum*), commentators interpret a vow (*votum*) as a promise made for a religious purpose or in favour of a church or of a pious cause.

It is a unilateral declaration of intent and a form of verbal contract distinct from the classical stipulation (*stipulatio*).

4. The phrase is *puberes sui iuris* and embraces both orphans under guardians, until they will have attained their majority (at fourteen years), and sons emancipated from the paternal power (*patria potestas*).

5. Though the Latin *paterfamilias* has been accepted in current Anglo-American usage, yet the Latin *filiusfamilias* still, it seems, waits for adoption and, until then, must be translated *minor son*. Such a one is described as *alieni iuris* (of another's status—i.e. legally dependent on his father) in contrast to the son characterized as *sui iuris* (of his own status) in the preceding note.

6. The practice of paying tithes ascends into Hebrew antiquity (Gen. 28. 22), wherein three types are found: (1) to Levites for their maintenance (Num. 18. 21), (2) for God's feasts and sacrifices (Deut. 14. 22–6), (3) for charity (Deut. 14. 28–9). Though tithing as such was not enjoined in early

Christian antiquity, yet some such contribution from Christians was commanded by St Paul (1 Cor. 9. 13-14; Gal. 6. 6).

According to Diogenes Laertius (*Vitae*, 1. 53) the Athenians as early as the sixth century B.C. paid a tenth of their property toward the cost of public sacrifices. Livy (*Ab Urbe Cond.* 5. 21. 2) reports that the Romans early in the fourth century B.C. dedicated to Apollo a tenth of what they took in war from their enemies.

Why the tenth part should have been selected among so many ancient peoples—for the custom was common also in Asia and Africa during antiquity—probably belongs to numerology, since the numeral ten contains within it all the lower numbers of the numerical system. Perhaps also it represents the totality of all types of property, which religious-minded persons regard as a gift from God, and, as all things come from God, so of his own then his worshippers give to him (1 Chron. 29. 14).

645. LETTERS OF POPE JOHN II AND JUSTINIAN I ON THEOPASCHISM, 533-4

(*CI* 1. 1. 8)

At least three versions of part of this curious document exist—curious because in his Code Justinian publishes with the force of law Pope John II's reply (534) to his letter sent to the pope (533). The latter is quoted in the former. In the Avellan Collection (*CSEL* 35. 320-8 and 344-7) are copies of the double correspondence and of the emperor's letter.

It appears that Justinian again revived in modified form the Theopaschite formula, which had been advanced in 519 to reconcile various heretical groups in the East, and requested John to rule on the doctrine. This the pope did by declaring for the proposition and by excommunicating its opponents.

The emperor's letter is noteworthy for its testimony to his theological attitude, which was accepted and approved by the pope's answer. By the insertion of both letters into the Code Justinian made his papally confirmed profession of belief legally binding upon his subjects.

John, bishop of the city of Rome, to Justinian Augustus, his most glorious and most clement son.

Amid the bright praises of your Gentleness' wisdom, most Christian of emperors, a certain constellation (so to speak) shines with purer light, because you, taught by ecclesiastical disciplines, through love for the faith and through zeal for love preserve reverence for the Roman see and to it you subject all things and you bring all things to its unity, to whose founder,[1] that is, the first of the apostles, was given the command, when the Lord spoke, "Feed my sheep".[2] And that this see is truly the head of all the churches both the fathers' regulations and the emperors' statutes declare and your Piety's most reverent addresses testify.[3] Therefore it is obvious that in you will be fulfilled what the Scriptures speak: "Through me kings reign and the mighty draft justice".[4] For there is nought which shines with brighter light than right faith in an emperor; there is nought which is so unable to be subject to downfall as true religion. For since each has regard for the author of life or of light, rightly they both reject darkness and know not how to be subject to failure. Wherefore, most glorious of emperors, with all prayers the Divine Power will be besought that it may preserve your Piety in this ardour of faith, in this devotion of mind, in this zeal for unimpaired religion, without its failure for longer times; for we believe this also to be expedient for the holy churches. For it is written: "By his lips a king rules"[5] and again "A king's heart is in God's hand and, where he shall have wished, he will turn it".[6] For it is this which strengthens your sovereignty; this which preserves your rule. For the Church's peace, religion's unity, guards with self-grateful tranquillity the sponsor of the deed who has been raised to the heights. For no little vicissitude is granted by Divine Power to him through whom the Church, divided by no wrinkles, is separated and is changed by no imported stains. For it is written: "That, when a just king shall have sat upon his seat, anything evil shall not oppose him".[7]

Accordingly your Serenity's letter we have received with customary reverence through Hypatius and Demetrius,[8] my most holy brethren and fellow-bishops, by whose report also we have learned that to your faithful peoples you have proclaimed an edict[9] through love for the faith for the intention of the heretics to be removed, according to apostolic doctrine, by the intervening consent of our brethren and fellow-bishops.[10] And this,[9] because it agrees with apostolic doctrine, by our authority we confirm.

Moreover the text of the letter is as follows:

Victor Justinian Pious, Fortunate, Renowned, Triumpher, Ever-August to the most holy John, archbishop of the genial city of Rome and patriarch.

Paying honour to the apostolic see and to your Sanctity (which ever has been and is in our prayer), as becomes those honouring as a father your Beatitude, we hasten to bring to your Sanctity's knowledge all matters which pertain to the churches' status,[11] since ever it has been our great desire that the unity of your apostolic see and the status of God's holy churches should be maintained, which status thus

645. THEOPASCHISM. 533-4

far continues and undisturbedly persists, because no opposition interposes. And so we have hurried both to subject and to unite to your Sanctity's see all bishops of the whole eastern region.

And at present, therefore, we have thought necessary that the matters which here are disturbed, although they are clear and undoubted and always maintained firmly and proclaimed by all bishops [12] according to your apostolic see's doctrine, should come to your Sanctity's knowledge. For we do not permit that anything which pertains to the churches' status, although it is clear and undoubted, and which is set in motion should not become known also to your Sanctity, because it is the head of all the holy churches. For by all means—as has been said—we hasten to increase your see's honour and authority.

Therefore we make known to your Sanctity that certain few persons, unbelieving and alien from God's Holy Catholic and Apostolic Church, have dared in Jewish fashion to speak against those matters which by all bishops [12] according to your doctrine are held rightly and praised and proclaimed, by denying that our Lord Jesus Christ, God's Only-Begotten Son and our God, incarnate from the Holy Spirit and Mary, the Holy Glorious Virgin and Mother of God, made man and crucified, is one of the Holy and Consubstantial Trinity, to be worshipped with and to be glorified with the Father and the Holy Spirit, consubstantial with the Father according to his divinity and the very same one consubstantial with us according to his humanity, suffering in his flesh and the very same one not suffering in his deity. For by refusing to confess that our Lord Jesus Christ, God's Only-Begotten Son and our God, is one of the Holy and Consubstantial Trinity, they seem to be following Nestorius' [13] evil doctrine, saying that according to grace he is God's son and saying that God the Word is one and Christ is another. But all the bishops [12] of the Holy Catholic and Apostolic Church and the most reverend archimandrites of the sacred monasteries, following your Sanctity and maintaining the status and the unity of God's holy Churches, which unity they have in regard to your Sanctity's apostolic see, changing nothing at all about the ecclesiastical status which hitherto has obtained and obtains, by one consent confess and praise, proclaiming that our Lord Jesus Christ, the Only-Begotten Son and Word of God and our God, before the ages [14] and without time [14] born from the Father, in the last days [15] decended from the skies and, having been incarnate from the Holy Spirit and Mary, the Holy and Glorious Virgin and Mother of God, having been born and having been made man and having been crucified, is one of the Holy and Consubstantial Trinity, to be worshipped with and to be glorified with the Father and the Holy Spirit. For we know not God the Word to be one and Christ to be another, but one and the very same consubstantial with the Father according to his divinity and the very same one consubstantial with us according to his humanity, suffering in his flesh and the very same one not suffering in his deity, for, as he is perfect in his divinity, so the very same one also is perfect in his humanity: for in one substance [16] we receive and confess unity, as the Greeks say "We confess unity according to hypostasis".[17] And since the Only-Begotten Son and Word of God, before the ages,[14] and without time [14] born from the Father, the very same also in the last days [15] decending from the skies, having been incarnate from the Holy Spirit and Mary, the Holy and Glorious Virgin and Mother of God, and having been made man, our Lord Jesus Christ is properly and truly God, therefore we say that Mary the Holy and Glorious Virgin, is properly and truly Mother of God:[18] not because God the Word took a beginning from her, but because in the last days [15] he decended from the skies and from her was incarnate and was made man and was born. And him we confess and believe (as has been said) to be consubstantial with the Father according to his deity and the very same consubstantial with us according to his humanity, recognizing the same one's miracles and sufferings, which voluntarily he endured in the flesh.

Moreover we receive four holy councils, that is, of the 318 holy fathers who assembled in Nicaea,[19] and of the 150 holy fathers who convened in this royal city [20] and of the holy fathers who assembled first in Ephesus [21] and of the holy fathers who convened in Chalcedon,[22] just as your apostolic see teaches and proclaims.

Therefore all bishops,[12] following your apostolic see's doctrine, so believe and confess and proclaim.

Wherefore we have hastened to bring these matters to your Sanctity's knowledge by Hypatius and Demetrius,[8] the most blessed bishops, that the things which by a certain few monks have been denied evilly and in Jewish fashion according to Nestorius' [13] disbelief may not escape your Sanctity's notice.

Therefore we ask your paternal Affection that by your letters, sent to us and to the most holy bishop and patriarch,[23] your brother, of this genial city,[24] since he himself has written by the same persons to your Sancity, hastening in all matters to follow your Beatitude's apostolic see, you should make known to us that your Sanctity receives all who confess rightly the aforesaid things and condemns the disbelief of those who in Jewish fashion have dared to deny the right faith. For thus both all persons' love for you and your see's authority increase the more and the unity of the holy churches—which is your concern—will be preserved undisturbed, when all the most blessed bishops shall have learned through your Sanctity's sincere doctrine of the matters which have been referred to you.

645. THEOPASCHISM, 533-4 1153

Moreover we ask your Beatitude to pray for us and to seek for us God's providence.

And by another hand:[25] May the Divinity guard you for many years, holy and most religious father.

Given on 6 June at Constantinople, our Lord Justinian Perpetual-Augustus being consul for the third time.

Therefore, most glorious emperor, it is clear—as the tenor of the reading and your legates'[8] report reveals—that you are desirous for apostolic instructions, when about the Catholic religion's faith you understand these things, you have written [26] these things, which—as we have said—both the apostolic see teachers and the fathers' venerable authority has decreed and we have confirmed in all points. Therefore it is timely to cry with prophetic voice: "The sky from above should take delight, the mountains should pour forth delight, and the hills shall be glad with gladness".[27]

Therefore it is fitting for the faithful to write these things in the tables of the heart,[28] to keep these things as the pupils of the eyes,[29] for there is not anyone, in whom Christ's love burns, who can be an opponent to the faith of your so right, so true confession, since in damning the impiety of Nestorius [13] and of Eutyches [30] obviously and of all heretics you preserve unshakenly and inviolably and with a mind pious and devoted to God the one, true, Catholic faith of our Lord and God, instituted by the Saviour Jesus Christ's instruction and diffused everywhere by prophetic and apostolic preachings and strengthened by the saints' confessions throughout the whole world, unified by the fathers' and the teachers' opinions and consistent with our teaching. For to your professions are opposed only those about whom the Divine Scripture speaks, saying: "They have set falsehood as their hope and they have hoped to be hidden by falsehood",[31] and again they are persons who according to the prophet say to the Lord: "Depart from us; we desire not to know your ways",[32] on account of which Solomon says: "They have roamed the paths of their own cultivation, but with their hands they collect fruitless things".[33]

This, therefore, is your true faith, this the sure religion, this all the fathers of blessed memory and the Roman Church's heads, whom in all things we follow, this the apostolic see has proclaimed hitherto and indestructibly has guarded: whoever has existed as a contradictor to this confession, to this faith, he himself has judged himself to be alien from the Holy Communion, alien from the Catholic Church. For in the Roman city we found Cyrus,[34] who was from a monastery of the Sleepless,[35] with his followers, whom by apostolic pleadings we hastened to recall to the right faith and as sheep, which, straying, had been lost, to the Lord's sheepfold,[36] that according to the prophet [37] the stammering tongues might know how to speak the things which pertain to peace. Moreover the first of the apostles [1] through us to them not believing speaks the words of the Prophet Isaiah: "Walk in the light of your fire and of the flame, which you have kindled",[38] but their heart was hardened,[39] as it is written, that they might not understand and the sheep, which were not mine, wished not to hear the shepherd's voice.[39] And since in these matters they maintained the things which have been ordained by their pontiff, we have not at all received them in our communion and we have ordered them to be alien from every Catholic church, unless, since their error has been damned, they shall have signified, after a canonical profession has been made, that they will follow our teaching as speedily as possible. Surely it is fair that those who do not adapt at all their obedience to our ordinances should be considered banished from the churches. But because the Church never closes her bosom to returners,[40] I beg your Clemency that if, when their previous error has been discarded and when their wicked intention [41] has been removed, they shall have wished to return to the Church's unity, you would remove the stings of your indignation from them, when received in our communion, and grant the pardon of a kindly spirit to us making intercession.

Moreover we beseech God and our Saviour Jesus Christ that he should deign to guard you for long and peaceful times in this true religion and unity and veneration for the apostolic see, whose pre-eminence you, as most Christian and pious, preserve in all matters.

Besides, most serene of emperors, we praise the persons of your legates, Hypatius and Demetrius,[8] our brethren and fellow-bishops, whom your Clemency's very selection has manifested that they will be pleasing.[42] For the weight of such a great case could not have been enjoined[43] upon persons unless perfect in Christ, but you would not at all deign to send addresses full of such great piety[44] and of such reverence[44] unless through loving persons.

And by another hand: The grace of our Lord Jesus Christ and the love of God and the communion of the Holy Spirit be always with you,[45] most pious son.

Likewise the subscription: May Almighty God guard your rule and safety [46] with perpetual protection, most glorious and most clement son, Emperor Augustus.[47]

Given on 25 March at Rome, our Lord Justinian Perpetual-Augustus for the fourth time and the most distinguished Paulinus the Younger being consuls.[48]

1. St Peter. See no. 442, n. 7.
2. John 21. 17.

3. See e.g. nos. 442, n. 7, and 637, n. 7. But in no. 618 (see n. 3 therein) Justinian asserts the primacy of the Constantinopolitan Church (on which see no. 375, n. 7).
4. Prov. 8. 15. The pope writes *scribunt* (write, draft) for the traditional *decernunt* (decree).
5. Prov. 16. 10.
6. Prov. 21. 1.
7. Prov. 20. 8. In the preceding sentence the idea that the *Church* has *no wrinkles* and *no stains* is borrowed from Eph. 5. 27.
8. The one was bishop of Ephesus and the other was bishop of Philippi. They carried the imperial letter to the pope.
9. Probably no. 636.
10. Perhaps the reference to the apostolic doctrine about heretics is to Titus 3. 10. See also *CA* 6. 18.
11. See no. 637, n. 7.
12. See no. 16, n. 4.
13. The Constantinopolitan patriarch, after whom Nestorianism is named.
14. See no. 569, n. 4.
15. See no. 569, n. 3.
16. The word is *subsistentia* rather than *substantia*, on which see no. 67, n. 17.
17. See no. 67, n. 17. The Greek quotation appears amid the Latin.
18. One version in *CSEL* has *genetrix* for *mater*, which the other version therein and *CI* have.
19. In 325.
20. At Constantinople in 381.
21. In 431, as opposed to the Ephesian *Latrocinium* of 449.
22. In 451.
23. Epiphanius.
24. Constantinople.
25. *CSEL* 35. 347 reads for this addition "Copy of the subscription", meaning thereby that the emperor signed the letter.
26. *CSEL* changes the tense to the present.
27. Editors note for this evolved quotation Isa. 45. 8, 44. 23, 55. 12; Ps. 96. 11 and 98. 8.
28. An allusion to 2 Cor. 3. 3.
29. An allusion to Prov. 7. 2, where the entire expression is singularized (*pupilla* being usually mistranslated as "apple").
30. Constantinopolitan archimandrite and author of Eutychianism.
31. Isa. 28. 15.
32. Job 21. 14.
33. Perhaps based on Wisd. 15. 4.
34. Not identifiable otherwise than chief of a monastic delegation to the pope in protest against Theopaschism.
35. The Akoimetoi, so called because of their system of successive relays of

monks devoted to perpetual prayer and to praise, were founded *c.* 400 on the Euphrates River. Later in the fifth century the Irenaion, their mother-house, was erected on the eastern shore of the Bosporus Strait, though its fame was overshadowed by the more famous Studium (also instituted in that century and in Constantinople), which, staffed by Akoimetoi, who, however, did not maintain the sleepless tradition, became the most influential monastery in the capital.

36. An allusion to John 10. 16.
37. An allusion to Isa. 32. 4 and Ps. 28. 3.
38. Isa. 50. 11.
39. For the thought see Mark 4. 10 with John 10. 26-7.
40. Such has been the Church's policy, based upon Biblical warrant, of which among many notable passages may be mentioned Isa. 30. 15, 55. 7; Ezek. 18. 23, 33. 11; Joel 2. 12-13; Luke 15. 11-32 (parable of the prodigal son). And the pope in announcing the Church's attitude here could point to the Roman Church's reception of the lapsed after the Decian persecution almost three centuries earlier, when a largely attended synod in Rome unanimously authorized return of such lapsed Christians as were sincere in their repentance (Eusebius, *HE* 6. 43. 2).
41. *CSEL* has "teaching".
42. A less likely translation, though more consonant with the Latin order of words, gives: "whom the very selection has manifested will be pleasing to your Clemency".
43. *CSEL* reads active voice here: "you could not have enjoined the weight" etc.
44. Or possibly "dutifulness . . . respect", if the pope is thinking of what a layman, though emperor, owes to his office.
45. Adapted from 2 Cor. 13. 14. *CSEL* inserts "amen" here.
46. Perhaps "health" or "life" (*salus* is the word, on which see no. 255, n. 3).
47. *CSEL* omits this paragraph.
48. *CSEL* gives simply the date.

646. MANDATES OF JUSTINIAN I ON THE OFFICE STAFF OF THE PRAETORIAN PREFECT OF AFRICA AND ON THAT DIOCESE'S ENTIRE STATUS, 534

(*CI* 1. 27. 1, 2)

These documents, which are of prime importance for the imperial organization of the government of the recently reconquered provinces of Africa [1] (seven grouped under a prefecture),[2] are remarkable also for the Christian cast of their introductions to the scheme's details (which are not translated as being devoid of ecclesiastical interest).[3] As part of the Empire's law, then, these imperial tributes to Christianity constitute notable testimony to the thought of the most accomplished theologian among Roman emperors.

I

In the name of our Lord Jesus Christ.

Emperor Caesar Flavius Justinian Alamannicus, Gothicus, Francicus, Germanicus, Anticus, Alanicus, Vandalicus, Africanus, Pious, Fortunate, Renowned, Victor and Triumpher, Ever-August to Archelaus, praetorian prefect of Africa.

What thanks and what praises we ought to present to our Lord God Jesus Christ neither our mind can conceive nor our tongue can proffer. Many bounties indeed even hitherto from God we have deserved and we confess his innumerable benefits toward us, for which we know that we have done nothing worthy: in comparison with all things, however, this, which now Almighty God through us has deigned to demonstrate for his own praise and for his own name, exceeds all miraculous works which in the world [4] have happened, that Africa through us in so short a time should regain its liberty, when it had been captured 105 years previously by Vandals,[5] who had been enemies at the same time of souls and of bodies.[6] For indeed they used to transfer the souls, not enduring various tortures and punishments, by rebaptizing to their own falsity;[7] moreover most harshly they used to subjugate to the barbarian yoke the bodies distinguished by free lineages. Also God's very sacrosanct churches they used to befoul with their own falsities;[7] but in the case of some they have made stables [8] from these. We have seen venerable men, who, though their tongues had been severed from the roots, used to speak miraculously about their punishments;[9] but others, dispersed through various provinces after various tortures, have passed their life in exile. With what speech, therefore, or with what works are we adequate to give worthy thanks to God, because through me, his latest servant, he has deigned to vindicate his Church's injuries and to snatch so many provinces' peoples from slavery's yoke?

Our predecessors, to whom not only it has not been permitted to liberate Africa,[10] but who also have seen Rome itself captured by the same Vandals [11] and all imperial ornaments transferred thence to Africa, have not deserved this benefit of God. But now God by his mercy not only has delivered Africa and all its provinces to us, but also has restored to us the very imperial ornaments, which from captured Rome had been taken forcibly.

Therefore after so many benefits, which God has conferred on us, from our Lord God's mercy we ask this: that he should guard the provinces, which he has deigned to restore to us, firm and unharmed and that he should cause us to govern these according to his will and pleasure and that all Africa should realize Almighty God's mercy and that its inhabitants should recognize how, since they have been liberated from harshest captivity and from the barbarian yoke, they have deserved to live in very great liberty under our most felicitous sovereignty.

This also we beseech, praying with prayers [12] of the Holy and Glorious Ever-Virgin and Mother of God, Mary, that whatever of our State is inferior God may restore through us, his latest servants, in his own name and may make us worthy to fulfil his services.

Accordingly, with God aiding, for our State's felicity we ordain through this divine law that all Africa, which God has offered to us, by his mercy should accept an excellent ordered state and should have its own prefecture, that, just as the East and Illyricum,[13] so also Africa may be adorned by our Clemency with the greatest praetorian power.

And we order its seat to be Carthage [14] and in the preamble of public papers to the other prefectures to be joined the name of it, which we decide that your Excellence now should govern.

And from it, with God aiding, should be arranged seven provinces with their own governors,[15] of which provinces Zeugi (which previously used to be called Proconsular Carthage [16]) and Byzacium and Tripolis should have consular rectors,[17] but the rest, that is, Numidia and the Mauretanias [18] and Sardinia,[19] should be governed by presidents [17] with God's aid . . .

We wish, therefore, that all our governors [15] should be eager so to govern their administrations according to God's will and fear and our selection and appointment, that none of them either should be surrendered to cupidity or himself should introduce or should permit his judges [20] to introduce any violences either upon their office staffs or upon any other contributors.[21] For although through all our provinces, God helping, we hasten that they may have unharmed contributors,[21] nevertheless we have particular regard for the African

646. THE STAFF OF THE PREFECT OF AFRICA, 534

diocese's tributaries, who after captivity of so long periods have deserved, God helping, through us to look upon the light of liberty. Therefore we order all violence and all avarice to cease and justice and truth to be preserved toward all our tributaries. For thus both God is placated and they themselves can be relieved and can flourish, just as our State's other contributors [21] . . .

And this is the list, God aiding: . . .[22]

The law was issued [23] at Constantinople, our Lord Justinian Perpetual-Augustus for the fourth time and the most distinguished Paulinus being consuls.

II

The same Augustus to Belisarius, master of the soldiers throughout the East.[24]

In the name of our Lord Jesus Christ we advance always to all plans and to all actions. For through him we have received the rights of sovereignty, through him we have confirmed peace with the Persians for eternity,[25] through him we have dejected very bitter enemies [26] and very strong tyrants,[27] through him we have overcome many difficulties, through him it has been granted to us both to defend Africa and to reduce it under our sovereignty, through him [28] also we trust that by our governance it may be governed rightly and may be guarded strongly.

Wherefore now through his grace we have constituted governors and office staffs of the civil administrations for each African province, assigning what emoluments each person ought to accept. Therefore, referring our purpose also now to his providence, we arrange to regulate the armed military forces and the dukes of the soldiers . . .[29]

The law was issued on 13 April at Constantinople, our Lord Justinian Perpetual-Augustus for the fourth time and the most distinguished Paulinus being consuls.

1. Although Alaric I, king of the Visigoths, in 410 and Wallia, his second successor, in 416 had prepared to invade Africa, it was not until 429 that the barbarians' third attempt succeeded under the leadership of Genseric (*al.* Gaiseric), king of the Vandals, who were accompanied by Alans. By 435 the conquest was sufficiently complete to permit Genseric and Valentinian III to conclude a treaty, which preserved the *status quo* on terms favourable to the Vandals. In 442 a second treaty surrendered more territory to the invaders, who extended their control eventually over the western Mediterranean islands (including Sicily).

After peace with Persia had been made in 532, Justinian started preparations for the reconquest of Africa—a plan which evoked no encouragement from his councillors, but which was hailed enthusiastically not only by the ecclesiastics, for they realized that its success would result in the rescue of the orthodox in Africa from their Arian overlords, who persecuted the native population and incarcerated their clergy, but also by the merchants, who reckoned the recovery of Africa as an advantage to their interests. In June 533 the Roman expeditionary force, commanded by Belisarius, Justinian's great general, sailed from Constantinople, landed at Caputvada (Ras Kapudia) in September, defeated the Vandals at Ad Decimum (near Tunis), occupied Carthage without opposition, destroyed the Vandal rule by a second victory at Tricamaron (near Carthage) in December.

The present document was issued in the following April.

2. The seven are named in the text after n. 15. "Diocese" is retained in the Code's title probably for antiquarian interest, since there was a diocese of Africa in the prefecture of Italy before the Vandalic conquest.

3. A confirmed bureaucrat would discover interesting reading in these details of an older bureaucracy (already ruinously expensive and irremediably corrupt), which numbered, recorded, regulated, and systematized everything. See Introd., n. 9 *ad fin.*

4. Or "in [our] age".

5. Cf. *supra* n. 1 *ad init.*, where the calculation tallies.

6. The Vandals were Arians and occasionally persecuted the Catholics in Africa. The best account of the atrocities is by Victor Vitensis, *Historia Persecutionis Africanae Provinciae*. It is *CSEL* 7. 1–114.

7. Literally "disbelief", but Arians believed in their version of Christianity, though it was not Catholic: hence heresy.

8. Procopius later confirms this and mentions horses and other animals stabled in churches (*De Bell.* 3. 8. 20).

The conversion of churches into stables may have amazed Justinian, but later Christians were to do the same and even far worse in the name of Christ, particularly in England, France, and Germany—not to extend the list by violating the (pagan) divine (Vergil, *Ecl.* 8. 75) and the (Christian) scholastic rule of three.

9. Evagrius (*HE* 4. 14), referring to this law, adds Procopius' testimony (*De Bell.* 3. 8. 4) that the latter personally saw in Constantinople such confessors, whose tongues Huneric, Genseric's son and successor, had excised, because they had refused conversion to Arianism.

10. E.g. Leo I's grand armada (over 1,110 vessels and 100,000 men) was half-destroyed near Carthage in 468.

11. In June 455 Genseric and his Vandals ransacked Rome for a fortnight.

12. The etymological figure is retained from the Latin.

13. After the prefectures of Gaul and of Italy had disappeared with the Western Roman Empire's fall (476), only these two remained in the Eastern Empire until the present erection of Africa.

14. Carthage, traditionally founded by Dido and colonists from Tyre (Vergil, *Aen.* 1. 12–14) anytime (according to ancient authors) between

646. THE STAFF OF THE PREFECT OF AFRICA, 534   1161

1234 B.C. (Appian, *Bell. Lib.* 1. 1 *in init.*) and 793 B.C. (Servius, *Comm. in Verg. Aen.* 4. 459), was destroyed in 146 B.C. by Publius Cornelius Aemilianus Scipio Africanus Minor (Florus, *Epit.* 1. 31. 7–18), was refounded as a Roman colony abortively by Gaius Sempronius Gracchus in 122 B.C. (Plutarch, *C. Gracch.* 11. 1, 13. 1), but was restored by Gaius Julius Caesar in 46 B.C. (Strabo, *Geog.* 17. 15; Plutarch, *Caes.* 57. 5), was captured by Vandals in 439 (Appian, op. cit., 20. 136; Procopius, op. cit., 3. 4. 1, 3. 5. 8), and was recovered by Belisarius in 533 (Procopius, op. cit., 3. 20. 17).

15. The word is *iudex*, but its meaning here must be distinguished from its significance *infra* at n. 20. See no. 234, n. 3.

16. Africa Proconsularis, the province wherein Carthage and Utica were the chief cities, had been beyond the jurisdiction both of the vicar of the diocese of Africa, in which it lay geographically, and of the praetorian prefect of Italy, which included North Africa west of Egypt administratively. The governor of Proconsular Africa reported directly to the emperor.

17. See no. 234, n. 3.

18. See no. 19, n. 22 *ad init.*

19. The reorganization thus is: Zeugitana (Proconsularis Carthago *sive* Africa), Byzacena, Tripolitana, Numidia, Mauretania Caesariensis, Mauretania Sitifensis, Sardinia.

20. The word is *iudex*, but its meaning obviously must differ from its significance *supra* at n. 15. See no. 161, n. 3.

21. Taxpayers (*collatores*), unless these are persons who pay voluntary contributions to the State. The drift is uncertain, for while officials' violence toward their office staffs is not unknown, it is more natural to couple office staffs with their superiors in violent acts upon citizens; but since in the next sentence it is certain that the Latin adjective characterizing *contributors* is passive in meaning and if any precision in use of conjunctions can be expected in late Latin, *office staffs* and *contributors* go together as objects of violence from governors and judges.

22. Here follows as elaborate schedule of office-holders and their salaries. From § 13 we learn that in the prefect's several bureaux were 396 men and that each of the seven provincial governors had a staff of fifty men: a total of 746 bureaucrats plus the eight superiors. Bury (1. 33, n. 1) estimates the civil administration's annual cost at nearly £11,000 (at the value of the pound sterling as of 1923). The cost of the military administration, which had a master of soldiers (*magister militum Africae*) at its head and included four dukes (*duces*), commanding mobile units and frontier garrisons, and their staffs (detailed in *CI* 1. 27. 2), Bury sets at £7,050 (loc cit.). The grand total, then, was annually about £18,050 (1923) or nominally about $50,540 at the current (1962) rate of exchange.

23. Since the next statute (*CI* 1. 27. 2), which treats the military organization of Africa, was promulgated on 13 April, it seems that the present law preceded it and that it may be assigned to the same month.

24. See no. 106, n. 4.

25. In the spring of 532 after a war which began in 527. But hostilities were resumed by the Persians in 540–5 and by the Romans in 549–57. In 562 peace was concluded finally.

26. A common phrase (*acerbissimi hostes*) in Cicero (e.g. *In Cat.* 4. 6. 13).

27. Probably the Vandals, who in the fundamental significance of the Greek word (transliterated into Latin and English) had usurped the government of Africa.

28. This concludes a notable series of six anaphoric phrases (*per ipsum*).

29. After this point Christian colour vanishes, save for such pious interpositions as "invoking God's aid by day and by night" (§ 4), "God favouring" (§ 4b), "God aiding us and our State" (§ 7), "after it shall have pleased God" (§ 10), "God helping" (§§ 10, 13, 18), "God assisting" (§ 13), "God willing" (§ 19). What remain are directions for the dukes and a schedule of salaries for their staffs.

647. EDICT OF JUSTINIAN I ON NON-CATHOLIC OWNERSHIP OF CHRISTIAN SLAVES, 534

(*CI* 1. 10. 2)

This law forbids non-Catholic ownership of Christian slaves and authorizes the freedom of such slaves and fines their masters thirty pounds as penalty.

Emperor Justinian Augustus.

A pagan [1] and a Jew and a Samaritan and everyone not orthodox cannot have a Christian slave, since both he is freed [2] and the possessor gives [2] thirty pounds to the private estate.[3]

Given on 28 June at Constantinople.

1. See no. 121, n. 3.
2. In English we should expect the future indicative.
3. Of the emperor.

648. MANDATE OF JUSTINIAN I ON LEGACIES TO ECCLESIASTICAL INSTITUTIONS, 534

(*CI* 1. 3. 55)

Justinian renews one of his earlier ordinances regulating the management of property willed to pious foundations (no. 612) and also by this supplement restricts further the commercial transactions of the controllers of these institutions, when they attempt to alienate property bequeathed in perpetuity to these.

The same Augustus to John, praetorian prefect.[1]

The present law is recalled to the recollection of another law written by us,[2] which indeed we have believed also ought to be confirmed anew with a certain better addition, by exhibiting a greater penalty against transgressors, not because we delight in increases of penalties (for nothing is so according our mind as benevolence), but that through fear of punishment we may bar from transgression persons preferring to sin.

Having written it, therefore, we know that the law says that there should be no licence to the most holy churches' stewards or to the directors of hostels or hospitals or almshouses or monasteries, whether of men or of women or of other such corporations (of which the preceding ordinance makes mention), to sell according to some agreement or for stated money [3] the things, which the laws call annuities,[4] bequeathed to them or to alienate these otherwise according to any way whatever and to take from persons succeeding them the ensuing consolation. And we added to the law suitable reasons, since no longer is the appellation of annuity [4] preserved because of this undertaking, if it would not be given year by year, but when bequeathed for once it would perish completely.

Renewing again this law with a certain addition, we ordain that if anyone of either the most devout stewards or managers of hostels or superintendents of hospitals or directors of almshouses or superintendents of homes for the aged or directors of nurseries or directors of orphanages or archimandrites or other persons embraced by our previous divine ordinance should have tried to change either in money [3] or in other properties what has been bequeathed in perpetuity to the holy houses, over which they preside, for that which does not seem to be in perpetuity, but by divisions [5] or sales or some other devices (contrary to the meaning of the divine law already made current by us against such matters) should have tried to stop the said property from continuing in perpetuity, he should have absolutely no authority to do this, but, even if he should have done it, what has happened should be invalid; and to him who shall take upon himself the said management after him or, if this one—as is likely—has been negligent, to all in succession should be authority to recall immediately what has happened and thus to declare it invalid (as if it has not proceeded in the beginning), so that in the interim the fruits and the interests and all gain may be brought wholly to the holy house—the things undertaken in the interim being void in every way.

1164   648. LEGACIES TO ECCLESIASTICAL INSTITUTIONS, 534

For to each man has been given by the Demiurge [6] one course of life, whose end is absolutely death;[7] but for the holy houses and their constitutions, being maintained immortal by God, it is not possible to contrive any limit even in respect to their possessions, but while the holy houses last (and they last even for ever and at least until the very end of the ages, while the Christians' name both exists and is venerated among men), it is just that the subsidies bequeathed in perpetuity or the immortal returns also should remain, ever subserving the pious actions which never cease at all.

But he who has committed any such transgression and has dared to deliver the property for money [3] or by any other motive should bring [8] (according to what has been said previously) no loss upon the houses against which he has done these things, but they should gain [8] profit from the money [3] or the property which they have accepted and should demand [8] that the bequest should be no less without any diminution at all, but he who has done this and his heirs and successors and his properties should be liable [8] to him with whom he has contracted and he should preserve [8] him [9] free from loss in respect to his own person and properties, in order that he may expect no restoration of the things given or confirmation of what has been done against the most holy house, which he has damaged for no needful purpose; but as far as it pertains to the person with whom he has contracted: he [9] should have all authority by the laws to proceed against him and his heirs and his properties and to collect what has been given, if he should have been able, in order that, if not with devoutness toward God, at least with fear for his own and his own heirs' substance they may be more hesitant toward such agreements, which admittedly they made for no useful purpose, but when they either are corrupted by money or are subservient to some passions.

And banning all these matters by this divine law and ordaining this to be inscribed in our sacred laws, we dedicate it to God, the lord of all things, and to our Saviour Jesus Christ, by bringing also this as a sacrifice fair and befitting him.

Given on 12 September at Constantinople, our Lord Justinian Perpetual-Augustus for the fourth time and the most distinguished Paulinus being consuls.

1. Of the East.
2. No. 612.
3. Literally "gold". The phrase in Greek represents the technical Latin expression *certa pecunia*.
4. See no. 612, n. 16.
5. Or "settlements", "compromises", "transactions".
6. It is rare to find such a philosophical word in legal language. In Platonism

the Demiurge (δημιουργός) first appears (especially in the *Timaeus*—in St Jerome's opinion Plato's darkest dialogue, which not even Cicero's Latin version, made with "golden mouth", could illumine for him [*Comm. in Amos*, 2. 5. 283 = *PL* 25. 1088])—as an inferior deity who created the cosmos, the architect and the artificer of the visible universe, the framer and the father of works, but not a creator *stricto sensu*, for he does not create things *ex nihilo*, but, acting as the Anaxagorean "Mind" (νοῦς) or active principle of the universe, imposes order on pre-existent Chaos.

But while the Jews and the Christian fathers use the word loosely to indicate the Creator and thus identify him with the Supreme Being, in Gnosticism of the early Christian era the Demiurge is the creator and the ruler of the material world, a subordinate being, very different from the Supreme Being. Some Gnostics made him the Satan of Gnosticism and other Gnostics equated him with Jehovah of the Old Testament to oppose him to Christ of the New Testament.

7. Perhaps the *course of life* is a reminiscence of Lucretius (*De Rer. Nat.* 2. 79), who concludes a passage on birth and death by likening generations of living creatures to runners who transmit the torch of life—a reference, doubtless, to the Greek torch race (λαμπαδηφορία), wherein each runner relayed a lighted torch to the next (Herodotus, *Hist.* 8. 98; cf. Plato, *Pol.* 1. 328A).

8. There are no principal verbs in this sentence, but those translated as such are infinitives depending on an understood construction of command.

9. The contractor with whom the transgressing ecclesiastic has dealt.

649. RESCRIPT OF JUSTINIAN I ON EPISCOPAL INTEREST IN ACTRESSES, 534

(*CI* 5. 4. 29)

This defective rescript,[1] addressed to civil magistrates (according to no. 650), authorizes provincial bishops, if provincial governors are unco-operative, to assist actresses in their desire to withdraw from the stage and to report such governors, that these may be punished severely.

The same emperor . . .
Every . . .
None either shall drag to the stage her who is undesiring or shall hinder her who voluntarily has entered it from afterward desiring to find rest or shall give encouragement and shall take securities from them concerning their non-departure later from the stage.
If anyone, therefore, being in whatever rank of life or officiating [2]

in whatever office,² should have done this, it shall be permitted for the woman to approach both the governor, unless he himself is one who uses force,³ and the bishop, that those men may avert him who forces the woman, on the ground that he knows that, if he should have resisted, he is ejected from the city and his property is confiscated. These things then, if anyone should have dragged anyone to the stage.

But if he hinders her who voluntarily has entered it from afterward departing, both the giving of securities shall be cancelled and, if the sureties have been demanded to give anything, they⁴ shall take double. Likewise also, if the women themselves have been demanded to furnish anything, they shall take double—the governor and the bishop executing these matters. And in the beginning it shall not even be permitted to demand securities for women who have entered the stage concerning their non-departure later.

The bishop has⁵ authority, if the province's governor is one who uses force,³ to oppose him and to preserve the sureties from payment. But if the governor does not yield, it shall be permitted to the bishop to declare it, so that the governor² should depart from his governorship² and his property should be confiscated and he should be exiled perpetually.

For such women there is⁵ authority also to engage in marriages and without a divine rescript.

Moreover this ordinance should prevail⁶ for its own times—all marriages formerly prohibited being prohibited, except this which now has been intended and which once needed a divine rescript but now no longer.⁷

The ordinance, having legislated all these matters, asserts that these then should prevail, while the women should remain discreet; for if after marriage they should have desired to become actresses again, not only they fall from the good standing which they had, but not even share in any aid either from this ordinance or from that of Justin of divine lot,⁸ for they lie under the charge of sexual crime.⁹

1. The superscription is restored, the opening part is lost, the subscription is missing. The date is conjectured to be the same as that of no. 650 or a little earlier. The last paragraph seems to be an interpretation of the statute.

2. The English translation preserves the etymological figure of the Greek.

3. Either to produce entrance or to prevent exit.

4. That is, the guarantors for her remaining an actress shall regain twice what they have been compelled to surrender in the category of securities forfeited by them because of her withdrawal.

5. This independently printed sentence in Greek has no principal verb in a finite mode. The genitive absolute construction is used.

6. This principal verb is an infinitive in Greek.

7. The editor of the Greek text suggests here the addition of the latter part of the fourth paragraph of no. 650, which regulates such marriages for ex-actresses—the exception here meant.

8. *CI* 5. 4. 23 (dated 520–3).

9. This word στοῦπρον is transliterated from Latin *stuprum*, which the Romans used widely to indicate unchastity of any kind within or without wedlock, always implying by it infliction of dishonour on the violator of the current sexual *mores* and often applying it to the worst type of sexual abnormality. Curiously, however, *stuprum* seems not to have been used to include commerce with prostitutes. Its Greek transliteration appears to be unrecorded in the standard Graeco-English dictionaries.

650. MANDATE OF JUSTINIAN I ON EPISCOPAL INTEREST IN ACTRESSES AND DANSEUSES, 534

(*CI* 1. 4. 33)

This constitution attracts provincial bishops' attention to another ordinance (no. 649), which with this authorizes them to intervene on behalf of women either compelled to become actresses or dancers or prevented from abandoning such activities. Particularly when provincial governors violate the law in this matter, the bishops then are to act and, if unable to secure adherence, then to report to the emperor that fact. Punishment for episcopal disobedience is threatened.

The same emperor to the most God-beloved bishops everywhere on earth.

We have made a divine ordinance,[1] permitting to none either to drag an unwilling woman, slave or free, into the drama or the dance [2] or to hinder her, if she wishes, from departing or to demand for her sureties on condition that they have promised a certain sum of gold concerning this matter.

But if any such thing should have occurred, we have ordered [1] that these things should be prevented both by the most distinguished governors of provinces and by the most God-beloved bishops in cities, having given to the most God-beloved bishops along with the most distinguished governor of the province permission to summon to themselves even against their will persons who have used force [3] or who hinder women from departing the profession [4] and to confiscate their property and to expel them from the city.

But if the province's governor [5] himself should be one who uses force[3] or hinders a departure from the said profession,[4] we have given permission[1] for her who suffers these things and for her surety to approach only the most God-beloved bishops and for them[6] to oppose themselves to him who has the rule and not to allow injury or, if they should not have been competent for this, to declare it to our Majesty, so that from us fitting punishment should be executed—the securities being cancelled absolutely and the sureties being preserved from payment; and we have given[7] permission[1] to such departing women, being free and well born, to enter upon lawful marriage, even if they who take these should happen to be adorned with the most august ranks, needing no longer an imperial rescript, but negotiating the marriage according to authority, the nuptial contracts, however, by every means being between them; and we have ordained[1] the same things in the case of actresses' daughters.

Therefore the said ordinance,[1] issued as a rescript to the civic magistrates, we have placed in the fifth book of all the ordinances of this book named after our Piety.[8]

Moreover, since it is necessary by the present legislation to make clear these matters also for you most God-beloved bishops everywhere on earth, we, having compressed, therefore, the matters legislated in that[1] with more diffuse narration, make this divine ordinance also for you, that you, maintaining the sacerdotal[9] gravity and adhering to discretion, should preserve these matters by reckoning then upon fear of the Great God and the imperial indignation, if you should have transgressed any of these.

Given on 1 November at Constantinople, our Lord Justinian Perpetual-Augustus for the fourth time and the most distinguished Paulinus being consuls.

1. No. 649.
2. Literally "stage (σκηνή) or orchestra (ὀρχήστρα)"; but to Greeks and Romans "stage" meant first the stage-building which was the background for the dramatic action and then the floor before the building, while "orchestra" meant the space where the chorus danced in front of the floor.
3. To compel women to become actresses or danseuses.
4. This is a euphemistic concession to modern opinion, for abundant references attest that the ancients regarded stagefolk of both sexes as plying a trade—and a low one at that. Patristic condemnation of the theatre is too well known to demand documentation and even in some contemporary Christian sects the chief fame which a "professional" actress or danseuse attains is definitely ill fame, since it sometimes seems that attainment of stardom is associated with sexual affability.

This law's irony is of no little interest, because Justinian chose for his consort (see no. 630, n. 6) an egregious ecdysiast and a heretical harlot, Theodora, whose intellect—even her antagonists, though they hated her for her humble birth, admitted—was not inferior to her pulchritude, over which many had slavered in her sensual strip-tease on the stage, with which some had acquired a better acquaintance in bed, and by which most maintained that she helped herself up the hill of history. But the theological talents of her accomplished emperor achieved expression not only in the construction of Hagia Sophia (the last great gift of Greek genius to us and on which see no. 505, n. 1), but also in the reconstruction of his empress' manners and morals. The conversion was obviously complete, since the Orthodox calendar commemorates her memory on 14 November. See also no. 630, n. 8 *ad fin.*

For a sympathetic biography of Theodora see P. I. Wellman, *The Female* (New York, 1953).

5. Literally "he who guides the province in a straight line".
6. Probably the bishops are meant.
7. In Greek this principal verb is a participle agreeing with the sentence's far-removed subject.
8. It (no. 649) is there and the book, of course, is his *Codex*.
9. See no. 526, n. 11.

651. MANDATE OF JUSTINIAN I ON EPISCOPAL JURISDICTION IN CLERICAL MISCONDUCT, 534

(*CI* 1. 4. 34)

This constitution concerns clerical gambling and attendance at popular spectacles, by forbidding these recreations to the clergy and by establishing episcopal procedure against violators. Penalties for violation of both the statute and its enforcement are announced.

The same emperor to Epiphanius, the most holy archbishop of this fortunate city [1] and ecumenical patriarch.

We exceedingly believe that the priests' [2] purity and good discipline and straining toward the Lord God and our Saviour Jesus Christ and the continual prayers uplifted by them procure much good will for our State and enlargement. And through these it is that we both rule over barbarians and are become lords of those places which formerly we had not. And by how much their dignity and decorum should be enlarged, by so much we believe also that our State increases. For if they should exhibit a life dignified and in every way blameless and should admonish all the rest of the people, so that they, looking toward their dignity, should refrain from many sins, it is evident that as a result both the souls will be better for all persons and easily to us will be granted by the Great God and our Saviour Jesus Christ a suitable benevolence.

Therefore to us who examine well these things it has been announced unexpectedly that some of the most devout deacons and even also indeed of the presbyters—for even beyond this we also blush to speak (we mean, of course, the grade of the God-beloved bishops)—that [3] of these some are not ashamed to handle dice of their own accord and thus to pursue a shameful sight [4] prohibited by us [5] for the most part [6] even for laymen themselves, but others do not engage actually in such a game, but either join the players or sit as spectators of a wicked play and with all craving watch the utmost wickednesses of all and hear blasphemous words, which in such affairs necessarily occur, and pollute both their hands and eyes and ears by thus condemned and prohibited games; and still others even undisguisedly either appear at horse races or even challenge [7] some persons on the defeat or the victory of horses or by themselves or by certain other persons indecorously play such games or are spectators at the amusements on the stage and in the orchestra [8] or are present at the fights of persons fighting [9] with beasts in theatres [10] and do not understand that they themselves preach to persons recently initiated [11] and deemed worthy of the venerable mysteries [12] that they should renounce both the service and all pomp of the Demon Adversary,[13] of which the least part are such things.

Often we have proclaimed to them to be on guard against such things; but, seeing that much information about these things is produced for us, we have come to the need to arrive at the present law because of our Piety's zeal and partly for the priesthood [14] itself and partly for the advantage to the common State.

And we ordain that none—either deacon or presbyter and (much more) bishop (and this also would seem incredible since in their ordinations both prayers are uplifted to Christ our God and invocation of the Holy and Venerable Spirit is made and on their heads or to their hands are imposed [15] or are delivered [15] the holiest of the mysteries [12] among us, that both all senses may be made pure for them and may be consecrated to God)[16]—none of these, therefore, henceforth after this our divine law should dare either to play any game of dice [17] whatever or to join persons playing it or to be seated by them and to enjoy himself and to be in sympathy with the things being done or to go to these popular spectacles, which we previously have mentioned, and to do any of the things prohibited in them, but henceforth to abstain from all participation in regard to these.

For as to what already has preceded: although one ought to investi-

651. JURISDICTION IN CLERICAL MISCONDUCT, 534

gate and to pursue properly, yet through benevolence we yield, imposing upon all persons for future time observance in accord with the present law. For it is proper for them to have time for fasts and for ceremonies and for exercises of the Divine Oracles [18] and for prayers for all persons, but not by abandoning these to fasten upon things altogether profane and prohibited.

And this also we ordain in the case of the rest of the clergymen—we mean subdeacons and lectors—who themselves are appointed assistants and servitors of the sacred table [19] and of all ornamentation concerning the most holy churches and, handling the Divine Oracles,[18] read the Sacred Writings [18] to us from our Holy Books and chant odes.[20]

But if anyone henceforth should have appeared to do any such thing and if this should have been denounced (either in this fortunate city [1] to your Holiness or in the provinces to the most God-beloved metropolitans appointed under you or to the rest of the bishops whose ordinations your Beatitude's see procures) and if any such complaint should have proceeded against a deacon or a presbyter and (much more) any of the most God-beloved bishops, here your Beatitude and in the provinces the most God-beloved metropolitans under you and the bishops under them should examine [21] with all exactness according to the order [22] of the priesthood [14] and should investigate [21] these matters and should not make [21] a cursory inquiry, but should hear [21] also witnesses worthy of belief and should go [21] by every road, so that they should seize the truth; for even as we exclude them from such things, so also we forbid them to be accused falsely by any persons.

And if, when from all sides the inquiry occurs with the Divine Oracles lying before them, the complaint should have appeared to be true and a deacon or a presbyter should have been proved either a dicer or joining dicers or seated by such vanities or going to the said spectacles or if even perhaps any of the most God-beloved bishops—and this we believe absolutely will not be—should have permitted any such spectacle or should have dared to be seated by and to be in sympathy with dicers henceforth, immediately by your Beatitude or by the metropolitan or at any rate the most God-beloved bishop under whom he has been stationed, if anyone should be of the so-called clergymen, such a one should be expelled [21] from the sacred ministry and on him should be imposed [21] canonical punishment and there should be determined [21] a time within which it is proper for him, employing both fasts and supplications, to propitiate the Great God for such an offence. And if during the determined time he should have continued, receiving such punishment and by tears and by penitence and by fast and by prayer to the Lord God asking for remission of the offence, then he under whom he has been stationed, having learned exactly and having investigated carefully these things should cause [21] common prayer to be made for him and should command [21] with all exactness him to abstain henceforth from such injury to the priesthood;[14] and if he should have believed that he has come sufficiently to penitence, then he shall share sacerdotal [23] benevolence with him.

But if even after excommunication he should have been found not truly employing penitence and contemning the affair and clearly possessed in his soul by the Adversary, this bishop [2] under whom he functions shall expel him from the sacerdotal [23] catalogues by deposing him absolutely. And he no longer shall have permission to enter into the sacerdotal [23] order;[22] but if he should have property, the senate of that city wherein he formerly was priest or, if the city should not have a senate, another senate of the province which especially needs a senator shall admit him to serve henceforth along with his property.[24] But if he should not have property, he shall be henceforth an apparitor of a provincial [25] office staff [26] instead of a priest [2] as formerly and, because he had deserted God's order,[22] he shall be a provincial [25] apparitor with this disgrace imposed upon himself instead of his former dignity.

Therefore we ordain that in this fortunate city [1] your Holiness and in each most holy church the defenders and the stewards should maintain all these matters, to whom it shall be a care to investigate and to denounce such matters and to deprive the convicted persons of both the sustenance and the subsidy given to them by the most holy churches, but in the provinces the most God-beloved metropolitans stationed under your Beatitude and besides the God-fearing bishops under them and their defenders of the churches and stewards themselves shall preserve careful guard by employing the same method —just as we previously have said—to the matter and by maintaining the sacerdotal [23] honour both blameless and unimpaired from all sides.

And also the most glorious prefects of our sacred praetorians—we mean those of the East over the peoples subjected to their jurisdiction— and the heads of the diocese of Illyricum and of Africa and the office staffs [26] obedient to them and the most distinguished governors of the provinces and the defenders of the municipalities shall maintain carefully these matters—the persons themselves who direct the great administrations being suspect in regard to our indignation and the office staffs obedient to them being suspect to fear a penalty of ten pounds of gold, but the provincial magistrates, both greater and lesser, and the office staffs [26] obedient to them and besides the defenders of the municipalities being afraid of a penalty of five pounds of gold apiece, if, having learned these matters, they themselves should not

651. JURISDICTION IN CLERICAL MISCONDUCT, 534

have denounced these to the priests,[2] that is, either to the most God-beloved bishops or to the most saintly metropolitans or to the most holy patriarchs of each diocese, in which place each should serve, so that [27] those, having learned these matters, according to what previously has been determined, may prosecute all persons and, whenever he who has been convicted in respect to such matters by them should have been condemned, may provide that this person should be delivered either to the city's municipal senate or to his order.[28]

And the most glorious prefect of this fortunate city [1] shall maintain carefully these matters, if in this our royal city [1] there should be any wrongdoing, along with the office staff obedient to him—he himself being suspect in regard to our indignation and his office staff being afraid of a penalty of ten pounds of gold.

But we have effected these things legislatively. And the following belongs to admitted things: that we have satisfied our conscience to God concerning the priests'[2] seriousness toward him. But if they [29] should transgress any of the established matters and should dissimulate and should not prosecute, but should have preferred a certain unpraiseworthy benevolence, they shall have besides our laws' penalties the penalties from heaven and the judgement thence, which in God's very tribunal shall happen both to convict and to punish the indecent dissimulation.

But if also any of the civil magistrates, both greater and lesser, or of apparitors or of defenders, having learned these matters, either should not have given information or should have neglected to prosecute, when possible, or even should have betrayed the matter for recompense,[30] he shall know that besides the penalties threatened by us he shall have punishment proceeding from the Great God and he shall be liable to all the curses contained in the Holy Books.

But just as these matters have been legislated by us for no other reason than for the Lord's service, so also we add the following: so that the investigations should occur with exactness and no calumniator [31] should rise against any persons and should accuse falsely or should witness falsely in such matters. For exactly as we have imposed such penalties on the priests,[2] if they should have done any such thing, so also we wish the persons who try to accuse them falsely to be subject to penalties from heaven and from our laws, if, having denounced, they should not have wished then to prosecute or should not have been strong to compose such accusations, since we support from all sides equity and justice, which in every action and especially in legislation we honour.

Given on 4 November at Constantinople, Justinian Perpetual-Augustus for the fourth time and the most distinguished Paulinus being consuls.

1. Constantinople.

2. See no. 16, n. 4.

3. An example of anacoluthon: Justinian forgets the construction with which he began (accusative subject of an infinitive yet to come) and starts anew (conjunction introducing a clause with a finite verb).

4. An editorial conjecture proposes "play" or "amusement".

5. Though in no. 593 Justinian legislated against laymen's gambling, already the *Constitutiones Apostolorum* (8. 47. 43-4) had prohibited both higher and lower clergymen from participation in such practice.

6. In *CI* 3. 43. 1. 4 (Latin interpretation) Justinian sets one solidus as the maximum stake in five games played with dice.

7. Perhaps in the sense of bet or wager, which the verb (προκαλεῖν) seems to stop just short of meaning with the construction used here.

8. Poetic plural in Greek. Since the Greek orchestra (see no. 650, n. 2) was that part of the theatre where the chorus danced around the altar (θυμέλη— the word used here) of Dionysus (the patron deity of drama), the word for altar by synecdoche often was used (as here) to indicate the dance floor. Derivatives of θυμέλη usually are associated with dancers and/or musicians rather than with actors (see no. 247, n. 4).

9. The English translation retains the Greek etymological figure.

10. Of course, these were what are called amphitheatres (ἀμφιθέατρον), though the simple Greek work for theatre (θέατρον) occasionally does duty for its compound.

11. This word, originally of pagan connotation, early in the Empire acquired also a Christian meaning: here "baptized".

12. See no. 75, n. 42.

13. For Satan as an adversary see 1 Tim. 5. 14-15 and 1 Pet. 5. 8.

Tertullian in his *De Spectaculis* associates spectacles with worship of pagan deities (5-13) and asserts that in Rome (cf. Rev. 18. 2, where Babylon [i.e. Rome] is called "a habitation of demons") the demons sit in conclave at these (7), which belong to the Devil and his pomp and his angels (4). With reference both to participation in the sacred mysteries and to presence at spectacles the apologist aptly quotes (13) St Paul's admonition against partaking "of the table of the Lord and of the table of demons" (1 Cor. 10. 21). And those Christians who think that the Scriptures do not require renunciation of spectacles he refers (3) to David's description of the godly man (Ps. 1. 1)—an ingenious interpretation.

14. See no. 158, n. 1.

15. The English translation preserves the synchysis or interlocked order of the Greek text.

16. Modern consecration and ordination retain from apostolic antiquity prayers for the candidate (Acts 1. 24, 6. 6, 13. 3; 1 Tim. 4. 14; 2 Tim. 1. 6). Although most ancient ordinals order a bishop's head and hands and a priest's and a deacon's hands (at least) to be anointed with oil, yet modern anointment

apparently is confined chiefly to Catholic Christianity, wherein no uniform rite appears because of the Church's division into several communions. The application of oil as a sign of separation of clergy to God's service descends from remote Jewish antiquity (Ex. 28. 41, 29. 7, 21, 29, 30. 30, 40. 13, 15; Lev. 4. 3, 6. 20, 22, 8. 12, 10. 7, 16. 32, 21. 10; Num. 3. 3, 35. 25).

17. The etymological figure in Greek is "to dice any game of dice", which, while allowable in English, is perhaps awkward.

18. That is, readings in the Bible.

19. The altar.

20. The ode (ᾠδή) in the Eastern Church at this time was a rather elaborate musical composition generally of rhythmical prose and beyond an ordinary hymn-singing congregation's ability to execute without extensive practice. On the odes in modern worship see R. M. French, *The Eastern Orthodox Church* (London, 1951), 126-7.

Specifically, however, Justinian may mean the so-called nine odes (αἱ ἐννέα ᾠδαί): (1) First Song of Moses, Ex. 15. 1-19; (2) Second Song of Moses, Deut. 32. 1-43; (3) Prayer of Hannah, 1 Sam. 2. 1-10; (4) Prayer of Habakkuk, Hab. 3. 2-16; (5) Song of Isaiah, Isa. 26. 1-19; (6) Prayer of Jonah, Jon. 2. 2-9; (7) Doxology of the Three Holy Children, Dan. 3. 52-6 (LXX) Three Children 29-34; (8) Song of the Three Holy Children (*Benedicite, Opera Omnia Domini*), Dan. 3. 57-90 (LXX) Three Children 35-68; (9) Song of Mary (*Magnificat*), Luke 1. 46-55, with Song of Zacharias (*Benedictus*), Luke 1. 68-79.

But these nine odes do not exhaust Scriptural canticles still used in Roman, Greek, Anglican, and certain Protestant Churches. Among these more important hymns may be mentioned: Song of Isaiah, Isa. 12; Song of Simeon (*Nunc Dimittis*), Luke 2. 29-32; all of the Psalms, particularly the *Venite* (Ps. 95). Other Biblical songs include, of course, Song of Solomon (Canticle of Canticles); Song of Deborah and Barak, Judges 5; Song of Judith, Judith 16. 2-17. Later compositions so classified are *Te Deum, Quicunque Vult* (the so-called Athanasian Creed), *Gloria Patri, Gloria in Excelsis, Trisagion* (*Ter Sanctus*), and *Ave Maria*.

21. This principal verb is an infinitive in Greek.

22. See no. 325, n. 6 *ad med*.

23. See no. 526, n. 11.

24. In compulsory public services.

25. The adjective connotes more of rural than of urban life and doubtless refers here to rustication in a remote region.

26. See no. 325, n. 6 *ad fin*.

27. The text of the consecutive clause is corrupt.

28. See no. 325, n. 6 *ad init*.

29. The bishops or the urban prefect's office staff.

30. The word *betrayed* (G. καταπροδοίη, L. *prodiderit*) is rather odd here.

The idea seems to be that an official has been bribed not to take action and thus has betrayed his trust.

31. See no. 334, n. 3.

652. MANDATE OF JUSTINIAN I ON ADMISSION TO RELIGIOUS LIFE, (?)534

(CI 1. 3. 54)

Several subjects are treated in this law: (1) disposition of betrothal gifts, when either of the affianced pair decides to embrace monachism; (2) removal of parents' power to compel children to relinquish monastic or clerical life and to disinherit them because of children's refusal to return to secular vocations; (3) award of all religious persons' property to the Church, if they desert the ecclesiastical establishment for life in the world; (4) prohibition against Jews' and pagans' and heretics' ownership of Christian slaves, who must be manumitted from such masters; (5) especial enforcement of this law in the civil diocese of Africa, where at least some of the offences touched in this law were rife.

The same Augustus to John, praetorian prefect.[1]

With God furnishing aid to us, we desire to establish by laws and to fulfil by works all things which for the Holy Catholic Church's honour we hasten to do for God's pleasure. And already indeed with his aid we have ordained many things which are suitable to be ordained for ecclesiastical doctrine, but at present we have considered with pious deliberation that this matter, which hitherto occurred contrary to God's fear, must be corrected.

For it has been known to us that, if any fiancé or fiancée, after earnests [2] had been given or accepted, should have wished to destine himself or herself to God's service and to retire from worldly living and to live a religious life and to persevere in God's fear, the man indeed was compelled to lose that which he had given in the category of earnests,[2] but the woman was compelled to repay double that which she had accepted. And to our Gentleness this has seemed quite contrary to religion.

Wherefore by the present law, which shall prevail in perpetuity, we order that if any fiancé or fiancée shall have desired, by despising this world's life, to live in religious living, the fiancé indeed should receive without any diminution all which he had given in the category of earnests [2] for the sake of future wedlock, but the fiancée should

652. ADMISSION TO RELIGIOUS LIFE, (?)534

restore to the fiancé not double, as hitherto, but only that which she had accepted in the category of earnests [2] and should be compelled to repay nothing more, except that which she shall have been proved to have accepted. For by an earlier law [3] already it has been provided by us in respect to husbands and wives who renounce the world that, if either a husband or wife for the sake of religion shall have retired from wedlock and shall have chosen a solitary life, each one of them should receive his or her own properties which he and she had offered either for dowry or by donation before marriage and should acquire in the category of profit from the one who shall have chosen a solitary life only that which one ought to exact legitimately or by agreement in event of death.

We also judge this, which is known to us, to be worthy of our correction: that if any man or any woman, established in parents' power, shall have chosen perhaps to be freed from legal power of this sort and shall have wished to join himself or herself to a monastery or to the clergy and to live religiously the remaining time of his or her life, it should not be permitted to parents either to withdraw the said persons by any means or to repel them, as if unacceptable, from their inheritance or succession because of only this cause, but it should be necessary for them by all means, when they compose their own last will (whether by writing or by other legitimate method) to bequeath indeed to them a fourth portion according to our laws; but if one shall have wished to bestow more, we grant this to one's wish. But if parents shall have been shown to have declared their last will neither by testament nor by other last record, the heirs, to whom it is due without will, should claim for themselves the entire substance according to our laws—no impediment for them being created as a result of religious living,[4] whether alone or with others they are called to the succession.

We wish those who shall have persevered in a monastery or the clericate to obtain this our perpetual law's benefits. For if any of them, about whom we have made the present law, shall have chosen a religious life, but shall have returned to worldly living, we order all their properties to belong to the legal rights of that church or monastery from which they shall have retired.

Since these matters thus have been disposed, by a repeated law [5] we order that no Jew or pagan or heretic should have Christian slaves. But if they shall have been found in such an offence, we ordain that by all means the slaves should be free according to our laws' previous tenor.[5] But in the present law we decree this further: that if anyone of the aforesaid Jews or pagans or heretics shall have had slaves not yet imbued with the Catholic faith's most holy mysteries [6] and if the aforesaid slaves shall have yearned to come to the orthodox faith, after they shall have been joined to the Catholic Church, by all means as a result of the present law they should be delivered to freedom; and the governors of provinces as well as the sacrosanct Church's defenders and also the most blessed bishops should defend them—their masters absolutely accepting nothing for their value.

But if perchance hereafter also their masters themselves shall have been converted to the orthodox faith, it should not be permitted to them to reduce to slavery those who have preceded them into the orthodox faith; but if anyone shall have practised such things, he shall lie under the gravest punishments.

Therefore all governors and the most religious bishops (whether of the African diocese—in which we have learned that offences of this sort are especially common—or of other provinces) should take care to observe diligently and very zealously all these matters, which with respect for piety our Eternity has ordained. For contemners shall be smitten not only with pecuniary fine, but also with capital punishment.

1. Of the East.
2. See no. 517, n. 2.
3. No. 629.
4. The religious life, in a sense remote from political activity in a city-state, reminds one of Aristotle's assertion that a person stateless by nature and not by fortune is like Homer's (*Il.* 9. 63) "clanless, lawless, hearthless" man (*Pol.* 1. 1. 9= 1253A). But Aristotle, of course, was not a Christian!
5. Nos. 616 and 647.
6. See no. 75, n. 42.

APPENDIX ON PERSECUTIONS

Perhaps here is as convenient a place as any to collect the important references to *reported* imperial legislation instigating persecution of Christians.

Ten principal persecutions are counted commonly:[1] (1) under Nero, 64; (2) under Domitian, 96; (3) under Trajan, *c.* 100–*c.* 113; (4) under Aurelius and Commodus, *c.* 161–*c.* 185; (5) under Septimius Severus and Caracalla, *c.* 202–*c.* 213; (6) under Maximin I, 235–8; (7) under Decius and Gallus, 249–52; (8) under Valerian, 257–60; (9) under Aurelian, 274–5; (10) under Diocletian, Maximian I, Galerius, and Maximin II, 303–13. But for only some of these are found imperial ordinances indirectly quoted.[2]

1. Under Nero: Sulpicius Severus, *Chron.* 2. 29. 3: "Also afterward by issued laws the religion was forbidden and by openly published edicts it was not lawful that a Christian should exist."[3]

2. Under Domitian: the tradition that Domitian, who popularly was regarded as a combined reincarnation of Tiberius (14–37) and Nero (54–68) and on whom the Senate passed a post-mortem sentence of *damnatio memoriae* (Suetonius, *Dom.* 23. 1), persecuted Christians rests chiefly on literary and archaeological evidence.[4]

But there appears to be one legislative testimony—and this, curiously enough, points to the cessation rather than to the inauguration of the persecution. Eusebius has from Hegesippus an ancient story (*HE* 3. 19—20. 7) to the effect that the emperor, when heretics had denounced Jesus' grand-nephews, summoned these surviving kinsmen of the Saviour to Rome, interrogated them about their property, learned that they were peasants, asked about Christ's kingdom, received the reply that it held no threat for his own sovereignty, despised them as simple persons, released them, and "by an edict ceased the persecution against the Church" (20. 5).[5]

3. Under Trajan: Pliny, *Ep.* 10. 97 (no. 1).[6]

See also Pliny's letter to the emperor (*Ep.* 10. 96), wherein he refers (§ 7) to his edict prohibiting "pursuant to your mandates" secret societies, among which Pliny puts Christian congregations.[7]

4. Under Aurelius: Eusebius, *HE* 5. 1. 47: "For Caesar had written

that they should be tortured to death, but that, if any should recant, these should be released."

From the celebrated *Letter of the Gallican Churches* (Vienne and Lyon) in 177, toward the end of Aurelius' reign, which was marked by martyrdoms elsewhere in the Empire, comes this reference to imperial instructions, which were sent as a rescript rather late in the Gallic persecution, wherein not a few had died for their faith, before the governor considered that he should consult his sovereign (§ 44).

See also no. 3 and Introd., n. 46 *ad init*.

5. Under Septimius Severus:[8] Scriptores Historiae Augustae: *Sev.* 17. 1: "Under heavy penalty he forbade persons to become Jews. Concerning Christians he also ordained the same."

While some African magistrates refused to enforce the edict (Tertullian, *Ad Scap.* 4), yet in Egypt, where the persecution principally raged (Eusebius, *HE* 6. 1. 1), the threat of persecution accounted for the suspension of the Catechetical School of Alexandria (Eusebius, *HE* 6. 3. 1), since it may be conjectured that the ordinance was aimed against converts to Christianity.

6. Under Maximin I: Eusebius, *HE* 6. 28: "Through rancour toward Alexander's [9] house, because it consisted of rather many of the faithful, he, having raised a persecution, ordered [10] the leaders of the Church alone, as responsible for the teaching according to the Gospel, to be destroyed."

7. Under Decius: Eusebius, *HE* 6. 41. 1: "The persecution did not begin among us from the royal edict, but it preceded it by a whole year." Cyprian, *Ep.* 43. 3: "... by an edict recently had been associated with the magistrates, that they might destroy our faith."

Although the edict has been lost,[11] yet from scattered sources (chiefly St Cyprian and Eusebius) Kidd has reconstructed with numerous references its objective and the procedure to be pursued: "... it provided for an universal proscription; and left nothing to local or personal initiative, whether of people or magistrate. It fixed a date ... for making profession of belief; and all who by this day had failed to declare their paganism were to be taken for Christians and so liable to persecution, not only in the large cities ... but in lesser towns ... in villages, and on private estates.... A commission of magistrates and notables for each locality summoned the populace to a temple.... Names were called. Each had then, in veil and crown, to offer a victim, or, at least, incense and a libation; to renounce Christ, and to partake in the sacrificial meal.... This done, the apostate bought a certificate or *libellus* [12] from the magistrate . . . . For those who neither apostatized nor took refuge in flight, but stood firm, there followed a trial before the Proconsul, and then grievous sufferings: long imprisonment in horrible dungeons, and repeated efforts to break down constancy. These were of all sorts, and from torture to threats . . . and not till they were exhausted came the final sentence of exile or death, with confiscation" (1. 431–3).

From the ancient testimony it is clear that the purpose of the persecution was to weaken the Church in two ways: (1) by attacking the leaders, so that the organization would collapse; (2) by making apostates, so that the prestige of the Church would decline.[13]

8. Under Valerian: two ordinances are known; of these the second probably was promulgated after the first had proved ineffective.

(a) Letter in August 257: Cyprian, *Acta Proconsularia*, 1, 3: "The most sacred emperors, Valerian and Gallien, have deigned to give to me a letter, whereby they have commanded that those who revere not the Roman religion must recognize the Roman religious rites . . . Therefore will you, pursuant to Valerian's and Gallien's command, go as an exile to the Curubitan city? . . . They have deigned to write to me not only about bishops, but also about presbyters . . . . They also have commanded that assemblies should not be held in any places and that cemeteries should not be entered. Accordingly, if anyone shall not have observed this so salutary command, he should be punished capitally . . . The most sacred emperors have ordered you to worship in Roman fashion (*caeremoniari*)."

(b) Rescript in July 258: Cyprian, *Ep.* 80. 1: ". . . Valerian wrote to the Senate that both bishops and presbyters and deacons should be punished immediately; but that senators and distinguished men and Roman knights, after they had lost their rank, also should be stripped of their goods and if, after their resources had been taken, they should have persevered in being Christians, they also should be punished capitally; that matrons, after their goods had been taken, should be relegated into exile; moreover that Caesarians,[14] whosoever either had confessed previously or now shall have confessed, should suffer confiscation of property and, when bound, should be sent, as assigned, to Caesar's estates. Emperor Valerian also subjoined to his address a copy of the letter which he wrote about us to the governors of the provinces."

The persecution was ended by Gallien's rescript (no. 4).

9. Under Aurelian: Lactantius, *De Mort. Pers.* 6. 2: "Not yet his

bloody writings had come to the more distant provinces, when he himself lay bloody on the ground."

However, Eusebius, *HE* 7. 30. 21: "But divine justice pursued him . . . when—one almost might say—he was signing writings against us."

The discrepancy between these accounts is obvious. Even if Eusebius should be preferred to Lactantius, historians number Aurelian's persecution as the ninth and to his principate martyrologists assign many martyrdoms.[15]

See also no. 5.

10. Under Diocletian: six laws are enumerated.[16]

(a) Edict of 24 February 303: Eusebius, *HE* 8. 2. 4–5: "This was the nineteenth year of Diocletian's sovereignty, in the month Dystrus (this would be called March,[17] according to the Romans), wherein, when the feast of the Saviour's Passion was approaching,[17] a royal letter was published everywhere; commanding to bring the churches to the ground, to destroy the Scriptures by fire, and ordering the persons who had held a post of honour to be dishonoured,[18] those in the households,[19] if they should have persisted in the profession of Christianity, to be deprived of freedom. And such was the first document against us."

Eusebius, *De Mart. Pal.*, praef. 1–2: "This was the nineteenth year of Diocletian's sovereignty, in the month Xanthicus (which would be called April,[20] according to the Romans), wherein, when the feast of the Saviour's Passion was nearing,[20] Flavian governed the people of the Palestines,[21] and a letter suddenly was published everywhere, commanding to bring the churches to the ground, to destroy the Scriptures by fire, and ordering the persons who had held a post of honour to be dishonoured,[18] those in the households,[19] if they should have persisted in the profession of Christianity, to be deprived of freedom. And such was the force of the first document against us."

Lactantius, *De Mort. Pers.* 13. 1: "On the next day [22] was posted an edict, wherein it was warned that persons of the celebrated religion should be deprived of all honour and rank, that they should be subjected to tortures, that they should come from any order or grade whatsoever, that every lawsuit should be valid against them, that they themselves should be unable to prosecute concerning wrongdoing, concerning adultery, concerning stolen property, that finally they should not have freedom and voice." [23]

This edict thus had two parts: one against things and one against

APPENDIX ON PERSECUTIONS 1183

persons. Lactantius may have omitted the first section for either of two reasons: (1) he had illustrated it in his previous chapter (12); (2) since the destruction of the church and of the Bible had occurred at Nicomedia before the edict's promulgation there, this section was not in the edict posted there.

It is possible that this edict contained as well other clauses. Eusebius says (*HE* 9. 10. 8): "It had been commanded by the most divine Diocletian and Maximian, our fathers, that the Christians' assemblies should be abolished." It appears that churches, houses, and lands belonging to Christians were confiscated and then either were sold or were donated to pagans according to Eusebius (*HE* 9. 10. 11; 10. 5. 9–11, 16–17). Rufinus in his translation of Eusebius says (*HE* 8. 2. 4): "If any of the slaves had continued as a Christian, he could not acquire freedom." [24]

It is noteworthy that Diocletian demanded that there should be no bloodshed in the execution of the edict (Lactantius, *De Mort. Pers.* 11. 8). But when someone tore down and then tore apart a copy of the edict at Nicomedia, he was arrested immediately and after torture was burned according to due process of law (Lactantius, *De Mort. Pers.* 13. 2–3; Eusebius, *HE* 8. 5. 1).

(b) Edict of (?) March 303: Eusebius, *HE* 8. 2. 5: "But with other letters not much later [25] added it was commanded that all the presidents of the churches in every place first should be surrendered to chains and then afterward by every device should be compelled to sacrifice."

Eusebius, *De Mart. Pal.*, praef. 2, repeats the above statement with an insignificant variation.[26]

Eusebius, *HE* 8. 6. 8: "Not long afterward [25] a royal edict was issued to confine the presidents of the churches everywhere in prisons and chains.[27]

This edict was inspired by two fires in Diocletian's palace, after Galerius had insisted that the Christians were guilty of this arson (Lactantius, *De Mort. Pers.* 14).

(c) Edict of 21 December 303: Eusebius, *HE* 8. 6. 10: "Moreover, when the first letter [28] had been overtaken by others, wherein it was commanded to let go into freedom the prisoners who had sacrificed, but to lacerate with myriad tortures those who had refused . . ."

This edict is associated by some scholars with the amnesty announced by Diocletian in honour of the twentieth anniversary of his reign (Vicennalia), when prisoners were released (Eusebius, *De Mart. Pal.*

2. 4)—the Christians, however, on the terms of this edict, which authorizes torture, perhaps, to induce them to accept release from crowded prisons. This view takes the edict as only a clause of the amnesty. Other scholars give the edict an independent status and suppose that it was enacted to clear the jails, which had been filled as a consequence of the second edict's enforcement.[29]

(d) Letter of Spring 304: Eusebius, *De Mart. Pal.* 3. 1: "While the second year had made its mark and the war against us had increased in intensity rather much, when Urban then was governing the province,[30] when at this time for the first a royal letter had been published, wherein by a universal edict it was ordered that all persons in a body in the several cities both should sacrifice and should pour libations to idols . . ."

Eusebius, *De Mart. Pal.* 3. 1:[31] "In the second year of the persecution the war against us increased in intensity (the governor of the province of Palestine being Urban, who at that time had superseded the governor Flavian), and imperial edicts arrived again for the second time, much worse than the first.[32] For the first gave commandment regarding the rulers of the Church of God alone, that they should sacrifice. But in the second there was a grievous command, which compelled all alike, that all the people in all the cities in a body—men and women and their children—should sacrifice and offer libations to the lifeless idols."

It is unclear whether the fourth law was promulgated late in April 304 by Maximian or in February 304 by Galerius. In any event the edict seems to have reached Palestine in March 305.[33]

It should be noted that, though Diocletian and Maximian had abdicated in May 305, the persecution continued, especially in the East under Galerius and his nephew Maximin II.

(e) Letter of 306: Eusebius, *De Mart. Pal.* 4. 8: "For indeed when a second uprising against us was made by Maximin in the third year of the persecution in our time and when the tyrant's letter was published for the first time, that in a body all persons at absolutely one time with the care and the eagerness of the magistrates in the several cities should sacrifice, and when through the entire city of the Caesareans heralds were calling men with women and children to the idols' temples in accordance with the gubernatorial order and in addition to these the chiliarchs [34] were summoning each person by name from the tax-register . . ."

Eusebius, *De Mart. Pal.* 4. 8:[35] "A second general attack, then, was

APPENDIX ON PERSECUTIONS 1185

directed during the third year of the persecution of our day, and a rescript from Maximin then for the first time reached us, in which he gave the order that the magistrates in the several cities should make it their earnest endeavour that all the people in a body should sacrifice and pour libations to the demons. Forthwith heralds in every city called men, and women and children too, to assemble at the temples of the idols; while the military tribunes and centurions went from house to house and from ward to ward making registers of the citizens: then they summoned each one by name and thus compelled him to do what was bidden."

This instruction reinforces the two-year-old ordinance, which perhaps had been permitted to lapse, or represents a periodical check on backsliders.[36]

Lactantius, *De Mort. Pers.* 21. 7: "For persons not having rank fire was the punishment. This execution he had permitted first against the Christians by issued laws, that after tortures the condemned persons should be burned by slow fires."[37]

Eusebius, *De Mart. Pal.* 8. 1: ". . . [and these things][38] ordered Firmilian, the successor of Urban, sent thither as governor, as if he commanded these in accordance with royal sanction."

(f) Edict of Autumn 308: Eusebius, *De Mart. Pal.* 9. 2: "Moreover suddenly Maximin's letter against us was republished everywhere. Both the governors in the several provinces and, besides, the person set in charge to command the army[39] by proclamations and letters and public ordinances urged curators[40] with duovirs and recorders in all the cities to carry to the limit the royal edict, which ordered that with all speed they should rebuild the fallen apparatus[41] of the idols, that they should be made careful that all in a body—men with their wives and house-servants, even nursing children—should sacrifice and should pour libations and should taste scrupulously the cursed sacrifices, and that the things for sale in market should be polluted utterly with libations from the sacrifices, and that guards should be stationed before the baths, in order that they might pollute with all-abominable sacrifices the persons cleaning themselves in these."

Eusebius, *De Mart. Pal.* 9. 2:[42] "And, on account of those things which happened, they[43] were urging the curators of the cities and the duovirs and the registrars[44] that they should build with speed what was fallen of the idol temples, and [that they should take care] that all the men with their wives and children and slaves, even babes at the breast, should offer sacrifice and libations to demons and that they should compel them even to taste the sacrifices; and it was ordered that every article which was bought in the market was to be defiled by libations and sprinkling of the blood of the sacrifices." [45]

This edict's objective thus appears to be a revival of paganism rather than an active persecution of Christianity, though Christian martyrs to flout the statute still were found (Eusebius, *De Mart. Pal.* 9. 4–13 et seq.).[46]

Eusebius, *De Mart. Pal.* 13. 2: "Then, when the person set in charge over the mines [47] had come, as if in accordance with royal sanction, he, having divided the multitude of the confessors, assigned to some to live in Cyprus and to others Lebanon, scattering some here and there in districts throughout Palestine, and ordered that all should be oppressed with various tasks . . ." [48]

After the Galerian Edict of Toleration in 311 (no. 7) and its author's death [49] Maximin II renewed the persecution so vigorously that it seemed much more severe than the previous pogrom.[50]

Eusebius, *De Mart. Pal.* 13. 10: "So, then, 39 in number were decapitated [51] in one day by the most all-accursed Maximin's sanction." [52]

Eusebius, *HE* 9. 2. 1: "At first he tried through a pretext to debar us from meeting in the cemeteries;[53] then through certain wicked men he sent to himself deputations against us, having incited the citizens of Antioch to ask to obtain from him, as in a very great boon, that he not at all would allow any of the Christians to live in their fatherland, and to cause that others should suggest the same thing." [54]

Eusebius, *HE* 9. 4. 1: "And when the tyrant had assented most readily to their acts [55] by a rescript, the persecution against us was rekindled again afresh."

Lactantius, *De Mort. Pers.* 36. 3–7: "First of all, he removed the indulgence granted by common title [56] to Christians by deputations from cities, which should ask that it might not be lawful for Christians to construct conventicles within their cities, that he might seem compelled by persuasion and impelled to do what he was about to do voluntarily. And by assenting to these he made high priests of a new character, each in each city from the principal persons, who both daily should make sacrifices for the sake of all their gods and, having been supported by the old service of the priests, should give attention that the Christians neither should build conventicles nor should assemble publicly or privately, but should compel them, when arrested by their own legal authority, to sacrifices or should bring them to judges. And, as if this were not enough, also over the provinces he placed individual pontiffs from a higher grade of rank and he ordered them all to appear dressed in white copes. Moreover he was preparing to do what he had been doing in the parts of the East; for, since he was professing clemency as far as a show, he forbade God's servants to be slain, but he ordered them to be mutilated. Accordingly in the case of confessors eyes were dug out, hands were chopped off, feet were lopped off, noses or ears were cut off."

Eusebius, *HE* 8. 14. 9: "Accordingly he also applied himself more vehemently and more constantly to the persecution against us than his predecessors, commanding temples to be erected in every city and sacred precincts, destroyed by length of time, to be restored with care and selecting priests of idols in every place and city and over these a high priest of each province—a certain one of those in political administration who with particular distinction had been conspicuous in every public service—with a military escort and bodyguard..." [57]

The Lactantian and Eusebian extracts present a composite picture of the emperor's endeavour to persecute Christians by an external reform of pagan religion. For the pontiffs must prevent construction of churches and meetings for worship, must see that Christians sacrifice or appear in court, and to assist them in their authority these civil-religious officials have armed soldiers.

Eusebius, *HE* 9. 5. 1: "Having forged, indeed, *Memoirs of Pilate and of Our Saviour*,[58] quite full of every blasphemy against Christ, by the will of the high authority, they sent these in different directions to every office under him, ordering through edicts that in every place, both fields and cities, they should exhibit these openly to all persons and that the schoolteachers should give these to the children instead of lessons to study and to commit to memory."

Eusebius, *VC* 1. 58: "And he himself indeed, as if having endeavoured to surpass the first [59] in a contest of evils, prided himself on the invention of newer punishments against us. For fire and sword and nailing or wild beasts and depths of the sea were not sufficient for him, but, having discovered a certain novel chastisement in addition to all these, he legislated that they must be blinded.[60] Thereupon a multitude, not only of men, but also of children and of women, after being disabled in respect to the sight of the right eye and to the joints of the feet by sword and by cautery, was consigned to hard labour in mines."

Maximin's persecution ended in 313 by a letter ordering its suspension to win Christian support against Constantine and Licinius, his rivals (no. 13), and in a final edict of toleration for the same purpose (no. 14).

Of the 249 years from the first persecution under Nero in 64 to the final peace under Constantine I in 313, it is estimated that Christians endured persecution about 129 years and enjoyed toleration about 120 years. But this calculation must be qualified by the circumstances that even in the periods of comparative peace Christians were ever exposed to pagan prejudice and hatred not only in Rome and in Italy, but also in the provinces, and that doubtless sporadic and spasmodic delation of Christians occurred not seldom before magistrates, who, if conscientious officials, obeyed the existing enactments and ordered the execution of Christians thus denounced.

In addition to accounts in modern histories of the early Church the literature on the persecutions is so vast and in so many languages and so specialized—some works attempt to cover all ten persecutions, others discuss a series of persecutions, others treat a single persecution, others explain the legal aspects of persecutions, others collect stories of martyrdoms, and others investigate individual or corporate martyrdoms—that only a selection of works will be made and particularly, wherever possible, for readers who are more familiar with English than with foreign languages.

(1) Of an encyclopaedic character is the *Dictionnaire général et complet des persécutions,* which is part of J. P. Migne's *Nouvelle encyclopédie théologique* (vols. 4 and 5, Paris, 1851). For a summary of the persecutions see E. C. E. Owen, *Some Authentic Acts of the Early Martyrs* (Oxford, 1927), 27-31.

(2) Of general works on the persecutions may be consulted: H. B. Workman, *Persecution in the Early Church* [2] (Cincinnati, 1906); E. G. Hardy, *Christianity and the Roman Government* [3] (London, 1925); W. D. Niven, *The Conflicts of the Early Church* (London, 1931); R. M. Grant, *The Sword and the Cross* (New York, 1955).

(3) Of general works on a series of persecutions may be mentioned: W. M. Ramsay, *The Church in the Roman Empire before A.D. 170* [7] (London, 1903)—to the Antonines; L. H. Canfield, *The Early Persecutions of the Christians* (New York, 1913)—to Hadrian; E. T. Merrill, *Essays in Early Christian History* (London, 1924), 49-201—to Trajan.

APPENDIX ON PERSECUTIONS 1189

(4) Of special studies on separate persecutions—and these appear overwhelmingly in periodicals—may be listed:

(a) under Nero: A. S. Barnes, *Christianity at Rome in the Apostolic Age* (London, 1938), 96–112.

(b) under Domitian: W. M. Ramsay, *The Letters to the Seven Churches of Asia and their Place in the Plan of the Apocalypse* (New York, 1905), 93–113.

(c) under Trajan and Hadrian: E. T. Merrill, op. cit., 202–16; H. M. Poteat, "Rome and the Christians" in *Classical Journal*, 33 (1937–8) 134–44.

(d) under Aurelius: W. F. Adeney, "M. Aurelius and the Christian Church" in *British Quarterly Review*, 77 (1883) 1–35; H. D. Sedgwick, *Marcus Aurelius* (New Haven, 1921), 207–45; C. B. Phipps, "Persecution under Marcus Aurelius" in *Hermathena*, 47 (1932) 167–201.

(e) under the Severi: P. Allard, *Histoire des persécutions pendant la première moitié du troisième siècle*[3] (Paris, 1905), 1–209.

(f) from Maximin I to Decius: P. Allard, op. cit., 210–75.

(g) under Decius and Gallus: J. A. F. Gregg, *The Decian Persecution* (Edinburgh, 1897); J. R. Knipfing, "The Libelli of the Decian Persecution" in *HTR* 16 (1923) 345–90.

(h) under Valerian: P. J. Healy, *The Valerian Persecution* (Boston, 1905).

(i) under Aurelian: F. Görres, "Die Märtyrer der aurelianischen Christenverfolgung" in *Jahrbücher für protestantische Theologie*, 6 (1880) 449–94.

(j) under Diocletian and his colleagues and successors: A. J. Mason, *The Persecution of Diocletian* (Cambridge, 1876); N. H. Baynes, "The Great Persecution" in *CAH* 12 (1939) 646–77 (see especially 665–77; see also 679–81 and 686–91); G. E. M. de Ste Croix, "Aspects of the 'Great' Persecution" in *HTR* 47 (1954) 75–113.

(5) Of studies on legal aspects of the persecution may be noted: W. E. Addis, *Christianity and the Roman Empire* (London, 1893), 53–92; T. Mommsen, "Der Religionsfrevel nach römischen Recht" in his *Gesammelte Schriften* (Berlin, 1907), 3. 389–422; O. Sild, *Das altchristliche Martyrium in Berücksichtigung der rechtlichen Grundlage der Christenverfolgungen* (Leipzig, 1920); J. Zeiller, "Nouvelles observations sur l'origine juridique des persécutions contre les chrétiens aux deux premiers siècles" in *Revue d'histoire ecclésiastique*, 46 (1951) 521–33.

(6) Of the martyrdoms the three chief collections of primary documents are noticed *supra* in n. 11 (Ruinart, Gebhardt, Knopf), to

1190   APPENDIX ON PERSECUTIONS

which may be added Owen's English translation of thirteen representative monuments (*supra* n. 1). Of studies may be noted: A. J. Mason, *The Historic Martyrs of the Primitive Church* (London, 1905);[61] D. W. Riddle, *The Martyrs: A Study in Social Control* (Chicago, 1931); H. B. Workman, *The Martyrs of the Early Church* (London, n.d.); G. Ricciotti, *The Age of Martyrs: Christianity from Diocletian to Constantine* (Milwaukee, 1959).

NOTES

1. For a summary of these consult the outline in E. C. E. Owen, *Some Authentic Acts of the Early Martyrs* (Oxford, 1927), 27–30.
See the end of this Appendix for a selected bibliography.
But the tradition of ten persecutions is without value: if it refers to the great pogroms, the number is too large; if it refers to all persecutions, the number is too little. It was Gibbon (2. 108) who conjectured that this calculation had been established by ecclesiastical writers of the fifth century from "the ingenious parallels of the *ten* plagues of Egypt [Ex. 7–12] and of the *ten* horns of the Apocalypse [Rev. 12. 3, 13. 1, 17. 3, 7, 12, 16] . . . in their application of the faith of prophecy to the truth of history". Sulpicius Severus appears to have been the first author to construct this computation (*Chron.* 2. 28. 1—2. 33. 3 [= *CSEL* 1. 82–7]), but he seems to have postponed the tenth and last persecution for the advent of the Antichrist.

2. See no. 4, n. 2 *ad init.*

3. *Christianum esse non licebat* is reminiscent of Tertullian's charge (*Apol.* 4. 4) that the Roman magistrates ruled that *non licet esse vos* (it is not lawful that you should exist).
Probably among these edicts was the *institutum Neronianum* against Christians, Nero's only constitution which was not abrogated after his suicide, according to Tertullian (*Ad Nat.* 1. 7 *ad init.*), and which, however, has not survived.
On Nero's attitude toward Christianity consult B. W. Henderson, *The Life and Principate of the Emperor Nero* (London, 1903), 249–53, 344–57, 434–49.

4. On this see Kidd, 1. 72–7, and J. Lebreton and J. Zeiller, *The History of the Primitive Church* (London, 1944), 2. 320–3.
On Domitian's attitude toward Christianity consult B. W. Henderson, *Five Roman Emperors* (Cambridge, 1927), 42–53.

5. Doubtless by *the Church* is meant the Church of Jerusalem, but Eusebius seems to have understood the word in a wider sense (as in *HE* 3. 32. 7–8).

6. On Trajan's attitude toward Christianity consult B. W. Henderson, *Five Roman Emperors* (Cambridge, 1927), 53–8.
For Hadrian's continuation of Trajan's policy see no. 2; for his attitude toward Christianity consult B. W. Henderson, *The Life and Principate of the Emperor Hadrian* (London, 1923), 221-31.

APPENDIX ON PERSECUTIONS 1191

Since only one martyrdom (if it can be called such, for μαρτυρεῖν need not mean that one dies for one's faith)—that of Pope St Telesphorus (125-36)—belongs to Hadrian's reign (Irenaeus, *Adv. Haer.* 3. 3. 3), though Eusebius erroneously assigns it to the principate of Antoninus Pius (*HE* 4. 10; 5. 6. 4), Hadrian hardly can be called a persecutor.

Similarly also for Antoninus Pius, Hadrian's successor. While isolated martyrdoms—Publius in Athens (Eusebius, *HE* 4. 23. 2); Ptolemy, Lucius, an unnamed third in Alexandria (Justin Martyr, *Apol. pro Christ.* 2. 2); Polycarp and his companions in Smyrna (*Martyrium Polycarpi*; Eusebius, *HE* 4. 15. 1-47)—are recorded, yet the emperor endeavoured to prevent "new measures" from being taken against Christians by writing letters to Larissans, Thessalonicans, Athenians, and all the Greeks (Eusebius, *HE* 4. 26. 10). See no. 3.

7. For a Christian view of illegal associations and how Christians constituted a corporation see Tertullian, *Apol.* 38. 1-2 and 39. See also no. 133, n. 1, for a résumé of governmental policy toward guilds in the Ante-Nicene era.

8. If we accept 197 as the received date for Tertullian's *Ad Nationes*, then Tertullian wrote this treatise early in this emperor's reign, when, according to the apologist, the *institutum Neronianum* (on which see *supra* n. 3 *ad med.*), Nero's constitution against Christians, apparently was still enforceable.

9. The reference to Alexander is to Alexander Severus, who was kindly disposed toward Christians (see no. 4, n. 2).

10. That the order was an edict (πρόσταγμα) seems probable from the verb *ordered* (προστάσσει), whence the noun is derived. At any rate, the ordinance was directed against the bishops—an innovation and a foreshadowing of future legislation against the Church rather than individuals.

11. But the fact that the original ordinance has not survived has led to a curious literary conclusion. B. Aubé in his *L'église et l'état dans la seconde moitié du troisième siècle* ² (Paris, 1886), 16-19, exposes the essay of a certain Bernard Médon at Toulouse in 1664 to supply such a statute. Médon, it seems, evolved his edict from Simeon Metaphrastes' (the late tenth-century Byzantine hagiologist) Greek tale of *The Holy Martyr Mercury's Contest* (*Certamen Sancti Martyris Mercurii*), which Luigi Cardinal Lippomano (Aloisius Lipomanus) had translated into Latin and had published in the fifth tome of his *Sanctorum Priscorum Patrum Vitae* (7 vols., Venezia and Roma, 1551-60). Re-edited by L. Surius, who had succeeded to Lippomano's labours, at Köln during 1570-5, this sylloge was expanded through several editions until in thirteen volumes at Torino during 1875-80 it found its final form, wherein (entitled *Surius: Historiae seu Vitae Sanctorum*) the Decian decree at the beginning of St Mercury's story (assigned to 25 November) appears (1879) in 11. 677. I have not seen Médon's forgery, called *Decii Augusti Imperatoris Edictum adversus Christianos* (Toulouse, 1664). Moreover, T. Ruinart regarded the *Acta Sancti Mercurii* as of so little authority that he did not admit it into his authoritative *Acta Primorum Martyrum Sincera et Selecta* (Paris, 1689; latest edition: Ratisbon, 1859).

M

However, relative to the Decian edict, from *acta* of saints Aubé prints two short texts (op. cit., 19, n. 1; 20, n. 1), of which the second, he says, has only "une valeur approximative", for "il n'a pas de caractère officiel". These he found *in manuscripto* in the Bibliothèque Nationale of Paris.

The first is a letter from Decius to Turcius Rufius Apollonius Valerianus, his praetorian prefect, and its Latin may be translated thus: "We urgently warn that, if you shall have found any Christians in the city, you should not delay to drag to tortures those who are unwilling to humble themselves before our gods and to offer sacrifices to them, in order that we can have them placated and can stand victoriously everywhere and the Roman liberty can be enhanced."

The second reads in translation thus: "When Decius, hateful to God, held the supremacy of Roman rule, he ordered all persons to be withdrawn from their own sect and those invoking Lord Jesus Christ's name to be called to unclean sacrifices. Moreover, if any should have refused, [he ordered them] to be brought before a judge and to be killed by powerful punishments."

With egregious exceptions (e.g. no. 42, the well-known *Martyrium Sancti Polycarpi* [the earliest history of a Christian martyrdom], the already cited *Epistola Ecclesiarum Viennensis et Lugdunensis*, the *Passio Martyrum Scillitanorum*, the *Passio Sanctarum Martyrum Perpetuae et Felicitatis* [containing autographic notes and an eyewitness's account], the already quoted Cyprianic *Acta Proconsularia*, the Eusebian *De Martyribus Palaestinae*) accounts of martyrdoms have received anciently such a large romantic element, so much rhetorical embroidery, such a great editorial redaction, in a pious effort to edify the reader—not to mention fabrication as well as forgery—that one should suspect automatically imperial *ipsissima verba* (such as in Aubé's first extract), while one can accept usually paraphrases or summaries (such as in Aubé's second extract).

Convenient selections of the more important—historically speaking—martyrdoms beyond the larger collections already mentioned in this section of the Appendix are either (1) O. L. von Gebhardt, *Acta Martyrum Selecta: Ausgewählte Märtyreracten und andere Urkunden aus der Verfolgungszeit der christlichen Kirche* (Berlin, 1902) or (2) R. Knopf, *Ausgewählte Märtyrerakten* [3] (Tubingen, 1929). Each gives over twenty documents in either Greek or Latin. For a good sample in English see Owen, op. cit. (*supra* n. 1), who translates thirteen monuments and whose "general introduction" gives an adequate classification of the literary material relating to the martyrs (11–15).

12. Of the *libelli* (preserved among papyri exhumed in Egypt) some forty have been catalogued and summarized by A. Bludau under the title "Die ägyptischen Libelli und die Christenverfolgung des Kaisers Decius" in Supplement 27 to *Römische Quartalschrift für christliche Altertumskunde und für Kirchengeschichte* (Freiburg im Breisgau, 1931).

J. A. F. Gregg, *The Decian Persecution* (Edinburgh, 1897), 155, gives a translated specimen of the *libelli*. A typical certificate has two parts: (1) petitioner's name, age, identifying marks; affirmation that the apostate "according to the edict's terms" sacrificed, poured libations, tasted the sacrificial victim; request for the commission's certification; signature; (2) commissioner's signature; emperor's name and titles; date.

Christians who had procured these *libelli* fraudulently and consequently had not sacrificed to the divinities were called *libellatici*. Although the Church condemned such chicanery, yet it treated its members who had been guilty of such circumvention more leniently than its members who actually had sacrificed to the deities and who thus were called *sacrificati*.

13. For the effect of this policy upon the Church, of which many were martyrs and more were apostates, see Kidd, 1. 435–6, and Lebreton and Zeiller, op. cit., 3. 653–4.

14. By *Caesarians* are meant probably either the employees on the imperial estates, which especially in North Africa were numerous and enormous, or "the saints of Caesar's household" (Phil. 4. 22), who were so many in Valerian's palace (professes Eusebius, HE 7. 10. 3) that it was a church of God, rather than the fiscal apparitors of the same appellation attached to the imperial treasury and serving in the provinces (on whom see CT 10. 7).

15. See F. Görres, "Die Märtyrer der aurelianischen Christenverfolgung" in *Jahrbücher für protestantische Theologie*, 6 (1880) 449–94.

16. That the persecution began even ere the emission of the first edict may be seen from Kidd's collection of incidents from various *Acta Martyrum* (1. 515), which relate how Christian soldiers were persecuted after they had refused to sacrifice (see also Eusebius, HE 8. 4), as well as from Lactantius' description (*De Mort. Pers.* 12) how on 23 February 303 Diocletian and Galerius, of whom the latter seems to have persuaded the former to persecution (Lactantius, *De Mort. Pers.* 10. 6—11. 8, 31. 1; Eusebius, HE 8. 16. 2, App. to 8. 1. 4; VC 1. 56–8), personally assisted at the destruction of the chief church in Nicomedia, which, after its Scriptures had been burned and its furnishings had been pillaged, was razed in a few hours by the praetorian guards armed with axes and other iron tools.

Notification of at least the first three edicts and instructions that their provisions should be enforced were sent to Maximian and Constantius in the West, where the one fully and the other partly complied (Lactantius, *De Mort. Pers.* 15. 6–7; cf. Eusebius, VC 1. 15).

17. There is no discrepancy in date. Since Easter in 303 fell on 18 April, March would be the month when Easter was approaching. Obviously Eusebius has in mind the date when the ordinance reached Palestine, where the historian resided.

18. The Greek paronomasia of τιμῆς and ἀτίμους is difficult to reproduce: he who had held a post of rank was to be degraded.

19. Probably the so-called Caesarians, on whom cf. *supra* n. 14.

20. Cf. *supra* n. 17. There is still no discrepancy in date, if, since the governor's name is mentioned, we can infer that Eusebius refers to the (usual) implementation of an imperial statute by the publication of a gubernatorial edict.

An interval of time must be allowed for the ordinance to leave Nicomedia late in February, to reach Palestine in March, to be proclaimed in April. Often not a few months intervened; for such a case see no. 301, n. 15.

21. See no. 470, n. 49.

22. That is, on 24 February, for Lactantius continues his narrative summarized *supra* in n. 16.

23. By *voice* is meant not vote (as some translators turn the word, since, when once freedom had been forfeited for servitude, there was no possibility of a slave's exercise of what little suffrage—and that apparently only in the Senate and in municipal senates and in what provincial assemblies remained—still survived from the Republic through the Principate into the Dominate, because by the end of the first century all general electoral and legislative voting of a popular character had ceased), but rather the right to protest vocally and legally against the enforcement of the edict or against the power of their masters, to whom they became slaves.

24. On the Rufinian addition see A. J. Mason, *The Persecution of Diocletian* (Cambridge, 1876), 344.

25. March is the month usually assigned for the second statute, but Mason, op. cit., 125, n. 2, holds that it could have "come anywhere between February and November, 303."

26. Eusebius here has "everywhere" (πανταχῇ) for "in every place" (κατὰ πάντα τόπον).

27. While Lactantius does not mention this ordinance specifically, he probably refers to it in *De Mort. Pers.* 15. 4–5, where he describes how the judges compelled all persons to sacrifice and where he says that the jails were full.

28. In reality the second statute, whose defect the third law was designed to repair.

29. Cf. *supra* nn. 27 and 28.

30. Palaestina Prima.

31. This passage is copied from the so-called Longer Recension in H. J. Lawlor and J. E. L. Oulton, *Eusebius: The Ecclesiastical History and the Martyrs of Palestine* (London, 1927), 1. 339. These translators explain how they have evolved this English version from Greek and Latin and Syriac (op. cit. [1928], 2. 46–50).

32. That is, the third edict.

33. For *pro* and *con* consult Lawlor and Oulton, op. cit., 2. 323–4.

34. Military tribunes: χιλίαρχος = *tribunus militum*, translated as "chief captain" in Acts 21. 31–3 *et al.*

35. From Lawlor and Oulton, op. cit., 1. 347. Cf. *supra* n. 31.

36. While it probably was not a legislative act, except so far as an emperor's will was the living voice of the law, it may be mentioned that on 20 November 307 (between the fifth and the sixth statutes) at Caesarea of Palestine in Maximin's presence was martyred one Agapius as part of that emperor's natal

celebration, for which Maximin had "boasted that he would display something new to all the multitudes of spectators who were gathered together on his account" and at which Maximin personally promised Agapius his freedom on condition that he would renounce the Christian religion (Eusebius, *De Mart.' Pal.* 6).

See Lactantius, *De Mort. Pers.*, for three personal episodes involving Diocletian: (1) in 302 he ordered his Christian attendants, who were watching him sacrifice, and all his Christian servants in his palace to be scourged, if they should have refused to sacrifice (10); (2) after the persecution had begun in 303, he presided at the torture of persons—some of whom doubtless were Christians—suspected of having set fire to his palace (14. 3–5); (3) in 303 he even compelled his wife and his daughter, who were Christians, to sacrifice (15. 1). Also Eusebius, *De Mart. Pal.* 2. 2–3, recounts how at Antioch in 303 Diocletian—apparently still averse from death as a penalty—saved from fire a condemned Christian, but commanded the novel punishment of excising the martyr's tongue.

37. In the Lactantian confused chronology this statement, which is amplified in the gruesome details of the rest of the chapter, is applied to Galerius and presumably pertains to the period after 305.

38. Eusebius describes how the Palestinian governor in 308 ordered 97 miners with women and infants—all Christians from Egypt—to be lamed in the left foot and to be blinded in the right eye.

39. Either the prefect of the camp (*praefectus castrorum*) or the master of the soldiers (*magister militum*) or the praetorian prefect (*praefectus praetorio*) in the Orient is meant.

40. On these officials see no. 8, n. 2.

41. Literally "the fallen things"—sufficiently wide to include statues, altars, shrines, temples, etc. pertaining to idolatrous cults.

42. From Lawlor and Oulton, op. cit., 1. 372. Cf. *supra* n. 31.

43. The persons meant are "the governors of districts and the dux who was the chief of the army of the Romans" (in Lawlor's and Oulton's translation), who correspond to *the governors in the several provinces and, besides, the person set in charge to command the army* in the shorter recension previously translated.

44. These are the *recorders* in the previous paragraph.

45. It should be noted that the longer recension is silent about an edict.

46. See Lawlor and Oulton, op. cit., 2. 330, for an epitome of this edict's end.

47. In the longer recension, which is very loose, "a Roman general, called a dux" (cf. the word in n. 43 *supra*) is sent. But the superintendent of the mines probably had some military authority, even if he was not an officer on detached service. A modern analogy is the peacetime duty of an officer in the United States Army Corps of Engineers.

48. Eusebius dates the episode late in 310.

49. Eusebius ends his *De Martyribus Palaestinae* with the words (13. 14):

"... quenching the conflagration against us by kindly edicts and by gentle mandates about us; and the palinode also must be recorded".

Here followed either Galerius' (no. 7) or Maximin's (no. 14) edict of recantation—probably the former's, for in this treatise Eusebius does not treat the latter's persecution beyond the fourth day after Galerius at Nicomedia promulgated the law which ended the persecution (cf. *infra* n. 52).

50. So Eusebius, *HE* 9. 6. 1, 4.

51. Literally "forty less one in number were cut off in respect to the heads".

52. Eusebius dates this last massacre on 4 May 311, only four days after Galerius issued the Edict of Toleration (no. 7).

53. While executed criminals' bodies ordinarily could be buried, if request had been made for these (e.g. Joseph of Arimathaea thus begged the body of Jesus from Pilate: Matt. 27. 57–60; Mark 15. 43–6; Luke 23. 50–3; John 19. 38–42), yet evidence exists for exceptions in the case of Christian martyrs (e.g. Eusebius, *HE* 4. 15. 41; 5. 1. 59, 61–3; 8. 7. 6; 10. 8. 17; *De Mart. Pal.* 9. 8–11; 11. 15–16; Lactantius, *De Mort. Pers.* 21. 11). It may be that governmental officials took a dim view of Christians foregathering at the graves of such champions of Christ and found that exclusion from cemeteries was an effective means to prevent a demotic demonstration.

54. For an example of this contrivance see no. 9 and n. 1 thereto as well as the next two extracts.

55. These were the municipal senates' resolutions (cf. no. 9, n. 3) sent to Maximin as petitions, as already told in the preceding paragraph. Eusebius later reports that copies of the petitions and of the rescripts were published on bronze tablets (*HE* 9. 7. 1).

56. The Galerian Edict of Toleration was promulgated in the name of all four emperors (no. 7, n. 2).

57. Eusebius (*HE* 9. 4. 2) briefly repeats the note about the appointment of pagan pontiffs.

58. These fabrications, apparently no longer extant, must be distinguished from the *Acts of Our Lord Jesus Christ Done in the Time of Pontius Pilate,* which is called sometimes either the *Gospel of Nicodemus* or (more simply) the *Acts of Pilate.* Eusebius earlier asserts that the former were of recent origin and were prepared particularly for Maximin's programme of (in this case, insidious) persecution (*HE* 1. 9. 3, 1. 11. 9). The latter is a Christian forgery, which— some scholars suppose—was composed as a counterblast to the pagan production.

The extant *Acts* survive in Greek, Latin, Coptic, Syriac, Armenian versions, with which allied documents, such as the correspondence between Tiberius and Pilate, are associated. A convenient translation of this material into English is by M. R. James, *The Apocryphal New Testament* (Oxford, 1924), 95–146, 153–65.

59. Galerius is meant by way of contrast to Maximin.

60. Literally "the sensory organs of light must be maltreated".

61. Mason's book contains also translations.

TABLE OF TITLES OF ADDRESS

The following complimentary titles appear in the constitutions. Those asterisked are not found in either Sister Lucilla Dinneen's *Titles of Address in Christian Greek Epistolography to 527 A.D.* (Washington, 1929) or Sister Mary Bridget O'Brien's *Titles of Address in Christian Latin Epistolography to 543 A.D.* (Washington, 1930).

Affection: L. *affectus
Angel: L. *angelus
Apostolicity: L. apostolatus
Authority: G. *αὐθεντία (authentia), ἐξουσία (exousia); L. *auctoritas, *dispositio
Beatitude: G. *μακαριότης (makariotes); L. beatitudo
Benediction: L. benedictio
Benevolence: G. φιλανθρωπία (philanthropia); L. benevolentia
Benignity: G. *εὐμένεια (eumeneia); L. benignitas
Brotherhood: G. *ἀδελφότης (adelphotes)
Carefulness: G. *ἐπιστρέφεια (epistrepheia)
Charity: L. caritas
Clemency: G. ἡμερότης (hemerotes); L. clementia
Conscience: L. *conscientia
Constancy: G. στερρότης (sterrotes)
Deliberation: L. *deliberatio
Devotion: G. *καθοσίωσις (kathosiosis); L. *devotio
Devoutness: G. εὐλάβεια (eulabeia)
Dignity: G. τιμιότης (timiotes); L. dignatio
Diligence: G. *ἐπιμέλεια (epimeleia); L. *diligentia

Disposition: G. διάθεσις (diathesis) L. *dispositio
Distinction: G. ἐνδοξότης (endoxotes)
Divinity: G. θειότης (theiotes); L. divinitas, numen
Eminence: L. culmen, eminentia
Eternity: L. aeternitas
Excellence: L. *dicatio, eximietas
Excellency: G. θαυμασιότης ([either] thau-masiotes [or] thaumasiotes, *ὑπεροχή (hyperoche), χρηστότης (chrestotes); L. spectabilitas
Experience: L. *experientia
Fairness: G. ἐπιείκεια (epieikeia)
Gentility: G. καλοκἀγαθία (kalokagathia)
Gentleness: G. πραότης (praotes); L. mansuetudo
Godliness: G. θεοσέβεια (theosebeia), θεοφιλία (theophilia)
Goodness: G. *φιλαγαθία (philagathia)
Grandeur: L. magnitudo
Gravity: G. *στιβαρότης (stibarotes); L. gravitas
Guidance: L. moderatio
Highness: L. celsitudo
Holiness: G. ἁγιωσύνη (hagiosyne), ἁγιότης (hagiotes); L. sanctimonia, sanctimonium

TABLE OF TITLES OF ADDRESS

Honour: L. *amplitudo*
Humanity: L. *humanitas*
Indulgence: L. *indulgentia
Ingenuity: L. *sollertia
Leniency: L. *lenitas
Liberality: L. *liberalitas
Love: G. ἀγάπη (*agape*)
Magnificence: G. μεγαλοπρέπεια (*megaloprepeia*); L. *magnificentia*
Majesty: G. βασιλεία (*basileia*), βασίλειον (*basileion*), καθοσίωσις (*kathosiosis*); L. *maiestas*
Memory: L. *recordatio*
Mightiness: G. κράτος (*kratos*)
Munificence: L. *munificentia
Patience: G. ἀνεξικακία (*anexikakia*); L. *patientia
Perpetuity: L. *perennitas*
Piety: G. εὐσέβεια (*eusebeia*); L. *pietas*
Providence: G. *πρόνοια (*pronoia*)
Prudence: G. φρόνησις (*phronesis*); L. *prudentia*
Purity: G. καθαρότης (*katharotes*)
Religiosity: L. *religiositas

Responsibility: L. *sollicitudo*
Reverence: G. σεμνότης (*semnotes*); L. *reverentia*
Sagacity: G. ἀγχίνοια (*anchinoia*)
Sanctitude: L. *sanctitudo*
Sanctity: G. ὁσιότης (*hosiotes*); L. *sanctitas*
Sapience: L. *sapientia*
Serenity: G. γαληνότης (*galenotes*); L. *serenitas*
Severity: L. *censura
Sincerity: G. *νηφαλιότης (*nephaliotes*); L. *sinceritas*
Sovereignty: L. *imperium
Splendour: G. λαμπρότης (*lamprotes*)
Sublimity: L. *sublimitas*
Superiority: L. *praestantia*
Tranquillity: L. *tranquillitas*
Venerability: L. *venerabilitas*
Veneration: L. *veneratio*
Wisdom: G. σύνεσις (*synesis*)
Worship: L. *religio*
Worthiness L. *dignitas*

GLOSSARY

It should be noted that only the commoner Greek and Latin equivalents are given in parenthesis as synonyms of an entry. For example, while the Latin for praetorian prefect (on which see no. 6, n. 4) is most commonly *praefectus praetorio,* there are at least 35 Greek phrases and circumlocutions for this title (see D. Magie's list in his *De Romanorum Iuris Publici Sacrique Vocabulis Sollemnibus in Graecum Sermonem Conversis* [Leipzig, 1905], 103-4); to reproduce all these—even in the case of the most important imperial minister—would be a waste of space. Moreover, since a Glossary ordinarily gives only words which seem to need explanation in the text to be glossed, one should not expect —to continue with the prefect—mention of all kinds of prefects, of whom more than thirty are known in Roman legal documents.

Wherever a reader may consider that the Glossary is deficient, it is suggested that he should consult the Glossary in C. Pharr, *The Theodosian Code and Novels and the Sirmondian Constitutions* (Princeton, 1952), 573-99, A. Berger, *Encyclopedic Dictionary of Roman Law* (Philadelphia, 1953), 338-785, and A. C. Johnson, P. R. Coleman-Norton, F. C. Bourne, *Ancient Roman Statutes* (Austin, 1961), 256-76, where he can find additional and usually accurate information.

abbess (L. *abbatissa, praefecta*; G. ἡγουμένη [*hegoumene*]). Head of a nunnery. See no. 614, nn. 2 and 4.

abbot (G. ἀββᾶς [*abbas*]; ἡγούμενος [*hegoumenos*] L. *abbas*). Head of a monastery. See no. 614, nn. 2 and 4.

account pertaining to provisions (L. *res annonaria*). See no. 301, n. 7.

accountant (G. λογοθέτης [*logothetes*]; L. *rationalis*). Supervisor of fiscal accounts, perhaps synonymous with catholicus.

acolyte (G. ἀκόλουθος [*akolouthos*]; L. *acoluthus, comes, sequens*). Clergyman in minor orders, who assisted a subdeacon.

actio communi dividundo (action for division of common property). See no. 641, n. 18.

actio de falso (action on forgery). See no. 204, n. 5.

actio ex empto or *empti* (action on purchase). See no. 641, n. 27.

actio ex lege condicticia (action according to condictal law). See no. 612, n. 13.

actio familiae erciscundae (action for division of family estate). See no. 641, n. 18.

actio hypothecaria (hypothecary action). See no. 604, n. 8.

actio in factum (action on a fact). See no. 598, n. 10.

actio in personam (action against a person). See no. 604, n. 6.

actio in rem (action for or over or to a thing). See no. 598, n. 8.

actio iniuriarum (action for injuries). See no. 334, n. 25.

actio mixta (mixed action). See no. 640, n. 7.

actio per condictionem (action by notice). See no. 598, n. 9.

actio pervasionis (action of forcible entry). See no. 478, n. 11.

actio sepulchri violati (action of violated sepulchre). See no. 641, n. 17 *ad med.*

Adelphians. See Enthusiasts.

Adiabenicus (L. *Adiabenicus*; G. 'Αδιαβηνιακός [*Adiabeniakos*]). Imperial title denoting victory over Adiabenians.

adquisitio miserabilis (miserable acquisition). See no. 631, n. 3 *ad fin.*

aedile, curule or plebeian (L. *aedilis curulis* or *aedilis plebeius*; G. ἀγορανόμος κουροὐλλιος [*agoranomos kouroullios*] or ἀγοράνομος τοῦ πλήθους [*agoranomos tou plethous*]). One of six annually elected magistrates, whose office can be traced to 494 B.C., when there were two plebeian aediles. Their chief concern was the care of the city of Rome, wherein they superintended maintenance of public works, supervised mercantile transactions, inspected weights and measures, managed public celebrations and amusements, licensed prostitutes, and organized the supply of grain until that function fell in the early Principate to the prefect of the grain supply.

The magistracy ceased in the late Principate, when imperial officials assumed aedilician duties.

Aegyptiacus (L. *Aegyptiacus*; G. Αἰγυπτιακός [*Aigyptiakos*]). Imperial title denoting victory over Egyptians.

Aetians. Adherents of the Arian Aetius, deacon of Antioch (see no. 103, n. 5), who taught that God the Father is wholly different in substance and in will from God the Son and God the Holy Spirit and that he alone has the true quality of deity.

Africanus (L. *Africanus*; G. 'Αφρικός [*Aphrikos*]). Imperial title denoting victory over (North) Africans.

agent, secret-service (L. *agens in rebus*). See no. 256, n. 3.

agnate (L. *agnatus*). Relative who traces his or her descent only through male line to a male ascendant who is (or was) his or her paterfamilias. See cognate.

agnation (L. *agnatio*). Relation wherein an agnate is related to other agnates. See no. 599, n. 5.

GLOSSARY

Alamannicus (L. *Alamannicus*; G. Ἀλαμανικός [*Alamanikos*]). Imperial title denoting victory over Alamans.

Alanicus (L. *Alanicus*; G. Ἀλανικός [*Alanikos*]). Imperial title denoting victory over Alans.

anchorite (G. ἀναχωρητής [*anachoretes*]; L. *anachoreta*). One who renounces the world for his soul's salvation and retires into solitary seclusion.

annona (L. *annona*; G. ἀννῶνα [*annona*], ἀννώνη [*annone*], σίτησις [*sitesis*]). See no. 301, n. 7.

annotation (L. *annotatio*). See no. 317, n. 2.

announcement of new work (L. *operis novi nuntiatio*). See no. 641, n. 31.

Anomoeans. A synonym for Aetians and Eunomians. They took their name from their distinctive dogma that God the Father is essentially or substantially different (G. ἀνόμοιος [*anomoios*]) from the other persons of the Trinity. Anomoeanism was the most intellectual expression of Arianism and therefore attracted few followers. See Aetians, Eunomians, Heteroousians.

Anticus (L. *Anticus*; G. Ἀντικός [*Antikos*]). Imperial title devoting victory over Antes.

apocrisiarian (G. ἀποκρισιάριος [*apokrisiarios*]; L. *apocrisiarius, responsalis*). Special ecclesiastical envoy, either permanent or temporary, usually representing either a major prelate or a particular church, to the court of either the emperor or a patriarch or a praetorian prefect. Apocrisiarians appeared perhaps by the mid-fourth century, certainly by the mid-fifth century (see no. 482, n. 6), and lasted into the eighth century. Papal apocrisiarians often were delegated to Constantinople from the fall of the Western Empire (476) and were empowered to observe ecclesiastical discipline, to resist spread of heresy, and to defend papal rights.

Apollinarians. Followers of Apollinaris the Younger, bishop of Laodicea in Syria, who, accepting the Platonic trichotomy of human nature (body, soul, mind), taught that Christ had a human body and a human soul, but not a human mind, for which was substituted the Divine Word (Logos). Apollinaris thus denied in Christ the union of perfect divine nature with perfect human nature. As a sect Apollinarianism had a short life in Asian provinces and in Egypt and became extinct soon after its condemnation at the Second General Council in 381 at Constantinople.

apostasy (G. ἀποστασία [*apostasia*]; L. *apostasia*). Abandonment of the Christian faith, especially with a view to adoption of a non-Christian religion.

Apostolics. See Encratitans.

Apotactitans. See Encratitans.

apparitor (L. *apparitor, officialis*; G. ὑπηρέτης [*hyperetes*], ὀφφικιάλιος [*ophphikialios*], ταξεώτης [*taxeotes*]). Member of a more important office staff. A typical panel of apparitors included one or more of the following:

accountant, archivist, attendant, auditor, bedel, carrier, cashier, chancellor, clerk, copyist, crier, messenger, recorder, registrar, secretary, summoner.

These men assisted magistrates and officials. At first they were appointed annually; but, since importance of an experienced public servant soon was seen, they easily became fixtures in a fairly permanent civil service to their temporary superiors and ere the end of the Republic, by which time they had been organized into groups of nominally ten men (decuries), even created a kind of class-consciousness for themselves.

Aquarians. See Encratitans.

archbishop (G. ἀρχιεπίσκοπος [archiepiskopos]; L. archiepiscopus). An early synonym for metropolitan. In some districts, however, the archiepiscopal office was not attached to the see of the metropolis of the civil province, but was held by the provincial bishop oldest either in age or in office.

archdeacon (G. ἀρχιδιάκονος [archidiakonos]; L. archidiaconus). Chief assistant to a bishop in diocesan administration, supervising other deacons in their management of ecclesiastical property, examining candidates for the priesthood, disciplining subordinate clergy and overseeing the discharge of their duties, making visitations among the rural clergy. On the spiritual side he seems to have been charged with the preservation of the faith in its primitive purity. Because of his experience an archdeacon often was chosen to succeed the bishop whom he had served.

archimandrite (G. ἀρχιμανδρίτης; L. archimandrites). Head of a monastery (G. and L. μάνδρα: mandra), sometimes of several monasteries. In orders he usually was a priest; even when he remained a deacon, he had precedence over secular priests. See no. 614, n. 2.

archpriest (G. ἀρχιπρεσβύτερος [archipresbyteros], πρωτοπρεσβύτερος [protopresbyteros]; L. archipresbyter). Chief priest of a church.

Arians. Adherents of Arius, priest of Alexandria, who tried to rationalize the mystery of the Trinity by denying the divinity of God the Son, whom he held inferior to God the Father and as created in time from a different, but similar, substance. Arianism, although the chief cause for the convocation of the First General Council in 325 at Nicaea, where it was condemned, was the principal heresy of the fourth century and has survived into the twentieth century as Unitarianism. See Anomoeans, Homoiousians, Heteroousians, Semi-Arians.

Armeniacus (L. Armeniacus; G. Ἀρμενιακός [Armeniakos]). Imperial title denoting victory over Armenians.

Armenius (L. Armenius; G. Ἀρμένιος [Armenios]). See Armeniacus.

as, asses (L. sing. as, L. plur. asses). The ancient Roman unit of base-metal currency. Originally a bar (one foot long) of aes (an omnibus term for copper and its alloys), finally a coin (weighing one pound) of bronze worth about $.17 (U.S.A. 1914) c. 269 B.C. Thereafter the as was reduced in weight

GLOSSARY 1203

and was depreciated in value until it weighed one-half ounce and was worth $.008 about the Social War (90-88 B.C.), soon after which it ceased to be struck. Augustus revived it c. 19 B.C. in copper.

Ascodrogitans. Fanatic followers of Montanus, a Phrygian prophet, whom they regarded as the Paraclete and with whose spirit in their opinion they were imbued when they danced around an altar, on which was laid a richly decorated and inflated wineskin (G. ἀσκός [askos]). Sometimes they were confused with Tascodrogitans from the similarity of name.

asiarch (G. ἀσιάρχης [asiarches]; L. asiarcha). See no. 3, n. 8.

Assembly (L. comitia; G. ἐκκλησία [ekklesia], τὰ ἀρχαιρέσια [ta archairesia]). Meeting of the Romans for electoral or judicial or legislative purposes, called in units and summoned by a magistrate with power of convocation, voting by units only on matters introduced by the presiding officer. The majority in each unit without discussion decided that unit's vote.

Assembly of Asia (L. commune Asiae; G. κοινὸν τῆς 'Ασίας [koinon tes Asias]). See no. 3, n. 8.

Assembly, Tribal (L. comitia tributa). Fourth oldest Roman Assembly, organized on a residential basis originally into four and finally into 35 units (each called a tribe [tribus]). Its principal activities were election of lower magistrates, legislation on apparently any subject, and decision in lawsuits conducted by an aedile.

assistant (L. administer). Provincial governor. See no. 5, n. 2.

association. See guild.

Audians. Adherents of Audius, a Mesopotamian bishop of irregular consecration, who held that God has a human form, adopted anthropomorphism as a religious tenet, inveighed against ecclesiastical laxity, and lived an ascetical life.

audientia episcopalis (episcopal hearing, i.e. a bishop's court). See no. 28, n. 1 *ad fin*.

auditor (L. *discussor*). Inspector or examiner of accounts, census (and income) records, and public works.

augur (L. *augur*; G. αὔγουρ [*augour*]). One of sixteen official diviners in Rome. Augurs professed to discover divine approval or disapproval of a proposed action by interpreting signs, which fell into five categories: (1) from birds, (2) from quadrupeds, (3) from celestial phenomena (particularly lightning), (4) from chickens, (5) from prodigies of various kinds.

Augusta (L. *Augusta*; G. Αὐγούστα [*Augousta*], Σεβαστή [*Sebaste*]). Title conferred by Senate ordinarily on an emperor's wife and occasionally on an emperor's female relatives (usually sisters and daughters).

Augustal (L. *Augustalis*, officially *sodalis Augustalis*). In Italian municipalities and colonies a priest of the cult of Augustus was one of six such ministers (*seviri Augustales*). See no. 6, n. 1.

Augustal prefect. See prefect, Augustal.

Augustus (L. *Augustus*; G. Αὔγουστος [*Augoustos*], Σεβαστός [*Sebastos*]). Title conferred by Senate on Octavian (Gaius Iulius Caesar Octavianus) on 16 January 27 B.C. and then held by all later emperors except Vitellius (69).

aureus (L. *aureus*). See no. 515, n. 18.

auxiliary bishop. See Introd., n. 42 *ad fin*.

Barbeliotes. See Borborians.

Batrachitans. An obscure sect of heretics who, thinking thus to appease divine anger, venerated the frogs (G. βάτραχοι [*batrachoi*]) of the Egyptian plague (Ex. 8. 1-15).

belt (L. *cingulum*; G. ζώνη [*zone*]). Girdle or sash of office. Symbolically the rank of a high military or civil official. See no. 476, n. 39.

beneficiarian (L. *beneficiarius*; G. βενεφικιάριος [*benephikiarios*]). A late title for an aide of a high military or civil official. See no. 14, n. 6.

bishop (G. ἐπίσκοπος [*episkopos*], ἱερεύς [*hiereus*], καθηγεμών [*kathegemon*], πρόεδρος [*proedros*], προεστώς [*proestos*], προστάτης [*prostates*]; L. *episcopus, antistes, praesul, sacerdos*). Generic term for the highest-ranking clergyman of the Church, of whose doctrine he was the custodian and of whose discipline he was the controller. Though the episcopate's origin and development are still controverted, it seems that the bishop was the chief clergyman of a city and of the circumjacent villages and countryside included in a city's territory, for most ecclesiastical dioceses in this sylloge's period consisted of a see city and its environs.

For various ranks within the episcopate, see archbishop, auxiliary bishop, exarch, itinerant bishop, metropolitan, patriarch, pope, primate, primate bishop, rural bishop, suffragan bishop. See also Introd., n. 42, and nos. 16, n. 4, and 158, n. 1.

Borborians. Nickname for Gnostics who properly were called Barbeliotes from their veneration of Barbelo (*al.* Barbeloth), the supreme female principle or aeon in Gnosticism. Borborians (Mud-Men; from G. βόρβορος [*borboros*]: "mud") lived licentious lives and disbelieved in a future judgement.

Breviarium Alaricianum (Alaric's Breviary). See Introd., n. 2.

brief (L. *brevis, breve*; G. βρεούιον [*breouion*]). See no. 15, n. 8.

bureau, secretarial (L. *scrinium*; G. σκρίνιον [*skrinion*]). See no. 256, n. 2.

Caelicolans. An obscure sect of Unitarians, who combined Christian and Jewish doctrines and ceremonies. Popularly called Caelicolans (Heaven-

Worshippers) for a now unknown reason, they were prevalent in North Africa. See no. 315, n. 1.

Caesar (L. *Caesar*; G. Καῖσαρ [*Kaisar*]). Imperial title derived from the cognomen (familial name) of Gaius Iulius Caesar, the real founder, though not the first emperor, of the Empire. See no. 28, n. 7, for its use also by male members of the emperor's family.

Caesarian (L. *Caesarianus*; G. Καισαριανός [*Kaisarianos*]). (1) Apparitor of the fiscal representative in charge of the fisc's administration. One of his duties was to take possession of property which either was ownerless or was confiscated by the imperial treasury. (2) Employee on imperial estates. (3) Servant in the imperial household. See App., n. 14.

calumny (L. *calumnia*). See no. 334, n. 3.

canon (G. κανών [*kanon*]; L. *canon*). (1) Regular and annual payment of a fixed amount as rent by a tenant to a landlord who has a long-term lease of land from the State. (2) Regular and annual tax or tribute on land paid to the State. (3) Ecclesiastical rule, especially an ordinance enacted by a Church council to regulate internal administration of the Church.

capitatio (capitation). See tax, capitation.

caput (head). (1) Person. (2) Civil or political life or status. (3) In the Dominate a tax unit assessed on the amount of land which normally could be cultivated in one year by one man or by two women as well as levied per head of farm animals, in which case several small animals normally were equated with one large animal. (4) Rations of grain for animals required as tax. See tax, capitation.

Carpicus (L. *Carpicus*; G. Καρπιανός [*Karpianos*]). Imperial title denoting victory over Carpians.

Cataphrygians. An early western name for Montanists, who originated in Phrygia.

catechumen (G. κατηχούμενος [*katechoumenos*]; L. *catechumenus*). One under Christian instruction preparatory to baptism. See no. 189, n.2.

catholicus (G. καθολικός [*katholikos*]; L. *catholicus, rationalis, rationalis summarum, rationalis summae rei*). (1) Supervisor of fiscal accounts whether in the imperial household or in the provinces. (2) Prefect of the State's treasury. (3) Head of the Abyssinian Church.

censor (L. *censor*; G. τιμητής [*timetes*]). One of two magistrates elected first c. 443 B.C. Censors assessed quinquennially citizens' property, revised the registers of senators and knights, allocated citizens in the Assemblies' units, managed the Republic's finances, and supervised public morals. Among republican magistracies the censorship was exceptional, for its tenure was for five years. After 22 B.C. the censors' functions were exercised by the emperor and by imperial officials. The census was taken at irregular intervals in imperial times. See no. 41, n. 2.

centurion (L. *centurio*; G. ἑκατόνταρχος [*hekatontarchos*]). Military officer commanding a century (nominally a hundred infantrymen) in a legion, to which sixty centurions nominally were assigned.

chamberlain (L. *cubicularius*; G. κουβικουλάριος [*koubikoularios*]). Official concerned with the comfort and the safety of the emperor and the empress. His duties were confined chiefly to the imperial bedchamber and were performed under the direction of the provost of the sacred bedchamber.

chanter (L. *cantor*; G. ψάλτης [*psaltes*]). Singer in divine worship and, as such, a cleric in minor orders.

chief imperial secretary. See chief of the notaries.

chief men (L. *primates, primores, priores, proximi*; G. προέχοντες [*proechontes*], πρωτεύοντες [*proteuontes*], πρῶτοι [*protoi*]). Prominent persons in municipalities, municipal wards, guilds, office staffs, and secretarial bureax.

chief of the notaries (L. *primicerius notariorum*; G. πριμικήριος τῶν νοταρίων [*primikerios ton notarion*]). Superintendent of the imperial secretariat. In his office was maintained a list (*laterculum*) of all imperial officials, whence has been derived our text of the *Notitia Dignitatum*—an invaluable document for administrative details about the Dominate.

chief of the office staff (L. *princeps, princeps officii*). Chief executive of an administrative office subordinate to its nominal head, who was a magistrate or an official. See no. 25, n. 9.

chiliarch (G. χιλίαρχος [*chiliarchos*]; L. *tribunus militum*). Military officer (on whom see App., n. 34), commander of nominally 1,000 soldiers.

chorepiscopus. See rural bishop.

Christmas (L. *dies natalis domini*; G. τὰ ἐπιφάνια [*ta epiphania*], θεοφάνεια [*theophaneia*], ἡ γενέθλιος [*he genethlios*]). See no. 220, n. 10.

Circumcellions. North African adherents of Donatism, mostly fugitive slaves and bankrupt peasants. Constituting Donatism's lunatic fringe and strong-arm squad, they were devoted fanatics and callous brigands, who for years roamed throughout North Africa and terrorized the Catholic population by committing atrocious outrages of refined cruelty particularly upon the orthodox clergy. Their name was derived from their vagrant movements as they wandered from place to place. See Donatists.

clergyman (G. κληρικός [*klerikos*]; L. *clericus*). Generic term for Christians ordained to the service of God in churches, but particularly applied to persons below the rank of bishop, such as priests and deacons and those in minor orders.

cleric. See clergyman.

clericate (L. *clericatus*; G. κληρικᾶτον [*klerikaton*]). Clerical office.

clerk (L. *cancellarius*). Official in the chancery of a high imperial functionary.

GLOSSARY 1207

clerk, chief (L. *primiscrinius*). Highest clerk in an imperial secretarial bureau (*scrinium*).

client (L. *cliens*; G. πελάτης [*pelates*]). Freeman, often a freedman, usually of low social and/or economic status, who entrusted himself to a patron's protection. Eventually this relation became hereditary and was regulated by law.

Codex Iustinianianus or (less correctly but more usually) *Codex Iustinianus* (Justinian's Code). See Introd., 1.

For Justinian I's first and extinct Code see Introd., n. 3.

Codex Repetitae Praelectionis (Code of Repeated Reading). See Introd., n. 3.

Codex Theodosianus (Theodosius' Code). See Introd., 1.

In the East it was abrogated by Justinian I's Code in 534, but it continued to be used in the West after that part of the Empire had fallen in 476 before the birth of Justinian, whose order about its abrogation had, of course, no effect there, and it had some influence on the chief three surviving barbarian codes of law: *Lex Romana Burgundionum, Lex Romana Visigothorum, Lex Romana Ostrogothorum*, on which see Introd., n. 2 *ad fin*.

Codex Vetus (Old Code). See Introd., n. 3.

cognate (L. *cognatus*). Relative usually by blood through either males or females, but occasionally by marriage and infrequently by blood through females only. See agnate.

cognation (L. *cognatio*). Relation wherein a cognate is related to relatives. See no. 599, n. 5.

cohortaline (L. *cohortalinus, cohortalis*; G. κορταλῖνος [*kortalinos*], ταξεώτης [*taxeotes*]). Member of a less important office staff. See no. 320, n. 5.

colonus (tenant farmer). See no. 528, n. 5.

commissary (L. *primipilus*). See no. 110, n. 5.

condiction (L. *condictio*). See no. 612, n. 13.

confessor (L. *confessor*; G. ὁμολογητής [*homologetes*]). See no. 46, n. 21.

consistory, sacred (L. *sacrum consistorium*; G. θεῖον κωνσιστώριον [*theion konsistorion*], θεῖον συνέδριον [*theion synedrion*]). Imperial council of the Dominate (in the Principate called *consilium* [council] after its prototype in the Republic, when a magistrate could avail himself of an advisory council). Its members, who were high-ranking dignitaries, departmental directors, and privileged personages, advised the emperor on administrative, financial, judicial, legislative, military, political matters, although the sovereign, who summoned them at will, was not obliged to accept their advice. The jurisconsults of this privy council, wherein the councillors stood in the presence of the seated prince, played a prominent part in the evolution of Roman law, for the consistory was also the supreme court of judicature.

constitution (L. *constitutio*; G. διάταξις [*diataxis*]). Generic term for imperial legislation such as (1) decree (L. *decretum*; G. κρῖμα [*krima*]), (2) edict (L. *edictum*; G. διάταγμα [*diatagma*], πρόσταγμα [*prostagma*]), (3) epistle or letter (G. ἐπιστολή [*epistole*], ἐπίσταλμα [*epistalma*], γράμματα [*grammata*], γραφή [*graphe*]; L. *epistola, epistula, litterae, scriptura, apices*), which may be also a rescript (L. *rescriptum*; G. ἀντιγραφή [*antigraphe*]) or a subscription (L. *subscriptio*; G. ὑπογραφή [*hypographe*]), (4) mandate (L. *mandatum*; G. διαταγή [*diatage*], ἐντολή [*entole*]).

See Introd., 2. See also edictal law, formulary, general law, pragmatic sanction, response, sanction.

consul (L. *consul*; G. ὕπατος [*hypatos*], στρατηγός [*strategos*], στρατηγὸς ὕπατος [*strategos hypatos*]). In the Republic one of two magistrates normally elected annually after 510 B.C. as the highest civil and military officials. In the Principate consuls lost their military duties and usually were nominated and then were appointed by the emperor, who sometimes served as a colleague and occasionally had several successive consular colleagues in a given year. In the Dominate the emperor appointed for each capital one consul, whose civil duties were nominal and who really enjoyed only an honorary position, for most of the consular powers had been transferred to imperial officers.

Romans dated their documents by consulships, of which each lasted for not more than one year.

consul suffectus (L. *consul suffectus*; G. σμικρότερος ὕπατος [*smikroteros hypatos*]). Substitute for a consul who was too sick to serve or died or resigned or served only during the first few months of a year.

consular (L. *consularis*; G. ὑπατικός [*hypatikos*]). Title of provincial governor in the Dominate.

consular rector. See rector, consular.

consulate (L. *consulatus*; G. ὑπατεία [*hypateia*]). Office of consul.

Continents (L. *Continentes*). (1) Popular term applied to monks, who were vowed to chastity in a period when other clerics could marry. (2) For heretics of this name see Encratitans.

contributor. See taxpayer.

contubernium (association). See no. 170, n. 3.

corporation. See guild.

Corpus Iuris Civilis (Body of Civil Law). Name given first in 1583 by Denys Godefroy (Dionysius Gothofredus) to Justinian I's codification of Roman Law. See Introd., n. 3 *ad fin*.

Corpus Iuris Canonici (Body of Canon Law). Name given first in 1582 by Pope Gregory XIII to the medieval compilations of the *ius canonicum*.

corrector (L. *corrector*; G. κουρήκτωρ [*konrektor*], διορθωτής [*diorthotes*],

GLOSSARY 1209

ἐπανορθωτής [epanorthotes]). (1) Imperial official governing a district (see no. 6, n. 1). (2) Provincial governor (see no. 18, n. 9).

council (L. *concilium, synodus*; G. σύνοδος [*synodos*]). Assembly of clergy convened to consider matters of doctrine and discipline affecting the Church locally or universally. Four general or nominally ecumenical councils occurred in this sylloge's period: Nicaea, 325; Constantinople, 381; Ephesus, 431; Chalcedon, 451.

count (L. *comes*; G. κόμης [*komes*]). Incumbent of a high imperial office, whether civil or military. Sometimes the title was conferred *honoris causa* on persons who never had held office.

count of the dispositions (L. *comes dispositionum*; G. κόμης τῶν διοποσιτιώνων [*komes ton dispositionon*]). Imperial official in charge of the bureau which arranged the emperor's tours through the Empire. See no. 256, n. 2.

count of the domestics (L. *comes domesticorum*; G. κόμης τῶν δομεστίκων [*komes ton domestikon*]). Commander of guards, both of infantry and of cavalry, who were stationed at the imperial court. See no. 547, n. 6.

count of the East or of the Orient (L. *comes Orientis*; G. κόμης τῆς ἀνατολῆς [*komes tes anatoles*]). Vicar of the diocese of the East or of the Orient, the only civil diocese to retain the title of count instead of that of vicar.

count of the private estates (L. *comes rerum privatarum*; G. κόμης τῶν πριβάτων κτημάτων [*komes ton pribaton ktematon*], κόμης τῶν θείων ἰδικῶν [*komes ton theion idikon*]). Late title for the procurator of the private estate of the emperor.

count of the sacred consistory (L. *comes sacri consistorii*; G. κόμης τοῦ θείου κωνσιστωρίου [*komes tou theiou konsistoriou*], κόμης τοῦ θείου συνεδρίου [*komes tou theiou synedriou*]). Member of the imperial council which advised the emperor.

count of the sacred largesses (L. *comes sacrarum largitionum*; G. κομης τῶν θείων λαργιτιώνων [*komes ton theion largitionon*]). Imperial official in charge of the central treasury as well as in control of mints and mines and customs. His curious title was derived from the duty assigned to his office at its institution: payment of donations to soldiers.

count of the sacred patrimony (L. *comes sacri patrimonii*; G. κόμης τῆς ἰδικῆς κτήσεως [*komes tes idikes kteseos*]). Chief administrator of the emperor's private property. See no. 519, n. 12.

count of the sacred treasury (L. *comes sacri aerarii*; G. κόμης τοῦ ἱεροῦ ταμιείου [*komes tou hierou tamieiou*]). Alternative title for either count of the private estates or count of the sacred largesses or count of the sacred patrimony.

cultivator, registered (L. *originarius*). See no. 478, n. 19.

curator (L. *curator*; G. κουράτωρ [*kourator*], ἐπίτροπος [*epitropos*], φροντιστής [*phrontistes*]). Generic term for a large variety of persons serving sometimes singly and sometimes as a group, with specific functions of supervisory character, whether publicly or privately. For some curators see following entries.

curator (L. *curator*; G. κηδεμών [*kedemon*]). Guardian of a ward. See guardian.

curator (L. *curator rei publicae, curator civitatis*; G. λογιστής [*logistes*]). Supervisor of municipal finances, with jurisdiction over matters pertaining to his office. Sometimes synonymous with father of the municipality.

curator of the imperial household (L. *curator dominicae [divinae] domus*). See no. 630, n. 1.

curial (L. *curialis*). Member of a municipality whose property made him eligible to serve in its local senate (*curia*) and as a municipal magistrate. The word often is synonymous with decurion.

Curials, who constituted the well-to-do, if not wealthy, upper and middle classes in the provinces, were reduced eventually to virtually universal bankruptcy, since the *curia* was responsible for the payment of such taxes as the municipalities could not collect—and there usually was an annual deficit. Propertied men were compelled to enroll in the curial class and to take their turn in office. Constantine I made the curial status hereditary (e.g. *CT* 12. 1. 12=*CI* 10. 39. 5; dated 325).

On curials (decurions) much legislation exists in the Codes: in *CT* 12. 1 are 192 constitutions from 313 to 436 and in *CI* 10. 32 are 68 laws from 259 to 529.

curule aedile. See aedile.

damnatio memoriae (damnation of memory). (1) Disgrace branding the memory of a person who either died under accusation of treason or after conviction of treason was executed. (2) Disgrace stigmatizing the memory of an emperor whom the Senate condemned because of the character of his life and administration.

Such condemnation entailed erasure of the person's name in documents and on monuments, invalidity of his will, and annulment of his donations made in view of his apprehension of imminent death.

deacon (G. διάκονος [*diakonos*]; L. *diaconus*). Member of the third and lowest rank of major orders—inferior to a bishop and a priest. While a deacon participated in the liturgical ministry, he particularly concerned himself with the temporal administration of a church and the relief of the congregational poor.

deaconess (G. διακόνισσα [*diakonissa*]; L. *diaconissa, diacona, ministra*). See no. 92, n. 1.

debtor, public (L. *debitor publicus*). Delinquent taxpayer.

decanicum (G. δεκανικόν [*dekanikon*]). See no. 258, n. 4.

decree. See constitution.

GLOSSARY 1211

decurion (L. *decurio*; G. δεκουρίων [*dekourion*], δέκαρχος [*dekarchos*], δεκάδαρχος [*dekadarchos*], δεκαδάρχης [*dekadarches*]). Member of a municipal senate. The word often is synonymous with curial.

decurion of the sacred palace (L. *decurio sacri palatii*). See nos. 353, n. 6, and 481, n. 1.

decurionate (L. *decuriatus*; G. δεκαρχία [*dekarchia*]). Office of decurion.

defender of the Church (L. *defensor ecclesiae*; G. ἔκδικος τῆς ἐκκλησίας [*ekdikos tes ekklesias*], ἐκκλησιέκδικος [*ekklesiekdikos*]). Laic agent of a church who represented it in legal and judicial matters.

defender of the municipality (L. *defensor civitatis*; G. ἔκδικος τῆς πολέως [*ekdikos tes poleos*]). Imperial official who protected the lower classes against the upper classes (particularly against powerful landowners) and all persons against provincial governors' oppression. He was an important officer with financial, judicial, and police powers and supervisory duties over all provincial officials. His post was elective and its tenure was for five years.

defender of the people (L. *defensor plebis*; G. ἔκδικος τοῦ πλήθους [*ekdikos tou plethous*]). Synonym for defender of the municipality.

defender of the place (L. *defensor loci*; G. ἔκδικος τοῦ τόπου [*ekdikos tou topou*]). Synonym for defender of the municipality.

Demiurge (G. δημιουργός [*demiourgos*]; L. *demiurgus*). See no. 648, n. 6.

denarism (L. *denarismus*; G. δηναρισμός [*denarismos*]). See no. 233, n. 5.

denarius (L. *denarius, denarium*; G. δηνάριον [*denarion*]). Roman silver coin worth about $.16 (U.S.A. 1914). In the Empire appeared a gold denarius and a bronze denarius, of which the former was worth about 25 silver denarii and was called an aureus and the latter was worth about 1/6000th of a solidus and was called sometimes a nummus.

diaconate (L. *diaconatus*; G. διακονία [*diakonia*]). Office of deacon.

diaconicum (G. διακονικόν [*diakonikon*]). See no. 258, n. 3.

dictator (L. *dictator*; G. δικτάτωρ [*diktator*]). Magistrate with absolute authority appointed by the consuls, usually at the Senate's advice, in times of external or internal crisis. His term was for six months, but normally he resigned earlier, if his business had been completed. Since the dictatorship as originally conceived in the early Republic ended in 202 B.C., the dictatorship of Sulla (82-79 B.C.) and of Caesar (49-44 B.C.) differed from the old conception in both purpose and scope and tenure and resembled the modern institution.

dies dominicus (Lord's Day). See *dies solis*.

dies solis (day of the Sun, i.e. Sunday). See no. 34, n. 5.

Digesta (or *Pandectae*) *Iustiniani*. (Justinian's Digest or Pandects). Justinian I's collection of excerpts from jurisconsults' writings. Compiled by a commission of jurists in the period 530-3, the Digest (or Pandects) was published on 16 December 533 in fifty books. It is the chief part of Justinian's *Corpus Iuris Civilis*. See Introd., n. 3 *ad init*.

dignitary (L. *honoratus*; G. ἀξιωματικός [*axiomatikos*]). See no. 495, n. 9.

diocese (G. διοίκησις [*dioikesis*]; L. *dioecesis*). (1) One of fourteen administrative subdivisions of the Dominate, a division of a prefecture and comprising several provinces. (2) District ruled by a bishop.
See Introd., n. 42 *ad init*.

diptych (G. δίπτυχον [*diptychon*]; L. *diptychum*). See no. 554, n. 1.

divorce (L. *divortium, repudium*; G. διαίσιον [*diaision*], ῥεπούδιον [*rhepoudion*]). See no. 629, nn. 20 and 22.

divus (deified *or* divine *or in* Christian parlance perhaps sainted). See no. 127, n. 6.

domestics (L. *domestici*; G. δομέστικοι [*domestikoi*]). Troop of guards, both foot and horse, who served as household guards at the imperial court, but who could be sent elsewhither for special purposes. Their total strength is not known, but they were organized in groups of nominally five hundred.
Sometimes Greek or Latin adjectives for "devoted" or "faithful" and occasionally formed in the superlative degree are prefixed to "domestics".

Dominate (L. *dominatus*). The later period of the Empire from 284, when the emperor was the "master" (*dominus*) of his subjects.

Donatists. Followers of Donatus (see no. 17, n. 7), who led the Donatist schism in North Africa. They maintained that sinners could not be members of the Church, that a clergyman's spiritual unworthiness impaired the validity of the sacraments which he administered, and that Christians who joined their sect must be rebaptized. See Circumcellions, Maximians, Montenses, Rupitans.

drachma (G. δραχμή [*drachme*]; L. *drachma*). Greek silver coin of about the same value as a Roman denarius.

drafter (L. *tabellio*). Professional writer who wrote legal documents for private persons. Such a secretary often had his stall (*statio*) in a public place and employed scribes (*scribae*).

duke (L. *dux*; G. στρατηγός [*strategos*]). Military governor, usually on the frontier, after the civil governor of a province had been relieved of military command in the Dominate, and subordinate to a master of the soldiers.

duke of the East or of the Orient (L. *dux Orientis*; G. στρατηγὸς τῆς ἕω [*strategos tes heo*]). See duke and no. 512, n. 1.

duovir (L. *duovir*; G. δύανδρος [*dyandros*]). One of a board of any two men, particularly magistrates in a colonial community.

duty, public. See service, public.

Easter (G. and L. πάσχα: *pascha*). See no. 52 nn. 3, 4, 29.

GLOSSARY 1213

edict. See constitution.

edict, praetorian. See praetor.

edictal law (L. *lex edictalis*). Late synonym for constitution.

Edictum Theodorici (Theodoric's Edict). See Introd., n. 2 *ad fin.*

elder (G. πρεσβύτερος [*presbyteros*]; L. *maior, senior*). See no. 23, n. 2.

elder, chief (G. and L. ἀρχιγέρων: *archigeron*). See no. 257, n. 1.

elder of the city (G. πρεσβύτερος τῆς πόλεως [*presbyteros tes poleos*]; L. *senior civitatis, senior urbis, maior natu civitatis*). See no. 23, n. 2 *ad fin.*

emancipation (L. *emancipatio*). Release of either a son or a daughter from a paterfamilias' paternal power (*patria potestas*), to be equated to, but not to be confused with, manumission (*manumissio*) of a slave from an owner's power (*manus*). See no. 37, n. 1.

emperor (L. *imperator, princeps*; G. αὐτοκράτωρ [*autokrator*], βασιλεύς [*basileus*]). Supreme sovereign of the Empire, sometimes with one or more colleagues. In him resided all powers once possessed by republican magistrates and officials. See no. 127, n. 7.

emphyteusis (G. and L. ἐμφύτευσις: *emphyteusis*). See no. 537, n. 6.

emphyteute (G. ἐμφυτευτής [*emphyteutes*]; L. *emphyteuta*). See no. 537, n. 6.

Encratitans (G. Ἐγκρατεῖς [*Egkrateis*], Ἐγκρατηταί [*Egkratetai*]; L. *Encratites, Continentes*). A puritanical sect which flourished chiefly in Asia Minor and Syria. These abstainers' or continents' excessive asceticism, eschewment of animal food and of wine, exaggerated morality, renunciation of marriage, abstention from property, repudiation of clericalism were derived chiefly from Gnostic views on the origin of matter.

Several groups have been distinguished: (1) Apotactitans (G. Ἀποτακτῖται [*Apotaktitai*]; L. *Apotactites*): Renunciators of marriage and of private property. (2) Apostolics (G. Ἀποστολικοί [*Apostolikoi*]; L. *Apostolici*): Professors of the apostolic way of life, they usually are considered synonymous with the Apotactitans. (3) Hydroparastatans or Aquarians (G. Ὑδροπαραστάται [*Hydroparastatai*]; L. *Aquarii*): Substitutors of water for wine in the Eucharist. (4) Saccophorians (G. Σακκοφόροι [*Sakkophoroi*]; L. *Saccophori, Saccofori*): Wearers of sackcloth as an outer symbol of inner austerity.

Enthusiasts. Known variously as Adelphians (from their first leader Adelphius, a Mesopotamian layman), Euchitans and Messalians (Praying Persons; from Greek and Aramaic verbs, respectively, meaning "to pray"), Lampetians (from their first priest Lampetius in Cappadocia), these heretics preferred to be called Enthusiasts (G. Ἐνθουσιασταί [*Enthousiastai*]; L. *Enthusiastae*) from their insistence on the immanence of the Holy Spirit, by whom they professed to be possessed (G. ἐνθουσιαζόμενοι). They regarded prayer as the sole means of salvation and attracted attention only in the East.

1214 GLOSSARY

ephor (G. ἔφορος [ephoros]; L. ephorus). See no. 540, n. 4.

episcopate (L. episcopatus, sacerdotium; G. ἐπισκοπή [episkope], ἱερωσύνη [hierosyne]). Office of bishop.

Epiphany (G. ἡ ἐπιφάνιος [he epiphanios], τὰ ἐπιφάνια [ta epiphania]; L. epiphania). See no. 220, n. 11.

epistle. See constitution.

Euchitans. See Enthusiasts.

Eunomians. Adherents of the Arian Eunomius, exiled bishop of Cyzicus and pupil of Aetius, whose doctrine he developed to such a degree that he discontinued trine immersion in and altered the formula of baptism. See Aetians and Anomoeans.

Eutychians. Followers of Eutyches, archimandrite of Constantinople, who taught that from the union of divine and human natures in Christ only one composite nature—and that divine—resulted. Thus they were the early Monophysites and were condemned at the Fourth General Council in 451 at Chalcedon. See Monophysites.

Ever-August (L. Semper Augustus; G. Ἀεὶ Σεβαστός [Aei Sebastos] or Ἀεισέβαστος [Aeisebastos], Αἰώνιος Αὔγουστος [Aionios Augoustos]). An imperial title.

exarch (G. ἔξαρχος [exarchos]; L. exarchus, primas). A synonym for patriarch and denoting a metropolitan whose jurisdiction was over other metropolitans in a civil diocese. It was a term in vogue more in the East than in the West and after 451 was restricted, it seems, in antiquity to the metropolitans of Asia (at Ephesus), of Cappadocia and Pontus (at Caesarea), and of Thrace (at Heraclea).

exception (L. exceptio). See no. 65, n. 9 ad fin.

exorcist (G. ἐξορκιστής [exorkistes]; L. exorcista). Clergyman in minor orders, whose duty was to deliver persons from demoniac possession.

Falcidian fourth (L. quarta Falcidia). See Lex Falcidia.

Falcidian proportion (L. ratio Falcidia). See Lex Falcidia.

farmer, tenant (L. colonus). See no. 528, n. 5.

fasces (L. fasces; G. φάσκης [phaskes], ῥάβδοι [rhabdoi]). See no. 439, n. 3.

Father of the Fatherland (L. Pater Patriae; G. Πατὴρ Πατρίδος [Pater Patridos]). An imperial title, but first conferred in the late Republic on outstanding statesmen and generals.

father of the municipality (L. pater civitatis; G. πατὴρ τῆς πόλεως [pater tes poleos]). Supervisor of municipal finances by imperial appointment. See curator.

fathers, conscript (L. patres conscripti; G. πατέρες ἔγγραφοι [pateres eggraphoi], πατέρες συγγεγραμμένοι [pateres syggegrammenoi]). The Roman or

GLOSSARY 1215

Constantinopolitan senators. Originally in Rome patrician senators were called *patres* (fathers) and plebeian senators were called *conscripti* (conscripts), but by 339 B.C. *patres (et) conscripti* was the phrase applied to all members. See senator.

federate (L. *foederatus, federatus*; G. φοιδεράτος [*phoideratos*]). See no. 567, n. 16.

fellow-traveller (G. συνοδείτης [*synodeites*]; L. *synodites*). See no. 272, n. 4.

fideicommissary (L. *fideicommissarius*). See no. 218, n. 7.

fisc (L. *fiscus*; G. φίσκος [*phiskos*]). Originally a basket woven of rushes or of twigs, next a basket for storage of money, then the emperor's treasury (*fiscus Caesaris*) as distinct from the State's treasury (*aerarium populi Romani* or *aerarium Saturni*—because it was in Saturn's Temple), finally and by the Dominate the imperial treasury, which absorbed all other public funds. See no. 395, n. 5.

flamen Dialis (L. *flamen Dialis*; G. φλάμιν Διᾶλις [*phlamin Dialis*], ἱερεὺς τοῦ Διός [*hiereus tou Dios*]). Priest of Juppiter (Zeus), the chief Roman deity. He was subject to an elaborate system of taboo.

follis (L. *follis*; G. φόλλις [*phollis*]). See no. 15, n. 7.

formulary (L. *forma*; G. τύπος [*typos*]). Late synonym for constitution.

Fortunate (L. *Felix*; G. Εὐτυχής [*Eutyches*]). An imperial title.

forum (L. *forum*; G. φόρον [*phoron*]). See nos. 62, n. 11, and 334, n. 5.

Francicus (L. *Francicus*; G. Φραγκικός [*Phragkikos*]). Imperial title denoting victory over Franks.

freedman (L. *libertus, libertinus*; G. ἀπελεύθερος [*apeleutheros*], ἐξελεύθερος [*exeleutheros*]). Ex-slave, who, though manumitted by his former master (now his patron, to whom he owed certain services), was debarred from magistracies, the senatorial and equestrian orders, and the armed forces.

Galileans. In Julian II's constitutions the Christians. See no. 112, n. 4.

general law (L. *lex generalis*). Late synonym for constitution.

Germanicus (L. *Germanicus*; G. Γερμανικός [*Germanikos*]). Imperial title denoting victory over Germans.

Gnostics. Generic name for members of many heretical sects mostly of Gentile provenance. Gnosticism generally professed to provide a purer statement of essential Christianity than that offered by the orthodox. As the rationalism of the early Church, it preached salvation by knowledge (G. and L. γνῶσις: *gnosis*), raised reason above faith, and was propagated from Asia Minor through Africa, where it lingered longest, to Portugal. Its syncretism of Oriental, Greek, and Christian elements tried to combine philosophy with religion. Its influence assisted both in the formation of the canon of the New Testament, because its exponents appealed to the authority of the writings (whether authentic or apocryphal) circulated as part of the New Covenant, and in the growth of asceticism, mysticism, sacramentalism, and celibacy.

The multiplicity and the divergence of Gnostic speculations make it difficult to detect a nucleus of stable doctrine; at most the heresy had some leading ideas more or less clearly traceable in its Syrian and Egyptian and Pontic schools. Perhaps next to its emphasis on exaltation of knowledge, Gnosticism's important stress was on the fundamental antagonism between good and evil. To maintain their dualism of purity of divine essence versus vileness of corporeal matter, Gnostics gainsaid any direct contact between the Godhead and the world. But to account for creation they posited essences called aeons (G. αἰῶνες [aiones]), which successively declined in purity as they emanated from the primal essence and eventually produced the material world. The chief agent in this creation was the Demiurge (see no. 648, n. 6, who was a limited and secondary God and who was aided by inferior deities. To deliver man from ignorance was the redemptive mission of Christ, in whom the real union of divinity and humanity was impossible.

See Borborians, Marcionites, Orphitans, Simonians, Valentinians.

Gothicus (L. *Gothicus*; G. Γοτθικός [*Gotthikos*]). Imperial title denoting victory over Goths.

governmental service. See service, governmental.

governor (L. *administer, administrans, administrator, cognitor, cognitor ordinarius, consularis, corrector, iudex ordinarius, moderator, praefectus, praepositus, praeses, praesidens, proconsul, propraetor, rector, strategus*; G. ἀνθύπατος [*anthypatos*], ἄρχων [*archon*], δικαστής [*dikastes*], ἔπαρχος [*eparchos*], ἡγεμών [*hegemon*], πραιπόσιτος [*praipositos*], προστάτης [*prostates*], στρατηγός [*strategos*]). (1) Generic term for chief executive and administrator of a province (see no. 234, n. 3). (2) Governor (G. στρατηγός [*strategos*]; L. *strategus*) of an Egyptian nome (see no. 8, n. 3).

gravedigger (G. κοπιάτης [*kopiates*]; L. *copiata, fossor*). See no. 97, n. 4.

Greatest (L. *Maximus*; G. Μέγιστος [*Megistos*]). An imperial title.

guardian (L. *tutor, curator*; G. ἐπιμελητής [*epimeletes*], κηδεμών [*kedemon*]). A guardian was appointed by will or by statute or—failing these—by magistrates for a person whose paterfamilias had died or had lost his citizenship.

In the Empire a tutor served for a male under fourteen years of age and for a female not yet twelve years old, unless she meanwhile had become a Vestal virgin. On tutors for women above twelve years of age see no. 621, n. 3.

A curator served for a male between fourteen and twenty-six years of age and without consideration of age for a person of either sex who was a spendthrift or whose mental or physical disabilities prevented proper performance of a juristic act.

A guardian served unpaid and as a public duty, but could refuse service

GLOSSARY 1217

for certain reasons, and could be prosecuted for dereliction of duty or for embezzlement of his ward's property, of which the administration was his primary function.

See nos. 621, nn. 2 and 3, and 628, n. 2.

guild (L. *cognatio, collegium, commune, consortium, contubernium, corpus, ordo, schola, societas, sodalicium, sodalitas, statio, studium, universitas*; G. αἵρεσις [*hairesis*], γερουσία [*gerousia*], δοῦμος [*doumos*], ἔρανος [*eranos*], ἐργασία [*ergasia*], ἔργον [*ergon*], ἑταιρία [*hetairia*], θίασος [*thiasos*], κλίνη [*kline*], κοινόν [*koinon*], οἶκος [*oikos*], πλῆθος [*plethos*], σπεῖρα [*speira*], συμβίωσις [*symbiosis*], συνέδριον [*synedrion*], συνεργασία [*synergasia*], συνέργιον [*synergion*], συνήθεια [*synetheia*], συνοδία [*synodia*], σύνοδος [*synodos*], συντέλεια [*synteleia*], συντεχνία [*syntechnia*], σύστημα [*systema*], σῶμα [*soma*], τάξις [*taxis*], φυλή [*phyle*]. Originally a voluntary organization, such as a trade group of almost every craft, an athletic association, a literary society, a burial society, a dining club, a fraternal association, a group bound by theoretical blood ties or by common worship of a deity or by service in the armed forces or in the government, a financial corporation—but later somewhat similar to a medieval guild and to a modern labour union. Often the members met to share a common meal. All guilds had religious rites, usually adopted a patron deity, and assembled to transact business in a temple. Some guilds were recognized as lawful (*collegia licita*) by the State; other guilds not so recognized (*collegia illicita*) were tolerated, but were subject to suppression on suspicion of subversion of the State.

From time to time repressed in the late Republic and in the early Empire because of their tendency to participate in politics and to disturb the public peace, in the late Empire guilds of artisans were recognized and were regimented, their labour being systematically conscripted for the State's service. Membership was made permanent and hereditary and sometimes was inflicted as a punishment. Most of the labouring classes were enrolled in guilds and were subjected to compulsory public services. Their property was obligated to their service and could not be alienated without special authorization. Since their lot was not a happy one, the tendency to avoid it was common—even to escape by flight or to sell themselves into slavery to private masters. Fugitives, when caught, were reduced to their former condition of economic servitude.

More than 35 guilds, public and private, are recorded for the fourth and fifth centuries in *CT* 13 and 14. Guilds may be divided roughly into higher and lower groups according to the degree of agreeability of their duties. Among the higher group were clerical workers, collectors of animals, grammarians, physicians, shipmasters, teachers. The lower group comprised armourers, bakers, colliers, limeburners, miners, porters, teamsters, transporters of wood, and others occupied in menial, but necessary, tasks. See no. 133, n. 1.

hegumen (G. ἡγούμενος [hegoumenos]; L. hegumenus). See no. 614, n. 2.

heir (L. heres; G. κληρονόμος [kleronomos]). See nos. 218, n. 9, 298, n. 6, 496, n. 12.

Hellenism (G. Ἑλληνισμός [Hellenismos]). See no. 121, n. 3.

heresy (G. αἵρεσις [hairesis]; L. haeresis). Religious opinion professed by a Christian in opposition to doctrines accepted and authorized by the Church and/or the State.

Belief divergent from commonly received dogmas and tending to foster dissension or division compelled the Church to examine the foundation of its creed, to formulate more systematically its faith, and to solicit the State's support in suppressing heresy as a sin against God. At the same time Christian emperors sought to extirpate heresy as a crime against the State for the reason that its propagation was hostile to national unity. Sometimes heresy (and more often schism) seemed to represent rebellion against the authoritarian State and/or Church rather than to denote deep doctrinal difference. See no. 7, n. 13 *ad fin*.

Hermeiecians. See Manichaeans.

Heteroousians. Arians who held that God the Father and God the Son are of a different substance (G. ἑτέρα οὐσία [hetera ousia]).

Homoiousians. Semi-Arians who held that God the Father and God the Son are of a similar substance (G. ὁμοία οὐσία [homoia ousia]). See no. 411, n. 14.

Homoousians. Orthodox Christians who held that God the Father and God the Son are of the same substance (G. ὁμὴ οὐσία [home ousia]). See no. 411, n. 14.

Hydroparastatans. See Encratitans.

hypothec (G. ὑποθήκη [hypotheke]; L. hypotheca). See no. 537, n. 5.

Imperator (L. *Imperator*; G. Αὐτοκράτωρ [*Autokrator*], Βασιλεύς [*Basileus*]). From the generic term for a military commander, who exercised *imperium* (supreme authority) and whom his soldiers thus saluted after a victory and who then added it to his name, the word became the *praenomen* (forename) of an emperor as early as Augustus, who first prefixed it to his name.

imperium (G. ἀρχή [*arche*], ἐξουσία [*exousia*], ἡγεμονία [*hegemonia*]). The Roman State's supreme authority in its dealings with divinity and humanity. This power of commanding, held by certain magistrates and officials throughout Roman antiquity, in the Empire was exercised by the emperor, by some imperial officers of high rank, by provincial governors, by commanders of the armed forces. One vested with this power could (1) take the auspices and supervise religious matters affecting political action, (2) represent the State in dealing with individuals and communities, (3) exercise civil and criminal jurisdiction, (4) punish persons who withstood constituted authority, (5) issue edicts, (6) command the armed forces, (7) summon the Senate and the Assemblies, (8) supervise administrative matters affecting public and private welfare.

The word in imperial times (1) sometimes means "sovereignty", when applied to an emperor, and (2) often means "empire", when denoting the Roman Empire.

indiction (L. *indictio*; G. ἐπινέμησις [*epinemesis*]). See no. 435, n. 9.

injury (L. *iniuria*). See no. 334, n. 25.

inspector (L. *inspector*). In the Dominate an administrative official authorized to investigate matters pertaining to the census.

Institutiones Iustiniani (Justinian's Institutes). Justinian I's introductory manual to the *Corpus Iuris Civilis*. Adapted from earlier textbooks of similar character by a commission of three jurists in 533, the *Institutes* was published on 21 November 533 in four books. See Introd., n. 3 *ad init*.

interdict (L. *interdictum*). See no. 641, n. 29.

interdictum de iure domini (interdict on an owner's right). See no. 641, n. 31 *ad fin*.

interdictum de mortuo inferendo (interdict on burying a dead person). See no. 641, n. 31 *ad fin*.

interdictum de sepulchro aedificando (interdict on building a sepulchre). See no. 641, n. 31 *ad fin*.

interdictum de vi (interdict on violence). See no. 478, n. 11.

interdictum de vi armata (interdict on armed violence). See no. 478, n. 11.

interdictum ne quid in loco sacro fiat (interdict lest anything in a sacred place should be made). See no. 641, n. 31 *ad init*.

interdictum ne quid in locum sacrum immittatur (interdict lest anything should be sent into a sacred place). See no. 641, n. 31 *ad med*.

interdictum quod in loco sacro factum est restituatur (interdict that what has been made in a sacred place should be removed). See no. 641, n. 31 *ad med*.

interdictum quod vi aut clam (interdict what by force or secretly). See no. 641, n. 31 *ad init*.

interpretation (L. *interpretatio*). A summary or a paraphrase occasionally appended to a constitution. Such interpretations originally formed no part of the *Codex Theodosianus* as issued in 438, but appear in the *Lex Romana Visigothorum* (called also the *Breviarium Alaricianum*), which was compiled partly from the Theodosian Code and the Post-Theodosian Novels and was promulgated *c*. 506 by Alaric II, king of the Visigoths, for the use of his Roman subjects.

Whenever an interpretation differs from the law which it interprets, it is supposed that the variance is due either to miscomprehension or to revision.

The probable sources of the interpretations are believed to have been jurist's private commentaries.

itinerant bishop (G. περιοδευτής [periodeutes]; L. circuitor, circumiens, visitator). Bishop who travelled a circuit of small scattered hamlets in the East. Such villages neither lay in the vicinity of a large city nor were large enough to provide the elements of a complete organization. Some scholars suppose that such a cleric was simply a priest who was sent on his rounds to minister to the spiritual needs of Christians living in a city's circumjacent territory. See bishop.

iugatio (jugation). See tax, jugation.

iuridicus (judge). Provincial official with juridical competence concurrent with that of a provincial governor.

ius accrescendi (right of accrual). See no. 496, n. 15.

ius canonicum (canon law). Corpus of canons collected from such varied sources as Biblical quotations, regulations ascribed to apostles, conciliar decisions, episcopal decrees, ecclesiastical customs, patristic opinions, papal rulings, Roman and barbarian law. The grand design is the direction of clergy and of laity in the duties of Christian life and in the best methods of ecclesiastical administration.

The first authoritative compilation of the *ius canonicum* in the West was made *c.* 1148 by Gratian, who called his compendium *Concordia Discordantium Canonum* (Concord of Discordant Canons), which organized the vast mass of abovementioned materials accumulated in earlier collections. Additions to Gratian's codification necessitated at last a revision, which was begun in 1904, was completed in 1917, and has been effective for Roman Catholics since 19 May 1918 as the *Codex Iuris Canonici* (Code of Canons Law).

In the East *c.* 883 the Νομοκάνων [*Nomocanon*] (Code of Canons) of Photius, who utilized earlier systematic collections, became the source of universal canon law for all Orthodox Catholics. Later accretions to it caused a revision, which was begun in 1852, was finished in 1859, and resulted in the Σύνταγμα τῶν θειῶν καὶ ἱερῶν κανόνων (Composition of Divine and Sacred Canons), the completest codification of Orthodox canon law and officially recognized by almost all the autocephalous churches of Eastern Christendom.

See no. 17, n. 3.

ius civile (civil law). See no. 65, n. 10.

ius exclusivae (right of exclusion). See Introd., n. 44 *ad fin*.

ius gentium (law of nations). See no. 599, n. 5.

ius honorarium (magisterial law). See no. 65, n. 10.

ius liberorum (right of children). See no. 31. n. 1.

GLOSSARY

ius postliminii (right of return behind one's threshold). See no. 308, n. 14.

ius praetorium (praetorian law). See no. 65, n. 10.

iusta causa (just cause). A requirement for certain juristic acts, such as manumission, or for exemption from certain civic duties, such as (compulsory) public services. In possession and in usucapion it also is important.

judge (L. *iudex*; G. δικαστής [*dikastes*]). (1) Provincial governor. (2) Judge of a court. (3) Any high administrator (see no. 134, n. 2). See next two entries.

judge, extraordinary (L. *iudex extraordinarius*). See no. 161, n. 3.

judge, ordinary (L. *iudex ordinarius*). See no. 161, n. 3.

jurisconsult (L. *iuris consultus*). See no. 308, n. 15.

jurisprudent (L. *iuris prudens*). See jurisconsult.

juristic person. A subject other than a natural person (human being) invested with proprietary capacity, such as a corporation (society), an institution (foundation), a community (municipality), the Church, and the State.

jus. See *ius*.

knight (L. *eques*; G. ἱππεύς [*hippeus*]. A person of equestrian rank (L. *ordo equester*), which ranked socially and financially below that of senators and above that of plebeians—the two other orders of citizens.

Traditionally organized in the Kingdom as cavalrymen with horses provided by the State and given various privileges, the knights by the late Republic developed into a social class, severed their connection with service as cavalrymen, became a capitalist nobility, and participated in politics and in administration. In the early Empire many of the principal bureaucratic posts were held by knights.

Lampetians. See Enthusiasts.

largesses, sacred (L. *sacrae largitiones*; G. θεῖαι λαργιτιῶνες [*theiai largitiones*]). Imperial treasury in the Dominate.

law, edictal. See edictal law.

law, general. See general law.

leaseholder (L. *conductor*; G. μισθωτής [*misthotes*]). Lessee of a large landholding, whether public or private. He sublet small portions of his holding to tenant farmers in exchange for rent and personal services.

lector (L. *lector*; G. ἀναγνώστης [*anagnostes*]). Reader of the Scriptures in divine worship and, as such, a cleric in minor orders. Admission to the lectorate in antiquity demanded a higher degree of education than that of several ecclesiastical offices.

legation (L. *legatio*; G. πρεσβεία [*presbeia*]). Delegation of envoys charged with a mission.

legion (L. *legio*; G. λεγιών [*legion*], τάγμα [*tagma*]). Largest unit of the Roman Army. In the Dominate about 1,000 infantrymen were in a legion, which in the late Republic was at its maximum of 6,000 soldiers.

legis actio (action of law, procedure according to statute).

Of the five ancient (republican) *legis actiones*—(1) *sacramento* (by solemn deposit), (2) *per iudicis arbitrive postulationem* (by demand for a judge or an arbiter), (3) *per manus iniectionem* (by laying on of hand), (4) *per pignoris capionem* (by seizure of pledge), (5) *per condictionem* (by notice)—only the last is mentioned in this sylloge, where see no. 598, n. 9. Though these ways of instituting a suit at law had become obsolete in the Principate (*GI* 4. 30), traces of their survival lingered into the Dominate.

letter. See constitution.

Levite (G. λευίτης [*leuites*]; L. *levites*). See no. 399, n. 3.

Lex Aebutia (Aebutian Law). This law of most debatable date—anywhere in the period 300-100 B.C.—and of unknown sponsorship—but by a certain Aebutius—reformed civil procedure.

Lex Aelia et Sentia (Aelian and Sentian Law). Sextus Aelius Catus and Gaius Sentius Saturninus, consuls in 4, by this statute completed restrictions established on manumissions by the *Lex Fufia et Caninia*. Among its provisions were minimal age-limits for both manumitting master (twenty years) and manumittable slave (thirty years).

Lex alearia (Dicing Law). See no. 593, n. 3.

Lex Aquilia (Aquilian Law). This law, enacted perhaps as early as 287 B.C. by an unidentified plebeian tribune named Aquilius, introduced the action for direct damage to property, whether caused intentionally or by negligence, but certainly not accidentally. One of its most noted provisions doubled the damages payable by the convicted defendant who had denied his liability.

Lex Augusta (Augustan Law). Any law emitted by an emperor.

Lex Caecilia et Didia (Caecilian and Didian Law). This statute of 98 B.C., carried by the consuls Quintus Caecilius Metellus Nepos and Titus Didius, provided an interval between announcement of and vote on a proposed bill. See no. 324, n. 7 *ad fin*.

Lex Cincia de donis et muneribus (Cincian Law on Gifts and Presents). Marcus Cincius Alimentus, plebeian tribune in 204 B.C., carried a plebiscite prohibiting donations above certain amounts to certain persons. See no. 31, n. 4.

Lex Clodia de collegiis (Clodian Law on Guilds). Carried by Publius Clodius Pulcher, plebeian tribune in 58 B.C., to revive corporations suppressed in 64 B.C. See no. 133, n. 1 *ad init*.

Lex Constantiniana (Constantinian Law). This law, promulgated by Emperor Constantine I in 335, ordered manumission for Christian slaves circumcised

GLOSSARY

by Jewish masters and forbade Jewish attacks upon Christian converts from Judaism. It is no. 76 in this sylloge.

Lex Cornelia de falsis (Cornelian Law on Forgeries). For this law, carried by the dictator Lucius Cornelius Sulla Felix in 81 B.C., see no. 204, n. 5.

Lex Cornelia de iniuriis (Cornelian Law on Injuries). For this law, carried by the dictator Lucius Cornelius Sulla Felix in 81 B.C., see no. 478, n. 11 *ad fin*.

Lex Cornelia nummaria (Cornelian Monetary Law). See *Lex Cornelia de falsis*.

Lex Cornelia testamentaria (Cornelian Testamentary Law). See *Lex Cornelia de falsis*.

Lex de imperio Vespasiani (Law on Vespasian's Power). The law which conferred on Emperor Vespasian (69-79) sovereign power. Several sections of this most important epigraphical document, which may have succeeded and preceded similar enactments in favour of other emperors, survive. See Introd., n. 9, *ad init*.

Lex Falcidia (Falcidian Law). In 40 B.C. this ordinance, introduced by the plebeian tribune Publius Falcidius, reserved for an heir at least one fourth of a testator's estate. See no. 392, n. 4.

Lex Fufia et Caninia (Fufian and Caninian Law). Gaius Fufius Geminus and Lucius Caninius Gallus, suffect consuls of 2 B.C., carried this statute restricting the number of slaves to be manumitted testamentarily by ordaining a sliding scale of manumission. For details see no. 392, n. 3.

Lex Furia (Furian Law). Proposed by Gaius Furius of unknown office, perhaps in 183 B.C., but certainly in the period 294-169 B.C., this law seems to have been the earliest enactment limiting legacies. By its terms no more than 1,000 asses could be willed to others than the testator's spouse or nearest relatives. See no. 392, n. 4 *ad fin*.

Lex Iulia de adulteriis coercendis (Julian Law on Adulteries to be Restrained). In 18 B.C. Augustus legislated against various sexual offences, fixed the forms and the terms of prosecution, and set penalties. Some scholars suppose that this statute was part of the *Lex Iulia de maritandis ordinibus*. See no. 214, n. 5.

Lex Iulia de collegiis (Julian Law on Guilds). A law issued by Gaius Julius Caesar *c*. 45 B.C., when dictator, to disband almost all Roman corporations. See no. 133, n. 1 *ad init*.

Lex Iulia de maiestate (Julian Law on Treason). This statute—usually ascribed to Gaius Julius Caesar in 46 B.C., though some suppose that Augustus was its author in 8 B.C. and others think that there was such a law by each in those years—seems to have prescribed both confiscation of property and death for one convicted of lese-majesty (*laesa maiestas*). The law was interpreted to include not only acts injurious to the State, but also words and deeds against the emperor's and his family's safety and dignity and honour.

Until Christianity was tolerated (no. 7) in 311, its profession was treated, when necessary, as a breach of this law.

Lex Iulia de maritandis ordinibus (Julian Law on Classes to be Married). In 18 B.C. Augustus promulgated a law regulating the marriages of the several orders of citizens. A special feature of this statute was the celebrated *ius liberorum* (right of children), on which see no. 31, n. 1.

Lex Iulia et Papia Poppaea (Julian and Papio-Poppaean Law). This statute (cited sometimes by shorter titles, such as *Lex Iulia, Lex Papia, Lex Papia Poppaea*) was carried by Marcus Papius Mutilus and Quintus Poppaeus Secundus, suffect consuls in 9, to revise the earlier *Lex Iulia de maritandis ordinibus* on regulation of marriage among the several orders of Roman society. See nos. 31, n. 1, and 496, n. 6.

Lex Iulia peculatus (Julian Law of Peculation). A penal law published probably in Augustus' reign (27 B.C.–A.D. 14).

Lex Leoniana (Leonine Law). This law, promulgated by Emperors Leo I and Anthemius in 472, regulated clerical wills. It is no. 514 in this sylloge.

Lex Licinia de sodaliciis (Licinian Law on Associations). Carried by Marcus Licinius Crassus Dives, consul in 55 B.C., to penalize persons who formed associations to procure electoral votes by bribery or by violence. See no. 133, n. 1 *ad init.*

Lex Plaetoria (Plaetorian Law). This law, passed perhaps in 192 B.C., but certainly in the period 254-184 B.C., protected persons below the age of twenty-five years and not under paternal power. Its sponsor was a plebeian tribune named Marcus Plaetorius (or Laetorius).

Lex Remmia (Remmian Law). Introduced *c.* 80 B.C. by a certain Remmius (otherwise unknown), this act legislated about false and tricky accusation. See no. 334, n. 3.

Lex Romana Burgundionum (Roman Law of Burgundians). See Introd., n. 2 *ad fin.*

Lex Romana Ostrogothorum (Roman Law of Ostrogoths). See Introd., n. 2 *ad fin.*

Lex Romana Visigothorum (Roman Law of Visigoths). See Introd., n. 2 *ad fin.*

Lex Voconia (Voconian Law). Proposed by Quintus Voconius Saxa, plebeian tribune in 169 B.C., this law legislated several important restrictions regarding wills. Among these it forbade a woman to be an heir to an estate valued above a certain amount, which is now unascertainable, but which scholars suppose was at least 200,000 asses. (Exceptions were when a woman became an intestate heir or an heir of a flamen Dialis or of a Vestal virgin.) This prohibition was designed to prevent large patrimonies from descending to women, who would be likely to dissipate these in luxurious living. Another restriction aimed to encourage an heir to accept an estate by allowing no

GLOSSARY 1225

legatee to receive more than the heir (or all joint-heirs). See no. 392, n. 4 ad fin.

libella (L. *libella*). See no. 312, n. 3.

libellus (inner bark of a tree, *used for writing-tablets; by transfer:* booklet, memorandum, notice, petition, accusation, certificate. libel). (1) Petition submitted to an official. (2) Accusation presented in a law-court. (3) Attestation issued by an official or by a private person (see App., n. 12).

lictor (L. *lictor*; G. ῥαβδοῦχος [*rhabdouchos*], δεκανός [*dekanos*]). Apparitor who carried the fasces before a magistrate and also a religious official, such as the flamen Dialis and a Vestal virgin. The number of lictors varied at various times and for magistrates, whom they escorted in public and in whose presence they maintained order. In the Empire the emperor had 24 lictors, the consuls twelve, the urban prefect probably twelve, a provincial praetor six, the urban praetor two. Lictors preceded their particular magistrate in a single file and cleared all persons except matrons and Vestal virgins from the path. See no. 439, n. 3.

liturgy. See service, public.

locus purus (unreligious place). See no. 641, n. 16.

Luciferians. Schismatic followers of Lucifer, bishop of Cagliari in Sardinia, who left the Church because repentant Arian clergy were not penalized for their past heresy by restriction to only laic communion.

lustration (L. *lustrum*). See no. 41, n. 2.

Macedonians. See Semi-Arians.

magistrate (L. *magistratus*; G. ἄρχων [*archon*]). Generic term for any municipal or provincial magistrate.

magistrate, chief (L. *principalis*; G. ἄρχων [*archon*]). Generic term for anyone of several principal magistrates in a municipality.

magistrian (L. *magistrianus*; G. μαγιστριανός [*magistrianos*]). Member of the staff of a governmental official, more particularly one of the secret-service men (*agentes in rebus*). In 430 there were 1,174 of these magistrians (*CT* 6. 27. 23)—so called as being under the control of the master (*magister*) of the offices—in the Orient.

mandate. See constitution.

Manichaeans. Disciples of the Persian Mani (*al.* Manes or Manichaeus), who professed a composite religion syncretized from Babylonian folklore, Buddhist ethics, Chaldaean astrology, Christian soteriology, Zoroastrian dualism, and various other Oriental elements. Spreading widely and rapidly through the Mediterranean world and regarded both as a rival religion to Christianity and as a Christian heresy (see no. 156, n. 1), Manichaeism was essentially a metaphysical dualism, which, like Gnosticism, recognized the eternal existence of good (God) and evil (matter), whose opposition and contest created the world. As an aeon, Christ came clothed in an ethereal body to teach men the distinction between the realm of light and the kingdom of darkness. Choicer spirits among the Manichees abstained from wine, were vegetarians, renounced marriage and property, refrained from ordinary work, and lived austerely.

Two Manichaean sects are mentioned in the sylloge: (1) Hermeiecians (probably more properly Hermeans), who followed the Persian Hermeas, principal pupil of Mani and the propagator of Manichaeism in Egypt. (2) Saccophorians, who affected sackcloth to symbolize their asceticism (see also Encratitans).

manumission (L. *manumissio*). Release of a slave from the power (*manus*) of his owner (*dominus*). The slave then became a freedman (*libertinus*, but *libertus* in relation to his ex-master, who then became his patron [*patronus*]) and a citizen (*civis*), though he had fewer political rights than had a freeborn person (*ingenuus*). See no. 26, n. 1.

A Roman jurist, therefore, would have called Lincoln's Emancipation Proclamation (1 January 1863) *Edictum Lincolnianum de manumissione*.

Marcellians. Adherents of Marcellus, bishop of Ancyra in Galatia, who taught that the terms Father and Son were only titles and unexpressive of essential characteristics and also that Christ was a mere man. After their condemnation at the Second General Council in 381 at Constantinople most Marcellians merged with Photinians.

Marcionites. Followers of Marcion, suffragan bishop of Sinope, whose quasi-Gnostic and anti-Semitic notions led him to reject the Old Testament and to revise the New Testament. They also denied the resurrection of the body, believed in metempsychosis, refused baptism to married persons, and were excessive fasters. Eventually Marcionites merged with Manichaeans.

master of each soldiery (L. *magister utriusque militiae*). See no. 106, n. 4.

master of each soldiery throughout the East (L. *magister utriusque militiae per Orientem*). See no. 106, n. 4.

master of the cavalry (L. *magister equitum*). See no. 106, n. 4.

master of the cavalry and of the infantry (L. *magister equitum et peditum*). See no. 106, n. 4.

master of the census (L. *magister census*; G. μαγιστρόκηνσος [*magistro kensos*]). Official subordinate to the urban prefect. He assessed taxes, intervened in opening of wills, registered certain donations, and supervised the conduct of students and of sojourners in Rome and in Constantinople. Pharr explains that "his apparently unrelated duties all derive from his ultimate function: to see that no person evaded his due tax payments by concealing or falsifying his place of residence or the amount of his property".

master of the infantry (L. *magister peditum*). See no. 106, n. 4.

master of the offices (L. *magister officiorum*; G. μάγιστρος τῶν ὀφφικίων [*magistros ton ophphikion*]). One of the highest imperial officials and the supervisor of various unrelated departments of the imperial bureaucracy. His principal duty was superintendence of the civil service, but he also managed the emperor's secretariat, conducted ceremonies at court, prepared the agenda for the sacred consistory, directed the public post, supervised the secret service, controlled the state factories of military matériel, administered some authority over military commanders in frontier provinces, commanded (through deputies) those imperial bodyguards called scholarians. Sometimes Greek or Latin adjectives for "sacred" or "divine" are prefixed to "offices".

master of the secretarial bureau (L. *magister scrinii*). See no. 256, n. 2.

master of the soldiers (L. *magister militum*). See no. 106, n. 4.

master of the soldiers throughout the East (L. *magister militum per Orientem*). See no. 106, n. 4.

master of the soldiery (L. *magister militiae*). See no. 106, n. 4.

Maximians. Schismatic adherents of Maximian, a Donatist deacon, who had himself consecrated bishop of Carthage and then deposed the Donatist bishop of that city. They differed from conservative Donatists in maintaining that baptism administered outside the Donatist sect was valid.

measure (L. *modius*). See no. 431, n. 1.

Medicus (L. *Medicus*; G. Μηδικός [*Medikos*]). Imperial title denoting victory over Medes.

Meletians (*al*. Melitians). Schismatic adherents of Meletius (*al*. Melitius), bishop of Lycopolis in Egypt, whose refusal to obey the patriarch of Alexandria ripened into schism. See no. 68, n. 2.

Messalians. See Enthusiasts.

metropolitan (L. *metropolitanus*; G. μητροπολίτης [*metropolites*]). Sometimes called archbishop, the bishop of the chief city (G. and L. μητρόπολις: *metropolis*) of a province with jurisdiction over all bishops in the province, after for various reasons his primacy had ripened into supremacy.

miliaresium (G. μιλιαρήσιον [*miliaresion*], μιλιαρίσιον [*miliarision*]; L. *miliarensis, milliarensis*). Silver coin in the Dominate. See no. 611, n. 7.

military tribune. See tribune, military.

minister (L. *minister*; G. ὑπηρέτης [*hyperetes*]). See no. 15, n. 3.

Mithras (G. Μίθρας [*Mithras*]; L. *Mithra*). The Persian god of light and wisdom. At first a solar worship, Mithraism was modified by syncretism in its westward wandering to Rome, which it reached shortly before the Flavians' reign (69-96), and was propagated in the Empire particularly by soldiers, for whom the militant Mithras provided a powerful attraction, as archaeology and patristic writings have proved. Mithras was the chief champion in the continuous conflict of light and darkness in the physical world and of good and evil in the spiritual realm. In this war, wherein there was no discharge (cf. Eccles. 8. 8), the devoted Mithraist was vouchsafed victory, for he had the help of the Unconquered Sun-God (L. *Deus Sol Invictus Mithra*; G. Θεὸς Ἥλιος Ἀνίκητος Μίθρας [*Theos Helios Aniketos Mithras*]), the captain of salvation (cf. Heb. 2. 10) who never lost a battle, the protector of holiness, of truth the defender, the antagonist of all wickedness, the guide who conducted the saved soul after death through the seven spheres of the sky to its heavenly home, at long last there to enjoy everlasting bliss and beatitude.

Among the mystery-cults contesting the Mediterranean area for converts in the Ante-Nicene period Mithraism was the strongest rival to Christianity, to which it showed several curious resemblances in its sacraments and ceremonies.

Monarchians. Heretics who denied the distinction of persons in the divine nature. They used the term monarchy (G. and L. μοναρχία: *monarchia*) in the sense of simple oneness to mean that the Godhead is so simple as to be indivisible. This ancient Unitarianism was a reaction against the polytheism of Gnosticism and the Christian dogma of the Trinity. See Paulianists.

monk (G. μοναχός [*monachos*], μοναστής [*monastes*], μονάζων [*monazon*]; L. *monachus*). Man dedicated to either cenobitical or eremetical life.

Monophysites. Generic term for the developers of Eutyches' heresy after they had separated from the Church subsequent to the condemnation of Eutyches at the Fourth General Council at Chalcedon in 451. Dioscore, patriarch of Alexandria, introduced into Eutychianism the modification that Christ's two natures (divine and human) were so united that these by their union became only one nature (G. μόνη φύσις [*mone physis*]). See Eutychians and Theopaschites.

Montanists. Adherents of Montanus, a fanatical, ecstatical, mystical, puritanical prophet of Phrygia, who claimed to have received a new revelation, introduced a dispensation of the Paraclete superseding that of Christ, inculcated rigorous conduct upon Christians, forbade second marriage and flight from persecution, denied the Church's power to absolve sinners. Montanism was a reaction in Asia Minor against Gnosticism and in North Africa against Catholic relaxation. See Ascodrogitans, Cataphrygians, Pepyzites, Phrygians, Tascodrogitans.

Montenses (*al.* Rupitans). Synonym for Donatists in Rome (see no. 290, n. 1).

mora (delay). See no. 612, n. 9.

municipal senate. See senate.

municipal senator. See senator.

mysteries (G. and L. μυστήρια: *mysteria*). See no. 75, n. 42.

GLOSSARY   1229

Neoplatonism. A Greek philosophy flourishing during the third to the sixth Christian centuries and combining nominally Platonic doctrines with Oriental conceptions. See no. 66, n. 7.

Nestorians. Followers of Nestorius, patriarch of Constantinople, who asserted that the Blessed Virgin Mary was only mother of the man Jesus and not the Mother of God (G. Θεοτόκος [*Theotokos*]) and thus implicitly denied the doctrine that there is only one person in Christ. Nestorianism was condemned at the Third General Council in 431 at Ephesus, but survives in certain churches of the Near and the Middle East.

nome (G. νομός [*nomos*]; L. *nomus*). See no. 8, n. 2.

notary (L. *notarius*; G. νοτάριος [*notarios*]). (1) One skilled in writing shorthand notes (*notae*). Such a secretary usually was a slave or a freedman. (2) Member of the imperial secretariat (L. *schola notariorum*; G. σχολή τῶν νοταρίων [*schole ton notarion*]). An imperial notary's duties included missions from the capital to the provinces, assistance to the master of the offices in his preparation of the sacred consistory's agenda, recording that council's *acta*, reading new legislation to the Senate.

Novatians. Adherents of Novatian, schismatic and then heretical bishop of Rome, who denied that the Church can confer absolution in certain cases. After starting schism by becoming anti-pope, Novatian passed into heresy, when he taught that the Church should not readmit those who had fallen from the faith (the lapsed: *lapsi*) during persecution and that forgiveness could not be given to Christians who had repented of adultery, fornication, idolatry, and murder.

Some Novatians, who called themselves Puritans (G. Καθαροί [*Katharoi*]; L. *Cathari*), also condemned remarriage for widowed persons and rebaptized converts from Catholicism. Others were called Protopaschitans in Phrygia, because they celebrated Easter at the time of the Jewish Passover. The latter group was called Sabbatians from their priest Sabbatius, a converted Jew, who introduced the heresy into the Balkans.

Novellae Iustiniani (Justinian's Novels). Justinian I's "new" laws issued mostly after 534, after he had codified Roman law in his *Codex, Digesta* (*Pandectae*), *Institutiones*. Now consisting of 168 statutes, of which seven were emitted by his two immediate successors, Justin II (565-78) and Tiberius II (578-82), the Novels constitute the fourth and final part of the *Corpus Iuris Civilis*. See Introd., n. 3 *ad med*.

nun (G. μοναχή [*monache*], μοναχοῦσα [*monachousa*], μονάστρια [*monastria*], μονάζουσα [*monazousa*]; L. *monacha, sanctimonialis*). Woman dedicated to either cenobitical or eremetical life. See virgin.

obol (G. ὀβολός [*obolos*]; L. *obolus*). See no. 606, n. 8.

office staff (L. *officium*; G. ὀφφίκιον [*ophphikion*], τάγμα [*tagma*], τάξις [taxis]). Most high imperial ministers, every diocesan and provincial governor, all higher commanders in the armed forces had a staff of assistants, called abstractly and collectively an office staff. See official and no. 34, n. 3.

official (L. *officialis*; G. ὀφφικιάλιος [*ophphikialios*], ταξεώτης [*taxeotes*]). Member of an office staff. Members of more important and of less important office staffs sometimes are called respectively apparitors and cohortalines.

Officials' duties were often so onerous and so poorly paid that many of them supplemented their wages by extortion of bribes from litigants and petitioners either to advance or to retard or even to suppress action.

official, chief (L. *principalis*). Highest official in a specific office or in municipal administration.

official, crown (L. *coronatus*). See no. 300, n. 3.

official, financial (G. διοικητής [*dioiketes*]; L. *dioecetes*). See no. 257, n. 2; accountant, catholicus, Caesarian, curator, rationalis, recorder, treasurer.

Constant change in officials' titles during the Dominate makes it difficult to distinguish certain officials especially in the involved financial administration.

official, governmental (G. στρατιώτης [*stratiotes*]; L. *militaris*). See official and no. 186, n. 4.

official, public (G. δημοσιεύων [*demosieuon*]; L. *minister publicus*). See no. 576, n. 8.

Ophitans. Egyptian heretics who combined Gnostic notions, Oriental myths, mysteries of Isis, and corrupt Christian doctrines into an obscure system, which emphasized their reverence toward the serpent (G. ὄφις [*ophis*]) of the Garden of Eden as the illuminator of mankind and their use of a serpent in their celebration of the Eucharist. See Gnostics.

oracle. See response.

order (L. *ordo*; G. τάγμα [*tagma*], τάξις [*taxis*]). (1) Class in the State, as senatorial, equestrian, patrician, plebeian. (2) Grade in the Church, as major (see no. 18, n. 11, for the three divisions) or minor (see no. 109, n. 3, for the many categories therein). (3) Often senators as a group, whether of Rome and of Constantinople or of municipalities.

See no. 325, n. 6.

ordinary (L. *ordinarius*; G. ὀρδινάριος [*ordinarios*]). See no. 540, n. 8.

pagan (L. *paganus*). See nos. 121, n. 3, and 148, n. 4.

palatine (L. *palatinus*; G. παλατῖνος [*palatinos*]). See no. 186, n. 3.

Papians. Heretical adherents of an unidentified Papias, whose doctrine is unknown, or of St Papias, bishop of Hierapolis in Asia Minor, who held chiliastic views.

parabalanus (sick-nurse). See no. 347, n. 1.

GLOSSARY

parish (G. παροικία [*paroikia*]: L. *paroecia, parochia*). Community of Christians living within a municipality or a district as distinct from non-Christians.

Passover (G. διάβασις [*diabasis*], ὑπερβασία [*hyperbasia*], πάσχα [*pascha*]; L. *pascha, phase, transitus*). See no. 52, nn. 3, 4, 29.

paterfamilias (L. *pater familias*). Citizen who is head of a family. His autocratic control over all persons under his paternal power (*patria potestas*) was limited only by custom and social tradition, until the ancient Roman conceptions were weakened by Hellenistic influence in the Principate and in the Dominate by Christianity.

paternal power. See *patria potestas*.

patria potestas (paternal power). A paterfamilias' absolute control over members of his family. This domestic control included (1) power of life and death, (2) power of sale into slavery, (3) power to give children in marriage and to require their divorce, (4) power to give children in adoption and to emancipate them from his authority, (5) ownership of nearly everything which his children might acquire. Paternal power ended when (1) a paterfamilias or his descendants died or suffered change in status, (2) a son became a flamen Dialis or a daughter became a Vestal virgin, (3) a son became an eminent personage in the Church or in governmental service, (4) a daughter became a nun. See no. 496, no. 6.

patriarch (G. and L. πατριάρχης: *patriarches*; L. *patriarcha*). (1) Spiritual leader of Palestinian Jewry (see no. 341, n. 2). (2) Spiritual leader of provincial Jews and subject to the Jewish patriarch of Palestine (see no. 23, n. 3). (3) Sometimes called exarch, the Christian bishop of the chief city of a civil diocese. Eventually the term was restricted to the incumbents of the five principal patriarchal sees: Alexandria, Antioch, Constantinople (after 381), Jerusalem (after 451), Rome.

A patriarch's primacy and jurisdiction over all ranks of clergy and all churches in large areas overcut provincial (Antioch and Jerusalem) and diocesan (Alexandria) and prefectural (Constantinople and Rome) frontiers. It began *de facto* and became *de iure*. Thus in our period the bishop (pope-patriarch-metropolitan) of Rome governed the churches in the city and its suburbs, those in seven Italian provinces, those in the islands of Sicily, Corsica, Sardinia, exercised metropolitical rights over all Italy, and had a primacy of honour due to long association of the city (*urbs*) as the capital of the world (*orbis*). This primacy was extended juridically at least by 378 (see no. 164) over the entire West, wherein the bishop of Rome seems to have been the only patriarch—not to mention the papal claim to universal primacy over Christendom (see no. 442, n. 7). On the other hand, the bishop of Carthage without the patriarchal title effectively controlled all North Africa from the Atlantic Ocean almost to Egypt.

When called ecumenical (G. οἰκουμενικός [*oikoumenikos*]; L. *oecumenicus*) the patriarch of Constantinople is meant (see no. 637).

1232 GLOSSARY

patriarchate (G. πατριαρχία [*patriarchia*]). (1) Office of a patriarch. (2) Territory under canonical jurisdiction of a patriarch (see no. 53, n. 3.)

patrician (L. *patricius*; G. πατρίκιος [*patrikios*], εὐπατρίδης [*eupatrides*]). (1) Member of the upper and privileged class of citizens as opposed to a plebeian. (2) In the Dominate a personal and honorific title imperially conferred on a high dignitary and for life only (see no. 106, n. 8).

patron (L. *patronus*; G. πάτρων [*patron*]). (1) Ex-master of an ex-slave, who in gaining his freedom became a freedman. (2) Protector of a client. (3) Legal adviser and sometimes pleader for a litigant.

patronage (L. *patrocinium*). See no. 241, n. 2 *ad fin.*.

patroness (L. *patrona*; G. πατρώνισσα [*patronissa*]). Female patron. Marriage of a patroness with her freedman was prohibited.

Paulianists. Adherents of Paul of Samosata, bishop of Antioch, who professed the unity of God without distinction of persons in the Godhead and that Christ was a mere man exalted above others by the immanence of the Logos, which descended upon and dwelt in him to such a degree that he ultimately was adopted into the Godhead. See Monarchians.

peculium (L. *peculium*). See nos. 337, n. 6, and 624, n. 3.

Pelagians. Followers of Pelagius, a British monk, who denied original sin (thus depriving mankind of an essential element of its heritage), baptismal regeneration, damnation of unbaptized infants, the necessity of grace, but asserted complete freedom of the human will and believed in the possibility of a perfectly sinless person. Pelagianism was condemned by the Third General Council in 431 at Ephesus.

Pentecost (G. ἡ πεντηκοστή [*he pentekoste*]; L. *pentecoste*). See no. 385, n. 6.

Pepuzians. See Pepyzites.

Pepyzites (*al.* Pepuzians). Montanists whose headquarters were at Pepyza (*al.* Pepuza) in Phrygia, wherein they located a celestial New Jerusalem.

peregrine (L. *peregrinus*). Non-Roman freeman, citizen of a state other than Rome. Such a person could marry a Roman or could conclude commercial transactions with a Roman if he had received from Rome either personally or through his state the right of marriage (*ius conubii*) or the right of trade (*ius commercii*). After Caracalla's grant (*Constitutio Antoniniana*) of citizenship to all free-born aliens in the Empire in 212, the legal difference between Romans and such persons disappeared with the result that only barbarians beyond the borders at first and then such barbarians as settled within the boundaries were considered peregrines.

Perpetual-Augustus (L. *Perpetuus Augustus*; G. Αἰώνιος Αὔγουστος [*Aionios Augoustos*]). A late imperial title.

Persicus (L. *Persicus*; G. Περσικός [*Persikos*]). Imperial title denoting victory over Persians.

GLOSSARY 1233

Photinians. Followers of Photinus, a Galatian deacon to Marcellus, bishop of Ancyra, and later bishop of Sirmium, who developed his master's Unitarianism (Marcellianism) along Monarchian lines to such an extent that his psilanthropist doctrine of Christ had much in common with Paulianism.

Phrygians. Synonym for Montanists who originated in Phrygia.

Pious (L. *Pius*; G. Εὐσεβής [*Eusebes*]). An imperial title.

pious causes (L. *piae causae*; G. εὐσεβεῖς αἰτίαι [*eusebeis aitiai*]). (1) Churches, oratories, monasteries, nunneries, asceteries. (2) Almshouses, asylums, gerontocomiums, hospitals, hostels, nurseries, orphanages. (3) Funds for relief of non-domiciled paupers and for ransom of prisoners of war.

Pneumatomachians. See Semi-Arians.

plebeian (L. *plebeius*; G. δημότης [*demotes*]). Member of the lower and underprivileged class as opposed to a patrician.

plebeian aedile. See aedile.

plebeian tribune. See tribune, plebeian.

policeman (L. *stationarius*; G. βιοκωλύτης [*biokolutes*]). See nos. 310, n. 8, and 568, n. 5.

pontifex (L. *pontifex*; G. ἀρχιερεύς [*archiereus*]). Often a shortened form of pontifex maximus. See no. 111, n. 1.

pontifex maximus (L. *pontifex maximus*; G. ἀρχιερεὺς μέγιστος [*archiereus megistos*]). (1) Chief of the college of pontiffs, a corporation of high priests not necessarily distinguished for piety, because admission to the pontificate was sought eagerly by politicians of dubious morality even by Roman standards. The college was instituted in the Kingdom with three members and gradually was increased in the Republic to sixteen priests, with which plenum it passed into the Empire. Plebeians were admitted after 300 B.C. The pontiffs regulated the calendar, chose Vestal virgins, compiled the civic annals, superintended the State's religious rites. (2) An imperial and papal title, on which see Introd., n. 26 *ad fin*.

pontiff. See pontifex.

pope (G. πάπας [*papas*]; L. *papa*). A term originally and often applied to any bishop, but by the end of our period used almost exclusively for the bishop of Rome. See no. 68, n. 1.

Porphyrians. Name given by Constantine I to Arians, because they copied the errors of the Neoplatonic philosopher Porphyry of Tyre (see no. 66, n. 7).

porter (L. *ostiarius*; G. πυλωρός [*pyloros*]). A clergyman in minor orders, who acted as doorkeeper of a church.

postliminium. See *ius postliminii*.

pound (L. *libra*; G. λίτρα [*litra*]). The Roman pound of twelve ounces is equated generally to twelve of the sixteen ounces of the Anglo-American pound avoirdupois, although English-speaking peoples usually use the Troy weight of twelve ounces to the pound when weighing precious metal.

praetor (L. *praetor*; G. πραίτωρ [*praitor*], στρατηγός [*strategos*]). The chief magistrate charged with administration of the law until the Dominate. A praetor was elected first in 366 B.C. to relieve the consuls of their jurisdictional duties. After Rome had acquired her first transmarine province (Sicily), a second praetor was added in 241 B.C. to adjudicate cases at Rome involving aliens with aliens or Romans. To preserve the distinction between the colleagues, the one was called urban (*praetor urbanus*) and the other was called peregrine (*praetor peregrinus*). The number of praetors increased as the State expanded. To omit intermediate increases, by 44 B.C. there were sixteen praetors at which strength the praetorship entered the Empire, where the college's maximal plenum was nineteen by 180. The ranking praetor was the urban; next came the peregrine. For some others we have epithets denoting the particular business with which they dealt during their tenure, which for all praetors was one year: *fiscalis* (cases concerning the fisc), *fideicommissarius* (cases concerning requests to heirs), *hastarius* (president of the centumviral court, whose sessional symbol was a spear [*hasta*]), *liberalis* (cases concerning freedom), *tutelaris* (cases concerning guardianship).

The urban praetor annually issued an edict, which was valid during his tenure and hence was called perpetual (*edictum perpetuum*). It served to aid, to supplement, to correct the statutory law. By this means the praetor, who may be considered the conserver of the people's conscience, determined in what cases strict law (*ius strictum*) should yield to equitable law (*ius aequum*). For the essence of the praetorian power resided in the exercise of remedies (announced in the edict), when the spirit of public opinion had outmoded the letter of the law.

But the great growth of the imperial power with its jealous intolerance of an inferior magistracy's prerogative, which permitted successive praetors (often in consultation with their legal advisers, for the praetors were primarily politicians and were lawyers secondarily) to reject or to alter or to accept their predecessors' edicts as well as to introduce their own ideas, decided Hadrian *c.* 129 to consolidate the praetorian edict into an imperial perpetual edict, alterable only at the prince's pleasure. This meant the end of what had been a living voice of the law for almost five centuries. Thereafter the praetorship declined in prestige until by the Dominate praetors lost their jurisdiction to imperial officials and were allowed to arrange spectacles and entertainments for Roman holidays.

Fragments of the praetorian edict are in *FIRA* I. 337–89. and are printed in English—for the first time, it is believed—in A. C. Johnson, P. R. Coleman-Norton, F. C. Bourne, *Ancient Roman Statutes* (Austin, 1961), 182–204.

praetorian prefect.   See prefect, praetorian.

GLOSSARY 1235

pragmatic sanction (L. *pragmatica sanctio, pragmatica forma*; G. πραγματικὸς νόμος [*pragmatikos nomos*], πραγματικὸς τύπος [*pragmatikos typos*]). Late synonym for (1) an imperial rescript to a corporation's or a community's petition with reference to its public affairs, (2) an epistle wherewith joint-emperors exchanged their enactments for promulgation in their colleagues' territory, (3) any fundamental law (see no. 460, n. 40) and, as such, a late synonym for a constitution.

prefect (L. *praefectus*; G. πραίφεκτος [*praiphektos*], ἔπαρχος [*eparchos*]). Generic term for the chief of an administrative office or for certain officers in the armed forces. Most prefects gradually acquired functions of the old republican magistrates, whose dignity and influence correspondingly decreased. A prefect's tenure was at the emperor's pleasure.

prefect, Augustal (L. *praefectus Augustalis, Augustalis*; G. ἔπαρχος Αὐγουστάλιος [*eparchos Augoustalios*], Αὐγουστάλιος [*Augoustalios*]). Vicar of the diocese of Egypt, directly responsible to the emperor and not to the praetorian prefect of the East—as were the vicars of the other eastern dioceses. See no. 489, n. 12.

prefect of aliments (L. *praefectus alimentorum*). See no. 474, n. 2.

prefect of the camp (L. *praefectus castrorum*). Commander of a military camp.

prefect of the city. See prefect, urban.

prefect of the grain-supply (L. *praefectus annonae*). See no. 141, n. 3.

prefect, praetorian (L. *praefectus praetorio*; G. πραίφεκτος τῶν πραιτωρίων [*praiphektos ton praitorion*], ἔπαρχος τοῦ πραιτωρίου [*eparchos tou praitoriou*]). (1) One of the normally two commanders of the praetorian guard (L. *cohortes praetoriae*), which served as the imperial bodyguard in the Principate. (2) One of the four highest officials in the Dominate, when each governed a prefecture. (3) After the fall of the Western Empire (476) one of the two highest administrators in the Eastern Empire, wherein one was prefect of the Orient (East) and the other was prefect of Illyricum, until the reconquest of Africa (533) caused the creation of a third praetorian prefect for that area (no. 646).

The praetorian prefects of the East and of Italy outranked their colleagues who governed Illyricum and Gaul and (later) Africa. Their functions were administrative, financial, judicial, legislative.

prefect, urban (L. *prafectus urbi, praefectus urbis*; G. ἔπαρχος τῆς πόλεως [*eparchos tes poleos*]). While this official represented in the Kingdom the king in his absence from Rome and in the Republic the consuls during their absence from the City, such a deputy practically disappeared after the creation of the urban praetorship in 367 B.C. But in the Principate Augustus re-established the office temporarily and Tiberius made it permanent. By the Dominate the urban prefect, who was a senator of consular rank and commanded the urban guard (L. *cohortes urbanae*), headed the civic administration in Rome (and also later in Constantinople) and had civil and criminal jurisdiction there and within a radius of a hundred miles. He had original jurisdiction in matters involveing senators and heard appeals from verdicts of local magistrates and officials who exercised jurisdiction within his area.

prefecture (L. *praefectura*; G. πραιφεκτωρία [*praiphektoria*], ἐπαρχότης [*eparchotes*]). (1) Office of a prefect. (2) One of the four highest divisions of the Empire—Orient (East), Illyricum, Italy, Gaul—until the loss of the Western Empire (476) left only Orient and Illyricum, to which two a third —Africa—was added after its reconquest (533). Each prefecture contained several dioceses, which were subdivided into provinces.

presbyter. See priest.

prescription (L. *praescriptio*; G. παραγραφή [*paragraphe*]). See no. 65, nn. 6 *ad fin.* and 9 *ad fin.*

prescription of forum (L. *praescriptio fori*; G. παραγραφὴ τοῦ φόρου [*paragraphe tou phorou*]). See no. 62, n. 11.

prescription of long time, of ten years, of twenty years, of thirty years, of very long time, of forty years, of a hundred years (L. *praescriptio longi temporis, decem annorum, viginti annorum, triginta annorum, longissimi temporis, quadraginta annorum, centum annorum*). See no. 65, n. 6 *ad med.*

prescriptive right (L. *usus*). See no. 641, n. 23 *ad init.*

president (L. *praesidens*; G. προεστώς [*proestos*], πρόεδρος [*proedros*]). (1) Bishop (see no. 16, n. 4). (2) Provincial governor (see no. 234, n. 3).

priest, Christian (G. ἱερεύς [*hiereus*], πρεσβύτερος [*presbyteros*], προεστώς [*proestos*]; L. *presbyter, sacerdos*). Officiating clergyman in charge of a parochial church, a member of the second rank in major orders, inferior to a bishop, superior to a deacon. See no. 16, n. 4.

priest, civil (G. ἱερεύς [*hiereus*]; L. *sacerdos, sacerdotalis*). See priesthood, high.

priesthood, Christian (G. ἱερωσύνη [*hierosyne*]; L. *sacerdotium*). See no. 158, n. 1.

priesthood, high (G. ἀρχιερωσύνη [*archierosyne*]). A pagan institution, on which see no. 208, n. 3.

primate. See exarch.

primate bishop (L. *primas episcopus*). See no. 326, n. 12.

principalis (chief magistrate). See magistrate, chief.

Principate (L. *principatus*). The earlier period of the Empire from 27 B.C. to A.D. 284, during which the emperor was the "first citizen" (L. *princeps*).

Priscillians. (1) Followers of Priscilla of Phrygia, one of the early prophetesses of Montanism and a disciple of Montanus. (2) Followers of Priscillian, bishop of Avila in Spain, who, influenced by Gnostico-Manichaean speculations, dabbled in magic, accepted several condemned apocryphal writings as authentic, fasted on Sundays, and inculcated a rigorous and somewhat indecent asceticism. Priscillian's chief claim to fame, however, is that he was the first heretic to be executed by civil authority (see no. 203, n. 1).

privilege (L. *privilegium*). See no. 528, n. 7.

privilege of forum (L. *privilegium fori*). See no. 62, n. 11.

proconsul (L. *proconsul*; G. ἀνθύπατος [*anthypatos*]). See governor.

procurator (L. *procurator*; G. διοικητής [*dioiketes*], ἐπίτροπος [*epitropos*]). (1) Manager or administrator of another's business or interests. (2) Agent of a municipal senate. (3) Advocate in court. (4) Any imperial overseer of such activities as customs, mines, post. (5) Assistant to prefect of the grain-supply. (6) Agent in a lawsuit.

procurator of the private estate (L. *procurator rei privatae, procurator rationis privatae, rationalis*; G. ἐπίτροπος τῶν κτημάτων [*epitropos ton ktematon*], ἐπίτροπος τῶν πριουάτων κτημάτων [*epitropos ton priouaton ktematon*]). Administrator of the emperor's private property and the income thereof. While such property consisted chiefly of large domains of real estate, it also comprised vacant inheritances and confiscated property of all kinds.
See count of the private estates.

Protopaschitans. See Novatians.

province (L. *provincia*; G. ἐπαρχία [*eparchia*]). Conquered or otherwise acquired territory governed by a magistrate or a promagistrate, each with *imperium*. See Introd., n. 42 *ad init.*

In the Principate provinces were either senatorial (governed by governors appointed by the Senate) or imperial (governed by governors appointed by the emperor), but the emperor could change any province's status. In the former category were generally older and insular and pacified territories; in the latter class normally were recently won regions, wherein either revolts still occurred or barbarian incursions were anticipated.

In the Dominate the emperor appointed all governors of provinces, which Diocletian had decreased in area to effect more efficient administration and thus had increased in number. Each province then became a subdivision of a diocese, which with other dioceses formed a prefecture.

provision, civil or military. See annona.

provost (L. *praepositus*; G. πραιπόσιτος [*praipositos*], ἄρχων [*archon*]). (1) Commander of troops (no. 8). (2) Superintendent of a granary (no. 109). (3) Overseer of the peace (no. 109). (4) Chamberlain of the sacred bedchamber in the imperial palace (no. 448, n. 2). (5) An ecclesiastic of some supervisory function (no. 579, n. 25).

public slave. See slave, public.

Puritans. See Novatians.

1238   GLOSSARY

Quadragesima (L. *quadragesima*; G. ἡ τεσσαρακοστή [*he tessarakoste*]). See no. 169, n. 3.

quaestor of the sacred palace (L. *quaestor sacri palatii*; G. ταμίας τοῦ ἱεροῦ παλατίου [*tamias tou hierou palatiou*]). The emperor's chief legal minister.

Quartodecimans. Heretics who celebrated Easter on the Jewish Passover (see no. 52, n. 3).

quindecimvir (L. *quindecimvir*; G. δεκάπεντε ἄνδρες [*dekapente andres*]). One of the nominally fifteen priests composing one of the great priestly colleges in Rome. Originally two in number and dating perhaps from the monarchical era, the college was increased to ten c. 367 B.C., when plebeians were eligible for election, then to fifteen c. 81 B.C., when their name became fixed, then to sixteen c. 47 B.C., and finally, some suppose, to 21 c. 17 B.C. The quindecimvirs, who stood to foreign cults much as the pontiffs stood to the national religion, guarded and interpreted the Sibylline Books and superintended certain religious ceremonies.

Quinquagesima (L. *quinquagesima*; G. ἡ πεντηκοστή [*he pentekoste*]). See no. 385, n. 6.

Quirites (citizens). See no. 358, n. 1.

rationalis. See catholicus.

reader. See lector.

recorder (L. *tabularius*; G. ταβουλάριος [*taboularios*]). Subordinate official of the fisc detailed for duty in military, municipal, and provincial administration, chiefly concerned with taxation. He often assisted individuals as a composer of documents in much the same way as a drafter (L. *tabellio*).

rector, consular (L. *consularis rector*). Provincial governor in the Dominate.

registrar (G. χαρτουλάριος [*chartoularios*], κομμενταρήσιος [*kommentaresios*]; L. *chartularius, commentariensis*). Record-keeper (1) in the Church of Hagia Sophia in Constantinople (no. 618), (2) in a secretarial bureau of the imperial administration (no. 618, n. 15), (3) in a prison (no. 312, n. 4).

Renowned (L. *Inclitus*; G. Ἔνδοξος [*Endoxos*]). An imperial title.

rescript. See constitution.

response (L. *responsum*; *oraculum*). (1) Imperial reply (*oraculum*) to a question submitted for solution (see no. 218, n. 5). (2) Jurisconsult's answer (*responsum*) to a question of law (see no. 308, n. 15).

res religiosae (religious things). See introd. to no. 641.

res sacrae (sacred things). See introd. to no. 641.

res sanctae (holy things). See no. 641, n. 2.

Rupitans. See Montenses.

rural bishop (G. χωρεπίσκοπος [*chorepiskopos*], χώρας ἐπίσκοπος [*choras* episkopos], ἐπίσκοπος τῶν ἀγρῶν [episkopos ton agron] or ἐν ταῖς κωμαῖς [en tais komais] or ἐν ταῖς χώραις [en tais chorais]; L. chorepiscopus). Bishop of a rural or a suburban community, commoner in the East than in the West, sometimes acting as suffragan or auxiliary bishop to the bishop of the nearest municipality. See bishop.

Sabbatians. See Novatians.

Saccophorians (al. Saccoforians). See Encratitans and Manichaeans.

sacerdotium (priesthood). See no. 158, n. 1, and also no. 16, n. 4.

sacrilege (L. *sacrilegium*). See no. 168, n. 1.

Samaritans. Descendants (1) of Israelites who c. 887 B.C. founded Samaria in Palestine and (2) of Chaldaeans, Cutheans, Syrians, and others who were sent to Samaria after the Assyrian capture of Samaria in 722 B.C. and (3) of Greeks and Syrians who were settled in Samaria by Alexander the Great in 332 B.C. Their peculiar variety of Judaism was a standing offence to orthodox Jewry throughout antiquity.

sanction (L. *sanctio*). (1) An ordaining as inviolable under penalty of a curse. (2) Clause in a law (a) to penalize violation of the statute, (b) to prohibit the statute's derogation by subsequent enactment, (c) to immunize a person who perchance violated another statute in complying with the provisions of the law containing the sanction. (3) Late synonym for constitution.

sanction, pragmatic. See pragmatic sanction.

Sanhedrin (G. συνέδριον [synedrion]; L. *concilium*). See no. 23, n. 2.

Sarmaticus (L. *Sarmaticus*; G. Σαρματικός [Sarmatikos]). Imperial title denoting victory over Sarmatians.

schism (G. and L. σχίσμα: *schisma*). Division of religious opinion leading to separation from the Church and to organization of a dissident sect within the Christian community. Frequently schism was a step on the way to heresy.

scholarian (G. σχολάριος [scholarios]; L. *scholaris*). See no. 547, n. 6.

school of the sacred palace (L. *schola sacri palatii*). See no. 547, n. 6.

secretariat. See bureax, secretarial, and notary.

secretary (L. *responsalis*). See no. 559, n. 10, and notary.

secret-service agent. See agent, secret-service.

see (G. καθέδρα [kathedra], θρόνος [thronos]; L. *cathedra, thronus, sedes*). Originally a bishop's seat or chair in a church, then in the chief church of the principal city in his (ecclesiastical) diocese, finally also the territory over which he exercised his jurisdiction. See also no. 311, n. 5.

Semi-Arians. Generic term for those Arians who denied either the divinity or the personality of the Holy Spirit. Sometimes they were called Pneumatomachians (Spirit-Fighters) or Macedonians (from Macedonius, Arian bishop of Constantinople, a leader, if not the founder, of this variety of Arianism).

Senate (L. *senatus, curia, ordo;* G. βουλή [*boule*], γερουσία [*gerousia*], κουρία [*kouria*], συνέδριον [*synedrion*], σύγκλητος [*sygkletos*]). (1) In Rome and in Constantinople (after 330) the advisory council of the emperors. Its plenum was six hundred. Members were appointed by the emperor and for life, but were subject to certain economic, financial, legal, moral, and political qualifications. The Senate formally elected emperors, to whom by the Dominate it surrendered almost all its previous vast powers and by whom it was regarded as of only nominal importance. (2) Local council of a municipality.

senator (L. *senator, curialis, decurio, municeps, vir ordinis*; G. βουλευτής [*bouleutes*], γερουσιαστής [*gerousiastes*], συγκλητικός [*sygkletikos*]). (1) Member of the Senate in Rome or (after 330) in Constantinople. See fathers, conscript. (2) Member of a municipal senate and, as such, usually then not called senator.

senator, hereditary (G. πατρόβουλος [*patroboulos*]). See no. 118, n. 2.

senatusconsult (L. *senatus consultum*; G. δόγμα συγκλήτου [*dogma sygkletou*]). The Roman Senate's considered opinion given to magistrates who had sought the Senate's advice. A senatusconsult usually was cited by its proposer's name and in the Principate had legislative force.

Senatus Consultum Claudianum (Claudian Senatusconsult). Of several senatusconsults of this name this senatorial legislation of 52 contained at least three provisions which are noted in no. 631, introd. and n. 1.

Senatus Consultum Persicianum (Persician Senatusconsult). This senatorial legislation of *c.* 34 and proposed by Paulus Fabius Persicus, consul in 34 and a notorious profligate, made permanently liable to previous penalties for celibacy men and women who had not married before the ages of sixty and fifty respectively.

serf (L. *adscriptitius, inscriptitius*; G. ἐναπόγραφος [*enapographos*]). See nos. 472, n. 23, and 528, n. 2.

service, extraordinary public. See service, public.

service, governmental (L. *militia*; G. στρατεία [*strateia*]). See no. 186, n. 4.

service, menial public. See service, public.

service, public (L. *functio, munia, munus, necessitas, officium*; G. λειτουργία [*leitourgia*]). An individual's obligatory duty or office or service to the State or to his birthplace or to the community of his domicile. Such service included maintenance of public works of all kinds, payment of taxes in cash or in kind, holding office as a municipal magistrate or a municipal senator, billeting soldiers and itinerant officials, providing building materials of various kinds, furnishing military supplies and transport, performing

GLOSSARY 1241

menial (on which see no. 186, n. 5) or extraordinary (on which see no. 226, n. 3) service. This conscription of labour and of money and of produce disrupted normal economic live and caused much hardship for those who could not win exemption from such services.

sevir (*al.* sexvir). See no. 478, n. 22.

sibyl (G. and L. σίβυλλα: *sibylla*). One of several female soothsayers in antiquity. The most celebrated sibyls were among the Greeks the Pythian at Delphi in Greece and among the Romans the Cumaean at Cumae in Italy. Sibyls in at least fifteen places are recorded.

silentiary (L. *silentiarius*; G. σιλεντιάριος [*silentiarios*]). See no. 448, n. 2.

Simonians. (1) Properly the followers of the protoheresiarch Simon Magus of Samaria, the earliest Gnostic. (2) Name given by Theodosius II to Nestorians, because they copied the errors of Simon Magus (see no. 422, n. 7).

sister (L. *soror*; G. ἀδελφή [*adelphe*]). See virgin, introduced.

slave, public (L. *servus publicus*; G. οὐικάριος [*ouikarios*]). Communities obtained public slaves by capture in war or by purchase from individuals or by legacy of townsfolk. Owned by the State, they were manumitted (nominally for meritorious service) either by the emperor or by a municipal senate. The position of public slaves was somewhat superior to that of privately owned slaves: they received an annual allowance for food, wore a special uniform, lived in houses built on public ground, could bequeath one half of their peculium, served as postmen, executioners, auctioneers, attendants in libraries and baths, servants in temples, secretaries in magisterial offices, labourers on aqueducts and roads, sweepers of sewers.

Sleepless (G. Ἀκοίμητοι [*Akoimetoi*] L. *Acoemeti*. Order of monks who maintained perpetual prayer by relays. See no. 645, n. 35.

sodalitas (brotherhood). See guild.

solidus (L. *solidus*; G. νόμισμα [*nomisma*]). See no. 433, n. 7.

sportula (fee). See no. 606, n. 20.

statute of limitations. See prescription.

steward of the church (G. οἰκονόμος τῆς ἐκκλησίας [*oikonomos tes ekklesias*]; L. *oeconomus ecclesiae*). Administrator and overseer of ecclesiastical property under episcopal supervision, sometimes also charged with relief of paupers.

stipulation (L. *stipulatio*). See no. 641, n. 25.

subdeacon (L. *subdiaconus*; G. ὑποδιάκονος [*hypodiakonos*]). Clergyman in minor orders and assistant to a deacon.

subscription. See constitution.

suffect consul. See consul suffectus.

suffragan bishop. See Introd., n. 42 *ad fin*.

Sunday. See *dies solis*.

surety (L. abstract *fideiussio*, concrete *fideiussor*). In the concrete sense one who guarantees a principal debtor's debt. In the abstract sense the guarantee itself. In all periods of Roman law suretyship was essentially the same, though it and the guarantor had different names corresponding to the formula pronounced by the voucher. Thus *sponsio* and *sponsor* and *fidepromissio* and *fidepromissor* existed with *fideiussio* and *fideiussor*. Justinian I welded *sponsio* and *fidepromissio* into *fideiussio* and then *fideiussor* superseded *sponsor* and *fidepromissor*. See no. 491, n. 6.

syndic (G. σύνδικος [*syndikos*]; L. *syndicus*). Representative of a corporate body, such as a municipality or a guild, usually in lawsuits.

synod. See council.

synod, domestic (G. σύνοδος ἐνδημοῦσα [*synodos endemousa*]; L. *synodus endemusa*). See no. 495, n. 1.

Syro-Roman Lawbook. See no. 32, n. 9.

Tascodrogitans. Fanatic followers of Montanus, a Phrygian prophet, who received their nickname from Phrygian words meaning peg (G. τασκός [*taskos*]) and nose (G. δροῦγος [*drougos*]), because during worship they inserted a finger in the nose. They repudiated revelation, rejected creeds, ridiculed sacraments. Sometimes they were confused with Ascodrogitans from the similarity of names.

tax, capitation (L. *capitatio*; G. ἐπικεφάλιον [*epikephalion*]). Poll-tax assessed on lower-class persons, especially on farmers and their helpers, for it was based on the amount of land (arable or plantable) ploughable by a yoke (L. *iugum*) of oxen in one day and which normally could be cultivated in one year by one man (L. *caput*) or by two women (L. *capita*), as well as on the number of farm animals on the farmer's farm.

tax equalizer (L. *exaequator, peraequator*; G. ἐξισωτής [*exisotes*]). Supervisor of tax assessments.

tax, jugation (L. *iugatio*). Land tax assessed on the amount of land which normally could be ploughed in one day by a yoke (L. *iugum*) of oxen. The unit was called *iugum*, on which see no. 107, n. 3.

tax, lustral (L. *collatio lustralis*; G. χρυσάργυρον [*chrysargyron*]). See no. 97, n. 1.

tax of the people (L. *exactio plebis*). See no. 149, n. 5.

taxpayer (L. *collator*). See no. 646, n. 21.

tax, poll. See tax, capitation.

tax unit: human (L. *caput*), land (L. *iugum*). The fiscal arrangement of the fourth century adopted as the unit of taxation a unit both of land and of labour, jugation (see tax, jugation) and capitation (see tax, capitation). The unit of land (*iugum*) was so much as could be cultivated by a farmer and the unit of labour (*caput*) was the farmer's work which could keep the plan in production. See nos. 67, n. 37, and 107, n. 3.

tenant (L. *inquilinus*). See no. 478, n. 19.

tenant farmer. See farmer, tenant.

Tessarescaedecatitans. Heretics who celebrated Easter on the Jewish Passover (see no. 52, n. 3).

testamentum inofficiosum (unduteous will). See no. 624, n. 4.

Tetraditans. Heretics who celebrated Easter on the Jewish Passover (see no. 52, n. 3).

Thebaicus (L. *Thebaicus*; G. Θηβαικός [*Thebaikos*]). Imperial title denoting victory over Thebans in the Egyptian Thebaid.

Theodosian Code. See *Codex Theodosianus*.

Theopaschites. Monophysites who insisted that Christ's divine nature suffered in the Crucifixion.

traditor (traitor). See no. 17, n. 4.

transportation (L. *translatio*). See no. 107, n. 13.

treasurer (L. *arcarius*; G. ἀρκάριος [*arkarios*]). Treasurer of a church, whether lay or clerical.

treasury, imperial. See fisc.

treasury, public (L. *aerarium*; G. τό δημόσιον [*to demosion*]). Any municipal treasury as distinct from the Roman State's treasury (L. *aerarium Saturni*), so called because of its location in Saturn's Temple in the Roman Forum.

tribune and notary (L. *tribunus et notarius*; G. τριβουνονοτάριος [*tribounonotarios*]). Chief confidential clerk in the imperial secretariat, often performing special missions for the emperor or for the imperial consistory, and probably deputy to the chief imperial secretary, who was the chief of the notaries.

tribune, military (L. *tribunus militum*; G. ταξίαρχος [*taxiarchos*], χιλίαρχος [*chiliarchos*]). In the Empire a legion's six military tribunes were drawn normally from the equestrian order and primarily performed administrative duties.

tribune, plebeian (L. *tribunus plebis*; G. δήμαρχος [*demarchos*]). One of ten officials (technically not magistrates) elected annually, perhaps as early as 494 B.C., to defend plebeian lives and property against patrician aggression. Tribunes survived the Republic, but their practical powers, which were extensive, passed to the emperors, who were vested with the tribunician power, and tribunes enjoyed merely an honorary distinction of office, whence they could pass into the Senate.

Tribunician Power (L. *tribunicia potestas*; G. δημαρχική ἐξουσία [*demarchike exousia*]). Phrase found among imperial titles. This power was conferred usually annually upon an emperor to signify that he held the full power and the personal inviolability which a plebeian tribune had enjoyed in the Republic. In effect it symbolized imperial control of domestic affairs.

Triumpher (L. *Triumphator*; G. Τροπαιοῦχος [*Tropaiouchos*]). An imperial title.

trust (L. *fideicommissum*). See no. 218, n. 7.

trustee. See guardian.

tutor. See guardian.

Unconquered (L. *Invictus*; G. Ἀνίκητος [*Aniketos*]). An imperial title.

urban prefect. See prefect, urban.

urban vicar. See vicar, urban.

unit, military (L. *numerus*; G. ἀριθμός [*arithmos*]). See no. 584, n. 8.

unit, tax. See tax unit.

use (L. *usus*). See usucapion.

usucapion (L. *ususcapio*). See no. 641, n. 23.

usufruct (L. *ususfructus*). See no. 602, n. 1.

usufructuary (L. *usufructuarius, fructuarius*). See usufruct.

Valentinians. Adherents of Valentine, an Alexandrian priest, the most important and most influential proponent of Gnosticism. See Gnostics.

Vandalicus (L. *Vandalicus*; G. Οὐανδαλικός [*Ouandalikos*]). Imperial title denoting victory over Vandals.

vicar (L. *vicarius*; G. οὐικάριος [*ouikarios*], βικάριος [*bikarios*]). Governor of a civil diocese. But the vicar of the diocese of the East or of the Orient was called a count.

vicar of the prefects (L. *vicarius praefectorum*; G. οὐικάριος τῶν ἐπάρχων [*ouikarios ton eparchon*]). See nos. 15, n. 12, and no. 54, n. 28.

vicar, urban (L. *vicarius urbis*; G. οὐικάριος [*ouikarios*] or βικάριος τῆς πόλεως [*bikarios tes poleos*]). Deputy of the urban prefect of Rome or of Constantinople.

vicariate (L. *vicaria*; G. οὐικαρία [*ouikaria*], βικαρία [*bikaria*]). Office of vicar.

Victor (L. *Victor*; G. Νικητής [*Niketes*]). An imperial title.

village, mother (G. μητροκωμία [*metrokomia*]; L. *metrocomia*). See no. 345, n. 4.

village, public (L. *vicus publicus*). See no. 345, n. 5.

virgin, introduced (L. *virgo subintroducta, agapeta*; G. παρθένος συνείσακτος [*parthenos syneisaktos*], ἀγαπητή [*agapete*]). Usually mentioned in the plural number, these so-called virgins contracted a kind of "spiritual" marriage with Christians, frequently with clergymen, lived with them as housekeepers ostensibly, and often became their concubines. See no. 372.

virgin, sacred or sacrosanct or sanctimonial (L. *virgo sacrata, virgo sacrosancta, virgo sanctimonialis*; G. ἱερὰ παρθένος [*hiera parthenos*]). See no. 92, n. 1.

virgin, Vestal (L. *virgo Vestalis*; G. Ἑστίας παρθένος [*Hestias parthenos*]). Priestess of the hearth-goddess Vesta (Hestia). Originally two or more, historically the Vestals numbered six. Candidates for vacancies among these official and animate symbols of chastity were chosen by the pontifex maximus from girls usually of patrician birth and between six and ten years of age. After thirty years' virginal service in the cult they could leave and then could marry. Of the few who retired—for they had more honours and privileges than matrons—fewer wed, because for them to do so was considered unlucky. The cult was suppressed in 382.

weaving establishment (G. γυναικεῖον [*gynaikeion*]; L. *gynaeceum*). One of several such manufactories maintained by the State for weaving garments to supply imperial needs.

widow (L. *vidua*; G. χήρα [*chera*]). See no. 92, n. 1.

INDEXES

The system of citation in the indexes employs this pattern:

When a word worthy of being indexed appears in a document's text, ordinarily no reference in the indexes, as an effort for economy, is made to its reappearance in the instrument's introduction or notes, save in several important instances, because it is believed that the reader normally will read the introduction and the notes to the text wherein he will have sought the reference. Thus: in Document 59 the word "basilica" occurs in both introduction and text and notes, but is indexed only to the text.

Note numbers are indicated by superior numerals. Reference to notes of the Table of Names and Dates of Emperors are prefixed "Tab". Those to the Introduction give the paragraph's or the note's number: thus "In, 6" or "In^{28}". Those to the Documents have the pertinent number, which is followed by a Roman numeral, if the constitution has several parts, or by "^{in}" if the instrument's introduction is indicated, or by superior numerals if attention is attracted to the law's note or notes; thus: "13"; "43 (I)"; "12^{in}"; "24^{2}"; "37^{7,9}". The Appendix on Persecutions is shown by "App"; its paragraphs and notes are cited after the same scheme as that of the Introduction. A citation from the Glossary is marked by "Gl". A comma separates non-consecutive references, but a hyphen connects two or more consecutive references; thus: 5^{in}, 25, 125^{5}, but 124–6, 175–90.

In the Index of Persons dates of their tenure, when known, are provided ordinarily for sovereigns, prelates, magistrates, public officials. For other persons their dates of birth and death are shown wherever possible; but the *floruit* is given whenever only that is ascertainable. This index contains also the names of non-Christian deities and the various Christian names (under the entry "God") for the Persons of the Trinity, but not the generic names of heretics and schismatics, which are combined with the names of their heresies and schisms (such as "Arianism *or* Arians" and "Donatism *or* Donatists") in the Index of Subjects.

The Index of Places, besides the names of regions, countries, communities, imperial administrative divisions, mountains, and rivers, lists also both religious and secular buildings and districts within communities as well as ethnic proper nouns and proper adjectives.

The Index of Subjects supplements minutely the Table of Contents, which latter should be consulted for the broader aspects of the laws.

In the remaining indexes collections and authors' works are cited either by the special abbreviations given in the List of Abbreviations or by conventional abbreviations.

The Index of Sources of Documents collects both ancient and modern sources, whether classical or patristic or secular, whence the documents come.

The Index of Legal Quotations and Allusions, as distinct from the primary references to the laws in the preceding index, contains references to legal matters, whether secular or ecclesiastical in origin.

The Index of Classical Quotations and Allusions, the Index of Patristic Quotations and Allusions, and the Index of Biblical Quotations and Allusions give references overwhelmingly to the introductions, the notes, the Appendix on Persecutions, and the Glossary. Occasionally, however, the composers of the documents quote from or allude to a classical author, a patristic writer, an ecclesiastical council's acts or canons, or the Sacred Scriptures, in which cases these references ordinarily are to the documents themselves.

SOURCES

AMBROSE
  Ep. 21. 2, **136**
AMERICAN JOURNAL OF
    THEOLOGY (AJT)
  9 (1905) 735–7, **527**; 739–40, **542**
ANALECTA SACRA SPICILEGIO
    SOLESMENSI PARATA
  4.452, **48** (II)
ANTE-NICENE CHRISTIAN
    LIBRARY
  20.2.92, **42**
ATHANASIUS
  Apol. ad Const. 23, **90** (I); 30, **98**; 31, **99**
  Apol. adv. Ar. 51, **84**; 54, **85**; 54–5, **86**; 56, **87**; 59, **72**; 61–2, **69**; 67–8, **68**; 70, **70**; 81, **74**; 85, **78**; 86, **75**; 87, **77**
  De Syn. 55, **105**
  Ep. ad Iov., App.³ **124**
  Hist. Ar. ad Mon. 23, **88**; 24, **90** (II); 33, **94**; 43, **100**
AUGUSTINE
  Cont. Cresc. 3.70.81, **21**; 71.82, **27**
  Cont. Litt. Pet. 2.97.224, **120**
  Ep. 88.4, **21**; 201, **368**
CASSIODORUS
  HE
  1. 19, **47**
  2. 2.2, **49** (I); 5.7, **49** (II); 15, **66**; 16.1–5, **64**; 22.5–16, **50**
  3. 7.2–13, **75**
  4. 2.2–6, **77**; 26–7.6, **84**; 30, **85**; 31, **86**; 32, **87**
  5. 17.2–26, **95**; 22.1–3, **105**
  7. 9.1–6, 8–11, **159**
  9. 7.2–5, **167**
CODEX CAN. ECCL. ET CONST.
    SANCTAE SEDIS APOST. (CA)
  26, **476**; 27, **477**; 28, **489**
CODEX IUSTINIANUS (CI)
  Const. Haec, **578**
  Const. Summa, **580**
  1. 1.1, **167**, 1.2, **173**; 1.3, **445**; 1.4, **476**; 1.5, **569**; 1.6, **636**; 1.7, **637**; 1.8, **645**; 2.1, **36**; 2.2, **181**; 2.3, **206**; 2.4, **319**; 2.5, **327**; 2.6, **375** (I); 2.7, **377**; 2.8, **384**; 2.9, **430**; 2.10, **431**; 2.11, **438**; 2.12, **474**; 2.13, **488**; 2.14, **510**; 2.15, **522**; 2.16, **526**; 2.17, **537**; 2.18, **538**; 2.19, **581**; 2.20, **584**; 2.21, **598**; 2.22, **595**; 2.23, **604**; 2.24, **618**; 2.25, **615**; 3.1, **83**; 3.2, **102**; 3.3, **107**; 3.4, **110**; 3.5, **126**; 3.6, **162**; 3.7, **178**; 3.8, **204**; 3.9, **225**; 3.10, **310**; 3.11, **270**; 3.12, **273**; 3.13, **276**; 3.14, **288**; 3.15, **285**; 3.16, **314**; 3.17, **347**; 3.18, **349**; 3.19, **372**; 3.20, **421**; 3.21, **436**; 3.22, **437**; 3.23, **479**; 3.25, **491**; 3.26, **498**; 3.27, **502**; 3.28, **507**; 3.29, **512**; 3.30, **508**; 3.31, **516**; 3.32, **515**; 3.33, **514**; 3.34, **518**; 3.35, **523**; 3.36, **528**; 3.37, **529**; 3.38, **530**; 3.39, **531**; 3.40, **565**; 3.41, **579**; 3.42, **580**; 3.43, **588**; 3.44, **613**; 3.45, **612**; 3.46, **614**; 3.47, **620**; 3.48, **623**; 3.49, **624**; 3.50, **625**; 3.51, **628**; 3.52, **629**; 3.53, **638**; 3.54, **652**; 3.55, **648**; 4.1, **127**, **128**; 4.2, **146**; 4.3, **180**, **201**; 4.4, **247**; 4.5, **257**; 4.6, **272**; 4.7, **271**; 4.8, **309**; 4.9, **312**; 4.10, **313**; 4.11, **308**; 4.12, **394**; 4.13, **490**; 4.14, **493**; 4.15, **506**; 4.16, **517**; 4.17, **534**; 4.18, **535**; 4.19, **541**; 4.20, **555**; 4.21, **582**; 4.22, **586**; 4.23, **589**; 4.24, **591**; 4.25, **593**; 4.26, **606**; 4.27, **608**; 4.28, **610**; 4.29, **611**; 4.30, **621**; 4.31, **627**; 4.32, **632**; 4.33, **650**; 4.34, **651**; 5.1, **56**; 5.2, **166**, **248**, **254**; 5.3, **258**; 5.4, **275**, **298**; 5.5, **395**; 5.6, **422**; 5.7, **429**; 5.8, **489**; 5.9, **492**; 5.10, **503**; 5.11, **533**; 5.12, **567**; 5.13, **570**; 5.14, **571**; 5.15, **572**; 5.16, **573**; 5.17, **574**; 5.18, **575**; 5.19, **599**; 5.20, **616**; 5.21, **622**; 5.22, **626**; 6.1, **158**; 6.2, **163**; 6.2, **335**; 6.3, **395**; 7.1, **91**; 7.2, **190**; 7.3, **230**; 7.4, **391**; 7.5, **429**; 7.6, **489**; 8.1, **393**; 9.3, **23**; 9.5, **188**; 9.6, **214**; 9.11, **303**; 9.12, **315**; 9.13, **332**; 9.14, **333**; 9.15, **341**; 9.16, **378**; 9.18, **429**; 10.1, **79**, **348**; 10.2, **647**; 11.5, **340**; 11.6, **382**; 11.9, **583**; 11.10, **600**; 12.1, **266**; 12.2, **315**; 12.3, **400**; 12.4, **413**; 12.5, **465**; 12.6, **501**; 12.7, **504**; 12.8, **505**; 13.1, **26**; 13.2, **35**; 24.2, **386**; 27.1, **646** (I); 27.2, **646** (II); 55.8, **311**; 55.11, **541**
  2. 2.4, **62**; 3.29, **625**; 4.41, **255**; 6.8, **506**; 15.2, **432**; 58.1, **592**; 58.2, **619**
  3. 1.13, **603**; 1.14, **605**; 2.4, **606**; 12.2, **34**; 12.5, **169**; 12.6, **220**, **385**; 12.7, **37**, **238**; 12.8, **302**; 12.9, **509**; 44.14, **206**
  4. 1.12, **594**; 63.1, **127**; 66.4, **632**
  5. 4.25.3–5, **610**; 4.26, **609**; 4.29, **649**; 9.3, **187**; 27.5, **525**; 70.7.5–6c, **608**
  6. 23.23, **565**; 24.12, **513**; 48.1, **585**
  7. 15.1.3, **602**; 15.2, **607**; 24.1, **631**; 37.3,

1249

630; *38.2*, 212; *40.2*, 627; *52.6*, 338; *62.29*, 272; *65.4a*, 146; *72.10*, 634
8. *50.20*, 308; *51.2*, 331; *51.3*, 591; *53.34*, 596; *53.35*, 601; *57.1*, 31
9. *4.6*, 586; *5.2*, 589; *13.1*, 638; *29.1*, 168; *47.25*, 369; *47.26*, 587
10. *15.1*, 521; *16.4*, 106; *16.12*, 384; *27.4*, 539; *30.4*, 606; *32.26*, 147; *32.52*, 263; *48.12*, 186; *49.2*, 438
11. *4.2*, 431; *18.1*, 430; *21.1*, 375; (I); *32.3*, 513; *41.6*, 394; *41.7*, 494; *48.20*, 597; *59.14*, 345; *75.4*, 377
12. *37.17*, 536; *50.21*, 434; *59.9*, 511; *60.7*, 532; *63.2*, 606

CODEX THEODOSIANUS (CT)
1. *27.1*, 28; *27.2*, 309
2. *4.7*, 318; *8.1*, 37; *8.18*, 209; *8.19*, 220; *8.20*, 236; *8.21*, 238; *8.23*, 279; *8.24*, 281; *8.25*, 316; *9.3*, 255
3. *1.5*, 199; *7.2*, 214; *8.2*, 187
4. *7.1*, 35
5. *3.1*, 421; *7.2*, 308; *9.2*, 331
8. *4.7*, 110; *5.46*, 202; *8.1*, 144; *8.3*, 209; *16.1*, 31
9. *3.7*, 312; *7.5*, 214; *16.12*, 313; *17.6*, 181; *17.7*, 206; *25.1*, 92; *25.2*, 126; *25.3*, 372; *35.4*, 169; *35.5*, 221; *35.7*, 302; *38.3*, 135; *38.4*, 145; *38.6*, 180; *38.7*, 198; *38.8*, 201; *40.8*, 132; *40.15*, 234; *40.16*, 272; *40.24*, 369; *45.1*, 241; *45.2*, 266; *45.3*, 273; *45.4*, 400; *45.5*, 413
10. *18.3*, 223
11. *1.1.*, 106; *1.33*, 384; *1.37*, 428; *7.10*, 144; *7.13*, 209; *16.15*, 186; *16.18*, 226; *16.21*, 262; *16.22*, 265; *24.6*, 345; *30.57*, 272; *36.20*, 146; *36.31*, 235; *39.8*, 178; *39.10*, 204; *39.11*, 230
12. *1.49*, 109; *1.50*, 114; *1.59*, 130; *1.63*, 147; *1.99*, 188; *1.104*, 193; *1.112*, 208; *1.115*, 210; *1.121*, 224; *1.122*, 229; *1.123*, 233; *1.163*, 280; *1.172*, 322; *5.3*, 263
13. *1.1*, 97; *1.4*, 114; *1.5*, 127; *1.11*, 165; *1.16*, 274; *10.6*, 149
14. *3.11*, 133
15. *3.6*, 377; *4.1*, 386; *5.2*, 243; *5.5*, 385; *7.1*, 154; *7.4*, 170; *7.8*, 177; *7.9*, 183; *7.12*, 247; *8.1*, 82; *8.2*, 394
16. *1.1*, 134; *1.2*, 167; *1.3*, 182; *1.4*, 205; *2.1*, 30; *2.2*, 29; *2.3*, 33; *2.4*, 37; *2.5*, 41; *2.6*, 55; *2.7*, 60; *2.8*, 83; *2.9*, 89; *2.10*, 32; *2.11*, 81; *2.12*, 96; *2.13*, 101; *2.14*, 102; *2.15*, 107; *2.16*, 108; *2.17*, 129; *2.18*, 148; *2.19*, 151; *2.20*, 150; *2.21*, 155; *2.22*, 157; *2.23*, 161; *2.24*, 162; *2.25*, 168; *2.26*, 173; *2.27*, 225; *2.28*, 227; *2.29*, 250; *2.30*, 261; *2.31*, 310; *2.32*, 269, 272; *2.33*, 270; *2.34*, 276; *2.35*, 288; *2.36*, 282; *2.37*, 285; *2.38*, 300; *2.39*, 307; *2.40*, 327; *2.41*, 334; *2.42*, 347; *2.43*, 349; *2.44*, 372; *2.45*, 375(I); *2.46*, 390; *2.47*, 387; *3.1*, 228; *3.2*, 237; *4.1*, 205; *4.2*, 216; *4.3*, 240; *4.4*, 283; *4.5*, 286; *4.6*, 287; *5.1*, 56; *5.2*, 57; *5.3*, 156; *5.4*, 160; *5.5*. 166; *5.6*, 173; *5.7*, 176; *5.8*, 179; *5.9*, 185; *5.10*, 191; *5.11*, 192; *5.12*, 194; *5.13*, 196; *5.14*, 213; *5.15*, 215; *5.16*, 217; *5.17*, 218; *5.18*, 219; *5.19*, 222; *5.20*, 232; *5.21*, 239; *5.22*, 245; *5.23*, 246; *5.24*, 248; *5.25*, 249; *5.26*, 251; *5.27*, 252; *5.28*, 254; *5.29*, 256; *5.30*, 258; *5.31*, 260; *5.32*, 260; *5.33*, 264; *5.34*, 268; *5.35*, 275; *5.36*, 277; *5.37*, 293; *5.38*, 292; *5.39*, 296; *5.40*, 298; *5.41*, 299; *5.42*, 304; *5.43*, 301; *5.44*, 305; *5.45*, 306; *5.46*, 310; *5.47*, 317; *5.48*, 320; *5.49*, 321 (I); *5.50*, 321 (II); *5.51*, 323, 339; *5.52* 329; *5.53*, 330; *5.54*, 337; *5.55*, 338; *5.56*, 339; *5.57*, 342; *5.58*, 343; *5.59*, 380; *5.60*, 381; *5.61*. 383; *5.62* 387, 388; *5.63*, 389; *5.64*, 387; *5.65*, 395; *5.66*, 422; *6.1*, 158; *6.2*, 163; *6.3*, 291; *6.4*, 289; *6.5*, 290; *6.6*, 335; *6.7*, 336; *7.1*, 175; *7.2*, 189; *7.3*, 190; *7.4*, 230; *7.5*, 231; *7.6*, 259; *7.7*, 391; *8.1*, 23; *8.5*, 76; *8.6*, 80; *8.7*, 91; *8.9*, 244; *8.13*, 267; *8.18*, 303; *8.19*, 315; *8.21*, 333; *8.22*, 341; *8.23*, 346; *8.25*, 376; *8.26*, 378; *8.28*, 392; *9.1*, 76; *9.2*, 79; *9.3*, 344; *9.4*, 348; *9.5*, 379; *10.7*, 184; *10.12*, 242; *10.13*, 253; *10.19*, 301; *10.20*, 340; *10.24*, 362; *11.1*, 278; *11.2*, 294; *11.3*, 324

CONSTITUTIONES
SIRMONDIANAE (CS)
1, 65; 2, 288; 3, 197; 4, 76; 6, 387; 7, 171; 8, 207; 9, 307; 10, 372; 11, 327; 12, 301; 13, 370; 14, 310; 15, 334; 16, 308

CORPUS SCRIPTORUM
ECCLESIASTICORUM
LATINORUM (CSEL)
26. *204–6*, 19; *208–10*, 20; *210–11*, 22; *211–12*, 24; *212*, 25; *212–13*, 39; *213–16*, 59
34. *410–11*, 21
35. *45–6*, 195; *46–7*, 211; *47–8*, 200; *48*, 137; *49*, 138, 140; *50*, 142; *50–1*, 143; *51–2*, 141; *52–3*, 152; *53–4*, 153; *54–8*, 164; *60–1*, 352; *65–6*, 353; *67–8*, 354; *68–9*, 356; *69*, 355; *69–70*, 357; *70–71*, 358; *71–2*, 359; *72*, 360; *73*, 361; *73–4*, 362; *76*, 363; *76–8*, 364; *79–80*, 365; *81–2*, 366;

SOURCES

82, 367; 83-4, 371; 90-1, 203; 320-8; 344-7, 645; 499-500, 545; 501-2, 544; 503-4, 547; 506-7, 548; 537-40, 546; 587-8, 549; 592-3, 550; 610-12, 554; 636-7, 556; 644-5, 541; 645-6, 553; 648-9, 552; 649-50, 558; 650-1, 557; 655-6, 562; 659-60, 563; 701-3, 560; 715-16, 561; 743, 564
52. 142, 120; 485-7, 21; 487, 27
57. 296-9, 368
65. 93-4, 104

DIGESTA (D)
Const. *Deo Auctore*, 617
Const. *Tanta*, 642; 12.2.5.3, 643; 50.12.2, 644

EUSEBIUS
HE
4. 9, 2; 13.1-7, 3
7. 13.2, 4
8. 17.3-10, 7
9. 1.3-6, 8; 7.3-14, 9; 9a.1-9, 13; 10.7-11, 14
10. 5.1-14, 12; 5.15-17, 10; 5.18-20, 17; 5.21-4, 18; 6, 15; 7, 16
VC
2. 24-42, 46; 46, 45; 48-60, 44; 64-72, 47
3. 12, 49 (II); 17-20, 52; 30-2, 54; 52-3, 63; 60-2, 61; 64-5, 40
4. 20, 38; 36, 64; 42, 73
EVAGRIUS
HE
2. 9, 495
3. 4, 524 (I); 7, 524 (II); 14, 527

FACUNDUS
Def. Trium Capit.
8. 3, 427
12. 2, 476; 4, 527
FONTES IURIS ROMAN ANTEJUSTINIANI (FIRA)
1. 466-7, 568

GELASIUS
HE
1. 11.23-31, 50
2. 4.1-13, 47; 7.39-41, 49 (II); 8.3, 49 (I); 36.1-2, 66; 37.1-9, 53; 37.10-22, 52
3. 3.1-4, 45; 4.1-5, 64; 5, 54; 14, 72; 15.1-5, 71; 16.1-3, 69; 17.1-7, 73; 18.1-13, 75; 19, 67; Suppl. 1, 50; Suppl. 2, 51
GESTA CONC. AQUIL. 3-4, 172
GREGORIUS PRESBYTER
De Conc. Nic. Prim. 49 (II), (III)

HAENEL (H.)
170, 5; 182, 6; 241, 399
HILARIUS PICTAVIENSIS
Excerpta ex Opere Hist. Deperdito, Ser. A, no. 8, 104

IMPERATORIS IUSTINIANI INSTITUTIONUM LIBRI QUATTUOR (II)
Const. *Imperatoriam Maiestatem*, 639
1. 20.5, 621
2. 1.7-9, 641 (I); 6.1, 641 (II)
3. 19.1-2, 641 (III); 23.5, 641 (IV); 27.7, 640 (I)
4. 6.19, 640 (II); 6.23, 640 (III); 6.26, 640 (IV); 15.1, 641 (V); 16.1, 640 (V)
INSCRIPTIONES LATINAE CHRISTIANAE VETERES (ILCV)
1. 14, 139; 23, 568; 1642 a and b, 566
IRENAEUS TYRIUS
Synod. 219, 427
ISIDORUS HISPALENSIS
Coll. Can. 476, 480, 489
ISIDORUS MERCATOR
Coll. Decr. 49 (I), 472 (I), 476, 480, 489

JULIAN
Ep. 376A-C, 121; 376C-D, 119; 377D-8C, 113; 378C-80D, 111; 380D-1A, 118; 398C-9A, 115; 404B-C, 112; 422A-4A, 116; 424B-5A, 123; 432C-5D, 122; 435D-8C, 117
JUSTIN MARTYR
Apol. pro. Christ.
1. 68.6-10, 2; App 3

LACTANTIUS
De Mort. Pers. 34, 7; 46.6, 11; 48.2-12, 12
LEGES NOVELLAE MAIORIANI (LNMaior)
6, 496; 7, 497; 10, 499; 11, 500
LEGES NOVELLAE MARCIANI (LNMarc)
5, 488
LEGES NOVELLAE THEODOSII II (LNT)
3, 429; 8, 431
LEGES NOVELLAE VALENTINIANI III (LNV)
3, 433; 7.3, 444; 10, 435, 13, 441; 17, 442; 18, 440; 20, 439; 23, 443; 35, 478
LIBERATUS
Breviarium, 17, 527

MANSI (M)
2. 930-9, 67
4. 1109-12, 398; 1112-16, 397; 1117-20, 401; 1377-80, 405; 1396-7, 406

5. *256*, **425**; *278–82*, **412**; *281–4*, **411** (III); *283–4*, **411** (I); *413*, **422**; *416–17*, **423**; *417–20*, **445**; *420*, **446**; *437–45*, **400**; *527–8*, **398**; *531–2*, **397**; *567–8*, **405**; *593–5*, **406**; *660*, **425**; *660–1*, **422**; *661–2*, **423**; *663–6*, **412**; *828*, **411** (II); *828–9*, **411** (III)
6. *551–4*, **464**; *553–4*, **464**, **467**; *555–6*, **466**; *557–8*, **468**; *559–62*, **469**; *587–90*, **449**; *593–4*, **450**, **451**; *595–6*, **453**; *597–8*, **454**; *597–600*, **455**; *599–600*, **458**; *619–20*, **457**; *731–4*, **448**; *935–8*, **470** (I); *951–5*, **470** (II); *1225*, **472**[31,35]
7. *47–50*, **470** (III); *59–62*, **470** (IV); *89–94*, **470** (V); *103–6*, **471**; *129–30*, **472** (I); *131–4*, **472**[2]; *169–74*, **472** (II); *173–8*, **472** (III); *177–8*, **472** (IV); *178*, **472**; *179–84*, **470** (VI); *189–90*, **470** (VII); *209–10*, **447**; *273–4*, **473**, **478**; *289–300*, **470** (VIII); *313–14*, **470** (IX); *355–8*, **470** (X); *451–4*, **470** (XI); *475–8*, **476**; *477–80*, **477**; *481–4*, **481**; *483–8*, **483**; *487–96*, **484**; *495–8*, **459**; *497–500*, **479**; *501–6*, **480**; *505–8*, **485**; *509–12*, **486**; *513–18*, **487**; *517–20*, **489**; *746–7*, **472**[1]; *757*, **468**; *758–9*, **469**
9. *249–50*, **422**; *250–1*, **459**; *364–5*, **559**

MARTYRDOM OF HABIB THE DEACON, 42

MONUMENTA ASIAE MINORIS ANTIQUAE (MAMA)
3, no. 197, **540**; 7, no. 305, **43**

NICEPHORUS
HE
3. *27*, **2**; *28*, **3**;
6. *12*, **4**
7. *23*, **7**; *31*, **13**; *38*, **14**; *41*, **12**; *42*, **10**, **15**, **16**; *43*, **17**, **18**
8. *13*, **47**; *16*, **49** (I, II); *25*, **52**, **66**; *27*, **45**, **64**; *28*, **54**; *47*, **58**; *48*, **72**; *50*, **75**
9. *3*, **77**; *21*, **84**; *25*, **85–7**; *36*, **103**
10. *7*, **111**
11. *30*, **159**
15. *18*, **495**
16. *3*, **524** (I); *7*, **524** (II); *12*, **527**

NOMOCANON
2.1, **585**

NOVELLAE (N)
155, **635**; App I Ed 2, **633**; App I Ed 10, **576**

OPTATUS
De Schis. Donat.
App 3, **19**; 5, **20**; 6, **22**; 7, **24**; 8, **25**; 9, **39**; 10, **59**

PALLADIUS
Dial. de Vita Chrys. 3, **284**, **295**; 11, **297**
PASSIO S. SABINI, 6[1]

PATROLOGIA GRAECA (PG)
25. *340–4*, **84**; *348*, **85**; *348–9*, **86**; *349–52*, **87**; *357*, **72**; *360–1*, **69**; *369–72*, **68**; *373*, **70**; *393–6*, **74**; *401* (I), **78**; *401–6*, **75**; *405–8*, **77**; *624*, **90**; *632–6*, **88**; *656–7*, **99**; *720*, **88**; *720–1*, **90** (II); *732*, **94**; *744*, **100**
26. *792*, **105**; *813*, **125**; *820–4*, **124**
47. *13*, **284**; *14–15*, **295**; *37*, **297**
65. *880–2*, **427**
77. *1448*, **411** (I); *1457–61*, **412**
83. *1473–6*, **407**
84. *595–6*, **402**; *596–7*, **403**; *597*, **404**; *618–19*, **410**; *625–6*, **408**; *631–2*, **409**; *656–7*, **411** (II); *657–8*, **411** (III); *740–1*, **414**; *758–9*, **415**; *788*, **416**; *796*, **417**; *796–7*, **418**; *797–8*, **419**; *798–9*, **420**; *802–3*, **426**; *849–50*, **427**
111. *429*, **49** (II); *433*, **49** (III)

PATROLOGIA LATINA (PL)
11. *1260–1*, **324**; *1261–3*, **325**; *1263–6*, **326**; *1367–8*, **324**; *1418–20*, **328**
13. *564–5*, **93**
16. *916–17*, **172**; *1045*, **136**
20. *679* [*leg. 769*]–*771*, **375** (II, III)
43. *816–17*, **324**; *817–19*, **325**; *819–21*, **326**; *840–1*, **328**
45. *1726–7*, **350**; *1727–8*, **351**; *1750*, **373**; *1751*, **374**
48. *379–86*, **350**; *392–4*, **351**; *404–7*, **373**; *408–9*, **384**
54. *899–900*, **461**; *903–6*, **462**; *905–8*, **462**; *970–4*, **475**; *1017–20*, **482**
56. *490–2*, **350**; *492–3*, **351**; *499–500*, **373**; *500*, **374**; *547–9*, **476**; *549–51*, **477**; *551–4*, **489**; *896–8*, **519**; *898*, **520**
67. *717–18*, **427**; *837*, **476**; *845–8*, **527**
68. *1023–4*, **527**
84. *173–4*, **476**; *174–6*, **480**; *176–8*, **489**
130. *254*, **49** (I); *303–4*, **472** (I); *314–15*, **476**; *315–17*, **480**; *317–20*, **489**

PATROLOGIA ORIENTALIS (PO)
4. *278*, **49** (I); *279–80*, **66**; *618*, **543** (I); *622–3*, **543** (II)
7. *546–7*, **48** (III); *550–1*, **66**
23. *204–5*, **48** (I); *207*, **49** (I)

PERRY (P)
3–7, **449**; *8–10*, **458**; *8*, n. † *ad fin.*, **458**; *10–13*, **456**; *39–40*, **452**; *364–70*, **459**; *370*, **460**; *374*, **459**; *402–4*, **449**; *405*, **451**; *406–7*, **457**; *407–9*, **453**; *409–11*, **455**

PITRA
2. *460*, **276**; *464*, **273**, **508**; *469*, **474**; *477*, **225**; *480*, **270**, **314**, **528**; *492*, **507**; *494*, **623**; *496*, **585**; *498*, **598**; *502*, **313**; *513*, **335**; *517*, **298**, **395**; *529*, **628**; *533*, **491**; *534–5*, **515**; *537*, **146**, **271**, **309**, **490**, **625**; *546*,

479; *556*, 396; *560*, **491**, **501**; *565*,
126; *577*, **230**; *595*, **528**, **529**; *598*,
247; *600*, **166**; *602*, **258**, **298**, **395**;
603, **214**; *634*, **26**, **35**; *638*, **393**

PLINY
  Ep. 10.97, **1**
P. LOND.
  878, **46**

RUFINUS
  HE
  4. *9*, **2**
  10. *2*, **49** (I)

SOCRATES
  HE
  1. *7*, **47**; *8*, **49** (I); *9*, **45**, **52-4**, **64**, **66**;
     25, **58**; *27*, **72**; *34*, **75**
  2. *3*, **77**; *23*, **84-7**; *37*, **105**
  3. *3*, **111**
  5. *22*, **52**
SOZOMEN
  HE
  1. *17*, **49** (I); *19*, **49** (II)

2. *22*, **72**; *28*, **75**
3. *2*, **77**
4. *14*, **103**
5. *7*, **111**
6. *7*, **131**
7. *4*, **167**
SUPPLEMENTUM EPIGRAPHICUM
    GRAECUM (SEG)
  4.517, **577**
SYRIAC MISCELLANIES
  1-2, **48** (II); 5-6, **48** (II); 6-7, **66**

THEODORET
  HE
  1. *7.12*, **49** (II); *10*, **52**; *15.1-2*, **45**;
     16.1-4, **64**; *17*, **54**; *20.1-10*, **50**; *27*, **69**;
     29.1-6, **73**
  2. *2*, **77**; *11*, **84** (II); *16*, **95**
  4. *8*, **159**

ZACHARIAS RHETOR
  Chron.
  3. *1*, **472** (I)
  4. *5*, **495**
  5. *2*, **524** (I); *8*, **527**

PERSONS

Abaddon, Judaeo-Christian demon, 159³⁷
Abednego, Hebrew hero (*flor.* 595 B.C.), 95³⁴
Abel, son of Adam (q.v.), 159³⁴
Abgarus (*al.* Acbarus, Augarus) V, Edessan king (4 B.C.–A.D. 7, 13–50), 42⁵
Abimelech, Gerarite king (*flor.* ?1750 B.C.), 223²
Abraham (*olim* Abram), Hebrew patriarch (*flor.* ?1750 B.C.), 53¹², 63, 76³
Ablabius (*al.* Ablavius), praetorian prefect (326, 330–3, 337), 43, 55, 65, 106⁵
Abundantius, Flavius, consul (393), 244
Acacius, St, bishop of Amida (400?–?31), 598¹³
Acacius, bishop of Arca in Armenia Secunda (*flor.* 431), 406
Acacius, bishop of Beroea in Syria Prima (381–437), 406, 411 (I, II), 412¹ⁿ
Acacius, bishop of Cotena (*flor.* 431), 406
Acacius, bishop of Melitene (431?–?8), 406
Acacius, bishop of Seleucia ad Tigrim (485-*ante* 500), 542
Acacius, patriarch of Constantinople (471–89), 524 (II), 526, 527¹ⁿ,², 544¹ⁿ, 550, 554, 560–3
Acacius, vicar of the East (330–2), 61 (III), 63
Achilles, Scythian monk (*flor.* 519), 551
Achilleus (*al.* Achilles), St, bishop of Spoleto (402–?20), 355–7, 358⁶, 364¹¹
Achitas (*al.* Achetas, Achitus), unidentified deacon (*flor.* 346), 84 (III)
Adam, the first man, 350²⁴,²⁶
Addeus, count and master of each soldiery throughout the East (393), 244
Adelphius, Mesopotamian laic and heresiarch (*flor.* 390), Gl s.v. Enthusiasts
Adelphius (*al.* Adelfius), Flavius, consul (451), 475¹³
Adiectus, Ursinian cleric (*flor.* 371), 152–3
Aelafius, vicar of Africa (*flor.* 313), 19
Aelianus, proconsul of Africa (313–15), 21
Aemilianus, Lucius Mussius, prefect of Egypt (257–61), 4¹
Aetheria (*al.* Etheria), Spanish abbess (*flor.* 380), 484²⁵
Aetius, bishop of Lydda (325?-*ante* 335), 61 (III)
Aetius, Anomoean heresiarch (*ob. c.* 367), 103 112, Gl s.vv. Aetians, Eunomians

Aetius, Constantinopolitan archdeacon (451), 472¹⁴
Aetius, urban prefect of Constantinople (419), 319; praetorian prefect of the East (425), 386
Aetius, Flavius, master of each soldiery (429–54), 413¹², 442
Aezanes, Auxumite king (*flor.* 357), 99
Afrodisius, tribune and notary (419), 352
Agapius, Palestinian martyr (*ob.* 307), App³⁶
Aginatius, urban vicar of Rome (368 or 370), 142–3
Agricola, praetorian prefect of the Gauls (418), 351; consul (421), 375 (I)
Agrippa Postumus, grandson of Augustus (12 B.C.–A.D. 14), 46¹⁶
Agrippina Minor, Julia, great-granddaughter of Augustus (15–59), 164⁸
Agroecius, Gallic priest (*flor.* 385), 203
Ahasuerus, unhistorical Persian king, 303¹. *See* Xerxes I
Alaricus I, Visigothic king (395–410), 308², 323¹ⁿ, 646¹
Alaricus II, Visigothic king (484–507), In², Gl s.v. interpretation
Albertus Magnus, St, German theologian (1193?–1280), 313¹
Albinus: praetorian prefect of the East (430), 399¹; praetorian prefect of Italy (445, 448), 440–1, 443, 446
Albinus, urban prefect of Rome (389), 219, 220
Albucianus, vicar of Macedonia (380), 169
Alexander, emperor (311), 44⁴
Alexander III Magnus, Macedonian king (336–323 B.C.), In²⁹, 42⁸, 62², 98, 111, 122, 127⁷, 495, 523², 614⁷, Gl s.v. Samaritans
Alexander, bishop of Apamea in Syria Secunda (*ob. post* 434), 406
Alexander, bishop of Arcadiopolis in Ionia (*flor.* 431), 406
Alexander, bishop of Cleopatris in Augustamnica Secunda (431–51), 406
Alexander, St, bishop of Constantinople (330?–?7), 71¹ⁿ
Alexander, bishop of Hierapolis in Phrygia Salutaris (431–4), 406, 407, 415 (I), 418–20
Alexander, bishop of Thessalonica (325?–?35), 74

PERSONS 1255

Alexander, St, patriarch of Alexandria (313–28), 47, 61 (III), 67^{14}, 71
Alexander Severus: *see* Severus Alexander
Alimentus, Marcus Cincius, plebeian tribune (204 B.C.), Gl s.v. *Lex Cincia*
Alpheus, bishop of Apamea in Syria Secunda (325–41), 61 (III)
Alypius, bishop of Thagaste (*flor.* 419), 362
Amatius, praetorian prefect of the Gauls (425), 387
Ambrosiaster, Biblical commentator (*flor.* 375), 164^{11}
Ambrosius, St, bishop of Milan (374–97), In^{21,31,49}, 52^{29}, 94^{1}, 136^{1n}, 150^{1}, 160^{1}, 172, 187^{1n}, 203^{1}, 205^{1n}, 242^{1n}, 326^{5}, 330^{1n}, 442^{7}, 465^{3}, 470 (I), 598^{13}
Amigetius (*al.* Amegetius, Megetius), imperial auditor (375), 159
Ampelius, urban prefect of Rome (370–2), 152, 154^{4}, 155, 156
Amphilochius, St, archbishop of Iconium (375–?400), 182
Amphion, bishop of Nicomedia (325–9, 339–), 50^{27}
Anastasius I, emperor (491–518), In^{31}, 65^{6}, 97^{1}, 464^{1}, 476^{1n}, 519^{12}, 523^{5}, 530^{1n}, 531^{1n}, 533–8, 540–8, 549^{1n}, 552^{2}, 554^{1n}, 557^{1n}, 560^{3,41,16}, 561, 611^{7}, 630^{1}
Anastasius II, pope (496–8), 560, 561^{8}, 562^{14}
Anastasius, bishop of Nicaea (*flor.* 451), 470^{61}
Anatolius, consul (440), 435; master of the soldiers (451), 470^{1}
Anatolius, patriarch of Constantinople (449–58), 463, 464, 470 (VIII), 471, 482^{5}, 492^{1}, 495
Anatolius, unidentified priest (*flor.* 455), 488
Anaxagoras, Greek philosopher (500?–?428 B.C.), 648^{6}
Andreas, St, disciple (*ob. c.* 60), 181^{5}
Andreas, bishop of Samosata (431-*ante* 449), 542
Andronicus, Cyrestene priest (*flor.* 520), 559
Annas, unidentified Jew (415), 344, 346
Annianus, Petronius, praetorian prefect of the Gauls (*flor.* 316), 25
Anthemius, consul (515), 545
Anthemius, Flavius, master of the offices (404), 283; consul (405), 289–92, 293^{5}, 294, 296; praetorian prefect of the East (405–15), 302, 303, 314, 320, 321 (I), 335–6, 345^{3}, 538^{2}
Anthemius (*al.* Antemius, Anthemus), Procopius, consul (455), 488, 489; emperor (467–72), Tab^{5}, 506, 508–10, 512, 514–18, Gl s.v. *Lex Leoniana*
O

Anthony: *see* Antonius
Antichrist, 7^{13}, 483, 485, 487, App^{1}
Antidius, diocesan vicar (381), 180
Antigonus I Cyclops (*al.* Monophthalmus), Asiatic king (306–301 B.C.), 48^{19}
Antiochinus, unidentified official (386), 207
Antiochus III Magnus, Seleucid king (223–187 B.C.), 23^{2}
Antiochus IV Epiphanes, Seleucid king (175–163 B.C.), 7^{3}, 95^{34}
Antiochus, bishop of Bostra (*flor.* 431), 406
Antiochus, provost of the sacred bedchamber (558), 618^{12}
Antiochus, Flavius, praetorian prefect of the East and consul (431), 400^{1,47,76}, 405,
Antoninus Pius, emperor (138–61), 3^{1n,3,30}, 4^{2}, 31^{4}, 76^{3}, 133^{1}, 577^{1}, App^{6}
Antonius, Flavius Claudius, consul (382), 185–7
Antonius, Marcus, triumvir (43–32 B.C.), 62^{2}, 122^{11}, 341^{2}, 593^{3}
Antonius of Padua, St, Portuguese monk (1195–1235), 223^{2}
Anulinus, proconsul of Africa (*flor.* 313), 10, 15–17, 19^{11}
Aphrodite, Greek goddess, 67. *See* Venus
Aphthonius, imperial secretary (419), 353
Apollinaris Maior, Laodicean priest (*ob. c.* 362), 116^{1}
Apollinaris Minor, bishop of Laodicea in Syria Prima (361–77) and heresiarch, 481, 483–7, 489, 542, 569, 636, Gl s.v. Apollinarians
Apollo, Graeco-Roman god, 44, 644^{6}
Apollodorus, proconsul of Africa (399–400), 278
Apollonius, consul (460), 500
Apolloris, confidant of Jovianus (*flor.* 364), In^{46}
Appius, bishop in (?) Gaul (*flor.* 376), 161
Aquilinus, bishop of Byblus (449?–51), 459^{14}
Aquilinus, urban vicar of Rome (378 or 379), 164
Aquilius, plebeian tribune (?287 B.C.): Gl s.v. *Lex Aquilia*
Arbitio, Flavius, consul (355), 96
Arcadia, sister of Theodosius II (400–44), 398^{3}
Arcadius, emperor (383–408), Tab^{3}, In^{3}, 171, 195, 197, 200–2, 204–5, 207, 211–12, 214, 216, 218–42, 244–94, 295^{1n}, 296–300, 307, 309, 319^{4}, 321^{1n,4}, 330^{6}, 381^{1n,5}, 443^{15}, 463^{1n}, 478, 488, 629
Arcadius, praetorian prefect of the East (486, 518), 536
Archelaus, Augustal prefect (397), 266

PERSONS

Archelaus, praetorian prefect of the East (524–7), 565, 568; praetorian prefect of Africa (534), 646 (I)
Ardaburius, consul (447), 393
Areius, Alexandrian philosopher (*flor.* 30 B.C.), 122
Ares, Greek god, 67
Arinthaeus (*al.* Arintheus, Arenteus, Aronteus, Arontheus, Arrontius), consul (372), 156, 157
Ariovindus (*al.* Aerobindus, Ariobindus, Arivendus), Flavius, consul (434), 421
Aristaenetus, consul (404), 283, 285–7
Aristides, Greek apologist (*flor.* 126), 2^{20}
Aristobulus I Philhellen, Jewish king (104–103 B.C.), 76^4
Aristolaus, tribune and notary (432), 411 (II), 412
Aristoteles, Greek philosopher (384–322 B.C.), 551^7, 583^1, 652^4
Arius, Alexandrian priest and heresiarch (256–336), 47, 50, 53, 58, 66, 67, $71-2^{1n}$, 156^1, 542, Gl s.v. Arians
Armasius, praetorian prefect of the East (469–70), 508–10
Armatus, consul (476), 525, 526
Arouet, François Marie: *see* Voltaire
Arsaces III, Armenian king (341 or 354–63), 106
Arsacius, patriarch of Constantinople (404–5), 284, 287
Arsenius, Egyptian bishop (*flor.* 335), 68^4
Artemis, Greek goddess, 397^1, 615^{1n}
Artemius, bishop of Embrun (374–), 161
Artemius, military governor of Egypt (361), $111^{12,14}$
Ascalesi, Alessio Cardinal (1872–1952), 364^{15}
Asclepiades, bishop of Chersonesus in Thrace (*flor.* 419), 369
Asclepiodotus, consul (423), 376–83; praetorian prefect of the East (423–5), 376–83, 385
Asmodeus, Jewish demon, 159^{37}
Aspar, Flavius Ardaburius, consul (434) 421, 476^4, 492^1
Aspiratus *or* Asporacius: *see* Sporacius
Asterius, bishop of Amida (*flor.* 431) 406
Atarbius, governor of the Euphrates (362), 119
Atarbius praetorian prefect of the East (528), 579
Athanasius, bishop of Perrha (445–51), 470 (X)
Athanasius, St, patriarch of Alexandria (328–36, 337–9, 346–56, 362, 364–5, 366–73), 20^1, 52^4, 53^{12}, 58^{1n}, 61^{21}, 67^{14}, 68–70, 71^{1n}, 72^{1n}, 73^{16}, 74–7, 78^{1n}, 84–8, 90, 93^{1n}, $94^{1n,1-2}$, 95, 98–100, 115, 121–2, 124 (I–III), 125, $195^{1n,3,5}$, 284^4, 470 (I), 481, 489, 569^5, 637^7, 651^{20}

Attalus, emperor (409–10, 414–16), 308^2, $323^{1n,1}$
Atticus, patriarch of Constantinople (406–25), 297, 375^{1n}
Atticus (*al.* Aetius), Constantinopolitan archdeacon *or* deacon (451), 469
Atticus Maximus, Nonius, consul (397), 261–7
Attila, Hunnish king (433 ?–53), 442^4
Audius, Syrian laic and heresiarch (*flor.* 350), Gl s.v. Audians
Augustinus, Aurelius, St, bishop of Hippo Regius (395–430), 1^3, 17^{11}, 27^{1n}, 28^1, 75^{42}, 206^7, 293^3, 313^1, 324^2, 326^5, 330^{1n}, 350^{1n}, 362, 368, 370^1, 406, 442^7, 515^3, 562, 598^{13}
Augustulus: *see* Romulus Augustulus
Augustus, emperor (27 B.C.–A.D. 14), Tab^5, In^{30}, 1^4, 4^2, 31^1, 46^{16}, 62^2, 122, 127^7, 140^1, 141^8, 203^4, 214^5, 218^7, 241^1, 256^3, 356^5, 382^1, 474^2, 550^2, 608^4, 626^3, 641^8, Gl s.vv. as, Augustus, Imperator, *Lex Iulia de adulteriis coercendis*, *Lex Iulia de maiestate*, *Lex Iulia de maritandis ordinibus*, *Lex Iulia peculatus*, prefect, (urban)
as Caesar Augustus, 122
Aurelianus, emperor (270–5), 5, App 9
Aurelianus, proconsul of Asia (395), 254; praetorian prefect of the East (414–16), 341–3, 345
Aurelianus, praetorian prefect of the East (399), 279; consul (400), 281, 282, 288^{20}, 293
Aurelianus Protadius, Dioscorus, praetorian prefect of (?) Illyricum (473), 520^1
Aurelius, emperor (161–80), Tab^1, $In^{14,46}$, 3, 36^1, 472^4, 608^4, 621^6, 641^{17}, App 4
Aurelius, St, bishop of Carthage (381/382–?430), 361, 367, 368
Ausonius, Decimus Magnus, consul (379), 165^8, 166^8, 248^5
Auxanius, Ursinian cleric (*flor.* 371), 152–3
Auxano, Ursinian cleric (*flor.* 371), 152–3
Auxentius (*olim* Mercurianus), Arian bishop of Silistria (*flor.* 386), 136^{1n}
Auxentius Draucus, Flavius Olbius, urban prefect of Rome (441, 445), 439
Auxonius, proconsul of Asia (381), 182
Auxonius: *see* Ausonius
Avienus (*al.* Habienus) Gennadius, consul (450), 461
Avitus, emperor (455–6) Tab^5
Azariah, Hebrew priest (*flor.* 760 B.C.), 95^{34}

PERSONS

Baal, Phoenician god, 9[6]
Babbutius, Numidian bishop (*flor.* 330), 59
Balbinus, emperor (238), 472[4]
Barachias, father of Zacharias (q.v.), 159[84]
Barbelo (*al.* Barbeloth), Gnostic aeon, Gl s.v. Borborians
Bardesanes, Gnostic writer (154–222) 542
Bardio, imperial chamberlain (*flor.* 363), 124 (IV)
Bardsuma: *see* Barsumas
Baris (*al.* Baruch, Bariscaeus), father of Zacharias (q.v.), 159[84]
Bark, William Carroll (1908–), 464[1]
Barsumas (*al.* Bardsuma), Syrian archimandrite (*ob. c.* 458), 450–51, 542[20]
Basilides, Roman soldier (*flor.* 215), 255[3]
Basiliscus, emperor (475–6), 411[8], 524, 526[1n,2-4], 542[8]
Basilius, Arian bishop of Ancyra in Galatia Prima (336–44, 353–60, 361–3), 159[43]
Basilius, bishop of Larissa in Thessaly (*flor.* 431), 406
Basilius, bishop of Seleucia in Isauria (448–58), 470 (I, III)
Basilius, Constantinopolitan deacon (*flor.* 451), 475
Basilius, Flavius Caecina Decius, praetorian prefect of Italy (458), 496, 497
Basilius Magnus, St, bishop of Caesarea in Cappadocia Prima (370–9), 94[1], 107[8], 470 (I)
Bassa, Palestinian abbess (*flor.* 453), 485
Bassianus, bishop of Ephesus (444?–9, 451–), 470 (VIII), 473
Bassus, Flavius, praetorian prefect of Italy (435), 423
Bassus, Flavius Anicius Auchenius, consul (408), 301–9
Bassus, Flavius Anicius Auchenius, count of the private estates (425), 387[3]; praetorian prefect of Italy (426), 391, 392; consul (431), 400[76], 405[12]
Bassus, Julius Annius, consul and praetorian prefect (331), 43 (II)
Bassus, Septimus, urban prefect of Rome (317–21, 326), 33, 57
Bauto (*al.* Baudo), Flavius, consul (385), 201–2, 204
Baynes, Norman Hepburn (1877–1961), 19[6,21]
Belisarius, Flavius, consul (535), 635, 646 (II)
Bencomalus: *see* Vincomalus
Benedictus XV, pope (1914–22), 617[6]
Benedictus of Nursia, St, Italian monk (480?–?543), 297[3]
Berechiah, father of Zechariah (q.v.), 159[84]

Berinianus, bishop of Perga in Pamphylia Secunda (*flor.* 431), 406
Bernicianus, Egyptian Arian (*flor.* 363), 124
Beronicianus, secretary of the sacred consistory (451), 471[1n], 472[20]
Bigelow, Poultney (1855–1954), 50[57]
Blandus, Roman priest (*flor.* 520), 558
Boethius, Anicius Manlius Severinus, consul (510), 223[2], 533[1]
Boethius, Flavius (?) Nar ... Manlius, consul (487), 533[1]
Bonaparte, Charles Joseph (1851–1921), In[32]
Bonaparte, Napoléon: *see* Napoleon I
Bonifacius I, St, pope (418–22) 352–4[1n,1,3], 355[1n,4], 356–7[1n,1], 358[1n,2], 359[1n,3], 362[10], 363[1n], 364[3,5], 365–7[1n], 371, 375[1n,3]
Bonifacius VIII, pope (1294–1303), In[31]
Borbonius, Matthias (*flor.* 1600), In[21]
Bosporius (*al.* Bosphorius), bishop of Gangra (*flor.* 431), 406
Brentesius (*al.* Brintisius), imperial auditor (375), 159
Burckhardt, Jakob (1818–97), 11[3], 38[3]
Bury, John Bagnell (1861–1927), In[31], 433[7], 513[5], 550[1]
Byron, George Gordon, Baron (1788–1824), 132[2]

Caecilianus, bishop of Carthage (311–?45), 10[1], 15–17, 19, 20[1n], 21, 22, 24, 27, 39[1n], 328
Caecilianus, praetorian prefect of Italy (409), 311–13
Caecilianus, Alfius, Aptungitan duovir (*flor.* 314), 21
Caelestius, Pelagian priest (380?–*post* 429), 350–1, 368, 373–4, 387
Caesar, Gaius Julius, dictator (49, 48–44 B.C.), 17[3], 62[2], 116[1], 122[10], 127[7], 133[1], 220[3], 334[5], 608[4], 624[3], 646[14], Gl s.vv. Caesar, dictator, *Lex Iulia de collegiis*, *Lex Iulia de maiestate*
Caesar Augustus: *see* Augustus
Caesarius, Flavius, praetorian prefect of the East (395–8), 252, 259–60, 267, 269; consul (397), 261–7
Calepius (*al.* Callepius, Calypius, Alypius), consul (447), 443, 444
Calibius Junior, Aptungitan civic curator (*flor.* 314), 21
Caligula (Gaius Julius Caesar Germanicus), emperor (37–41), 164[8], 619[7]
Callistratus, jurisconsult (*flor.* 220), 133[1]
Callistus (*al.* Calixtus) I, St, pope (217–22), In[26], 364[15]
Calopodius, (?) praetorian prefect of Italy (554), 618[18]
Candidianus, Flavius, count of the domestics (431), 401–5, 406[1n], 407[6], 408[2]

PERSONS

Capito, Donatist bishop (*flor.* 316), 25

Caracalla (Marcus Aurelius Antoninus), emperor (211–17), 65[6], App *ante* 1, Gl s.v. peregrine

Carolus Magnus: *see* Charlemagne

Cassianus, Donatist bishop in Africa (362), 120

Cassiodorus Senator, Flavius Magnus Aurelius (consul 514), 544

Catafronius (*al.* Cataphronius), (?) vicar of Italy (376–7), 162[1]

Catilina, Lucius Sergius, praetor (68 B.C.), 133[1]

Cato Maior Censorius Sapiens, Marcus Porcius Priscus, consul (195 B.C.), 59[4]

Cato Minor Uticensis, Marcus Porcius, praetor (54 B.C.), 65[13]

Catullinus (*al.* Catulinus) Philomathius, Fabius Aco, consul (349), 89

Catus, Sextus Aelius, consul (4), Gl s.v. *Lex Aelia et Sentia*

Celestinus (*al.* Coelestinus) I, St, pope (422–32), In[43], 388[3], 406, 411[15], 412, 477, 480, 484, 486, 524[14]

Celidonius (*al.* Chelidonius, Cheldonius), bishop of Besançon (*flor.* 445), 442[1n,1]

Celsus, Domitius, vicar of Africa (315–16), 24, 25

Cephas: *see* Petrus

Charlemagne, Carolingian emperor (800–814), Tab[5], 492[1]

Charles I the Great: *see* Charlemagne

Charles III the Fat, Carolingian emperor (876–87), Tab[5]

Charlevoix, Pierre François Xavier de (1682–1761), 522[4]

Charon, Graeco-Roman mythical character, 395[15]

Charybdis, Graeco-Roman maelstrom, In 8

Chrestus, bishop of Syracuse (*flor.* 314), 18, 19[1n,15-18,23,29], 20[1n]

Chronopius, Italian ex-bishop (*flor.* 369), 146

Chrysaphius, chief of the sacred bedchamber (*ob.* 450), 459, 463[2]

Chrysippus, Greek philosopher (280?–?207 B.C.), 223[2]

Chrysostomus, Dio, Greek orator (40?–*post* 112), 577[1]

Chrysostomus, Joannes, St, patriarch of Constantinople (398–404), 94[1], 228[1], 246[1], 283[1n], 284[1n,1-4], 285[1n,2,3,6], 295, 297[1n], 302[2], 372[2], 481[3], 515[3], 527[76]

Churchill, Sir Winston Leonard Spencer (1874–1965), 62[2]

Cicero, Marcus Tullius, consul (63 B.C.), In[1,54], 59[4], 220[2,4], 223[2], 509[6], 593[3], 625[12], 648[6]

Ciceronius, imperial auditor (375), 159

Claudianus, Donatist bishop in Rome (*flor.* 377), 164

Claudius I, emperor (41–54), 164[8], 631[1n,1]

Claudius II Gothicus, emperor (268–70), 472[4]

Claudius Hermogenianus Caesarius, urban prefect of Rome (369, 374–5), 146; proconsul of Africa (370), 148

Clearchus, urban prefect of Constantinople 396–9, 400–2), 258, 274

Clearchus, Flavius, consul (384), 196, 198–9

Clemens I, St, pope (88–97), 1[4], 61[11], 75[42]

Clemens of Alexandrina, Greek theologian (150?–?215), In[52], 189[2], 613[4]

Cleopatra VII Thea Philopator, Egyptian queen (51–49, 48–30 B.C.), 122[10,11]

Clicherius (*al.* Glycerius), count of the East (381), 179

Commodus, emperor (177–93), Tab[1], 474[2], App *ante* 1

Conon, St, Pamphylian martyr (*ob. c.* 250), 523

Constans I, emperor (337–50), In[17], 32[1], 38, 43[1,18], 65[6], 77[1], 78[4], 79–80[8], 81, 84 (I), 90, 95–6, 214[5]

Constans, Roman general (*ob.* 409), 308[2]

Constans, Flavius, consul (414), 337, 338

Constantia, Flavia Valeria, sister of Constantinus I (*ob. c.* 329), 58[1n], 106[5]

Constantianus, vicar of Pontus (382–3), 191

Constantinus I Magnus, St, emperor (306–37), Tab[5], In 1, 4[9,14,17,18,29,30,33,36,43,46,50], 7, 9[1n], 10–11[1n], 12, 13[1], 14[1n], 15–24, 26–41, 42[1n,1], 43–7, 48[1n (II, III)], 49–61, 62[1n,2], 63–77, 84[27], 89[1n], 91[6], 95[41], 97[1], 103[12], 106[1n,4-6,8], 111[11], 115[1], 116[11], 117[1n], 119[5], 124 (II), 127[7], 131[1], 136[1], 141[3], 150[1n], 163, 186[5], 211[1n], 214[3,5], 225[1n], 228[2], 233[7], 241[3], 267, 285[2], 303[3], 309[1n], 313[1], 324[2], 328, 331[5], 341, 364[12], 375[14], 382[1], 406, 421[5], 422, 433[7], 442[3], 463[5], 470[61], 472 (I), 474[2], 484[24], 495, 522[4,6], 523[2], 524 (I), 525, 528[5], 537[6], 543 (II), 550[1], 551[10], 578[5], 614[13], 617[10], 624[3], 638[10,13], App 10 (f), Gl s.vv. *Lex Constantiniana*, Porphyrians

Constantinus II, emperor (337–40), In[17], 28[8], 31–8, 43, 75[1n], 77, 78[4], 95[46]

Constantinus III, emperor (407–11), 308[2]

Constantinus, Constantinopolitan deacon (520), 561

Constantinus, Flavius, praetorian prefect of the East (456), 490, 491; consul (457), 492

Constantius I Chlorus, emperor (305–6), 34[5], 44[3], 46, 91[6], 525[1], 581[4], App[16]

PERSONS 1259

Constantius II, emperor (337–61), In^{17}, 32^1, 33^4, 38, 43, 55–7, 65^6, 77^1, 78^4, 79–112, 113^5, 115, 117^{3,5}, 119^5, 123^4, 124 (II), 127^{1n}, 148, 163, 171^1, 205, 214^5, 267, 285^2, 407^8, 463^5, 637^7

Constantius, Flavius, consul (414, 417, 420), 337–8, 348, 361^1, 372; as Constantius III, emperor (421), 373, 387^9

Constantius Gallus, Flavius Claudius (Julius), (known also as Constans and Gallus), consul (352, 354), 91^6, 92, 112^5

Cornelius, St, pope (251–3), 523^1

Crassus Dives, Marcus Licinius, consul (70, 55 B.C.), Gl s.v. *Lex Licinia*

Crescentius, Numidian bishop (*flor.* 330), 59

Crispus Caesar, consul (318, 321, 324), In^{14}, 28–9^2, 34–8, 43^{18}, 63^2

Cullman, Oscar (1902–), 442^7

Curtius, praetorian prefect of Italy (407–8), 301

Cybele (Magna Mater), Asiatic goddess, 397^1, 442^7

Cynegius (*al.* Cynigius), Flavius Maternus, praetorian prefect of the East (384–8), 195^{1n}, 196, 199, 202, 206, 210, 213–14, 217; consul (388), 213–17

Cyprianus, Thascius Caecilius, St, bishop of Carthage (248–58), 17^5, 154^2, 523^1

Cyrillus, St, bishop of Jerusalem (350–7, 379–86), 167^9, 303^3

Cyrillus, St, patriarch of Alexandria (412–44), 284^4, 347^{1n,13}, 349^{1n,1}, 397–8, 402, 405^3, 406, 408–9, 411 (III), 412, 418^{1n}, 445–6, 458, 470 (I), 477, 480–1, 484, 486, 489, 524^{14}, 527, 542

Cyrus I Magnus, Persian king (550–529 B.C.), In^{23}

Cyrus, Achaean bishop (*flor.* 431), 406

Cyrus, bishop of Aphrodisias in Caria (431–49), 406, 428, 542

Cyrus, bishop of Marcopolis (*flor.* 431), 406

Cyrus, Asiatic presbyter (*flor.* 448), 447^3

Cyrus, unidentified monk (*flor.* 534), 645

Cyrus, Flavius, urban prefect of Constantinople (439), 430, 538^2; praetorian prefect of the East (439–41), 434

Dalmatius, bishop of Cyzicus (427?–*post* 431), 406

Dalmatius (*al.* Delmatius), Flavius Julius, consul (333), 65

Damascius, tribune and notary (448), 447

Damasus I, St, pope (366–84), 137^{1n}, 138, 146^2, 150, 159^{46}, 164, 167, 200^{1n}, 375^{1n,5,7,11}

Damasus (*al.* Damascus), imperial auditor (375), 159

Daniel, Hebrew prophet (*ob. post* 535 B.C.), 95^{34}

Daniel, bishop of Carrhae (*ob. post* 449), 447

Daniel Stylites, St, pillar saint (409–93), 411^3

Dares, mythological pugilist, 429^{30}

Darius, unhistorical Persian king, 95^{34}

Darius, praetorian prefect of the East (436–7), 428

Datianus, consul (358), 106

David, Hebrew king (1013?–?973 B.C.), 546, 651^{13}

Dawson, Christopher (1889–), 375^7

Decius, emperor (249–51), In 4^8, 523^6, 645^{40}, App 7,^{11}

Decius (*al.* Decitius), Flavius, consul (529), 586–97

De Clercq, Victor Cyril (1913–), 48^2

Delehaye, Hippolyte (1859–1941), 228^2

Demetrius, bishop in (?) Egypt (*flor.* 260), 4

Demetrius, bishop of Philippi (533–6), 645

Demosthenes, Greek orator (384–322 B.C.), 116

Demosthenes, Flavius Theodorus Petrus, praetorian prefect of the East (529), 591–9

Denny, Edward (1853?–1928), 95^1

Denticulus, Licinius, Roman gambler (*flor.* 44 B.C.), 593^3

Deogratias, bishop of Carthage (454–?8). 598^{18}

Deuterius, African bishop (*flor.* 419), 362

Devil *or* Demon, 20, 39^5, 49 (II), 53, 59, 66^2, 67, 416, 418, 457, 483, 487, 651. *See* Satan. *See* Index of Subjects, s.v. devil *or* demon

Dexianus, bishop of Seleucia in Isauria (*flor.* 431), 406

Dexter, count of the private estates (387), 212

Diana: *see* Artemis

Didascalus, unidentified Jew (*flor.* 415). 344, 346

Didius, Titus, consul (98 B.C.), Gl s.v. *Lex Caecilia et Didia*

Dido, mythical Carthaginian queen, 646^{14}

Dill, Samuel, Sir (1844–1924), 137^2

Diocletianus, emperor (284–305), In^{9,43}, 6^1, 7^4, 13, 14, 15^7, 44^{2,4,10,15}, 62^2, 68^2, 156^1, 203^4, 313^1, 395^{10}, 414^6, 446, 515^{18}, 528^5, 641^{14}, App 10 (a)–(d),^{16,36}, Gl s.v. province

Diodorus, bishop of Tarsus (379–94), 182, 459^{28}, 542, 559

Dionysius, bishop in (?) Egypt (*flor.* 260), 4

Dionysius, master of the soldiery *or* master of the soldiers (c. 434), 415–16^{1n}, 417, 419

1260   PERSONS

Dionysius, Flavius, count (*flor.* 335), 73, 74
Dionysius Exiguus, Scythian monk (*flor.* 525), 52[4]
Dionysius Magnus, St, bishop of Alexandria (247?–?65), 4[5], 68[1], 189[2]
Dionysus, Graeco-Roman god, 651[8]
Dioscorus, anti-pope (530), In[43]
Dioscorus I, patriarch of Alexandria (444–51), 284[4], 449, 458–9, 470 (I, X), 481, 489, 524[14], 560, 562, Gl s.v. Monophysites
Dioscorus, Roman deacon (520), 556, 558
Dioscorus, praetorian prefect of the East (472), 516, 518, 520
Dioscorus (*al.* Dioscurus), Flavius, consul (442), 436
Diotimus, Flavius Pionius, proconsul of Africa (405), 294, 296
Dius, St, Cappadocian martyr (*ob. ante* 314 or 325), 568[2]
Dominator, vicar of Africa (398–9), 275
Domitianus, emperor (81–96), 1[5], 46[16], App 2,[4]
Domitianus, quaestor of the sacred palace (*c.* 434), 414
Domnus I, bishop of Antioch in Syria (269–74), 5[1]
Domnus II, patriarch of Antioch in Syria (442–9), 459
Donatianus, African bishop (*flor.* 419), 362
Donatus, Numidian bishop (*flor.* 330), 59
Donatus, proconsul of Africa (408), 305
Donatus Magnus, bishop of Negrene (*ante* 313), of Carthage (313–55), 17[1n,7], 19[8], 328, Gl s.v. Donatists
Dorotheus (*al.* Theodorus), bishop of Dodona (*flor.* 431), 406
Dorotheus, bishop of Marcianopolis (430–?4), 406
Dorotheus, bishop of Myrrhina (*flor.* 431), 406
Dorotheus, governor of Palaestina Prima (453), 484, 486–7[25]
Dorotheus, professor of law in Beirut (*flor.* 534), 639[9], 640[1]
Dracilianus, vicar of the East (326), 54, 56
Drummond, William (1585–1649), In[30]
Dulcitius, tribune and notary (412), 329[8]
Dvornik, František (1893–   ), 48[2]
Dynatus (*al.* Donatus), bishop of Nicopolis in Epirus Vetus (425?–?33), 406

Ecdicius, prefect of Egypt (362), 113, 121–2[1n]
Eleusius, unidentified bishop (*flor.* 431), 406
Elisha, Hebrew prophet (*ob. c.* 790 B.C.), 206[6]
Elizabeth II, British queen (1952–   ), 472[4]

Elpidius (*al.* Helpidius), count of the sacred consistory (449), 453–4, 457
Ennius, Quintus, Roman poet (239–169 B.C.), 139[8]
Enoch, Hebrew patriarch (*aet. inc. sed ante* 1200 B.C.), 313[1]
Ennodius, Magnus Felix, St, bishop of Pavia (511–21), 546
Entellus, mythological pugilist, 429[30]
Ephesius, Luciferian bishop (*flor.* 395), 254[2]
Ephraim, patriarch of Antioch in Syria (526–45), 635[1n,1]
Epictetus, bishop of Civitavecchia (*flor.* 355), 95
Epinicus, consular (474), 521
Epiphanius, St, bishop of Constantia (*olim* Salamis) in Cyprus (368/9–403), 52[29], 67[1,2,8,11,12], 159[84]
Epiphanius, patriarch of Constantinople (520–35), 560[18], 579–80, 637, 645[23], 615
Erastus, Thomas (1524–83), In[34]
Erythrius, praetorian prefect of the East (466, 472), 501–3, 513–15, 516[2], 517
Esther, unhistorical Persian queen, In 4
Eucherius (*al.* Eucerius, Eutherius, Euterius), Flavius, consul (381), 173–84
Euclio, dramatic character, 223[2]
Eudocia (*olim* Athenais), consort of Theodosius II (401?–60), 398
Eudocia, daughter of Valentinianus III (439?–*ob. post* 461), 435[4]
Eudoxia, Aelia, consort of Arcadius (*ob.* 404), 284[1n], 319[4]
Eudoxia, Licinia, consort of Valentinianus III (422–*ob. post* 462), 435[4]
Eudoxius, bishop of Germanicia in Augusta Euphratensis (330?–57), patriarch of Antioch in Syria (357–60), bishop of Constantinople (360–70), 103
Eudoxius, Flavius, praetorian prefect of the East (427 or 447), 393
Eudoxius, Flavius, consul (442), 436
Euhodius, African bishop (*flor.* 419), 362
Eulalius, anti-pope (418–19), In[48], 352–4[1n,1,2], 355[1n,4], 356–7[1n,1], 358[1n,2], 359[1n,4], 363[1n], 364–7[1n], 371[1n]
Eulogius, bishop of Terenuthis (*flor.* 431), 406
Eulogius, Asiatic presbyter (*flor.* 448), 447
Eulogius, secret-service agent (*flor.* 519), 551[4], 553
Eulogius, tribune and notary (449), 453–4
Eulogius, tribune and notary (520), 563
Eumalius (*al.* Eumelius), vicar of Africa (316), 27[1n]
Eunomius, bishop of Cyzicus (360–1), 542, Gl s.v. Eunomians
Eunomius, bishop of Nicomedia (449–?60), 470[61]

PERSONS

Euphemia, St, Chalcedonian martyr (*ob.* 307), 472 (III)
Euphemia, consort of Justinus I (*ob. ante* 527), 563[8], 630[6]
Euphemius, patriarch of Constantinople (489–95), 560[3]
Euphronius, patriarch of Antioch in Syria (330–2), 61 (III)
Euprepius, St, Arabian martyr (*ob.* 303), 410[2]
Eurichus (*al.* Euricus), Visigothic king (466–84), Tab[5]
Euripides, Greek dramatist (485?–?406 B.C.), 472[29]
Eurydicus, bishop in (?) Gaul (*flor.* 376), 161
Eusebius, bishop of Ancyra in Galatia Prima (*ante* 446–*ante* 458), 470 (I, III)
Eusebius, bishop of Aspona (*flor.* 431), 406
Eusebius, bishop of Beirut (*ante* 319), of Nicomedia (319–25, 329–39), of Constantinople (339–42), 50–51, 58[1n], 61[7,11], 71[2], 72[1n], 74
Eusebius, bishop of Clazomenae (*ante* 431–*post* 451), 406
Eusebius, bishop of Dorylaeum (448–51), 459, 470 (I, II), 479
Eusebius, bishop of Heraclea in Honorias (*flor.* 431), 406
Eusebius, bishop of Magnesia (*flor.* 431), 406
Eusebius, bishop of Nilopolis (*flor.* 431), 406
Eusebius, bishop of Pelusium (*ante* 431–*post* 457), 406
Eusebius, St, bishop of Vercelli (340?–55, 361–*post* 371), 93
Eusebius, father-in-law of Constantius II (*ob. post* 349), 106
Eusebius, chief of the sacred bedchamber (*flor.* 355), 95, 124[22]
Eusebius, Flavius, consul (359), 104
Eusebius Pamphili, bishop of Caesarea in Palaestina Prima (315?–?38), In[29,46], 2[1n,5-7,20], 3[1n,3], 4[1n,5], 5[1], 7[1n,1,2], 8[1n], 9[1n], 10[1n], 12[1n], 13[1n], 31[1n], 38[2], 42[1,4,5], 45, 46[26], 49[1,21,26], 53[12], 61, 64, 415[6], App 2, 9, 10 (a)
Eusignius (*al.* Euscinus), Flavius, praetorian prefect of Italy (386–7), 205
Eustathius, bishop of Beirut (451–8), 447, 456, 470 (I, III, V)
Eustathius, St, bishop of Beroea in Syria Prima (*ante* 323), patriarch of Antioch (324/5–c. 331), 61[1n,7-9,11,16]
Eustathius, praetorian prefect of the East (505–6), 541
Eustathius, Flavius, consul (421), 375 (I)
Eutherius, bishop of Stratonicia (*flor.* 431), 406

Eutherius, bishop of Tyana (*flor.* 431), 406
Eutherius (*al.* Euterius, Eucherius, Eucerius), Flavius, (?) urban prefect of Rome (367?–?75), 139
Eutropia, Galeria Valeria, mother-in-law of Constantinus I (*flor.* 332), 63[2]
Eutropius, praetorian prefect of the East (380/1), 171, 173, 175–6
Eutropius, consul (387), 212
Eutropius, consul (399), 246[1n,1]
Eutyches, Constantinopolitan archimandrite and heresiarch (378–?455), 448[1n], 449[1n], 453, 455, 459, 463[2], 469–70 (I), 476[1n], 477, 479–87, 489, 524 (II), 527, 542, 546, 569, 636–7, 645, Gl s.vv. Eutychians, Monophysites
Eutychianus, Flavius, praetorian prefect of the East (396–9, 404–5), 264, 268–9[1], 270–3, 277, 280, 287; consul (398), 268–73, 330[11]
Eutychus, secret-service agent (407), 301
Euzoius, Arian patriarch of Antioch in Syria (361–78), 71, 124 (IV)
Evagrius, praetorian prefect (?315, ?325, 326, ?329, 331, ?339), 23, 79–80
Evagrius Scholasticus, ecclesiastical historian (536?–*post* 594), 97[1]
Evodius (*al.* Eubodius), Flavius, consul (386), 205–10, 243
Ezra, Hebrew priest and scribe (*flor.* 458 B.C.), 173[11]

Facundus, bishop of Hermiane (*flor.* 550), 476[1n]
Facundus, Tettius, consul (336), 76
Falcidius, Publius, plebeian tribune (?40 B.C.), Gl s.v. *Lex Falcidia*
Farrer, Austin Marsden (1904–), 442[7]
Fausta, Flavia Maxima, consort of Constantinus I (306?–37), 63[2]
Faustinus (*al.* Faustus), bishop of Thuburbo Maius (*flor.* 314), 17[4]
Faustus, Luciferian priest (*flor.* 383), 195
Faustus, Anicius Acilius Glabrio, urban prefect of Rome (*ante* 423, 425, *ante* 438), 388
Felicitas, St, Roman martyr (*ob.* 162), 364[5]
Felix II, anti-pope (355–65), In[43], 95[1n,27], 102, 137[1n]
Felix III (II), St, pope (483–92), In[31], 527[1n], 544[1n], 550[9], 560[3], 562[14]
Felix, bishop of Aptunga (*flor.* 312), 17[1n], 21, 328
Felix, Numidian bishop (*flor.* 330), 59
Felix, Roman deacon (*flor.* 520), 558
Felix, urban prefect of Rome (398, ?412), 330
Felix, Flavius Constantius, consul (428), 394, 395
Felix, Furius, praetorian prefect (333–5), 76

Festus, Porcius, procurator of Judaea (55?–?6), 1[5], 5[1]
Festus, Rufius Postumius, consul (439), 430–31[12], 432–3
Fidentius, Donatist bishop (*flor.* 316), 25
Firmilianus, governor of Palaestina Prima (308), App 10 (e)
Firminus, praetorian prefect of Italy (449–52), 478
Firmus, bishop of Caesarea in Cappadocia Prima (*ante* 431–8), 406
Flacillus, Arian patriarch of Antioch in Syria (333 ?–?42), 74
Flavianus, bishop of Philippi (*flor.* 431), 406[1]
Flavianus, St, patriarch of Constantinople (447–9), 284[4], 448[1n], 449[1n], 455, 459, 463, 470 (I, II), 472 (I), 479, 524[1,14]
Flavianus, governor of Palaestina Prima (303), App 10 (a), (d)
Flavianus, Virius Nicomachus, vicar of Africa (376–8), 163; praetorian prefect of Italy (388–93), 230–31
Florentius, bishop of Pozzuoli (*c.* 355, 370–), 164
Florentius, Augustal prefect (384), 208
Florentius, consul (515), 544–5
Florentius, praetorian prefect of the East (428–9, 438–9, 445), 394–5, 429, 431–2, 437, 448
Florentius, Flavius, consul (361), 108–10
Florianus, consular of Venetia (368–73), 144
Florianus, count of the sacred largesses (447), 444
Florianus, vicar of Asia (377), 163
Florus, count of the private estates (531), 630
Florus, praetorian prefect of the East (381, 383), 184–5, 187
Fortuna, Roman goddess, 223
Fortunatus, bishop of Catania (*flor.* 515), 546
Francis II, Holy Roman emperor (1792–1806), Tab[5]
Francis Joseph I, Austrian emperor (1848–1916), In[44]
Fravitta (*al.* Fravitas, Flavita), patriarch of Constantinople (489), 560[3]
Frederick I Barbarossa, Holy Roman emperor (1152–90), Tab[5]
Frumentius, St, bishop of Aksum (*ob. c.* 383), 99
Fundanus, Gaius Minucius, proconsul of Asia (*flor.* 121), 2
Furius, Gaius, Roman magistrate (?183 B.C.), Gl s.v. *Lex Furia*

Gabriel, St, archangel, 546[3]
Gainas, master of the soldiers (*ob.* 400), 246[1]
Gaius, jurisconsult (*ob. c.* 180), 94[1], 133[1], 392[3,4], 598[3], 621[2], 640[1]
Gaius: *see* Caligula
Galerius, emperor (305–11), In[17], 7–8[1n], 10[1n], 13[1n], 14[1n], 17[1n], 44[4], 67[37], 106[5], App 10 (b), (d), (f),[16,37,49,52,56,59]
Gallicanus, Flavius, consul (330), 60
Gallicus, Numidian bishop (*flor.* 330), 59
Gallienus, emperor (253–68), Tab[2], 4, App 8 (a)
Gallio, Lucius Junius Annaeus, proconsul of Achaea (*c.* 52), In 4
Gallus, emperor (251–3), App *ante* 1
Gallus, Lucius Caninius, suffect consul (2 B.C., Gl s.v. *Lex Fufia et Caninia*
Gallus: *see* Constantius Gallus
Gamaliel VI, Jewish patriarch (*ob.* 425), 341
Gaudentius, magistrian (*flor.* 333), 67
Gaudentius, Ursinian cleric (*flor.* 371), 152, 154
Gavin, Frank Stanton Burns (1890–), 550[2]
Gelasius I, St, pope (492–6), In[31], 95[1], 375[7], 560[16], 562[14]
Geminus, Gaius Fufius, suffect consul (2 B.C.), Gl s.v. *Lex Fufia et Caninia*
Genius, Roman deity, 242, 255[3]
Genius Augusti, 242[7]
Genius Caesaris, 255[3]
Gennadius, Augustal prefect (396), 257
Geisericus (*al.* Gensericus *et al.*), Vandal king (428–77), 646[1,9,11]
George, St, patron saint of England (*aet. inc.*), 98[15]
Georgius, Arian bishop of Laodicea in Syria Prima (335–*ante* 363), 61 (III)
Georgius, Arian patriarch of Alexandria (357–61), 98–9, 111, 113, 124 (I, III)
Georgius, Cyrestene deacon (*flor.* 520), 559
Georgius, proconsul of Africa (425), 389, 390
Gerasimus, bishop in (?) Gaul (*flor.* 376), 161
Germanus, St, bishop of Capua (518–*c.*41), 558
Gibbon, Edward (1737–94), In[2], 98[15], 218[11], 411[3], 505[1], App[1]
Gildo, count of Africa (385–98), 293[1n]
Glycerius, emperor (473–4), Tab[5], 519, 520
God, Tab[5], In[28,29,31,32], 1[3], 3[24–6], 4[2], 7, 11[1n], 12[2], 18[1n], 20, 21[1n], 22–4, 31[1n], 38–40, 44–7, 48 (II, III), 49 (I, II), 50–4, 58–9, 61–2[11], 63–4, 66–71, 73, 75, 76[3], 81[4], 85–6, 92–3, 98–9, 117, 122[14], 124 (III, IV), 125–6[5], 127[7], 159, 164, 166–7[1n,5], 168[1], 172, 176[10], 184, 188, 194–5, 203, 206[7], 212[1], 215,

PERSONS

223², 230, 247, 280, 288–99, 301, 308, 313¹, 315, 324, 335, 343, 350–51⁶, 354, 360–61, 367–8, 372–3, 375 (III), 375⁷, 385–6¹ⁿ, 397–400, 405, 409, 411–12, 413³, 414⁷, 415 (II), 416, 418, 423, 427, 429, 442⁷, 443, 445, 447–51, 453–5, 458–9, 461, 464, 466–9, 470 (I–III, VIII), 472 (II), 475, 477, 479–88, 489⁴⁰, 495¹⁴, 496, 498², 502, 508, 516, 519, 521, 522⁴, 523¹, 524 (I), 526–7, 530, 542, 545–8, 550–1, 553, 555⁴, 558–9, 562, 567, 569, 573, 575, 577, 579, 590, 598¹³, 603, 605, 606¹⁸, 609, 612, 614, 617, 619–20, 629–30⁸, 633², 636–9, 641 (I), 642, 644⁶, 645, 646 (I), 648, 651, App¹¹
  Father, 47¹ⁿ, 49 (II), 50, 67, 86, 95⁴³, 103, 131¹ⁿ, 159, 167, 182, 218¹¹, 422⁷, 449, 481, 527, 542, 546, 548⁵, 561–2, 569, 636–7, 645, Gl s.vv. Aetians, Anomoeans, Arians, Heteroousians, Homoiousians, Homoousians, Marcellians
  Son, 44, 47¹ⁿ, 49 (II), 50, 53¹⁸, 67, 75⁴², 103, 131¹ⁿ, 159, 167, 173, 182, 218¹¹, 335, 422⁷, 481, 483–7, 527, 542, 546, 548⁵, 553, 561–2, 569, 636–7, 645, Gl s.vv. Aetians, Arians, Heteroousians, Homoiousians, Homoousians, Marcellians
  Only-Begotten, 49 (II), 69
  Only-Begotten Son of God, 524 (I), 527, 569, 636–7, 645
  Spirit 49 (II), 330¹ⁿ
    All-Holy, 49 (II)
    Divine, 46, 554
    Holy, 49 (II), 53, 71, 95⁴³, 159, 167, 173, 182, 400, 422⁷, 460, 481, 483–7, 524 (I), 527, 542, 546, 555⁴, 561–2, 569, 577, 636–7, 645, Gl s.vv. Aetians, Enthusiasts, Semi-Arians
    Vivifying, 49 (II)
    as Comforter, 156¹
    as Holy Ghost, 519¹
    as Paraclete, 156¹, Gl s.v. Montanists
  Trinity, In²⁶, 49 (II, III)²⁸, 53⁷, 67¹⁷, 75⁴², 159, 167, 173, 182, 292, 325, 411³, 418, 422⁷, 470 (VI), 483, 487, 519, 524 (I), 527, 542, 550⁷, 551¹ⁿ, 552¹ⁿ, 553–4, 556, 560–2, 569, 575, 579, 617, 636–7, 641⁴, 642¹¹, 645, Gl s.vv. Anomoeans, Arians, Monarchians. *See in* Index of Subjects, s.v. Godhead, Persons in Godhead
God, All-Overseeing, 53
  Almighty, In³¹, 19–20, 22, 24, 39, 52, 53¹⁵, 63, 171, 173, 195, 251, 255, 294, 299, 301, 362, 371, 385, 400, 403, 464, 475, 482, 489, 495–6, 503, 519, 544, 546, 578, 590, 599, 617, 628, 638, 645, 646 (I)
  Benevolent, 579–80, 588, 600
  Great, 15, 17, 46, 400, 527, 612, 650–51
  Greatest, 46, 400
  Highest, 45, 154, 307
  Holy, 11, 44
  Holy, Supreme, 11
  Living, 561–2
  Mightiest, 44
  Most High, In²³,³¹, 19
  Most Holy, 19
  Most Powerful, 19
  Omnipotent, 18, 46, 480
  One and Highest, 173
  Saviour, 44–5, 49 (II), 51, 54⁸, 64
  Supreme, 11, 24, 39, 44, 59, 125, 203, 313¹
  Supreme, Holy, 11
  as All-Benefactor and Saviour, 52⁵⁸
  as Almighty, 46–7, 49 (II), 53, 85–6, 99, 103, 412, 423, 449, 453, 455, 457, 469, 472 (II), 483–4, 486
  as Alpha and Omega, 159²⁵
  as Author, Supreme, 173
  as Being, Supreme, 648⁶
    True, 45
  as Clemency, Divine, 411 (III), 520
  as Creator, 648⁶
  as Deity, 16, 47, 67³⁵, 159¹⁶, 167, 415 (II), 429⁹, 617
  as Demiurge, 50, 122¹³, 648, Gl s.v. Gnostics
  as Divinity, 12, 15–17, 24, 46, 49 (II, III), 50, 61 (II), 63, 76, 86, 90 (I), 104, 164, 182, 203, 211, 289, 400, 414, 422, 440, 442–3, 472 (I), 475, 477, 480¹⁰, 483, 501, 519, 551, 561, 563, 645
  as Divinity, Celestial, 415
  Eternal, 207, 461
  Gracious, 20
  Heavenly, 22, 557
  Highest, 302, 556
  Most High, 19
  Most Sacred, 274
  Supernal, 386, 393, 429, 442
  Supreme, 24, 39
  as Eternity, 562
  as Eternity, Supernal, 563
  as First and Last, 159
  as God and Lord, Holy, True, Just, and Supreme, 59
  as God and Saviour, Great, 47⁷³
  as God of God, 173, 569
  as God our Saviour, 398
  as God the Word, 457, 527, 542, 569, 636–7, 645
  as Highest, 49 (I)
  as Immortal, 3

PERSONS

as Jehovah, In²³, 648⁶
as Judge, 49 (I)
as King, 49 (II), 159
as King, Great, 159
    Supernal, 159³⁵
as Light from Light, 173
as Logos, In²⁹, 67¹⁶, 71, 75⁴², 122, 159³,
    Gl s.vv. Apollinarians, Paulianists
as Lord, In⁸¹, 44, 48 (I), 49–50, 67, 159,
    206⁶, 223², 325, 410, 427¹ⁿ, 481, 483¹⁵,
    484, 489⁵⁰, 543, 561-2, 641⁴, 645, 651
as Lord God, 543 (II), 575, 579, 606,
    614, 629, 642, 646 (I), 651
as Lord God of Heaven, In²³
    of Israel, In²³
as Lord and God, 645
as Lord and Saviour, 49 (II)
as Lord the Saviour, 20
as Majesty, 519–20, 561
as Majesty, Celestial, 617
    Divine, 53, 475, 520
    Eternal, 562
    Ever-Excellent, 350
    Highest, 509
    Supernal, 429, 520, 546, 549,
        564
as Name, Supernal, 190
as Power, Divine, In²⁹, 45, 52, 223, 480⁴,
    484, 645
    Holiest Heavenly, 16
    Supernal, 20
as Providence, 85, 397, 416
    All-Seeing, 85
    Divine, In⁸¹, 17, 47, 50⁴⁴,
        51-3, 75, 77, 90 (II),
        152-3, 411 (III), 449
    Fairest and Divine, 47
    Heavenly, 20
as Saviour, 20, 45³, 47, 48¹⁹, 49 (II), 52,
    63, 73, 86³³, 462
as Virtue, Divine, 414
as Word, 122, 159, 484
as Word, Divine, Gl s.v. Apollinarians
as Word God, 527⁸⁷, 542
as Word of Life, 71
Christ, In²¹,³¹,³², 1², 4², 7¹³, 17³, 20,
    48 (I), 49 (I, II), 50, 54⁸, 64⁵,
    67, 73, 75⁴², 95⁴³, 103¹ⁿ, 119⁵, 159,
    166⁴, 167⁵, 173, 220⁶,¹⁰, 373, 385,
    395⁷, 398⁶, 399, 403, 418, 422⁶,
    442⁷, 448¹ⁿ, 464¹ⁿ, 470¹², 471¹,
    472⁴, 483–7, 503³, 523¹, 524 (I),
    527¹ⁿ,⁸⁴, 542, 553, 555⁴, 569,
    579⁹, 614⁷, 636–7, 645, 646⁸,
    648⁶, App 2, 7, 10 (f), ⁵³, Gl s.vv.
    Apollinarians, Eutychians, Gnostics, Manichaeans, Marcellians,
    Monophysites, Montanists, Nestorians, Paulianists, Photinians, Theopaschites

Christ, Omnipotent, 475
Christ Jesus, 166⁴
Christ our God, 651
Christ our God and Lord, 548
Christ our Lord, 543 (I), 553
Christ the Lord, 466
Christ our Saviour, 398⁶
Christ the Saviour, 20, 125, 472 (II)
God and Saviour Christ, 527¹⁰⁴
Lord and Saviour Christ, 469, 481,
    485–6, 559
Lord Christ, 615
Lord Christ our God, 579
Lord God and Saviour Christ, 50
Saviour Christ, 393, 449, 483–7
Jesus, In²³, 7¹³, 12³³, 17³, 42⁵, 52¹⁶,³⁷,⁵¹,
    53¹², 54⁶, 75⁴², 116¹³, 117¹⁸, 122,
    156¹, 159²⁷,³⁴, 169³, 206⁶, 220¹¹,
    313¹, 397¹, 411³, 442⁷, 457¹³,
    472⁴, 483, 485, 487, 543 (III),
    569⁵, App 2,⁵³, Gl s.v. Nestorians
as Bambino, 397¹
as Lord, In⁸¹, 20, 34⁵, 52, 67, 209,
    220, 325, 372¹, 375⁷, 457, 487¹⁴,
    509, 543, 645
as Saviour, In⁴³, 42⁵, 53–4, 61 (I), 75⁵³,
    103, 159²⁷, 167¹ⁿ, 370¹, 457, 484,
    527, 545–6, App 10 (a), (f)
as Saviour and Lord, 636
Jesus Christ, In²¹,³⁶, 7¹³, 41, 75⁴²,
    95⁴³, 156¹, 159, 442⁷, 486, 527,
    577⁵, 615¹ⁿ, 636
God and Saviour Jesus Christ, 524 (I)
God and Saviour Jesus Christ, Great,
    642, 651
Lord Jesus Christ, In³¹, 472³, 527,
    542, 546, 550, 561-2, 569, 615,
    636-7, 639, 645-6, App¹¹
Lord God Jesus Christ, 646 (I)
Lord God and Saviour Jesus Christ,
    642, 651
Lord and God Jesus Christ, 642
Lord and Master Jesus Christ, 486
Lord and Saviour Jesus Christ, 472
    (I), 483–5, 487, 636
Saviour Jesus Christ, 445, 527, 645, 648

Godefroy, Denys (Gothofredus, Dionysius) (1549–1621), Gl s.v. *Corpus Iuris Civilis*
Gordianus I, emperor (238), 472⁴
Gordianus II, emperor (238), 472⁴
Gracchus, Gaius Sempronius, plebeian tribune (123–122 B.C.), 141³, 646¹⁴
Gratianus, emperor (375–83), In²⁶, 135,
    137-43, 145-6; 149–50, 152-5, 157,
    159–70, 171², 172-7, 179–94, 196,
    198-9, 201, 203³, 204–5¹ⁿ, 206, 208–10,
    213, 215, 217, 220⁹, 243, 278¹ⁿ, 288,
    331⁴, 375¹ⁿ, 429³¹, 442¹ⁿ, 488

PERSONS 1265

Gratianus, Joannes, Italian monk and canonist (*flor.* 1148), Gl s.v. *ius canonicum*
Gratus, count of the sacred consistory and master of the secretarial bureau of the records (518), 549–50, 560
Graves, Robert Ranke (1895–), In[26]
Greenidge, Abel Hendy Jones (1865–1906), 65[13]
Grégoire, Henri (1881–), 47[1]
Gregorius I, St, pope (590–604), 52[2], 297[3], 330[2], 442[7]
Gregorius VII, St, pope (Hildebrand) (1073–85), 95[62]
Gregorius XIII, pope (1572–85), In[52], Gl s.v. *Corpus Iuris Canonici*
Gregorius, bishop of Elvira (357?–92), 195
Gregorius, St, bishop of Nyssa (371–94), 182, 470 (I)
Gregorius, jurisconsult (*flor.* 294), 578[5]
Gregorius Illuminator, St, patriarch of Armenia (302–?32), 106[6]
Gregorius Nazianzenus, St, bishop of Constantinople (380–1), 470 (I)
Gundobadus (*al.* Gundebadus), Burgundian king (474–516), In[2]

Habib, Telzehan deacon (*flor.* 323), 42[1n]
Hadrianus, emperor (117–38), In 1, 1[3], 2, 3[1n,30,31], 4[2], 54[6], 67[37], 76[3], 150[3], 223[3], 483[15], 523[2], 578[5], 590[1n], 631[1], 641[14], App[6], Gl s.v. praetor
Hadrianus I, pope (772–95), Tab[5]
Hadrianus, praetorian prefect of Italy (401–5), 281, 288–90, 293
Haines, Charles Reginald (1856?–1935), 3[4]
Haman, unhistorical Persian premier, 95[34], 303[1,3,4]
Hatch, Edwin (1835–89), In[52], 107[8]
Hecebolius, Edessan official (362 or 363), 123[1]
Hecebolius, Greek sophist (*ob. post* 363), 123[1]
Hegesippus, St, Greek theologian (*ob. post* 174), App 2
Helena, Flavia Julia, St, mother of Constantinus I (*ob. c.* 328), 54[6], 303[3], 525[1]
Helena, Flavia Maximiana, consort of Julianus II (*ob.* 360), 111[11]
Helias, (*al.* Elias), bishop of Caesarea in Cappadocia Prima (*flor.* 520), 557
Helios, Greek god, 117[17], 122
Helladius, bishop of Adramytium (*flor.* 431), 406
Helladius, bishop of Caesarea in Cappadocia Prima (379–94), 182
Helladius, bishop of Ptolemais in Phoenicia Prima (*flor.* 431), 406
Helladius, bishop of Tarsus (*c.* 430–4), 406, 414, 415 (I), 418
Hellanicus, bishop of Rhodes (*flor.* 431), 406

Helpidius, (?) deputy of praetorian prefect (321–9), 34, 37, 41
Hemerius, Flavius, catholicus in Egypt (*flor.* 337), 78
Henry VIII, English king (1509–47), 641[8]
Hephaestus, Greek god, 67[12]
Hera, Greek goddess, 411[3]. *See* Juno
Heraclas, St, bishop of Alexandria (231?–?246), 68[1]
Heraclianus, unidentified priest (*flor.* 520), 561
Heraclianus, count of Africa (410–15), 323, 338
Heraclidas, bishop of Oxyrhynchus (*flor.* 384), 195
Heraclides, procurator of imperial estate (*flor.* 313), 15
Heraclius, emperor (610–41), 538[3]
Herasius, proconsul of Africa (381), 183
Herculanus, Flavius Bassus, consul (452), 478
Hercules (*al.* Heracles), Graeco-Roman god, 2, 9[6]
Herculius, praetorian prefect of Illyricum (410–12), 321
Hermeas, Persian Manichaean (*flor.* 300), Gl s.v. Manichaeans
Hermes, Greek god, 116, 223[2]
Hermogenes, master of the offices (531–5), 631, 638
Hermogenianus, praetorian prefect (*flor.* 301), 6
Hermogenianus, jurisconsult (*flor.* 365), 578[5]
Herodes Agrippa I, Jewish king (41–4), 7[3], 487[14]
Herodotus, Greek historian (485?–?425 B.C.), 116
Heros, bishop of Arles (409?–411/412), 350[1n]
Hesiodus, Greek poet (*flor.* ? 8th cent. B.C.), 116
Hesperius, Decimus Hilarianus, proconsul of Africa (376 or 380), 160[2]; praetorian prefect of Italy (377–80), 160, 165–6
Heuresius (*al.* Euresius), Asian bishop (*flor.* 395), 254[2]
Hezekiah, Jewish king (720?–?692 B.C.), In[23]
Hibas: *see* Ibas
Hierius, vicar of Africa (395), 250
Hierius, Flavius, praetorian prefect of the East (425–8, 432), 413; consul (427), 393
Hieronymus Sophronius, Eusebius (Jerome), St, Pannonian monk (340?–420), In[54], 105[2], 150[1], 167[7], 330[1n], 350[1n], 442[7], 629[6], 648[6]
Hilarianus, master of the offices (470), 511
Hilarius, St, archbishop of Arles (429–49), 442

PERSONS

Hilarius, St, bishop of Poitiers (353?–6, 360–7/8), 104^{1n}, 470 (I)
Hilarius, chief of office staff (*flor.* 316), 25
Hilarius, notary and papal legate (515), 546
Himelco, Felix, praetorian prefect of Italy (473), 519, 520
Himerius, bishop of Nicomedia (*flor.* 431), 406
Hinschius, Paul (1835–98), In^{39}
Hippolytus, St, anti-pope (217–35), In^{43}, 95^1, 97^4
Hippolytus, St, aporcyphal Roman martyr (*ob. c.* 250), 397^1
Hippolytus, dramatic character, 397^1
Hisac (*al.* Isaac), converted Jew (*flor.* 378), 164
Hobbes, Thomas (1589–1679), Tab^5
Homerus, Greek poet (*flor.* ? 9th cent. B.C.), 116, 150^1
Honoria, Justa Grata, sister of Valentinianus III (417?–*post* 452), 435^4
Honorius, emperor (393–423), Tab^3, In 3, 188^8, 21^{1n}, 62^2, 120^1, 205–10, 235, 241–83, 285–96, 298–324, 326–7, 328^{1n}, 329–50, 352–60, $361^{1,5}$, 362^8, $363^{1n,1,3}$, 364–6, 368–72, 373^1, 375–83, $387^{1,9}$, 443^{15}, 476, 629
Horatius Flaccus, Quintus, Roman poet (65–8 B.C.), In 4, 150^1
Hormisdas, St, pope (514–23), 544–7, $548^{1,9}$, 549, 550^{1n}, 551, $552^{1n,3}$, $553^{1n,4}$, 554, 556–8, 560–1, 562^{1n}, $563-4^{1n,1}$
Hormisdas, praetorian prefect of the East (448–50), 445^2, 446^1
Hosius (*al.* Ossius), bishop of Córdoba (296–357), In^{14}, 15, 16^8, 35, 47^4, 100^{1n}
Hunericus (*al.* Hugnericus, Hunerix), Vandal king (477–84), 7^3, 646^9
Hypatia, Greek philosopher (*ob.* 415), 98^{14}, 228^1, 347^{1n}, 488^2
Hypatia, unidentified widow (*ob. c.* 455), 488
Hypatianus, bishop of Heraclea in Thrace (356–65), 131^{1n}
Hypatius, bishop of Ephesus (*c.* 520–*post* 536), 645
Hypatius, aide to master of the soldiers (*c.* 434), 420
Hypatius, Augustal prefect (383, 392), 235
Hypatius, master of the soldiers in the East (520), $559^{1n,8}$
Hypatius, Flavius, consul (359), 104; praetorian prefect of Italy (382–3), 186, 188, 190
Hyrcanus I, Jewish king (134–104 B.C.), 76^3

Ibas (*al.* Hibas), bishop of Edessa (436–49, 451–67), 447, 450^2, 456, $459^{12,14}$, 542^{17}

Iconius, bishop of Gortyna (*flor.* 431), 406
Iddo, grandfather of Zechariah (q.v.), 159^{34}
Ignatius, St, bishop of Antioch in Syria (67?–?108), 75^{42}
Indacus, bishop of Corycus (*flor.* 503), 540
Ingentius, Ziquensian decurion (*flor.* 314), 21
Innocentius I, St, pope (401–17), 285^6, 295^{1n}, 350^{1n}
Innocentius III, pope (1198–1216), In^{31}, 181^6
Irenaeus, St, bishop of Lyon (177?–201/2), 167^{1n}
Irenaeus, count (431–6, bishop of Tyre (444–8), 401, 426, 445–6, 459^{14}
Irenianus (*al.* Herennianus, Berrenianus, Serenianus), bishop of Myra (*flor.* 431), 406
Irnerius, Italian glossator (1050?–?1130), In^2
Isaiah, Hebrew prophet (760?–?701 B.C.), 645
Ischyras, bishop of Maerotis (*flor.* 343), $68^{5,7}$, 78
Isidorus, St, archbishop of Seville (599–636), 476^{1n}
Isidorus, Flavius Anthemius (praetorian prefect of Illyricum (424), 384; praetorian prefect of the East (431, 435–6), 410^1, 423–6; consul (436), 425, 428
Isidorus Mercator, French (?) literary forger (*flor.* 850), 472^{1n}, 476^{1n}
Isis, Egyptian goddess, 111^4, 122, Gl s.v. Ophitans
Isocrates, Greek orator (436–338 B.C.), 116

Jacob, Hebrew patriarch (*flor.* ?1650 B.C.), 399^3
Jacobus: *see* James
James, St, apostle and bishop of Jerusalem (*ob.* 44), 487^{14}
James, St, apostle and bishop of Jerusalem (*ob.* 62), 487^{14}
James I, English king (1603–25), In^{30}, 64^{21}, 577^9
James, unidentified archimandrite (449), 452
Januarius, Numidian bishop (*flor.* 330), 59
Jehoiada, Hebrew priest (*ob. ante* 800 B.C.), 159^{34}
Jerome: *see* Hieronymus Sophronius, Eusebius, St
Joannes I, St, pope (523–6), 567^{1n}
Joannes II, St, pope (533–5), 553^4, 636^{1n}, 645
Joannes XII, pope (956–64), Tab^5
Joannes I, bishop of Augustopolis in Palaestina Tertia (*flor.* 431), 406

PERSONS 1267

Joannes I, patriarch of Antioch in Syria (429–42), 401[12], 402, 404, 406, 409, 411 (II, III), 412, 414, 415 (II), 416, 417[3], 418[1n], 419–20, 427
Joannes II, patriarch of Alexandria (496–505), 542
Joannes II, patriarch of Constantinople (518–20), 549, 554, 558
Joannes, bishop of Aureliopolis (*flor.* 431), 406
Joannes, bishop of Damascus (*flor.* 431), 406
Joannes, bishop of Hephaestum (*ante* 431–49), 406
Joannes, bishop of Mytilene (*flor.* 431), 406
Joannes, bishop of Proconnesus (*flor.* 431), 406
Joannes, bishop of Sycamamazon (*flor.* 431), 406
Joannes, bishop of Theodosiopolis in Osrhoëne (*flor.* 448), 447
Joannes, unidentified bishop and papal legate (*flor.* 520), 558, 560–61, 563
Joannes, Scythian monk (*flor.* 519), 551–2
Joannes, Syrian monk (*flor.* 507/18), 543[1n,4]
Joannes, emperor (423–5), 387[1n,1]
Joannes, consul (456), 490, 491[9]
Joannes, count of the sacred largesses (429–31), 405[7], 406, 407[6], 408
Joannes, imperial decurion (*flor.* 452), 481
Joannes, praetorian prefect of Italy (412–13, 421), 332
Joannes, praetorian prefect of the East (531–3, 534–41), 620–9, 633–4, 648, 652
Joannes Archaph (*al.* Arcaph), bishop of Memphis (*flor.* 335), 70
Joannes of Egea, heretical priest (*flor.* 483), 542
Joannes of Ephesus, Monophysite historian (*flor.* 530), 630[8]
Joannes: *see* Chrysostomus, Joannes; John the Baptist; St; John the Divine, St
John the Baptist, St, Jewish reformer (4 B.C. ?–?A.D. 26), 159[34]
John the Divine, St, apostle (*ob.* ?100), 46[16], 159[21], 519[1], 568, 577[6,8,9,13]
John: *see* Joannes
Jordanes, consul (470), 510
Josaphat, St, unhistorical Indian King, 28[15]
Joseph, Hebrew patriarch (1680?–?1570 B.C.), 206[6]
Joseph, St, spouse of Blessed Virgin Mary (*ob. post* 9), 223[2]
Joseph of Arimathaea, St, Judaeo-Christian Sanhedrinist (*flor.* 29), App[53]
Jovianus, emperor (363–4), In[46], 116[1n], 124–30, 148[1]
Jovinianus, heretical monk (*ob. ante* 409,) 330
Jovinus, Flavius, consul (367), 135

Jovius, praetorian prefect of Italy (409), 315–18
Judas Iscariot, apostle (*ob. c.* 29), 543 (II), 579[7], 614[10]
Jugurtha, Numidian king (118–106 B.C.), 19[22]
Julia, daughter of Augustus (39 B.C.–A.D. 14), 46[16]
Julian: *see* Salvius Julianus Aemilianus
Julianus II Apostata, emperor (361–3), In[18,43,46], 43[5], 91, 93[1n], 95[41], 97, 98[15], 101–2, 107–8, 111–23, 124 (II), 125[1n], 126[1], 127[1n,7], 148[1n,1,2,6], 158[1n], 168[1], 205[1n], 208[3], 293, 393[1], 397[1], 606[20], Gl. s.v. Galileans
Julianus, bishop of Cos (448–58), 482[6]
Julianus, bishop of Larissa in Syria Secunda (*flor.* 431), 406
Julianus, bishop of Sofia (*flor.* 431), 406
Julianus, count of the East (*ob.* 363), 111[24], 127[2], 128
Julianus, praetorian prefect of the East (530–1), 601–15, 619
Julianus, Anicius, proconsul of Africa (297 or 302), 156[1]
Julianus, Julius, praetorian prefect of the East (316–24), 25
Julianus, Quintus Sentius Fabricius, proconsul of Africa (412–14), 337–8
Julianus, Sextius Rusticus, proconsul of Africa (371–3), 158
Julius I, St, pope (337–52), 94[1], 95[25], 482[3]
Julius, secret-service agent (407), 301
Juno, Roman goddess, In[26]. *See* Hera
Juppiter (*al.* Jupiter), Roman god, In[26], 9[8], 54[6], 223[2], 483[15], Gl s.v. flamen Dialis. *See* Zeus
Justina, consort of Valentinianus I (*ob.* 388), 205[1n]
Justinianus I Magnus, St, emperor (527–65), In 1, 2[18,43,50], 1[5], 3[34], 4[2], 16[1n], 26[1], 32[9], 34[5], 65[6], 94[1], 114[2], 204[3,5], 212[1n], 369[4], 375[7], 392[3,4], 426[1n], 436[1n], 463[5], 470[70], 476[1n], 483[21], 491[7], 505[1], 515[1n,5], 523[5], 525[3], 538[4], 544[1n], 549[1n], 550–3, 555[1n,3], 560[18], 561–4, 567–652, Gl s.vv. *Codex Iustinianianus; Codex Theodosianus; Corpus Iuris Civilis; Digesta Iustiniani; Institutiones Iustiniani; Novellae Iustiniani;* surety
Justinus I, emperor (518–27), 530[1n], 531[1n], 542[1n], 549, 550[1n,1,2], 552[2–4], 554–60, 561[1,2,9], 562[1,2,5,6,8,12], 563[1,7,8], 564[1n,1,2], 565, 567–8, 575[5], 604[8], 630[6], 649
Justinus II, emperor (565–78), In[3], Gl s.v. *Novellae Iustiniani*
Justinus Martyr, St, Greek apologist (*ob. c.* 165), In[46], 2, 3[1n], 34[5]

1268   PERSONS

Juvenalis, bishop (421-51) and patriarch (451-8) of Jerusalem, 406, 451[1], 458, 460, 470 (I, III, VI), 483-4, 486-7

Kemp, Eric Waldram (1915-), 181[5]
Kidd, Beresford James (1864-1948), 1[5], 5[1], 94[1], App 7

Laban, Hebrew patriarch (*flor.* ?1700 B.C.), 223[2]
Labienus, Titus, Roman orator (*ob. c.* 7), 382[1]
Lactantius, Lucius Caelius Firmianus, Latin theologian (*flor.* 320), In[14], 11[1n,3], 12[1n], 44[10], 67[37], 167[11], 212[1], App 9, 10 (a)
Lagus, father of Ptolemaeus I (*flor.* 367 B.C.), 122
Lampadius, Flavius, consul (530), 601-17, 619-30, 634
Lampetius, Cappadocian priest and heresiarch (*flor.* 460), Gl s.v. Enthusiasts
Lampon (*al.* Dialampon), imperial auditor (375), 159
Lar Familiaris, Roman god, 223[2], 242
Laocoon, mythological priest, 614[10]
Largus, proconsul of Africa (418-19), 366-7
Latourette, Kenneth Scott (1884-), In[40]
Latronianus, Domitius, corrector of Sicily (313-14), 18
Laurentius, anti-pope (498, 501-5), In[43]
Lazarus, bishop of Aix (409?-11/12), 350[1n]
Leo I, emperor (457-74), In[15], 492-8, 500-3, 506-19, 520[2], 521, 561, 624[3], 646[10], Gl s.v. *Lex Leoniana*
Leo II, emperor (474), 521
Leo I Magnus, St, pope (440-61), In 4, 203[1], 440, 442, 459[1], 461-4, 468, 470 (I, IV, VII, VIII), 471[1n], 472 (I), 473[1n], 475, 476[1n], 479, 482, 484, 514, 542, 546, 551, 561
Leo III, St, pope (795-816), Tab[5], 211[1], 492[1]
Leo XII, pope (1823-29), 211[1]
Leo XIII, pope (1878-1903), In[31,44], 76[4]
Leonitius, unidentified official (357), 101
Leontius, Novatian bishop in Rome (*flor.* 387), 370[1]
Leontius, Scythian monk (*flor.* 519), 551-2
Leontius, Ursinian cleric (*flor.* 371), 152-3
Leontius, praetorian prefect of the East (503 or 504), 540
Leontius, urban prefect of Constantinople (435), 422[2]
Levi, Hebrew patriarch (*flor.* ? 1600 B.C.), 399[3]

Libanius, Flavius, governor of Euphratesia (*c.* 434), 420
Liberius, pope (352-66), 93[1n], 95, 101[1n], 102[1], 137[1n], 637[7]
Licinius, emperor (307-24), In[17], 7, 9[1n], 11[1n,3], 12, 13[1], 14[1n], 21, 23, 28[8], 29[2], 38[2], 41[5], 42, 44[4,5], 45[1n,3,6,7], 46[1n,5,12,13,24], 47[5,8,9,13,14], 48[1n,3,19], 49[18], 50[6,12,20], 54[9], 106[5], App 10 (f)
Licinius Caesar, (315-26), 29-30
Limenius, Ulpius, consul (349), 89
Lincoln, Abraham (1809-65), Gl s.v. manumission
Livius, Titus, Roman historian (59 B.C.-A.D. 17), 95[1]
Lollianus, Quintus Flavius Maesius (*al.* Messius) Egnatius, consul (355), 96
Longinianus, prefect of Egypt (341-3), 81
Lucianus, Donatist bishop (*flor.* 316), 25
Lucianus, unidentified bishop (*flor.* 451), 475
Lucifer, bishop of Cagliari (353?-?70), 195[1n,5,6], Gl s.v. Luciferians
Lucius, Alexandrian martyr (*ob. ante* 161), App[6]
Lucius, Arian patriarch of Alexandria (373-8), 124, 124 (III, IV)[2], 147[5]
Lucius, consul (413), 335-6
Luke, St, evangelist (*ob. ante* ?100), 116
Lupicinus, Flavius, consul (367), 135
Lutharis, unidentified heretic (*flor. ante* 505), 542
Lysanias, governor of Osrhoëne (*c.* 323), 42[1n]
Lysias, Greek orator (459?-?380 B.C.), 116
Lysimachus, Macedonian king in Asia Minor and the Balkans (306-281 B.C.), 48[19]

Macarius, St, bishop of Jerusalem (311?-33), 54, 63
Macarius, bishop of Pharan (Mt Sinai), (451?-?3), 475, 479
Macarius, Egyptian priest (*flor.* 335), 68[7], 78[2]
Maccabees, Jewish patriots (167-134 B.C.), 23[2], 95[34]
Macedonius I, Arian bishop of Constantinople (342-60), 542, Gl s.v Semi-Arians
Macedonius II, patriarch of Constantinople (496-511), 543 (II), 560[3]
Macedonius, bishop of Mopsuestia (325?-?59), 95[22]
Macedonius, curator of the imperial household (531), 630
Macedonius, master of the offices (382-3), 288[15]
MacGregor, Geddes (1909-), 95[43]
Macrianus, emperor (260-1), 4[1]

PERSONS 1269

Macrobius, Ambrosius Theodosius, Afro(?)-Roman antiquarian (*flor.* 400), In⁵⁴
Magi, three legendary kings (*flor.* 4 B.C.), 220¹¹, 223², 313¹
Magna Mater: *see* Cybele
Magnentius, emperor (350–3), 90², 95
Magnus, consul (460), 500
Magnus, Flavius Anastasius Paulus Probus Moschianus Probus, consul (518), 549
Magnus, silentiary (448), 448²
Majorianus, emperor (457–61), Tab⁵, 478, 496–7, 499–500
Majorinus, Donatist bishop of Carthage (312–?13), 17ⁱⁿ,⁵
Mamertinus, Flavius Claudius, consul (362), 114
Mammarius, Donatist priest (*flor.* 316), 25
Mani (*al.* Manes, Manichaeus), Persian sage (216?–?76), 156¹, 542, Gl s.v. Manichaeans
Manning, Henry Edward, Cardinal (1808–92), 95⁴³
Maras, Asiatic presbyter (*flor.* 448), 447³
Marcellinus, St, pope (296–308), 68¹
Marcellinus, Luciferian priest (*flor.* 383), 195
Marcellinus, Flavius, tribune and notary (*ob.* 413), 324–6, 328, 338
Marcellus, bishop of Ancyra in Galatia Prima (314–36, 344–53), Gl s.vv. Marcellians, Photinians
Marcellus, master of the offices (395), 256
Marcianus, emperor (450–57), 48¹², 459, 461–2, 463ⁱⁿ, 464–5, 466ⁱⁿ, 467–9, 470ⁱⁿ,⁸,⁷⁰, 471–7, 479–84, 485ⁱⁿ, 486ⁱⁿ, 487–91, 492¹
Marcianus, unidentified diocesan vicar (384), 198
Marcianus, Aelius, jurisconsult (*flor.* 225), 641¹³,¹⁷
Marcianus, Flavius, consul (469, 472), 508–9, 513–18
Marcion, suffragan bishop of Sinope and Gnostic heresiarch (110?–*post* 155), 542, Gl s.v. Marcionites
Marcus, emperor (475–6), 524
Marcus, St, pope (336), 17, 19⁶
Marcus, Arian bishop of Arethusa (341?–?62), 119⁵
Marcus Aurelius: *see* Aurelius
Marina, sister of Theodosius II (403–4), 398⁸
Marinianus, Flavius Avitus, consul (423), 376–83
Marinus, bishop of Arles (313–14), 17
Maris, bishop of Chalcedon (325–62), 95
Mark, St, evangelist (*ob.* ?62), 53²
Marmarius (*al.* Martyrius), bishop of Marcianopolis in Moesia Inferior (*flor.* 381), 182

Martinus, St, bishop of Tours (371?–?99), 203¹, 297³, 370¹
Mary, Blessed Virgin (*ob.* ?48), 95¹, 159, 330ⁱⁿ, 397ⁱⁿ,¹, 481, 483–7, 497³, 524 (I),546, Gl s.v. Nestorians
 as Holy and Ever-Virgin and Mother of God, 524 (I), 569, 636
 as Holy and Glorious Virgin, 645
 as Holy and Glorious Virgin and Mother of God, 645
 as Holy and God-bearing Virgin, 542
 as Holy Ever-Virgin, 569, 636–7
 as Holy Glorious Ever-Virgin and Mother of God, 569, 573, 636–7, 646 (I)
 as Holy Mother, 577
 as Holy Virgin, 542
 as Holy Virgin and Mother of God, 527, 542
 as Mater Dolorosa, 561², 397¹
 as Mother of God, 481, 483, 485–7, 527, 542, 546, 579, 637, 645, Gl s.v. Nestorians
 as Our Lady of the Atom, 397¹
 as Queen of Heaven, 397¹
 as Regina Coeli, 397¹
 as *Theotokos*, 397¹, 542³¹
 as Virgin, 546, 561, 562
 as Virgin and Mother of God, 527
Masinissa, Numidian king (201–149 B.C.), 19²²
Maternus, bishop of Köln (313–?15), 17
Maternus, Julius Firmicus, Christian astrologer (*flor.* 337), 313¹
Matthew, St, evangelist (*ob. ante* ?90), 116
Matthias, St, apostle (*flor.* 29), 543 (II)
Mauritius, Scythian monk (*flor.* 519), 551
Mavortius (*al.* Maburtius), Flavius Vettius Agorius Basilius, consul (527), 568
Maxentius, emperor (307–12), In¹⁷, 38², 44⁴
Maximianus I, emperor (286–305, 306–10), In¹⁷, 6, 13–14, 44²,⁴, 525¹, 641¹⁴, App 10 (a), (d),¹⁶
Maximianus, Donatist bishop of Carthage (393–*post* 394), Gl s.v. Maximians
Maximianus, patriarch of Constantinople (431–4), 412¹
Maximinus I, emperor (235–8), 472⁴, App 6
Maximinus II Daia (*al.* Daza), emperor (307–13), In¹⁷, 7ⁱⁿ, 8ⁱⁿ, 9, 11ⁱⁿ, 13–14, 21, 44⁴,⁵, App 10 (d)–(f)³⁶,⁴⁹,⁵⁵,⁵⁹
Maximinus, bishop of Anazarbus (423?–?35), 415 (I)
Maximinus, civil priest (445), 441
Maximinus, Flavius, urban vicar of Rome (370–2), 152–3
Maximus I, emperor (383–8), 203, 215ⁱⁿ, 370¹

PERSONS

Maximus II, emperor (455), Tab[5]
Maximus II, patriarch of Antioch in Syria (449–55), 470 (VI, X)
Maximus, bishop of Assos (431–51), 406
Maximus, bishop of Cyme (*flor.* 431), 406
Maximus, praetorian prefect of Italy (439–41), 433, 435
Maximus, secret-service agent (407), 301
Medea, mythological sorceress, 135[5]
Melanthius, Greek tragedian (*flor.* 419 B.C.), 111[7]
Melchizedek, Salemite king (*flor.* ?1750 B.C.), In[31]
Meletius, bishop of Lycopolis (305?–?35 or 310?–?25), 53[1], 68[2], Gl s.v. Meletians
Meletius, bishop of Mopsuestia (427?–?34), 416–17
Melitius, praetorian prefect of Italy (410–12), 327, 331, 334
Melito, St, bishop of Sardis (*ob. c.* 190), In 4, 3[30], 4[2]
Melkart, Phoenician god, 9[6]
Memnon, bishop of Ephesus and exarch of Asia (431–40), 406, 408–9
Menalius, Donatist bishop (*flor.* 315), 24
Menander, Greek dramatist (343?–?291 B.C.), 223[2]
Menas, praetorian prefect of the East (528–9), 581–2, 586–90
Mensurius, bishop of Carthage (303?–11), 17[1n]
Merobaudes (*al.* Moerobaudes, Merobaudus), Flavius, consul (377, 383, 388), 162–3, 188–94
Merocles, St, bishop of Milan (304–15), 17[10]
Meshach, Hebrew hero (*flor.* 595 B.C.), 95[34]
Militiades (*al.* Melchiades), St, pope (311–14), 17, 18[1n], 19[6]
Minerva, Roman goddess, In[26]
Mithras, Persian god, 34[5], 116[16], 117[17], Gl
Modestinus, Herennius, jurisconsult (*flor.* 240), 214[5]
Modestus, Flavius Domitius, praetorian prefect of the East (369–77), 147, 151; consul (372), 156–7
Mohammed II, Turkish sultan (1451–81), 463[5]
Monaxius, Flavius, praetorian prefect of the East (416–20), 347–9, 351, 369; consul (419), 368[7], 369–70
Monimus, unidentified bishop (*flor.* 431), 406
Montanus, Phrygian prophet (*flor.* 156 or 172), Gl s.vv. Ascodrogitans, Montanists, Priscillians, Tascodrogitans
Monteglas, Maximilian Joseph von, Count (1759–1838), In[21]
Mordecai, cousin of Esther (q.v.), In 4, 95[34]

Moses, Hebrew legislator (1355?–?1235 B.C.), 23[2], 399[3], 400[9]
Moss, Henry St Lawrence Beaufort (1896–1960), 121[8]
Mus, Publius Decius, consul (340 B.C.), 479[6]
Mus, Publius Decius, consul (295 B.C.), 479[6]
Mus, Publius Decius, consul (279 B.C.), 479[6]
Muses, Graeco-Roman goddesses, 116
Mutilus, Marcus Papius, suffect consul (9), Gl s.v. *Lex Iulia et Papia Poppaea*

Napoleon (*olim* Napoleone Buonaparte, Napoléon Bonaparte) I, French emperor (1804–15), Tab[5]
Narcissus, Arian bishop of Neronias (314?–?58), 61 (III)
Narses I, Persian king (294–303), 106[5]
Nasutius, Donatist bishop (*flor.* 316), 25
Nations, Gilbert Owen (1866–1950), In[31]
Nebuchadnezzar II, Chaldean king (605–562 B.C.), In[23], 95
Nectarius, patriarch of Constantinople (381–97), 182
Nemesinus, (?) notary (*flor.* 363), 124 (III)
Neoterius (*al.* Neuterius), Flavius, praetorian prefect of Italy (385), 201; praetorian prefect of Illyricum (390), 223; consul (390), 223–9
Nepos, emperor (473–80), Tab[5], 520[2]
Nepos, Quintus Caecilius Metellus, consul (98 B.C.), Gl s.v. *Lex Caecilia et Didia*
Nepotianus, Flavius Popilius Virius, consul (336), 76
Nero, emperor (54–68), I[4,5], 5[1], 164[8], 472[4], 505[1], App 1, 2,[3,8]
Nerva, emperor (96–8), In[9], 472[4], 577[1]
Nestorius, patriarch of Constantinople (428–31) and heresiarch, 284[4], 397, 398[2,3], 401–2, 405–6, 408[5], 410, 411[1n,13,15,16], 412, 414[1n,3], 416[1n], 422–3, 425–6, 427[1n], 445–6, 448, 450–5, 457–9, 470 (VII), 477, 480–1, 483–7, 489, 524, 527, 542, 546, 559, 569, 636–7, 645, Gl s.v. Nestorians
Nestorius, prefect of Egypt (345–52), 87–8
Nevitta (*al.* Nebitta, Nebidda, Nebietta), Flavius, consul (362), 114
Nicasius, (?) notary (*flor.* 313), 19
Nico, unidentified priest (*flor.* 472), 518
Nicostratus, unidentified bishop (*flor.* 520), 557
Nicostratus, praetorian prefect of the East (468), 506–7
Nitentius (*al.* Nicentius), tribune and notary (*flor.* 380), 163[7]
Nomus, consul (445), 437–42

PERSONS   1271

Nonnus (al. Photius), bishop of Tyre (449–51), 456⁵
Novatianus, anti-pope (251–7/8), In⁴³, 57⁸, Gl s.v. Novatians
Novatus, African bishop (flor. 419), 362
Novellus, bishop of Tyzica (flor. 314), 17⁴
Numa Pompilius, Roman king (716–693 B.C.), 399¹¹

Octavianus, Rufinus, corrector of Lucania and Brutii (319), 28
Odoacer (al. Odovacar), Herul king in Italy (476–93), Tab⁵
Odysseus (Ulysses), mythical Ithacan king, 150¹
Olybrius, emperor (472), Tab⁵
Olybrius, Flavius Anicius Hermogenianus, consul (395), 249–56
Olybrius, Quintus Clodius Hermogenianus, urban prefect of Rome (369–70), 141–3, 145; consul (379), 165–6
Olympians, Graeco-Roman deities, 122
Olympias, consort of Arsaces III (flor. 360), 106⁵
Olympius, bishop of Claudiopolis in Honorias (flor. 431), 406
Olympius, master of the offices (408), 304
Opilio (al. Opilianus), Flavius Rufius, consul (524), 565
Optatus, St, bishop of Milevis (370?–?85), In²¹, 19¹, 20¹ⁿ,⁹,¹⁰, 203¹
Optatus, Augustal prefect (384), 197; urban prefect of Constantinople (398, 405), 285³
Optimus, bishop of Antioch in Pisidia (381–?400), 182
Orestes, Augustal prefect (412–15/16), 347¹ⁿ
Orestes, prefectural aide (436), 426
Orestes, Flavius Rufius Gennadius Probus, consul (530), 601–17, 619–30, 634
Orfitus, Memmius Vitrasius, urban prefect of Rome (353–6, 357–9), 92
Origenes, Alexandrian theologian (185?–?254), 189², 313¹
Orosius, Paulus, Iberian priest and historian (flor. 415), 350¹ⁿ, 525¹
Osiris, Egyptian god, 111⁴, 220¹¹. See Serapis
Ossius: see Hosius
Otreius, bishop of Melitene (366–82), 182
Otto (al. Otho) I the Great, Holy Roman emperor (926–73), Tab⁵
Ovidius Naso, Publius, Roman poet 43 B.C.–?A.D. 17), 523³

Pales, Italic god, 220⁴
Palladius, bishop of Amasea (flor. 431), 406
Palladius, bishop of Helenopolis in Bithynia Prima (400–5), of Aspona (417–ante 431), 228¹, 284¹ⁿ,²⁻⁴, 285²,⁶, 295¹ⁿ,³,⁵, 297¹ⁿ, 330⁴, 446¹⁰, 599⁷
Palladius, Arian bishop of Ratiara (flor. 381), 172¹ⁿ
Palladius, count (445), 441
Palladius, magistrian (flor. 431), 405
Palladius, praetorian prefect of the East (450–5), 474, 476⁴, 477, 479, 480³,⁷⁴, 488–9
Palladius, Flavius Junius Quartus, praetorian prefect of Italy (415–20), 350–1, 372; consul (416), 346–7
Pancratius, urban prefect of Constantinople (381–2), 181
Pantius, Numidian bishop (flor. 330), 59
Papias, St, bishop of Hierapolis (ob. c. 130), Gl s.v. Papians
Papinianus, Aemilius, jurisconsult and praetorian prefect (ob. 212), 168¹, 641 (I)
Parker, Thomas Maynard (1906–), 17⁶
Paschasinus, bishop of Lilybaeum (449–post 451), 470 (IV, VIII)
Patalas, Alexandrian lawyer (flor. 363), 124 (III)
Paterius, prefect of Egypt (flor. 333), 67
Patricius, consul (452), 476⁵⁵
Patricius, master of the soldiers (503–18), 545
Patricius, vicar of Africa (flor. 313), 15
Patricius, Flavius Julius, consul (459), 498
Patroclus (al. Patrocles), archbishop of Arles (412–26), 387
Paul, St, apostle (ob. 64 or 67), In 4,²³, 1⁵, 5¹, 9⁴, 17³, 32⁹, 41⁴, 53¹⁶, 67²⁰, 73¹⁷, 75⁴², 107⁸, 140¹, 150¹, 164¹¹, 166⁴, 167², 181⁵, 200¹, 211, 214², 225²,¹²,¹³, 337⁸, 359⁴,⁷,⁸, 361³, 372¹, 414⁶, 445¹⁴, 465³, 484, 486, 496¹¹, 523¹, 546, 551¹³, 577¹⁵, 579¹²⁻¹⁴, 620², 644⁶, 651¹³
Paul: see Paulus
Paulinus, Augustal prefect (?385), 204
Paulinus, defender of the church (519), 552
Paulinus, governor of Epirus Nova (372), 157
Paulinus, Milanese deacon (flor. 411), 350¹ⁿ
Paulinus, urban prefect of Rome (380), 170
Paulinus, Aelius, vicar of Africa (313–14), 19²
Paulinus, Meropius Pontius Anicius, St, bishop of Nola (409–31), 359
Paulinus Minor (al. Junior), Flavius Decius Theodorus, consul (534), 645–6, 648, 650
Paulus II, pope (1464–71), In²⁶
Paulus II, patriarch of Antioch in Syria (519–21), 559
Paulus, Julius, jurisconsult and praetorian prefect (flor. 200), 36¹, 641¹⁴

Paulus of Samosata, bishop of Antioch in Syria (260?–69), 5[1], 542, Gl s.v. Paulianists
Paulus: *see* Paul
Pelagius, St, bishop of Laodicea in Syria Prima (363–72, 375?–81), 182
Pelagius, British monk and heresiarch (*ob. post* 418), 350–1, 368, 373[1n], Gl s.v. Pelagians
Pelikan, Jaroslav (1923–), 397[1]
Penates, Roman deities, 242
Pergamius: *see* Pregmius
Perigenes, bishop of Corinth (419?–35), 406
Persicus, Paullus Fabius, consul (34), Gl s.v. *Senatus Consultum Persicianum*
Persius Flaccus, Aulus, Roman satirist (34–62), 508[7], 598[13]
Peter, St, apostle (*ob.* 64 or 67), In[23,43,46], 53[2], 140[1], 167, 181[5], 359[4], 372[1], 375[7], 422[7], 442[1], 475[6], 519[1], 545–6, 551[13], 561, 562[15], 645[1]
Petrus II, patriarch of Alexandria (373–80), 167
Petrus III Mongus, Monophysite patriarch of Alexandria (482–9), 527[2], 560, 562
Petrus III, patriarch of Antioch in Syria (1052–4), 53[3]
Petrus, bishop of Crusa (*flor.* 431), 406
Petrus, bishop of Oxyrhynchus (*flor.* 431), 406
Petrus, bishop of Parembolae (*ante* 428–*ante* 451), 406
Petrus, bishop of Trajanopolis (*flor.* 431), 406
Petrus, curator of the empress's household (531), 630
Petrus, Flavius, consul (516), 547–8
Petrus Fullo, Monophysite patriarch of Antioch in Syria (471, 476–7, 485–9), 560, 562
Pfister, Pierre (1895–), In[31]
Phaedria, dramatic character, 223[2]
Pharaohs, Egyptian kings, 349[1]
Pharr, Clyde (1883–), 433[7], 618[15], 625[12], Gl s.v. master of the census
Philippus, praetorian prefect of Illyricum (?412, ?418, 420–21), 333, 375 (I)
Philippus (*al.* Filippus), Flavius, consul (408), 301–9
Philomenus (*al.* Philumenos), master of the offices (*flor.* 334), 68[5]
Photinus, bishop of Sirmium (347?–9), 483, 485, 487, Gl s.v. Photinians
Photius, bishop of Tyre (449–51), 447, 456, 470 (V)
Photius, patriarch of Constantinople (857–67, 877–86), Gl s.v. *ius canonicum*
Photius, Nestorian propagandist (436), 426

Phritilas (*al.* Fritilas), bishop of Heraclea in Thrace (*flor.* 431), 406
Pilatus, Pontius, procurator of Judaea (26–36), 4[2], 52[51], 67[35], 99[2], 159, 636, App 10 (f)[53,58]
Pinianus Severus, Valerius, (?) vicar of Rome (385), 200[1n]
Pinnas, bishop in (?) Egypt (*flor.* 260), 4
Pirie, Valérie (*ob. c.* 1959), 76[3]
Pius IX, pope (1846–78), In[31], 95[43], 350[1n]
Pius X, St, pope (1903–14), In[44]
Pius XI, pope (1922–39), 76[1]
Pius XII, pope (1939–58), Tab[5], 551[1]
Pius, bishop of Pessinus (*flor.* 431), 406
Placidia, daughter of Valentinianus III (441?–*ob. post* 461), 435[4]
Placidia, Galla, daughter of Theodosius I Magnus, consort of Constantius III, mother of Valentinianus III (*ante* 393–450), 361–2, 435[4]
Placidus, Marcus Maecius Memmius Furius Baburius Caecilianus, consul (343), 82, 83
Plaetorius (*al.* Laetorius), Marcus, plebeian tribune (?192 B.C.), Gl s.v. *Lex Plaetoria*
Plato, Greek philosopher (427?–347 B.C.), In[54], 135[4], 551[7], 583[1], 648[6], Gl s.vv. Apollinarians, Neo-Platonism
Plautus, Titus Maccius, Roman dramatist (254?–184 B.C.), 223[2]
Plinius Caecilius Secundus Minor, Gaius, propraetorian legate of Bithynia et Pontus (111?–?113), 1, 2[1n], 12[33], 150[1], 236[3]
Plinta (*al.* Plenta), consul (419), 368[7], 369–70
Plotinus, Greek philosopher (203?–62), 66[7]
Plutarchus, Greek littérateur (46?–?127), 65[13], 220[4], 472[29]
Polycarpus, St, bishop of Smyrna (106 or 117–56), 206[7], 577, App[6]
Pompeianus, Gabinius Barbarus, proconsul of Africa (400–1), 282
Pompeius Magnus, Gnaeus, consul (70, 55, 52 B.C.), 414[6], 509[6]
Pontius, Donatist bishop in Africa (362), 120
Pontius Pilate: *see* Pilatus, Pontius
Porphyrius, patriarch of Antioch in Syria (404–13), 284, 287, 297
Porphyrius, Alexandran notary (362), 113[4]
Porphyrius, Greek philosopher (233–304), 66, 382[1], 422, 445–6, 459, Gl s.v. Porphyrians
Porphyrius Proculus, Caelius Pompeius, proconsul of Africa (407–8), 299–301
Poseidon, Greek god, 614[10]
Possidius, St, bishop of Calama (397–*post* 437), 28[1]

PERSONS

Postumianus, praetorian prefect of the East (383), 189, 192-4
Postumianus, Rufius Praetextatus, consul (448), 445¹³, 449
Potamius, Augustal prefect of Egypt (392), 240
Praetextatus, Vettius Agorius, urban prefect of Rome (367-?9), 137-8, 140
Pregmius (al. Pergamius), Augustal prefect of Egypt (482), 527²
Primianus, Donatist bishop of Carthage (391-411), 328
Principius, praetorian prefect of Italy (385-6), 209
Priscilla, Montanist prophetess (flor. 205), Gl s.v. Priscillians
Priscillianus, bishop of Avila (380?-5), 203¹, 370¹, Gl s.v. Priscillians
Probatius, imperial chamberlain (flor. 363), 124 (IV)
Probianus (al. Probinianus), Caelius Aconius, consul (471), 512
Probianus, Petronius, proconsul of Africa (315-16), 21
Probinus, Flavius Anicius, consul (395), 249-56; proconsul of Africa (397), 263
Probus, emperor (276-82), In⁹, 472⁴
Probus, Sextus (?) Anicius Flavius Petronius, consul (371), 154-5
Proclianus, proconsul of Africa (?360), 106
Proclus, St, patriarch of Constantinople (434-47), 427, 637
Proclus (al. Proculius), proconsul of Asia (449), 453⁸, 454
Procopius, Greek historian (ob. 565), 550¹, 575¹, 646⁹
Proculus (al. Proclus), urban prefect of Constantinople (392), 236
Proemptor, unidentified Constantinopolitan (flor. 519), 552
Promotus, Flavius, consul (389), 218-22
Protadius, praetorian prefect of the Gauls (473), 520¹
Protadius, Aurelianus, praetorian prefect (473), 520¹
Protadius, Dioscorus Aurelianus, praetor (473), 520¹
Proterius, patriarch of Alexandria (452-7), 470³⁵, 489, 495⁴
Proteus, Graeco-Roman god, 148⁴
Protogenes, bishop of Sofia (316?-343/4), 26
Protogenes, Flavius Florus, consul (449), 451-2, 455
Ptolemaeus I Soter, Egyptian king (304-?283B.C.), 122, 189²
Ptolemaeus XI Neos Dionysos (Auletes), Egyptian king (80-51 B.C.), 122¹⁰
Ptolemaeus XIV Philopator Philometor Caesar (Caesarion), Egyptian king (44?-30 B.C.), 122¹⁰
Ptolemaeus, Alexandrian martyr (ob. ante 161), App⁶
Ptolemies, Macedonian sovereigns of Egypt (304-30 B.C.), 122, 133¹, 349¹
Publius, St, bishop of Athens (ob. ante 126), App⁶
Pulcher, Publius Clodius, plebeian tribune (58 B.C.), 133¹, Gl s.v. Lex Clodia
Pulcheria, St, sister of Theodosius II, consort of Marcianus (399-453), 347ⁱⁿ, 398, 461¹, 462, 466, 472ⁱⁿ,⁴, 476⁴, 484², 485-6
Pupienus Maximus, emperor (238), 472⁴
Pythian: see Apollo

Quadratus, Greek apologist and (?) bishop of Athens (flor. 126), 2²⁰
Quietus, emperor (260-1), 4¹
Quirinius, Aurelius, administrator of the treasury (flor. 260), 4
Quirites, 358¹. See in Index of Places s.v. Romans

Radin, Max (1880-1950), 133¹
Rambulus (al. Rabbulas), bishop of Edessa (412-36), 406
Rampolla del Tindaro, Mariano Cardinal (1843-1916), In⁴⁴
Reginus, Flavius Simplicius, praetorian prefect of Illyricum (435), 423
Regulus, Marcus Aquilius, Roman delator and orator (ob. post 96), 150¹
Remmius, Roman magistrate (c. 80 B.C.), Gl s.v. Lex Remmia
Rhampsinitus (? Rameses III), Egyptian pharaoh (1179-1147 B.C.), 68⁴
Rheticius, St, bishop of Autun (313?-34), 17
Richomeres (al. Ricomeres, Ricomedes, Rigomedes, Rhochomeris, Rhinchomeres, Richomerius), Flavius, consul (384), 196, 198-9
Ricimer (al. Ricemer, Recimer, Rechimer, Recemer, Recimerus, Rechimerus, Reccimirus, Ricimirus, Ricimerius), Flavius, master of each soldiery (460), 500
Rienzi, Cola di, Roman patriot (1313-54), In⁹
Rogatianus, Donatist bishop in Africa (362), 120
Romanus, Syrian monk (flor. 507), 543ⁱⁿ,⁴
Romulus, Roman king (753-716 B.C.), Tab⁵, 140¹
Romulus, Flavius Pisidius, consul (343), 82-3
Romulus, Flavius Pisidius, count of the sacred largesses (392), 241

1274 PERSONS

Roosevelt, Franklin Delano (1882-1945), 12[2]
Rufinus, Ursinian cleric (*flor*. 371), 152-3
Rufinus, Flavius, consul (392), 233-42; praetorian prefect of the East (392-5), 242-3, 246-9, 251, 253, 255
Rufinius, Gaius Vettius Cossinius, consul (316, 323), 26, 41
Rufus, bishop of Thessalonica (410-*post* 431), 406
Rufus, Ursinian cleric (*flor*. 371), 152-3
Rufus, consul (457), 492
Rusticius (*al*. Rusticianus), Flavius, consul (520), 556-60, 562

Sabbatius, Novatian bishop of Constantinople (*flor*. 380), Gl s.v. Novatians
Sabellius, Libyan heresiarch (*flor*. 220), 542
Sabinianus, bishop of Perrha (445-9, 451–), 470 (X)
Sabinianus, Flavius, consul (505), 541
Sabinus, Antonius Caecina (?), consul (316), 26
Sabinus, Peucetius, praetorian prefect (311), 9, 13, 14[1n,7,9]
Sade, Donatien Alphonse François de, Comte (Marquis de Sade) (1740-1814), 154[1]
Sallustius, urban prefect of Rome (386), 211
Salvius Julianus Aemilianus, Lucius Octavius Cornelius Publius, jurisconsult and consul (148), 375, 625[12]
Samuel, Asiatic presbyter (*flor*. 448), 447[3]
Sapidianus, vicar of Africa (399), 276
Sappius (*al*. Sapricius), bishop of Paphos (*flor*. 431), 406
Sarus, Visigothic general (*ob*. 412), 308[2]
Sassanids, Persian kings (226-641), 106[5]
Satan, 50[5], 66[1], 416[3], 457[1], 483[4], 522[4], 527[45,52], 562[9], 648[6], 651[13]. See Devil
Saturnus, Roman god, Gl s.vv. fisc; treasury, public
Saturninus, Aptungitan civic curator (*flor*. 314), 21
Saturninus, Flavius, consul (383), 188-94
Saturninus, Gaius Sentius, consul (4), Gl s.v. *Lex Aelia et Sentia*
Saul, Hebrew king (*ob*. c. 1013 B.C.), 472[4]
Saxa, Quintus Voconius, plebeian tribune (169 B.C.), Gl s.v. *Lex Voconia*
Sazanes, Auxumite king (*flor*. 357), 99
Scipio Africanus Minor Numantinus, Publius Cornelius Aemilianus, consul (147, 134 B.C.), 646[14]
Scylla, mythical monster, In[8]
Sebastianus, praetorian prefect of the East (476-80, 484), 525-6, 528-9

Sebastianus Thrax, prefect of Egypt (353-4), 81[6]
Secundianus, Arian bishop of Singidunum (*flor*. 381), 172[1n]
Secundus, Arian bishop of Ptolemaïs in Libya Prima (321?-5), 20[1], 53[1], 67[30]
Secundus, bishop of Tigisis (*ob*. *post* 311), 17[5]
Secundus, Quintus Poppaeus, suffect consul (9), Gl s.v. *Lex Iulia et Papia Poppaea*
Secundus Salutius, Saturninus, praetorian prefect of the East (361-6), 114, 126-7, 128[1]
Selene, Greek goddess, 122
Seleucus I Nicator, Syrian king (301-280 B.C.), 523[2]
Seleucus, bishop of Amasea (448-58), 406
Seleucus, praetorian prefect of Italy (412, 414-15), 329
Senator, urban prefect of Rome (407), 298
Senator, Flavius, consul (436), 428
Senator: see Cassiodorus Senator
Serapis (*al*. Sarapis), Egypto-Greek god, 111, 121-2, 220[11]. See Osiris
Serennius Granianus: see Silvanus Granianus Quadronius Proculus
Sergius I, bishop of Cyrus (*al*. Cyrrhus) (518?-?20), 559
Servilius Vatia Isauricus, Publius, consul (79 B.C.), 523[5]
Severianus, St, bishop of Scythopolis (451-2), 483-4, 487
Severianus, count of the sacred consistory (516), 547-8
Severianus, proconsul of Achaea (349), 89
Severus, patriarch of Antioch in Syria (512-18), 543
Severus, urban prefect of (?) Constantinople (343), 82
Severus, unidentified official (355), 96
Severus, Acilius, consul (323), 41
Severus, Flavius Messius Phoebus, consul (470), 510
Severus, Libius, emperor (461-5), Tab[5], 44[4], 496[1n]
Severus, Lucius Septimius, emperor (193-211), 65[6], 186[4], 474[2], 476[39], 641[13], App 5
Severus, Sulpicius, ecclesiastical historian (360?-?410), 297[3]
Severus Alexander, emperor (222-35), In[9], 4[2], 31[4], 133[1], 341[2], 472[4], 498[2], 508[7], App 6
Shadrach, Hebrew hero (*flor*. 595 B.C.), 95[84]
Shakespeare, William (1564-1616), 267[10]
Sherwin-White, Adrian Nicholas (1911–), 1[3]
Sibyl, Erythraean, 67

PERSONS 1275

Sicininus, unidentified ecclesiastic (*ob. ante* 367), 138³
Sidonius, Gaius Sollius Modestus (?) Apollinaris, St, bishop of Clermont (472 ?–*post* 483), 519⁵
Silvanus, emperor (355), 95
Silvanus, African bishop (*flor.* 419), 362
Silvanus Granianus Quadronius Proculus, Quintus Licinius, proconsul of Asia (120–1), 2⁷
Silvester (*al.* Sylvester) I, St, pope (314–35), 208, 364¹²
Silvia (*al.* Sylvia) Aquitana: *see* Aetheria
Simeon Stylites, St, pillar saint (388–459), 376¹ⁿ, 411 (I, III), 412¹ⁿ
Simon Magus, Samaritan protoheresiarch (*flor.* 37), 422, 459, 485, 487, 519¹, Gl s.v. Simonians
Simplicius, Flavius, urban vicar of Rome (374), 164
Siricius, St, pope (384–99), 200, 205, 211³, 330¹ⁿ, 372⁴
Sixtus III, St, pope (432–40), 95¹, 414¹ⁿ
Sol Invictus, Perso-Roman god, 34⁵, 220¹⁰, Gl s.v. Mithras
Solomon, Hebrew king (973 ?–?933 B.C.), 223², 472⁴, 505¹, 645
Solon, Athenian statesman (638 ?–?559 B.C.), 98³
Solon, public slave (*flor.* 314), 21
Sophronius, Eusebius Hieronymus: *see* Jerome, St
Soterichus, bishop of Caesarea in Cappadocia Prima (512–36), 557²
Sperantius, Numidian bishop (*flor.* 330), 59
Sporacius (*al.* Sporatius, Sphoracius, Aspiratus), consul (452), 476–7, 479–80
Stachys, St, bishop of Byzantium (*flor.* 60), 181⁵
Stephanus, bishop of Ephesus (449–51), 470 (VIII), 473¹ⁿ
Stephanus, prefectural aide (436), 426
Stephanus Protomartyr, St (*ob. c.* 33), 566, 577¹³
Stephen: *see* Stephanus
Stilicho (*al.* Stillico, Stellico), Flavius, consul (400, 405), 281–2, 288–94, 296
Strabo, Greek geographer (63 B.C. ?–?A.D. 21), 17³
Strategius, count of the private estates (410), 321 (II)
Strategius, Flavius, praetorian prefect of the East (354–7), 61 (III)
Studius, urban prefect of Constantinople (404), 285–6
Stylites: *see* Simeon Stylites, St
Suetonius Tranquillus, Gaius, Roman biographer (69 ?–?140), 207³, 641⁸
Sulla Felix Epaphroditus, Lucius Cornelius, dictator (81–79 B.C.), 7³, 382¹, Gl s.vv. dictator; *Lex Cornelia de falsis*; *Lex Cornelia de iniuriis*
Superius, centurion (*flor.* 314), 21
Syagrius (*al.* Siagrius, Suagrius), Flavius, consul (381), 173–84
Syagrius, Flavius Afranius, consul (382), 185–7
Symmachus, St, pope (498–514), 562¹⁴
Symmachus, Aurelius Anicius, urban prefect of Rome (418–19), 352–3, 356, 363–5
Symmachus, Valerius Tullianus, consul (330), 60
Symmachus Eusebius, Quintus Aurelius, consul (391), 230–3, 370¹, 429³¹
Symmachus Phosphorius, Lucius Aurelius Avianus, urban prefect of Rome (364–5), 132–4
Syncletius, magistrian (*flor.* 333), 67

Tacitus, emperor (275–6), 472⁴
Tacitus, Cornelius, Roman historian (55 ?–*post* 115), In⁴⁵, 3¹⁵, 106⁶, 214⁵
Tatianus, urban prefect of Constantinople (452), 477, 479–80
Tatianus, Quintus Flavius Eutolmius, praetorian prefect of the East (388–92), 216, 218, 221–2, 224–9, 233–4, 237–9; consul (391), 230–3
Taurus, Flavius, consul (428), 394–5; praetorian prefect of the East (434, 445), 421, 438
Taurus Aemilianus, Flavius Palladius Rutilius, praetorian prefect of Italy (353–61), 97, 107–10
Teiresias, legendary Theban seer, 150¹
Telesphorus, St, pope (125–36), 470⁶⁶, App ⁶
Tennyson, Alfred, Lord (1809–92), 46⁹, 411³
Terennius (*al.* Gerontius), bishop of Tomi (*flor.* 381), 182
Tertullianus, Quintus Septimius Florens, Latin apologist and theologian (160 ?–?235), In²⁶,⁴⁶,⁵², 1³, 2²⁰, 4², 16⁴, 34¹, 75⁴², 167⁵,¹¹, 214², 225¹³, 247¹³, 422¹¹, 569¹, 651¹³, App³,⁸
Thaddaeus, St, apostle (*flor.* 30), 42⁵
Thalassius, exarch of Caesarea in Cappadocia Prima (438–52), 458, 470 (I, III)
Thalassius, praetorian prefect of the East (*ob.* 353), 91
Themistius Euphrades, urban prefect of Constantinople (384), 159¹⁶
Theodora, St, consort of Justinianus I (527–48), 630¹ⁿ,²,⁴,⁶⁻⁸, 650⁴
Theodora, Flavia Maximiana, stepmother of Constantinus I (*flor.* 292), 63², 91⁶, 525¹

Theodorus, bishop of Heraclea in Thrace (335–51), 95
Theodorus, bishop of Mopsuestia (c. 392–428), 427[1n,2], 459[17,28], 542, 559
Theodorus, bishop of Tarsus (flor. 325), 61 (III)
Theodorus, bishop of Trimuthus (flor. 680), 295[3]
Theodorus, Flavius, consul (505), 541
Theodorus, Flavius Mallius, praetorian prefect of Italy (397–9, 408–9), 261–2, 265, 306–10; consul (399), 274–80
Theodoretus, bishop of Cyrus (al. Cyrrhus) (423–49, 451–7), 407, 415 (I), 418, 449, 458–9, 463[3], 470 (VII), 479, 542, 559
Theodoricus Magnus, Ostrogothic king (474–526), In[2], 528–9, 533[1], 548[8], 550[13], 567[1n]
Theodosius I Magnus, emperor (379–95), Tab[3], In 3,[33,43,49], 12[1], 62[2], 106[4], 116[11], 139[1], 165–71, 172[3], 173–202, 204–48, 249[1n], 251[3], 252[3], 253[1n,5], 256[6], 280[3], 370[1], 375[1], 381[1n,4], 429[31], 443[15], 475, 488
Theodosius II, emperor (408–50), In 1, 3, 65[6], 114[2], 205[1n], 242[2], 283, 286–92, 293[4], 294, 296, 298–306, 308[1,26], 309–24, 327, 329–50, 368–70, 372, 375–401, 402[2,10], 403[1n,5], 404[3,5], 405–9, 410[1n], 411–13, 414[1n,5], 415[1n,8,13], 416[1n,7,9], 417[6], 418[2], 419[1], 420[5], 421–3[4], 424, 426–45, 446[2], 447–56, 457[2], 458–60, 461[1n,1], 463[1n,2], 464[1], 470[39], 472[4], 473[1n], 476[4], 484[2], 505[1], 524 (I), 578[6], 629, Gl s.v. Simonians
Theodosius, heretical patriarch of Jerusalem (452–3), 483–5, 486[1n,2], 487
Theodotus, Arian bishop of Laodicea in Syria Prima (ante 325–post 355), 51, 61 (III)
Theodotus, bishop of Pergamum (flor. 152), 470[66]
Theognius (al. Theognis, Theogonius), Arian bishop of Nicaea (324?–325, 328–ante 344 or 354), 50–1, 95
Theonas, bishop of Marmarica (flor. 325), 20[1], 53[1], 67[30]
Theophilus, unidentified bishop (flor. 431), 406
Theophilus, patriarch of Alexandria (385–412), 284, 287, 295, 297, 481, 489, 527[76]
Theophilus, professor of law in Constantinople (ob. c. 536), 639[9], 640[1]
Theopompus, count of the domestics (516), 547–8
Thomas, unidentified bishop (flor. 520), 557
Thomas, praetorian prefect of the East (442), 436, 629

Thomas, secret-service agent (flor. 520), 559
Thrasyllus, Alexandrian and Rhodian astrologer (ob. 36), 313[1]
Thucydides, Greek historian (457?–?400 B.C.), 116
Tiberius I, emperor (14–37), 1[4], 3[15], 4[2], 31[1], 164[8], 241[1], 313[1], 621[6], App 2,[58], Gl s.v. prefect, urban
Tiberius II, emperor (578–82), In[3], Gl s.v. Novellae Iustiniani
Tibullus, Albius, Roman elegist (48?–19 B.C.), 140[1]
Timasius, Flavius, consul (389), 218–22
Timotheus I, patriarch of Alexandria (380–85), 182, 197
Timotheus II Aelurus, Monophysite patriarch of Alexandria (457–60, 475–7), 495, 524 (I), 526[1n], 560, 562
Timotheus III Salophacialus, patriarch of Alexandria (460–75, 477–82), 523[1]
Timotheus II, bishop of Briula (flor. 431), 406
Timotheus, St, bishop of Ephesus (ob. c. 97), 523[1], 577
Timotheus, bishop of Thermae (flor. 431), 406
Timotheus, bishop of Tomi (flor. 431), 406
Timotheus, bishop of Termessus et Eudocias (flor. 431), 406
Timotheus, patriarch of Constantinople (511–18), 560[8]
Tiridates III Magnus, Armenian king (259–314), 106[6]
Tischendorf, Konstantin von (1815–74), 64[18,21], 483[21]
Titus, emperor (79–81), 207[3], 624[3]
Titus, bishop of Bostra (361–?4), 117
Titus, St, bishop of Crete (ob. ante 100), 523[1]
Titus, Flavius, count of the domestics and vicar of the master of the soldiers (434–5), 415 (I), 416, 417[7], 418, 419[1n], 420
Toynbee, Arnold Joseph (1889–), Tab[5], In[52], 1[1], 411[3]
Trajanus, emperor (98–117). 1, 2[1n], 3[31], 141[3], 577[1], App 3,[6]
Tranquillinus, bishop of Antioch in Pisidia (flor. 431), 406
Tribonianus (al. Tribunianus), jurist and quaestor of the sacred palace (530–32, 535–?45), 505[2], 617, 639[9], 640[1], 642
Trifolius, praetorian prefect of the East or of Italy (388–9), 215
Trinity, Capitoline, Roman deities, In[26]
Triton, Graeco-Roman god, 148[4]
Troilus, bishop of Constantia (olim Salamis) in Cyprus (ante 431), 406

PERSONS

Tullia, daughter of Marcus Tullius Cicero (78?–45 B.C.), 220[4]
Tuscianus, count of the East (381), 174

Ulpianus, Domitius, jurisconsult and praetorian prefect (ob. 228), In[9], 4[2], 31[4], 332[5], 347[13], 615[1n], 641[31], 643[1n], 644[1n]
Unconquered Sun: see Sol Invictus
Urania, Graeco-Roman muse, 116[9]
Uranius, bishop of Himeria (445–51), 447, 456
Urbanus, bishop of Parma (flor. 378), 164[13]
Urbanus, governor of Palaestina Prima (304), App 10 (d)
Ure, Percy Neville (1879–1950), In[32]
Ursacius, bishop of Singidunum (335?–?69), 95
Ursinus, anti-pope (366–7), In[43], 137[1n,3], 138[1n,1,3], 140, 146[2], 152–3, 164, 200
Ursus, unidentified bishop (flor. 431), 406
Ursus, Ursinian cleric (flor. 371), 152–3
Ursus, catholicus of Africa (flor. 313), 15
Uzziah, Jewish king (780–740 B.C.), 95[34]

Valens, emperor (364–78), 55[2], 116[1n], 127–30, 132–5, 137–63, 205[1n], 267, 331[4], 470[61], 488
Valens, Arian bishop of Mursa (335?–?67), 95
Valens, count of the domestics (408), 304
Valentinianus I, emperor (364–75), 55[2], 62[2], 116[1n], 118[1], 126[1], 127–59, 163, 165, 165[5], 190, 205[1n], 248[4], 267, 331[4], 470[61], 488
Valentinianus II, emperor (375–92), Tab[3], 62[2], 136[1n], 139[1], 146, 160–71, 172[3], 173–7, 179–202, 204–34, 236–40, 243, 488
Valentinianus III, emperor (423–55), Tab[5], 168[1], 361[1], 363[1], 373, 385–401, 402[10], 403[5], 404[5], 405–6, 408, 412–13, 420[6], 421–2, 423[4], 424, 427–44, 445[2], 449, 452, 456, 459[17], 461, 464, 467–9, 470[1n], 472[4], 473–6, 478–80, 482, 488[16], 489, 629, 646[1]
Valentinianus, praetorian prefect of Illyricum (452), 477, 479–80
Valentinus, bishop of Mallus in Cilicia Prima (431–4), 406
Valentinus, bishop of Mutlobaca (al. Mutlublaca), (flor. 431), 406
Valentinus, Egyptian Gnostic (ob. c. 160), 123, 483–7, Gl s.v. Valentinians
Valentinus, Marcus Aurelius Valerius, consular of Numidia (flor. 330), 60
Valerianus, emperor (253–60), Tab[2], In[43], 4[1n,3], App 8,[14]
Valerianus, St, bishop of Aquileia (369–88), 172[1n]

Valerianus, urban prefect of Rome (381), 177
Valerianus, Turcius Rufius Apollonius, praetorian prefect (flor. 250), App[11]
Valerius, consul (432), 413
Varanes (al. Barnes), Flavius, consul (410), 320–4, 328
Varanes, Joannes, consul (456), 490, 491[10]
Varronianus, Flavius, consul (364), 126–30
Vasiliev, Alexander Alexandrovich (1867–1953), In[2], 34[5], 550[1,2], 567[1], 630[3]
Venantius, priest and papal legate (515), 546
Venus, Roman goddess, 54[6], 483[15], 641[8]. See Aphrodite
Venustianus, Augustal of Tuscia (flor. 301), 6[1n]
Vergilius Maro, Publius, Roman poet (70–19 B.C.), 641[17]
Verinus, Lucrius, vicar of Africa (318–21), 324[2]
Verres, Gaius, propraetor of Sicily (73–70 B.C.), 1[5]
Verus, emperor (161–9), Tab[1], 641[17]
Verus, vicar of Africa (315), 21
Vespasianus, emperor (69–79), In[9], 159[34], 186[6], 631[1], Gl s.v. Lex de imperio Vespasiani
Vesta, Roman goddess, Gl s.v. virgin, Vestal
Victor I, St, pope (189–99), 5[1], 52[3], 470[66]
Victor, Numidian bishop (flor. 330), 59
Victor, St, bishop of Vita (ob. c. 490), 598[13], 646[7]
Victor, consul (424), 384
Victor, proconsul of Africa (394), 245
Victor, Flavius, consul (369), 146
Victorinus, Numidian bishop (flor. 330), 59
Vinatius, unidentified bishop (flor. 431), 406
Vincentius of Lérins, St, Gallic monk (ob. c. 450), In[52]
Vincomalus (al. Vincomallus, Bencomalus), Joannes, master of the offices (452), 477, 479–80
Virus, praetorian prefect of the East (430), 399
Vitalianus, Flavius, consul (520), 544[1n], 545[4,5], 552, 556–8
Vitalius, deacon and papal legate (515), 546
Vitellius, emperor (69), Gl s.v. Augustus
Vitulus, imperial clerk (flor. 419), 363
Viventius, urban prefect of Rome (364–7), 135, 154; praetorian prefect of the Gauls (368–71), 149, 154[4]
Vivianus, praetorian prefect of the East (459–60), 498
Voltaire (1694–1778), Tab[5]

1278 PERSONS

Volusianus, Rufius Antonius Agrypnius, urban prefect of Rome (416, 421), 373-4
Volventius, (?) proconsul of Spain (382-3), 288[15]

Wallia, Visigothic king (415-18), Tab[5], 646[1]
Wolff, Hans Julius (1902-), In[9]
Wolsey, Thomas Cardinal (1475?-1530), 641[8]
Wordsworth, William (1770-1850), 148[4]

Xenophilus: *see* Zenofilus
Xenophon, Greek historian (430?-354 B.C.), 606[2]
Xerxes I, Persian king (485-465 B.C.), 303[1]

Zacharias, St, pope (741-52), 297[3]
Zacharias, father of St John the Baptist (*flor.* 4 B.C.), 159[34]
Zacharias, Hebrew prophet (*ob.* ?800 B.C.), 159[34]
Zacharias, Jewish defendant (*ob.* 68), 159[34]
Zacharias, unidentified Jew, 159[34]
Zacharias Rhetor, bishop of Mytilene (*flor.* 536), 472[1n]
Zealots, Jewish patriots (35 B.C. ?- ?A.D. 70), 159[34]
Zechariah, Hebrew prophet (*flor.* 520 B.C.), 159[34]
Zeno, Flavius, consul (469), 508, 509, 513[8]; master of the soldiers throughout the East (469-71), 512; emperor (474-91), Tab[5], In[31], 411[1], 476[1n], 521-3, 524[1n], 525-9, 530[1n], 531[1n], 533, 537[6], 542, 544[1n], 545[2], 549[1n], 554[1n], 560[3], 601[1n], 630[1]
Zeno, Flavius, consul (448), 445[13], 449
Zenobia, Palmyrene queen (267-72), 5[1]
Zenofilus, Domitius, consul (333), 65
Zeus, Greek god, 9, 122, 223[2], 400[9], Gl s.v. flamen Dialis. *See* Juppiter
Zeuzius, Numidian bishop (*flor.* 330), 59
Zosimus, St, pope (417-18), 350[1n], 352, 387[9]
Zosimus, Greek historian (*ob. post* 425), 97[1], 525[1]
Zoticus, unidentified cleric (*ob. ante* 472), 518

PLACES

Abyssinians, 99^{1n}. See also Ethiopians
Achaea, In 4, 89, 234^3, 375^1, 384
Acheron, 44
Actium, 127^7
Ad Decimum, 644^1
Adiabenians, Gl s.v. Adiabenicus
Adrianople, 38^2, 42^6, 49^{18}, 105^4, 246^6
Adriatic Sea, 330^9
Aegean Sea, 46^{16}
Aelia (Capitolina), 54^6, 75^3, 313^1, 483^{15}, 474–6, 523^2. See also Jerusalem
Aelians, 483–5. See also Jerusalemites
Africa, Tab^5, 10^{1n}, 15, 16^2, 17^{1n}, 18, 19, 20^{1n}, 22, 24, 25, $27^{1n,3}$, 39, 47, 52, 60^2, 95^{46}, 107, 120^{1n}, 158^{1n}, 164, 168^1, 203^1, 225^{13}, 276^4, 293^{1n}, $294^{1n,1}$, 308^2, 310, 315^1, 322, 325, 326^{1n}, $329^{7,8}$, 339, 350^{1n}, 369^3, 474^2, 598^{13}, 615^1, 638^5, 639, 642^{17}, 644^6, 646, Gl s.vv. Gnostics, prefect (praetorian), prefecture
Africans, 164^{16}, 220^{10}, 293^{1n}, 294, 310, 326^4, 329, 350^{1n}, 360, $362^{1n,3}$, 366, 367, 369^3, 470^2, 646 (II), 652, App 5, Gl s.vv Africanus, Circumcellions
Africa (diocese), $15^{6,12}$, $19^{1n,22}$, 20, 21, 24, 25, $27^{1n,3}$, 163^1, 250, 275, 276, 294^2, 310, $324^{2,12}$, 325^{13}, 326^{12}, 646 (I), 652
— (prefecture), 646 (I), Gl s.v. prefecture
— (province), 10^{1n}, 15^{16}, $16^{2,8}$, 17, $19^{22,26}$, 21, 59, 106^2, 120^2, 148, 156^1, 158, 160^2, 183, 234^2, 263, 278, 282, 293^3, 294, 296^1, 299, 300, 305^1, 310, 324^{12}, 337, 338, 364, 367^{1n}, 389, 390, 566^1, 646^{16}
— Proconsularis, $646^{16,19}$
— North, 648^{16}, App^{14}, Gl s.vv. Caelicolans, Circumcellions, Donatists, Montanists, patriarch
Agrippina, see Köln
Aix, 350^{1n}
Aksum, see Auxume
Alamans, Tab^5, Gl s.v. Alamannicus
Alans, Tab^5, 308^{1n}, 492^1, 646^1, Gl s.v. Alanicus
Albania, 547^7
Aleppo, 411^3
Alexandria, In^{11,43,52}, $4^{1,5}$, 20^1, 29^1, 47^{1n}, 52^4, $53^{1n,1}$, 61 (III), 62^2, 67, $68^{1n,2}$, 69, 70^{1n}, 72^{1n}, 73^{16}, 74^{1n}, 75^{1n}, 77, 78^{1n}, 84 (III), 85^{1n}, 86, 87^{1n}, 94^{1n}, 95, $98^{1,3,4,7}$, $99^{1n,4,5}$, 111^{1n}, 112^{1n}, 113^{1n}, 115^{1n}, 121^{1n}, 122^{1n}, 124–5, 147^5, 156^1, 167, 172^{1n}, 187^2, $193^{1n,3}$, $195^{1n,5}$, $228^{1n,1}$, 255^2, 257, $284^{1n,4,5}$, 295, 297^{1n}, $347^{1n,1,18}$, $349^{1n,1}$, $375^{5,7}$, 393^1, 397–8, $403^{1n,1}$, 405^3, 406^{1n}, 409, 411 (III), 412, 418^{1n}, 442^7, 446^5, 449–51, 458, 459^{16}, 470 (I), 473^{1n}, 481, $484^{18,19}$, 486^7, 489^{21}, $495^{1n,4,14}$, $523^{1,2}$, $524^{2,7,14}$, 526^{1n}, 527, 542, 546, 550^9, $560^{3,7-10}$, 569^5, 584^1, 613^3, 621, App ^{56}, Gl s.vv. Arians, Meletians, patriarch
— Library, 98^5; Monastery of Metanoia, 584^1; Museum, 189^2; Serapeum, 111^{13}; Temple of Good Success, 257^6
Alexandrians, 50, 53, 67^{31}, $69^{3,10}$, 77^3, 85^1, $86^{1,2,15,35}$, 95^{22}, 98, 111, 115, 119^5, 122, 182, 257^1, 345, 347, 349, 408, 409, 412^{1n}, 445, 459^{12}, 470 (IV), 477, 480, 481, 488^2, 489, 495, 524 (I), 527, 562, $621^{6,8}$, 637^7, Gl s.v. Valentinians
Algeria, 59^{10}
Ali-Faradin-Yaïla, 568^{1n}; Oratory of St John the Apostle, 568
Alpes Maritimae, 203^4
Alps, 203^4
Amalfi, 181^4; Basilica of Sant' Andrea, 181^4
Amida, 598^{12}
Amidenes, 636
Anazarbus, 415^4
Ancore, 48^{19}
Ancyra, 48 (II, III), $159^{42,43}$, 470 (I), Gl s.vv. Marcellians, Photinians
Ancyrans, 636
Angles, Tab^5
Angora, see Ancyra
Ankara, see Ancyra
Antes, Gl s.v. Anticus
Antigoneia, 48^{19}
Antioch (Caria), 159^{42}
— (Pisidia), 182^3
— (Syria), In^{11,43}, 5^1, 48 (III), 53^3, 61 (II), 71^{1n}, 74^3, 75^{42}, 84^{1n}, 103, 108, 111^{12}, 112^4, 113^4, 117, 119^5, 124, 125^2, 126, $159^{16,42}$, 167^2, 194^7, 284^5, 297^4, $375^{5,7}$, 401^{12}, 402^4, 405, $410^{2,4}$, 411 (I)^3, 412, $414^{1n,8}$, $415^{1n,6,12}$, 416, 417^3, 418^{1n}, $419^{1n,2}$, 420^4, $427^{1n,6}$, 442^7, 459, $470^{44,62,64,69}$, 473^{1n}, 512^{1n}, 523^2, 527^{1n}, 542^{11}, 543^{1n}, 559, $560^{1n,7,10}$, $635^{1n,1}$, App 10(f), ^{36}, Gl s.v. Aetians, patriarch, Paulianists. See also Theopolis. Great Church (Domus Aurea), 119^5; Monastery of Euprepianum, 410^2

1279

PLACES

Antiochenes, 13[11], 47[1n], 61, 103[4], 108, 124 (III), 376[1n], 402, 404, 405[1n,3-5], 411, 412[1n], 414, 415 (II), 417[1n], 427[1n], 459, 470 (VI, X), 512, 559, 562. *See also* Theopolitans
Antium (Anzio), 64[5]
Apamea, 428
Apameans, 636
Apennines, In[7]
Aphrodisias, 428[1n], 542[18]
Aphrodisians, 428
Aptunga, 17[1n], 21[1n], 328[9]
Aptungitans, 21, 328
Aquileia, 84[8], 129, 130, 133, 165, 172[1n], 177, 209, 295, 387–90
Aquileians, 172
Aquitania, 203[4]
Arabia, 117[1n], 273[2], 470 (VI)
Arabs, 442[7]
Arethusa, 119[5]
Arethusians, 61 (III)
Argentina, 1[4]
Arimathaea, App[53]
Ariminum, *see* Rimini
Arles, 17[12], 18, 19, 20[1n], 21[1n], 22[1n], 25, 95[21], 350[1n], 387[9], 442, 500
Arlesians, Arletans, 17, 432
Armenia, In[43], 3[7], 103[1], 106[5,6], 417, 637[18]
Armenians, 106, 637, Gl s.v. Armenaicus
Armenia Minor, 416[1n]
Arycanda, 9[1n]
Arycandans, 13[11]
Aržer Palanca, *see* Ratiara
Asia, 28[1], 46[16], 52[48], 397, 406[1n], 449, 452, 551[1], 547[1], 615[1], 642[17], 644[6]
— (diocese), 43 (II), 52, 159, 163, 182, 410[4], 470[70], 471, 475[1n], 618, Gl s.v. exarch
— (province), 2, 3[8], 182, 234[3], 243, 254, 454, 470[53]
— Minor, In[43], 3[8,21], 5[1], 18[3], 43[1n], 48[9], 52[2,3], 107[7], 117[6], 159[1n], 303[2], 350[1n], 428[1n], 489[21], 523[5], 568[1n], 577[1n,13], Gl s.v. Encratitans, Gnostics, Montanists, Papians
Asians, 410[4], 470 (XI), 471, 560, Gl s.v. Apollinarians. *See also* Asiatics
Asiatics, 3[8], 5[1], 167[1n], 397[1]. *See also* Asians
Aspona, 84[1n]
Assyrians, Gl s.v. Samaritans
Asturia et Gallaecia, 19[27]
Athens, In[11], 73[17], 98[7], 111[7], 582[1], 606[2], App[6]
Athenians, 3[20], 644[6], App[6]
Atlantic Ocean, Gl s.v. patriarch
Augustamnica (Augustomnicha), or Augustamnichus, 87
Austria, In [44], Tab[5], 308[1n]
Autun, 17[12]
Auxume (Auxumis), 99

Auxumites, 99[1n]
Avignon, 140[1]
Avila, 103[1], Gl s.v. Priscillians
Axoum, Axum, *see* Auxume

Babylon, 651[13]
Babylonians, 303[1], Gl s.v. Manichaeans
Baetica, 19[27]
Bagai, 328[5]
Baleares, 19[27]
Balkans, 52[48], 181[4], 545[4], Gl s.v. Novatians
Baltimore, In [32,42]
Beirut, In[11], 61[11], 147, 447[1n], 456, 470 (I), 640[1]
Beirutians, 447
Belgium, Tab[5]
Belgrade, *see* Singidunum
Berlin, In [44]
Beroea, 61[11], 95[1n], 406, 411 (II), 412[1n]
Besançon, 442[1n]
Bethlehem, 313[1]
Bithynia, 1[1n], 45[1], 47[102], 48 (I, II), 117, 133[1], 212[1], 466, 468[6], 470 (IX). Monastery of Irenaion, 645[35]
Bithynians, 1[5], 131[1n], 464, 525[1]
Black Sea, 523[3]
Bologna, In[2]
Bordeaux, 203[1,8]
Bosporus, 476[1], 645[35]
Bostra, 117[1n,14], 123[3]
Bostrans, 117
Braga, 203[1]
Brescia, 276
Brindisi, 220[3]
Britain, Tab[5], 46[9], 52, 203[3]. *See also* Britannia, England
Britannia, 52[47]
— Inferior, Prima, Secunda, Superior, 52[47]
Britons, 46, 350[1n], Gl s.v. Pelagians
Brooklyn, In[42], 472[30]
Bruttii, 16[2], 30
Bua, 330
Bulgaria, 84[1], 172[1n]
Burgundy, Tab[5]
Burgundians, In[2], Tab[5], 519[1n]
Byblus, 459[14]
Byzacena, 646[19]
Byzacenes, 118, 129, 130
Byzacium, 19, 118[1], 566[1], 646 (I)
Byzantium, *see* Constantinople
Byzantines, 118[1], 228[2]

Cabarsussi, 328[5]
Caesarea (Cappadocia), 61 (III), 107[7], 113[5], 119[5], 182[4], 458[3], 470 (I), 557[1n,3,4], Gl s.v. exarch
— (Palestine), In[11], 44[1n], 61[1n,6], 64[1n], 470[49], App 10(e),[36]
Caesareans (Cappadocia), 119[5], 557
— (Palestine), 61 (I, II)
— (Cappadocia or Palestine), 636

PLACES 1281

Cagliari, 37, 195^{1n}, Gl s.v. Luciferians
Camden, In^{42}
Campania, 46^{13}, 365^7
Canaanites, 457
Cappadocia, In^{14}, 61 (III), 98^{15}, 113, 124 (I), 182^4, 458^3, 470 (I), 557^{1n}, Gl s.v. Enthusiasts, exarch
Cappadocians, 98^{15}, 107^7, 119^5, 568^2, 620^1
Caputvada, 646^1
Caria, 119^1, 428^{1n}
Carophrygia, 159
Carpians, Gl s.v. Carpicus
Carrhae, 447^{1n,5}
Carrhaeans 447
Carthage In^{11,26,52}, 4^4, 10^1, 15, 16^8, 17^{1n,5}, 19^{8,28}, 20^{1n}, 21^{1n}, 24^{1n}, 27^{1n}, 47^{14,16}, 68^1, 76, 140^1, 183, 301, 324^{1n,5,12}, 325, 326, 328, 338^{1n}, 350^{1n,4}, 361^{1n}, 367, 368^{1n}, 409^5, 523^1, 642, 646 (I)^{14}, Gl s.v. Maximians, patriarch. Baths of Gargilius, 326; Forum, 301
Carthaginians, 17, 19, 21^{10}, 325, 326, 340^{1n}, 361, 397^{10}
Carthaginiensis, 19^{27}
Carthago Proconsularis, 646^{19}
Casae Nigrae, 17^{1n,7}, 328^6
Castle of Simeon, 411^3
Centumcellae, 95^{27}
Chalcedon, In^{34,43}, 16^{1n}, 53^3, 228^{1n,2}, 246^1, 284^4, 275^7, 407, 408^{1n}, 409, 412^1, 447^{1n}, 449^{1n,7}, 456^{1n}, 461^{1n}, 464^{1n,1}, 466^{1n}, 467^{1n,1}, 468, 469^{1n}, 470^{1n,44,70}, 471^{1n}, 472^{1n,14,30}, 473, 475-7, 479^{1n,11,13,14}, 480, 481, 482^{1n,4,5}, 483^{1n}, 484^{1n}, 485-7, 489^{1n,21}, 495, 524, 527, 542, 543^6, 546, 548, 551^2, 559^{11}, 560, 569^5, 577^{1n}, 591, 592^7, 606, 613^{1,4}, 637, 645, Gl s.vv. council, Eutychians, Monophysites. Church of St Euphemia, 471^{10}, 472^{27}
Chalcedonians, 465^3, 466, 468, 469, 470^{1n}, 473 (III), 476, 477, 479, 480, 482-4, 486, 489, 527^{1n}, 543^9, 546
Chaldaeans, 207^{10}, Gl s.v. Manichaeans, Samaritans
Châlons-sur-Marne, 442^4
Chersonesus, Tauric, 369^3, 495^{1n}
Chicago, In^{42}
China, 1^4
Cilicia, 52, 104^{1n}, 107^7, 414^6, 416^8, 417^2, 427^{1n}, 540^{1n}
— Prima, 414^6
— Secunda, 95^{22}, 414^6, 417
Cilicians, 67^{37}, 414
Cirta, 19^{22}, 59^{10}
Civitavecchia, 95^{27}
Colonia Agrippina, see Köln
Commagene, 420^2
Concordia, 230, 231
Constanta, 523^3. See also Tomi
Constantia, 43^{1n}

Constantiana, 523^3. See also Tomi
Constantina (Gaul), 18^8
— (Numidia), 59
Constantinople, In^{11,30,34,43,52}, Tab^{3,5}, 28, 32, 38^{1n}, 43 (II), 47^{102}, 50^{1n}, 53^3, 55^2, 61^{7,11}, 62^{1n,2,4}, 64^3, 65, 71^{1n}, 75, 76^{4,5}, 82^1, 98^{15}, 103^1, 106, 107^{10}, 112^1, 114, 118^{1,3}, 120^5, 127, 128, 140^1, 141^3, 159^{16}, 163, 167, 173-6, 178, 179, 181^{1n,1,2,5,6}, 184, 185, 186^2, 187, 189, 191-4, 196, 197, 205-8, 210, 212, 217, 220, 222^{1n,2}, 223, 228^{1n,1,2}, 233-42, 244, 245, 248, 250, 251, 260, 264, 266, 268, 274, 277, 279, 283, 289^{1n,4,5}, 285-7, 295^{1n,6}, 302, 303, 319^{1n,1,2,4}, 320, 322, 333, 335, 341-3, 347-9, 369, 372^2, 375^{1n,5,7,8,13}, 376-82, 384, 385, 395, 397, 398^{1,4}, 399^4, 400^{44,76}, 401^{15}, 402^{1n}, 405^{1n,3,4}, 406^{1n}, 409, 410^{1n,2}, 411^{16}, 412^{1n,2}, 413, 422^{2,3,19}, 424, 426^{1n}, 427^{1n,2}, 429, 430^1, 431, 432, 434^3, 435-7, 439^3, 442^7, 445^{1n,13}, 446^{1n}, 447, 448^{1n,9}, 449, 450^3, 451^8, 452, 453^{2,6}, 455, 456, 457^{1n,4}, 458^{1,6}, 459, 461, 455, 456, 457^{1n,4}, 458^{1,6}, 459, 461, 463-5, 467^1, 468^{1n,3}, 470 (VIII, IX), 471^{1n,8}, 472^{14,17}, 473^{1n}, 474-7, 479, 480 482, 483^9, 484^{16,20}, 485^9, 486^5, 487^{8,27}, 488, 489, 490^2, 491^{2,5,7}, 492, 495, 497^2, 501, 502, 505^{1,3}, 506-10, 513^3, 516-19, 523^2, 524$^{1,3,12-15,32}$, 526^{6,8,10}, 527, 528, 529^8, 537^{1,8}, 538, 542, 543^{1n,6}, 544, 545, 546^{13} 547, 549, 550, 551^{1n,2}, 552^3, 553^{1n,2}, 554, 556-9, 560^{2,3,6,18,19}, 561^{5,10}, 562^7, 563^{6,7}, 565, 567^{1n,14}, 568, 569^{5,6}, 577^2, 578-80, 584^{4,8}, 583^2, 585^1, 586, 587, 589, 590, 592, 593, 594^6, 595^7, 596^{12}, 597^8, 600^4, 601, 603-5, 608-17, 618$^{1-3}$, 619-25, 627, 628^5, 629, 630, 632^{4,7}, 634, 635, 636^2, 637-9, 640^1, 645-8, 650, 651, Gl s.vv. apocrisiarian, Apollinarians, Council, Eutychians, Marcellians, master of the census, Nestorians, order, patriarch, prefect (urban), registrar, Semi-Arians Senate, senator, vicar (urban)
— as Eternal City, 62^{1n}, 617^{10}; as New Rome, 62^2, 181^5, 325^7, 442^7, 470 (IX)^{22}, 527^{1n}, 544^{1n}, 554, 557^3; as Younger Rome, 475; Blachernae, 538; Ceras (Chrysoceras), 120^5 (see also Golden Horn); Church of the Holy Twelve Apostles, In^{30}, Tab^5, 181^5, 463^5, 551^{10}, 568^1; Church of the Holy Wisdom or Hagia Sophia, 236^3, 246^1, 285^7, 503^1, 518^4, 537^1, 538^1, 579^{18}, 616^7, 617^2, 650^4, Gl s.v. registrar; Forum Augusteum, 595^7; Galata, 538^4; Golden Gate, 595^7; Golden Horn, 120^5, 538^{2,4} (See also Ceras); Hebdomon, 595^7; Hippo-

1282 PLACES

drome, 236²; House of Hormisdas, 541¹⁰; House of Justinian, 541¹⁰; Milion, 595⁷; Monastery of Studium, 645³⁵; Senate House, 276²; Sycae, 120⁵, 538
Constantinopolitans, 120⁵, 127⁶, 167, 181, 225¹ⁿ, 236³, 295, 297¹ⁿ, 345, 375 (I), 398⁷, 408⁴, 411³, 412¹, 449¹ⁿ, 459, 470¹ⁿ,⁷⁰, 472 (I), 474², 475, 476¹ⁿ,⁴, 477¹,¹⁶, 479¹,¹², 483⁵,²³, 485¹⁰, 486⁸, 487⁴, 489, 490¹ⁿ, 495¹ⁿ,⁵, 510¹ⁿ, 524³,²⁸,³², 526¹ⁿ, 527⁷², 530⁹, 538¹ⁿ, 546¹⁴, 551¹ⁿ, 552¹ⁿ, 554, 558³, 560, 562, 565¹ⁿ, 569⁵,⁷, 578¹ⁿ, 580¹ⁿ, 618¹ⁿ, 636, 637³, 645. Gl s.v. fathers (conscript)
Copts, In⁴³
Corcyra, 137¹
Córdoba, In¹⁴, 15⁹, 16⁸, 47⁴, 100¹ⁿ
Corinth, 225¹³
Corinthians, 41⁴, 620²
Corsica, 46¹⁶. Gl s.v. patriarch
Coryciotes, 540
Corycus, 540¹ⁿ,⁷
Cos, 482⁶
Creta, 375¹
Cretans, 523¹
Crete, 52⁴⁸, 523¹
Crimea, 495¹ⁿ
Crimean Peninsula, 369³
Ctesiphon, 156¹
Cumae, Gl s.v. sibyl
Curubitans, App. 8(a)
Cutheans, Gl s.v. Samaritans
Cyprus, 246¹, App. 10(f)
Cyrenaica, 52⁴⁸
Cyrenaica et Creta, 52⁴⁸
Cyrenenses, 1⁴
Cyrestenes, 559
Cyrus (Cyrrhus), 407, 415⁶, 449, 458, 459¹², 463³, 470⁵⁰, 479¹ⁿ, 541¹⁴, 559
Cyzicenes, 676
Cyzicus, 117, 120⁵, 542²⁶, Gl s.v. Eunomians

Dacia, 84¹, 375¹, 523³. See also Romania
— Mediterranea, 375¹
— Ripensis, 375¹
Dalmatia, 375¹
Danube, 464¹, 523³, 545⁴
Dardanelles, 49¹⁸
Dardania, 375¹
Delphi, 44⁸, Gl s.v. Sibyl
Diospolis, 350¹ⁿ
Dorylaeum, 459¹⁰, 470⁶, 479¹ⁿ
Dyrrhachium (Durazzo, Durrës), 547⁷

Eboracum, 52⁴⁷
Eden, Garden of, Gl s.v. Ophitans
Edessa, 42¹ⁿ,⁴,⁵, 84 (III), 123, 447¹ⁿ, 450², 456, 459¹², 542¹⁷. Church of St Thomas the Apostle, 123⁴

Edessans, 42⁵, 123, 447, 456¹ⁿ
Edom, 425¹ⁿ
Egea, 542
Egypt, In³¹, 41, 8¹ⁿ,²⁻⁴, 15⁷, 17³, 23², 42⁴, 52, 53¹ⁿ, 67, 68², 70¹ⁿ, 74¹ⁿ, 78¹ⁿ, 81, 85¹, 87¹ⁿ, 95³⁷, 98¹,³,⁴, 99, 111, 113, 121, 122, 124¹¹, 127⁷, 133¹, 147, 182, 195⁶, 197¹ⁿ, 208¹ⁿ, 220¹⁰, 255², 256³, 257¹ⁿ,², 273², 284², 313¹, 330⁴, 425², 442⁷, 446⁹, 450⁵, 456¹ⁿ, 470³¹, 481¹ⁿ, 489²⁶, 527, 544¹, 560⁹, 562¹¹, 584¹, 638, 646¹⁶, App 5,¹,¹²,³⁸, Gl s.vv. Apollinarians, Manichaeans, Meletians, patriarch, prefect (Augustal)
Egyptians, 28¹, 52⁴, 53¹ⁿ,¹, 68⁵, 98³,⁴, 111⁴, 122, 146⁴, 173¹ⁿ, 189², 220¹⁰, 228¹, 257¹, 284²,⁴, 397¹, 410⁷⁸, 418¹ⁿ, 488², 489, 495, 527¹ⁿ,¹, 549¹ⁿ, 604², Gl s.vv. Aegyptiacus, Batrachitans, Gnostics, governor, Ophitans, Thebaicus
Eire, In⁴³
Elvira, 195⁶, 372⁴
Elysium, 46⁶
Embrun, 161¹
England, 52²,⁴⁷, 98¹⁵, 646⁸. See also Britain
Ephesus, 3, 73¹⁷, 284⁴, 350¹ⁿ, 397, 388¹ⁿ,¹¹, 401¹ⁿ,¹⁴, 402, 403¹ⁿ,⁴, 404¹ⁿ,⁷, 405, 406¹ⁿ, 407-10, 411¹ⁿ,¹, 414¹ⁿ, 415¹ⁿ, 416⁵, 417¹ⁿ, 418¹ⁿ,¹, 420¹ⁿ, 422, 426¹ⁿ, 442⁷, 445, 447¹ⁿ, 448, 449¹ⁿ,⁷, 450¹ⁿ, 451¹ⁿ, 452-6, 457¹ⁿ, 458, 459, 463², 470 (I, VIII), 473¹ⁿ, 476¹, 477, 479¹ⁿ, 480, 484, 486, 489²¹, 523¹, 524 (I), 527⁶⁹,⁷¹,⁷⁶, 542, 551², 559¹¹, 568¹, 577¹ⁿ,¹,⁶,¹³,¹⁵, 613¹, 630⁸, 637, 645, Gl s.vv. council, exarch, Nestorians, Pelagians. Church of Hagia Maria, 397¹, 403³; Oratory of St John the Apostle, 568
Ephesians, 397, 401, 402, 405, 406, 408, 409, 446, 449-51, 455, 460², 470 (VIII), 489, 523¹, 524 (I), 527, 577¹,³, 615¹ⁿ, 636
Epirus Nova, 157, 375¹, 547⁷
— Vetus, 375¹
Erythraeans, 67
Ethiopia, In⁴³, 99⁴
Ethiopians, 99¹ⁿ,². See also Abyssinians
Etruria, 365⁷
Etruscans, 242⁵, 439²
Eudoxiopolis, 319, 383
Euphratensis, 559
Euphrates, 119¹ⁿ, 645³⁵
Euphratesia, 420
Europe, Tab⁵, 281¹, 48 (II), 52⁴⁸, 62², 369³, 382¹ⁿ, 472⁴, 476³⁹, 544, 545⁴, 615¹, 642¹⁷

Flavia Caesariensis, 52⁴⁷
Fonte-Avellana, In⁷. Abbey of Santa Croce, In⁷
Forum Flaminii, 221

PLACES 1283

France, Tab[5], 238[1], 308[1n], 476[39], 646[8]
Franks, Tab[5], Gl s.v. Francicus
Galatia, 18[3], 48 (II, III), 117, Gl s.v. Marcellians
Galatians, 448, 488, Gl s.v. Photinians
Galileans (= Christians), 112, 113, 115-19, 122, 123, Gl
Gallia Aquitanica, Belgica, Bracata, Celtica, Circumpadana, Cisalpina, Citerior, Comata, Lugdunensis, Narbonensis, Togata, Transalpina, Transpadana, Ulterior, 203[4]
Galliae, 203[4]
Gallicans, see Gauls
Gangra, 495[1n]
Gaul, 3[4], 17[1n], 18, 19, 25, 52, 75[1n], 77, 95[51], 106[4], 107[7], 138[1n,1], 149[2], 152, 153, 154[4], 159, 161[2], 164, 165, 203[3,4], 308[2], 351[1], 387, 442, 484[25], 519[1n], 520[1], Gl s.vv. prefect (praetorian), prefecture
Gauls, 159[46], 161[1], 167[1n], 203[1n,1,4], 350[1n], 366, 442, App 4
Gaza, 43[5]
Gentiles, 75[42], 167[2], 214[2], 310, 422[7], 442[7], Gl s.v. Gnostics
Gerastus, 56
Germanicia, 103[1]
Germans, 225[13], 369[3], Gl s.v. Germanicus
Germany, Tab[5], 14, 646[8]
Goths, 246[1], 528[8], 567, Gl s.v. Gothicus
Graeco-Romans, 641[4]
Greece, 1[4], 52, 181[4], 215[1n], 273[2], 641[4], Gl s.v. Sibyl
Greeks, 2[23], 3[30], 26[4], 67[31], 111, 117, 135[4], 181[6], 223[2], 225[13], 241[1], 313[1], 397[1], 414[2], 422, 496[5], 505[1], 537[5], 567[1n], 614[8], 648[7], 650[2], 651[8], App[5], Gl s.v. Samaritans, sibyl

Hades, 46[8], 150[1]
Hadrumetum, 118[3], 566[3]
Hebrews, 122, 206[6], 223[2], 241[2], 472[4], 543 (II), 644[6]. See also Israelites, Jews
Hebron, 63[6]
Helenopolis, 284[1n,2], 285[6], 295[1n]
Helicore, 48[19]
Hellenes (= pagans), 121[3], 476[35], 477[23]
Hellespontines, 131[1n]
Heraclea Perinthus, 131[1n], 181, 182, 243, 247, 269, 544[1n,2], Gl s.v. exarch
— Thraciae (see Heraclea Perinthus)
Heracleans, 544
Heruls, Tab[5]
Hierapolis (Phrygia), 82, 151, Gl s.v. Papians
— (Syria), 407[1n], 411[3], 415[5], 418[1n], 419[1n], 420[1n,8]. Temple of Hera, 411[3]
Hierapolitans, 407, 420
Himeria, 456
Himerians, 447

Hippo Regius, 326[5], 362[2], 368[1n], 406[1]
Hispania, see Spain
— Citerior, Ulterior, 19[27]
Hispellum, 45[1]
Huns, Tab[5], 442[4], 461[1n], 464[1], 467[1], 468[1n,7], 475[5]
Hypepe, 463[4]

Iberians, 350[1n]
Iconium, 182
Idumaeans, 76[4]
Illyricum, 67[13], 105[11], 106[4], 107[7], 159, 165, 184[5], 223[1], 322, 332, 375, 384, 462, 463, 467[1], 468[1n], 469, 471, 475[5], 477, 479, 520[1], 638, 646 (I), Gl s.vv. prefect, praetorian, prefecture
Illyrians, 159[46], 172[1n]
Intherallum, 451[7]
Ionia, 67[27,31], 397[1]
Ireland, In[43]. See also Eire
Irene Secontarurus, 78
Isauria, 470 (I), 523[5,6]
Isaurians, 302, 523, 630[1]
Isaurica, 414[6]
Isauropolis, 523
Israel, In[23], 111[13]
Israelites, 16[4], 23[2], 206[6], 214[2], 242[7], Gl s.v. Samaritans. See also Hebrews, Jews
Istanbul, see Constantinople
Italy, In[7,53], Tab[5], 1[4], 5[1], 6[1], 15[12], 16[8], 17[1n], 19[28], 20[15], 23[1], 24[1n,3], 29[1n], 31[1], 45[1], 46[16], 48 (II), 52, 65[6], 93[1n], 95[27,46], 97[3], 104[1n], 106[4], 107, 109[1], 110[1], 133[1], 160[2], 162[1], 164, 165, 166[2], 172, 181[5], 186[2], 188[1], 190[1], 201[2], 203[4], 205[2], 209[2], 215[1n], 217[7], 220[3], 230[1], 231[1], 261[1], 262[1], 265[1], 281[1], 288[1], 289[1,2], 293[1], 301[1], 306[1], 307[2], 308[1n,1], 309[2], 310[2], 311[1], 312[1], 313[2], 315[2], 316[1], 317[1], 318[1], 326[5], 327[2], 329[1], 331[1], 332[2], 334[1], 350[1n,15], 351[1], 362, 372[5], 391[1], 392[1], 433[1], 435[1], 443[2], 446[1], 461[1n], 474[2], 478[2], 496[1], 497[1], 519, 520[1,2], 528[7], 544[1n], 548[8], 561, 618[13], 646[1,16], App 10(f), Gl s.vv. patriarch, prefect (praetorian), prefecture, sibyl
Italians, 5[1], 17[1n], 104, 141[3], 146[1], 159[46], 172[1n], 173[1n], 220[3], 295[3], 297[3], 341[2], 365[7], 375[7], 397[1], 440[5], Gl s.vv. Augustal, patriarch
Ithaca, 450[1]
Ituraeans, 76[4]

Jerusalem, In[29,31,43], 41[4], 53[3], 54[1n,2,3], 63[1], 73[1n], 75[2], 122[9], 159[34], 167[9], 303[3], 375[7], 451[1], 458, 460, 470 (I), 472[4], 483[1n,15], 484[1n,1,3,5,22], 485[1n,1], 486[1n,1,2], 487[1n,1,14], 523[2], 527[1n], 543 (II), 560, Gl s.v. patriarch. See also Aelia. Church of the Holy Sepulchre, 54, 73[1n]; Holy Sepulchre, 54[1n,6], 483[15]; Temple, Jewish,

1284   PLACES

111^{13}, 159^{34}, 483^{15}; Temple of Jupiter, 54^6, 483^{15}; Temple of Venus, 54^6, 483^{15}
Jerusalemites, 470 (VI), 480^1, 487, 636. See also Aelians
Jews, In 5 (7), 1^4, 17^3, 23, 52, 76, 79, 80, 91, 98^4, 107^7, 116^{13}, 122^9, 148^4, 164^{11}, 188, 209, 214, 225^{13}, 241^2, 244, 266, 267, 303, 305, 310, 315, 332, 333, 341, 344, 346, 348, 376, 378, 379, 382, 385, 387, 392, 397^1, 422^7, 429, 442^7, 476, 477, 483^{15}, 546, 567, 570, 577^{13}, 586^3, 622, 637, 645, 647, 648^5, 651^{16}, 652, App 5, Gl s.vv. Caelicolans, Novatians, patriarch, Quartodecimans, Samaritans, Tessarescaedecatitans, Tetraditans
Judaea, 1^5, 4^2, 159^{27}
Judah, In^{23}
Jugoslavia, see Yugoslavia.
Justinianopolitans, 636
Jutes, Tab^5

Kairwan (Kairuân), $566^{1n,1}$. Abbey of St Stephen the Martyr, 568
Köln, 17^{12}, 95^{51}, 164

Lampsacus, 131^{1n}, 159^{42}
Laodicea, 51^{1n}, 61^{20}, 182^2, 481^4, 483^7, 484^{10}, 485^7, 486^{10}, 487^6, 489^7, 542^{22}, 569^8, 636^{12}, Gl s.v. Apollinarians
Larissans, 3^{30}, App ^{5}
Latins, 313^1
Latin-Americans, 1^4
Lebanon, App 10(f)
Leontopolitans, 523
Levantines, 524^{31}
Libya, Tab^5, 52, 67, 87, 442^7, 527, 642
— Inferior, Superior, 52^{48}
Libyans, 67^{30}
Long Island, In^{42}
Loreto, 397^1
Lucania, 16^2, 30
Lusitania, 19^{27}. See also Portugal
Lycia, Lycians, 9^{1n}
Lycopolis, 53^1, 68^2, Gl s.v. Meletians
Lydia, 426^{1n}, 463^4
Lydians, 479^4
Lyon, 3^4, App 4

Macedonia, 169, 375^1, 384
— Salutaris, 375^1
Macedonians, 111^4, 122
Macellum, 113^5
Maiuma, 43^{1n}
Mambre, 63
Marche, In^6
Marcianopolis, 182
Mareotis, 78, 95
Marmara, Sea of, 120^5, 181^5, 228^2, 538^2, 595^6. See also Propontis
Marmarica, 20^1, 53^1, 67^{30}
Marseille, 19^{28}

Maryland, In^{42}
Mauretania, 15, 19. See also Moors
— Caesariensis, $19^{22,26}$, 646^{19}
— Sitifensis, $19^{22,26}$, 441^2, 646^{19}. See also Moors, Sitifensian
— Tingitana, $19^{22,27}$
Mauretanias, 646 (I)
Maxima Caesariensis, 52^{47}
Medes, 95^{43}, Gl s.v. Medicus
Mediterranean Sea or area, In^{27}, 28^1, 127^6, 195^6, 203^4, 313^1, 328^3, 400^9, 646^1, Gl s.v. Manichaeans, Mithras
Melitene, In^{14}, 182, 416^{1n}, 417
Mesopotamia, 42^{1n}, 112^{10}, 313^1, 598^{12}
Mesopotamians, 52^4, Gl s.v. Audians, Enthusiasts
Milan, In^{21,33,49}, Tab^3, 7^{23}, 9^{1n}, 10^{1n}, 12, 13^{1n}, $14^{1n,13}$, 15^{12}, 18^{1n}, 21^{1n}, 22^{1n}, 23^5, $24^{1n,6}$, 27^{1n}, 39^{1n}, 41^{1n}, 42^{1n}, 47^9, 62^2, 84^7, 91, 93, 94^{1n}, $95^{1n,3}$, 101, 102, 107, 134, 136^{1n}, 160^1, 166, 170, 172^{1n}, 186^2, 187^{1n}, 188, 198, 200–2, 203^1, 205, 218, 220^4, 222, 224–6, 242^{1n}, 250, 261–3, 265, 271, 275, 282, 326^5, 330, 350^{1n}, 375^7, 470^{19}, 495^1. Basilica Portiana (Church of San Vittore al Corpo), 136^{1n}, 205^{1n}
Milanese, 172
Milevis, In^{21}, 19^1, 203^1, 350^{1n}
Milvian Bridge, In^{14}, 10^{1n}, 13^1, 38^2, 44^{17}
Misenians, 3^{25}
Mnizus, 269^4, 270, 271^6, 272, 273
Moesia, 52^{48}
— Inferior, 545
— Prima, 375^1
Moors, 293^{1n}, 598^{12}
— Sitifensian, 441
Mopsuestia, 95^{22}, $416^{1n,8}$, 417^{1n}, 427^{1n}, $459^{7,28}$, 542^{13}, 559^3
Mopsuestians, 417
Murgillum, 23
Mysian Peninsula, 120^5

Nacolaea, 43^4
Nacolaeaus, 43
Naples, 364^{14}
Narbo Marcius, 203^4
Narbonensis, 203^4
Narbonne, 203^4
Nazianzus, 470^{15}
Negrene, $17^{1n,7}$
New Epirus, see Epirus Nova
— Jersey, In^{42}
— Jerusalem, Gl s.v. Pepyzites
— York City, In^{42}, 281, 472^{30}
Newark, In^{42}
Nicaea, In^{14}, 15^9, 17^3, 19^{1n}, $20^{1,11}$, 47^{1n}, 48, 49^1, 50, $51^{1n,2,3}$, 52, 53, 71, 72^{1n}, 94^1, 95, 103^7, 159, 169^3, 181^5, 182^9, 368^5, 375^5, 406^{10}, 442^7, 445, 446, 448,

PLACES 1285

455, 458–60, 461[1n], 464[1n], 466[1n], 467–9, 470[1n] (I), 472[1n], 475[2], 476[1,31], 477, 480, 481, 483[11,24], 484[14], 486[4], 487, 523[1], 524 (I), 527, 542, 543[9], 546, 551[2], 554[1], 559[11], 569[5], 613[1,3], 637, 645, Gl s.vv. Arians, council
Nicaeans (Nicenes), 52[5], 53, 182, 368, 459[18], 464, 466, 470[61,70,74], 472[7], 489, 569[5]
Nicomedia, 7[1n], 12[9], 13, 15[12], 47[10], 51[1], 58[1n], 61[7,11], 71[2], 72[1n], 212[1], 411[1n], 412[1n], 470 (IX), 472[30], App 10(a),[16,20]
Nicomedians, 13, 47, 50, 412, 472 (III)
Nile, 1[3], 67
Nish, 84[7]
Nisibis, 542[20]
Nola, 359[1n]
Nolans, 359
Noricum Mediterraneum, Ripense, 375[1]
Novempopuli, 203[4]
Numidia, In[21], 15, 17[5], 19, 59, 60, 326[5], 441[2], 646 (I)
— Cirtensis, 19[22]
Numidians, 60[1n], 441
Nursia, 297[3]
Nyssa, 182, 470[15]

Oppidum Ubiorum, see Köln
Orcistus, Orcistans, 43
Orontes, 167[1n]
Osrhoëne, 42[1n], 476
Ostrogoths, In[2], Tab[5], 308[1n], 519[1n], 520[2], 528[7], 544[1n], 567[1n]
Oxford, 641[8]. Christ Church, 641[8]
Oxyrhynchus, 195[6]

Pactiana, 159
Padua, 190, 278
Palaestina Prima, 45[14], 54[28], 64[20], 470[49], 484[22], 486[14], App[30]. See also Palestine
— Secunda, 470[49], 483[15], 484[6]. See also Palestine
— Tertia, 470[49]. See also Palestine
Palestine, 4[2], 46, 47[11], 61[1n], 63, 64[1], 174[1n], 341[2], 350[1n], 397[1], 470 (VI), 483, 484[25], 485, 486[1n,2], 487, App 10 (a), 10 (d), 10 (f)[17,20,36], Gl s.vv. patriarch, Samaritans
Palestinians, 23[3], 63[1n], 341[2], 487[1n], App[38], Gl s.v. patriarch
Palmyra, 5[1]
Pamphylia, 523[6], 568[1n]
Pamphylians, 9[1n]
Pandataria, 46[13]
Pannonia Prima, Secunda, 375
Pannonians, 519[1n]
Paphlagonia, 117, 495[1n]
Parma, 164
Parthia, 106[6]
Parthians, 3[7]
Paterson, In[42]

Patmos, 46[13]
Patras, 182[4]
Pentapolis, 442[7], 527
Pepuza, Pepyza, Gl s.v. Pepyzites
Pergamum, 470[86]
Perinthus, 11[1n], 544[2]
Perrha, Perrhenes, 470 (X)
Persia, 105[5,6], 542[20], 627[1]
Persians, 4[1], 34[5], 95[43], 117[17], 119[17], 156[1], 303[1], 542, 551[10], 598[12], 642, 646 (II), Gl s.vv. Manichaeans, Mithras, Persicus
Petra, 425, 426, 470[49]
Pharan, 483[2], 487[22]
Philippi, 406[1], 626[8]
Phoenice, 470[48]
— Libanensis, 470[48]
Phoenicia, 43[1n], 63, 470 (VI)
— Prima, 470 (V)
Phoenicians, 9[6], 59[10], 447
Phrygia, 43[1n], 119[5], Gl s.vv. Cataphrygians, Montanists, Novatians, Pepyzites, Phrygians, Priscillians
— Salutaris, 470[6]
Phrygians, 43[4], Gl s.vv. Phrygians, Tascodrogitans
Pisidia, 182[3], 205[6]
Planasia, 46[13]
Po, 203[4]
Poitiers, 104[1n], 470[18]
Poland, 1[4]
Pompeii, 3[25]
Pontics, 410, 470 (XI), 471, 542[29], 547, Gl s.v. Gnostics
Pontus, 1[1n], 52, 133[1], 182, 410[4], 470[70], 475[1n], 568[2], 615, 618, Gl s.v. exarch. Martyry of St Dius, 568[2]
Portugal, Tab[5], 1[4], 19[27], Gl s.v. Gnostics. See also Lusitania
Pozzuoli, 164
Praevalitana, 375[1]
Propontis, 319[4], 544[1n,2]. See also Marmara, Sea of
Provincia, 203[4]
Ptolemais, 20[1], 53[1], 67[30]
Pyrenees, 203[4]

Quadians, Tab[5], 105[11]
Quinque Provinciae, 203[4]

Ratiara, 172[1n]
Ravenna, 62[2], 186[2], 220[4], 281, 288–94, 296, 304–8, 310–13, 315–18, 323[1], 324, 327, 329, 331, 332, 334, 337, 340, 344, 346, 350, 352, 353[2], 354[1n], 355[2], 356[1n], 357[1n], 358[4], 359[1n,1], 361[2], 362, 365[1,2], 366[3,4], 368, 370, 372, 375[7], 389[1], 391, 393, 399, 434, 435, 495[1], 496, 497, 519
Ravennates, 353
Reggio, 199
Reims, 135[6]
Rhaetia, 188[2]

Rhine, 203^4
Rhône, 18^8
Rimini, 104, 105, 159^{42}, 205
Rockville Center, In^{42}
Romania, 523^3. See also Dacia
Rome, $In^{9,11,14,26,42,43,45,52}$, $Tab^{3,5}$, $1^{2,3}$, 5^1, 15^{12}, 17, 18^{1n}, 19, 20^{1n}, 21^{1n}, 22^{1n}, 28¹, 31, 36, 38^2, 45^1, 52, 53^3, 55^2, 57^3, $62^{1,2}$, 65^6, 68^1, 76^3, 82^1, 84^7, 92^3, 95, 97, 98^7, 101, 102^1, 106^5, 118^3, 127^6, 131^{1n}, 132^1, $133^{1,2}$, 134^1, 135, 137^4, 138, $139^{1n,3}$, 140, $141^{1n,2,3}$, 142, $143^{1n,1-4}$, 145^1, 146^{1n}, 150, 152, 153, 154^4, 155^2, 156^2, 159, 164, $167^{1n,2,3}$, 168^1, 169^1, 173^{1n}, 177^2, 180, 181^4, 183^{1n}, 186^2, 200^2, 203^2, 206^6, 209, $211^{1n,1,7}$, 219, 220, 232, 236^2, 285^5, 290^1, 293^{1n}, 295, 298–301, 313, $330^{1n,7,8}$, 334^4, 338, 341^2, $350^{1n,31,34}$, 351^2, $352^{1n,7}$, 353^1, $355^{1n,3}$, $356^{1n,1,3,5}$, $357^{1n,2}$, $358^{3,5}$, 359^{1n}, 360^1, 361, 362, 363^{1n}, $364^{1n,1,3-5,8,11,14}$, $365^{1n,1,2,4,7}$, $366^{2,4}$, 367, 368, 371^1, $373^{1n,3}$, 374^{1n}, 375 (I)^{5,7,9}, 388, 397^1, $399^{4,11}$, 409^5, 413, 435^2, 439–44, 461–4, 468, 471, 472 (I), $475^{1n,9}$, 478, 479, 480^{27}, 482, 492^1, 495^1, 496^4, 497^2, 499^{1n}, 500^{11}, 505^3, 520, $523^{1,5}$, 524^{14}, 527^{1n}, $544^{1n,1}$, 545^{1n}, 546^1, $547^{4,8}$, 548, 549^{1n}, $551^{1n,1}$, $552^{3,6}$, $553^{1n,3}$, 554^3, 557^{1n}, 558^1, $560^{2,10}$, 561, 563, 564, 598^{12}, 614^6, 617, 637^7, 641^8, 645, 646 (I), 651^{13}, App 2, 10 (f), Gl s.vv. aedile, augur, fathers (conscript), master of the census, Montenses, order, patriarch, peregrine, pope, praetor, prefect (urban), quindecimviv, Senate, senator, vicar (urban)
—, as Catholic Rome, 489^{39}; as Elder Rome, 470 (I, VIII), 637; as Eternal City, 140, 200, 350, 356, 366, 371, 374; as Great Rome, 484; as Old Rome, 62^2, 181^4, 375 (I)^{7,8}, 442^7, 470 (VII, XI), 544^{1n}, 617, 628; Altar of Victory, 231^1, 429^{30}; Basilica Liberiana, 97; 138^3; Basilica Sicininiana, 138; Basilica of San Giovanni in Laterano, 352^2, 364^{11}; Basilica of San Paulo fuori le Mura, 200^1; $211^{1n,1}$, 551^{13}, 618^{13}; Basilica of San Pietro in Vaticano, Tab^5, 139^{1n}, $551^{1,13}$; Basilica of Santa Maria Maggiore, 95^1, 138^3; Capitol, 341^2; Catacomb of San Callisto, In^{26}, 97^4; Catacomb of Maximus, 364^4; Cemetery of Santa Felicita, 364^4; Cemetery of Santi Mareo, Marcelliano e Damaso, 97^4; Church of San Bonifacio, 364^4; Church of San Callisto, 364^{14}; Church of Santa Felicita, 364^4; Circus Maximus, 236^2; Forum Romanum, 241^1, 324^7, 334^4, Gl s.v. treasury (public); Forum Traianum, 443; Quirinal, 220^3; Regina Coeli, 397^1; Temple of Safety, 220^3; Temple of Saturn, Gl s.vv. fisc, treasury (public); Temple of Venus Genetrix, 624^8; Vatican Library, In^7

Romans, $1^{2,5}$, 2^{22}, 3, 5^1, 7, 8, 16, 17, 35, 38^3, 44, 45^{14}, 52, 62^2, 76, 99, 106^8, 122, 126^5, 127^6, 135^4, 137^{1n}, 140^1, 150^1, 156^1, 159^{34}, 167, 187, 200, 203^4, 204^3, 211, 218^5, 220^3, 223^2, 236^2, 241^1, 242^5, 295, $308^{14,22}$, 315^1, 320, 324^7, 341^2, $358^{1n,1}$, 369^{1n}, 370^1, 371, 375 (II), 394^4, 395, 399^1, 404^{1n}, 409^1, 411 (I), 414^6, 422, 435^3, 442, 459, 468, 470^{70}, 471^{1n}, 474^2, 475, 477, 479^4, 480, 483^{15}, 484, 489^{39}, 495, $496^{5,11}$, 505^1, 515^{17}, 519, 527, 528^7, 537^5, 544^{1n}, 548^{1n}, 552^3, 555^{1n}, 561, 567^{16}, 572^3, 578, $623^{2,6}$, 639, $641^{1n,7,12,17}$, 642, 650^2, App, 8, 10 (a)^{11,43,47}, Gl s.vv. as, Assembly, consul, fathers (conscript), imperium interpretation, manumission, paterfamilias, peregrine, pontifex maximus, praetor, sibyl

Rugians, Tab^5
Russia, 1^4

Sahara, 52^{48}
Samaria, 422^7, 457^{14}, Gl s.vv. Samaritans, Simonians
Samaritans, In^{45}, 392, 422^7, 429, 484, 486, 567, 570, 574, 575, 599, 622, 647, Gl
Samosata, 5^1, 117, 542, Gl s.v. Paulianists
Sardica, see Sofia
Sardinia, In^{39}, 195^{1n}, 646 (I), Gl s.vv. Luciferians, patriarch
Sardis, In^4, 3^{20}, 4^2
Sarmatians, 105^{11}, Gl s.v. Sarmaticus
Savia, 375^1
Saxons, Tab^5
Scutari, 49^{18}
Scythia, 182, 544, 545
— Minor, 523^4, 551^{1n}
Scythians, 369^3, 523, $551^{1n,7}$, $552^{1n,6}$, 553, 560^{16}, 636^{1n}
Scyths, 545^4
Scythopolis, 470^{49}, 484^6
Scythopolitans, 483, 487
Sebastenes, 636
Seleucia, $104^{1n,2,3}$, 159^{42}, 205^6, 470 (I)
— -on-the-Tigris, 542^{21}
Selymbria, 319^4
Serdica, see Sofia
Sevastopol, 369^3
Sicily, In^{53}, 1^5, 8, $9^{24,28}$, 646^1, Gl s.vv. patriarch, praetor
Sidon, 483^{23}, 487^{27}
Silistria, 136^{1n}

PLACES 1287

Sinai, 64[18] 483, 484[22], 487
—, Monastery of St Catharine, 483[21]
Sinaitics, 483
Singidunum, 172[1n]
Sinope, Gl s.v. Marcionites
Sirmium, 15[12], 41, 159[42], 164, 483[6], 485[6], 487[5], Gl s.v. Photinians
Smyrna, 206[6], 577[1n,3,13], App[6]
Smyrnans, 577
Sofia, 26[2], 31, 59, 60, 84[1,7], 95
Spain, In[42], Tab[5], 1[4], 19, 52, 107, 164, 195[6], 203[1], 369[8], 372[4], Gl s.v. Priscillians
Spanish, 249[1], 288[14], 370[1], 484[25]
Spartans, 540[4]
Spoleto, 57, 355[1n,2], 356[1n], 357, 358[6], 359, 360[1n], 361[1n,3], 362[1n], 364
Spoletans, 355, 356, 360, 364
Sporades, 46[13]
Stobi, 215, 216
Sueves, Tab[5], 308[1n]
Switzerland, Tab[5], 308[1n]
Syracuse, 18, 19[1n]
Syracusans, 18
Syria, In[42], 17[3], 51[1n], 61[20], 94, 108[1n], 112[4], 117[6], 119[5], 167[2], 182[2], 410[4], 411[3], 416[8], 426, 470[62], 481[4], 483[7], 484[10], 485[7], 486[10], 487[6], 489[7], 527[1n], 542[22], 544[1], 560[9], 562[11], 569[8], 620[12], Gl s.vv. Apollinarians, Encratitans
Syrians, 52[1,4], 61[20], 94[1], 167[1n], 410[1n], 476[1n], 527[1n], 543[1n], 549[1n], 560[16], Gl s.vv. Gnostics, Samaritans
Syrophoenicians, 457[15]

Tangier, 19[27]
Tarraconensis, 19[27]
Tarsus, 107[7], 182, 414, 415[3], 459[28], 542[12], 559[2]
Tarsians, 636
Tartarus, 46[6]
Telezeha, 42[1n]
Thagaste, 362[2]
Thamugada, 21[1n]
Thebaïd, 53[1] 68[2], 87, Gl s.v. Thebaïcus
Thebans, Gl s.v. Thebaïcus
Thebans (Boeotia), 150[1]
Theodosiopolis, 447
Theopolis, 35[1]. See also Antioch (Syria)
Theopolitans, 635, 636. See also Antiochenes
Theoupolis, see Theopolis
Therallum 451
Thessalia, 375[1]
Thessalonica, In[45], 74[5], 167-9, 213, 214, 217[7], 295, 375[1n,5,13], 384[1n,1]
Thessalonicans, 3[30], 375[3], 384, App[5]
Thisbeans, 341[2]
Thrace, 95[1n], 106[4], 131[1n], 462, 463, 469, 470[70], 471, 475[1n], 618, Gl s.v. exarch
Thracians, 319[4], 470 (XI), 492[11], 544[2]
Thuburbo Maius, 17[4]

P

Thuringians, Tab[5]
Tiber, 1[3], 167[1n], 211
Tiberias, 341[2]
Tigisis, 17[5]
Tingis, see Tangier
Tingitana, 19[27]
Toledo, 372[4]
Tomi, 182[5], 523. See also Constanta
Tours, 203[1], 297[3]
Transjordan, 425[1n]
Trapezuntians, 636
Trenton, In[42]
Trèves, 15[12], 25, 35[5], 62[2], 75[1n], 77, 84[7], 140, 144, 148, 149, 154, 156-8, 160, 161, 203[1,7,8]
Tricamaron 646[1]
Trimuthus 295[3]
Tripolis 19, 52[48], 646 (I)
Tripolitana 646[19]
Troy, 62[2], 617[10]
Tunis 566[1] 646[1]
Tunisia, 17[1n], 566[1n]; Monastery of St Stephen the Protomartyr, 566
Turkey, 1[4], 28[1], 489[9]
Turks, 29[1], 61[2], 220[3], 505[1]
Tuscia, 6[1]
Tyre, 9, 68[4], 70[1n], 73, 74[1n], 75, 95, 273[2], 401[18], 426[1n], 445, 446[1n], 447[1n], 456, 470[39], 646[14], Gl s.v. Porphyrians
Tyrians, 9[4], 13[11], 75[1], 273[2], 445-7, 470 (V)
Tyzica, 17[4]

Ulster, In[42]
Umbria, 6[1], 45[1]
United States, In[1,42], 62[11], 83[5], 357[1n], 472[30]
Utica, 646[16]

Valentia, 52[47]
Vandals, Tab[5], 308[1n], 369[8], 470[2], 597[12], 642, 646 (I), Gl s.v. Vandalicus
Venetia, 144
Venetians, 181[4]
Vercelli, 93[1n]
Verona, 227-9
Vesuvius, 3[25]
Via Ostiensis, 200[1], 211[5]
— Salaria, 364[4]
Vienna, In[44]
Vienne, 3[4], 62[2], 238[1], App 4
Viennensis, 203[4]
Visigoths, In[2], Tab[5], 308[1n], 323[1n], 350[1n], 646[1], Gl s.v. interpretation

Washington, In[42]
Westminster Abbey, 472[4]
Whitby, 52[2]

York, see Eboracum
Yugoslavia, 1[4], 172[1n], 330[9]

Zaragoza, 203[1]
Zeugi, 646 (I)
Zeugitana, 646[19]
Ziquensians, 21

SUBJECTS

a censibus, 256²
a cognitionibus, 256²
a commentariis, 256²
a consiliis, 256²
a diplomatibus, 256²
a dispositionibus, 256²
a libellis, 256²
a memoria, 256², 511²
a rationibus, 256²
a studiis, 256²
ab epistulis, 256²
Abba Salama, 99¹
abbess, 484²⁷, 614, Gl
abbot, 116¹⁶, 405³, 450¹ⁿ, 531, 566, 614, Gl
absolution, Gl s.vv. Montanists, Novatians
Abuna, 99¹
accession, 341², 510
acclamation, 448⁶, 465³, 470¹²,⁵⁸, 471³, 472⁴,¹⁴,¹⁶,¹⁹,²⁶, 475⁶, 519
accomplice, 638
accounts, public, 15⁸, 606
accrual, 496¹⁵
accusation *or* accuser, In⁴⁶, 1, 2¹ⁿ, 3, 4², 9⁹, 15, 17, 19, 21, 22, 24, 27, 46, 49 (I), 50, 61 (I), 62, 64, 67–9, 74, 75²⁷, 88, 91, 94¹ⁿ, 95, 96, 99, 102, 111, 117, 124 (I–III), 135, 136¹, 150, 159³⁴, 164, 185, 190, 214, 242, 266, 268, 298, 299, 319, 328, 334, 344, 347, 350, 351, 372, 391, 392, 399–401, 413, 432, 437, 440, 443, 445, 447¹,⁴, 470 (X), 478, 479, 490, 496, 500–2, 507–9, 511, 515, 519, 522, 570, 573, 579, 582, 586, 592, 605, 611, 612, 627, 640 (V), 651, App 10(a), Gl s.vv. *damnatio memoriae, Lex Remmia, libellus*. *See also* litigant; plaintiff; prosecutor
acephali, 527¹ⁿ
acolyte, 32⁴, 109³, Gl
 regional, 356⁶
acropolis, 400
acta:
 conciliar *or* synodal, 17³, 95¹ⁿ, 107², 159, 397, 403, 406¹, 408¹ⁿ, 414¹ⁿ, 448⁴, 451¹, 452¹, 453¹ⁿ,¹, 455¹ⁿ, 456, 457¹⁹, 459¹ⁿ, 469⁴, 470 (I, XI), 477, 479, 480, 482, 483, 485¹ⁿ, 486¹ⁿ, 495¹⁴, 524 (I), 546
 conferential, 324¹ⁿ, 328²
 judicial, 203⁷
 martyrial, App¹⁶
 proconsular, 21, App 8 (a)
actio hypothecaria, 604

in factum, 598, 641²¹
in personam, 598⁸⁻¹⁰, 604, 612¹³
in rem, 598, 604, 612¹³
legis. *See legis actio*
per condictionem, 598
action, 504, 640¹ⁿ
 debarment of, 65⁶, 185⁸, 190⁸, 209, 238, 255, 598, 622, 630, 632, App 10 (a)
 for adultery, 190⁸, App 10 (a)
 for damages, 625¹⁴, 640 (III, V), Gl s.v. *Lex Aquilia*
 for division of common property, 641¹⁸
 for division of family estate, 641¹⁸
 for exaction of interest, 598
 for falsehood, 204
 for injuries, 334, 394⁵, 440, 478
 for recovery of payment of non-existent debt, 640²
 for recovery of price, 598
 for sacrilege, 392
 mixed, 640 (II–V)
 of forcible entry, 478
 of violated sepulchre, 641¹⁷
 of voidance, 190
 on contract, 501, 625⁹, 648
 on corrupting slaves, 640 (III)
 on delict, 509¹
 on deposit, 640 (III)
 on informal promise, 522¹ⁿ
 on obligation, 168¹, 509¹, 625⁹
 on purchase, 641 (IV)
 on robbery, 593³
 on stolen property, App 10 (a)
 on theft, 640 (III)
 right of, 387, 421, 604¹ⁿ, 623, 648
 undefended, 603
actor *or* actress, 154, 170, 177, 183, 247, 493, 629⁶, 649, 650, 651⁸. *See also* ex-actress; orchestra; spectacle, theatrical; stage; theatre
Adelphians, Gl
administration *or* administrator:
 civil, 376, Gl s.v. judge
 military, 582, 646²². *See also* governor, military
 of leased ecclesiastical property, 618
 of pious causes, 612, 623, 648¹ⁿ
 provincial, 582, 646. *See also* governor, provincial
 public, 41, 575, 605, 628³, 650, App 10 (f)
adoption, 26¹, 67, 577, Gl s.v. *patria potestas*

SUBJECTS

adoration, 206^7, 386^{1n}
adultery *or* adulterer, 63^2, 65^6, 67^{12}, 135, 145, 168^1, 171^1, 180, 190^8, 198, 201, 207, 214, 225^{13}, 593^3, 638^{14}, App 10 (a), Gl s.vv. *Lex Iulia de adulteriis coercendis*; Novatians
Advent, Second, 159
adviser, ecclesiastical, to emperor, In, 3, 6^{14,18,44,49}, 15^9, 16^8, 23^4, 31^{1n}, 46^{26}, 47^{1n,17,26}, 50^{1n}, 71^2, 72^{1n}, 95^{27}, 126^1, 158^{1n}, 160^1, 172^{1n}, 242^{1n}, 372^6, 376^{1n}, 406, 447^{1n}, 524^2, 526^{1n}
advocate. *See* lawyer
aedile, 141^3, 382^1, Gl and therein s.v. Assembly, Tribal
aeon, Gl s.vv. Borborians, Gnostics, Manichaeans
Aetians, 179, Gl and therein s.v. Anomoeans
affidavit, 456
aged, the, 133^1, 515^5, 595, 604, 612, 648
agency *or* agent, 478, 606, 619^{1n}, 625^{1n}, Gl s.v. procurator
agent, secret-service, 256, 301, 433, 511, 547^6, 551, 553, Gl s.vv. magistrian, master of the offices
agnation *or* agnate, 421, 599, 608, 628^2, Gl. *See also* cognation *or* cognate
agriculture, Tab^5, In^9, 9, 34, 107^3, 148^4, 223^2, 239^{1n}, 422^4, 427^{1n}, 429, 527, 530, 606^3. *See also colonus or colona*; cropland *or* crops; cultivator, registered; farm *or* farmer; field; food *or* drink; grain; orchard; peasant; plantation; plough; serf; tenant farmer; vineyard; viniculture
air. *See* phenomena, natural
Akoimetoi *or* Acoemeti, 636^{1n}, 647^{35}, Gl s.v. Sleepless
alien, 287, 484; 527, Gl s.vv. peregrine, praetor. *See also* peregrine
almshouse, In 5 (d), 515, 519, 522, 537, 579, 581, 585, 595, 604, 612, 623, 630, 648, Gl s.v. pious causes
  assistant in direction of, 537
  director of, 537, 579, 648
  superintendent of, 579
altar:
  Jewish, 159^{34}
  heterodox, 160, 215, Gl s.v. Ascodrogitans
  orthodox, In^{8,9,52}, 68^5, 95^1, 98^{15}, 127^7, 206^7, 225, 246^1, 258^3, 372^4, 400, 413, 429, 443, 508, 515, 551, 554^1, 629^6, 651^{13,19}
  pagan, 41^4, 63, 117, 189, 190, 206^7, 231^1, 242, 301, 400, 424^3, 429^{31}, 651^8, App^{41}. *See also* cloth, altar
Aman, 303
ambassador *or* envoy, imperial, 547^{1n,5,8}, 548, 552, 558^{1n}, 560, Gl s.vv. apocrisiarian, legation. *See also* legate
ambo, 554^1
amnesty, In 5 (g), 85^9, 112^{1n}, 115^{1n}, 135^{1n}, 145^{1n}, 168^1, 171, 180^{1n,5}, 198^{1n}, 201^{1n}, 207, App 10 (c), App^{36}. *See also* pardon
amphitheatre, 132^2, 154^{1n}, 168^1, 243^2, 629^6, 651^{10}. *See also* arena; circus; combat (gladiatorial); games; spectacle (amphitheatrical)
amusements, In, 5 (g)^{26}, 52, 141^3, 154, 316, 385^{1n}, 651, Gl s.vv. aedile, praetor. *See also* games; spectacle
anathematization *or* anathema, 159, 173^1, 205^1, 411^{1n}, 412, 427^{19}, 445, 455^{1n}, 470 (VII), 481, 483–7, 524, 527, 530, 542, 546, 549, 636, 637
anchor, 98
anchorite, 411 (I), 483^{21}, Gl. *See also* hermitage *or* hermit; monk; nun; solitary; solitary life
angel, 7^{13}, 11^{1n}, 63, 127^7, 159, 223^2, 522, 543 (II), 651^{13}. *See also* archangel
Angel, 416, 551
  Holy Guardian, 242^7
animals:
  collector of, Gl s.v. guild
  domesticated, 646^8; ape, 214^5; ass, 410^4; bull, 429^{30}; cattle, 301^7; chicken, 214^5, Gl s.v. augur; dog, 111, 214^5; horse, 75, 112, 113, 124 (I), 186^5, 236^3, 279, 410^4, 426, 484, 646^8, 651, Gl s.v. knight. *See also* cavalry; ox, 107^3, Gl s.vv. *caput*; tax, capitation; tax, jugation; sheep, In, 4, 61^1, 107^8, 524 (I), 561^{19}, 645. *See also* sheepfold; shepherd
  farm, Gl s.vv. *caput*; tax, capitation; tax, jugation
  livestock, 522^3, 588^4, 604^4, 623^6
  transport, 112, 186^5, 301^7, 410$^{4-6}$, 426, 434, 438, 530
  wild, 67, 84 (I), 113, 243, 509, 651, App 10 (f); bird, 113, Gl s.v. augur; caged, 370^3; chase of, 243, 509^6, 651; elephant, 509^6; frog, Gl s.v. Batrachitans; horse, 397^1; leopard, 641^4; lion, 67, 243^2; murex, 273; serpent, 44^{16}, 67, 614^{10}, 641^4, Gl s.v. Ophitans; (dragon), 44; (python), 44^{16}; (viper), 67, 214^5; wolf, 67, 112
anniversary^2
  of colony, 220^4
  of Constantinople, 220
  of emperor, 220, 236, 243, App^{36}
  of reign, 73^{1n}, 220, 243, 316, 341^2, App 10 (c)
  of Rome, 220
annona, 301^7, 535^{1,3}, 536^3

SUBJECTS

annotation, 43 (I), 317, 329, 417, 428, 431, 448
Annuario Pontificio, 364^{15}
annuity, 612^{16}, 648
Annunciation, 546^{2}
anointment, 651^{16}
Anomoeanism *or* Anomoeans, 103^{1n}, 112^{1n}, Gl
anthropomorphism, Gl s.v. Audians
anti-bishop, 17^{1n}. *See also* bishop
anti-pope, In^{43}, 57^{3}, 95^{1n,1}, 102^{1}, 138^{1n,1}, 146^{2}, 152^{1n,2}, 164^{5}, 200^{1n}, 371^{1n}, 545^{2}, Gl s.v. Novatians. *See also* pope
anti-Semitism, 52^{14}, 244, Gl s.v. Marcionites
apartment, women's, 46
apocrisiarian *or* apocrisiarios, 512, 559^{10}, Gl
Apollinarianism *or* Apollinarians, 194, 196, 213, 264, 395, 411^{1}, 478, 481^{4}, 483^{7}, 484^{10}, 485^{7}, 486^{10}, 487^{6}, 489, 542^{22}, 569^{8}, 636^{12}, Gl
apology *or* apologist, 2^{20}, 9^{9}, 66^{7}, App^{8}
apostasy *or* apostate, In, 5 (9)^{45}, 80, 91^{1n}, 111^{1n}, 119^{5}, 159, 168^{1}, 175, 177, 189, 190, 230^{1n}, 231^{1n}, 259, 315^{1n}, 387^{16}, 391, 429, 573, App 4, 7^{12,13,36}, Gl. *See also* ex-Christian
apostle, 17^{3}, 41^{4}, 49 (II), 61 (III), 95^{43}, 112^{4}, 127^{7}, 140^{1}, 156^{1}, 163, 167, 181, 206^{6}, 211, 225, 270^{3}, 284^{4}, 313^{1}, 350, 359, 362, 372^{1}, 382^{1}, 442^{7}, 449, 463, 470^{53,66}, 471^{3}, 472 (I), 476, 477, 484, 486, 487, 515^{1n}, 516^{1n}, 522, 523^{1}, 524, 545, 546, 550, 551, 554, 561-3, 569, 577, 579, 613^{4}, 614^{10}, 645, 651^{16}, Gl s.v. *ius canonicum*
apostole, 341^{2}
Apostolics, Gl
Apotactitans, 176, 192, 395^{6}, Gl
apparel, 95^{1}, 107, 247, 273^{2}, 308, 385, 501, 531^{8}, Gl s.v. weaving establishment. *See also* cloth; crown; diadem; factory; insignia; jewelry; mitre; sceptre; tiara
belt, 283, 284^{3}, 411^{3}, 439^{4}, 444, 476, 480, 489, 515, 529^{2}, 567, 625, 629, Gl
breeches, 203^{4}
fillets, 229, 242, 496, 520
garland, 223^{2}, 242
lappets, episcopal, 520; imperial, 630
pallium, 541^{14}
robe, 95^{51}, 247^{3}, 273^{2}, 506^{3}
sackcloth, Gl s.vv Encratitans; Manichaeans
toga, 203^{4}, cf. 506^{3}
tunic, 236^{3}
veil, 405, 496, App^{7}
vestment, ecclesiastical, 68^{5}, 598; pagan priestly, App, 10 (f)
apparition, 514. *See also* ghost
apparitorship *or* apparitor, 34^{3}, 37^{7}, 81^{4}, 95^{41}, 134, 164, 181^{3}, 253, 308, 318, 324, 383, 429, 440, 489, 491, 509, 511, 536, 540^{8}, 591^{3}, 606^{20}, 651, App^{14}, Gl and therein s.vv. Caesarian, lictor, official. *See also* ordinary
appeal, 5^{1}, 17^{8}, 19-22, 28, 65, 74^{1n}, 75^{1n}, 146, 159^{1n}, 164, 168^{1}, 203^{1}, 213, 234, 235, 272, 309, 328^{1n}, 478^{30}, 504, 505, 603, 611, 638^{10}
apse, 258^{3}
Aquarians, Gl
aqueduct, 43^{13}, 606, Gl s.v. slave, public
arbiter, 17^{3}, 136^{1n}, 209, 220^{8}, 263, 271, 478, 605, 625. *See also* judge; referee
archangel, 546, 615. *See also* angel
archbishop, In, 5 (a)^{42}, 28^{1}, 53^{3}, 66^{1}, 119^{5}, 125, 364^{15}, 375^{8}, 387^{9} 393^{1}, 409^{1n}, 416, 420, 427, 442^{1n}, 458, 461-3, 468, 470 (I, IV, VII, VIII, XI), 471, 472^{30}, 482, 490, 491, 504, 505, 510, 524, 527, 537^{3}, 542, 545, 551^{14}, 554, 567, 577, 579, 580, 611, 612, 635, 637, 645, 651, Gl and therein s.v. metropolitan
archdeacon, In^{26}, 17^{1n,10}, 95^{1n,27}, 102^{1}, 352^{1n}, 469, 472^{14}, 497, 500, Gl
archdiocese, In^{42}, 472^{30}
archiepiscopate, 479
archimandrite, 448^{1n}, 450-3, 455, 456, 463^{2}, 476^{1n}, 477^{16}, 480^{1}, 484, 486, 487, 489, 524^{4}, 527, 546^{14}, 569^{8}, 614^{2}, 629, 636^{3}, 637, 645, 648, Gl and therein s.v. Eutychians
architect, 211, 648^{6}
archives:
  ecclesiastical, 621
  municipal, 26, 42^{4,5}
  papal, 95^{25}
  public, 576^{3}
archon, 234^{3}
archpriest, 375^{8}, 579, Gl
arena, 132^{1n}, 236^{3}. *See also* amphitheatre; circus
Arianism *or* Arians, In^{43}, 20^{1}, 47, 48^{1n}, 49^{1n}, 50^{1n,16,48}, 51^{1n}, 53^{1n}, 58^{1n}, 61^{20}, 65^{9}, 66^{1n,3,7,18}, 67, 68^{2}, 69^{1n}, 70^{1n}, 71^{2}, 73^{7}, 74^{1n}, 75^{1n}, 84^{1n}, 85^{1n}, 93^{1n,5}, 94^{1n}, 95^{21,22,27}, 98^{15,16}, 99^{5}, 100, 103^{1n}, 104^{1n}, 105^{1n,2}, 107^{4}, 111^{1n}, 112^{1n}, 113^{1n}, 117^{5}, 119^{5}, 120^{5}, 123, 124, 131^{1n}, 136^{1n}, 147^{5}, 159^{1n,3,16,37,42,43,46,53}, 172^{1n}, 173, 179, 192, 194, 195^{1n,3}, 196, 205^{1n,1,3,8,9}, 217, 350^{1n}, 380, 381, 395, 422, 492^{1}, 533^{1}, 542^{25}, 567^{1n}, 646^{1,6,9}, Gl and therein s.vv. Anomoeans, Eunomians, Heteroousians, Homoiousians, Luciferians, Porphyrians, Semi-Arians
armourer, Gl s.v. guild
arrest, 5, 42^{1n}, 50, 215, 273, 277, 313, 330, 343, 350, 364, 399, 408^{5}, 416, 440, 453, 489, 573, 638, App 10 (a)

SUBJECTS 1291

arsenal, 186⁵
arson, App 10 (b). See also fire
art. See fresco; icon; image or statue; mosaic; painter; sculptor
  Christian, 53¹², 181⁷, 546³
  pagan, 424³, 478²⁹
artificer, 54, 190, 648⁶
artisan, 34, 54, 133¹, 186⁵, 257, 284³, 350¹⁸, 641¹², Gl s.v. guild. See also workman
as, Gl and therein s.vv. Lex Furia, Lex Voconia
Ascension, 75⁴², 159, 636
ascetery, In, 5 (d), Gl s.v. pious causes
asceticism, 330¹ⁿ, 411¹ⁿ,³, 614, 628, Gl s.vv. Audians, Encratitans, Gnostics, Manichaeans, Priscillians. See also monachism; solitary life
Ascodrogitans, 429, Gl and therein s.v. Tascodrogitans
Ash Wednesday, 169³
asiarch, 3⁸
assault, 68, 334²⁵, 465, 470 (VIII). See also entry, forcible; injury or insult or outrage; molestation; violence
assemblies. See meetings, tumultuous
  Christian, 1², 4²,⁴, 12, 14, 26⁴, 32, 36⁴, 42¹, 49 (II), 117, 138, 148⁴, 641⁴, App 8 (a), 10 (a), (f)
  Greek, 614⁷
  heretical or schismatical, 40, 69, 142, 143, 156, 160, 163, 164, 166, 173, 176, 185, 190–2, 194, 196, 213, 215, 217⁵, 222, 232, 239, 248, 251, 253, 258, 264, 268, 275, 277, 287, 289, 290¹, 306¹ⁿ, 323, 328, 335⁸, 336, 339, 342, 343, 422, 423, 459, 477, 481, 484, 489, 559, 567, 571, 573, 616. See also sepulchre = assembly
  Jewish, 23, 91, 244
  provincial, App. ²³
  Roman, In⁹,²⁶, 65⁶, 523¹, 614⁷, 641¹², Gl s.vv. Assembly; Assembly, Tribal; censor
  sacrilegious, 330
assembly, right of, 1², 7, 12, 13¹ⁿ, 14, 40, 42¹, 103, 117, 131¹ⁿ, 137, 142, 143, 164, 166¹, 167¹ⁿ, 173, 176, 185, 191, 192, 194, 196, 205, 213, 215, 217⁵, 239, 248, 251, 253, 258, 268, 277, 287, 293, 301, 306, 323, 326, 336, 337, 339, 342, 343, 395, 422, 423, 459, 465, 476, 477, 480, 484, 489, 567, 571, 616, App 8 (a), 10 (a), 10 (f)
Assembly:
  of Asia, 3
  of the Saints, 49¹
  Tribal, 523¹, Gl
assessment, 606, 618
assessor, judicial, 6¹

assistant = provincial governor, 5, 234³
astrology or astrologer, 23⁴, 171¹, 207¹⁰, 313, 382¹, 387, 388, Gl s.v. Manichaeans See also astronomy; divination or diviner
astronomy, 52⁴, 116⁹, 207¹⁰, 313¹. See also astrology or astrologer
asylum, In 5 (d), 515¹ⁿ, Gl s.v. pious causes right of, In, 5 (f), 241¹ⁿ,¹,³, 246¹, 400⁹. See also fugitive; refuge; sanctuary, right of
atheism or atheist, 3, 13³, 567
athlete, Gl s.v. guild
Atonement, 75⁴²
auction or auctioneer, 46, 519, 520, Gl s.v. slave, public
Audians, 395, Gl
auditor or accountant, 606, Gl and therein s.v. apparitor
augury or augur, In²⁶, 168¹, 231¹, 375⁷, 523¹, 617, Gl.See also divination or diviner
Augusta = empress, 438, 463, 472⁴, 630, Gl
Augustal, 6¹ⁿ,¹,², 527², Gl
aunt, 613⁴
aureus, 433⁷, 515, 641¹⁴ Gl s.v. denarius
auspices, In²⁶, 13, 242, 301⁷, 617¹⁰. See also divination or diviner
authors, pagan, 116, 646¹⁴. See also literature, pagan
autocephality, 577³
avarice, 508, 646 (I)
Ave Maria, 651²⁰
axe, 439³, 443

Babylonian Captivity, 140¹
baker, 133, 186⁵, Gl s.v. guild
banditry or bandit, 2¹³, 50, 51, 67–9, 302, 484, 495³, 523⁵. See also brigandage or brigand; robbery or robber
banker, 629¹⁷. See also money-changer
banquet, 243, 301, 593³, 616
baptism, 112⁴, 116¹⁴, 121, 154⁵, 158, 163, 164¹⁷,¹⁸, 166, 167¹ⁿ, 187³, 203, 220¹¹, 230, 289, 290, 330¹ⁿ, 343, 346, 385, 481, 524, 527, 530, 560¹⁶, 571, 600, 609, 616, 651¹¹, Gl s.vv. catechumen; Marcionites; Maximians; Pelagians heretical, 158⁴, 395, 571, 616, Gl s.v. Eunomians. See also rebaptism
barbarians, In, 4²,⁹,⁴³, Tab⁵, 34⁵, 44, 66¹⁸, 75, 98, 105, 140¹, 173¹ⁿ, 308, 369, 400, 435¹ⁿ, 484²², 507, 513⁵, 523, 527¹ⁿ, 528⁵,⁸, 567¹⁶, 646 (I), 651, Gl s.vv. Codex Theodosianus; ius canonicum; peregrine; province
Barbeliotes, Gl
basilica, Tab⁵, 54 59, 63, 95¹, 123⁴, 136¹ⁿ, 138³, 139¹ⁿ, 200¹, 205¹ⁿ, 211, 352², 364⁵,¹², 463, 551, 618¹³

basket, Gl s.v. fisc
bastard, 19[22], 29[2], 122[10], 525[1n]. *See also* concubine; legitimation
baths, 43 (I), 63[2], 312, 326, 400, 606, App 10 (f), Gl s.v. slave, public
Batrachitans, 395[6], Gl
beggar. *See* mendicant
belt. *See* apparel
Benedicite, Opera Omnia, 651[20]
Benedictinism, 297[3]
benediction, 645
Benedictus, 651[20]
beneficiarian, 13, 110, Gl
bequest, In, 4, 5 (d), 26, 31[1,2], 36, 46, 117[8], 150, 157, 176, 218[4,8], 225, 227, 321 (I), 343, 395, 480, 488, 515[1n], 579, 583, 585, 595, 604, 606, 612, 615, 629, 640 (IV), 648, 652, Gl s.v. slave, public. *See also* legacy
betrothal, 478[30], 496[1n], 517, 567, 595[5]. *See also* earnests, betrothal; fiancé *or* fiancée
Bible, In, 5 (g)[8], 1[3], 7[13], 17[3], 21, 23[2,4], 45[2], 47[25,79], 49 (I, II), 53, 59, 60, 61[12], 64, 67, 95[34], 116[1], 122, 124[5], 159, 163, 164[11], 167[2], 203[5], 313[1], 328[3], 370[1], 399[3], 407, 457[11], 483, 491[7], 513, 520[7], 532[1n,1,2], 537, 543[10,13] 545, 546, 555, 577[9], 592, 594, 600, 603, 605, 606, 608, 614, 619, 634, 640[13], 645, 648[6], 651, App 6, 10 (a)[16], Gl s.vv. Gnostics, *ius canonicum,* lector, Marcionites, Priscillians. *See also* Index of Biblical Quotations and Allusions
Epistles, 167[2], 484, 486
Gospels, In[32,36], 49 (II), 116, 159, 163, 167, 470 (VIII), 491[7], 546, 555, 574[8], 605, 606, 614, 619, 634, App 6
Apocalypse, 159[21], 577[9]
Canticle of Canticles, 651[20]
Psalms, 651[20]
Codex Sinaiticus, 64[1n,15,18], 483[21]
copies of, 64
billboard, 364
billeting, 83, 168[1], 186[5], 432[1n], 606[24], Gl s.v. service, public
birthday, 220[4], 236, 243, 279, 316, 509, App[36]. *See also* anniversary
birthright, 631
bishop, In, 5 (a)[31,42], 4, 5[1], 16[4], 17–22, 25, 26, 28,32, 35, 39, 42[1], 45, 47[1n], 48, 49 (I)[26], 50, 52, 53, 58[1n], 59, 60[1n], 61, 63, 64[2], 65–7, 68[1,2], 69–71, 73, 74[1n], 75, 77, 78[2], 81, 84[2,20,29], 85–8, 90, 93–6, 99, 100[1n], 102–5, 107, 109 111[23], 112, 116[1,16], 117, 119[1,5], 120, 124 (I, III), 131[1n], 136[1n,1], 138, 146, 150, 154, 157–9, 160[1], 161, 162[2], 163[2], 164[1n], 166, 167, 172, 173, 178, 181[5], 182 187[1n], 194[3], 197, 200, 203, 205, 211, 213, 222, 225, 235, 241, 242[1n], 248, 251, 254, 269–72, 277, 280, 284[1n,2,3], 285, 287, 288, 295, 297, 300, 301, 303[3], 306, 307, 308[20], 309–13, 324, 325, 326, 327[4], 328–31, 334–7, 342, 347, 349, 350[1n], 352–62, 364–71, 375, 387, 394, 397–409, 410[4], 411, 412, 414–22, 426–9, 436, 443, 445–7, 448[1,8], 449–52, 455, 456, 458, 459, 461–4, 466, 467[1n], 468, 470, 471, 472 (I, III), 473[1n], 475–84, 486–9, 490[4], 491, 493, 495, 497, 498, 500, 501, 507, 508, 510, 514, 515, 516[1n], 519, 520, 522–4, 526–8, 530, 531, 534, 535, 537, 539–41, 543 (II), 544, 546, 547, 549–51, 554, 557–64, 567, 569, 574–6, 577[13,15], 579, 580, 582, 583, 586–9, 591, 593, 598, 606, 608, 610–12, 614, 618, 620, 621, 623, 624, 627–30, 632, 637, 641[7], 645, 649–51, App 8[10], Gl and therein s.vv. archbishop, archdeacon, chorepiscopus, clergyman, deacon, diocese, metropolitan, patriarch, pope, president, priest, primate bishop, rural bishop, see. *See also* archbishop; brother = bishop; episcopate; exbishop; father = bishop; hierarchy; metropolitan; patriarch; pontiff; pope; prelate; president = bishop; primate = bishop; and *infra* auxiliary; itinerant; primate; rural; suffragan; titular; heretical *or* schismatic
auxiliary, In[42], Gl s.v. rural bishop
itinerant, 530, 579, Gl
primate, 326
rural, 579, Gl s.v. rural bishop
suffragan, In[42], 17[5], 78[3], 284[2], 285[6], 397, 456, 459, 470[39,49,66], 472[30], 483[1n], 530, 557[4], 580, Gl s.vv. Marcionites, rural bishop
titutlar, In[42]
heretical *or* schismatic, 5[1], 17, 19, 20[1], 22, 24[4], 25, 50, 51, 58[1n], 68, 70 71, 74, 75[1n] 95[1,27], 103[1], 105[2], 111[1n], 112[1], 119[5], 120, 124[2], 136[1n], 137[1n], 138[1], 140, 146[2], 147[5], 152[1n], 153, 158[1n], 164, 166, 172[1n], 194[3], 196, 200, 205[1], 213, 222, 245, 248, 251, 254, 277, 288[1n], 324, 325, 326, 328, 329, 336, 337, 342, 352, 368, 370[1], 387, 395[3], 416[1n], 417[1n], 427[1n], 440, 445, 446, 448[9], 450–2, 456, 459, 470[51], 480, 481[4,5], 483, 484[10], 485[6,7,9], 486[5,10], 487, 489, 495[3], 524[14], 527, 542[11–13,16–18,20–22,26,27], 543[1n], 546[13], 554[1n], 558[1n], 560[5], 562[10], 563, 569[6,8], 616, 636[2,12], 637[2], Gl s.vv. Eunomians, Luciferians, Maximians, Nestorians, Novatians, Paulianists, Photinians, Priscillians, Semi-Arians
consecration of, In, 5 (a), 17[1n,6], 21, 99,

112^1, 137^{in}, 200, 213, 245, 328^9, 352^{in}, 354^{in}, 371, 410^2, 412, 420, 442, 459, 470 (IV, VIII, X, XI), 480, 483, 487, 489, 495^2, 500, 508, 519, 523^1, 537^3, 579, 601, 620, 651, Gl s.v. Audians
court of. *See* court, episcopal
deposition of, In^{34,44}, 5^1, 50, 51, 61^{in}, 72, 74^{in}, 75^{in}, 95^{19}, 99, 103, 115, 117^{14}, 121, 137, 146^2, $158^{in,4}$, 163^2, 164, 203^1, 213, 225, 284, 288, 295, 297, 328^5, 352, 368, 387, 406^{in}, 408, 410^3, 411 (III), 412, 414, 416^{in}, 417^{in}, 420, 426^{in}, 442, 445, 446, 447^{in}, 448, $449^{in,7}$, 455^{in}, $456^{in,5}$, 459, 463, 470 (I, II, VIII, X), 473^{in}, 477^{15}, 479, 481^{12}, 483, 484, 487, 489^{21}, 495^3, 508, 519, 524 (I), 526, 527, 543^{in}, 557, 559^{in}, 579, 580, 637^7, Gl s.v. Maximians
duty of. *See* duty, episcopal
election of, In, 5 (b)^{44}, 61, 124^{in}, 137^{in}, 246^1, 326^5, 352–67, 371, 470 (XI), 473^{in}, 475^{in}, 508, 519, 520, 523^1, 526, 557, 559, 579, 620, Gl s.v. archdeacon
investigation by. *See* investigation, episcopal
jurisdiction of. *See* jurisdication, episcopal
translation of, 61, $61^{7,11}$
as civil administrator, In, 5 (f), 117, 271, 301, 349, 398^{14}, 493, 507, 523, 534, 535, 539–41, 574–6, 582, 588, 591, 593, 606, 608, 610, 627, 628^3, 632, 635, 649–51. *See* jurisdiction, episcopal
as defendant, 96, 136^1, 146, 164, 172^{in}, 195, 197, 437, 478, 515, 611
as donee, 630
as heir, 623^7
as judge over emperor, 136^1
as proprietor, 109, 514, 579
as witness, 26, 65, 178, 331
as interested in actresses, 649, 650; in debtors, 627; in danseuses, 650; in detention of property, 627; in disputed loans, 582, 628^3; in exiles, 587; in foundlings, 331, 591; in gamblers, 593; in guardianship, 608, 621, 628^3, 635; in heirs, 612; in illegal exactions, 606; in inspection of accounts, 606; in judication in suretyships, 606; in management of ecclesiastical property, Gl s.v. steward of the church; in municipal administration, 606, 628^3; in paupers, 623; in payment of rent, 632; in prenuptial settlements, 610, 628^3; in prisoners, 312, 369, 370, 507, 585, 589, 623; in probate of wills, 612; in prostitutes, 394; in reception of legislation, 606; in slaves, 652; in supervision of public works, 606
blasphemy, 47, 49 (II), 53, 75, 95^{43}, 99, 453–6, 459, 481, 524 (I), 543 (II), 546, 573, 637, 651, App 10 (f)
bodyguard, imperial, 44, 186^3, 400, 547^6, Gl s.vv. master of the offices; prefect, praetorian. *See also* praetorian guards for pagan high priest, App 10 (f)
bond (document), 618, 628^2
bone, $206^{6,7}$, 641^{31}
Bonifacians, $352^{2,5}$, 353^2
book, 113, 328^3, 382^1, 422, 423, 446, 459, 480, 481, 484, 489, 573, 617
Biblical, 21, 651. *See also* Bible
legal, $642^{11,13}$, 650
liturgical, 68^5, 258^3, 651. *See also* Book of Common Prayer; Breviarium Romanum
philosophical, 66, 113, 382^1
rhetorical, 113
theological, 66, 113, 268, 573
book-burning, 21, 66, 68^5, 113, 268, 313, 382^1, 422, 423, 445, 459, 480, 489, 524 (I), 573, App 10 (a)^{16}. *See also* fire
Book of Common Prayer, 75^{42}
booty, In^{9,26}
Borborians, 395, 429, 575, 599, 600, 622, Gl
borrower, $582^{3,5,6,10}$, 604^8. *See also* creditor; debt; debtor; leader; loan
bosom, Church's, 35, 645
God's, 577
boundary or frontier, 143, 415^2, 640^7
boy, 146, 205–10, 243, 331. *See also* son
bread. *See* food *or* drink
breeches. *See* apparel
bribery *or* bribe, 519, 532, 566^4, 625^{14}, $633^{in,6}$, Gl s.vv. *Lex Licinia de sodaliciis*; official; venality
bride, 613^4. *See also* wife
bridge, 186^5, 538^4, 606
construction or care of, 327, 377, 606
brief, 8
brigandage *or* brigand, In^9, 69, 528^5, 568^{in}, Gl s.v. Circumcellions. *See also* banditry *or* bandit; piracy; robbery *or* robber
bronze, App^{55}, Gl s.vv. as, denarius
brothel, 82, 440. *See also* prostitution *or* prostitute
brother, Tab^1, 84 (I), 90, $95^{34,46}$, 187, 189, 214^3, 252^3, 259, 295^{in}, 298^6, 361, 362, 398^3, 463^{in}, 487^{14}, 496, 514, 525, 552, 579, 624^4, 638^3
brother = bishop, 20 39, 45, 48 (II), 51, 54, 59, 61 (II, III), 63, 64, 68, 71, 73, 93, 645
brother = fellow-Christian, 39, 50, 52, 53, 61 (I), 66^{23}, 69, 70, 77, 95

SUBJECTS

brother = official, 25, 99, 444. *See also* cousin = official; father = official
brother-in-law, 363¹ⁿ
brotherhood, 39, 49 (II), 133¹
Buddhists, Gl s.v. Manichaeans
building. *See* property; building *or* house; villa
   private, 606¹⁴
   public, 59, 498, 641⁹
   religious, 498. *See also* churches; mosque; oratory; place, religious; shrine; temple
   sacred, 641 (I)³⁰. *See also* churches; mosque; oratory; place, sacred; shrine; temple
   demolition of, 606, 641 (I)
bureau, imperial, In, 3¹¹, 19¹³, 186³,⁴, 256², 353⁶, 433, 444¹ⁿ, 478, 511², 549, 560, 568⁷, 618, Gl s.vv. chief men; clerk, chief; knight; registrar
   prefectural, 646²²
bureaucracy, In, 4⁹, 110⁶, 186⁴, 476³⁹ 646³,²², Gl s.v. master of the offices
Byzantine Empire, 28¹, 181⁶, 398⁷, 618³, 646¹³
Byzantinism, 471¹ⁿ

Caelicolans, 301, 315, Gl
Caesar *or* Caesars (as symbol), In, 4¹⁴,²³,³², 1⁴, 3³⁴, 4², 5²⁵¹, 62²,¹¹, 159, 255³, App 4, 8 (b)¹⁴. *See also* Caesarism
Caesarian, App 8 (b)¹⁴,¹⁹, Gl
Caesarism, 94¹, 397¹ⁿ. *See also* Caesar *or* Caesars
Caesaropapism, In, 1³⁴,⁴³, 104⁴, 455¹ⁿ
calendar, In⁵², 52⁴,²⁹, 99², 106⁶, 194⁴, 220¹ⁿ,³ Gl s.v. pontifex maximus
calumny *or* calumniator, 2, 27³, 164, 334, 344², 432, 485, 487, 515, 521, 592, 619, 651. *See also* slander *or* libel
cannibal, 495⁴
canon:
   apostolic, 445
   conciliar, In⁸,⁴³,⁴⁴, 16¹ⁿ, 52⁴, 57¹, 58¹ⁿ, 61¹¹, 94, 95⁴³, 112⁴, 169³, 203⁵, 205⁹, 350¹ⁿ,¹¹, 370¹, 372³,⁴, 375⁵,⁷, 442⁷, 448⁸, 458, 470 (I, V, VIII, XI)²²,²⁴,⁴¹,⁴⁴, 61,70,74, 472⁷,²⁰, 475¹⁰,¹², 476¹ⁿ, 477¹ⁿ, 480, 482¹ⁿ,³,⁵, 485¹ⁿ,¹⁶,³¹, 526⁸, 527¹ⁿ, 542⁸, 577², 613¹ⁿ,⁴, Gl and therein s.v. *ius canonicum. See also* canon, ecclesiastical
   divine, 600, 613
   ecclesiastical, 86, 95⁴³, 375, 397, 411¹⁰, 474, 480³², 481–3, 487, 491, 579, 611–13, 632³, Gl and therein s.v. *ius canonicum. See also* canon, conciliar
canonization, In⁵², 17¹⁰, 95¹, 98¹⁵, 99¹,², 159²⁷, 200¹ⁿ, 362², 459¹¹, 481², 533¹, 650⁴. *See also* saint

cantor, 109⁸, 613, 651, Gl s.v. chanter. *See* musician
captive. *See also* prisoner of war
Carolingian Empire, Tab⁵, 492¹
Cassatis quae, 21¹ⁿ, 329¹ⁿ
castration. *See* eunuch
catacomb, In²⁶, 97⁴, 206⁷, 290¹, 364⁵. *See also* Index of Places s.v. Rome
catalogue. *See* register
Cataphrygians, 40, Gl
catechetical school *or* catechist, 98⁴, 109³, 189²
catechumenate *or* catechumen, In⁸⁷, 189, 189², Gl
Cathari, 57¹
Catholicism *or* Catholics, In³¹,⁵⁶, 10¹ⁿ, 15¹¹, 17⁶, 20, 25⁵, 52², 58¹ⁿ, 59, 120²,⁸, 148⁴, 159¹ⁿ, 164, 167¹ⁿ,⁹, 172¹ⁿ, 173¹¹, 185, 187¹ⁿ, 193–5, 203, 212¹ⁿ, 239, 249¹, 293¹ⁿ, 301, 324, 325, 326¹ⁿ, 328, 329, 338¹ⁿ, 350–3, 368, 375 (II), 387–9, 397¹ⁿ, 416, 418, 427, 449, 456¹ⁿ, 459, 477¹, 481, 491, 550, 553, 554, 646⁶,⁷, Gl s.v. Novatians. *See also* Christendom; Christians, Catholic; Church, Catholic
Catholics:
   Orthodox, Gl s.v. *ius canonicum. See also* Christendom, Eastern; Christendom, Orthodox; Christians, Orthodox
   Roman, In²⁶,⁴²⁻⁴, 75⁴², 95¹,⁴³, 223², 242⁷, 442⁷, 470⁷⁰, 472³⁰, 523¹, 579⁹, Gl s.vv. Circumcellions, *ius canonicum. See also* Christendom, Roman Catholic; Church, Roman Catholic
catholicus:
   ecclesiastical, 99⁴, Gl
   imperial *or* provincial, 15, 64, 78¹ⁿ, 124 (III), Gl
cavalry, 90², 106⁴, 559¹², 567¹⁶, Gl s.vv. count of the domestics, domestics, knight. *See also* soldier; Stabilisians
celibacy *or* celibate, 31, 330¹ⁿ, 372¹ⁿ,⁴, 613¹ⁿ,⁴, 620², 629, Gl s.vv. Gnostics, *Senatus Consultum Persicianum. See also* chastity; continence; nun; Vestal; virginity *or* virgin
cemetery:
   Christian, 4⁸, 97⁴, 364⁵, App 8 (a), 10 (f). *See also* catacomb
   Manichaean, 176⁵
   Novatian, 57
   pagan, 641¹ⁿ
censor, 26¹, 174³, 234², Gl
census, 26¹, 41², 174³, 421, 516, 537, 565, G s.vv. censor, inspector, master of the census
centurion, In¹⁴, 21, App 10 (e), Gl
ceremony, religious, 139, 169, 263³, 267, 299, 301, 303, 315¹, 359¹ⁿ, 364¹ⁿ, 400, 429, 641²,¹²,¹⁴, 651, Gl s.vv.

SUBJECTS 1295

Caelicolans, Mithras, quindecimvir. *See also* rites; worship
chamberlain, 95^{1n}, 186, 246^1, Gl. *See also* ex-chamberlain
Chaos, 648^6
charcoal, 186^5
chariot *or* charioteer, 236^3, 247^{1n}, 279^{1n}, 397^1, 559
charity, 515^{1n}, 520^7, 644^6. *See also* pious causes; poor, the; prisoner of war
chastity, 92, 126^6, 150^2, 168^1, 177, 201, 334^{25}, 397^1, 496, 638^1, Gl s.v. Continents. *See also* celibacy *or* celibate; continence; unchastity; virginity *or* virgin
chicanery, 223^3, 344, 513, App^{12}. *See also* fraud
chief captain, 337^6
centurion, 110^5
of office staff, 25, 272, 310, 478, 540
of secretarial bureau, 478
child, 9, 31^1, 32, 44^{10}, 47^{70}, 49 (I), 65^6, 116, 127^6, 176, 187^{1n}, 189, 247, 289, 298, 303^4, 331, 334^{25}, 335^6, 347^{13}, 392, 397^1, 421, 474^2, 496, 497, 500, 517^4, 525, 527^{101}, 528^5, 543 (II), 548, 567, 570, 572, 575, 579, 599, 600, 610, 619^7, 624^4, 627^2, 629, 631^1, 635^2, App 10 (d)–(f), Gl s.v. *patria potestas. See also* daughter; grandchild; granddaughter; grandson; infant; minor; son; ward
emancipated, 602, 609^2, 644^4
emancipation of, 38^{1n}, 602^4
exposed, 331
illegitimate, 613
legitimate, 572^3
of clergyman, 32, 102, 372^4, 421, 433, 497, 514, 579, 613, 620, 624^4
of deaconess, 225
of decurion, 33, 322
childlessness, 31, 624^4, 629
chiliarch, App 10 (e), Gl
Chiliasm, Gl s.v. Papians
choirs, papal, 76^4
chorus, 650^2, 651^8. *See also* theatre
Christendom, In, 4^{43}, 39^6, 47^{1n}, 49^{21}, 52^2, 112^{1n}, 169^3, 185^6, 195^4, 442^7, 470^{70}, 548^{10}, 551^{1n}, 556^1, 641^4, Gl s.v. patriarch
African, 338^{1n}
Eastern, 47^{1n}, 58^{1n}, 61^{11}, 62^2, 66^{18}, 148^4, 167^{1n}, 181^6, 258^3, $284^{1n,4}$, 411^{1n}, 418^2, 546^{20}, 550^2, Gl s.v. *ius canonicum. See also* Orthodoxy, Eastern
Orthodox, In^{43}
Roman Catholic, 618^3
Western, 47^{1n}, 61^{11}, 62^2, 66^{18}, 140^1, 148^4, 167^{1n}, 181^6, 442^7, 564^{1n}
Christian Empire, Tab^5, 41^3
Christianity *or* Christians, In, 4–7, $9^{8,9,14}$, 18,21,25,26,29,30,32,33,36,37,40,42,44-648,49,52,

1–3, $4^{1n,2-4,8-10}$, 5–8, $9^{1n,1,4,9}$, 10, 12–14, 15^3, $16^{1n,2,6,10}$, $17^{1n,3,4,8}$, 18^{1n}, $20^{1n,4-6}$, 21^{10}, 22^{1n}, $23^{1n,4}$, $24^{1n,\ 4,10}$, 26, $28^{1n,1}$, 31^{1n}, 33^{1n}, $34^{1,5}$, $38^{1n,3}$, $39^{1n,4}$, 40^{1n}, $41^{1n,2,4}$, $42^{1n,1,5}$, 43^{1n}, 44, $45^{1n,1,3,6}$, $46^{1n,6,7,12,16}$, $47^{11,17}$, 48^{1n}, 49^1, 50, $52^{1,2,4,10,29,39}$, $53^{1n,12,16}$, 58^{1n}, 62^2, $65^{1n,13}$, $66^{3,7}$, 68^1, $72^{6,7}$, 73^{17}, 75^{42}, 76, 77^5, 78^3, 79, 80, 82, 91, 95, 96^{1n}, 97^4, $98^{4,7,15}$, $103^{1n,12}$, 106^6, $112^{1n,4,5}$, 114, 115^6, $116^{1n,1,11,12,18}$, 117–19, 120^5, 121^3, 122, $123^{1n,2,3}$, $124^{9,24}$, 125, 127, 128, 129^1, 132, 133, 134^{1n}, 135^5, 136^1, $139^{1n,5}$, 141^{1n}, 142–4, $148^{1,4}$, 149^6, 150^{1n}, 152, 153, 154^{1n}, 156^1, 159^{16}, 163, 166, $167^{1n,8}$, 168^1, 170^{1n}, 173^{11}, 175, 176^8, 177^{1n}, 183, 186^5, 187^{1n}, 188^{1n}, 189, 190, 197, 199, 203^5, 205^{1n}, $206^{6,7}$, 208, 211, $212^{1n,1}$, 214, 220^6, 223^2, 225^{13}, 229^3, 231^{1n}, 233, 236, 239^{1n}, $241^{1n,2}$, 242^{1n}, 247^{1n}, 249^1, 253^{1n}, 255^3, 257, 259, 263^3, 266^{1n}, 267^3, 271^1, 272^4, 276^4, 285^6, 288, 300^3, 301, 303, 308, 310, 312, $313^{1n,1}$, 315, 326, 327, 330, 332, 333^{1n}, 334, 336^3, 340, 341, 344, 346, 365^8, 368, 375 (II, III), 376^{1n}, 378, 379, 382, 385, 387, 391, 392^{1n}, 393^1, 396, $397^{1n,1}$, 399^3, 406, 411^3, 412, 422, 428, 430^{1n}, 442^7, 443^6, 445, 446, 459, 463, 471^{1n}, $472^{3,4}$, 476, $483^{15,21}$, 487, 492^1, 498^2, 506^{1n}, 510^2, 511^{1n}, 515^{1n}, $516^{1n,1}$, 517^4, 520^6, 521^2, 522^{1n}, 525, 526, 527^{1n}, 532^{1n}, 537^{16}, $541^{1n,3}$, 546, 555, 560, 567, 569^5, 573, 575, $577^{1,13}$, 583^1, 586^4, 600, 602, 607^{1n}, 615^{1n}, 616, $617^{1n,10}$, 620, 628, 629^6, 631^{1n}, 636, $641^{1n,4,7}$, 643^{1n}, $644^{1n,6}$, 645, $646^{1n,7,8,29}$, 647, 648, 650^4, 651^{11}, 652, App *passim*, Gl s.vv. Gnostics, *Lex Constantiniana, Lex Iulia de maiestate*, Manichaeans, Mithras, paterfamilias. *See also* Church, Christian; Galileans
Catholic, 167, 641^7, 651^{16}
Christianos ad leonem, 1^3
Christians:
Latin, 181^4
Orthodox, 555, 573, 575
Christmas, 220, 281, 385. *See also* Nativity
chrysargyron, 97^1
Church:
claims of, In, 4^{18}, 46
concessions to, In, 4, $5^{32,46}$, 32^9, 34^5, 59, 101, 107, 186, 250, 261, 262, 265, 276, 300, 327, 375 (II, III), 387, 390, 437, 474, 499^{1n}, 518
exemption from extraordinary public service, 262, 265; from menial public service, 226, 262, 265, 327; from taxation, 106, 107, 314, 384, 595

gift and/or bequest to, In, 5 (d), 36, 42¹, 395, 488, 499¹ⁿ, 510, 518, 522⁴, 585, 595, 604, 630, 652; recission of, 117
manumission in, 26, 35, 602, 607
persecution of, In, 4, 5^{8,40}, 1^{3,5}, 3, 4$^{\text{in},3}$, 5^{in}, 6, 7^{in}, 8$^{\text{in},5}$, 9, 12$^{\text{in},2}$, 13$^{\text{in},5,7}$, 14^{in}, 17$^{\text{in},4}$, 21^{in}, 24^{in}, 40^{in}, 42$^{\text{in},1}$, 44–6, 50, 68², 73⁷, 103¹², 117, 119, 123³, 127⁷, 156¹, 159, 167⁷, 189², 195^{in}, 203¹, 212¹, 411³, 483²¹, 544^{in}, 562, 630⁸, 645⁴⁰, 646 (I), App *passim*, Gl s.vv. Montanists, Novatians; bibliography, selected, on App *ad fin.*
protection of, 50, 250, 536
recognition of, In, 4, 5 (d)⁴⁸, 4, 5¹, 12, 31^{in}, 33^{in}, 44, 167^{in}, 173¹¹, 241^{in}, 267³, 515^{in}, 641^{in}
sale to, 604
subjection to public service, 377, 434
subsidy to, 15
toleration of, 7, 12
as Christ's mystical body, 53¹⁶, 75⁴²
as defendant, 318
as depository of disputed revenue, 597
as donee, 488, 515^{in}, 581, 595, 613
as heir, 46, 421, 488, 515^{in}, 615, 623; debarment of, 225
as juristic person, In, 4, 5 (d), 4$^{\text{in},4}$, 10, 12, 36^{in}, 46, 106^{in}, 133¹, 186⁵, 226^{in}, 329, 515^{in}, 536⁵, Gl s.v. juristic person. *See also* corporation
as legatee, 488, 499^{in}, 510, 515^{in}, 585, 595, 615, 640
as lessor, 618
as mother, 510, 526, 527, 618
as proprietor. *See also* property, ecclesiastical
as sanctuary for fugitive, In, 5 (f), 168¹, 241, 246¹, 266, 273, 289, 315, 370, 400, 413, 497, 501, 576, 633². *See also* asylum, right of; fugitive; refuge; sanctuary, right of
as subordinate to priesthood, 49 (I)
Abyssinian, Gl s.v. catholicus
Anglican, 75⁴², 148⁴, 476^{in}, 651²
Armenian, 553⁴, 637¹⁸
Catholic, In^{31,33,52}, 10, 15–17, 21, 26, 30, 36, 39, 40, 49 (II), 50, 52, 53, 59, 69, 73, 75⁵³, 77, 85, 86, 105, 163, 164⁶, 167⁹, 258⁵, 298, 306, 310, 319, 337, 395, 399, 412, 415 (II), 425, 429, 469, 470 (I), 481, 486, 527, 551, 553, 567, 651¹⁶, 652. *See also* churches, Catholic
Catholic and Apostolic, 63, 542, 575
Catholic and Apostolic Orthodox, 524 (I)
Christian, 17$^{\text{in},3}$, 20⁵, 39³, 49^{in}, 167^{in}, 300^{in}, 555⁴, 561

Coptic, 481^{in}
Eastern, 614², 651²⁰. *See also* Orthodoxy, Eastern
Egyptian, 189²
Episcopalian, 75⁴²
Ethiopian, 99$^{\text{in},1,4}$, 159²⁷
Greek, In^{30,41}, 28¹, 92¹, 651²⁰. *See also* Orthodoxy, Eastern
Holy Catholic, 652
Holy Catholic and Apostolic, 527, 569, 636, 637, 645
Holy Orthodox Catholic Apostolic, 28¹. *See also* Orthodoxy, Eastern
Lutheran, 92¹
Methodist, 92¹
Presbyterian, 92¹
Roman Catholic, In⁵², 95⁴³, 98¹⁵, 109²
of Christ, 17⁶, 32⁹, 442⁷, 503³, 509¹
of God, 49 (II)¹, 67, 69, 167^{in}, 212¹, 400, 412, 427, 455, 460, 466, 484, 546, 637, 646 (I), App 10 (d)¹⁴
of the Lord 543 (I)
in Africa, 10^{in}, 17⁶, 350^{in}, 397¹⁰
of Alexandria, 52⁴, 69, 75¹⁷, 77, 86, 442⁷, 527
of Antioch, 5¹, 61 (II, III), 103, 442⁷, 459, 470 (VI)
of Arles, 442
of Beroea, 411 (I)
of Caesarea, 61 (III)
of Carthage, 16
of Constantinople, 64, 182, 225^{in}, 319, 425, 469, 475, 479, 491, 510, 518, 526, 537, 538, 552^{in}, 554, 558³, 560, 561, 579, 616, 618, 645; privileges of, 518, 524 (II), 526, 530, 537, 557³, 618, 645, 651
of Edessa, 42⁵, 123
of Egypt, 284⁴
of Epheseus, 470 (VIII), 577$^{\text{in},13}$
of Jerusalem, 54, 313¹, 470 (VI), 560, App⁵
of Nicomedia, 50, 212¹
of Perrha, 470 (X)
of Rome, In⁴⁶, 17³, 76⁴, 92¹, 101, 109³, 138$^{\text{in},4}$, 167$^{\text{in},2}$, 200^{in}, 220¹⁰, 262, 295, 359^{4,5}, 360, 371, 375 (II, III), 397^{1,10}, 442, 462, 475, 489³⁹, 552, 560, 618³, 645, 651²⁰; privileges of, In^{31,46}, 101, 164, 375, 470⁷⁰, 475, 563, 618³, 637, 645, Gl s.v. patriarch
of Smyrna, 206⁷, 577$^{\text{in},13}$
of Thessalonica, 384
of Tyre, 456
Church and State, *passim*, but esp. Tab⁵, In, 1, 4–7, 9, 4², 5¹, 10², 15, 17^{in}, 18^{in}, 167^{in}, 375⁷, 398⁷, 415 (II), 544^{in}, 613^{in}
Churches:
Orthodox, 75⁴², 148⁴, 650⁴
Protestant churches, 75⁴², 92¹, 651²⁰.

SUBJECTS 1297

See house, God's = church; house of prayer = oratory; martyry; oratory; temple = church
closure of, 42[1], 119[5]
confiscation of, 4[10], 6, 7, 10, 12, 14, 18[1n], 40, 123, 160, 179
consecration of, 641[6]
construction of, In 5 (g)[44], 7[23], 13[1n], 14[13], 44, 45, 54, 59, 63, 64, 78, 95[1], 120[5], 179, 186[5], 200[1], 206, 211, 364[12], 395, 489, 568[1], 612, App 10 (f)
conversion into stables, 646[8]
destruction of, 42[1], 44, 120[5], 200[1], 212[1], 285[2], 463[5], App 10 (a)[16]
disturbance in, In 5 (g), 68[5], 310, 400, 413, 465, 466[1n], 484, 485, 495, 504, 505, 524 (I), 551
enlargement of, 45, 211
epithets of: apostolic, 167[5], 524 (II); Catholic, 106, 182, 289, 310, 465, 468, 489, 490, 524 (II), 527[91], 554; holy, 59, 64, 375, 400, 412, 418–20, 427, 448, 455, 457, 459, 460, 466–8, 482–7, 495, 523, 524 (I), 526, 527, 530, 545, 546, 551, 552, 561, 569, 579–81, 588, 600, 612, 613, 615, 620, 621, 634, 637, 645, 648, 651; orthodox, 395[26], 491, 495, 609; religious, 421, 510; sacred, 552, 556; sacrosanct, 287, 319, 384, 421, 430, 434, 437, 438, 465, 474, 488, 490, 501, 510, 515, 526, 536, 550, 561, 562, 604, 623, 628, 630, 640 (I, II), 646 (I), 652; titular, 364[15]; universal, 546; venerable, 334, 340, 377, 395, 546, 569, 557, 558, 560, 562, 563, 595
heretical or schismatic 40, 57, 59, 120[1n,5], 123[4], 138, 160, 163, 167, 179, 182, 191, 192, 194, 213, 258, 301, 324, 325, 328, 329, 336, 337, 342, 395, 416[1n], 417[1n], 484, 489
names of. See in Index of Places s.vv. Amalfi, Antioch, Chalcedon, Constantinople, Edessa, Ephesus, Jerusalem, London, Milan, Rome
repair of, In[44], 44, 45, 186[5], 211[1], 463[5], 478
reunion of, 414[1n,5], 418[2], 546[1n], 548[10], 550[1n], 551[1n], 554[1n], 556[1n,1,3], 557[1n], 560[1n], 563[2]
surrender: by heretics or schismatics to orthodox, 5[1], 40, 59, 138, 163, 173, 182, 258[8], 301, 324, 325[9], 328, 329, 337, 342, 395; by orthodox to heretics or schismatics, 120[1n,4], 123[4], 325, 395; by pagans to Christians, 4, 7, 10, 12, 14
Circumcellions, 17[6], 276[4], 328, 329, Gl. See also Donatism or Donatists

circumcision, 53[12], 76, 79, 341[7], 378, Gl s.v. Lex Constantiniana
circus, 236, 243, 385, 509, 629[6]. See also amphitheatre; arena; games; spectacle, amphitheatrical
citizens:
lower-class, 127[6], 204[3], 242, 497[5], 646[8], Gl s.vv. client; defender of the municipality; patrician; plebeian; tax, capitation
upper-class, 127[6], 204[3], 242, 394[4], 435[6], Gl s.vv. curial, defender of the municipality, patrician
citizenship, Roman, 1[2], 35, 46, 92[2], 167[1n], 184[3], 234[2], 308[14], 358[1], 607, 623[3], Gl s.vv. guardian, peregrine
city-state, 73[17], 614[7], 652[4]
Claudians, 164[16]. See also Donatism or Donatists
clergy or clergyman, Tab[5], 16, 24, 29, 30, 32, 33, 35, 41, 45[14], 46[25], 50[20], 55, 59, 60, 62, 67[40], 81–3, 85, 87, 89, 95[41], 97, 101, 102, 106[1], 107, 108[1n], 109[1n], 114[1], 117, 119[5], 120, 127[4], 128[1n], 129[1], 130, 133[1n,3], 136[1n], 137, 1n, 146[3], 150, 152[7], 161, 165, 188, 197, 202[1n], 204, 210, 213, 216[2], 222, 227, 228[1n], 225, 233[1n], 239, 241, 258, 260, 267–70, 272, 273, 276, 280, 284[3], 285, 300, 307, 310[3,13], 311, 314, 325[9], 329, 331, 334, 336, 342, 343, 347, 350, 351, 352[2], 364, 371, 372, 387, 390, 399, 400, 408[4], 410[4], 412, 413, 421, 432, 433, 436[1n], 437, 439, 443, 444, 447, 448[1n], 456, 466, 470 (XI), 472, (II, III), 476, 478, 480, 487[1n], 488–91, 494, 495, 497, 500–3, 510, 514[1n], 515, 516[1n], 518[3], 519, 522[4], 523[1], 524 (I), 526–8, 530, 537, 540, 541, 554, 559, 560, 565, 576, 579, 580, 584, 585, 598[13], 611–13, 623, 624[3], 625[1n], 628, 629, 641[6], 646[1], 651. Gl and therein s. vv. archdeacon, Continents, Donatism, exorcist, lector, patriarch, priest, subdeacon, virgin, introduced. See also ex-clergyman; presbyter; priest, Christian
heretical or schismatic, 24, 57, 68, 69[1n], 107[4], 120, 152, 153, 196, 213, 222, 239, 248, 251, 258, 260, 268, 325[9], 326, 329, 336, 337, 343, 395, 445, 480, 489, 542, 560[18], 616, Gl s.v. Luciferians. See also bishop, heretical or schismatic; deacon, heretical or schismatic; priest, heretical or schismatic
benefit of, 62[11], 96[1n], 152[7]
deposition of, In, 5 (b), 225[14], 307, 334, 342, 472 (III), 476, 478, 480, 524 (I), 579, 613, 629
encouragement of convicted person's appeal, 235, 272

exclusion from residence: in or near Constantinople, 196, 222, 258, 285; in or near Rome, 152, 164
exemption: from billeting, 83; from compulsory public service, In, 5 (c), 16, 17^{1n}, 29, 30, 32, 33, 55, 56, 59, 60^2, 67^{40}, 81, 85, 87, 89, 102, 107, 108^{1n}, 114^1, 129^1, 188, 202, 210, 274, 282^1, 629; from extraordinary public service, 515; from menial public service, 41, 102, 107; from municipal senate, 60, 81, 89, 118^1, 151, 155, 267; from personal public service, 162
prohibition: on defending debtors, 241; on intervening in probate of wills, 565; on paying debtors' debts, 241
forfeiture of property on admission to clericate, 193, 224, 233, 273, 629; to another person, 188, 210; to children, 109, 110, 433, 497; to municipal senate, 109, 130, 280, 433, 497, 629; to provincial office staff, 110; to public post, 202; to relatives, 109, 130, 433, 497
immunity: from guardianship, 628; from pagan ceremonies, 41, 117; from taxation, In, 5 (c); 32, 83, 97, 102, 107, 130^{1n}, 165, 174, 282; from torture as witness, 204; from transfer of property to municipal senate, 109, 193, 280, 322, 433, 629
interference in execution of sentence in criminal case, 234, 235, 237^2, 272, 370
migration of, 270^3, 472 (III)
ordination of, In, 5 (a), 33, 55, 103, 109, 194, 203, 239, 269, 270, 273, 478, 480, 500, 537^3, 579, 613, 629, 651
privilege of, 441^{1n}, 478
privileges for, 56, 101, 102, 107, 202, 204, 280, 282, 300, 387, 390, 491^7, 651
recall from clericate: to civic duties, 33, 109, 110, 114, 118, 130, 151, 155, 273, 280, 307, 322, 478, 497, 629, 651; to governmental service, 444; to guild, 133, 307, 439, 497
recall from exile, 58, 61^7, 67^{13}, 71^{1n}, 77, 84–7, 93^{1n}, 95, 98^{13}, 101^{1n}, 112, 115^{1n}, 117, 120, 124, 125, 137, 463, 524^2
recruitment of, In, 5 (g), 33, 55, 103, 109, 130, 269, 270, 272, 528
subjection: to municipal senate, 118, 151, 322; to public post, 202; to public service, 107, 118, 280, 438; to taxation, 106^1, 107, 127, 435; to transport provisions, 107
subsidy to, 15, 651
as banker, 107^8
as caretaker of ecclesiastical property, 472 (III)

as civilian official, 16^{1n}, 60, 540, 541
as defendant, 62, 102, 150, 161, 197, 334, 387, 399, 490, 491, 515, 611, 625^{1n}
as donee, 488, 612; debarred as donee, 225, 488
as farmer, 107^8
as heir, 488; debarred as heir, 225, 488
as landowner, 17^6, 107
as leaseholder, 472 (III)
as legatee, 488, 612
as manager of property, 472 (III)
as owner of property. See property, owned by clergy
as physician, 107^8
as shepherd, 107^8
as silversmith, 107^8
as tentmaker, 107^8
as tradesman, 32, 83, 102, 107, 127^4, 128^{1n}, 165, 274, 282^{1n,1}, 478; debarred as tradesman, 478
as victualler, 282
clericalism, Gl s.v. Encratitans
clericate, 33, 55, 103, 109, 110, 282, 314, 322, 372, 397, 433, 441, 478, 497, 500, 502^{1n}, 514, 579, 652, Gl
persons debarred from: baker, 133; beneficiarian, 110; cohortaline, 629; commissary, 110; cultivator, registered, 478; curial, 433; decurion, 33, 478; decurion's relative, 33, 55; farmer, 314^3; goldsmith, 478^{21}; guildsman, 439, 478; heretic, 103, 192, 193, 196, 213, 239, 251; magistrate-elect, 109; municipal senator, 478, 629; patron, 478^{21}; peculator, 110; provost of granary, 109; provost of the peace, 109; receiver of taxes, 109, 478; rich, the, 33, 55, 129; slave, 478, 528, 529; tenant, 478, 528; tenant farmer, 441^6, 478; treasury official, 118
clerk:
chief to urban prefect, 364
conciliar, 470^2. See also secretary, conciliar
imperial, 363, 387^1, Gl. See also notary; scribe, imperial; secretary, imperial
ordinary, Gl s.v. guild
cleromancy, 614^{10}. See also divination or diviner; lot; sortition
client, 39^5, 50, 127^6, 605, 606^{20}, Gl and therein s.v. patron. See also patronage or patron or patroness
climate. See phenomena, natural
cloth, 301^7, 432. See also apparel
altar, 551
clothes or clothing. See apparel
cloud. See phenomena, natural
coadjutrix, 122

SUBJECTS 1299

codicil, 225, 298, 488, 510. *See also* will *or* testament
cognation *or* cognate, 421, 572, 575, 599, Gl. *See also* agnation *or* agnate
cognitor, 234³
cohabitation, 170³, 497, 631^{1n,3}, 635². *See also* coitus
coheir, 592, 640⁷. *See also* heir
cohortaline, 383, 567, 576, 629, Gl and therein s.v. official
governmental service, 320, 395, 429, 480, 488
coin, In²³, 1⁴, 15, 34⁵, 38², 95⁶², 116, 165, 204⁵, 239³, 312, 433, 456⁷, 464¹, 470 (VIII), 491, 515, 555, 581, 596, 606, 611, 621, 651⁶, Gl s.vv. as, aureus, denarius, drachma, follis, libella, milaresium, obol, solidus. *See* the above items, *also*: coinmaker; currency; depreciation of; farthing; medallion; mint; money; nummus; pound; shilling
coinmaker, 430. *See also* counterfeiting *or* counterfeiter
coitus, 517⁴. *See also* cohabitation
collector, 515
College of Cardinals, 364¹⁵
collier, Gl s.v. guild
colloquy, 95, 124, 150¹, 407. *See also* dialogue
collusion, 513. *See also* connivance
colonus or colona, 497³, 528⁵, 618⁴. *See also* serf
colony, 220⁴, 313¹, 646¹⁴, Gl s.vv. Augustal, duovir
combat, gladiatorial, 132². *See also* arena; gladiator
comedy:
  Greek, 67²⁵, 116¹,⁷, 223². *See also* drama; mime
  Roman, 67³³, 223². *See also* drama; mime
comet. *See* phenomena, natural
commander, military, 555
commandment, God's, 20, 46, 47, 54, 59, 61 (II), 155³, 159, 195, 350
commerce, Tab⁵, In⁹, 32, 83, 102; 107; 127, 274, 282, 472 (III), 478, 616^{1n}, Gl s.v. peregrine. *See also* industry; merchant, tradesman
commissary, 110, 383, 502
commission:
  = document, 511
  = errand, 512
  = group, 617⁴, App 7. *See also* delegation
  = mandate, 561¹⁸
commissioner, 74^{1n,9}, 93, 95²², 104, 324^{1n}, 347^{1n}, 400^{1n}, 401^{1n}, 402^{1n}, 403^{1n}, 404^{1n}, 405^{1n,7}, 406^{1n}, 407⁶, 408², 447^{1n}, 448⁵, 453^{1n}, 454^{1n}, 457^{1n}, 470$^{1n,1,4,12,27,38,39,44,50,53,55-57,60,61,70}$, 471^{1n,5}, 505², 556³, 578⁷, App¹². *See also* delegation; legate
Commissum nobis, In⁴⁴
communication *or* communion, 17⁶, 19, 47, 50, 67¹³, 70, 71, 72^{1n}, 85, 87, 94^{1n,1}, 95, 122, 154², 167⁷, 182, 194, 231, 284, 287, 295, 297, 301, 310, 328, 337, 364, 368, 375^{1n}, 388, 407, 414, 415 (II), 416, 417^{1n,3}, 418, 419^{1n}, 420, 427^{1n}, 472 (III), 489, 527, 551, 559, 560^{11,16}, 561, 562, 564^{1n}, 616, 645, Gl s.v. Luciferians
Communion, Holy, 75⁴², 206⁷, 364⁸, 527, 559¹⁵ 588, 645. *See also* Eucharist; Liturgy, Divine; Lord's Supper; Mass, Holy; Sacrifice, Christian
concordat, In⁹
concubine, 63², 525, Gl s.v. virgin, introduced. *See also* bastard; legitimation; mistress; "sister"
condiction, 612
Conference of Carthage (411), 324^{1n}, 325^{1n}, 326^{1n}, 328^{1n}, 338^{1n}
confession *or* confessor, 7²², 46, 50, 127⁷, 463, 646⁹, App 10 (f)
Congress, United States, 357^{1n}
connivance, 164, 181³, 194, 234, 239, 242, 248, 253, 258, 268, 272, 289, 298, 301, 307, 308, 310, 312, 324, 337, 368, 382, 395, 413, 440, 506, 513, 534, 536, 573, 616. *See also* collusion; dissimulation; fraud; negligence
consecration:
  of bishop. *See* bishop, consecration of
  of churches. *See* churches, consecration of
  of sacred things, 641^{8,11}
consistory, In, 3, 136^{1n}, 178, 186, 197, 226, 453, 454, 457^{1n}, 471^{1n}, 472²⁰, 547, 548², 549, 594-7, Gl and therein s.vv. master of the offices, notary, tribune and notary
conspiracy, 1⁴, 3, 67, 68, 70^{1n}, 74^{1n}, 78^{1n}, 145, 215, 295, 326, 330, 371, 375 (II, III), 470 (VIII), 496
constitution, In, 2$^{6,11-14,17,44,46,49}$, 4², 9^{1n}, 12⁶⁶, 32⁹, 33, 34⁵, 39¹, 59¹⁰, 61⁵, 76, 86³⁵, 94¹, 95^{41,43}, 108¹, 120², 121³, 126¹, 133¹, 159^{1n}, 163, 166⁷, 168¹, 176, 204^{3,5}, 214⁶, 238¹, 248, 253^{1n}, 256², 273², 285⁶, 287^{1n}, 289, 292, 301¹⁴, 308, 310⁴, 313, 315¹, 320⁶, 324^{2,3}, 325, 328³, 331⁴, 338^{1n}, 339^{1n}, 375^{1n}, 380, 399⁴, 400, 421, 422, 425, 429, 435, 436^{1n}, 439, 440, 443¹⁵, 444-6, 456^{1n}, 459²⁰, 474, 476, 477, 488, 489, 496, 501, 502, 508¹, 510, 525, 526, 528, 565, 578, 585³, 586-8, 590, 599, 604, 606, 613^{1n}, 615^{1n}, 617⁶, 619-21, 632, 638¹⁴, 639⁸, 640 (I, V), 641 (I)^{13,22,24,28},

App^{3,8}, Gl s.vv. interpretation, pragmatic sanction, sanction. *See also* law

decree, In, 2, 18^{1n}, 27^{1n}, 49, 94^1, 145, 190, 289, 311, 328^{1n}, 347, 353, 368, 373, 414, 415 (II), 422^{13}, 459, 470, 472, 479, 506, 520, 524 (I), 546, 625^9, 641^{13}

decree, pragmatic, 426

edict, In, 2^{46}, 1^{2,4}, 3^{1n,5}, 7, 8^{1n,5}, 9^{1n}, 10^{1n}, 11, 12^{2,4,7,29}, 13, 14, 28, 31, 32, 36, 38, 44^{12}, 46, 47^9, 65, 66^1, 71, 94, 95^{34}, 108, 111^{1n}, 115, 116^{1n}, 117, 118, 119^1, 123, 129, 130, 150, 164, 167, 168, 178, 223^3, 284, 285, 288, 291-4, 301, 307, 308, 310, 324-6, 328, 340, 341^2, 351, 358, 370, 372, 374, 375^{1n}, 400, 402, 404, 405^3, 422, 423, 429, 431, 433, 440, 441, 443, 446, 459, 460, 465, 466^{1n}, 472^{19}, 476-80, 488, 489, 492-4, 496, 497, 501, 508^1, 519, 520, 523, 524, 526^4, 551^7, 555, 566, 568^1, 569, 575, 577, 578, 618, 625^9, 633^1, 636, 637, 639, 642, 645, 647, App 1-3, 5-7, 10 (a)-(c), (f), Gl s.v. praetor

epistle *or* letter, In, 2^{31,46}, 3, 4^{1n}, 6-8, 10-20, 22, 24, 25, 27, 39, 40, 41^4, 42^5, 43 (I), 44, 48, 50-4, 58, 59, 60^{1n}, 61, 63, 64, 66, 68, 69, 71-8, 83-6, 88, 90, 93, 94^1, 96, 98-100, 103, 104, 105^{1n}, 107, 111, 112, 116, 116^{16}, 119, 125, 137, 139, 150, 152, 153, 159, 161, 164, 171, 197, 200, 207, 232, 288, 295, 296, 301, 305, 307, 308, 310, 311, 324, 327, 350^{1n}, 352, 353^6, 354, 356, 359-68, 371-3, 375 (II), 397, 398, 401-3, 405-12, 414-16, 418-20, 426, 427, 431, 433, 435, 440, 433, 444, 449-53, 455, 458-62, 464, 466, 467, 470 (I, V, VII), 473, 475, 478, 480-3, 485-9, 495-7, 511, 519, 524, 527, 542-54, 556-8, 560-4, 577, 580, 600, 606, 617, 637, 645, App 8, 10, Gl s.v. pragmatic sanction

formulary, In, 2, 12, 182, 205^1, 217, 495, 526, 530, 536, 540, 567, 568, 584, 597, 606

formulary, pragmatic, 600, 633, 635

mandate, In, 2, 1^2, 5, 23, 26, 27^3, 29, 30, 33-5, 37, 40, 55-7, 60, 71, 79-82, 87-9, 91, 92, 97, 104, 106, 109, 110, 113, 114, 121, 126-8, 132-5, 140, 145-9, 151, 154-8, 160, 162-6, 169, 170, 172-7, 179-94, 196, 198, 199, 201, 202, 204-6, 208-10, 212-17, 219-31, 233-83, 285-7, 289, 290, 293, 294, 298-300, 302-4, 306, 309, 311-24, 325^9, 328^{1n}, 329-39, 341-9, 355, 366, 369, 375 (I), 376-83, 385-95, 399, 400, 413, 417, 421, 424, 425, 428, 430, 432, 434, 436, 437, 447, 448, 453, 454, 456, 457, 471, 473, 474, 479, 488^{16}, 490, 491, 498, 500-3, 506-18, 525, 526, 528, 529, 536, 540, 548^{1n}, 558, 559, 565, 572, 576, 579, 581, 582, 586-99, 601-16, 619-31, 634, 638, 642^{11}, 646, 650-2, App 3^{49}

memorandum, 411 (II, III), 414, 447, 453, 457^{19}, 560

oration, 49, 357, 363^3, 472

ordinance, In^{5,31}, 3, 4, 4^{4,8}, 10, 12-14, 29, 32^9, 41, 42^{1n}, 44, 46, 61 (I, III), 62, 76^{1n}, 78^{1n}, 85, 87, 88, 95, 103, 104, 115, 116, 122, 152-4, 155^1, 158, 160, 164, 166, 176, 180, 181^2, 195, 203, 207, 215, 217, 246^1, 249, 253, 265, 293^3, 301, 308, 310, 324, 325, 326, 328, 350, 364, 368, 372, 375 (II), 378, 397, 402, 415 (II), 419, 422, 424, 427^{16}, 431, 442, 445, 449^{1n}, 451^{1n}, 456, 458^{1n}, 459, 463, 466, 469, 473, 477-80, 483, 485, 487, 489, 520, 522, 524 (II), 530, 538, 554, 560, 568^6, 576, 579, 584, 589, 606, 613, 619, 629, 633, 645, 648-50, App 5, 8, 10 (f)

rescript, In, 2, 1, 2, 3^{1n,34}, 4, 4^2, 9, 12, 12^{10}, 21, 42, 43 (II), 64^{24}, 65, 67, 70, 72^{1n}, 76^4, 105, 119^{1n}, 120, 122, 136, 141-3, 156^1, 158^1, 164, 166, 172^3, 173, 195, 203, 211, 218, 284^3, 288, 293, 297, 314, 323^{1n}, 327, 350, 352, 353, 365, 371, 375 (III), 384, 395^{26}, 415 (I), 439, 441, 442, 463, 468, 484, 486, 489^{61}, 498^2, 505^2, 523, 553, 568, 584^2, 633, 635, 641^{16}, 649, 650, App 4, 8 (b), 10 (e), (f), Gl s.v. pragmatic sanction

response, 218, 288, 323, 324^3, 372, 375 (III), 391, 417, 431, 438, 444, 520 568, 622, Gl

sanction, 76, 83, 107, 146, 163, 187, 225, 233, 254, 261, 267, 276, 289, 299, 308, 329, 334, 343, 346, 372, 380, 381, 413, 418, 428, 433, 443, 480^2, 488, 489, 496, 565, 568, 626, 641^2, App 10 (e), (f); Gl

sanction, pragmatic, In, 2, 329, 431, 439, 444, 446, 470 (V, VI), 474, 518, 526, Gl

statute, 31^{1n}, 59, 60^{1n}, 76, 94^1, 95^{34}, 104, 117^{1n}, 133^1, 144, 149^4, 157, 166, 168^1, 176, 186, 204^5, 218, 225, 248^5, 253, 267^9, 273^2, 285^3, 288, 293^3, 301, 312, 315^5, 316^{1n}, 317, 324^7, 335, 337, 339^{1n}, 340, 346, 364, 387, 390^2, 393, 400, 431, 433, 440, 443, 459, 478, 497, 502, 510, 515^{1n}, 520, 524, 536, 546, 557, 568, 581, 628^2, 640,

SUBJECTS 1301

641, 644, 645, App[20], Gl s.v. sanction
subscription, 131
interpretation of, 29, 35, 37, 92, 96, 146, 161, 169, 187, 199, 201, 204, 209, 214, 214[6], 220, 255, 308, 312, 318, 331, 332[1n], 372[25], 395[26], 400, 409[3], 417, 421, 425, 426, 429, 459, 478, 488, 497, 500, 587, 589, 649[1], 651[6], Gl; independent, of, 62, 532, 538, 574, 593[1n,1]; unneeded, 76[5], 80[3], 91, 126, 278, 288, 440, 443
paraphrase *or* translation, Arabic, of, 32[9], 48 (III), 49[11], 66[1,2], 543[1n]; Armenian, of, 32[9], 527, 542; Ethiopic, of, 543; Greek, of, 2, 4, 7-10, 12-18, 26[6], 32[9], 35[1n], 38, 44, 49, 87, 90, 105, 119[1], 126[1n], 146[4], 158[3], 163[2], 166[7], 214[6], 225[3], 230[6], 247[3], 257[7], 270[4], 271[6], 273[7], 276[1n], 298[13], 309[9], 313[4], 314[3,4], 335[6], 375[8], 393[6], 395[26], 411, 432[5], 459[2], 474[1n], 475[1n], 476, 479[11], 490[1n], 491[5,7], 501[7], 507[1n], 508[1n,1], 515[1n,12,14,16], 528[1n], 529[1n,2], 568[1n], 576[7], 585[1n], 593[1n], 598[1n], 623[1n], 625[12], 628[1n]; Latin, of, 47, 48[17], 50, 64, 66, 75, 77, 84-7, 95, 119[1], 159, 397, 398, 400, 405, 406, 411, 412, 422, 423, 425, 447[2,5,6], 449[2,3], 450[4,5], 451[4], 454[4,7], 457[8,10], 11,16,18, 459[1n,17], 462[1], 468[1], 469[1], 470[1n], 472[1,2], 473[3], 477, 479[1,2], 480, 481[1,6,15], 484[11], 486[15], 487[2], 489, 527, 532[1,2], 534[4], 555[5,6,8], 567[15], 579[22,23], 593[1n], 606[11], 611[2,7,13], 612[22], 614[5,11], 615[5], 618[14], 621[4,7,10], 635[3], 642[1n,11,13,15-17]; Syriac, of, 32[9], 42, 48 (I, II), 49[9], 66[3], 449[1n], 450[1n], 451[1n,6], 452, 453[1n], 455[1n], 458[1n,6], 459, 460, 472[3], 495[1n], 524, 527
publication of, In[6], 8, 9[1n], 11[1n], 12, 13, 27[1n], 52[1n], 68, 76, 111, 120[1], 122, 126[1], 153, 288, 293, 294, 301, 307, 308, 310, 350, 364, 368, 371, 372, 377, 400, 422, 429, 431, 433, 435, 440, 441, 443, 446, 478-80, 488, 489, 496, 497, 519, 520[1,2], 554, 588, 633, App 10 (a), (f)[20,55]
constitutiones principum, In, 2
consubstantiality, 47[1n], 50, 67, 103, 131[1n], 156[1], 159, 173, 481, 527, 546, 569, 575, 636, 637, 645
consul, 3, 7, 23, 26, 28-37, 41, 42[6], 55, 65, 76, 79-83, 89, 91, 92, 96, 97, 101, 102, 104, 106-10, 114, 126-30, 132-5, 139, 144-51, 154-8, 160-3, 165-70, 173-7, 179-94, 196, 198, 199, 201, 202, 204-10, 212-81, 283, 285-94, 296, 298-324, 327, 329-50, 368[7], 369, 370, 372, 375 (I), 376-95, 399, 400[1,76], 405, 413, 421, 422, 424, 425, 428-33, 436-44, 445[13], 474-8, 480[82], 488-90, 491[10], 492, 496-8, 500-2, 506-10, 512-19, 521, 528, 529, 533, 541, 544, 545, 547-9, 556, 558-60, 562, 565, 568, 578-81, 586-97, 601-17, 635-9, 642, 645, 646, 648, 650, 651, Gl and therein s.vv. dictator, *Lex Aelia et Sentia*, *Lex Caecilia et Didia*, *Lex Licinia de sodaliciis*, lictor, praetor, prefect (urban), *Senatus Consultum Persicianum*. *See also* consul, suffect; consul-designate; consular; consular rank; consulate; ex-consul; proconsul
consul, suffect, 127[8], Gl and therein s.vv. *Lex Fufia et Caninia*; *Lex Iulia et Papia Poppaea. See also* consul; consulate
consul-designate, 477, 479, 480. *See also* consul; consulate
consular, 6[1], 59, 60, 144, 234[3], 466, 521[1], 646 (I), Gl. *See also* consul
consular rank, 73, 74[1], Gl s.v. prefect (urban). *See also* consul
consulate, 104, 140, 146[5], 178, 233, 280, 282, 328, 397, 435, 449 451, 452, 455, 461, 464, 479, 480, 525, 526, 528[8], 552[2], 557, 619-30, 634, 642, Gl. *See also* consul
continence, 169[1]. *See also* celibacy *or* celibate; chastity; virginity *or* virgin
Continents, 150, 488, Gl
contract, 289, 298, 320, 337, 421[4], 510, 515, 517[2], 537, 582, 593, 598[8], 604[6], 613, 618, 622, 625[1n,9,12], 641[24], 644[3]
of deposit, 634
of rent, 618
of sale, 510, 513, 516, 604[1n], 641[27-9]
nuptial, 650
quasi-contract, 604[6], 640[1n]
right of, 289, 298, 320, 337, 440
contractor, 236[3], 301[7], 648
contributor = taxpayer, 646 (I)
convent. *See* nunnery
conventicle, 7, 167, 176, 329, 336, 342, 395[15], 489[47], App 10 (f)
conversion *or* convert, In[14,33,37,43], 16[2], 17[3,6] 42[5], 76, 80, 91, 106[6], 148[4], 154, 166[4], 195, 313, 350[1n], 392, 395, 525, 573, 600, 629, 646[9], 650[4], App 5, Gl s.vv. *Lex Constantiniana*, Mithras, Novatians
Jews, 33, 76, 164[11], 392, App 5, Gl s.v. *Lex Constantiniana*
slaves, 264[4], 652
conveyance *or* vehicle, transport, 18, 19, 58, 64, 70, 84 (II), 95[41], 112, 186[5], 410[6], 434[2], 438. *See also* public post
cook, 498[2]
copper, Gl s.v. as
copyist, 64, 180, 326, Gl s.v. apparitor
coronation, Tab[5], 472[4], 476[4], 492[1]. *See also* crown

1302 SUBJECTS

corporation:
Christian, In, 4, 5 (d), $4^{1n,4}$, 12, $36^{1n,4}$, 106^{1n}, 133^1, 186^5, 226^{1n}, 395, 515^{1n}, 537^6, 612, 648, App^7, Gl s.v. juristic person. See also guild or guildsman
pagan, In^9, $36^{1n,1}$, $133^{1n,1,6}$, 186^5, 300^{1n}, 495^{11}, 536, 537^6 619, 629, Gl s.vv. juristic person, Lex Clodia de collegiis, Lex Iulia de collegiis, pontifex maximus, pragmatic sanction. See also guild or guildsman
corpse, 68^4, 97^4, 117, 119^1, 139, 171^1, 181, 206, 334^{25}, 443, 463, 484, 495^4, 641 (I), App^{53}
carrier of, 319, 430, 437
transfer of, 206, 641^{13}
corrector, 234^3, Gl
of Lucania and Bruttil, 29
of Sicily, 18
of Tuscia and Umbria, 6^1
cosmos, 648^8
council, ecclesiastical, In, 5 (b)^{44}, $17^{3,5}$, 18, 19, 36^4, 39^{1n}, 47^{1n}, 48, 49, $68^{4,7}$, 73^{17}, 93, $94^{1n,1}$, 95, 104^{1n}, 112^4, 159^{42}, 164, 172, 203, 288, 325, 354^{1n}, 356, 358, 366, 367^{1n} 375 (I), 401^{12}, $403^{2,4}$, 404^4, 411^9, 416, 442^{1n}, 467, $470^{2,66}$, 519^{19}, 526, 542, 546, 554, 559, Gl and therein s.v. canon. See also council (ecumenical), synod
behaviour at, 73, 402, 405, 407, 464, 466, $470^{3,4,12}$, 471^3, $472^{1n,4,34}$
convocation of, In^{44}, 47, 73, 93^{1n}, 95^{1n}, 104^{1n}, 172^{1n} 205^1, 295, 353, 354^{1n}, 359-62, 366, 367, 397, 401, 402, 406, 408, 409, 449-55, 458, 459, 461-4 468^{1n}, 470^{1n}, 473, 476, 477, 483, 543^9, 544, 545
procedure in, In^{44}, 17-20, 48 (I), 49, 53, 73, 104, 105, 326, 401-5, 448-58, 466, 467, 469-73
ecumenical, 460, 470 (XI), 613^{1n}, Gl s.v. council; First, of Nicaea (325), In^{14}, 15^9, 17^3, 19^{1n}, $20^{1,11}$, 47^2, 48, 49^{1n}, 50, 51^{1n}, 52, 53, 57^{1n}, 58^{1n}, $61^{7,11}$, 67^{33}, 71, 94^1, 95, 103^7, 159^{49}, 169^3, 173^{1n}, 182^9, 368, 372^{1n}, 375^5, 406^{10}, 442^7, 445, 446^4, 448^7, 455^3, 458^4, 459^6, 460^1, 469^2, $470^{13,34,41,44,61,70,74}$, 472 (I), $476^{1,31}$, 477, 480, 481^8, $483^{11,24}$, 484^{14}, 485^5, 486^4, 487^{24}, 489^{14}, 523^1, $524^{10,16}$, 527, 542^2, 543^9, 546^{16}, 551^2, 554^4, 559^{11}, 569^5, 577^{1n}, $613^{1,4}$, 637^{13}, 645^{19}, Gl s.vv. Arians, council; Second, of Constantinople (381), In^{34}, 47^2, 173^{1n}, 205, $375^{5,7}$, 442^7, 469^2, $470^{14,22,34,70}$, $475^{7,9,10}$, $476^{1,31}$, 477^{10}, 480^{23}, 484^{16}, 489^{15}, 495^5, $524^{13,16}$, 526^8, 527, 542^4, 551^2, 559^{11}, 569^5, 577^2, 613^1, 618^3, 637^{14}, 645^{20}, Gl s.vv. Apollinarians, council, Marcellians; Third, of Ephesus (431), 284^4, $397^{1n,1}$, 398^{1n}, 401^{1n}, 402^{1n}, 403^{1n}, 404^{1n}, 405^{1n}, 406^{1n}, 407^{1n}, 408^{1n}, 409^{1n}, 410^{1n}, 411^{1n}, 414^{1n}, 415^{1n}, 416^7, 417^{1n}, $418^{1n,1}$, 420^{1n}, 422, 426^{1n}, 442^7, 445, 446^7, 448^8, 453^3, 454^8, 455^4, 458^5, $459^{7,24}$, 460^2, 469^2, $470^{21,34,44}$, 476^1, 477, 480, 484, 486, 489, $524^{14,16}$, 527, 542^5, 551^2, 559^{11}, 613^1, 637^{15}, 645^{21}, Gl s.vv. council, Nestorians, Pelagians; Fourth of, Chalcedon (451), $In^{34,43}$, 16^{1n}, 53^3, 228^{1n}, 284^4, 375^7, 411^1, 447^{1n}, $449^{1n,7}$, 456^{1n}, 461^{1n}, 464^{1n}, 465^{1n}, 466^{1n}, 467^{1n}, 468^{1n}, 469^{1n}, 470^{1n}, 471^{1n}, $472^{1n,14}$, 473, 475-7, 479^{1n}, 480-7, 489, 495, $524^{17,27,31}$, $527^{1n,2}$, $542^{1n,8,19}$, 543^6, 546, 551^2, 559^{11}, 569^5, 577^{1n}, $613^{1,4}$, 637^{16}, 645^{22}, Gl s.vv. council, Eutychians, Monophysites; Fifth, of Constantinople (553), 427^3; Seventh, of Nicaea (787), 48^{12}; Twelfth, of the Lateran (1215), 470^{70}; Twentieth, of the Vatican (1869-70), $95^{1,43}$
local: Africa (410), 324^4, 325^1; Alexandria (321), 47^{31}; (363), 195^2; Ancyra (358), 159^{42}; Antioch (ante 100), 112^4; (330), 61^7; (341), 159^{42}; (367), 159^{42}; (436), 427; (455), $470^{62,64}$; Aquileia (381), 172; Arles (314), 18, 19, 20^{1n}, 21^{1n}, 22^{1n}, 25^{1n}, 27^{1n}, 328^7; (353), 95^{21}; Bagai (394), 328^5; Besançon (444), 442^{1n}; Bordeaux (384), 203^1; Braga (563), 203^1; Cabarsussi (393), 328^5; Carthage (411) 350^{1n}; (416), 350^{1n}; (417), 350^{1n}; (418), 350^{1n}; Constantinople (448), 448^{1n}, 449^{1n}, 453^6, 455^{1n}, 457^{1n}, $459^{1n,10}$, 470^6, 479^8; (458), 495^{1n}; Elvira (ca. 300), 372^4; Ephesus (Robber or Latrocinium [449]), 284^4, 411^1, 447^{1n}, 449^{1n}, 450^{1n}, 451^{1n}, 452^{1n}, 453^{1n}, 454^{1n}, 455^{1n}, 456^{1n}, 457^{1n}, 458^{1n} 459^{1n}, 460^2 463^2, $470^{4,27,50,62,63,69}$, 479^{1n}, 480^{19}, 489^{21}, 524^{14}, 637^{15}, 645^{21}; Heraclea (514), 544; Illyricum (375), 159; Jerusalem (ca. 29), 470^{66}; (ante 35), 470^{66}; (ca. 49), 17^3, 470^{66}; (ca. 56), 470^{66}; (335), 67^{13}, 94^1; (415), 350^{1n}; Lampsacus (364), 131^{1n}, 159^{42}; Lydda (415), 350^{1n}; Milan (355), 93, 94^{1n}, 95^{1n}; Milevis (416), 350^{1n}; Palestine (453), 487; Ravenna (419), 354 355^2 356, 357^{1n}, 359^{1n} 361^1, 362^6, 364^8, $365^{1,2}$, $366^{3,4}$; Rimini (359), 104, 107, 159^{42}, 205; Rome (251), 645^{40}; (313), 17, 18^{1n}, $19^{6,8}$, 20^{1n}

21^{1n}, 22^{1n}, 27^{1n}, 328^7; (340), 84^{1n}; (371), 159; (378), 164^{1n}; (405), $295^{1n,3}$; (417), 350^{1n}; Sardica (343), 84^1, 95^{24}, 370^1; Seleucia (359), 104^{1n}, 159^{42}, 205^7; Sirmium (357), 100^{1n}, (358), 159^{42}; Spoleto (419), 359^{1n}, 360, 361^{1n}, 362^{1n}; Thessalonica (405), 295; Toledo (400), 372^4; Tyre (335) 68^4, 73, 74^{1n}, 75, 95; Whitby (633/4), 52^2; Zaragoza (380) 203^1
Hebrew, 23^2
imperial, In, 3, 67^{41}, 646^1, Gl s.vv. consistory, count of the sacred consistory. *See also* consistory,
count, 61 (III), 63, 244, 337, 363, 405^7, 415 (I), 417^7, 418^{1n}, 426, 442, 484, 486, 500, 523^5, 547^6, Gl
  of Africa, 293^{1n}, 310, 323, 339
  of the dispositions, 256^2
  of the domestics, 304, 401, 402, 404, 405, 420, 547, 548^2, Gl
  of the East, 63^5, 111^{24}, 127^2, 128, 147, 174, 179, 234, 272, 638^7, Gl and therein s.v. vicar
  of the private estates, 212, 311, 321 (II), 387^3, 555, 575, 616, 628, Gl and therein s.v. count of the sacred treasury
  of the sacred consistory, 186, 226, 453, 454, 457^{1n}, 547, 548^2, 549, Gl
  of the sacred largesses, 241, 311, 406, 407, 408^3, 444, 521^1, Gl and therein s.v. count of the sacred treasury
  of the sacred patrimony, 519, 630^1, Gl and therein s.v. count of the sacred treasury
  of the sacred treasury, 567, 575, Gl
counterfeiting *or* counterfeiter, 168^1, 171^1, 180, 198, 201, 204^5, 207. *See also* coinmaker
courier, 98, 168^1, 256^3, 363, 371, 402^4, 543 (II), 551^4
court:
  centumviral, Gl s.v. praetor
  episcopal, In, 5 (e), 17^3, 28, 62^{11}, 161^{1n}, 164, 197, 307, 334, 387, 490, 491, 500^{1n}. *See also* investigation, episcopal; jurisdiction, episcopal
  imperial, $In^{14,34}$, 20, 21, 38^2, 48 (I), 50, 58, 69^{1n}, 70, 71^2, 74^{1n}, 75, 84, 88, 94^{1n}, 95^{1n}, 104, 107, 112, 186, 226^{1n}, 288, 304, $349^{1n,1}$, 350^{1n}, 353^6, 363^{1n}, 398^7, 401, 405, $412^{1n,9}$, 434^{1n}, 447^{1n}, 449^{1n}, 456^{1n}, 463^2, 480, 481^1, 489, 495, 519, 543^{1n}, 549, Gl s.vv. count of the domestics, domestics, master of the offices. *See also* household, imperial; palace, imperial; courtiers, In, 3^{29}, 38^2, 63^2, 75, 126^1, 284^{1n}, App^{36}

military, 483, 487
non-State, 17^3, 341^5
papal, 440, 442, 500^{12}
praetorian prefectural, 491, 506, 515
provincial, 506, 513, 515
courtyard, 400
cousin, 113^5, 214^3, 435^3
  = official, 6, 65, 138, 140–2, 152, 195, 203, 211, 288, 301, 307, 308, 310, 352, 353, 356, 364, 365, 373, 429, 431, 433, 435, 439, 440, 442, 443, 488, 489, 496, 519. *See also* brother = official; father = official
covenant, 159, 509, 613, 625^9, 629
crafts, 34, 107^8, Gl s.v. guild
creditor, 241^1, 324^7, 501, 537, 582, 623, 627, 634. *See also* borrower; debt; debtor; lender; loan
creed, 100^{1n}, 105^2, 148^4, $250^{1,8}$, 459, 460^{1n}, 483, 489, 527, 569^5, Gl s.vv. heresy, Tascodrogitans. *See also* faith
  Apostles', 350^{20}, 569^5
  Athanasian, $546^{4,8,10}$, 569^5, 651^{20}
  Nicene, $50^{1n,57}$, 58^{1n}, 67^{17}, 93^{1n}, 95, 159, 173^{1n}, 481, 483–7, 524 (I), 527, 546^4, 569^5, 637
cremation, 443^4, 495^4. *See also* fire; punishment: death, by cremation
crier, court, 509, Gl s.v. apparitor
crime *or* criminal, In^{49}, $1^{2,3}$, 2, 3, 5, 12^{33}, $17^{3,8}$, 21–3, 39, 40, 44, 46, 50^{57}, 52, 59, 70^{1n}, 76, $92^{2,5}$, 98, 111, 117, 127^6, 135, 141, 145, 161, 164, 168^1, 169, 171, 173, 176, 180, 184, 185, 190, 196, 198, 199, 201, 203, 204, 207, 214, 230, 234, 237^2, 241^1, 242, 253, 260, 268, 272, 276^4, 288, 289, 298, 299, 301, 302^{1n}, 307, 310, 315, 325, 328, 333–6, 339^3, 343, 346, 350, 365, 368, 370, 372, 374, 387–9, 391, 392, 394, 395, 399, 401, 413, 424, 429, 432, 437, 440, 442, 443, 459, 470 (X), 476, 478, 483, 484, 487, 489, 496, 500, 504, 519, 520, 570, 576^{1n}, 583, 592^5, 611, 638, 641^{25}, 649, 651, 652, App^{53}, Gl s.vv. heresy, Lex Iulia de adulteriis coercendis
cropland *or* crops, 107^3, 220, 429^1, 627^4
Cross, In^{14}, 23^4, 38^2, 53^{12}, 54^6, 62^2, 303, 393^{1n}, 424^{1n}, 498, 546, 569, 636. *See also* Crucifixion; Passion
crown, 341^2, App 9. *See also* coronation; diadem; tiara
Crucifixion, 52^{16}, 53^{12} $54^{2,6}$, 75^{42}, 636, 637, 645, Gl s.v. Theopaschites. *See also* Cross; Passion
Crusade, Fourth, 181^5
cult:
  Christian, 23, 155, 334, 415, 489. *See also* religion, Christian; worship, Christian

foreign, Gl s.v. quindecimvir
imperial, In^{26,30}, 1^2, 6^1, 127^7, 300^3, 386^3, Gl s.v. Augustal. *See also* deification; worship, pagan
cultivator, registered, 47
Cunctos populos, In^{33}, 12^1, 167
curator:
  civic, 21, 154, 310, 325, App 10 (f). *See also* ex-curator
  financial, 8, App, 10 (f)
  of imperial household, 630
  of pious causes, 613
  of ward, 149, 255^2, 516, 608, 610, 619, 621^{1,3,5,8}, 627, 628, 638, Gl s.v. guardian. *See also* guardianship *or* guardian; tutor
curial, 43 (I), 81, 89, 109, 110, 118^1, 130, 151, 188, 193, 214, 229, 233, 242, 253, 263, 273, 306-8, 311, 320, 337, 349, 421, 426, 429, 432, 433, 478^{23}, 497, 513, 541, Gl. *See also* decurion; senator, municipal
curialate, 233, 433^4. *See also* decurionate
currency, depreciation of, 15^7, 301^7, 433^7. *See also* coin
cursing *or* curse, 1^2, 651
custom, In^{15}, 1^{1n,4,5}, 5^1, 7, 8, 10, 13, 14, 17^{5,15}, 26^4, 28^{1n}, 30, 31, 39, 41^2, 52, 59, 61 (I), 83^5, 90, 116, 117, 119^1, 139, 148^4, 161, 180, 181^{1n}, 186, 201, 203, 207, 225^{13}, 241^{1n}, 273, 278, 298, 310, 324, 341^2, 352, 355, 358, 361, 375 (I), 386, 400, 410^4, 423, 435, 442, 449, 470 (IV), 472^4, 476^{39}, 477, 478, 482, 487-9, 491, 492, 496, 502, 505, 511, 518, 519, 520^1, 530, 548, 579^7, 614^7, 617, 618, 629, 641,^{6} 642, 644^6, 645, Gl s.vv. *ius canonicum*, paterfamilias
Cynics, 124 (III)

damnatio memoriae, 127^7, 427^{19}, App 2; Gl
damnation, 59, 645, Gl s.v. Pelagians
dance *or* dancer, 49^{16}, 303^4, 493, 650, 651^8, Gl s.v. Ascodrogitans. *See also* theatre
daughter, 122, 187, 259, 331, 372, 392, 394, 435^3, 442^4, 463^{1n}, 496, 497, 567, 599, 602, 609, 650, App^{36}, Gl s.vv. Augusta, emancipation, *patria potestas*. *See also* child; foster-daughter
day. *See* Feast; festival; holiday; market-days; paschal days; Sabbath; Sunday; unlucky days; weekday
deacon, 17^3, 18^{11}, 42^{1n}, 45, 50, 64, 84 (III), 103^5, 109, 124^{20}, 158^4, 162, 166, 200^{1n}, 222, 224, 258^3, 280, 295, 310^{13}, 334^2, 336^2, 337, 342, 397^{10}, 399, 421, 436, 469^5, 478, 484, 488, 496, 497, 514, 510^{20}, 546, 551, 554^1, 556^3, 558, 559, 561, 588, 613, 628, 651, App 8 (b), Gl and therein s.vv. archdeacon, archimandrite, clergyman, priest, subdeacon heretical *or* schismatic, 95^{1n}, 103^5, 166, 222, 336^2, 337^1, 342, 350^{1n}, 352^{1n}, 559, 616, 624, Gl s.vv. Aetians; Maximians, Photinians
regional, 356^6
deaconess, 1^2, 82^1, 225, 227, 421, 488, 613^4, 638
  rape of, 92, 638
  as donee, 612
  as legatee, 612
deaconry, 258
deaf, the, 621^3, 628
deanery, 258
debauchery, sexual, 198, 201^4. *See also* adultery *or* adulterer; brothel; cohabitation; coitus; fornication; incest; lust; necrophilism; prostitution *or* prostitute; rape *or* rapist; seduction; "sister"; unchastity
debt, 209, 220, 266, 273, 324^7, 392^4, 501, 509^4, 515^{10}, 537, 567, 623, 634, 640^2, 641^{10}, Gl s.v. surety. *See also* loan
debtor, 241, 273, 324^7, 501^9, 519, 576^3, 582^{1n}, 604^8, 634^{1n}, Gl s.v. surety. *See also* borrower; creditor; lender
decree. *See* constitution
decretal, papal, 164^{1n}, 375^7, 472^{1n}
Decretals, False, 472^{1n}
decurion, 21, 33, 81^5, 114, 273, 329, 337, 353^6, 426, 481, 495^{10}, Gl. *See also* curial; senator, municipal
decurionate, 59, 229^{1n}, 263^{1n}, Gl. *See also* curialate
decury, Gl s.v. apparitor
dediticii, 23^4
defendant, 1^5, 2, 3, 17, 49 (I), 62, 65, 74, 95, 96, 102, 135^3, 146, 176^{13}, 234, 318, 328, 334, 347, 353, 399^6, 447^{2,4}, 470 (X), 478, 480, 491^7, 515, 528, 582^5, 598^{9,10}, 603, 611^9, 612^{14}, 619, 640 (V), Gl s.v. *Lex Aquilia*. *See also* bishop, as defendant; clergy *or* clergyman, as defendant; litigant
defender:
  of Church, 478, 491, 501, 505, 515, 565, 579, 651, 652, Gl
  of municipality, 242, 253, 289, 298, 306, 311, 394, 395, 426, 429, 480, 489, 516, 535, 537, 540, 541, 559, 567, 571, 586, 591, 593, 606, 619, 621, 627, 632, 634, 651, Gl
  of region, 356^5
deification, In^{26}, 127^7. *See also* cult, imperial
deity *or* divinity, pagan, 1, 2^{22}, 3, 4^2, 5-9, 12, 13, 26^4, 34^5, 41^4, 42^{1n}, 44, 49 (III), 54^6, 67, 111, 116, 117, 119, 121, 122, 124^8, 127^7, 148^4, 168^1, 184^{1n}, 206^7, 214^2, 220^{4,10,11}, 223^2, 242, 255^3, 259, 301

SUBJECTS

386^3, 442^7, 483^{15}, 484, 486, 521^2, $615^{1n,1}$, $641^{1n,4,8,9}$, 648^6, $651^{8,13}$, App 10, (f)^{11}, Gl s.vv. flamen Dialis, guild, Mithras. *See also* idolatry *or* idol; worship, pagan

delation *or* informer, $1^{2,3}$, 3, 42^{1n}, 150^1, 185, 223^3, 311, 372, 440^6, 443, 507, 573

delegation, 324, 341^2, 347, 375 (II), 384, 401^{12}, 402^{1n}, 404^{1n}, 407^{1n}, 408^{1n}, 429^1, 441, 470^2, 471^{1n}, 544^{1n}, 547, 550^{1n}, 562, 563^{1n}, 645^{34}, App 10 (f). *See also* commission = group

delict, 161, 334^5, 431, 509^1, 519, 598^7, 604^6
quasi-delict, 604^6

demon. *See* devil

denarism, 233

denarius, 95^{62}, 233^5, 312^2, Gl and therein s.v. drachma
double, 15^7
half, 515^{18}

desert, 46, 52^{48}, 98^{12}, 147^5, 169^3, 228, 237^2, 341, 442^7, 446

devil *or* demon, 7^{13}, 41^4, 44^{21}, 135^5, 148^4, 159, 411 (II, III), 457, 527^{45}, 651^{13}, App 10 (e), (f). *See* in Index of Persons s.vv. Devil, Satan

diaconate, 225^{1n}, 497, Gl

diadem, 400. *See also* crown; tiara

dialogue, 95, 228^1, 284^{1n}, $295^{1n,5}$, $297^{1n,3}$, 407. *See also* colloquy

dicast, 234^3

diece *or* dicer, 593, 651. *See also* gambling

dictator, 1^4, 7^3, 624^3, Gl and therein s.vv. Lex Cornelia de falsis, Lex Cornelia de iniuriis, Lex Iulia de collegiis

dignitary, 341^2, 349, 435, 456, 495, 513, 601, Gl s.vv. consistory, patrician. *See also* persons

dignity, 226, 229, 242, 426, 429, 434, 443, 459, $470^{44,54}$, 472^{30}, 488, 589, 608, 614, 629, 631, 638, 651

diocese:
ecclesiastical, In 5 (a), 20^1, 68^2, 75^{1n}, 449, 472^{30}, 611, 612, Gl and therein s.vv. bishop, see
imperial, 76, 172, 180^1, 198^2, 203^4, 234^3, 288, 443^{19}, 470^{71}, 471^7, 475^{1n}, 618^{10}, 646^2, 651, Gl and therein s.vv. exarch, patriarch, prefect (Augustal), prefecture, province, vicar; Africa, $15^{6,12}$, $19^{1n,2,22}$, 20^5, 250, 275, 276, 294^2, 324^{12}, 325^{13}, 646 (I), 651, 652; Asia, 43 (II), 52, 159, 182, 410^4, 470 (XI), 471, 475^{1n}, 618^{10}, Gl s.v. exarch; Carophrygia, 159; Cilicia, 52; Dacia, 375^1, 471^7; East, the, 45^{14}, 52^{48}, 54^{28}, 56^1, 63^5, 64^{20}, 234^3, 471, 489^{12}, 618^{10}, Gl s.v. count of the East; Egypt, 197, 234^3, 470 (IV), 489, 495, Gl s.v. prefect (Augustal);

Galliae, 203^4; Illyricum, 375^1, 651, Macedonia, 375^1, 471^7; Moesia, 52^{48}, Pactiana, 159; Phrygia, 159; Pontus, 52, 182, 191, 410^4, 470 (XI), 471, 475^{1n}, 618^{10}, Gl s.v. exarch; Spain, In^{42}, 19^{27}; Thrace, 470 (XI), 471, 475^{1n}, 618^{10}, Gl s.v. exarch; Viennensis, 203^4

diploma, 341

diplomacy, 520^2

diptych, 550^9, $554^{1n,1}$, 558^{1n}, 560, $561^{1n,11}$, 562^{10}, 563^{1n}, 637

disarmament, 606

disciple, 17^3, 75^{42}, 122, 359, 373^{1n}, 411^3, 484, 577

discipline:
apostolic, 167, 375 (III)
Catholic, 185, 227
ecclesiastical, In^{43}, 19, 61 (II, III), 68^3, 203^5, 501, 645, 651, Gl s.vv. apocrisiarian; archdeacon; bishop
public, 311, 498. *See also* public order

disease, 7^{1n}, 9, 40, 42^5, 44, 46, 47, 67, 93^5, 111, 116, 117, 203, 328, 402^4, 429, 480, 562, 567, 572, 575, 600, 616, 636. *See also* epidemic; medicine; pestilence; phthiriasis; physician; plague

disherison, 496, 525^7, 608, 624^4. *See also* heir; inheritance; will *or* testament

dissimulation, 160, 298, 310, 321 (II), 328, 395, 443, 519, 618, 619, 651. *See also* collusion; connivance; fraud; negligence

ditch, 14^6, 34

divination *or* diviner, 223^2, 242. *See also* astrology *or* astrologer; augury *or* augur; auspices; cleromancy; horoscope; lot; necromancer; numerology; prophecy *or* prophet; seer; sibyl; soothsaying; sortition

divinity (as opposed to humanity), 400, 484, 569, 636, 637, 645, Gl s.vv. Gnostics, *imperium*, Monophysites

divorce, In, 5 (g), 28^1, 372^{1n}, 478^{30}, 629, Gl s.v. *patria potestas*. *See also* marriage

Docetists, 7^{13}

Doctors of the Western Church, 326^5, $330^{1n,2}$, 362^2, 442^7

document, 17, 88, 293^3, 325, 326, 328, 334, 353, 382^1, 401^{12}, 444^9, 472^{1n}, 489, 503, 509, 510^{10}, 511^1, 527^2 560, 577^1, 606, 646 (I), App 10 (a), Gl s.vv. *damnatio memoriae*, drafter, recorder
papal. *See* Annuario Pontificio; Breviarium Romanum; Casti connubii; Commissum nobis; Decretals, False; epistle, encyclical, papal; Praeclara gratulationis; Providentissima Mater Ecclesia; Syllabus of Pius IX; Tome of Leo; Unam sanctam; Vatican Decrees

dogma, 159^{41}, 166^8, 167, 172, 179, 222, 253, 289, 290, 301, 317, 343, 350, 351, 368, 397^1, 401, 405, 406, 411 (III), 422, 423, 446, 453, 454, 459, 480, 489, 512, 524 (I), 567, 573, 577, 579^9, 637, 641, Gl s.vv. heresy, Monarchians

dole, 141^3, 301^7, 528^5. *See also* subsistence, public

domestics, Gl

Dominate, In, 2, 4^9, 15^8, 44^2, 52^{48}, 133^{1n}, 141^3, 168^1, 186^3, 301^7, 313^1, 324^{12}, 325^6, 330^9, 345^{1n}, 472^{23}, 511^1, 523^5, 528^5, 532^{1n}, 535^5, 547^6, 584^8, 596^{1n}, 606^{20}, App^{23}, Gl and therein s.vv. *caput*, chief of the notaries, consistory, consul, consular, diocese, duke, fisc, guild, inspector, largesses, legion, *legis actio*, milaresium, official (financial), paterfamilias, patrician, praetor, prefect (praetorian), prefect (urban), province, rector (consular), Senate

Dominus, In^9, 34^5

donation *or* gift, In, 4, 5 (d), 4^{10}, 9, 12, 14, 31^4, 46, 79^1, 83^4, 95^{62}, 130, 150, 157, 176, 218^{11}, 225, 227, 242, 277, 289, 321 (I), 329, 342^2, 343, 348, 391, 395, 478^{30}, 478, 496^{1n}, 510, 513, 514, 515^{1n}, 517^{1n,2}, 518, 522, 525, 530, 567, 572, 574, 579, 581, 583, 595^{1n,5,6}, 596, 599, 601, 604, 606, 610, 612, 613, 624^3, 629, 630, 641 (I), 644^6, 652, Gl s.vv. count of the sacred largesses, *damnatio memoriae*, *Lex Cincia*, master of the census

Donation of Constantine, In^{46}, 364^{12}

Donatism *or* Donatists, In^{43}, 10^{1n,1}, 15^{11}, 16^{1n,3,8}, 17^{1n,6,7}, 18^{1n}, 19^{1n,1,8}, 20^{1n,3,8,10}; 21^{1n,10}, 22^{1n}, 24$^{1n,3-5}$, 25^{1n}, 27^{1n,3}, 29^1, 30^1, 39^{1n}, 47^{7,12,14,16}, 59^{1n}, 60^2, 65^9, 73^7, 120^{1n}, 148^6, 158^{1n}, 163^6, 164^{3,16,17}, 166^4, 276^4, 289, 290, 292, 293, 294^1, 296, 298, 299, 301, 305, 310, 315^1, 323^{1n}, 324, 325, 326, 328, 329 ,337, 338, 339^{1n}, 395, Gl and therein s. vv. Circumcellions, Maximians, Montenses

dowry, 223^2, 478^{30}, 496^8, 525, 567, 582, 595^6, 599, 610, 629, 652. *See also* marriage

doxology, In^8

Doxology and Song of Three Holy Children, 651^{20}

drachma, 116, Gl

drama, 98, 170, 183, 223^2, 243, 279, 303^4, 397^1, 423, 650, 651^8. *See also* comedy; mime; tragedy

dream, 11^{1n}, 95^1, 223^2

drink. *See* food *or* drink

drought. *See* phenomena, natural

dualism, Gl s.v. Manichaeans

duke, 638, 646 (II), Gl

dumb, the, 621^3, 628

duovir, App 10 (f), Gl. *See also* ex-duovir

duty, episcopal, 90, 109, 115^{1n}, 125^2, 178^8, 195^3, 272, 278, 300, 301, 308, 309, 312, 331, 366, 367, 371, 437, 457, 459, 493, 507, 531, 534, 535, 537, 539–41,567, 579, 580, 582, 583, 586–9, 591, 593, 605, 608, 610, 612, 614, 621, 623, 627, 628^3, 632, 635, 649–52

Dyophysites, 527^{1n}

earnests, betrothal, 517, 652. *See also* betrothal; dowry; fiancé *or* fiancée; marriage

earth. *See* phenomena, natural

earthquake. *See* phenomena, natural

easement, 598^8, 606^{14}

Easter, 5^1, 48^{1n}, 52, 135, 145, 169^3, 171, 180, 185, 194, 198^3, 201, 207^2, 220, 238, 285^6, 335, 355, 356, 358, 359^{1n}, 364, 382, 385, 397, App^{17}, Gl s.vv. Novatians, Quartodecimans, Tessarescaedecatitans, Tetraditans

Eastertide, In, 5 (g), 38^2, 52^{39}, 171^{1n}, 180^{1n}, 201^3, 205^{1n}, 207^{1n,8}, 220, 238, 302, 355^1, 356, 357^4, 358^6, 365^2, 385^5. *See also* paschal days

ecclesiastic, 41, 82, 117^{13}, 150, 155, 326, 411^{1n}, 435, 437, 462^1, 488, 510^1, 646^1

edict. *See* constitution

edict, praetorian, 150^8, 375^7, 443^4, 593^3, 625, 641^{30}

Edict:
of Milan, In^{33}, 7^{25}, 10^{1n}, 12, 13^{1n}, 14^{1n,13}, 41^{1n}, 42^{1n}, 47^9, 167^{1n}, 267^3
of Prices, 15^7
of Toleration: Galerian, 7, 8^{1n}, 10^{1n}, 12^{8,29}, 13^{11}, 14^{1n}, 17^{1n}, App 10 (f)^{52,56}; Honorian (?), 324^4; Maximinian, 14, App 10 (f)

education. *See* professor; school; teaching *or* teacher
religious, 98^{3,4}, 122, 189^2, 546^{19}, 550^1
secular, 98^{3,5}, 116, 186^6, 189^2, 525^2, 615, 639, App 10 (f)

effigy, burning in, 303^3

elders:
Christian, 41^4, 257, 480^{21}
civic, 22^2, 257, 325, 328, 497
Jewish, 23, 341^5, 344, 346

embezzlement *or* peculation, 301^7, 519^7, 576^{1n}, Gl s.v. *Lex Iulia peculatus*

emancipation, 37, 394, 609^2, Gl. *See also* manumission

embryo, human, 606^5

emperor, unknown, 62, 504, 505, 530–2, 539, 566

emphyteusis *or* emphyteute *or* emphyteuticary, 337, 537, 618, 632. *See also* lease *or* leaseholder

Empire:
 Byzantine. *See* Byzantine Empire
 Carolingian. *See* Carolingian Empire
 Christian. *See* Christian Empire
 Holy Roman. *See* Holy Roman Empire
 Roman. *See* Dominate; Principate; Roman Empire
Encratitans, 176, 185, 192, 395⁶, Gl
enthusiasm, religious, In, 4, 111¹ⁿ, 228¹ⁿ
Enthusiasts, 395, Gl
entry, forcible, 334²⁵. *See also* trespass
eparch, 334³
ephor, 540
epic, Greek, 116¹
Epicureans, 422¹¹
epidemic, 522⁴. *See also* pestilence; plague
Epiphany, 220, 281, 385
episcopate, In 5 (a), (b)⁴³, 21, 61 (III), 158¹ⁿ,¹, 166, 167²,⁷, 203¹, 288, 310, 366, 387, 408, 410, 440⁵, 459, 461, 463, 470, (X, XI), 478, 483, 484, 487, 495³, 508, 519, 520, 523, 526⁵, 530, 544, 545, 557, 558, 575, 577, 579, 620, 629, Gl and therein s.v. bishop. *See also* hierarchy
epistle *or* letter. *See* constitution
epistle, encyclical, papal, 350¹ⁿ
epitaph, In⁸
equinox. *See* phenomena, natural
equity, 334, 375 (III), 488, 501, 641²⁴, 651
Erastianism, In³⁴
error, In³¹, 9, 16, 24, 39, 40, 44–7, 49 (I), 50–3, 54²⁰, 59, 67, 69, 73, 86, 98, 116, 122, 152, 155, 163, 164, 190, 192, 194–6, 222, 232, 239, 272, 288, 289, 291, 298¹³, 299, 307, 313, 324, 328, 337, 350, 351, 358, 364, 381, 385, 387, 389, 400, 406¹, 411 (II), 422, 423, 429, 449, 459, 461, 463, 470 (I), 472 (I, II), 476, 477, 480, 481, 484–7, 489, 533, 546, 554, 559, 562, 563, 567, 572, 573, 575, 600, 626, 633, 636, 637, 640², 645. *See also* falsehood *or* falsity; truth
escheat, 642
essence, 50, 67, 67¹⁷, 103. *See also* hypostasis; ousia; substance
estate:
 division of, 28¹, 168¹, 488
 lease of, 119⁵
estates, private, imperial. *See* property, imperial
Eucharist, 75⁴², Gl s.vv. Encratitans, Ophitans. *See also* Communion, Holy; Liturgy, Divine; Lord's Supper; Mass, Holy; Sacrifice, Christian
Euchites, 395, Gl
Eulalians, 352², 364¹ⁿ, 371¹ⁿ
Eunomianism *or* Eunomians, 166¹,³, 173, 179, 192, 194, 196, 218, 230⁵, 246, 249, 252, 260, 268, 277, 321 (I), 336, 343, 380, 381, 383, 395, 429, 542²⁶, Gl and therein s.v. Anomoeans
eunuch, 95, 124 (IV), 218, 246¹, 448², 459¹ⁿ, 463². *See also* castration
Eustathians, 617
Eutychianism *or* Eutychians, 453⁶, 455¹ⁿ, 457¹ⁿ, 463¹, 464¹ⁿ, 467¹ⁿ, 469¹ⁿ, 470³⁴, 471¹, 472⁵, 475⁵, 477¹⁶, 480¹ⁿ, 482⁴, 483⁵, 484⁸, 485¹⁰, 486⁸, 487⁴, 489, 524¹⁴,¹⁷, 527⁷², 542²³, 546¹⁴, 569⁷, 636³, 637¹ⁿ,³, 645³⁰, Gl and therein s.v. Monophysites
evangelist, 49 (II), 159³⁴, 163⁵, 173¹¹, 350
exarch, In, 5 (a), 406¹ⁿ, 458³, 571, 579, 616, Gl and therein s.v. patriarch
exception, 65⁹, 582
exchange, 510, 537
excommunication, 5¹, 17³, 47³¹, 52³ 67¹⁴, 68², 71¹ⁿ, 182, 195¹ⁿ, 203¹, 313¹, 364⁷, 407, 455, 527¹ⁿ, 530, 546, 550⁹, 560³, 645, 651
executioner, Gl s.v. slave, public
executor, 392⁴. *See also* heir
exile, recall from, 46, 117. *See also* clergy *or* clergyman (recall from exile)
Exodus, 23²
exorcism *or* exorcist, 109³, 135⁵, 162, 224, Gl
extortion, 13, 14, 325
ex-actress, 649⁷. *See also* actor *or* actress
ex-aide, 534¹ⁿ
ex-bishop, 146, 417. *See also* bishop
ex-chamberlain, 186. *See also* chamberlain
ex-Christian, 199. *See also* apostasy *or* apostate
ex-clergyman, 307, 529², 629. *See also* clergy *or* clergyman
ex-consul, 106, 448³, 470¹, 483, 487, 521¹, 642. *See also* consul
ex-curator, 21. *See also* curator
ex-duovir, 21. *See also* duovir
ex-magistrate, 472⁴. *See also* magistrate
ex-master, Gl svv. manumission, patron. *See also* master
ex-master of the cavalry and of the infantry, 106. *See also* master
ex-minor, 65⁶. *See also* minor
ex-monk, 530. *See also* monk
ex-official, 242, 502. *See also* official
ex-patriarch, 411¹³. *See also* patriarch, Constantinopolitan *or* ecumenical
ex-prefect, 448³, 590. *See also* prefect, praetorian, of the East; prefect, urban, of Constantinople
ex-quaestor of the sacred palace, 642. *See also* quaestor of the sacred palace
ex-slave, 337⁶, Gl s.vv. freedman, patron. *See also* slave
ex-vicar, 164. *See also* vicar, urban, of Rome

faction:
  ecclesiastical, 10¹, 17–19 21, 30, 44, 47, 49 (II), 50, 61 (I), 69, 73, 74⁹, 86, 98, 103¹², 112¹ⁿ, 117, 123¹ⁿ, 137, 138¹ⁿ, 140¹ⁿ,², 142¹ⁿ, 143, 173, 195, 273⁴, 293¹ⁿ, 325, 350, 352¹ⁿ, 353², 354, 356, 357, 362, 363, 401, 402⁶, 403¹ⁿ, 404⁸, 406¹ⁿ, 407, 408⁴, 409, 459, 464, 472 (I), 527¹ⁿ
  sporting, 236³
factory:
  linen, 46. See also apparel
  military matériel, Gl s.v. master of the offices
  weaving, 80, Gl s.v. weaving establishment. See also apparel
faith:
  apostolic, 71, 95, 163, 462, 477, 481, 524
  august, 487
  Catholic or Christian, 12, 18, 20, 24, 39, 40, 46, 47, 48 (I), 49–53, 59, 61 (I, III), 64¹,², 67, 69, 71, 72⁴, 73, 79, 95, 99, 100¹, 103–5, 106⁶, 108¹ⁿ, 124 (III), 125, 127⁵, 131¹ⁿ, 136, 163³, 167¹ⁿ,⁵, 170, 182, 183, 189², 194, 195, 203, 205, 230, 239, 289, 293, 294, 299, 303–5, 315, 318, 324, 325, 326, 328, 336, 346, 358, 368⁵, 374, 375 (II), 378, 387, 393, 395, 396, 398, 402, 405–8, 411 (II, III), 419, 423, 425, 427, 429, 440, 442, 448, 457–9, 461–4, 467, 469, 470 (I, IV, VIII), 471, 472 (I, II), 475–7, 479, 480, 482–7, 489, 496, 508, 511, 523¹, 525–7, 533¹, 546, 550, 551, 553, 554, 556, 559, 560, 562, 564, 636, 637, 645, 652, App 4, 7, Gl s.vv. archdeacon, Novatians
  correct, 408, 524 (I), 569, 579
  divine, 374, 453 454, 461, 484
  faultless, 527, 637
  holy, 402, 453, 455, 459, 460, 469, 480, 483–5, 487, 527⁶⁴, 552, 567
  immaculate, 481, 559
  Nicene, 95, 173, 182, 546
  one, true, Catholic, 645
  orthodox, 95 125, 195⁴, 335², 402, 404, 412, 436, 445, 448–53, 455, 458, 459, 466, 468, 469, 470 (I, II), 471, 472 (I), 477, 480–7, 489, 501–3, 514, 515, 524 (II), 530, 549, 567, 575, 583, 616, 652
  pagan, 9
  pure, 480, 484, 485, 567, 575
  religious, 475
  right, 411 (III), 527, 542, 546, 573, 616, 645
  sacred, 423
  sacrosanct, 514
  salutary, 575

sure, 325
true, 408, 411 (II), 423, 456, 468, 470 (II), 471, 472 (I), 475, 480–3, 485, 487, 502, 524⁹, 527, 544, 546, 549, 559, 573, 575, 600, 645
umblemished, 569
venerable, 525
addition to, 397, 458–60, 481, 483–5, 487, 489, 524 (I), 569, 636
confession of, 48 (I), 100¹, 159, 182, 255³, 299, 350¹ⁿ, 368, 442⁷, 463, 475⁶, 546¹ⁿ, 553, 560¹ⁿ,¹⁸, 569, 636, 637, 645, App 8
definition of, In⁴³, 459, 460, 470 (VII), 471¹ⁿ, 472¹⁴,¹⁹, 480, 481¹ⁿ, 484¹ⁿ, 524 (I) 527, 542, 637
subtraction from, 458–60, 481, 483–5, 487, 489
Falcidian fourth or portion, 392, 496, 623
falsehood or falsity, 40, 44, 50, 59, 68, 75²⁷, 98, 116, 204, 295, 328, 350, 373, 395, 476, 481, 484, 485, 487, 496, 548, 553, 559, 598¹⁰, 636, 645, 646 (I). See also error; truth
falsification:
  of fiscal account, 110, 606
  or ordinance, 532
  of report to emperor, 405¹,³,⁴, 406⁹
famine, In⁹, 1³, 429³¹
fanaticism or fanatic, In, 4, 228¹ⁿ, 276⁴, 347¹, 472²⁰, 527¹ⁿ, Gl s.v. Circumcellions
farm or farmer, 9, 34, 107³, 314³, 429, 472²⁴, 478²⁰, 510⁴, 528, 530, 535, 568¹ⁿ, 618⁴, 627³, Gl s.vv. tax (capitation), tax unit. See also agriculture; cropland or crops; cultivator; registered; food or drink; grain; orchard; peasant; plantation; serf; tenant farmer; vineyard; viniculture
farthing, 312
fasces, 43 (I), 439, 443
fasting or fast, 52, 169¹,³, 281, 472 (III), 651, Gl s.vv. Marcionites, Priscillians
father, Tab², 3, 44, 59, 77, 103, 136¹ⁿ, 187, 214³, 229, 233, 249, 251–3, 256, 259, 280, 321 (I), 363¹, 373, 381, 392, 394, 406, 408, 429⁷, 435³, 441⁶, 457, 459, 479⁶, 485, 496, 590, 514, 516, 518, 525, 567, 575, 579, 599, 608, 609¹ⁿ,³, 613, 620, 621³, 624³, 629, 635², 644, 645. See also foster-father; parent
= bishop, 32⁹, 48⁹, 49 (II)¹, 52⁴,²³, 71, 90, 95⁴³, 104, 203, 359, 361, 367, 368, 397, 398, 402, 405¹ⁿ, 418, 419, 427, 445, 448, 450–5, 457–9, 464, 465³, 468¹ⁿ, 469, 470 (I, II, V, XI), 471³, 472 (I, II), 475–7, 480, 481, 483–7, 489, 524 (I), 526, 527, 542, 543⁹, 546, 551, 553, 554, 557, 561, 563, 577¹³, 579, 637, 645

= emperor, 3, 13, 14, 77, 136^{1n}, 164, 249, 251-3, 256, 280, 321 (I), 375 (II, III), 381, 433, 575, App 10 (a)
= monk, 543^3
= official, 6, 266^5. See also brother = official; cousin = official
of the municipality, 567, 571, 591, 593, 606, Gl and therein s.v. curator
Father of the Fatherland, 3^9, 7, 548, Gl
fathers:
  Church, In^{46}, 154^{1n}, 442^7, 648^6
  conscript, 357, 548, Gl. See also senator, Roman
  Semi-Arian leaders, 159^{43}
fatherland, 75^{15}, 141, 159^9, 164, 220^4, 507, App 10 (f)
favour, divine, 85, 375 (II), 411 (III), 475, 482, 519, 547, 579, 590, 595, 617, 639, 642^{1n,13,16}, 646^{29}
Feast:
  of St Andrew, 181^5
  of St Hippolytus, 397^1
  of St Peter's Chains, In^{46}
  of SS. Peter and Paul, 167^2
  of the Assumption, 397^1
  of the Queen of Heaven, 397^1
  of the Saviour's Passion, App 10 (a)
federates, Tab^5, 528^8, 567
fee, 168^1, 491, 515, 606, 611
feebleminded, the, 621^3
festival. See Feast; holiday
  Christian, 34^5, 37, 52, 167^2, 171, 220, 285^6, 385^{1n}, 386, 397^1, 505, 509, App 10 (a). See also Angel, Holy Guardian; Annunciation; Ascension; Ash Wednesday; Assumption; Christmas; Conception, Immaculate; Crucifixion; Easter; Eastertide; Epiphany; Feast; Good Friday; Holy Week; Lent; Marian Year; Nativity; Passion; Pentecost; Quadragesima; Quinquagesima; Resurrection; Sunday
  Jewish, 303, 644^6. See also Aman; Passover; Purim; Sabbath
  pagan, In^{26}, 3^8, 31^4, 220^{2,4,10,11}, 243^4, 303^1, 386, 397^1, 600. See also Parilia; Sacaea; Suovetaurilia; Tricennalia; Vicennalia
fiancé or fiancée, 517, 610^{3,5}, 638^{1n}, 652. See also betrothal
fiction, legal, 150^1, 603^{1n}, 634^5
fideicommissary, 218, 225, 507
fideiussor, 491^6
field, 9, 34, 46, 194, 223^2, 242, 336, 422, 472^{24}, 543 (I), App 10 (f). See also agriculture
filicide, 52^{13}
filiusfamilias, 624^3, 644^5
fillets. See apparel
fire. See phenomena, natura

first-fruits. See food or drink; oblation; offering
fisc, 6, 12, 59, 65^6, 79, 91, 107, 117, 146, 150, 156, 163, 176, 179, 185, 186^3, 194, 218, 223^3, 234, 235, 239, 241^{1n}, 242, 253, 256^2, 258, 264, 268, 277, 289, 308, 310, 321 (I), 328, 329, 332, 337, 341^2, 343, 370, 395^5, 399, 440, 489, 499^{1n}, 501, 503, 519, 574, 576^9, 599, 641^{13}, Gl and therein s.vv. Caesarian, praetor, recorder. See also treasury, imperial
fishing or fisher, 273, 606^3
flagitia cohaerentia nomini, 1^3, 12^{33}
flamen, In^{26}
flamen Dialis, 399^{11}, Gl and therein s.vv. Lex Voconia, lictor, patria potestas
flattery, 508^1
Flavian gens, 21^1, 45^1, 139
flint-stone, 393
flood. See phenomena, natural
foederati. See federates
follis, 15
folly, 7, 9, 39, 44, 47, 50, 67, 69, 115-17, 119
food or drink, 41^4, 107, 308, 312, 330^4, 350, 400, 474^2, 475, 501, 593^3, 606^{19}, Gl s.vv. Encratitans, guild, slave (public). See also rations; vegetarianism
  bread, 186^5, 301^7, 537
  first-fruits, 530
  flour, 186^5
  fodder, 301^7, 536^4
  grain, 9, 107^3, 141, 301^7, 429, 431^1, 584^7, Gl s.vv. aedile, caput. See also granary; distribution of, 141^{1n,3}, 301^7, 474^2; export of, 75^{1n}; purchase of, 534, 539, 606
  grape, 107^3
  herb, 180
  lard, 301^7
  meat, 41^4, 95^{34}, 98^{15}, 301^7, 330^{1n}, Gl s.v. Encratitans
  oil, 301^7, 584^7, 641^8, 651^{16}
  olive, 107^3
  salt, 133^1, 301^7, 474^2
  vinegar, 301^7
  water, 44, 159, 330, 606, Gl s.v. Encratitans; supply of 43 (I), 606. See also aqueduct
  wine, 1^2, 223^2, 242, 301^7, 330^4, Gl s.vv. Encratitans, Manichaeans. See also vineyard; viniculture
forgery, In, 6, 3^{34}, 19^{28}, 21, 49^1, 65^6, 204^5, 217, 241^3, 364^{12}, 472^{1n}, App^{11}
formula:
  baptismal, 230^{1n}
  doctrinal, In^8, 401, 471^{1n}, 472 (IV), 481^{1n}, 551^{1n}, 553^{1n,4}, 560^{18}, 563^4, 564^{1n}, 636^{1n}, 637, 645^{1n}

honorific, 577¹
Hosian, 100¹ⁿ
legal, 598¹⁰, 619⁸, Gl s.v. surety
praetorian, 334⁴
reunion, 561³
Semi-Arian, 159⁴²
Trinitarian, 158⁴
formulary. See constitution
fornication. Gl s.v. Novatians. See also debauchery, sexual
fortress, 108, 442⁷
forum:
of defendant, 478, 491
prescription of, 62, 625, 638
privilege of, 62¹¹, 478
fossor. See gravedigger
foster-daughter, 609
foster-father, 516, 518, 609³
foundling, 515⁵, 591¹ⁿ,², 595². See also orphan
Fourteenthers, 52³
fraud, 65⁶, 109, 173, 176, 185, 268, 321 (I), 343, 344, 391, 431, 440, 470 (VIII), 496, 511, 619, App¹². See also chicanery; collusion; connivance; dissimulation; negligence
freedman or freedwoman, 6¹, 31¹,⁴, 65⁶, 76, 324²⁵, 337⁶, 421⁵, 488, 501, 585¹ⁿ, 631, 638¹ⁿ, Gl and therein s.vv. client, manumission, notary, patron, patroness. See also ex-slave
freedom or liberty, 26, 35, 46, 76, 79³, 289, 308, 337⁶, 348, 370, 392³, 493, 497, 528, 548, 602, 607, 609, 631, 646 (I), 652, App 10 (a)¹¹,²¹, Gl s.vv. patron, praetor
of speech, 606, App 10 (a)
of procedure, 641²⁴
of will, Gl s.v. Pelagians
fresco, 97⁴
fugitive, In, 5 (f), 44, 46, 68², 168¹, 241, 266, 273, 335, 470², 483¹ⁿ,²¹, 501, 528⁵, 576⁷,⁸, 638, App 7, Gl s.vv. Circumcellions, guild, Montanists. See also asylum, right of; refuge; sanctuary, right of
funeral, In, 5 (g), 9, 119¹, 133¹, 139, 408⁴, 484, 492, 538, 618¹³, Gl s.v. guild. See also cemetery; cremation; grave or sepulchre or tomb; interment
furniture, 227

gallows, 303³. See also punishment: death, by hanging
gambling or gambler, In, 5 (f), 593¹ⁿ,¹,³, 651¹ⁿ,⁵. See also dice
games, 3⁸, 303⁴, 386, 651. See also amusements; spectacle
Circensian, 236³
public, 132, 208³, 236³, 243

gardens, Christian, 10, 400
garland. See apparel
garrison, 535, 547⁶, 568, 584⁸, 618¹¹, 646²²
ghost, Tab⁵. See also apparition
general, 341², 635, 638⁸, 646¹, App⁴³,⁴⁷, Gl s.vv. Father of the Fatherland, Imperator, imperium, office staff
gerontocomium, In, 5 (d), 515¹ⁿ, 595³ 604, 612, 648, Gl s.v. pious causes
superintendent of, 612, 648
gift. See donation
gladiator, 495³. See also combat, gladiatorial
Gloria in Excelsis, 651²⁰
Gloria Patri, 651²⁰
Gnosticism or Gnostics, 7¹³, 31¹ⁿ, 123⁵, 161², 422⁷, 483⁸, 484⁹, 485⁸, 486⁹, 487⁷, 542²⁹,³⁰, 648⁶, Gl and therein s.vv. Borborians, Encratitans, Manichaeans, Marcionites, Monarchians, Montanists, Ophitans, Priscillians, Simonians, Valentinians
godfather, 459¹ⁿ
godson, 463²
Godhead, 50, 67¹⁷,²⁰, 182, 495, 527, 645, Gl s.vv. Gnostics, Monarchians, Paulianists
Persons in, In, 4⁴⁸, 50², 53⁷, 67, 103, 156¹, 159, 167, 173, 182, 218¹¹, 397¹ⁿ, 448¹ⁿ, 464¹ⁿ, 471¹, 481, 483–7, 524¹⁷,²⁸, 527, 542, 546, 553, 561, 562, 569, 636, 637, 645, Gl s.vv. Apollinarians, Arians, Eutychians, Monarchians, Monophysites, Nestorians, Paulianists, Photinians. See in Index of Persons s.v. God: Trinity
gold, 54, 68⁵, 97¹, 113, 121, 133¹, 165, 181, 223², 225, 233⁵, 234, 235, 239, 242, 243, 247³, 258, 272, 276, 282, 284,³ 286, 289, 298, 301, 307, 308, 310, 312, 327, 329, 341², 370, 395, 399, 428, 429, 432, 433, 437, 440, 442, 464¹, 470 (VIII), 478, 480, 489, 491, 500, 506, 508, 530, 534, 536–8, 555¹⁰, 565, 567, 575, 586⁷, 597, 598¹³, 606, 611⁷, 612¹⁸, 616, 618, 621, 629, 633, 648³, 650, 651, Gl s.v. denarius
coronary, 341²
goldsmith, 478²¹
Good Friday, 49¹, 470⁴
governor:
diocesan, Gl s.v. office staff. See also vicar, diocesan
military, 111, 523⁵, Gl s.v. duke
nomic, 8, Gl
provincial, 1¹ⁿ,³,⁵, 2¹ⁿ, 3, 4¹⁰, 5, 7, 8¹ⁿ,³, 12¹ⁿ,¹⁰,²⁹, 13–15, 18⁹, 19²⁴, 29, 31¹, 34⁵, 42⁵, 45, 54, 59, 64²⁰, 65⁶, 66², 76, 86, 87, 95⁴¹, 106, 109, 110 119¹ⁿ,¹,

SUBJECTS 1311

154, 157, 159^{27}, 160, 161^3, 164, 168^1, 182^{1n}, 190, 194, 201, 227, 234, 235^{1n}, 242, 243, 253, 257^6, 263, 268, 278^1, 287, 288^{15}, 289, 290, 293^3, 298, 300–3, 307, 308, 309^8, 310, 312, 324^{12}, 325, 327, 337, 341, 343, 344, 346, 377, 382, 386, 394, 395, 405, 409, 417, 420, 426, 429, 432, 433, 441–4, 466, 478, 480, 483, 484^{22}, 486^{14}, 487^{25}, 489, 497, 506, 507, 515, 516, 521^1, 523^5, 528, 532, 536, 540^8, 567, 568, 574^2, 575, 584, 586^2, 588, 591, 593, 597, 606, 608, 610, 612, 616, 621, 627, 631–4, 638, 641^{11,13}, 646, 649–52, App 4, 8 (b), 10 (a), (d)–(f)^{38,43}, Gl and therein s.vv. assistant, consular, corrector, defender of the municipality, duke, *imperium*, *iuridicus*, judge, office staff, president, province, rector (consular)
grace, divine, 85, 112^4, 158^3, 290, 350^{1n}, 458, 562, 580, 636, 645, 646 (II), Gl s.v. Pelagians
grager, 303^4
grain. *See* food *or* drink; granary
grammarian, 116, 186, 226, Gl s.v. guild
granary, 109, 301^7. *See also* grain
grandchild, 392, 579
grand-daughter, 259, 298^6, 599
grandfather, 298^6, 381, 392, 408, 475^9, 479^6, 514, 521^5
grandmother, 298^6, 392
grandnephew, 608^4, App 2
grandson, 259, 298^6, 479^6, 521^5, 599
grape. *See* food *or* drink
grave *or* sepulchre *or* tomb, 97^4, 135^3, 139, 167^2, 176^{15}, 181, 200^1, 206, 211^1, 641, (I), App^{53}. *See also* cemetery; funeral; interment
   accessibility to, 641^{16,30}, App^{53}
   boundaries of, 139
   construction of, 641^{16,30}
   destruction of, 641^{13,30}
   donation of, 139
   interment in, 181, 206, 443^4, 641^{23,30}
   ownership of, 139, 641^{23}
   protection of, 139
   purchase of, 139
   repair of, 641^{30}
   rites at, 139, 206^7
   use of, 641^{16,30}
   violation of, 135^3, 168^1, 181^7, 198, 201, 443, 641^{13,16}
gravedigger, 97, 107, 109^2
great-grandfather, 514
great-great-great-great-grand-daughter, 572^3
great-great-great-great-grandson, 572^3
Greek, use of, In, 2, 9^{11,43,52,56}, 2^{1n}, 49^{1,21}, 53^{12}, 61^5, 67^{31}, 104^{1n}, 173, 186^7, 226^{10}, 256^2, 284^{1n}, 297^3, 313^1, 350^{1n}, 422, 446^9, 461^{1n}, 470^{1n,2}, 472^{1n,1}, 515^5, 537^{3,5,6}, 645^{17}
guard, App 10 (f), Gl s.vv. count of the domestics, domestics, prefect (urban). *See also* bodyguard
guardianship *or* guardian, 26^1, 28^1, 31^1, 149^4, 225, 516, 608^{1n,12}, 610^4, 619^{1n}, 621, 627^2, 628^2, 635, 638, 644^4, Gl and therein s.v. praetor. *See also* curator; tutor public, 518^3
guest, 612
guild *or* guildsman, 36^1, 133^{1n,1,6}, 274, 286, 301^7, 307, 319, 347, 430, 435, 439, 478, 497, 506, 535, 573, 584, 585, App^7, Gl and therein s.vv. chief men, syndic. *See also* corporation; primate = guild official

hail. *See* phenomena, natural
hair, 44, 67, 203^4, 207, 225, 310. *See also* tonsure
harbour, 606
heart, 604^3, 645
heaven. *See* phenomena, natural; sky
hegemon, 234^3
hegumen, 537, 614^2
heir, In, 5 (g), 26^1, 28^1, 46, 65^6, 107^3, 168^1, 176, 185^{3,4}, 187^{1n}, 190^6, 218, 225–7, 230, 246, 298, 334^{25}, 392^4, 488, 495^1, 496, 507, 510, 514, 522, 570^{1n}, 575, 579, 601, 604, 606, 608, 612, 615, 618, 623, 625(a), 629, 633, 640^{5,12}, 644, 648, 652, Gl s.vv. *Lex Falcidia*, *Lex Voconia*, praetor. *See also* coheir; disherision; executor; inheritance.
hell, 442^7, 569^5
Hellenism, 121^3, 624^5. *See also* paganism *or* pagans
Henoticon, 411^1, 527, 542, 544
herald, App 10 (e)
herb. *See also* food *or* drink
heresy *or* heretics, In, 5 (b)^{18,32,43,45}, 5^1, 7^{13}, 17^8, 24^{1n}, 30, 40, 47, 49, 53^{1n}, 56, 57^{1n}, 58^{1n}, 59, 60, 66^{1,2,18}, 68^2, 71, 95^{1n,1}, 100, 103, 111^{23}, 112^{1n}, 115^{1n}, 117, 123^{4,5}, 124^{1n}, (III), 156^1, 158^4, 159^{34}, 161^2, 164^{17}, 166, 167^{1n}, 168^1, 173, 176, 179, 182, 185, 189^2, 191, 192, 194^7, 195, 196, 203^1, 205^{1n,9}, 213, 215^{1n}, 216^{1n}, 222, 230^3, 232, 239, 240^{1n}, 245, 246, 248, 249, 252^3, 253, 254, 256, 258, 260^{1n}, 264^{1n}, 268, 275, 276, 289, 296, 298, 299, 301, 304^{1n}, 305, 306^{1n}, 310, 315, 317, 320^{1n}, 323, 324^2, 329, 330^{1n,9}, 335, 337, 339, 343, 350^{1n}, 368, 370^1, 373^{1n}, 378, 380–3, 387–9, 395, 397^{1n}, 398^4, 402, 407, 411^{14}, 422, 423, 425, 427^{1n}, 429, 440^{1n}, 448^{1n,9}, 450^3, 451^3, 455^{1n,5}, 457^4, 459, 463^{1,2},

470⁴,²⁷,⁵¹, 471¹, 472 (I), 476, 479¹², 480, 481¹ⁿ,³⁻⁵, 482⁷, 483-7, 489, 492, 495³,¹², 503, 515¹⁶, 519¹, 524, 527¹ⁿ,⁴⁵, 542, 543 (II), 546, 551¹ⁿ, 554¹ⁿ, 556¹ⁿ, 559, 562¹⁰, 567, 569, 570, 573¹ⁿ, 575, 599, 616, 622, 626, 633, 636, 637, 643¹ⁿ, 645, 646⁷, 650⁴, 652, App 2, Gl and therein s.vv. apocrisiarian, Manichaeans, Monarchians, Monophysites, Novatians, Ophitans, Papians, Priscillians, Quartodecimans, schism, Tessarescaedecatitans Tetraditans. See *acephali*; chiliasm; heterodoxy *or* heterodox; schism *or* schismatic; sect, heretical; sect, schismatical
   debarment from administrative office, 343, 383¹ⁿ, 567, 571, 575; from church, 72, 173; from cities, 173, 176, 192, 194, 480, 616; from civil service, In, 5 (g); from commerce within ecclesiastical precincts, 616; from governmental service, 249, 256, 304¹ⁿ, 320, 343, 382, 440, 480, 489, 567, 575; from managing real esate, 571; from military service, In, 5 (g); from owning orthodox slave, 616, 647, 652; from provincial governorship, 343; from teaching, 575
   evidence in court, In 5 (g), 622
   readmission to church, 71, 72, 205⁹
Hermeiecians, 395⁶, Gl
hermitage *or* hermit, 487, 518, 527, 614, 638. *See also* anchorite; solitary
hero, 95³⁴, 98¹⁵
heterodoxy *or* heterodox, In, 3 5 (b)¹⁸,³², 24¹ⁿ, 49 (III), 100¹ⁿ, 103¹ⁿ, 236³, 382¹, 476¹ⁿ, 553⁴, 575, 647. *See also* heresy *or* heretic
Heteroousians, Gl
hierarchy, 167⁷, 228¹ⁿ, 412⁵, 635¹ⁿ. *See also* episcopate
hill *or* hillside. *See* phenomena, natural
Hill Folk, 290¹, 301⁴
hire, 537⁶
historian, In⁹,⁵⁹, 116⁷, 246¹, 449⁷, 463³, 470⁵⁰, 484²⁶, 482³, 522⁴, 525¹, 538², 542¹⁴, 559¹ⁿ, 630⁸, App 9
holiday, 31⁴, 37¹ⁿ, 65⁶, 132², 220, Gl s.v. praetor. *See also* anniversary; festival; New Year's Day
   harvest, 220
   Jewish, 303⁴
   vintage, 220
Holy Roman Empire, Tab⁵
Holy Week, 52⁴. *See also* Eastertide
homicide, 135, 145, 171¹, 198, 201, 207, 413. *See also* murder
Homoeans, 217⁴
Homoiousianism *or* Homoiousians, 411¹⁴, Gl

homoousian, 524 (I), 527⁸⁴
Homoousianism *or* Homoousians, 411¹⁴, Gl
homousion, 546⁹
horoscope, 207¹⁰. *See also* divination *or* diviner; soothsaying
hospital, In 5 (d), 515¹ⁿ, 522, 579, 581, 612, 623⁹, 648, Gl s.v. pious causes
   director of, 648
   superintendent of, 579, 581, 648
hostel, In 5 (d), 515, 518, 522, 537, 579, 581, 585, 595, 604, 612, 623, 630, 648, Gl s.v. pious causes
   assistant director of, 537
   director of, 537, 648
   guest-master of, 623¹⁰
   manager of, 579, 612, 623, 648
   superintendent of, 579
   warden of, 515, 623¹ⁿ
house:
   God's = church, 400, 641⁶
   holy = pious cause, 648
   venerable = pious cause, 623
   of prayer = oratory, 522, 584, 615
household, imperial, In¹⁴, 127, 128, 328, 329, 337, 430⁵, 434, 435, 438, 630, App¹⁴, Gl s.vv. Caesarian, catholicus, domestics. *See also* court, imperial; palace, imperial
housekeeper, 372¹ⁿ
humanitas, 1⁵, 44³
humanity (as opposed to divinity), 181, 400, 431, 469, 636, 637, 645, Gl s.vv. Gnostics, *imperium*, Monophysites
hurricane. *See* phenomena, natural
husband, 31, 176, 187, 214³,⁶, 225¹³, 329, 361¹, 372, 461¹, 466¹ⁿ, 485, 486, 497, 517⁴, 596², 621³, 629, 641⁸, 652. *See also* wife
Hydroparastatans, 176, 185, 192, 395, 429, Gl
hymn, In⁷, 651²⁰. *See also* ode; prayer; psalmody *or* psalm; song
hypostasis, 67, 159, 569, 636, 637, 645. *See also* essence; *ousia*; substance
hypothec, 537, 598, 608, 634¹ⁿ. *See also* mortgage

ice. *See* phenomena, natural
idolatry *or* idol, In, 5 (g), 3²⁰, 41⁴, 44, 49 (III), 54, 63, 69⁵, 86, 111, 116¹³, 135⁵, 214², 242¹ⁿ, 259, 301⁸, 400, 424³, 600, App 10 (d)-(f)⁴¹, Gl s.v. Novatians. *See also* deity *or* divinity, pagan; image *or* statue, pagan; polytheism; worship, pagan
ignorantia legis neminem excusat, 310⁴
image *or* statute:
   angel's, 63⁴
   bishop's, 559

emperor's, In^{23}, 1^{2,4}, 38^2, 180, 241^1, 247^{1n}, 386, 400, 606
pagan, In^{26}, 1^2, 13, 54^6, 95^{34}, 111, 124^{19}, 242, 301, 386^3, 489, 641^5, App^{41}
immortality, In^{37}, 39, 42, 49 (II), 50, 52, 67, 75^{42}, 76, 443^9
imperium, In, 4^{9,17}, 476^4, 619^5, 641^{28}, Gl and therein s.vv. Imperator, province
imperium in imperio, In, 4
impiety, 1^{3,4}, 9, 44, 46, 49 (II), 59, 63, 66, 67, 95, 98, 99, 103, 116, 117, 143, 163, 203, 215, 259, 350, 385, 408, 422, 423, 425, 426, 429, 446, 450, 451, 453–7, 459, 461, 476, 480, 481, 483–7, 496, 530, 572, 573, 583, 599, 601, 609, 616, 636, 645. *See also* piety
IN HOC SIGNO VINCES, 38^1
in partibus infidelium, In^{42}
incantation, 135^5, 183. *See also* sorcery *or* sorcerer; witchcraft
Incarnation, 50, 67, 75^{42}, 159, 210^{11}, 325, 472, 481, 484, 524 (I), 527, 542, 546, 569, 636, 637, 645
incense, 1^2, 95^{34}, 223^2, 242, App 7
incest, 171^1, 180, 201
indolence, 228^2, 536
industry, Tab^5, In^8, 32, 102, 228^2, 236^3, 273^2, 337^6. *See also* commerce; merchant; tradesman
infallibility:
  conciliar, 94^1
  ecclesiastical, 95^{43}
  papal, 95^1, 397^1
infamy, 176, 190, 209, 225^{13}, 231, 234. *See also* punishment: infamy
infant, 607^4, 627^2, 629, App 10 (f)^8, Gl s.v. Pelagians. *See also* child; minor; ward
infantry, 106^4, Gl s.vv. centurion, count of the domestics, domestics, legion. *See also* soldier
infidel, 67, 214^2, 480
inflation, 15^7, 433^6
informer. *See* delation
inheritance, In, 5 (g), 28^1, 31^{1,2}, 46, 117, 150, 176, 189, 190, 218, 219, 230, 298, 321 (I), 343, 348, 391, 392, 421, 440, 496^{15,16}, 513, 514, 525, 537, 570^{1n}, 572, 575, 592, 595^6, 602^7, 604, 612, 615, 623, 626, 640^7, 644, 652, Gl s.v. procurator of the private estate. *See also* coheir; executor; heir; succession
iniquity, 497. *See also* sin
injury *or* insult *or* outrage, 2, 3^{24}, 13, 23, 39, 44, 46, 50, 53^{12}, 67, 68, 70, 76, 79, 82, 111, 117, 119, 123, 145, 168^1, 180, 190, 195, 198, 201, 204, 207, 276^4, 284^3, 308, 310, 324, 325, 327, 328, 334, 334^{25}, 341, 351, 370, 378, 382, 394^5, 395, 400, 402, 407^2, 412, 414, 429, 440, 442, 449, 453, 454, 459, 463^4, 465, 470 (VIII), 476, 478, 480, 484, 500, 515, 520, 524^{14}, 527^{54}, 531, 548^1, 568, 593^3, 602^1, 638, 641^{28}, 646 (I), 650, 651, App 10 (a), Gl s.v. Circumcellions. *See also* assault; molestation; slander *or* libel
inquisitor, 185
insane, the, 608, 610, 621^3, 628
insanity *or* madness, 1^2, 7^{19}, 15, 20, 23, 24, 39, 46, 47, 50, 52, 59, 63, 67, 69, 103, 116, 117, 142, 164, 167, 173, 184, 215, 248, 249, 260, 292, 301, 328, 334–6, 356, 381, 382, 385, 395, 400, 423, 429, 443, 445, 457, 476, 477, 480, 481, 483, 484, 487, 569, 572, 573, 600, 608^2, 616, 622, 627, 636, 637
inscription, In^{8,9}, 9^{1n}, 25^{1,2}, 28^8, 38^2, 43^{1n}, 45^1, 48^9, 68^1, 97^4, 133^1, 139^{1n,2}, 163^1, 211^{1,6}, 255^3, 364^{12}, 431, 540, 566, 568, 577, 618^{13}, Gl s.v. *Lex de imperio Vespasiani*
insignia:
  imperial, Tab^5, 34^5, 95^{51}, 400, 431^{1n}, 461^1, 520^6, 550, 630^9, 646 (I)
  of dignities, 229, 429
inspector, 154
institution, charitable. *See* pious causes
intercession, 206^6, 234, 235, 272, 370, 375 (II), 501, 540, 548, 626
interdict, 144, 380, 391, 478^{11}, 627^4, 641 (V)
interest, payment of, 612^8, 648
interment, 119^1, 181, 492, 636, 641 (I), App^{53}. *See also* cemetery; funeral; grave *or* sepulchre *or* tomb
  in church, Tab^5, In^{30}, 167^2, 188, 200^1, 211^1, 463, 551^{13}
  in city, 181, 641^{13}
interpreter, 350^{1n}, 500^{14}
intestacy, 46, 189^3, 218^6, 225, 321 (I), 343, 391, 392, 421, 489, 507, 525, 570, 572, 574, 575, 599, 608, 652, Gl s.v. *Lex Voconia*. *See also* testation, right of; will *or* testament
invasion, Tab^5, In^{43}, 107^{10}, 203^4, 215^{1n}, 228^{1n}, 302^2, 308^{1n}, 369^{1n,3}, 435^{1n}, 442^4, 461^{1n}, 464^1, 467^1, 468^{1n}, 472^{25}, 475^5, 513^5, 519^{1n}, 520^2, 523, 646^1, Gl s.v. province. *See also* barbarians; war
inventory, 608
investigation:
  episcopal, 17–20, 21^{1n}, 22^{1n}, 27^{1n}, 39^{1n}, 53, 96, 99, 136, 159, 164, 271, 278, 309, 350^{1n}, 354, 357, 358, 366, 440^5, 447, 456^{1n}, 459, 470, 473, 490, 491, 495, 534, 586, 593, 612, 651. *See also* court, episcopal; jurisdiction, episcopal
  judicial, 1–3, 5, 20–2, 24, 27, 28, 39^{1n}, 68, 69^{1n}, 96, 136^1, 159, 164, 185, 256^2, 271^{1n}, 278, 302, 325, 326, 338, 344, 350, 353, 391, 440^5, 489, 501,

528, 532, 583, 605. *See also* trial, court
iron, 67, 400, 443
irreligion, 601
Isapostolos, In^{30}
Islam, In^{43}, 28^1, 67^{35}, 140^1, 338^{1n}, 442^7, 566^1
island. *See* phenomena, natural
iugum, Gl s.vv. tax (capitation), tax (jugation), tax unit
iuridicus, Gl
ius canonicum, 17^3, Gl
ius civile, 65^{10}
ius commercii, Gl s.v. peregrine
ius connubii, Gl s.v. peregrine
ius exclusivae, In^{44}
ius gentium, 599^6
ius honorarium, 65^{10}
ius liberorum, 31^1, Gl s.v. *Lex Iulia de maritandis ordinibus*
ius postliminii, 308^{14}
ius praetorium, 65^{10}
iusta causa, Gl

Jacobites, In^{43}
jailor, 312, 370^3, 429
janitor, 134^3, 370. *See also* porter
Jesuits, 614^7
jewelry, 215, 247^3, 598^5
Jewry *or* Judaism, 1^4, 7^{15}, 13^3, 23^3, 91^{1n}, 168^1, 190, 199, 267, 270^3, 315^{1n}, 346, 387^{16}, Gl s.vv. *Lex Constantiniana*, Samaritans. *See also* sect, Jewish, and in Index of Places s.v. Jews
Jews:
debarment from governmental service, 387, 429, 567; from judgeship, 429; from ownership of Christian slaves, In, 5 (g), 76, 79, 199, 341, 344, 379, 387, 647, 652, Gl s.v. *Lex Constantiniana*
evidence in court, In, 5 (g), 622
jockey, 236^3
Johnnites, 285^3
Judaism. *See* anti-Semitism; Jewry *or* Judaism
udge, 17^{1n}, 20, 22^{1n}, 24^{1n}, 28, 31^1, 34, 37^1, 44, 46, 49 (I), 59, 62, 65, 68, 75^{1n}, 95, 96, 98, 111, 117, 132, 134, 136, 143, 164, 168^1, 235, 248, 254^{1n}, 255, 272, 273, 309, 318, 324, 325, 326, 328^{1n}, 334, **338**, 341, 347, 350, 351, 354, 357, 362, 370, 382^1, 387, 394^3, 398, 400, 424, 429, 437, 443, 444, 453, 457, 465, 476, 478, 490, 491, 500, 501, 506, 509–11, 515, 528, 561, 565, 567, 573, 582, 583, 590, 592, 594, **595**, 602, 603, 605, 607, 611, 614^{18}, 616, 619, 621, 622, 625, 630, 631, 634, 638, 641^{19,24}, 646 (I), App 10 (f)^{11,27}, Gl. *See also* arbiter;

investigation, judicial; referee; trial, court
extraordinary, 161, 197
ordinary, 134^2, 152^8, 161, 197, 234, 278, 515
petty, 625
judgement, last, 49 (I), 159^{51}, 325, 364, 561–3, 575, 612, 614, 651, Gl s.v. Borborians
juger, 107^3
jurisconsult *or* jurisprudent *or* jurist, In^9, 4^2, 6^3, 65^9, 133^1, 168^1, 204^3, 214^6, 308, 334^5, 372^4, 478^{18}, 508^1, 515^{12}, 598^3, 617^{1n,7,8}, 621^3, 638^{14}, 639^8, 641^{12,13,16,28}, 642^{11}, 643^{1n}, 644^{1n}, Gl s.vv. consistory, *Digesta*, *Institutiones Iustiniani*, interpretation, manumission, response. *See also* lawyer
jurisdiction:
archiepiscopal, 490, 491
civil, 3^8, 23^2, 28, 65^{6,9}, 143^4, 161, Gl s.vv. *imperium*, prefect (urban)
criminal, 24^2, 65^6, 161, Gl s.vv. *imperium*, prefect (urban)
episcopal, In, 5 (e)^{42}, 17, 17^3, 28, 39^{1n}, 62^2, 65, 96, 117, 136^{1n}, 161, 164, 197, 203, 271, 278, 288, 307, 309, 334, 368^3, 387^{1n}, 413, 442^{1n}, 472^{30}, 478, 491, 611, 625^{1n}, 651, Gl s.v. see. *See also* court, episcopal; investigation, episcopal
metropolitical, Gl s.vv. metropolitan, patriarch
papal, 17, 164, 375^{1n,3,11}, 442, 499^{11}, Gl s.v. patriarch
patriarchal, 375^{1n}, 490^{1n}, 524^{32}, Gl s.vv. patriarch, patriarchate
religious, 23^2, 49 (I), 161, 375
Roman, 1^3
juror, 65^{13}, 605

kathegemon, 116^{16}
kingdom:
Abyssinian, 99^{1n}
client, 99^{1n}
Ethiopian, 99^{1n}
Numidian, 19^{22}
Roman. *See* Roman Kingdom
of Christ, App 2
of God, 75^{42}
of heaven, 123
kings, Jewish, In^{23,44}, 645
knight, App 8 (b), Gl and therein s.vv. censor, freedman, order, tribune (military)

labarum, 44^{17}, 119^5
labour:
conscripted, 226^3. *See also* public service, menial

SUBJECTS   1315

public, 282
laboratories, Alexandrian, 98⁵
laesa maiestas, 497¹⁰. *See also* treason *or* traitor
laity *or* layman, 16⁴, 17, 24, 47, 62¹ⁿ, 65⁹, 66, 68²,⁷, 73¹⁷, 82, 86, 94¹ⁿ, 113⁵, 114¹, 119⁵, 129¹, 131, 136¹ⁿ, 137¹ⁿ, 148⁴, 152⁹, 208³, 210³, 243⁷, 254¹ⁿ, 269¹ⁿ, 297¹ⁿ, 300¹ⁿ, 326, 329, 347¹, 350, 351, 352², 364, 372¹¹, 401, 408⁴, 426⁴, 436¹ⁿ, 442¹, 443¹, 445, 448¹ⁿ, 450-2, 456, 459¹¹, 466, 478, 519¹⁶, 523¹, 524 (I), 527, 529², 530, 547², 552³, 560, 579, 611, 645⁴⁴, 651, Gl s.vv. Enthusiasts, Luciferians
lake. *See* phenomena, natural
Lampetians, Gl
landlord, 107³, 337⁶, 421⁵, 443, 528⁵, 537⁶, 632¹ⁿ, Gl s.v. canon. *See also* tenant; tenant farmer
landowner. *See* property, ownership of; proprietor
lappets. *See* apparel
lapsed, the, 645⁴⁰
lard. *See* food *or* drink
largesses, 186³, 241, 311, 337, 521¹, 618¹⁴, Gl
Latin, use of, In, 2, 9¹¹,⁴³,⁵²,⁵⁶, 2¹ⁿ, 49¹,²¹, 67³¹,³³, 104¹ⁿ, 186⁷, 226¹⁰, 256², 422, 446⁹, 461¹ⁿ, 470¹ⁿ,², 472¹ⁿ,¹, 515⁵, 606⁶, 612⁴,⁵,⁹⁻¹³, 615⁴, 621⁶, 629²², 633⁸,⁹, 641²⁴
Latrocinium. *See* council, ecclesiastical, local, Ephesus
lavabo, 67³⁵
law = Christianity *or* Christian religion, 16-20, 28, 39, 41, 46, 54, 56, 63, 65, 69, 75, 77, 81, 82, 93, 105, 108, 109, 123, 138, 141, 148, 149, 155, 167, 168, 170, 183, 195, 199, 236, 266, 267, 271, 287, 288, 303, 310, 315, 323, 324, 328, 334, 335, 339, 350, 352-4, 360, 365, 375 (I), 387, 389, 429, 476. *See also* law, canon; law, Catholic; law, Christian; law, ecclesiastical
  = Judaism, 188, 199, 346, 429. *See also* law, Mosaic; law, Jewish
Augustan, 195, Gl s.v. *Lex Augusta*
barbarian, In², 578⁵
canon, 16¹ⁿ, 17³, 61 (II, III), 62¹¹, 68, 73, 94, 95, 99, 158¹, Gl s.v. *ius canonicum*
Catholic, 19, 20, 56, 81, 389
ceremonial, 206⁶
Christian, 28, 65¹³, 82, 108, 170. *See also* law = Christianity *or* Christian religion
civil, 16¹ⁿ, 65, 94¹, 150, 161, 204³, 496¹², 599⁵, 613. *See also ius civile*
common, 99, 246, 478, 626

Constantinian, 441, Gl s.v. *Lex Constantiniana*; cf. 76
corporation, 133¹
criminal, 127⁶, 161, 204³
divine, 46, 47, 49 (I, II)²⁶, 53, 67, 69, 75¹⁷, 139, 163, 166, 168, 195, 197, 203¹, 214⁶, 225, 248², 374, 375⁸, 382¹, 484, 604, 641 (I)
ecclesiastical, 68
edictal, In, 2, 440, 442, 478, 496
emphyteutic, 119⁵
equitable, Gl s.v. praetor
general, In, 2, 422, 459, 488
human, 641 (III)
Jewish, 188, 199, 267
Leonine, 624, Gl s.v. *Lex Leoniniana*, cf. 514
Medo-Persian, 95⁴³
military, 626
Mosaic, 65¹³, 122³
national, 400
natural, 400, 528
of nations, 599⁵, 631¹
praetorian, 65, 496¹²
pragmatic, 530, 567, 572, 576, 633
private, 204⁵, 309¹ⁿ, 526²
public, 68, 204⁵, 278, 333, 372, 470 (X), 478, 589
retroactive, 155, 176, 218¹ⁿ,³
Roman, In, 1-3, 5, 6⁵⁵, 1⁵, 7, 17³, 23⁴, 28¹, 31⁴, 65⁶,¹³, 94¹, 108¹, 133¹, 135⁴,⁵, 156¹, 176, 186⁵, 189, 204³,⁵, 218⁷, 219², 220⁶, 308¹⁵, 324⁷, 334³, 391⁴, 429, 478⁵,¹⁶, 491⁶, 522¹ⁿ,⁴, 525², 537⁵, 578⁵, 579⁷, 593³, 595⁵, 599⁵, 602, 605, 611⁹, 617⁷, 624³, 627²,⁴, 631¹, 641⁴,¹², Gl s.vv. consistory, *ius canonicum*, *Novellae*, surety
sacral, In²⁶, 264⁴, 644³
secular, 613¹ⁿ
strict, Gl s.v. praetor
obedience to, 2, 5, 10, 12-15, 18, 20, 28, 39, 42, 46, 48 (III), 52, 59, 63, 65, 67, 69, 71¹ⁿ, 73, 75¹ⁿ, 76, 86, 87, 95, 111, 115, 117, 121, 122, 132, 152, 153, 159, 164, 167¹ⁿ, 168¹, 176, 181³, 192, 194, 195, 197, 205, 207, 212, 214⁵, 216, 231¹, 234, 240, 242, 243, 248, 253, 254, 256-8, 267, 272, 276, 283, 288, 289, 298, 299, 301, 303, 307, 308, 310, 312, 315, 317, 321 (II), 324, 328, 344, 346, 363, 364, 366, 373, 382, 393, 395, 412, 415 (I), 416, 418-20, 422-4, 426, 429, 431, 433, 442, 444⁹, 445, 446, 449, 454, 459, 465, 478, 480, 483, 484, 486, 487, 489, 500¹⁴, 501, 509, 510, 522, 523, 530, 534, 536, 565, 567, 568, 574¹ⁿ, 575, 579, 580, 587-9, 592⁴, 605, 606,

631, 641^{28}, 648–52, App 10 (f), Gl s.v. sanction
recision of, In^{39}, 7, 8, 12, 31, $65^{8,13}$, 85, 87, 107^{13}, 116^{1n}, 130^{1n}, 148^{1n}, 158^{1n}, 166, 205^{1n}, 215^{1n}, 217, 218^{1n}, 225^{1n}, 227, 228^{1n}, 237, 246^{1n}, 249, 252^{1n}, 277, 288^{14}, $293^{1n,3}$, 302, 321, 323, 324, 354, 375^{1n}, 376^{1n}, 379^{1n}, 392^3, 459^{1n}, 478, 479, 488, 496^{1n}, 522^6, $524^{1n,3,28,32}$, 526, 635, 638^{14}
re-enactment of, 65, 76, 114, 126, 209, 226, 238^{1n}, 239^{1n}, 242^{1n}, 243, 246^{1n}, 252^{1n}, 253^{1n}, 263^{1n}, 273^2, 301, 368, 373, 376^{1n}, 378, 429, 431, 433, 443, 489, 525, 565, 567, 648
lawcourt, 629, Gl s.v. *libellus*
lawsuit, 20, 26^1, 37, 62, 65, 96, 111, 161, 164^2, 178, 204^{1n}, 209, 220, 238, 255, 278, 309^{1n}, 318, 332, 334^{25}, 341, 350, 387, 391, $399^{1n,5}$, 421, 431, 444, 478, 490, 491, 500, 504, 507, 509^1, 515, 516, 522^{1n}, 567, 578, 586^7, 589, 592, 594^{1n}, 597, 598, 605, 611, 612, 619, 622, 625, 640^4, App 10 (a), Gl s.vv. Assembly (Tribal), procurator; syndic. See also accusation or accuser; action; calumny or calumniator; court, episcopal; defendant; delation or informer; investigation, judicial; judge; juror; litigant; plaintiff; trial, court; witness or testimony
lawyer, 6^1, 65^{13}, 124, 220^2, 300, 350^{1n}, 421^3, 478, 491, 506, 509, 515, 567, 575, 585, 605, 617^4, 619, 629^{21}, 639^{1n}, 640^3, Gl s.v. praetor. See also juriscounsult or jurisprudent or jurist; orator
layman. See laity or layman
lead, 69, 92^2, 289, 298, 330, 399
lease or leaseholder, 119^5, 239, 289, 298, 308, 328, 329, 337, 472 (III), 480, 489, 510^6, 528^5, 537^6, 568, 606, 618, 632^{1n}, Gl and therein s.v. canon. See also cultivator, registered; tenant farmer
lector, 59, 60, 109^3, 162, 200^{1n}, 222, 280, 513, 651, Gl
ledger, 444
legacy or legatee, 218, 225, 392^4, 488, 507, 510, 513, 572, $595^{1n,6}$, 604, 612, 615, 618, 623, 626, 640, Gl s.vv. Lex Furia, Lex Voconia, slave (public). See also bequest
legacy-hunting, 150, 225^{1n}
legate, 19^{28}, 95^{1n}, 397^{10}, 404^7, 406^1, 409^5, 468^4, $470^{2,38}$, $471^{1n,9}$, 475^9, 480^{27}, 482^6, 484^{18}, 486^7, 527^{1n}, 546, 549^{1n}, 550^{1n}, 551^{1n}, 552^3, 556^1, 557, 558, 560^{19}, 562^5, 560, 564, 645, Gl s.vv. apocrisiarian, legation. See also ambassador or envoy; commission = group; commissioner; delegation
legend, 95^1, 422^7

legion, Gl and therein s.vv. centurion, tribune (military)
Legion, Twelfth Thundering, In^{14}
legis actio, 598^8, Gl
legislation:
  imperial, In 2, 3, App *passim*, esp.^{6}. See also constitution
  popular, In^9
legitimation, 525^{1n}. See also bastard; concubine
legum nutrix, In^{11}
lender, $582^{2,3,5,10}$, 604^8. See also borrower; creditor; debt; debtor; loan
Lent, 52^4, $169^{1n,3}$, 221^{1n}, 282^{1n}, 302^{1n}, 356^{1n}, 365^1, 385^6
letter or epistle. See constitution
letter, commendatory, 270^2, 437, 580^3. See also public post, warrant for
Levite, 399, 644^6
libation, 1^2, 117, App 7, 10 (d)–(f). See also oblation; offering
libella, 312^3
libellus, App 7, Gl
library, Gl s.v. slave (public). See in Index of Places s.vv. Alexandria; Rome
  patriarchal, 98^{15}, 111^{1n}, 113
lictor, 439^3, Gl
lightning. See phenomena, natural
lights, 242
lime or limeburner, 186^5, Gl s.v. guild
litany, 117, 258
literature:
  Christian, 459
  Hebrew, 315^1
  pagan, 49^1, 67, 116, 382^1, Gl s.v. guild. See also authors, pagan; comedy; drama; epic; mime; orator; poet; tragedy
litigant, 2, 17^3, 28, 37, 62, 65, 164, 197, 204, 227, 235^{1n}, 271, 324^7, 347, 478, 506^5, 509, 515, 592, 603, 605, 606^{20}, 611^{1n}, 619, 622, $625^{13,14}$, 640^{1n}, Gl s.vv. official, patron. See also accusation or accuser; defendant; lawsuit; plaintiff; trial, court
lithomania, 481^2
liturgy:
  = public service. See public service
  Coptic, 99^{1n}
  Ethiopic, 99
  Greek, 470^4, 554^2
  Roman, 67^{35}, 470^4
Liturgy, Divine, 75^{42}, 579, 580, 588, Gl s.v. deacon. See also Mass, Holy
loan, 537, 580, $582^{1n,3}$, 604. See also borrower; creditor; debt; debtor; lender
lodgings, appraisal of, 606
Lord's Day. See Sunday
Lord's Supper, 75^{42}. See also Communion,

Holy; Eucharist; Liturgy, Divine; Mass, Holy; Sacrifice, Christian
lot, 614. *See also* cleromancy; sortition
lucerna iuris, In²
Luciferians, 195^{1n,3,6}, 254², Gl
lumber, 186⁵. *See also* tree; wood
lust, 631
lustration, 41, 67³⁵, 117, 214⁵

Macedonianism *or* Macedonians, 192, 194, 196, 380, 381, 395, 542²⁷, Gl s.v. Semi-Arians
madness. *See* insanity
magic *or* magician, 68⁴, 135, 145, 171¹, 198, 201, 203¹, 207, 521³, Gl s.v. Priscillians. *See also* sorcery *or* sorcerer; witchcraft
magistracy, 229, 439², 567, 575, 586², 616, 621⁶, Gl s.vv. censor, freedman, official. *See also* office, governmental
magistrate:
  chief, 194, 289, 298, 329, 382⁶, 497, 505³, 535, Gl
  Constantinopolitan, 439³, 480, 505³, 565^{1n}, 567, 583, 585, 586, 618, 626³, 628², 640 (IV), Gl s.vv. lictor, magistrate, prefect
  local, 21, 31¹, 37^{1n}, 43 (I), 117, 119⁵, 161³, 166⁷, 208³, 239^{1n}, 271^{1n,1}, 275, 309⁹, 310, 325, 372²³, 382¹, 424, 442¹, 447, 456, 480, 488², 493, 504, 509¹, 534^{1n}, 540⁴, 573, 574, 582¹¹, 583–6, 589, 606, 621$^{6-8}$, 632, 650, 651, App 5, 7, 10 (e), (f), Gl and therein s.vv. curial, duovir, prefect (urban), public service
  Roman, Tab⁵, In²⁵, 26¹, 31¹, 34³, 37^{1n}, 164, 334²⁵, 356⁵, 364⁹, 413⁶, 439³, 472⁴, 505³, 592⁴, 608¹², 619⁵, 626³, 628², 641^{13,28}, App³, Gl s.vv. aedile, apparitor, Assembly, Assembly (Tribal), censor, consistory, consul, dictator, guardian, lictor, magistrate, praetor, prefect, province, senatus-consult, tribune (plebeian). *See also* ex-magistrate; primate = magistrate
magistrate-elect, 109
magistrian, 67, 405, Gl
Magnificat, 497², 651²⁰
maid, 496. *See also* spinster
manager, 325, 329, 395, 421, 472 (III), 480, 568
  of estate, 239, 253, 268, 277, 289, 298, 308, 342, 489, 571, 608, 619
mandate. *See* constitution
mandate *or* mandator, 478¹³, 501, 602, 619
manor, 503, 510. *See also* plantation; villa
Manichaeism *or* Manichaeans, 117¹³, 156, 164¹, 176, 185, 190, 192, 203, 218^{1n}, 219, 275, 292, 298, 299, 301, 380, 382, 387, 388, 395, 429, 440, 480, 489, 533, 542²⁸, 567, 572, 573, 575, 599, 600, 622, Gl and therein s.vv. Marcionites, Priscillians
manumission, In 5 (g), 26, 35, 37, 76, 79, 113, 199, 218⁹, 337⁶, 392^{3,4}, 394, 493, 494, 528, 529, 602, 607^{1n,1,3,4}, Gl and therein s.vv. emancipation, freedman, *iusta causa*, *Lex Aelia et Sentia*, *Lex Constantiniana*, slave (public). *See also* emancipation
marble, 54, 95¹, 393, 443, 577^{1n}
Marcellianism *or* Marcellians, 395, Gl and therein s.v. Photinians
Marcionites, 40, 95, Gl
Mariolatry, 397¹
market, App 10 (f)
market-days, 324⁷
marriage, In 5 (g), 28¹, 31, 92, 126, 150, 170³, 187, 214, 225¹³, 227, 308¹⁴, 330^{1n}, 372, 442⁴, 445, 454⁵, 461¹, 496, 497⁵, 517, 525, 567, 575, 596, 609, 610, 613, 629–31, 635², 649, 650, 652, Gl s.vv. Continents, Encratitans, *Lex Iulia de maritandis ordinibus*, *Lex Iulia et Papia Poppaea*, Manichaeans, Marcionites, Montanists, Novatians, *patria potestas*, patroness, peregrine, *Senatus Consultum Persicianum*, virgin (introduced), virgin (Vestal). *See also* divorce; dowry; earnests, betrothal
martyrdom *or* martyr, In⁸, 17^{1n}, 24, 34⁵, 39, 42^{1n}, 46, 46²¹, 54², 97⁴, 117¹⁹, 127⁷, 140¹, 167², 181, 203¹, 206, 364⁴, 411³, 471, 472 (III), 487¹⁴, 497, 522, 523, 559, 568², 577, 615, App 4, 9, 10 (f)^{6,11,13,36,53}. *See also* protomartyr
martyry, 46, 54, 206, 526, 559, 568²
  as donee, 488
  as heir, 488, 615
  as legatee, 488
  name of. *See* in Index of Places s.v. Pontus
Mass, Holy, 67³⁵, 68⁵, 75⁴², 78², 554^{1,5}, 598². *See also* Liturgy, Divine
massacre, 236³
master:
  of a secretarial bureau, 256², 549, 560
  of a slave, 26, 35³, 76^{1n}, 170³, 218⁹, 241¹, 289, 298, 329¹⁰, 331, 337⁶, 344, 364, 387, 394, 413, 421⁶, 443, 473 (II), 478, 484¹², 501, 528, 529, 586⁷, 592⁵, 602¹, 607, 631, 644, 647, 652, Gl s.vv. emancipation, freedman, guild, *Lex Constantiniana*, manumission. *See also* ex-master
  of each soldiery, 106⁴, 442, 499
  of each soldiery throughout the East, 106⁴, 244
  of the cavalry, 106⁴

of the cavalry and of the infantry, 106⁴, 311. *See also* ex-master of the cavalry and of the infantry
of the cavalry and of the infantry in the presence, 106⁴
of the census, 516, 537, 565, Gl
of the infantry, 106⁴
of the offices, 256, 283, 288¹⁵, 304, 311, 341, 406², 408, 477, 479, 480⁸⁶, 511, 631, 638, 640¹, 642⁷, Gl and therein s.vv. magistrian, notary
of the soldiers, 106⁴, 246¹, 415 (II), 416¹ⁿ, 417, 418¹ⁿ, 419¹ⁿ, 420⁹, 470¹, 476⁴, 512, 545⁵, 635³, 638, 646²², App³⁸, Gl s.v. duke
of the soldiers throughout the East, 106⁴, 483, 487, 512¹, 559¹ⁿ,⁸, 635¹ⁿ, 646 (II)
of the soldiery, 106⁴, 415 (I), 420
mathematician, 387¹³
matron, 247³, 488, 619⁵, App 8 (b), Gl s.vv. lictor, virgin (Vestal). *See also* wife
rape of, 638¹ⁿ
Maximians, 326, 328, Gl. *See also* Donatism *or* Donatists
meadow, 9
measure = weight, 431. *See also* weights and measures
meat. *See* food *or* drink
medallion, 34⁵. *See also* mint
medicine, 39, 44, 107⁸, 111, 313¹, 328, 480. *See also* physician
meetings, tumultuous, 59, 142, 283, 285, 286, 292. *See also* assemblies; public order; riot
megalopolis, 284⁴, 405, 445, 458, 470 (IV, X), 481, 524 (I), 527¹
Meletians, 68, 70¹ⁿ, 78¹ⁿ, Gl
memorial, 606
memorandum. *See* constitution
mendicant, 97¹, 133¹, 515, 565
merchant, 9⁷, 32, 67²⁴, 165, 329, 464¹, 646¹. *See also* commerce; industry; tradesman
Messalianism *or* Messalians, 395, Gl
metal-worker, 133¹
metempsychosis Gl s.v. Marcionites
meterorite.
metran, 99⁴
metropolis, 9, 42⁵, 118, 123¹ⁿ, 164³⁰, 397, 398, 401, 402, 405, 449, 456, 468⁶, 470 (V, XI), 472 (III), 475¹ⁿ, 480, 489, 523, 524 (I), 577¹, 580, 588, 611, 615, Gl s.vv. archbishop, metropolitan
metropolitan, In 5 (a), 16⁸, 66², 99⁴, 164, 326², 387⁹, 397, 405, 406¹ⁿ, 442¹ⁿ, 449, 456, 459, 470 (IX, XI), 471, 495, 523⁴, 526, 530, 537³, 567, 577¹ⁿ,³, 579⁷, 580, 588, 597, 611, 612, 651, Gl and therein s.vv. archbishop, exarch

Middle Ages, Tab⁵, In²,³¹, 303⁴
milestone:
from Constantinople: 7th, 594-7
from episcopal see: 100th, 288
from Rome: 20th, 142, 143, 164⁶
from Rome: 100th, 164, 373, 388
miliaresium, 611⁷, Gl
mill, 186⁵
water, 43 (I)
millstone, 393⁶
mime, 247, 493, 593³. *See also* comedy; drama
Mind, Anaxagorean, 648⁶
minerals. *See* phenomena, natural
mining *or* mine *or* miner, 133¹, 606³, App 10 (f)³⁸, Gl s.v. count of the sacred largesses, guild, procurator. *See also* punishment
superintendent of, App⁴⁷
ministry *or* minister, 15, 47, 49 (I, II), 61 (II), 107⁸, 148⁴, 166, 168¹, 179, 194, 196, 224, 239¹ⁿ, 248, 277, 303¹, 307, 310, 329, 334, 336, 337, 372, 375 (II), 387, 433, 443, 502, 519, 522⁴, 526², 566, 586², 598¹³, 614, 629, 633², Gl s.vv. Augustal, office staff
minor, 65, 71, 255², 496, 516, 600, 621, 629, 635¹ⁿ, 644, Gl s.v. *Lex Plaetoria*. *See also* child, ex-minor; infant; ward
mint, 186⁵, 456⁷, Gl s.v. count of the sacred largesses. *See also* coin; medallion, money; pound
miracle, In³⁶, 46²¹, 54, 527, 569, 637, 645, 646 (I)
mistress, 630⁶. *See also* concubine; "sister"
Mithraism, 116¹⁶, Gl s.v. Mithras
mitre, 520⁶. *See also* tiara
mob, 52, 98¹⁴,¹⁵, 111¹ⁿ, 292, 473¹ⁿ, 484. *See also* meetings, tumultuous; riot
Modalism, 542²⁴
moderator, 234³
molestation. *See* assault; injury *or* insult *or* outrage
of Christians, 3, 8, 13, 23, 29, 30, 39, 42¹, 76, 81, 102, 117, 119⁵, 123, 134, 332, 486, 515, 567, 568, 576¹ⁿ,
of heretics or schismatics, 57, 325, 328, 484
of Jews, 244, 333, 378, 382
of pagans, 119¹, 382
monachism, 31¹ⁿ, 147⁴, 228¹,², 284², 330⁴, 436¹⁰, 472 (III), 529, 531², 614⁷. *See also* asceticism
Monarchianism *or* Monarchians, 5¹, 542¹¹, Gl and therein s.v. Photinians
monastery, In 5 (d), 116¹⁶, 124¹⁹, 148⁴, 228², 405³, 410, 421, 478, 483¹ⁿ,²¹,²³, 484-6, 487²⁷, 489, 512, 515, 518, 528-31, 537, 543¹ⁿ, 566, 584, 588, 595, 604, 614, 628, 630³, 637, 638¹¹, 645, 648,

SUBJECTS

652, Gl s.vv. abbot, archimandrite, pious causes. *See also* asceticism; monachism; nun; nunnery
construction of, 472 (III), 480, 594
as donee, 612, 630³, 652
as heir, 421
as legatee, 612, 630³, 652
as recipient of property of ex-monk, 530, 652
names of. *See* in Index of Places s.vv. Alexandria, Antioch, Bithynia, Constantinople, Fonte-Avellana, Sinai, (Mt) Tunisia
money, In^{9,15,43}(II), 95^{62}, 123, 168¹, 195, 201, 284, 312³, 341², 401, 433⁷, 447⁴, 472 (III), 474², 507, 508, 510², 503, 515^{1n}, 516, 519, 520, 526², 532, 535, 538^{1n}, 566, 576, 579, 580. 582, 586, 592⁴, 593³, 597, 598⁹, 604, 606^{20,24}, 612, 618, 623, 629, 630⁶, 634, 640 (II), 648, 650, Gl s.vv. fisc, pious causes, public service. *See also* coin; mint; pound
money-changer, 286, 430², 629¹⁷. *See also* banker
monk, 48 (III), 98^{12,14}, 147, 148⁴, 150^{1,2}, 228, 237, 258⁴, 269, 272, 284², 330^{1n}, 401, 411³, 421, 437, 446, 450¹, 456, 463², 466, 472 (III), 478, 479⁸, 480, 481, 483, 484, 485^{1n}, 486-9, 494, 495^{1n}, 498, 512^{1n}, 515, 524 (I), 526-8, 529^{1n}, 537, 543^{1n,3}, 551, 552, 566, 588, 613⁴, 614, 628, 630, 636^{1n}, 645, Gl and therein s.vv. Continents, Sleepless. *See also* Akoimetoi; anchorite; Continents; ex-monk; monachism; monastery; nun; nunnery
heretical, 483, 484¹⁰, 485^{1n,10}, 487, 542²³, 543^{1n}, 551^{1n}, 552, 553, 560¹⁶, 569⁷, 636^{1n,3}, 637³, Gl s.vv. Eutychians, Pelagians
discipline of, In, 5 (g), 472 (III), 486, 513, 531, 551, 588, 629
recall to public services, 147, 629
transfer of property to curials, 147, 629
as donee, 488, 629, 630
as heir, 488, 629
as legatee, 488, 629
as missionary, 148⁴
monogram, In⁸
of Christ, 119⁵
Monophysitism *or* Monophysites, In⁴⁸, 411³, 449⁷, 476^{1n}, 481^{1n}, 495^{1n,12}, 524^{2,17}, 526^{1n,2,4}, 527^{1n}, 542^{1n,8}, 543^{1n}, ^{9,15}, 544^{1n,1}, 546^{1n,2}, 549^{1n}, 550^{9,12}, 551^{1n}, 552^{1n}, 553^{1n}, 560^{3,5,10}, 562¹¹, 564^{1n}, 630⁸, Gl and therein s.vv. Eutychians, Theopaschites
monotheism, 38³, 641^{1n}
Montanism *or* Montanists, 17⁶, 40¹, 268, 289, 320, 342, 395, 429, 575, 599, 616, 622, Gl and therein s.vv. Cataphrygians, Pepyzites, Phrygians, Priscillians
Montenses, Gl
Monumentum Ancyranum, 48⁹
monument, Gl s.v. *damnatio memoriae*
funereal. *See* grave *or* sepulchre *or* tomb
moon. *See* phenomena, natural
morals, 195, 301, 372, 398, 496, 520, 649⁹, 650⁴, Gl s.vv. censor, Encratitans, Manichaeans, Montanists, pontifex maximus
mortgage, 65⁶, 537⁵, 608¹⁷, 634^{1n}. *See also* hypothec
mosaic, 95¹
mosque, 505¹
mother, 187, 259, 303³, 372, 392, 397^{1n,1}, 435³, 496, 500, 510, 526, 527, 546, 560, 567, 575, 577, 599, 602⁴, 613, 618, 629, 635. *See also* parent
mother-in-law, 526²
mountain. *See* phenomena, natural
mourning, 225¹³
mummery, 303⁴
municipality, 83⁵, 147, 179, 228^{1n}, 237, 260, 280, 306³, 307, 310, 313, 322, 334⁵, 341², 343, 394⁴, 395, 433, 481¹, 497, 567, 571, 591, 593, 606, 615, 619, 627, Gl s.vv. Augustal, chief men, curator, curial, defender of the municipality, defender of the people, defender of the place, juristic person, magistrate, order, parish, rural bishop, Senate, syndic
murder, 19²², 29², 31⁴, 42¹, 43¹⁸, 46, 50, 52¹³, 62², 63², 68⁴, 91⁶, 98^{14,15}, 111, 119⁵, 120^{1n}, 127⁷, 135, 137^{1n,1}, 138³, 145, 159³⁴, 171¹, 180, 238¹, 276⁴, 315, 347^{1n}, 413, 442⁴, 483, 484, 487, 495⁴, 527, 546, 552², 586, 592⁵, Gl s.v. Novatians. *See also* filicide; homicide; nepoticide; parricide; patricide; uxoricide
musician, 247⁴, 493, 651⁸. *See also* hymn; ode; psalmody *or* psalm; song
mystagogue, 75⁴²
mysteries = sacraments, 47³¹, 75⁴², 139⁵, 164¹⁸, 173, 176, 194, 215, 225, 229, 230, 233, 236, 239, 251, 277, 280, 289, 311, 315, 325, 327, 334, 335, 337, 342, 343, 346, 356, 358, 364, 376, 395, 415 (II), 420, 433, 443, 476, 477, 503, 506, 519, 530, 541, 554, 559, 598², 616, 628⁴, 651, 652. *See also* sacrament
mystery religions, In³⁷, 13³, 34⁵, 75⁴², 111, 111⁴, 116, 116¹⁶, Gl s.vv. Mithras, Ophitans
mysticism, Gl s.v. Gnostics
myth, Oriental, Gl s.v. Ophitans

name, Christian, 560, 628, 648, cf. 1³ and 12³⁰
Nativity, 472 (I). *See also* Christmas

SUBJECTS

Nature, In^{43}, 44, 152, 242, 372^{24}, 429, 642
necromancer, 135, 145^{1n}. *See also* divination *or* diviner
necrophilism, 135^3
negligence *or* carelessness. *See* chicanery; collusion; connivance; dissimulation; fraud
  ecclesiastical, 618, 648
  episcopal, 109, 397, 442, 575, 612
  magisterial, 164, 181, 194, 234, 242, 248, 253, 276, 289, 298, 301, 308, 310, 312^{1n}, 324, 373, 413, 420, 443, 454, 478, 480^{78}, 489, 532, 555, 567, 575, 586, 589, 606^{18}, 616, 625, 651
neopaedagogy, 62^{11}
Neo-Platonism *or* Neo-Platonists, 66^7, 117^{17}, 445^{1n}, 459^{26}, Gl and therein s.v. Porphyrians
nephew, 514, 524^{1n}, 550^2, 560^{18}, 630^6, App 10 (d)
nepoticide, 52^{13}
Nestorianism *or* Nestorians, 397^{1n}, 398^{9,16}, 400^5, 402^{1n,6}, 403^{1n}, 407^{1n,5}, 408^{1n}, 411^{1n,5,7}, 412^{1n}, 414^{1n,4}, 415^{1n}, 416^{1n,5}, 417^{1n,3}, 418^2, 420^{1n}, 422^{1n}, 426^{1n}, 445, 452^{1n,6}, 453^3, 455^5, 456^{1n}, 457^6, 459, 470^{34}, 480^{25}, 481^5, 483^9, 484^{20}, 485^9, 486^5, 487^8, 489^{18}, 524^{14,15}, 527^{70}, 542$^{6,12,16-21}$, 569^6, 636^2, 637^{1n,2,18}, 645^{13}, Gl and therein s.v. Simonians
"New Empire" of Egypt, 256^3
New Year's Day, 220
Nicolaitanes, 7^{13}
nimbus, 34^5
niece, 514
nobleman *or* noblewoman, 231^{1n}, 236^3, 472^{1n}, 496, 552^3, Gl s.v. knight
nolo episcopari, 508^9
nome, 8^2, Gl s.v. governor
notary, 19^{13}, 109^3, 113, 124^{16}, 163^7, 186, 324^{1n}, 326, 328, 329^8, 352, 412, 447, 453, 454, 472^{14}, 546, 563, 618^{13}, Gl and therein s.v. tribune and notary. *See also* clerk; scribe; secretary
  regional, 356^5
nous, 648^6
Novatianism *or* Novatians, In^{43}, 17^6, 40, 57, 120^5, 335, 370^1, 380, 388^4, 395, Gl
numerology, 644^6, cf 53^{12}. *See also* soothsaying
nummus, Gl s.v. denarius
nun, In^{26}, 31^{1n}, 92^1, 149^1, 247^{1n}, 421^3, 488, 496^{1n,10}, 588, 613^4, 614^8, 638^{1n}, Gl. *See also* anchorite; asceticism; monachism; monastery; monk; nunnery
  rape of, In, 5 (g), 92^1, 126, 372, 440^6, 496, 638
  as donee, 612, 629
  as heir, 629
  as legatee, 612, 629
Nunc Dimittis, 651^{20}
nunnery, In, 5 (d), 485^{1n}, 496^7, 588, 604, 614^{1n}, 629^{22}, 638, 648, Gl s.vv abbess, pious causes. *See also* monastery
nursery, In, 5 (d), 515^{1n}, 579, 595, 604, 612, 648, Gl s.v. pious causes
  director of, 579, 612, 648
  superintendent of, 579

oath, In, 5 (g), 2^{23}, 121, 255, 320, 444, 470 (IV), 491, 501, 511, 513^{1n}, 532^{1n}, 541, 555^{1n}, 559, 586^7, 592, 594, 603^{1n,2}, 605, 606, 608, 614^8, 619, 634, 635^2, 640 (V), 643
oblation, 407, 515^3, 530, 537^{16}. *See also* offering
obol, 606
observance. *See* religion; worship
  Catholic, 166, 194, 195, 337
  Christian, 12, 46, 208
  heretical, 195, 323
  Jewish, 303^4, 332
  religious, 192, 207
  sacred, 356
observer = informer, 215. *See also* delation
ode:
  Christian, 651^{20}. *See also* hymn; psalmody *or* psalm; song
  Greek, 116^1
offering. *See* oblation
  commemorative, 341^2
  purificatory, 117
  thank, 46; 48^{19}
  unspecified, 342, 395^4, 400, 530, 641^{1n,9}
  votive, 111, 119^5, 376, 598
office, governmental, 476. *See also* magistracy
office staff. *See* staff, office
official:
  chancery, 511
  crown, 300
  ecclesiastical, 421^{15}, 530^9
  public, 6^1, 8^{1n}, 14, 24^3, 30^{1n}, 31^1, 43 (I), 66^1, 67^{43}, 74^{1n}, 83^5, 95^{41}, 119^1, 127^6, 141^3, 161^3, 165^8, 186^4, 205^{1n}, 242, 253^{1n}, 256^2, 284^3, 301^7, 324, 332, 357^{1n}, 414^{1,9}, 432^{1n}, 438^6, 470, 471, 472 (II, IV), 476, 495, 511^{1n}, 519^7, 527^1, 528^8, 534, 539, 572^{1n}, 576, 586^7, 592^4, 606^{20}, 621^6, 624^3, 629^5, 646^{21}, 649, Gl s.vv. apparitor, chief of the office staff, *libellus*, office staff, praetor, prefect (praetorian), prefect (urban), public service, tribune (plebeian). *See also* ex-official
oil. *See* food *or* drink

SUBJECTS 1321

olive. See food or drink
OMNIVM VRBIS ET ORBIS ECCLE-
  SIARVM MATER ET CAPVT, 364¹²
Ophitans, 395⁶, 429, 575, 599, 622, Gl
oracle:
  celestial 324
  pagan, 44, 67³¹, 218⁵. See also sibyl
Oracula Sibyllina, Gl s.v. quindecimvir
oraculum. See rescript
oration. See constitution
orator, 116⁷, 284¹ⁿ, 295¹ⁿ, 515. See also
  lawyer
oratory (building), In, 5 (d), 40, 400, 465²,
  471, 484, 503, 522, 568, 584¹ⁿ,⁵, 594,
  615, Gl s.v. pious causes
  names of. See in Index of Places s.vv.
  Ali-Faradin-Yaila, Ephesus
orchard, 107², 472²⁴. See also farm or
  farmer
orchestra, 650², 651
order, 32, 49 (I), 62, 85¹², 167⁷, 211, 224,
  229, 325⁶, 429, 433, 497, 500, 529²,
  534, 555⁸, 567, 629
orders, holy, 16¹ⁿ, 18¹¹, 109³, 280¹ⁿ, 490⁴
  major, 16⁴, 18¹¹, 61 (III), 270³, 613¹ⁿ,
  624¹ⁿ,³, Gl s.vv. deacon, order, priest
  minor, 109², 280¹ⁿ, 334, 478²⁶, 641⁶,
  Gl s.vv. chanter, clergyman, exorcist,
  lector, order, porter, subdeacon
ordinance. See constitution
ordinary = apparitor, 540
ordination, 33¹ⁿ, 61 (III), 68², 103, 166⁷,
  194, 200, 203, 213, 248, 269, 270, 342,
  343, 350¹ⁿ, 352-4, 371, 372, 395, 412,
  420, 442, 457, 459¹⁵, 466, 470 (IV, V,
  X, XI), 478, 480, 483, 489, 500, 508,
  520, 523¹, 524 (II), 530, 537³, 560¹⁶, 571,
  579, 611, 613, 620, 629, 651
orphan, 133¹, 496, 515⁵, 516, 518, 595²,
  644⁴. See also foundling; orphanage
orphanage, In 5 (d), 515¹ⁿ, 518, 537, 579,
  581, 595, 604, 612, 648, Gl s.v. pious
  causes. See also orphan
  director of, 579, 612, 648
  superintendent of, 579
orthodox, In, 3, 5 (b)¹⁸,³²,⁴³,⁴⁵, 16³,
  40¹ⁿ, 47¹⁷, 50, 53⁴,⁵, 56, 58¹ⁿ, 70¹ⁿ,
  71¹, 74¹ⁿ, 75²⁷, 90¹ⁿ, 93¹ⁿ, 94¹ⁿ, 95,
  100¹, 103¹ⁿ, 104¹ⁿ, 105², 107⁴, 112¹ⁿ,
  115¹ⁿ, 117⁵, 120²,⁵, 124¹ⁿ(III)²², 125,
  129¹, 136¹ⁿ, 147⁵, 156¹, 159¹⁶, 164¹⁷,
  166⁴, 172¹ⁿ, 173, 176¹⁵, 182¹ⁿ, 197, 205¹ⁿ,
  230¹ⁿ, 240¹ⁿ, 248³, 272⁴, 276⁴, 289⁷,
  298¹³, 301¹ⁿ, 308⁶, 332, 335, 336³,
  342, 395, 396, 397¹ⁿ,⁴, 407⁵, 415, 416,
  422, 429⁹, 445, 448⁶, 450, 451, 456,
  459, 460¹ⁿ, 467, 469, 470²⁴, 472⁴, 475⁶,
  476, 477, 480, 481, 483, 495, 515, 524,
  526², 527¹ⁿ,⁷,⁷⁶, 542, 543⁶, 544, 546,
  551¹ⁿ, 552¹ⁿ, 553¹ⁿ,⁴, 555, 567, 570, 574,
  575, 599, 600, 613⁴, 620, 622, 643¹ⁿ,
  646¹, Gl s.vv. Circumcellions, Gnostics,
  Homoousians
orthodoxy, conformity with, In, 5 (b),
  16³, 50⁶, 53, 70, 98¹², 105¹ⁿ, 167⁷,
  173¹ⁿ, 195¹ⁿ, 205¹ⁿ, 236³, 239¹ⁿ, 254¹ⁿ,
  284⁴, 301¹ⁿ, 350¹ⁿ, 398¹, 406¹ⁿ, 411 (II)³,⁹,
  416¹ⁿ, 418⁴, 448, 455, 458-60, 470²⁴,
  472, 476¹ⁿ, 480, 481, 483-6, 489,
  495¹², 511¹ⁿ, 526¹ⁿ, 542, 549¹ⁿ, 555¹ⁿ,
  564¹ⁿ, 567, 569, 575, 645
Orthodoxy, Eastern, 140¹. See also
  Christendom, Eastern; Church, Eastern;
  Church, Greek; Church, Holy Orthodox Catholic Apostolic; Churches,
  Orthodox
ousia (essentia), 67¹⁷, 159⁴⁷, 173, 569². See
  also essence; hypostasis; substance
outrage. See injury or insult or outrage
overseer, 325, 328, 641¹¹, Gl s.v. procurator
  of estate, 298, 308, 489
owner. See property, ownership of

pact, 255, 509, 510, 525, 612, 625
paganism or pagans, In, 5 (g), 9²⁶,⁴³,⁴⁵,
  1³, 3²⁰,²⁵, 4²,⁷, 7¹³, 9⁹, 11³, 12, 13⁹,
  14¹³, 16¹⁰, 20, 23⁴, 38¹ⁿ,³, 41, 48², 49 (II),
  63, 67, 73¹⁷, 86, 111¹ⁿ,¹², 112¹ⁿ, 115⁷,
  116¹ⁿ, 117, 119⁴,⁵, 121³, 122⁵, 124 (III),
  126⁵, 135⁵, 137¹ⁿ, 139¹ⁿ,⁴, 148, 146⁸, 159¹⁶,
  168¹, 175, 190², 208¹ⁿ,⁴, 212¹ⁿ, 220¹⁰,¹¹,
  223², 225¹³, 231¹, 241², 242¹ⁿ,¹,², 253,
  255², 259¹ⁿ, 285³, 300¹ⁿ, 301, 304¹ⁿ,
  310, 340¹ⁿ, 370¹, 372¹, 375¹⁴, 378, 382,
  385, 387, 389, 397¹, 400², 424, 429, 440,
  443⁹, 476, 477, 484, 489, 515¹ⁿ, 520⁶,
  523¹, 567, 575, 577¹³, 583, 599, 604³,
  614⁷, 615¹ⁿ,¹, 617¹⁰, 622, 629⁶, 641¹ⁿ,⁶,
  644¹ⁿ, 646⁸, 647, 651¹¹, App 7, 10 (f).
  See also Hellenism
pagans' debarment from governmental
  service, In, 5 (g), 304¹ⁿ, 387, 567; from
  ownership of Christian slaves, In, 5 (g),
  647, 652
  evidence in court, In, 5 (g), 622
  preference over Christians, 119
painter, 168¹, cf 393
palace:
  Christ's = Church, 399
  imperial, 186, 304, 405, 414¹ⁿ, 430⁵,
  448², 472⁴, 480, 489, 505², 538³, 547,
  554¹ⁿ, 594-7, 618¹¹, 642, App 10 (b)¹⁴,³⁶,
  Gl s.vv. provost, quaestor of the sacred
  palace. See also court, imperial; household, imperial
palatine, 168¹, 186³, 256, 444, 547⁶, 575
pallium. See apparel
palm, 496
panel, 54

Papacy, Tab^5, In^{9,26,31,39,46}, 95^{43}, 137^{1n}, 140^1, 164^{1n}, 181^6, 200^{1n}, 203^1, 363^{1n}, 366, 372^4, 562^{1n}. *See also* archives, papal; choirs, papal; Church, of Rome: privileges of; council, ecclesiastical, ecumenical: Twelfth, Twentieth; council, ecclesiastical, local: of Rome; court, papal; documents, papal; infallibility, papal; jurisdiction, papal; Mariolatry; papalism; patriarch, Roman; patriarchate, Roman; Peter (as symbol); pope = bishop of Rome; prerogative, papal; right *or* rights, papal; tiara; Vatican Church–State; Vatican Decrees; vicar, papal
  election to, In^{44}, 137^{1n}, 200^{1n}, 352–67, 371. *See also ius exclusivae*
papalism, 5^1, 442^{1n}. *See also* Papacy
Papians, 395^6, Gl
papyri, In^8, 28^1, 46^{1n,1,2}, 68^2, 328^3, 435^8, App^{12}
pardon, 1, 7, 46, 49 (I), 51, 53, 59, 75^{42}, 95, 137, 171^1, 177, 180, 195^8, 201, 207^{1n}, 289, 302, 310, 352, 358, 369^{1n}, 398, 419, 429, 485, 501, 569, 573, 645, 651. *See also* amnesty
parent, 189, 225^{1n,13}, 334^{25}, 372^4, 392, 421, 496, 500, 517, 525^{1n,7}, 567, 570, 579, 599, 602, 608, 613, 615, 624^4, 638, 652. *See also* father; mother; paterfamilias; paternal power
Parilia *or* Palilia, 220^4
parish, Gl
parricide, 171^1, 180, 201^8, 214^5, 495^3, 496. *See also* patricide
partner, 501, 509^1, 641 (I)
paschal days, 37^6, 52^4, 169, 201, 205^{1n}, 207^2, 220 238, 281, 356^{1n}, 358^{1n}. *See also* Eastertide
Passion, 52, 54, 67, 159, 220^6, 385, 527, 542, 546, 553, 561, 562, 569, 636, 637, 645, App 10 (a), Gl s.v. Theopaschites. *See also* Cross; Crucifixion
Passover, 50, Gl s.vv. Novatians, Quartodecimans, Tessarescaedecatitans, Tetraditans
patents of nobility, 341^2, 436^1, 586^2. *See also* persons
paterfamilias, 435^3, 602^5, 644, Gl and therein s.vv. agnate, emancipation, guardian, *patria potestas*. *See also* child; daughter; father; parent; paternal power; son
paternal power, 31^4, 32^9, 37^1, 187, 218^9, 289, 394, 496, 514^{1n}, 525, 602^5, 609^2, 621^3, 644^4, 652, Gl s.vv. emancipation, *Lex Plaetoria*, paterfamilias, *patria potestas*. *See also* child; daughter; father; parent; paterfamilias; son
patria potestas, Gl. *See also* paternal power

patriarch:
  Alexandrian, 4^5, 52^4, 67^{14}, 68^{1n}, 69^{1n}, 70^{1n}, 71^{1n}, 72^{1n}, 73^{16}, 74^{1n}, 77, 78^{1n}, 85^{1n}, 86^{1n}, 87^{1n}, 90^{1n}, 94^{1n}, 95^{1n}, 98^{1n}, 99^{1n}, 111^{1n}, 112^{1n}, 113^{1n}, 115^{1n}, 121^{1n}, 122^{1n}, 124^{1n,2,6}, 147^5, 167^{3,4}, 173^{1n}, 182, 189^2, 195^{1n}, 197^{1n,6}, 284^{1n,4,5}, 287^{1n}, 295^8, 297^{1n}, 347^{1n,13}, 349^{1n,1}, 393^1, 397^{1n}, 398^{1n,4}, 402^{1n}, 405^3, 406^{1n}, 409, 411^{1n}, 412^{1n}, 418^{1n}, 446^5, 449^{1n}, 451^{1n}, 458^{1n}, 459^{16}, 470^{4,17,20,27,38,62}, 473^{1n}, 481^{2,12}, 484^{18,19}, 486^7, 489^{21}, 495^{1n,4}, 523^1, 524^{2,14}, 526^{21}, 527^{1,2,76}, 542^8, 560$^{6-8}$, 562^{11}, Gl s.vv. Meletians, Monophysites
  Antiochene, 53^3, 61^4, 71^{1n}, 74^3, 103^1, 124^{20}, 284^5, 287^{1n}, 297^4, 401^{12}, 409^1, 411^{1n,12}, 412^{1n}, 414^{1n,8}, 415^{1n,12}, 416^{1n,6}, 417^3, 418^{1n}, 419^{1n,2}, 420^4, 427^{1n}, 459^{12}, 470^{44}, 473^{1n}, 543^{1n}, 559^9, 560^7, 562^{11}, 635^{1n,1}
  Armenian, 106^6
  Christian, In, 5 (a)^{34}, 53^3, 412^9, 470^{66}, 611, 614, 632, 651, Gl and therein s.vv. apocrisiarian, exarch
  Constantinopolitan *or* ecumenical, 28^1, 182, 283^{1n}, 284^{1n,4,5}, 287^{1n}, 295^{1n}, 297^{1n}, 375^{1n,7}, 397^1, 398^{1,4,7}, 402^{1n}, 405^{1n,3}, 406^{1n}, 410^{1n}, 411^{1n,13}, 412^{1n}, 423^3, 426^{1n}, 427^{1n}, 445^{1n}, 446^{1n}, 448^{1n,9}, 449^{1n}, 450^3, 451^3, 452^6, 453^2, 454^3, 455^{1n,5}, 457^4, 458^1, 459^{1n,2,17}, 463^2, 464^{1n}, 470^{4,5,51,62,70,73}, 471^{1n,8}, 473^{1n}, 477^{15}, 479^{1n}, 480^{25}, 481^{2,5}, 482^5, 483^9, 484^{20}, 485^9, 486^5, 487^8, 489^{18}, 490^{1n,4}, 491^7, 492^1, 495^{1n,1}, 510^{1n}, 524^{1,3,14,15}, 526^5, 527^{1n,70}, 530^{1n,9}, 542^{6,27}, 543^{1n}, 544^{1n}, 546^{13}, 549^4, 550^9, 553^{1n}, 554^{1n,6}, 558^3, 559^4, 560^{3,6,18}, 561^{10}, 562^{11}, 563^6, 567, 569^6, 579, 580, 618, 636^2, 637, 645^{13,23}, 651, Gl s.vv. Nestorians; patriarch. *See also* ex-patriarch
  Coptic, 28^1, 99^4
  ecumenical. *See* patriarch, (Constantinopolitan *or* ecumenical)
  erusalemite, 470^{49}, 483^{1n}, 484^5, 486^2, 487^1
  Jewish, 23, 267, 341^{2,3}, Gl s.v. patriarch. *See also* patriarch (Palestinian)
  Montanist, 616
  Palestinian, 23^3, 341^2. *See also* patriarch (Jewish)
  Roman, 484, 545, 554, 637, 645. *See also* pope *or* bishop *or* archbishop of Rome
patriarchate, In^{34,43}, 181^5, Gl
  Alexandrian, In^{43}, 53^{1n}, 69^{1n}, 125^{1n}, 228^1, 284^{4,5}, 345^{1n}, 349^1, 375^{5,7}, 470^{70}, 527^{1n,76}, 557^4, 637^7, Gl s.v. patriarch

SUBJECTS   1323

Antiochene, In^{43}, 53^3, 284^6, 375^{5,7}, 411^{16}, 417^{1n}, 470^{44,62,70}, 527^{1n}, 557^4, 560^{1n}, Gl s.v. patriarch
Constantinopolitan, In^{34,43}, 53^3, 181^5, 246^1, 284^{4,5}, 285^{1n,6}, 345^{1n}, 372^2, 375^{1n,7}, 412^1, 427^{1n}, 470^{70}, 475^{1n}, 482^{1n,5}, 495^{1n,5}, 524^{32}, 526^{1n}, 527^{1n,76}, 554^{1n}, 557^4, 558^3, 560^3, 618^3, Gl s.v. patriarch
Jerusalemite, In^{43}, 53^3, 375^7, 470^{44,70}, 483^{1n}, 487^1, 527^{1n}, 557^4, 560^{1n}, Gl s.v. patriarch
Palestinian, 23^2, 341^2, Gl s.v. patriarch
Roman, In^{43}, 53^3, 375^{5,7}, 442^7, 476^{70}, 527^{1n}, Gl s.v. patriarch
rivalry of, In, 4^{43}, 53^3, 181^5, 284^4, 349^1, 375^7, 398^4, 412, 442^7, 449^{1n}, 459^{12}, 470^{44,70}, 495, 527^{1n,76}
patrician, 106^{4,8}, 421, 442, 448, 470^1, 478, 483, 487, 492^1, 500, 590, Gl and therein s.vv. fathers (conscript), order, plebeian, tribune (plebeian), virgin (Vestal)
patricide, 52, 67. *See also* parricide
patrimony, 55, 81, 109, 151, 181, 193, 210, 224, 226, 233, 298, 307, 322, 347, 399^7, 433, 478, 497, 502, 509, 510, 515, 599, 623, Gl s.v. *Lex Voconia*
of church, 510
of emperor, 519
of the poor, 515^3
patronage *or* patron *or* patroness, 5^1, 34^5, 39^5, 43^{1n}, 62^2, 127^6, 203, 241^2, 319, 322, 331, 334^{25}, 345^{1n,1}, 421, 430^6, 484, 497, 501, 506, 519, 520, 540, 579, 606^{20}, 651^8, Gl and therein s.vv. client, freedman, manumission. *See also* client
Paulianism *or* Paulianists, 40, 395, Gl and therein s.v. Photinians
pauper. *See* poor, the
pax Augusta, 127^7
peasant, 618^4, App 2, Gl s.v. Circumcellions. *See also* farm *or* farmer; serf
peculation. *See* embezzlement
peculium, 337, 421, 478, 510, 514, 624, Gl s.v. slave (public)
Pelagianism *or* Pelagians, 324^{10}, 350^{1n,1,14}, ^{20,25}, 351^3, 368^{1n}, 373^{1n}, 387, 542^{13}, Gl
penalty. *See* punishment
peninsula. *See* phenomena, natural
penitence, 1, 39, 46, 50, 69, 70^{1n}, 230, 299, 481, 486, 496, 554, 573, 645^{40}, 651
pension, 470 (VIII), 473^{1n}, 474
Pentecost, 52^4, 285^2, 385, 397
Pepyzites *or* Pepuzians, 380, 382, 395^6, Gl
peregrine, In^{45}, Gl. *See also* alien
perfidy, 173, 190, 194, 293, 381, 389, 391, 429, 475, 496
perjury, 52, 592^4

persecution. *See* Church, persecution of
Persian Empire, 256^3
personality, legal, 522, 596^2, 604^6, Gl s.v. juristic person
persons:
admirable, 329
distinguished, 311, 337, 435, 541, App 8 (b)
eminent, 186^1
honorable, 334, 489, 495^9
illustrious, 329, 435, 436, 438
more powerful, 43 (I), 127^6, 164, 242, 255, 345^{1n}, 497, 504, 509^1, 632
most distinguished, 329, 432, 528
nobler, 443, 610. *See also* nobleman *or* noblewoman
notable, App 7
principal, 501, 619. *See also* litigant
prominent, 65^6
public, 621
rather humble, 127^6, 370
religious, 601
pestilence, In^9, 1^3, 98, 173, 305, 343, 522^4. *See also* epidemic; plague
Peter (as symbol), In, 4
petition, In, 2^8, 3, 5^1, 9, 13, 17^{1n}, 43, 50, 55, 57, 59, 75, 78, 95, 117, 120, 122^{1n}, 124, 131^{1n}, 138, 164, 168^1, 172^{1n}, 177, 195, 197, 213, 218, 255, 256^2, 276^3, 288, 295^{1n}, 317^2, 325, 344, 347, 352^2, 353, 354^3, 369, 370, 378, 389, 417^{3,4}, 431, 441^{1n}, 442^3, 468, 470 (IV), 473, 484, 486, 495, 505, 510, 521, 527, 540, 549, 551^{14}, 556, 557, 559, 560, 568, 577^{1n}, 618, 627, 635^{1n,2}, App 10 (f)^{55}, Gl s.vv. *libellus*, official, pragmatic sanction
phenomena, natural. *See also* epidemic; famine; pestilence; plague
air, 9, 48 (II), 214^5, 359, 370, 527
climate, 9, 48 (II, III)
cloud, 315^1, 326
comet, 124 (IV)
drought, 1^3
earth, 9, 44, 46, 54, 76^4, 95, 159, 195, 214^5, 236^2, 242, 329, 393, 395, 399, 400, 422^4, 429, 496, 527, 560, 567, 575^{19}, 579, 628, 650
earthquake, 1^3, 3, 9, 538^2, 635^1, 641^{12}
equinox, 52^{4,29}
fire, 9, 23, 42, 44, 61 (I), 63, 66, 67, 117, 211^1, 214^5, 236^3, 242, 268, 285, 303, 313, 376, 378, 382^1, 423, 445, 459, 476^{1n}, 480, 483, 484, 487, 489, 505^1, 524 (I), 645, App 10 (a), (b), (e), (f)^6. *See also* arson; book-burning; cremation
flood, 1^3, 98, 641^{12}
hail, 1^3

1324 SUBJECTS

heaven, In²³, 20, 38², 400, 442⁷, 524 (I), 527⁶⁰, 549, 577, 617, 651, Gl s.v. Mithras. *See also infra*, sky
hill *or* hillside, 107³, 645, 650⁴. *See also infra*, mountain
hurricane, 9
ice, 1³
island, 3³⁴, 46, 330, 337, 646¹, Gl s.v. patriarch
lake, 369²
lightning, 1³, Gl s.v. augur
minerals. *See* baetylus; bronze; coin; copper; flint-stone; gold; iron; jewelry; lead; lime *or* limeburner; metal-worker; millstone; mining *or* mine *or* miner; monument; pillar; silver; stone-worker
moon, 44, 52⁴, 122¹³, 124 (IV)
mountain, 9, 46, 443, 483¹ⁿ, 487, 528⁵, 632. *See also supra*, hill *or* hillside
peninsula, 369³
plain, 9, 38¹ⁿ, 107³
planet, 124¹⁹, 313¹
rain, 1³, 9, 67
river, 369²
sea, 9, 44, 46, 62², 84 (I), 95, 124 (IV), 214⁵, 236³, 366, 400, 406, 495¹¹, App 10 (f)
seasons, 34, 44, 122, 207, 220, 236³, 429, 527³⁶
sky, 1³, 9, 48 (I), 236³, 315¹, 429, 453, 569, 636, 637, 645. *See also supra*, heaven
snow, 1³, 95¹, 236³
star, 44, 67, 207, 313¹, 443, 626
sun, 23⁴, 34, 37, 44, 46, 115¹⁷, 122¹³, 124 (IV), 144, 209, 220, 236, 243, 313¹, 316
tempest, 1³, 9, 84 (I), 124 (IV)
thunder, 1³, 577
tree, 63, 242, 285⁶, 538⁴. *See also* lumber; wood
water. *See* food *or* drink
wind, 9, 44, 124 (IV), 167¹ⁿ, 495⁴, 527³⁶
philosophy:
  Christian, In²⁹, 4², 65¹ⁿ, 551⁷, 648⁶
  ethical, 116
  Greek, In²⁹, 47, 49¹, 66⁷, 98³, 113, 115¹⁷, 116⁷,¹¹⁸, 119⁵, 122¹², 159¹⁶, 189², 223², 231¹, 313¹, 551⁷, 583¹, 648⁶, Gl s.vv. Gnostics, Neo-Platonism, Porphyrians. *See also* Neo-Platonism *or* Neo-Platonists; Platonism *or* Platonists
  Jewish, 23⁴
  political, 116
Photinianism *or* Photinians, 166¹, 173, 395, 429, 483⁶, 485⁶, 487⁵, Gl and therein s.v. Marcellians

Phrygians, 298, 380, 395, 429, Gl
phthiriasis, 7³
physician, In, 5 (c), 347¹³, 562, 585, Gl s.v. guild. *See also* disease; medicine
physis (natura), 67¹⁷
piety, 8, 9, 46, 47, 52, 53³, 63, 66⁸, 67, 115¹⁷, 116, 119⁵, 187, 197, 200¹ⁿ, 327, 373, 397, 398, 400, 401, 405, 406, 411³, 415 (I), 423, 443, 445, 449, 454, 457, 463, 467, 480, 486, 496, 507, 518, 524 (I), 579, 581, 595, 596, 612, 623, 640 (I), 645, 652, Gl s.v. pontifex maximus. *See also* impiety; irreligion
pilgrimage *or* pilgrim, In⁸, 411³, 484²⁵, 515⁵
pillar, 54, 95¹, 200¹, 246¹, 364¹⁵, 376¹ⁿ, 411¹ⁿ,³
pious causes, In, 5 (a), 65⁶, 301⁷, 515¹ⁿ,⁵, 522, 530⁶, 536, 579, 581, 585¹ⁿ, 595, 596, 601, 604¹ⁿ, 612, 623¹ⁿ, 630³, 644³, 648, Gl. *See also* almshouse; asylum; gerontocomium; hospital; hostel; nursery; orphanage; poor, the; prisoner of war
  curator of, 612
  custodian of, 612
  privileges of, 518, 595
piracy, In⁹
place:
  religious, 641 (IV)
  sacred, 641 (IV, V)
  venerable, 640 (I-V)
places, holy (Palestinian), 174
plague, 40, 543 (II), App¹, Gl s.v. Batrachitans. *See also* epidemic; pestilence
plain. *See* phenomena, natural
plaintiff, 65⁶,⁹, 334¹ⁿ,⁴, 399¹ⁿ⁵,⁶, 478, 490, 491, 504, 515, 582⁵, 598⁹,¹⁰, 603, 611⁹, 619, 640⁴,¹⁴, App 10 (a). *See also* accusation *or* accuser; litigant; prosecutor
planet. *See* phenomena, natural
plantation, In⁹, 46, 239¹ⁿ, 528⁵. *See also* farm *or* farmer; manor; villa
Platonism *or* Platonists, 422¹¹, 648⁶
plebeian, 329, 351⁴, 413, 432, 443, Gl and therein s.vv. fathers (conscript), knight, order, patrician, pontifex maximus, quindecimvir, tribune (plebeian)
plebiscite, 625⁹, Gl s.v. *Lex Cincia*
pleroma, 67²⁰
plough, 139
Pneumatomachians, 192, 395⁶, Gl s.v. Semi-Arians
poet, 116⁷, 165⁸
poison *or* poisoner, 40, 53, 67, 135, 145, 171¹, 173, 180, 198, 201, 207, 395¹⁰, 480, 489. *See* virus
police, 194⁷, 204³, 207⁸, 240¹ⁿ, 310, 483²³, 487²⁷, 568¹ⁿ,⁵

SUBJECTS 1325

politician, Gl s.vv. pontifex maximus, praetor
politics, ecclesiastical, 228[1n], 527[76]. *See also* patriarchate, rivalry of
polytheism, 67[15], 115[17], 242[2], 567, 641[1n], Gl s.v. Monarchians. *See also* idolatry *or* idol; paganism; worship, pagan
pontifex maximus, In[26], 3, 7, 111[1], 119[1], 476[4], 523[1], Gl and therein s.v. virgin (Vestal)
pontiff:
  Christian, 86[5], 95[2], 167, 459, 544[1n], 550[9], 557, 558[1n], 561, 564[1], 641[6], 645
  pagan, In[26], 523[1], 598[13], 623[7], 641 (I), App 10 (f), Gl s.vv. pontifex maximus, quindecimvir
pontificate, 196, 200[1], 375[7], 553, 561[19], 563, Gl s.v. pontifex maximus
poor, the, In[9], 33, 81, 123, 127, 128, 139, 141[3], 146, 223[2], 226, 228[1n], 347, 356[5], 370, 399, 435, 474, 488, 515, 518, 519, 579, 585, 595[3], 616, 618, 623
  patrimony of, 515[3]
  relief of, In, 5 (d), 32, 54, 55, 102, 123, 127, 128, 141[3], 146, 312, 474[2], 501, 520, 579, 612, 615, 623, Gl s.vv. deacon, pious causes, steward of the church
  superintendent of, 515, 579
  as heir, 623
pope:
  = bishop of Alexandria, 53[3], 68[1]
  = bishop of Rome, Tab[5], In[26,31,44,46], 5[1], 17–19, 48[2], 53[3], 68[1], 76[4], 95, 95[43], 102[1], 138[4], 150, 164, 167[2], 173[1n], 181[5], 200[1n], 211[1,3], 262, 284[4], 295, 330[1n], 350[1n], 352[1n], 353, 354[1], 355[4], 356, 357[1], 358[1n,1], 359[1n,4], 361, 362, 364[2,3,6], 365[1n], 366, 367, 371, 375[1n,7,13], 388, 412, 461–4, 468, 470 (I, VII, XI), 472 (I), 473[1n], 475[1n], 479, 492, 500, 523[1], 527[1n], 544–54, 556–8, 560, 561, 562[1n,5,12,14], 563, 564[1n,1], 637, 645, Gl and therein s.vv. Novatians, patriarch, pontifex maximus. *See also* Papacy; papalism; patriarch, Roman; patriarchate, Roman
  election of, In[44], 200, 352–67, 371
pork. *See* food *or* drink
Porphyrians, 66, 422, Gl
porter, 109[3], 162, Gl and therein s.v. guild. *See also* janitor
portico, 400. *See also* stoa
post, public. *See* public post
postliminium, 308, 641[16]
potestas iurisdictionis, In[4]
potestas magisterii, In, 4
pound, 121, 146, 181, 234, 235, 239, 242, 258, 272, 276, 286, 289, 298, 301, 307, 308, 310, 312, 329, 337, 370, 395, 399, 429, 432, 433, 437, 440, 442, 478, 480, 489, 491, 500, 506, 530, 534, 536–8, 555, 565, 567, 575, 586,[7] 606, 616, 618, 646[22], 647, 651, Gl. *See also* coin; mint; money
Praeclara gratulationis, In[31]
praetor, 218[4], 489[2], 520[1], 548, 608[4], 621, 625, 641[28,29], Gl and therein s.vv. lictor, prefect (urban). *See also* propraetor
praetorian guards, 186[3], App[16], Gl s.v. prefect (praetorian). *See also* bodyguard
praetorium, 515
pragmatic sanction. *See* constitution
praying *or* prayer, In[8], 1, 11, 20, 38–40, 44, 47, 49 (II, III), 52, 67, 67[35], 73, 86, 90, 117, 125, 159, 167[1n], 184, 198, 207, 223[2], 258[3], 313[1], 327, 328, 366, 385, 395, 400, 407, 411, 414, 419, 453–5, 465, 472 (II, III), 475, 477, 479, 484, 485, 487, 508, 515, 519, 521, 527, 547, 551, 552, 554, 556–8, 561, 563, 579, 637, 645[35], 651, Gl s.vv. Enthusiasts, Sleepless
  by emperor, 11, 20, 38, 44, 47, 49 (II), 475, 476, 483, 485–7, 495, 527[26], 543 (I), 550, 642, 645, 646 (I)
  for emperor, 1[4], 7, 49[26], 86[35], 125, 139[8], 313[1], 371, 407, 411 (III), 461, 468, 482, 485, 487, 545, 546, 549, 551, 637, 645
  house of prayer, 522, 584, 615
Prayer:
  of Habakkuk, 651[20]
  of Hannah, 651[20]
  of Jonah, 651[20]
preaching, In[29], 122, 255[3], 327, 350[1n], 407[2], 459, 524 (I), 553, 559, 561, 569, 651
  apostolic, 472 (I)
  prophetic and apostolic, 645
precept, apostolic, 163, 225
prefect, Gl
  Augustal = of Egypt, 197, 204, 208, 234, 235, 239, 257, 266, 272, 347, 489[12], 527[2], Gl. *See infra*, prefect, of Egypt
  municipal: of Milan, 15[12]; of Nicomedia, 15[12]
  prefect, praetorian, In[9], 4[2], 6[3,4], 8[1n], 13[1n], 14[1n], 15[12], 23[1], 25[1], 33[1], 34[2], 43[1n], 45[14], 54, 55, 65, 76, 79[1], 95[41], 106[5], 161[4], 168[1], 172[8], 272[8], 293[2], 298[1], 309[6], 311, 333[1], 410, 423[1n], 426[1], 443[19], 445[2], 491[5], 520, 572[1], 584[3], 586[4], 606, 632, 638, 641[12], 651, App[11], Gl and therein s.v. apocrisiarian
  of Africa, 646 (I), Gl s.v. prefect (praetorian)
  of Illyricum, 223, 322, 332, 375 (I, III),

384, 423^3, 477, 479, 480, 520^1, 638, Gl s.v. prefect (praetorian)
of Italy, 15^{12}, 23^1, 97^3, 160^2, 164, 165^2, 166^2, 172^{1n}, 186^2, 188^1, 190^1, 201^2, 205^2, 209^2, 230^1, 233^1, 261^1, 262^1, 265^1, 281^1, 288^1, 289^1, 290^2, 293^1, 301^1, 306^1, 307^2, 308^1, 309^2, 310^2, 311^1, 312^1, 313^2, 315^2, 316^1, 317^1, 318^1, 324^1, 327^2, 329^1, 331^1, 332^1, 334^1, 350^{15}, 351^1, 372^5, 391^1, 392^1, 423^2, 433^1, 435^1, 440^3, 441^1, 443^2, 446^1, 478^2, 496^1, 497^1, 519, 520^1, 618^{13}, 640^{16}, Gl s.v. prefect (praetorian)
of the East, 25^2, 45^{14}, 61^{13}, 91^2, 114^4, 126^2, 127^2, 128^1, 147^1, 151^1, 171^2, 173^2, 175^1, 176^1, 184^2, 185^1, 187^1, 189^1, 192^1, 193^2, 194^2, 195^{1n}, 196^2, 199^2, 202^1, 206^3, 210^2, 213^2, 214^1, 215^2, 216^1, 217^3, 218^1, 221^1, 222^1, 224^1, 225^1, 226^1, 227^1, 228^3, 229^1, 233^1, 234^1, 237^1, 238^2, 239^1, 242^3, 243^1, 246^2, 247^1, 248^1, 249^2, 251^1, 252^1, 253^1, 255^1, 259^1, 260^1, 264^1, 267^1, 268^1, 269^2, 270^1, 271^3, 272^1, 273^1, 277^1, 279^1, 280^1, 287^1, 302^1, 303^2, 314^2, 320^1, 321^1, 335^1, 336^1, 341^1, 342^1, 343^1, 345^2, 347^2, 348^1, 349^2, 351^1, 369^1, 376^3, 377^1, 378^2, 379^1, 380^1, 381^1, 382^2, 383^1, 385^2, 386^2, 393^2, 394^1, 395^1, 399, 400^1, 410^1, 413^1, 421^1, 423^1, 424^1, 425^1, 426^5, 427^1, 429^1, 431^2, 432, 434^1, 436^2, 437^1, 438^1, 446^1, 474^1, 477, 479^2, 480^3, 488^1, 489^2, 490^1, 491^1, 498^1, 501^1, 502^1, 503^1, 506^1, 507^1, 508^2, 509^2, 510^3, $513^{1,3}$, 514^2, 515^8, 516^2, 517^1, 518^2, 520^1, 525^6, 526^1, 528^1, 529^1, 536^1, 538^2, 540^2, 541^1, 565^1, 568, 579^1, 581^1, 582^1, 586^1, 587^1, 588^1, 589^1, 590^3, 591^1, 592^1, 593^2, 594^1, 595^1, 596^1, 597^1, 598^1, 599^1, 601^4, 602^3, 603^1, 604^1, 605^1, 606^1, 607^1, 608^1, 609^1, 610^1, 611^1, 612^1, 613^3, 614^1, 615^2, 619^1, 620^1, 621^1, 622^1, 623^1, 624^1, 625^1, 626^1, 627^1, 628^1, 629^2, 633^3, 634^1, 648^1, 651, 652^1, App^{39}, Gl s.vv. prefect (Augustal), prefect (praetorian). See also ex-prefect
of the Gauls, 25^2, 149^2, 154^2, 164, 351^1, 387, 520^1, Gl s.v. prefect (praetorian)
prefect, urban, 15^{12}, 161^4, 183^3, 354^3, 363, 439^3, 505^3, 621, Gl and therein s.vv. lictor, master of the census
of Constantinople, 159^{16}, 181^1, 236^1, 258^1, 274^1, 285^1, 286^1, 319^1, 422^2, 430^1, 477^{32}, 479^3, 480^{84}, 505^3, 538^2, 590^4, 608^{13}, 610^6, 638, 651^1, Gl s.vv.

prefect (urban), vicar (urban). See also ex-prefect
of Rome, 33^1, 92^3, 132^1, 133^2, 134^1, 135^1, 137^{1n}, 138, 139^3, 140^{1n}, 141^{1n}, 142^1, $143^{1n,5}$, 145^1, 146^{1n}, 152^{1n}, 153^{1n}, 154^4, 155^1, 156^2, 170^1, 177^2, 183^{1n}, 211^{1n}, 219^1, 220^1, 298^1, 323^1, $330^{1n,7}$, 352, $353^{1n,1}$, $356^{1n,3}$, 364^1, 365^{1n}, 373^{1n}, 374^{1n}, 388^2, 439^1, 505^3, Gl s.vv. prefect (urban), vicar (urban); deputy of, 142, 143^5

prefect:
of aliments, 474^2
of camp, App^{38}, Gl
of Egypt, 8^3, 67, 81, 87, 88, 113, 121, $122^{1n,12}$, 349^{1n}, 489^{12}, 527^2, 638. See supra, prefect (Augustal)
of grain-supply, 141^3, 301^7, Gl and therein s.v. aedile
of province, 234^3
of soldiers, 11^{1n}
of treasury, 4^{10}, Gl s.v. catholicus
prefecture:
honorary, 341
praetorian, 15^{12}, 45, 106^4, 172^6, 311^4, 375^1, 520^1, 646 (I), Gl and therein s.vv. diocese, patriarch, prefect (praetorian), province; of Africa, 646 (I), Gl s.v. prefecture of Illyricum, 15^{12}, 106^4, $375^{1n,1,3,11}$, 471^7, 520^1, 646 (I), Gl. s.v. prefecutre; of Italy, 15^{12}, 20^{15}, 106^4, $311^{4,5}$, 375^1, $646^{2,13}$, Gl s.v. prefecture; of the East, 15^{12}, 54^{28}, 106^4, 280^6, 311^{11}, 471^7, 489^{12}, 511, 646 (I), Gl. s.v. prefecture; of the Gauls, 15^{12}, 25^9, 106^4, 520^1, 646^{13}, Gl s.v. prefecture
urban, 141, 143, $608^{7,13}$
prelate, $In^{8,43}$, 5^1, 61^{11}, 84^{27}, 284^5, 337, 398^{1n}, 402^{1n}, 405^{1n}, 406^1, 408^5, 409^{1n}, 411^3, 414^{1n}, 415^{1n}, 416^{1n}, 417^{1n}, 442^7, 455^{1n}, 457^{1n} 463^3, $470^{2,4,29,56,70}$, 471^{1n}, $472^{1n,14}$, 480^{30}, 492^1, 508^{11}, $524^{13,17}$, 527^{76}, 556^{1n}, 558^{1n}, 560^5, 562^{10}, 567, 598^{13}, 606^{1n}, 614^{13}, 635^{1n}, Gl s.v. apocrisiarian
prerogative, 102, 139, 186, 229, 326, 375 (I), 431, 442^7, 470^{70}, 472 (III), 495^8, 526, 528^7, 595, 625, 630
papal, 284^1, 470^{70}, Gl s.vv. patriarch, pontifex maximus, pope. See also Papacy; pope = bishop of Rome
presbyter, 107^8, 158^4, 352^{1n}, $447^{1n,1}$, 452, 519^{20}, 523^1, 651, App 8. See also clergy or clergyman; priest, Christian
prescription. See forum; time
president:
= bishop, In^{31}, 16, 398, App 10 (b)
= provincial governor, 234^3, 646 (I)

priest:
  cardinal, 364¹⁵
  Christian, In³¹, 16⁴, 17³, 18¹¹, 20¹¹, 25, 45, 47, 48 (I), 49 (I, II), 50, 58¹ⁿ, 59, 61 (III), 66¹,², 67⁴⁰, 68²,⁷, 78, 84 (III), 85, 109, 110¹⁰, 119¹,⁵, 131, 150¹, 161, 162, 166, 194, 195¹ⁿ, 196, 203, 204, 222, 224, 280, 284³, 295, 300⁶, 308, 310¹³, 312, 334, 337, 342, 350, 352, 353, 354³, 372, 398, 399, 411 (I), 412, 421, 425, 436, 451, 459, 468, 478, 480, 484, 487–90, 495¹⁴, 497, 514, 515, 518, 519, 523¹, 524 (I), 527, 546, 554¹, 558, 559, 566, 568¹ⁿ, 579, 580¹ⁿ, 588, 613, 624, 628, 629, 636, 637, 651, Gl s.vv. archimandrite, clergyman, deacon, itinerant bishop. *See also* clergy *or* clergyman; priesthood, Christian
  heretical *or* schismatic, 25, 47¹ⁿ, 53, 58¹ⁿ, 66, 67, 71, 72¹ⁿ, 166, 194, 195¹ⁿ, 222, 336², 337, 342, 350¹ⁿ, 352¹ⁿ, 373¹ⁿ, 395, 425, 445, 448¹ⁿ, 449¹ⁿ, 455¹ⁿ, 459¹ⁿ, 463², 470⁴,²⁷, 479, 480, 483, 489, 542, 559, 561, 606², 616, Gl s.vv. Enthusiasts, Novatians, Valentinians. *See also* clergy *or* clergyman, heretical *or* schismatic
  Jewish, 23², 159³⁴. *See also* Levite
  pagan, In, 5 (c), 3⁸, 16¹⁰, 41⁴, 46, 116¹⁶, 119¹, 206⁷, 208³, 242¹, 397¹, 399¹⁰, 400, 411³, 520⁶, 523¹, 614¹⁰, 619⁵, App 10 (f), Gl s.vv. flamen Dialis, quindecimvir. *See also* Augustal; flamen; flamen Dialis; pontifex maximus; pontiff, pagan; priesthood, pagan; sevir; civil, 208³, 329, 337, 441, App 10 (f); high, 208³, App 10 (f), Gl s.v. pontifex maximus
priestess, 44, 397¹, Gl s.v. virgin (Vestal)
priesthood. *See also* episcopate; hierarchy
  Christian, 16⁴, 48 (I), 49 (I), 110⁸, 112⁴, 118¹ⁿ,¹, 129¹ⁿ, 155¹ⁿ, 158, 163², 182, 195¹ⁿ, 203, 208³, 270¹ⁿ, 314, 334, 372, 397, 398, 408, 457, 459¹⁵, 466, 483, 484, 526⁵, 530, 576, 577, 613, 625, 629, 651, Gl s.v. archdeacon
  pagan, 523¹; high, 208
primacy, In³⁴, 53³, 375⁷, 442, 461, 470 (IX, XI), 475, 482¹ⁿ, 495⁵, 526, 550⁹, 557³, 560³, 563, 577¹ⁿ,¹, 618³, 637, 645, Gl s.vv. metropolitan, patriarch
primate:
  = bishop, In, 5 (a), 17⁴, 455. *See also* bishop
  = guild official, 430³. *See also* guild *or* guildsman
  = magistrate, 356⁵, 364⁸. *See also* magistrate, Roman

R

Principate, In⁹, 65⁶, 133¹, 186², 281⁶, 313¹, 341², 400⁹, 496⁶, 511², 515¹⁸, 537⁵, 592⁴, App²³, Gl and therein s.vv. aedile, consistory, consul, guild, knight, *legis actio*, paterfamilias, prefect (praetorian), prefect (urban), province, senatusconsult
principum placita, In, 2. *See also* constitution
Priscillianism *or* Priscillians, 161², 203¹ⁿ,¹,⁹, ¹⁰, 288¹ⁿ,⁹,¹⁴,¹⁵, 298, 311, 320, 380, 395, 429, Gl
prison *or* prisoner, 135, 145¹ⁿ, 171, 180, 198, 201, 207, 258⁴, 285, 295⁶, 308, 312, 370, 429, 463⁴, 473¹ⁿ, 479⁸, 483, 484, 487, 524¹⁴, 533¹, 586, 589, App 10 (b), (c)²⁷, Gl s.v. registrar
prisoner of war:
  ransom of, In, 5 (d,g), 5 (7), 127⁵, 308¹ⁿ, ⁶,¹⁴, 488, 507, 510², 585, 598, 604, 612, 623, 641 (I), Gl s.vv. pious causes, slave (public)
  as heir, 623
privilege, 528⁷. *See also* Church of Constantinople, privileges of; Church of Rome, privileges of; clergy *or* clergyman, privilege of, privileges for
privy purse, imperial, 148¹, 395⁵, 618¹⁴
prize, 243
proceeds, 510
proconsul, 4², 7, 17¹⁶, 164, 234, 272, 294², 301, 337, 367, 548, 638, 641²⁹. *See also* consul
  of Achaea, In, 4, 89, 234³
  of Africa, 10¹ⁿ, 15, 16², 17, 19¹¹, 21, 106², 120², 148, 156¹, 158, 160², 183, 234³, 263, 278, 282, 294, 296¹, 299–301, 305¹, 324¹², 337, 338, 366, 368¹ⁿ, 389, 390, App 7
  of Asia, 2, 182, 234³, 245, 254, 453, 454
proconsular, 328
procurator, 1⁵, 4², 159²⁷, 273, Gl
  of grain-supply, 301⁷, Gl s.v. procurator
  of private estate, 15, Gl and therein s.v. count of the private estate
  as representative of litigant, 501, 619, Gl
procurer, 97¹, 374, 593³
prodigy, Gl s.v. augur
professor:
  Christian, In¹⁴, 116, 617⁴, 640¹. *See also* education; teaching *or* teacher
  pagan, In, 5 (c), 98³, 116¹ⁿ, 122. *See also* education; teaching *or* teacher
progress, imperial, 434, 438, Gl s.v. count of the dispositions
proletariat, 141³, 474²
promagistrate, Gl s.v. province
promise *or* vow, 517, 520, 522, 543,

544^{1n}, 547, 560, 601^{1n}, 605, 608, 641^{8,24}, 644
promotion, 606
property:
  alienation of, 4^{10}, 12, 14, 46, 109, 123, 139, 187^{1n}, 212, 337^6, 391, 433, 435^4, 497, 503, 510, 514, 516, 574, 579, 598, 604, 612, 623, 630, 634, 641^{11}
  bequest of. *See* bequest; legacy *or* legatee; to churches, 36, 225, 227, 395, 488, 595, 624; to clerics, 150, 157, 225, 227, 488; to virgins, 157
  community of, 4^4, 641^{14}
  confiscation of. *See* punishment: property, confiscation of
  detention of, 627, 634, 641^{22}
  donation of. *See* donation *or* gift; to churches, 225, 227, 329, 595, 604; to clerics, 150, 157, 225, 227, 601; to paupers, 225, 227; to virgins, 157
  ownership of, 46, 185^2, 223^3, 239, 242, 255, 268, 270, 277, 285^6, 289, 298, 301^7, 308, 314, 328, 329, 336, 342, 343, 395, 421, 431, 435^6, 436, 464^1, 472 (III), 480, 489, 502, 510, 528, 535, 567, 572, 593^3, 597, 608, 610, 619, 624^3, 627, 631, 632, 640^7, 641^{2,13,22,27,28,30}, 644, 648, 652, Gl s.vv. curial, master of the census, *patria potestas*; by Church. *See infra*, property, ecclesiastical; by city, 513, 606; by clerics, 17^6, 106^1, 107, 109, 110, 130, 147, 151, 193, 202, 224, 233, 277, 280, 284, 297, 307, 337, 342, 343, 421, 425, 432, 433, 488, 514, 515, 568, 579, 624, 629, 652; by deaconess, 225, 227; by pagan temple, 615^{1n}, 641^{1n}; by remarried widow, 187^{1n}; by remarried widower, 187; by State, 537^6; by ward, 150, 153, 516, 608, 621, 635^2, Gl s.v. guardian; by widow, 150, 153, 187^{1n}, 225-7, 488, 489, 629, 630^{1n}, 635^2, 652, App 8 (b). *See also supra*, bequest of: to virgins; donation of: to virgins; ownership of: by deaconess, by remarried widow, by ward, by widow; claim against, 46, 65^6, 595^6, 597, 641^{22}
  possession of, 4^2, 65^6, 139, 218, 308^{14}, 432, 435^4, 478^{11}, 503, 510, 606, 612, 627^4, 634^{1n}, 641^{4,22,23,28}, Gl s.v. *iusta causa*
  renunciation of, Gl s.vv. Encratitans, Manichaeans
  restoration of: when confiscated by fisc, 46, 65^6; when exiles returned, 46, 84 (I), 112^{1n}, 117; when illegally alienated, 65^6; when illegally owned or occupied, 212; when illegally possessed, 65^6, 478^{14}, when illegally seized, 382, 395
  rights of, 167^{1n}, 337^6, 478^{14}, 624^3, 634, 638, 641^{30}
  surrender of: by heretics without orthodox survivors to fisc, 599; by pagans to Church, 301, 340; by pagans to cities, 583; by pagans to fisc, 600; for nonfulfillment of promise, 255; on becoming a defender of the Church, 478; on entering clericate or ascetic life, 109, 110, 130, 147, 193, 202, 210, 224, 225, 227, 233, 280, 322, 433, 629
  building *or* house, 9, 14, 40, 46, 124 (III), 156, 163, 185, 191, 192, 194, 242, 258, 264, 268, 275, 277, 284^3, 285, 289, 298^9, 336, 342, 343, 372, 374, 377, 393^1, 395, 399^{11}, 422, 429^{36}, 442^7, 459^{15}, 472 (III), 478^{11}, 483, 484, 489, 510, 513, 593^3, 594, 613^4, 616, 641^7, App 10 (a,e). *See also* almshouse; ascetery; asylum; building; churches; gerontocomium; hermitage; hospital; hostel; house; martyry; monastery; nunnery; nursery; oratory; orphanage; palace; stable; synagogue; temple; villa
  buried, 223, 521
  ecclesiastical, Gl s.v. archdeacon. *See also* apparel; cemetery; gardens; vessel; administration of, 447^4, 510, 518, 522, 530, 579, 612, 618, 623, 630^6, 638, 648, 651, Gl s.v. steward of the church; division of, 588, 648; donation of, 4^{10}, 12, 14, 46, 510, 515^{1n}, 537, App 10 (a); emphyteusis of, 537; exchange of, 510, 537, 648; hypothec of, 537, 598; lease of, 618; nonalienation of, 503, 510, 537, 568^2, 579, 598, 641 (I), 648; pledge of, 598, 641 (I); possession of, 4^2, 10, 12, 46, 57, 345, 579, 638; purchase of, 4^{10}, 10^{1n}, 12, 14, 46, 57, 212, 503, 510, 515^{1n}, 537, 598, 641^{10}, 648, App 10 (a); surrender of: by fisc to churches, 46; by Christians to pagans, App 10 (a); by illegal owners or occupiers, 212, 484, 486; by pagans to Christians, 4, 4^8, 7, 10, 12, 14; violation of, 168^1, 289, 310; confiscated by emperor, 119^5, 123, 148^1, App 10 (a); exempted from public services, 107, 327; from taxation, 107, 327, 395; nonexempted from capitation tax, 345; from public services, 438; owned by heretics or schismatics; 57; seized by heretics or schismatics, 59, 395, 484, 486; by orthodox bishops, 124 (III)

immovable, 501, 503, 522, 530, 536, 588, 600, 604, 606, 615^{1n}, 618, 623, 629, 641^{22}. See also supra, property, building or house; infra, property, landed
  imperial, 15, 106, 107^3, 123, 186^2, 223^3, 239, 253, 298, 301, 321 (II), 329^{7,9}, 337, 340^1, 377, 387^3, 421^4, 432^5, 555, 567, 575, 630, 647, App 8 (b)^{14}, Gl s.vv. Caesarian count of the private estates, count of the sacred patrimony, count of the sacred treasury, procurator of the private estate
  landed, 10, 14, 46, 65^6, 107, 124 (III), 148^1, 163, 168^1, 179, 212, 239, 242, 268, 270, 277, 289, 298, 308, 314, 327–9, 336, 337, 342, 343, 421, 472^{23,24}, 474^2, 480, 489, 497, 503, 510, 528, 568, 597, 632, 641^{13}, App 10 (a), Gl s.vv. canon, caput, leaseholder
  lost, 223^2
  movable, 501, 520, 522, 530, 537, 588, 600, 604, 615^{1n}, 623, 641^{10,22}
  ownerless, 168^1, 218, 223, 233, 521, 641^4, Gl s.v. Caesarian
  private sacred, 168^1, 641^{13}. See also things, religious, sacred, sanctioned; place, religious, sacred
  public sacred, 168^1, 615^{1n}, 641^{13,30}. See also things, religious, sacred, sanctioned; place, religious, sacred
  self-movable or self-moved, 522, 588, 604, 623
  stolen, App 10 (a)
prophecy or prophet, 7^{13}, 9^7, 44^{6,8}, 67, 98^{14}, 156^1, 159^{34}, 382^1, 398^6, 468^7, 484, 522, 546, 645, App^1, Gl s.vv. Montanists, Priscillians, Tascodrogitans. See also divination or diviner; seer; sibyl; soothsaying
propraetor, 234^3. See also praetor
proprietor, 220, 301, 308, 329^{10}, 337, 641 (I). See also landlord; property, ownership of
prosecutor, 329. See also accusation or accuser; litigant; plaintiff
proselytism (by Jews), 80, 341, 345, 348
prosopon (persona), 67^7
prostates, 234^3
prostitution or prostitute, 80^2, 82, 97^1, 198^4, 247^3, 394^{1n,5}, 457, 493, 494, 649^9, Gl s.v. aedile. See also brothel
protectorate, 106^5
Protestantism or Protestants, 75^4, 92^1, 140^1
protoheresiarch, 422^7, 487^9. See also heresy or heretic
protomartyr, 566^{1n}. See also martyrdom or martyr

Protopaschitans, 335, Gl s.v. Novatians
proverb, 1^3, 3^{15}, 59, 65^{13}, 66^{18}, 95^1, 117, 310^4, 350^4, 429^5, 573^1, 641^{30}
Providentissima Mater Ecclesia, 617^6
province:
  ecclesiastical, In, 5 (a), 397
  imperial, Tab^5, In^{42}, 1^1, 4^2, 8^2, 15, 16, 17, 19, 23^3, 31^1, 32, 46^{11}, 52^{47,48}, 54, 59^{1n}, 62, 64^{20}, 65^6, 73, 83^{3,5}, 93, 106, 117, 117^6, 118^{1n}, 119^{1n,5}, 124 (III), 133^1, 141^2, 159^{27}, 164, 168^1, 203, 204^3, 220, 234^3, 243^2, 253, 258^8, 287, 288^{15}, 289, 290, 298, 300–3, 307, 308, 310, 324^{12}, 325–7, 337, 341, 343, 344, 346, 353, 366, 368, 369^3, 375, 377, 382, 387, 395, 400, 405, 408, 411 (I), 414, 415 (II), 417, 420, 422, 426, 429, 434^{1n}, 435, 438, 440–4, 447, 456, 464, 470 (V, IX, XI)^{2,49,66,71}, 474^2, 476–8, 480, 483, 487, 489, 497, 506–8, 513, 515, 516, 521^1, 523, 524 (II), 526, 527^{1n}, 528, 530, 532, 536, 537, 543, 544, 546, 537, 551^{1n}, 556, 559, 566^{1,3}, 567, 568, 575, 576, 579^7, 580, 582, 583, 585, 586, 588, 591, 593, 600, 606, 608, 610–12, 618^{10}, 619, 621, 629, 631–4, 638, 639, 641^{11,22}, 646, 649–52, App 8 (b), 9, 10 (d), (f)^{16,43}, Gl and therein s.vv. archbishop, catholicus, curial, duke, master of the offices, metropolitan, notary, patriarch, praetor, prefecture
  provincials, Tab^5, 2, 7, 12^{69}, 13, 14, 44, 46, 67^{37}, 121^2, 141^3, 168^1, 243^2, 308, 341^2, 382, 384^{1n}, 422, 434^{1n}, 513, 515, 616^8, 651, Gl s.vv. archbishop, patriarch
provisions, 301, 410, 495^{11}
  civil, 301^7, 510, 513, 537, 584^1
  extra transport, 32, 102, 107^{13}, 226^3, 434, 438
  military, 14^6, 110^5, 113^5, 301, 535, 536, 584, Gl s.v. public service
  transport, 19^{28}, 25, 107, 410, Gl s.v. public service
provost, 579
  of granary, 109, Gl
  of public post, 168^1
  of school, 547^6
  of soldiers, 8, Gl
  of the peace, 109, Gl
  of the sacred bedchamber, 448^2, 618^{12}, Gl and therein s.v. chamberlain
psalmody or psalm, 559, 579. See also hymn; ode; song
public conveyance. See conveyance or vehicle, transport
public order, 7, 12, 68, 69, 86, 105, 117, 123, 137, 138, 140–3, 152, 153, 205, 220^2, 235, 240, 243, 272^{10}, 283^{1n}, 288,

1330 SUBJECTS

310, 326, 328, 347^{1n,1,3}, 352, 355-8, 373, 374, 401, 404, 408, 409^4, 414, 415 (I), 427, 465, 466, 469, 476, 478, 483, 484, 487, 495, 629, 641^{28}, Gl s.v. guild. *See also* discipline, public; meetings, tumultuous; mob; riot

public post, 18, 19, 25, 32, 43^{11}, 48^2, 58, 64, 70, 84 (II), 95, 95^{41}, 110, 112, 119^5, 186^5, 202, 256^{2,3}, 410^5, 426^8, Gl s.vv. master of the offices, procurator, slave (public). *See also* conveyance *or* vehicle, transport; letter, commendatory
  provost of, 168^1
  warrant for, 95^{41}, 256^2
public service, compulsory, In^9, 109, 110, 114, 118, 129^1, 147, 208, 210, 233, 262, 265, 273, 280, 282^1, 307, 332^4, 345, 346^3, 377, 430, 433. 435, 436, 478^{24}, 497, 502, 612, 629, 651^{24}, Gl and therein s.v. guild
  exemption from, Tab^5, In, 5 (c), 16, 17^{1n}, 29, 30, 32, 33, 55, 56, 59, 60^2, 67^{40}, 81, 85, 87, 89, 102, 107, 114^1, 129^1, 162, 170, 186, 188, 202, 210^3, 226, 233, 261^2, 262, 265, 267, 345^{1n}, 377, 434, 435, 438, 441, 515, Gl s.vv. *iusta causa*, public service; extraordinary, 102, 226, 262, 265, 434, 515; menial, 41, 102, 107, 170, 183, 186, 226, 262, 265, 327, 377, Gl s.v. public service; exemption from, 14^6, 32; municipal, 322; personal, 162, 429; rural, 314
public works, In, 5 (f), 46, 59^{10}, 168^1, 186^5, 606, 641^8, Gl s.vv. aedile, auditor, public service
publican, 457. *See also* tax collector; tax receiver
punishment, In, 4, 5 (b)^{46,49}, 1-3, 4^2, 5, 6, 8, 13, 17^{3,8}, 20, 23, 24, 31, 44, 46, 47^{1n}, 50, 51, 59, 63, 66-9, 76, 85^{1n}, 86, 92, 98, 111^{23}, 113^4, 115-17, 127^6, 137, 140, 143^5, 144^3, 145, 152, 153, 156, 159, 161, 167, 168^1, 171, 173, 185, 190, 195, 198, 199, 203^1, 204, 205, 207, 214-16, 223^3, 225, 230^6, 234, 242, 249, 253, 254^{1n}, 261, 265, 272, 275, 286, 288, 290, 292^3, 299, 301, 303, 305, 315, 320, 324, 325, 327-9, 330^{1n}, 331^4, 334, 335, 337, 342, 344, 347, 350, 352, 356, 369, 374, 380-2, 389, 392, 393, 395, 397^{12}, 399, 412, 413, 416^{1n}, 420, 422, 423, 429, 431, 440, 443, 457, 459, 470 (I, VI), 472 (I), 476, 477, 480, 481, 483, 484, 486, 487, 489, 494^2, 501, 504, 505, 520, 523^8, 524 (I), 530, 554^1, 560, 567, 569-71, 573, 574, 576, 579, 583, 586, 588, 593^3, 599-601, 606, 612, 616, 618, 638, 640^{1n}, 646 (I), 648, 652, App 5, 8 (b), 10 (f), Gl s.vv. *imperium*, *Lex Iulia de adulteriis coercendis*, sanction, *Senatus Consultum Persicianum*
  conditioned by rank, 337
  conditioned by rank, age, sex and by time and circumstance of crime, 168^1
  assignment: to guild, Gl s.v. guild; to imperial estates, App 8 (b); to mines, 44, 168^1, 207, 298, 308, 310, 394, 395, 418^{1n}, App 10 (f); to public games, 132, 168^1; to public works, 46
  beating: with cudgels, 41, 119, 239, 489; with rods, 480; with scourges, 21^9, 289, 298, 329, 330, 337, 395, 399^{10}, App^{36}
  blinding, App 10 (f)
  blood, 323, 339, 346, 429, 443, 560
  branding, 164, 173^{10}, 176^3, 231, 255, 334^3, 337, 443
  cancellation of exemption from public service, 67, 118
  canonical, 651
  capital, 66, 79, 80, 92^2, 126, 127^6, 134, 159^{27}, 168^1, 171^1, 203^1, 207^{1n}, 268, 272, 310, 324^7, 348, 369, 373, 396^{1n}, 400, 429, 439^3, 443, 445^{12}, 459, 478, 483, 497, 500^{14}, 501, 515^{16}, 532, 533, 571^1, 573^{1n}, 589, 625^{14}, 638, 641^2, 652, App 8. *See also infra*, death; last; loss of citizenship
  castigation, 631
  castration, 76^3
  censure, 132, 167^{11}, 173^{11}, 242, 288. *See also infra*, reprimand
  chains, App 8 (b), 10 (b). *See also infra*, custody; imprisonment
  condemnation, 194, 354^{1n}, 365
  contumacy, 478. *See also infra*, disgrace; dishonour; ignominy; infamy
  corporal, 127^6, 204, 221, 439^3, 555, 575, 606^{23}. *See also supra* beating; blinding; blood; branding; castigation; castration; *infra*, mutilation
  custody, 453. *See also supra*, chains; *infra*, imprisonment
  death, 2^{1n}, 3, 6, 7^{18}, 24, 42^1, 46, 66, 79, 80, 92^2, 98, 117, 119, 159, 167^{1n}, 168^1, 185, 201^9, 203^1, 204^5, 205, 214^5, 268^2, 277^4, 299^2, 305^3, 310, 323, 335^5, 364, 395^{10}, 399^{10}, 424, 432, 443, 465^4, 480^{72}, 489^{68}, 515^{23}, 573^2, 600^3, 638, App 7^{11,36}, Gl s.vv. *damnatio memoriae*, *Lex Iulia de maiestate*, Priscillians. *See also supra*, capital; *infra*, last; by cremation, 23, 42, 92^2, 95^{34}, 123, 168^1, 214^{41}, 395^{10}, 562, 638^{13}, App 10 (a), (e); by crucifixion, App 10 (f); by decapitation, 66^3, 164^{12}, 205, 246^1, 255^3, App 10 (f)^{51}; by drinking molten

SUBJECTS

lead, 92²; by drowning, 214⁵, App 10 (f); by hanging, 168¹, 303³; by sword; 42, 44, 123, 159²⁷, 214⁵, 562, App 10 (f); by torture, App 4; by wild beasts, App 10 (f)

debarment: from bequeathing, 480, 489, 575; from bequest, 31¹, 176, 249, 395, 480, 489, 575; from buying, 298; from contracting, 289, 298, 320, 337, 440, 575; from donating, 298, 343, 391, 395, 489, 575; from donation, 289, 298, 343, 395, 489; from inheriting, 31¹, 176, 249, 298, 440; from residing in or near cities, 164, 173, 176, 194, 213, 232, 260, 268, 288, 313, 368, 387, 395, 415 (II), 440, 459, 480, 519, 649, 650; Alexandria, 115, 121, 122; Constantinople, 196, 222, 256, 258, 264, 285, 472 (II), 476, 480, 616; Rome, 140, 152, 153, 164, 219, 313, 350–2, 356, 364–6, 368, 371, 373, 374, 388; from selling, 298; from testation, 117, 167¹ⁿ, 175, 176, 185, 189, 190, 218, 230, 249, 259, 277, 289, 343, 391, 395, 440, 489, 575

demotion in rank, 413, 426, 472 (II), 478, 575, App 10 (a)

deportation, 137, 168, 194, 204⁵, 207, 239, 240, 268, 277, 288, 298, 308, 310, 313, 327, 335, 342, 343, 372, 387, 432, 443, 480, 489, 543¹ⁿ. *See also infra,* exile

disgrace, 46, 66, 288, 651, Gl s.v. *damnatio memoriae. See also supra,* contumacy; *infra,* dishonour; ignominy; infamy

dishonour, 523, App 10 (a). *See also supra,* contumacy; disgrace; *infra,* ignominy; infamy

excommunication, 17³, 52³, 67, 164, 173¹¹, 182, 286¹ⁿ, 297, 368, 415 (II), 445, 459, 530

exile, In⁴⁸, 3,³⁴, 9, 13, 18¹ⁿ, 20¹, 42¹, 46, 50, 51, 58¹ⁿ, 67¹³, 68, 72, 73, 74¹ⁿ, 75¹ⁿ, 77¹ⁿ, 93¹ⁿ, 94, 95, 98, 99, 103, 112, 115, 117, 121–3, 124 (I, II), 137, 140, 152¹,⁶, 153, 159¹⁶, 164, 167¹ⁿ, 168¹, 192, 195⁵, 205¹, 207, 214⁵, 230, 246¹, 260, 284²⁻⁴, 288⁹, 289, 295¹ⁿ, 297¹ⁿ, 306, 325⁹, 329, 330, 337, 342, 343, 350, 353, 378, 382, 394, 395, 416¹ⁿ,⁷, 417, 418, 419¹ⁿ, 420, 425, 426, 429, 445, 457⁵, 459, 463, 480, 489, 495¹ⁿ, 506, 510, 523³, 524 (I), 533, 562, 567, 576¹ⁿ, 587¹ⁿ, 592⁴, 600, 606¹²,²³, 637⁷, 646 (I), 649, App 7, 8. *See also supra,* deportation

expulsion: from clericate, 443, 459¹⁵, 472 (III), 476, 524 (I), 530, 576, 579, 611, 613, 629, 651; from damaged property, 618; from ecclesiastical administration, 530, 579, 618; from episcopate, 284, 297, 508, 518, 524 (I), 543¹ⁿ, 559¹ⁿ, 575¹⁹, 576, 579, 580, 588, 611, 620, 629; from equestrian order, App 8 (b); from governmental service, 509, 511, 529², 567, 575, 600; from guardianship, 621; from legal practice, 506, 567, 575; from provincial governship, 443, 532, 606¹²,²³, 649; from public administration, 575; from registrate, 618; from sacerdotal rank, 618, 651; from stewardship, 510; from trial court, 619

fine, 41, 119⁵, 121, 132, 146, 167¹ⁿ, 181, 234, 235, 239, 242, 253, 258, 272, 276, 284³, 286, 289, 298, 301, 307, 308, 310, 312, 329, 337, 364, 382, 395, 429, 432, 433, 437, 440, 442, 478, 480, 489, 500, 506, 530, 532, 534, 536–8, 555, 565, 567, 575, 580, 586⁷, 589, 606, 616, 618, 641¹³,²⁰,²⁸, 647, 651, 652

imprisonment, 21¹ⁿ, 42¹, 46²¹, 117, 207, 255³, 285, 369, 447¹ⁿ, 589, 641⁸, 646¹, App 7, 10 (b). *See also supra,* chains; custody

ignominy, 156, 613. *See also supra,* contumacy; disgrace; dishonour; *infra,* infamy

infamy, 156, 164, 167, 176, 209, 231, 255, 289, 324, 337, 443, 478, 480, 489, 508. *See also supra,* contumacy; disgrace; dishonour; ignominy

last = death, 480, 501, 515. *See also* death

loss: of belt, 283, 284³, 476, 480, 489, 515, 529², 567. *See also infra* loss of office *or* of rank; of citizenship, 92², 478. *See also supra,* capital; of freedom, 631, App 10 (a); of military privileges, 555¹ⁿ; of money accepted in lieu of bequest or of donation, 612; of office *or* of rank, 231, 310, 325, 341, 478, 510, 529², 567, 575. *See supra,* loss of belt; of rations, 555¹ⁿ

mutilation, App 10 (f)³⁶,³⁸

payment: of costs and expenses to defendant clergyman by convicted calumniator, 515; of embezzler's peculation for failure to surrender embezzler, 576; of illegal tax deficit, 106; of loss to churches from alienation of ecclesiastically owned property, 510; of rental, 337; of soldiers' guard-duty expenses from personal property, 536; of valuation of leased

property, 618; double: of amount extorted on cost of appeal, 611; of bequest by delaying heirs, 612; of valuation of leased property, 618; for delay to pay legacy or trust, 640, (II–IV); for denial of guilt, 612, Gl s.v. *Lex Aquilia*; for denial of liability to pay legacy, 640 (IV); double or triple, for denial of liability to pay legacy, 640 (V); triple: by extortionate guardian, 621; of presents extorted from heretics, 633
poverty, 289, 290, 426, 600. *See also infra*, property, confiscation of
property: assignment to accuser, 496; assignment to Church, 425; confiscation of, 4^{10}, 6, 10^{1n}, 14, 40, 42^1, 46, 65^6, 84, 91, 117, 119^5, 123, 124 (III), 134, 150, 156, 157, 160, 163, 176, 179, 181, 184^3, 185, 194, 218, 219, 239, 242, 258, 264, 268, 277, 283–5, 289, 290, 297, 298, 306, 308, 310, 328, 329, 336, 337, 340, 342, 343, 348, 351, 372, 378, 382, 389^{1n}, 395, 422, 426, 429, 432, 443, 459, 478, 480, 489, 503, 509–11, 515, 523, 524 (I), 567, 572, 574, 575, 583, 586^6, 589, 600, $606^{12,23}$, 629, 638, 649, 650, App 7, 8 (b); Gl s.vv. Caesarian; *Lex Iulia de maiestate*; procurator of the private estate. *See supra*, poverty; large amount of, 519; one fourth of, 629; one half of, 506, 629; one third of, 496, 500, 640^{21}; two thirds of, 629^{22}; forfeiture of for nonfulfillment of promise, 255; repair of damage to, 618; restoration of stolen plus triple or quadruple damages, 382
proscription, 323, 335, 336, 339, 374, 389, 394, 429, 443, 496, 506, 511
reprimand, 288. *See also supra*, censure
restriction to one's city, 53^1, 445, 480, 489
restoration of betrothal gift on dissolution of betrothal, 517
restoration of betrothal gift and of quadruple its value on dissolution of betrothal, 517^2
ship, confiscation of, 431
statutory, 379
suspension of judicial function, 119^1
taxation: increase of, 67; on celibates, 31^1
torture, 1^2, 3^4, 5, 21, $42^{1n,1}$, 44, 46^{21}, 95^{36}, 113, 119^5, 124 (IV), 169, 197, 201, 204, 223^3, 284^3, 299^2, 302, 310, 443, 484, 559, 560, 646 (I), App 4, 7, 10 (a), (c), (e)^{11,36}
purification, 117, 119^1, 424
Purim, $303^{1,3,4}$
Puritans, 57^3, Gl s.v. Novatians
purple:
 cloth, 432^1
 dye, 273^2
 ink, In, 3
 robe, 95^{51}, 247^3, 273^2
Pythagoreans, 422^{11}
Python, 44^{16}

Quadragesima, 169, 221, 281, 302
quadruped, Gl s.v. augur. *See also* animals
quaestor, 617
 of the sacred palace, 414^{1n}, 505^2, 640^1, Gl. *See also* ex-quaestor of the sacred palace
quartermaster, 301^7
Quartodecimans, 52^3, Gl
Quicunque Vult, 651^{20}
quindecimvir, In^{26}, 523^1, Gl
Quinquagesima, 385^6
quitrent, 632

race:
 horse, 236^3, 279, 651. *See also* games
 torch, 648^7
rain. *See* phenomena, natural
ransom. *See* prisoner of war, ransom of
rape *or* rapist, 92, 126, 135, 145, 171^1, 180, 201, 372, 440^8, 496, 638
rationalism, Gl s.v. Gnostics
rations, 301^7, 536, 555^{1n}. *See also* food *or* drink
reader. *See* lector
rebaptism *or* rebaptizer. In 5 (g), 16^6, $158^{1n,4}$, 163, 164, 166^4, 230^{1n}, 289–91, 335, 336, 343, 646 (I), Gl s.vv. Donatists, Novatians. *See also* baptism, heretical
recidivist, $180^{1n,5,6}$. *See also* crime *or* criminal
recorder, 444, 516, 618^{1n}, 627, 634, App 10 (f)^{44}, Gl and therein s.v. apparitor
records. *See* accounts; *acta*
 civic, 606
 conciliar, 19, 397
 fiscal, 110^6, Gl s.v. auditor
 legal, 293, 510, 522, 530, 536, 581, 596, 601, 608, 612, 618^{1n}, 621, 652
 personal, 227, 234, 537^{11}, 541, 592
 public, 26, 338, 497, 537^{11}, 567
 of conference, 326
 of defender, 537, 559
 of master of census, 537, Gl s.v. auditor of secretarial bureau, 549
rector = provincial governor, 234^3, 646 (I)
REDDITOR LVCIS AETERNAE, 34^5
referee, 625. *See also* arbiter; judge
Reformation, the, In^{31}
refuge *or* refugee, 136^{1n}, 168^1, 289, 315, 370, 400, 413, 437, 442^7, 483^{1n}, 497,

SUBJECTS

501, 633², App 7. *See also* asylum; fugitive; sanctuary, right of
cities of, 241², 400⁹
regeneration, baptismal, 116¹⁴, 527, Gl s.v. Pelagians
register:
 citizens', App 10 (e)
 civic, 234²
 ecclesiastical, 554¹
 equestrian, Gl s.v. censor
 financial, 78
 guild's, 497
 lawyers', 557
 military, 555
 official, 353⁶, 432
 prefectural, 88
 registrars', 618
 sacerdotal, 85¹², 487, 618, 651
 senatorial, 46, 497, Gl s.v. censor
 tax, App 10 (e)
 tradesmen's, 107
registrar, 124¹⁶, 312, 618, App 10 (f), Gl and therein s.v. apparitor
relics, 117, 139, 181¹ⁿ,⁵,⁶, 206⁶,⁷, 443¹, 479, 497, 551, 577¹³. *See also* saint
religio:
 illicita, 1⁴
 laesa, 641²⁵
 licita, In, 3⁴⁴, 3³⁴, 4¹ⁿ, 5¹, 7²⁰, 33¹ⁿ, 67³⁷, 114¹, 267³, 515¹ⁿ
religion:
 Catholic, 15, 18–20, 21¹⁰, 30, 40, 41, 56², 58¹ⁿ, 138, 160, 167, 173, 192, 203, 248⁵, 253, 254, 282, 289, 290, 304, 313, 389¹, 395, 429, 433, 461, 484, 489, 506, 645. *See also* sect, Catholic
 celebrated, App 10 (a)
 Christian, In²¹, 3, 6–8, 12–14, 16–21, 23, 24, 27, 42⁵, 43 (I), 44, 46, 47, 51, 52, 65, 66⁸, 86, 93, 104, 119¹, 134, 137, 139–41, 150, 152, 153 159, 161, 163, 164, 169, 170, 173, 176, 177, 183, 185, 187, 189, 190, 194, 196, 202, 209, 211, 215, 222, 231, 244, 247, 256, 261, 265, 272, 274, 278, 281, 287³, 298, 308, 310, 312, 326, 327, 340, 344, 345, 348, 360, 365, 372, 375 (III), 392, 397, 398, 400, 402, 411 (I), 412, 413, 415 (I), 422–7, 429, 431, 435, 437, 442, 443, 445, 446, 449, 459, 462, 470 (II), 475, 476, 478, 480, 488, 496, 497, 515, 519, 554, 558, 561, 563, 631, 640 (I), 652, App 1³⁶, Gl s.v. Gnostics. *See also* cult, Christian; faith; law = Christianity *or* Christian religion; observance, Christian; sect, Christian; services, divine; worship, Christian
 divine, 324, 361, 385, 459, 496, 564, 598

holy, 164, 398, 413, 427, 467, 472 (II), 483, 484, 486
orthodox, 298¹³, 311, 313⁴, 396¹ⁿ, 401, 406, 446, 464, 467, 474, 483, 486, 489⁴⁰, 503, 526, 541, 544, 550, 599. *See also* sect, orthodox
pious, 422, 500
pure, 422
Roman = Christian, 411 (I)
sacred, 307, 425, 429, 443, 462, 562
sacrosanct, 327, 433, 519
State's (Christian), In, 4³³, 12¹, 167¹ⁿ, 212¹ⁿ, 643¹ⁿ, 644¹ⁿ; (pagan), In, 4²⁶, 1⁴, 139, App 8 (a), 10 (f), Gl s.vv. pontifex maximus, quindecimvir
sure, 645
true, 299, 400, 412, 422, 429, 486, 645
uimpaired, 645
venerable, 360, 387, 424, 433
difference in, 517
discussion of, 47, 216, 283¹ⁿ, 422, 472 (II), 476, 477, 489, 512, 554, 561. *See also* speech, freedom of
disturber of, 240, 288
rent, 632, Gl s.vv. canon, leaseholder
rentier, 239, 308, 310, 311, 347¹³, 470 (XI), 489, 513, 532, 534, 540, 541, 606
report (to emperor), 2, 3, 4², 6, 17, 19, 21¹ⁿ, 24, 54, 61 (II, III), 63, 121, 141, 142, 211, 285, 288, 324, 327, 347¹ⁿ, 352, 353, 354³, 365, 403, 405¹ⁿ,¹,³,⁴,⁶, 406⁹, 431, 439, 442, 456, 459, 470 (I), 483, 484, 559, 567, 575, 579, 580, 583, 588, 606, 633, 646¹⁶, 649, 650
republic, Latin-American, 1⁴
requisition, 497⁵
Res Gestae Divi Augusti, 48⁹
rescript. *See* constitution
 papal, 350¹ⁿ
response *or* reply of jurisconsult, 168¹, 204³, 308¹⁵, 334, 639⁸
responsum. *See* constitution
restitutor, 50⁷
Resurrection, 7¹³, 75⁴², 159, 509¹, 569, Gl s.v. Marcionites
revelation, 75⁴², Gl s.vv. Montanists Tascodrogitans
revenues:
 ecclesiastical, 470 (VIII), 510, 515³, 519, 520, 530, 537, 538, 576, 579, 580
 municipal, 606
 public, 583
 of decedents' estates, 612
rhetoric *or* rhetorician, 113, 116, 159¹⁶ 186, 226
rich, the, 33¹ⁿ, 55, 118¹ⁿ, 127⁷, 129¹, 150¹, 204³, 341², 347, 399, 435, 618, Gl s.v. curator
right *or* rights:
 civic, 35, 46, 308¹⁴, 593³, 638¹²

1334   SUBJECTS

divine, 483, 485, 598
human, 483, 485
Italic, 375⁷
legal, of churches, 10, 12, 510, 524 (II), 630, 652; of cities, 513, 523; of citizens, 35, 136, 603, 625, 630; of monasteries, 652; of pious causes, 623, 630; of the State, 194, 212; of temples, 212; of tenant farmers, 618
obligatory, 598⁸, 604⁶
papal, Gl s.v. apocrisiarian
political, 523, Gl s.v. manumission
public, 212², 239, 306
real, 598⁸
riot, 50, 53, 59, 68, 73¹⁷, 86, 98⁷, 103¹², 111, 117, 123, 133¹, 137, 138, 141, 142, 153, 205, 220², 228¹ⁿ, 236², 283, 285, 286, 288, 289⁷, 292, 341, 347¹, 352, 356, 358, 359¹ⁿ, 363¹ⁿ, 364, 365, 371, 397¹, 400, 427¹ⁿ, 465, 466, 469, 470⁵³, 472 (II), 476¹ⁿ, 487, 512, 527¹ⁿ, 546²⁰. *See also* meetings, tumultuous; mob; public order
Nika, 236³, 505¹
rites. *See* ceremony, religious; worship
familial, 214⁶, 602⁵
heretical, 426, 489
orthodox, 455
pagan, 139, 623⁷, App 8, Gl s.vv. guild, pontifex maximus. *See also* worship, pagan
river. *See* phenomena, natural
road, 20, 68, 75, 122, 186⁴, 211, 328, 410, 446, 483, 551, 595⁷, 605, 645, 651
construction *or* care of, 327, 377, 606, Gl s.v. slave, public
robbery *or* robber, 198, 457, 593³, 611¹². *See also* banditry *or* bandit; brigandage *or* brigand
robe. *See* apparel
Rock Dweller, 290¹
Roma Aeterna, 140¹. *See* in Index of Places s.v. Rome: as Eternal City
Roma locuta est; causa finita est, 350⁴
Roman Empire, Gl s.v. *imperium*. *See also* Dominate; Principate
(Christianized), In, 1, 4, 6³⁸, 41², 65⁶, 116¹¹, 126⁶, 150¹, 154¹ⁿ, 159²⁸, 167¹ⁿ, 208³, 300³, 315, 478²⁸, 515¹ⁿ, 615¹ⁿ
(pre-Christian), In, 1, 4, 1⁴, 127⁷, 241¹ⁿ, 440
decay of, In⁹
division of, Tab³, In, 3⁴³, 62², 77¹, 106⁴, 375¹, 475⁹
fall of western part, Tab⁵, In²,⁴³, 353³, 544¹ⁿ, 646¹³, Gl s.vv. apocrisiarian, *Codex Theodosianus*, prefect (praetorian), prefecture
reunion of, Tab⁵
safety of, 7, 11–13, 16, 38², 41², 46, 313¹, 375 (III), 397, 411 (III), 415 (II), 423, 425, 427, 442, 449, 453–5, 461, 462, 464, 468, 475, 478, 482, 485, 487, 496, 524 (I), 525, 527, 544, 546, 557, 558, 579, 580, 588, 637, 645, 646 (I), 651
Roman Kingdom, 28¹, 358¹, 439³, Gl s.vv. knight, pontifex maximus, prefect (urban), quindecimvir
Roman Republic, 31⁴, 41², 127⁷, 133¹, 204³, 218⁷, 220², 392³,⁴, 439³, 472⁴, 509⁶, 515¹⁸, 537⁵, 592⁴, 605³, 606²⁰, 624³, 625¹⁴, App²³, Gl s.vv. apparitor, censor, consistory, consul, dictator, Father of the Fatherland, guild, knight, legion, pontifex maximus, prefect, prefect (urban), tribune (plebeian), Tribunician Power
rule, apostolical, 73
Rupitans, Gl

Sabbath, 34⁵, 332, 586³
Sabbatians, 380, 395, Gl s.v. Novatians
Sabellianism. *See* Modalism
Sacaea, 303¹
Saccophorians (*al.* Saccoforians), 176, 185, 192, 395⁶, Gl
sackcloth. *See* apparel
sacrament, In³⁷, 17⁶, 47³¹, 75⁴², 154, 158, 163, 164¹⁷,¹⁸, 166⁴, 199, 305, 425, 527⁵⁸, 559¹⁵, Gl s.vv. Donatists, Mithras, Tascodrogitans. *See also* mysteries = sacraments
sacramentalism, Gl s.v. Gnostics
Sacrifice:
Christian, 258³, 519. *See also* Communion, Holy; Eucharist; Liturgy, Divine; Lord's Supper; Mass, Holy
Hebrew, 644⁶
pagan, In²⁶, 1⁴, 3²⁰, 5, 6, 9, 41, 42, 63, 116, 117, 168¹, 184, 206⁷, 231, 242, 253, 391, 424, 429, 521, 600, 644⁶, App 7, 10 (b)–(f)⁻¹¹
sacrilege *or* sacrilegious, 1⁴, 4², 16, 29, 59, 78², 91, 111, 120¹ⁿ, 135², 152, 164, 168, 168¹, 171¹, 173, 176, 179, 180, 184, 190, 198, 201, 209, 232, 283, 289, 298, 299, 301, 303, 308, 310, 327, 329, 344, 350, 368, 370, 387, 389, 391, 400, 422, 429³⁰, 433, 440, 443, 476, 489, 496, 510, 520, 546
sacristy, 258³
safety of emperor, 1⁴, 242, 255³, 313¹, 325, 403, 461, 462, Gl s.v. *Lex Iulia de maiestate*. *See also* Roman Empire, safety of
sailor, 584¹ⁿ
saint, In⁸,¹⁴,⁵², 17³, 34⁵, 47¹ⁿ, 50⁵⁷, 95¹, 97⁴, 98¹⁵, 99⁷, 127⁵,⁷, 167¹ⁿ, 181¹ⁿ,⁵, 195⁴, 203¹, 206, 297¹ⁿ,³, 330¹ⁿ, 397¹,

SUBJECTS 1335

411^{1n}, 415^{14}, 433^1, 484, 568^2, 615^{1n}, 641, 645, App^{11,14}. See also canonization; relics
salary. See wage
sale, fictitious, 343, 391
salt. See food or drink
salvation, In, 4, 18–20, 24, 40, 44, 47, 49^{26}, 50, 59, 66^2, 67, 68, 99^7, 104, 125, 139^8, 154, 159, 166^4, 176, 203, 255^3, 292, 317, 328, 416, 427, 481, 487, 524 (I), 546, 548, 553, 561, 569, 575^{1n}, 579, 636, Gl s.vv. Enthusiasts, Gnostics, Mithras
Samaritans. See in Index of Places s.v. Samaria
   debarment from governmental service, 567
sanction. See constitution
   pragmatic. See constitution
sanctity, apostolic, 167
sanctuary:
   Christian, 168^1, 310, 370, 400, 508, 519^1, 619
   Jewish, 399^3
   pagan, 424
   asylum, right of, In, 5 (f), 241, 246^1, 266, 273, 289, 315, 370, 399^{1n}, 400, 413, 497, 500^{14}, 501^{1n}, $576^{1n,7}$, 633. See also right of; fugitive; refuge or refugee
Sanhedrin, 23^2
Saturn (planet), 23^4
scandal, 215^{1n}, 448, 456, 459, 460, 546
sceptre, 527, 562^3, 642
schedule, 15^8
schism or schismatic, In 5 (b)^{18,32,43,45}, $10^{1n,1}$, 15, $16^{3,8}$, 17–19, 20^{1n}, 21^{1n}, 22^{1n}, 24^{1n}, 27^{1n}, 39^{1n}, 40, 47, 50, 53, 56, 57, 59, 61^{1n}, 68^2, $69^{1n,12}$, 70^{1n}, 95^{1n}, 112^{1n}, 120^5, 137^{1n}, 138, 153, 158^4, $164^{2,3,16,17,26}$, 166^4, 167^{1n}, 168^1, 181^6, 182^{1n}, 195^{1n}, 203, 276^4, 289, 290, $301^{1n,5}$, 304^{1n}, 306^{1n}, 310^{1n}, 324^2, 325^2, 328, 329^{1n}, 338^{1n}, 352^{1n}, 353^{1n}, 354^{1n}, 356^{1n}, 359^{1n}, 365^6, 370^1, 371^{1n}, 375^{1n}, 387–9, 395^{1n}, 402, 422, 459, 472 (I), 482^{1n}, 524^3, $527^{1n,45}$, 543 (II), 544^{1n}, 545^2, 546^2, $547^{1n,8}$, $548^{1n,1}$, 549^{1n}, 550^9, $551^{1n,8}$, 552^2, 553^3, 554^6, 556^1, $558^{1n,3}$, $560^{1n,3,19}$, $561^{10,19}$, 562, $563^{1n,6}$, 643^{1n}, Gl and therein s.vv. Donatists; heresy; Maximians; Meletians; Novatians. See also heresy or heretic; Hill Folk; Rock Dwellers; sect, schismatical
scholar or scholarian, 547^6, Gl s.v. master of the offices
scholarch, 116^{16}. See also professor; teaching or teacher
school, 116, 122, 547, App ^{6}. See also education; teaching
   catechetical (Alexandrian), 98^4, 189^2
   imperial, 547^6, 575

philosophical, 583^1
theological (Antiochene), 459^{28}
science, 52^4, 98^3, 116^9, 284^4, 313^1, 347^{13}
scribe:
   ecclesiastical, 326, 472^4
   imperial, In^{14}, 20^{1n}, 159^{37}, 177^2. See also clerk, imperial; notary; secretary, imperial
   Jewish, 23^2
Scripture or Scriptures. See Bible
sculptor, 67, cf 393
sea. See phenomena, natural
seafaring, 606^3
seal, 632, 634
search:
   for Christians, 1^3, 42^{1n}
   for criminals, 1, 42^{1n}, 310 483, 486
   for heretics, 260, 275
   for sacrilegious persons, 168^1
seasons. See phenomena, natural
secretary:
   conciliar, 469^4
   episcopal, 559
   imperial, In^{14}, 11^{1n}, 103^{13}, 176^{15}, 256^2, 353^6, 434, 471^{1n}, 472^{20}, 511^2, 549, 559^{18}, 560, Gl s.vv. chief of the notaries, master of the offices, notary, registrar, tribune and notary. See also clerk, imperial; notary; scribe, imperial
   papal, In^{31}
sect:
   Catholic, 41, 304, 305, 329, 335. See also religion, Catholic
   Christian, 1^4, 7^{13}, 12, 14, 96^{1n}, 112^{1n}, 387, 422^{12}, 650^{14}. See also religion, Christian
   heretical, 167^{1n}, 176, 215, 216^{1n}, 249, 299, 368, 381, 387, 388, 395^{1n}, 429, 489, 503, 559, 575^{1n}, 599. See also heresy or heretic
   Jewish, 23, 244, 348
   orthodox, 342. See also religion, orthodox
   schismatical, 167^{1n}, 289, 290, 387, 388, 395^{1n}, Gl s.v. schism. See also schism or schismatic
security, 608, 619, 621, 634, 649, 650
seduction, 63^2, 171^1
see, apostolic, 360, 371, 375 (II), 472 (I), 475, 482, 484, 500, 551, 557, 558, 560, 562, 563, 645, cf 181^5, 284^4
seer, 150^1. See also divination or diviner; prophecy or prophet; sibyl; soothsayer
Semi-Arians, Gl. See also Arianism or Arians
Senate:
   Constantinopolitan, 399^9, 461, 470 (I, II), 488, 492^1, 497^2, 578, 585, 608^{13}, 642, Gl and therein s.v. *imperium*

Roman, In^{9,26,46}, 3^{34}, 4^2, 36^1, 48^2, 67^{41}, 118^2, 127^7, 133^1, 211, 231^1, 241^1, 357^{1n}, 363^3, 399^9, 429^{81}, 440, 472^4, 497^2, 548, 631^{1n}, 641^{11}, App 2, 8 (a)^{23}, Gl and therein s.vv. Augusta, Augustus, *damnatio memoriae*, dictator, *imperium*, notary, province, senatusconsult, tribune (plebeian)

senate, municipal, 9^4, 33, 43 (II), 46^{14}, 55, 60, 67^{41}, 89, 109, 118, 124 (III), 130, 151, 155, 168^1, 193, 208^3, 210, 224^{1n}, 229, 233, 257^1, 280, 301, 307, 310, 312, 320, 322, 325, 328, 347, 395, 421, 426, 433, 436, 478, 497, 500^7, 529^2, 536, 585, 595^4, 629, 651, App^{23,55}, Gl s.vv. curial, decurion, procurator, Senate, senator, slave (public)

senator:
  Byzacene, 118
  Constantinopolitan, 127^6, 236^3, 337, 470^{1n}, 476^4, 481^1, 554^{1n}, Gl s.vv. fathers (conscript), freedman, knight, notary, order, prefect (urban), senator
  hereditary, 118
  municipal, 55, 60^2, 67^{41}, 114^{1n}, 118, 124 (III), 156^{1n}, 188^{1n}, 210^{1n}, 229, 263, 273^3, 280^{1n}, 322^2, 325, 328, 329, 347^{13}, 443, 478, 481^1, 534^{1n}, 629, 651, App 8 (b), Gl s.vv. order, public service. *See also* curial; decurion
  Roman, 95, 127^6, 334^{25}, 337, 370^1, 472^4, 481^1, 499^{1n}, 548^{1n}, App 8 (b), Gl s.vv. censor, fathers (conscript), freedman, knight, order, prefect (urban), senator. *See also* fathers, conscript
  exemption: from military service, Tab^5; from senatorial service, 267; from torture as witness, 21, 204^3

Senatus Populusque Romanus (SPQR), In^9, 46, 211^6, 241^1, 341^2

senatusconsult, In^9, 31^1, 133^1, 204^5, 341^2, 593^3, 615^{1n}, 625^9, 631, Gl. *See also Senatus Consultum Claudianum* and *Senatus Consultum Persicianum* in Index of Legal Quotations and Allusions

seniority, 614

sepulchre. *See* grave *or* sepulchre *or* tomb

sepulchre = assembly, 176

serf, 107^3, 239^{1n}, 443^{15}, 472 (III), 501, 528, 568, 631. *See also colonus or colona*; peasant

separatism, ecclesiastical, In^{43}, 17^6, 476^{1n}, 527^1, 542^{1n}, 544^1, 548^{10}, 560

servant, 97^1, 387^{1n}, 483, 484, 501, 546, App 10 (f) ^{36}, Gl s.v. slave (public)
  of clergyman, 18, 32, 102, 580
  of God, 20, 39, 44–7, 50, 54, 59, 73, 75, 93, 359, 646 (I), App 10 (f)
  of governor, 417^8

service:
  civil, 186^4, 236^3, 320^5, 511^2, Gl s.v. master of the offices
  God's, 651, 652
  governmental, 46^{17}, 62, 119^5, 186^{3-5}, 205^{1n}, 226^6, 249, 256, 304, 307, 320, 343, 383, 387, 395, 429, 433, 435, 439–41, 444, 472 (II), 476^{39}, 480, 489, 502, 509, 511, 515^{16}, 529^2, 534, 567, 573, 575, 600, 625, 629, Gl s.vv. guild, *patria potestas*; cohortaline, 320, 383, 395, 480, 489; frontier, 480, 489; dismissal from, 119^5; exemption from, 320
  military, 186^4, 624, 629, Gl s.v. guild. *See also* soldier; Christians in, In^{14}, 42^1, 46; debarment from, In, 5 (g); demotion in, 42^1; discharge from, 42^1, 46, 383; exemption from, Tab^5; expulsion from, 629; recruitment for, Tab^5, 50
  personal, 186^5, 488, 606^{20}, Gl s.vv. freedman, leaseholder
  public. *See also* public service

services, divine = worship, 301, 366^5, 387, 412, 497, 628, 629, 641^{1n}, 651^{16}. *See also* worship, Christian

sevir, 478

sewer, 606, 641^{30}, Gl s.v. slave (public)

sheepfold, 645. *See also* animals, domesticated: sheep; shepherd

shepherd, In, 4^{43}, 61 (I), 68^2, 107^8, 125, 210^4, 248^3, 561, 645. *See* animals, domesticated: sheep; sheepfold

shilling, 555^7

ship *or* vessel, In^9, 61 (I), 67^7, 95^{42}, 124 (IV), 285, 301^7, 369, 431, 495^{11}, 646^{10}
  confiscation of, 431

shipmaster, Gl s.v. guild

shipowner, 133^1, 495, 584^7

shipwreck, 400

shipwright, 369^{1n}

shrine, 159^{34}, 206^7, 212^{1n}, 242, 253, 301, 424, 483^{15}, 508, App^{41}

sibyl, 67, Gl. *See also* divination *or* diviner; prophecy *or* prophet; seer; soothsaying

Si quis igitur, 472^{19}

sick, the, 133^1, 206^6, 347^1, 349, 370, 515^5, 612, 621^3, 623

sick-nurses, 347, 349

signatures, In^3, 46^{26}, 326, 331, 406^1, 459, 511, 568, 618, 645^{25}

silentiary, 448^2

silver, 1^4, 97^1, 133^1, 146, 223^2, 225, 312^3, 329, 337, 399, 598^{13}, 611^7, Gl s.vv. denarius, drachma, milaresium

silversmith, 430

Simonians, 422, 423, 459, Gl

simony, In, 5 (g), 137^{1n}, $508^{1n,11}$, $519^{1n,1}$, 520^{1n}

SUBJECTS

sin, In^{37}, 1^3, 39, 49 (I), 61 (I), 63, 67, 68, 75^{42}, 137, 168^1, 195, 206^6, 207, 229, 281, 288, 289, 307, 310, 324, 327, 330^{1n}, 334, 335, 350, 391, 394, 399^{11}, 400, 422, 429, 443, 457^{13}, 476, 484, 487, 496, 504, 519, 520, 546, 559, 567, 600, 613, 614, 638, 648, 651, Gl s.vv. Donatists, heresy, Montanists, Pelagians. See also iniquity

singer. See cantor; musician

sister, 187, 259, 298^6, 361^1, 372, 398, 435^3, 461^1, 476^4, 484^2, 514, 525^{10}, 579, 613^4, 619^7, 624^4, 638^3, Gl s.v. Augusta

"sister", 372, Gl s.v. virgin (introduced). See also concubine; mistress

sky. See phenomena, natural

slander or libel, 334^5, 382^1, 488^2. See also calumny or calumniator; injury or insult or outrage

slave, In^9, 1^{2,4,5}, 29^2, 46, 65^6, 79, 82, 107^3, 122, 127^5, 133^1, 168^1, 170^3, 204^{3,5}, 218^9, 225^{13}, 227, 239, 241^1, 273, 286, 289, 298, 315, 329, 331^5, 337, 364, 379, 387^{1n}, 392^2, 394, 395, 413, 421^6, 429, 432, 443, 472 (III), 476^{43}, 478, 484^{12}, 493, 494, 497, 501, 510, 513, 528, 529, 586, 592, 602, 607, 612^{13}, 616, 631, 638^{1n,13}, 640^5, 644, 647, 650, 652, App 10 (a), (f)^{23}, Gl s.vv. Circumcellions, emancipation, manumission, notary. See also ex-slave

public, 21, 46, 341^2, 478, Gl

as heir, 218^9

of clergyman, 35, 83

of Jew, In, 5 (g), 76, 79, 199, 341, 344, 348, 379, 387^{1n}, 392, 647, Gl s.v. Lex Constantiniana

of treasury, 46, 79

flogging of, 329

gift of, 79^2, 348

manumission of, In, 5 (g), 26, 35, 37, 46, 76, 79, 199, 218^9, 289, 348, 392^3, 493, 494, 528, 529, 602, 607, 647, 652, App 10 (a), Gl s.vv. emancipation, freedman, Lex Constantiniana, Lex Fufia et Caninia, slave (public)

prostitution of, 168^1, 394, 493, 494

purchase of, 79, 82, 199, 348, 616, Gl s.v. slave (public)

rape of, 638^{1n}

torture of, 204^3, 592^{1n,5}

slavery, 65^6, 76, 122, 199, 324^7, 337^6, 487, 501^{10}, 529, 616^5, 631, 646 (I), 652, App^{23}, Gl s.vv. guild, patria potestas

Sleepless, Gl. See also Akoimetoi

snow. See phenomena, natural

soldier, In^{14,45}, 8^4, 11^{1n,3}, 14^6, 38^{1n,2}, 42^1 44, 46, 47, 50, 77^1, 83^5, 90^2, 95^{51,62}, 110^5, 111, 121, 122^{11}, 123, 124 (I)^1, 127^{6,7}, 186$^{3-5}$, 203^1, 220^9, 225^{13}, 228^1, 246^1, 255^2, 285^6, 301, 310, 383, 387^1, 395, 417, 420, 432, 435^{1n}, 442, 453, 461, 474^2, 476^{39}, 482^{1n}, 483^{20}, 484, 486, 492^1, 520^2, 530^3, 534, 536, 555^{1n,10}, 559, 567^6, 568, 584^{1n}, 585, 592^4, 614^7, 617, 624^3, 626, 641^{11}, 646 (II)^{1,10,22}, App 10 (f)^{16,43}, Gl s.vv. centurion, chiliarch, count of the domestics, count of the sacred largesses, domestics, freedman, Imperator, legion, Mithras, office staff, prefect, public service. See also cavalry; infantry; legion; service, military; staff, military; unit, military

demotion of, 42^1

discharge of, 42^1, 46, 119^5, 555, Gl s.v. Mithras

exemption of, Tab^6

recruitment of, Tab^5, 50, 186^5, 555^{4,7,9}

solidus, 165, 433, 433^7, 464^1, 491, 515, 555^6, 581, 596, 606^{11}, 611^7, 621^{4,5,8,10}, 651^6, Gl s.v. denarius

solitary, 527. See also anchorite; hermitage or hermit

solitary life, 185, 228, 237^2, 388, 421, 472 (III), 486, 528, 529, 629, 652. See also asceticism

son, Tab$^{1-3}$, In^{14}, 26^1, 43^{1n,18}, 76^4, 187, 259, 331, 359^1, 361^1, 364^5, 392, 442^4, 472^4, 479^{36}, 495^{11}, 497, 500, 524^{1n}, 527, 561-4, 567, 577, 599, 602, 614^{10}, 624^3, 644, 645, Gl s.vv. emancipation, patria potestas. See also boy; child

of clergyman, 81, 89, 150, 233, 497

of decurion, 229, 233

son-in-law, 512^1

song, 67, 303^4, 559, 651^{20}. See also hymn; ode; psalmody or psalm

Song:

of Deborah and Barak, 651^{20}

of Judith, 651^{20}

of Mary, 651^{20}

of Simeon, 651^{20}

of Solomon, 651^{20}

of Zacharias, 651^{20}

Songs:

of Isaiah, 651^{20}

of Moses, 651^{20}

Sonship, 527^{86}

soothsaying, 242^1. See also astrology or astrologer; augury or augur; auspices; cleromancy; divination or diviner; horoscope; lot; necromancer; numerology; prophecy or prophet; seer; sibyl; sortition

sophism or sophist, 67, 103, 116, 214^6, 480

sorcery or sorcerer, 135^4, 145^3, 156^1, 171^1, 198^4, 201^6, 203^1, 268. See also magic or magician; witchcraft

sortition, 523^1. See also cleromancy; lot

soteriology, Gl s.v. Manichaeans
spectacle:
  amphitheatrical, 168¹, 170, 236, 243, 279, 281, 509, 651¹³. *See also* amphitheatre
  public, 208³, 220², 347, 349, 385, 472⁴, 651, Gl s.v. praetor. *See also* amusements; games
  theatrical, 154, 170, 243, 281, 493, 651¹³. *See also* theatre
speech, freedom of, 73¹⁷, 458, 459. *See also* religion, discussion of
spendthrift, 621³, Gl s.v. guardian
spinster, 149¹, 435³. *See* maid
spirit, evil, 616. *See* devil *or* demon
sport, 303
spy, 50, 256³. *See also* agent, secret-service
Stabilisians, 559. *See also* cavalry
stable, 646 (I)
staff:
  military, 555⁸, 646²²,²⁹
  office, 12³¹, 14⁶, 25, 34³, 45¹⁴, 67⁴³, 109, 110, 132, 181, 194, 234, 235, 242, 253, 257, 258, 272, 283, 289, 298, 301, 306, 308–10, 312, 320⁵, 321 (II), 324, 325⁶, 364, 370, 373, 382, 432, 440, 478, 480, 491, 506, 536, 555⁸, 565⁴, 567, 568, 575, 585, 586, 591, 597, 606, 616, 629, 646, 651, Gl s.vv. apparitor, chief men, chief of the office staff, cohortaline, office staff, official, slave (public)
stage, 650²,⁴, 651. *See also* actor *or* actress; dance *or* dancer; orchestra; spectacle; theatre
star. *See* phenomena, natural
state, Frankish feudal, 181⁶
statue. *See* image *or* statute
status:
  clerical, 62¹ⁿ, 133⁵, 237, 325, 353, 364, 576⁹, 613
  curial, Gl s.vv. client, curial
  ecclesiastical, 526, 577¹ⁿ, 611, 629, 637, 645
  municipal, 43, 263, 456⁷, 470³⁹,⁴³,⁴⁴,⁶¹, 472 (III), 523
  personal, In⁹,³¹, 28¹, 31¹ⁿ, 41, 46, 62¹¹, 92¹,², 96¹, 136, 137, 164¹², 167¹ⁿ, 168¹, 170, 174³, 190⁸, 204³,⁵, 230, 231, 233, 234, 239, 242, 256², 273, 277, 282, 289, 298, 307, 308, 322, 325⁶, 334²⁵, 337, 341, 394, 395, 413, 421, 429, 435, 443¹⁵, 472 (III), 478, 497, 498, 501, 502, 528, 567, 589, 597, 631, 638, 644, 649, Gl s.v. *patria potestas*
  provincial, Gl s.v. province
statute. *See* constitution
statute of limitations, 65⁶, 151¹ⁿ, 185⁸, 212¹ⁿ, 272⁶, 308, 315, 324, 325, 391¹ⁿ, 478³⁰, 582¹¹, 627⁶, 630, 632, 634³
stenography, 326
stepbrother *or* stepsister, 187⁵
stepdaughter, 525¹
sterilization, eugenic, 76⁴
steward:
  of church, 109³, 273, 421, 490, 491, 501, 510, 515, 522, 537, 579, 598, 615, 618, 623, 634, 648, 651, Gl
  of God, 159
  of person, 492¹
  of pious causes, 612
  of rural estate, 185³, 239¹ⁿ
  of urban house, 277, 472 (II)
stipulation, 168¹, 348, 501, 515, 522¹ⁿ, 601¹ⁿ, 641 (III), 644³
stoa, 606. *See also* portico
Stoicism *or* Stoics, 223², 330⁵, 350²⁰
stone-worker, 133¹, 566⁵
strategus, 234³
stylite, 411³
subdeacon, 59, 60, 109, 162, 280, 356⁵, 421, 439, 613, 628, 651
  regional, 356⁵
subscription, In, 2. *See also* constitution
  to conciliar acts, 95, 100¹ⁿ, 406¹, 448⁸
  to creed, 459, 460, 463, 472¹⁴, 484, 524 (I)
  to law, 373, 524 (I), 544¹ⁿ
  to petition, 618, 627
subsistence, public, 575, 600. *See also* dole
substance, 67, 156¹, 159, 173, 182¹, 542, 546, 569, 636, 645, Gl s.vv. Arians, Heteroousians, Homoiousians, Homoousians. *See also* essence; hypostasis; *ousia*
substitute, 30, 33, 55, 109, 130, 188, 210, 280, 314, 319, 347, 349, 355², 430, 433, 436, 478, 488, 579⁷, 629, 635²
succession, 31¹, 46, 109, 150, 185, 187, 189, 225, 233, 259, 298, 321 (I), 343, 391, 392, 478³⁰, 488¹⁸, 496, 507, 525, 537, 561¹⁸, 574, 575, 579⁹, 599, 602, 604, 606, 613, 648, 652. *See also* inheritance
  intestate, 298⁶, 321 (I), 343, 391, 496¹², 507, 525, 574, 575, 599, 652
  universal, 631³
suicide, 122¹⁰, 614¹⁰, App³
summons *or* summoner, 44⁹, 62, 75¹ⁿ, 95, 144, 159²⁹, 164, 172¹ⁿ, 204, 271, 310, 324, 325, 353, 360-2, 382, 397, 402, 406, 408, 412¹ⁿ, 442, 449-52, 461, 470 (X), 478, 491, 500, 501, 515, 543 (II), 544, 550, 559, 586⁷, 611, 619⁵, 640 (II, IV), 650, App, 2, 7, 10 (e)
sun. *See* phenomena, natural
Sunday, 17³, 23⁴, 34, 37, 38¹ⁿ, 52¹ⁿ,³,⁴, 127⁵, 144, 169³, 209, 220, 236, 243, 279, 312, 316, 385, 509, Gl s.v. Priscillians

SUBJECTS 1339

observance of, In, 5 (g), 34, 37, 38^{1n}, 236, 243, 279, 385, 509, Gl s.v. Priscillians
Suovetaurilia, 41^2
superstition:
  Christian, $1^{1,2}$, 3^{34}, 6, 13, 45^1, 118, 122
  heretical or schismatic, 7^{13}, 40, 166, 191, 195, 230^3, 268, 296, 315, 320, 321 (I), 323, 324, 325, 328, 330, 337, 339, 373, 387, 395, 422^4, 440, 616
  Jewish, 348, 392, 622
  pagan, 3^{34}, 41, 63, 242, 259, 301, 340^{1n}, 341^4, 389, 400, 429
  Samaritan, 392
supplication, surreptitious, 205
suretyship or surety, 470 (IV), 491, 501, 509, 515, 516, 586^7, 597, 606, 608, 619, 621, 649, 650, Gl
surreption, 431, 506, 606
"swords, the two", In^{31}
Syllabus of Pius IX, In^{31}
synagogue, 23^2, 214^6, 244, 267, 303^4, 333, 341, 344^1, 376, 378, 429, 575
  construction or repair of, 341, 376, 429
  destruction of, 333, 341, 376, 378, 574
  rulers of, 23^2, 267
  seizure of, 376^{1n}, 378, 429
syndic, 347, Gl
synod, 12^{61}, 17-19, 22^{1n}, 42^1, 47, 48 (II, III), 49 (II), 50-2, 53^{1n}, 61 (III), 67, 73, 75, 95, 103, 104^{1n}, 146^2, 159, 161, $164^{1n,26}$, 172^{10}, $295^{1n,3}$, $350^{1n,9}$, 354-6, 359, 361, 362, 364-6, 375^8, 397, 398, 401-6, 408-10, 418, 420, 422, 427, 442, 445, 448-56, 458-64, 466-9, 470 (I, II, IV-VI, VIII-XI), 471-3, 475-7, 479, 480, 482-7, 489, 495, 524 (II), 527, 544, 546, 551, 571, 611, 637, 645^{40}. See also council, ecclesiastical

Tabernacle, Jewish, 399^3
Tascodrogitans, 191, 395, 429^{33}, 575, 599, 622, Gl and therein s.v. Ascodrogitans
tares, 341^2, 524 (I)
tax:
  capitation, 32^9, 67, 67^{37}, 107^3, 149^5, 174, 270, 314, 345, 384, 421^5, 435, Gl
  coronary gold, 341^2
  extraordinary, 226^3, 327
  gold, 478
  lustral, 32^9, 97^1, 127^3, 165
  poll. See supra, capitation
  superindictional, 226^3
  for grain-supply, 220^9
  in kind, 301^7, 530, 535, 597, Gl s.v. public service
  on agriculture, 428
  on celibates, 31^1
  on land, 107^3, 435, 464^1, Gl s.vv. canon, tax (jugation)
  on livestock, 97^1
  on property inherited or donated, 233^5
  on business receipts, 97^1
  on tools, 97^1
  on trades, 133^1, 165, 282
  account, fictitious, 168^1
  assessment of, Gl s.vv. master of the census, tax equalizer. See also tax equalizer
  collection of, 106, 107, 121^2, 133^1, 168^1, 186^5, 220^9, 233^5, 497^5, 509^4, 535. See also tax collector; tax receiver
  collector, 29, 30^3, 78, 144, 432^{1n}, 457^{13}, 497, 633^{10}. See also publican; tax, collection of; tax, payment of
  debarment of claim for, 65^6
  equalizer, 606, Gl. See also tax, assessment of
  immunity from, In, 5 (c), 31^1, 32, 83, 97, 102, 106, 107, 127, 165, 314, 327, 384^4, 428, 435; cancellation of immunity from, 106^1, 107, 127
  lawsuit about, 65^6
  payment of, 159, 226^3, 241^4, 270^4, 327, 341^2, 345^{1n}, 535, 597^{1n}, 632^3, 633, Gl s.vv. curial, master of the census, public service. See also tax collector; tax receiver; taxpayer
  receiver, 29, 30^3, 107^{13}, 109, 478, 633. See also publican; tax, collection of; tax, payment of
  relief from, 384^{1n}
  remission of, 31^1, 106, 168^1
  unit, 107, 327, Gl and therein s.v. caput
taxation, In^9, 119^5, 121^2, 127, 444, 576^3, 618, Gl s.v. recorder
taxpayer, 568, 633, 646^{21}. See also tax, payment of
teaching or teacher, 42^1, 44, 47, 49 (II), 50, 64, 67, 69, 90, 98, 99, 116, 117, 122, 124 (III), 125, 131^{1n}, 152, 156, 159, 163, 164, 166, 167, 172, 184, 189^2, 194-6, 248, 260, 264, 268, 272, 284^4, 288, 301, 306, 310, 313^4, 324, 344^1, 352, 385, 387, 396, 397^1, 411 (II), 412, 422^4, 427^{1n}, 428, 445, 449, 456, 457, 459, 463^3, 464, 470 (II), 472 (I), 476, 480, 481, 483, 484, 486, 515, 524 (I), 527, 542, 546, 551, 552^{1n}, 553, 569, 575, 577^{13}, 579, 585, 600, 616, 629, 636, 637, 645, App 6, 10 (f), Gl s.vv. catechumen, guild, Manichaeans. See also education; professor
teamster, Gl s.v. guild
Te Deum, 651^{20}
tempest. See phenomena, natural
temple:
  = church, 212^1, 400, 463, 502, 503, 508
  of equity = lawcourt, 619^{10}
  of justice = Digesta, 617

pagan, In, 5 (f)²⁶, 3²⁶, 9, 26⁴, 41⁴, 44, 45¹, 54⁶, 63, 111, 116, 119⁵, 123, 134, 148¹, 168¹, 184, 189, 190, 206⁷, 208, 212¹ⁿ, 220⁴, 241¹, 242, 253, 257⁶, 301, 341⁴, 386³, 397¹, 400, 424, 478²⁹, 483¹⁵, 615¹ⁿ, 641¹ⁿ,⁸, App 7, 10 (e), (f)⁴¹, Gl s.vv. guild, slave (public); appropriated to public use, 301, 424³; Christian janitor of, 134; confiscation of, 424³, 478²⁹; construction or repair of, 119⁵, App 10 (f); conversion into church, 424³; demolition of, 119⁵, 341⁴, 424, 478²⁹; slave of, 26⁴; theft from, 168¹; names of. See also in Index of Places s.vv. Alexandria, Hierapolis, Jerusalem, Rome
tenant, In, 8, 478, 568¹ⁿ, 627⁴, Gl s.v. canon. See also landlord
tenant farmer, 212, 329, 337, 421⁵, 441, 443, 472²³, 478, 497, 501, 510, 528, 568, 597, 618⁴, Gl s.v. leaseholder. See also agriculture; lease or leaseholder
tentmaking, 107⁸
Ter Sanctus, 651²⁰
territory, 306, 320, 343, 397, 489, 523, 530, 531, 535, 550, 552, 554, 615, 619, 646¹, Gl s.vv. bishop, itinerant bishop, patriarchate, province, see
Tessarescaedecatitans, 52³, 395⁶, Gl
testation, right of, 117, 167¹ⁿ, 175, 176, 185, 189, 190, 218, 230, 246, 249, 252, 259, 277, 298, 337, 343, 391, 395, 421, 489, 510², 514, 572, 574, 575, 579, 624. See also intestacy; testator; will or testament
testator, In, 5 (g), 26¹, 218⁴,⁶,⁷,⁹, 392³,⁴, 496¹²,¹⁶, 507, 570¹, 572³, 608⁶, 612, 623, 628, Gl s.vv. Lex Falcidia, Lex Furia
testis unus, testis nullus, 65¹³
Tetraditans, 52³, 395⁶
theatre, 73¹⁷, 154, 170, 177, 183, 243, 247³ 279, 385, 472⁴, 493, 509, 649–51. See also actor or actress; chorus; dance or dancer; orchestra; spectacle, theatrical; stage
theft or thief, 113⁴, 168¹, 301⁷, 457¹², 484, 519, 593³, 611¹², 618
theology or theologian, In⁹, 98⁴, 284⁴, 341², 442⁷, 470²⁴, 550², 577, 637¹ⁿ, 641⁴, 645¹ⁿ, 646¹ⁿ, 650⁴
Theopaschism or Theopaschites, 551¹ⁿ,⁷, 552¹ⁿ,⁵,⁶, 553¹ⁿ, 560¹⁸, 561⁷, 562¹ⁿ, 563⁴, 564¹ⁿ, 636¹ⁿ, 637¹ⁿ, 645¹ⁿ,³⁴, Gl
things:
religious, 641 (I–III). See also place, religious
sacred, 641 (I–III). See also place, sacred; property, private sacred, public sacred

sanctioned, 641 (I)
thunder. See phenomena, natural
son of, 577
tiara, In³¹. See also crown; diadem; mitre
time, prescription of, 65, 164, 168¹, 176¹³, 185, 190, 212, 597, 604, 612, 627, 641²²
tithe, 644⁶
toga. See apparel
toleration, In, 4⁴⁶, 7, 12, 13, 14, 16¹⁰, 39, 41¹ⁿ, 44, 47, 57, 59, 117¹ⁿ, 159¹ⁿ, App 10 (f)
tomb. See grave or sepulchre or tomb
Tome:
of Leo, 470³⁴, 471¹ⁿ,¹, 475⁶, 524, 542, 546¹⁸
of Proclus, 427¹ⁿ, 637¹⁸
tonsure, 300³. See also hair
totalitarianism, In⁹
trade, right of, Gl s.v. peregrine
tradesman, 32, 83, 97, 102, 107, 127, 128, 133¹, 274, 282¹, 478. See also commerce; industry; merchant
tradition:
apostolic, 49 (II), 61 (II, III), 163, 167¹ⁿ, 375⁷, 524 (I)
patristic, 75⁴², 442⁷, 637
social, Gl s.v. paterfamilias
traditor, 17¹ⁿ,⁴,⁶
tragedy, 400. See also drama
Greek, 116¹,⁷
traitor. See treason or traitor
transportation, Tab⁵, 18, 19, 25, 32⁸, 48², 58, 64, 70, 84²⁷, 95, 107, 112, 141³, 186⁵, 301⁷, 327, 410, 426⁸, 431, 434, 438⁶, Gl s.v. public service. See also conveyance or vehicle, transport; public post; ship
traveller, 133¹, 272⁴, 426⁸, 484²⁵, 515⁵
treason or traitor, In³², 1⁴, 3, 4², 59¹⁰, 135, 145, 150¹, 159³⁴, 168¹, 171¹, 180, 198, 201, 204³, 205, 207, 242, 298, 315, 370¹, 483, 487, 618, Gl s.vv. *damnatio memoriae*; *Lex Iulia de maiestate*. See also *laesa maiestas*
treasure or treasure-trove, 59, 223, 521
treasury or treasurer:
diocesan, 43 (II)
ecclesiastical, 4⁴, 618, 634
imperial, 4, 46, 59, 110⁴, 307, 321 (I), 337, 341², 343 395, 399, 424³, 426³, 435, 567, 575, 576, 600, 633, App¹⁴, Gl s.vv. Caesarian, count of the sacred treasury, fisc, largesses. See also fisc; officials of, 110; slaves of, 46
military, 474²
municipal, 257, 597, Gl s.v. treasury (public)
public, 536, 572, 592⁴, 629, Gl and therein s.vv. catholicus, fisc
treaty, 646¹

SUBJECTS 1341

tree. See lumber; phenomena, natural; wood
trespass, 478^{11}. See also entry, forcible
trial, court, 1–3, 21, 22, 27^2, 28, 37, 42^{1n}, 62, 65, 95, 96, 99, 111, 119^1, 144–6, 150, 152, 159, 161, $164^{1n,2}$, 169, 185, 190, 197, 203, 204^3, 209, 215, $220^{2,3}$, 225, 242, 254^{1n}, 271, 274, 278, 288, 296^{1n}, 299^2, 302, 308^7, 309, 310, 318, 325, 326, 333, 334^5, 347, 349, 357, 364, 365, 374, 382, 399, 401, 421, 430, 440^5, 476–8, 484, 491, 506^5, 509, 528, 598, 603–5, 607, 611, 619, $625^{1n,14}$, 638^9, 640 (II), App 7. See also investigation, judicial; juror; lawsuit
tribe, 523^1, Gl s.v. Assembly (Tribal)
tribunal, divine, 561
 papal, 440^5, 442
tribune, 163^7, 324^{1n}, 328, 329^8, 352, 412, 441, 454, 547^6, 563, Gl s.v. tribune and notary
 military, 11^{1n}, 492^1, App 10 (e)^{34}, Gl
 plebeian, 548, Gl and therein s.vv. Lex Aquilia, Lex Cincia, Lex Falcidia Lex Plaetoria, Lex Voconia, Tribunician Power
 preatorian, 447, 453
Tribunician Power, 3, 7, 476^4, 548, Gl and therein s.v. tribune (plebeian)
tribute, In, 8, 106^5, 148, 464^1, 632^3, Gl s.v. canon
 public, 6, 32^9
tributary, 646 (I)
Tricennalia, 73^{1n}
Trinitarianism, 422^7, 641^{1n}
Trisagion, 470^4, 553^4, 651^{20}
triumph, 341^2, 472^4, 475, 523^5
trophy, 38^1, 49 (II)
trust, 218^7, 225, 348, 488, 507, 510, 513, 575, 595^6, 604, 607, 612, 615, 626, 640 (I, II). See also trusteeship or trustee
trusteeship or trustee, 150^1, 510^2, 612. See also trust
truth, 1^2, 20, 22, 24, 40, 44, 47, 49 (I, II), 50, 52–4, 61 (I), 65, 67–9, 73, 75, 98, 99, 103, 116, 122, 125, 167^{1n}, 169^2, 172, 204, 322, 324, 325, 326, 328, 350, 360, 365, 395, 401, 402, 405, 414, 415 (II) 419^1, 422^6, 442^7, 459, 464, 469, 472 (I), 475–7, 481, 483–7, 507, 524 (I), 527, 544, 546, 548, 554, 559, 569, 583, 592, 598^{10}, 605, 615, 618, 636, 637, 646 (I), 651, App^1, Gl s.v. Mithras. See also error; falsehood or falsity
tunic. See apparel
tutor, 149, 608, 619, $621^{1,3,5,6,8}$, 627, 628, Gl s.v. guardian. See also curator; guardianship or guardian
Twelve Chapters of Cyril, $411^{1n,1}$, 527, 542
tyranny or tyrant, 8^{1n}, 13, 14, 46, 49 (II), 50, 111, 117, 387, 519^5, 526, 646 (II), App 10 (e), (f)

Unam sanctam, In^{31}
unchastity, 493, 517^4, 649^9. See also chastity; debauchery, sexual
uncle, 214^3, 549^{1n}, 550^{1n}, 552^2, 555^{1n}, 561^{1n}, 562^{12}, 568^{1n}, 575^1, 579
uncle-in-law, 526^2
union, labour, Gl s.v. guild
unit, military, 584, 585^{1n}, 646^{22}
Unitarianism, Gl s.vv. Arians, Caelicolans, Monarchians, Photinians
unity, ecclesiastical, In, $4^{30,43}$, 17–19, 21, 24, 39, 44, 47, 48 (I), 49, 50, 52, 53, 59, 61, 67–71, 73, 75, 85, 86, 93, 98, 99, 104, 112^{1n}, 120^2, 137, 138, 140, 141^{1n}, 142, 143^{1n}, 152, 153, 159, 164, 166, 167, 168^{1n}, 172, 173, 182, 288, 292, 294, 295, 324, 325, 328, 350, 353–5, 368, 371, 373, 375^7, 397, 398, 401, 402, 406, 408, 409, 411, 412, 414–16, 418–20, 427, 442, 449, 453–5, 457, 460–4, 466–9, 470 (II, VI), 471, 472 (I), 475, 476, 483, 486, 495, 524 (I), 527, 542, 544–54, 556–8, 560–4, 637, 645
unlucky days, 65^6
Ursinians, $137^{1n,3}$, $138^{1n,3}$, 140, 141^{1n}, 142^{1n}, 143^{1n}, 152^{1n}, 153^{1n}
usucapion, 443^4, 641 (II), Gl s.v. iusta causa
usufruct or usufructuary, 435^4, 496^{1n}, 497, 510, $602^{1n,1}$, 638, 641 (I)^{30}
usurpation of undue rank, 103, 168^1, 196
usurper, Tab^1, 387, 495^3, 526^3
uxoricide, 52^{13}

vagrant, 528^5
Valentinians, 40, 395, Gl
Vatican Church-State, Tab^5
vegetarianism, Gl s.v. Manichaeans. See also food or drink
veil. See apparel
venality, 497, 508, 519. See also bribery or bribe
veneration, 7, 9, 24, 38, 46^{21}, 48 (III), 82, 93, 192, 206, 211, 288, 375 (II), 400, 413, 480, 496, 577^{13}, 645
vengeance, 5, 39, 59, 86, 167, 195, 290, 310, 320, 325, 333, 334, 469, 484, 496, 600
Venite, 651^{20}
vessel, sacred, 17^4, 68, 119^5, 537, 598
Vestal, In^{26}, 126^6, 399^{11}, 621^3, Gl s.vv. guardian, Lex Voconia, lictor, patria potestas, pontifex maximus, virgin (Vestal). See also virginity or virgin
vestment. See apparel
vicar:
 diocesan, 12, 76^6, 95^{41}, 106, 168^1, 172^6,

180, 198, 234, 272, 294^2, 337, 443^{19}, 489^{12}, 586^2, 638, Gl; of Africa, 15^{12}, 19^{1n}, 21, 24, 26, 28^{1n,3}, 250, 275, 276, 324^{12}, 646^{16}, 651; of Asia, 163; of Britain, 52^{47}; of Egypt, Gl s.v. prefect (Augustal); of Illyricum, 651; of Italy, 162^1; of Macedonia, 169; of Pontus, 191; of the East, 45^{14}, 54^{28}, 56^1, 63^5, Gl s.v. count of the East
papal, 375^{1n}, 387^9
urban: of Constantinople, Gl s.v. vicar (urban); of Rome, 142^2, 143^{1,5}, 152, 153, 164, 200^{1n}, Gl s.v. vicar (urban). *See also* ex-vicar; of master of the soldiery, 415 (I), 417, 418^{1n}, 420^{1n}
vicariate = diocese, 20^{15}
vice, 44, 69, 154^{1n}, 177^{1n}, 246^1, 307, 330^{1n}, 359, 361, 362, 496, 519. *See also* virtue
Vicennalia, App 10 (c)
viceroy, 544^{1n}, 548^8
villa, 194, 239, 422^{18}. *See also* manor
village, 78^3, 117, 232, 270, 314, 345, 507, 530, 568^{1n}, 589, 615, 619, App 7, Gl s.vv. bishop, itinerant bishop
vinegar. *See* food *or* drink
vineyard, 107^3, 472^{24}
viniculture, 34, 107^3. *See also* agriculture; farm *or* farmer; vineyard; wine
violence, 24, 220^2, 289, 310, 382, 443, 478^{11}, 485^{1n}, 593^2, 646 (I), 649, 650, Gl s.v. *Lex Licinia de sodaliciis*. *See also* assault
virginity *or* virgin, 31^{1n}, 92, 117^7, 149^1, 157, 180, 247, 330^{1n}, 372, 463^{1n}, 484, 488, 496, 604, 614, 629, 638, Gl. *See also* celibacy *or* celibate; chastity; continence; nun; Vestal
introduced virgin, Gl s.v. virgin (introduced)
marriage proposed to virgin, 126, 496
rape of virgin, 92, 126, 180, 201^5, 372, 496, 638
virtue, 44, 46^{21}, 49 (II), 50, 77, 108, 126^6, 154^{1n}, 330^{1n}, 361^3, 411 (II), 472 (I), 479, 496, 519, 579. *See also* vice
virus, 163, 350
vote, 61^7, 73^{17}, 95, 95^{43}, 111, 133^1, 137^{1n}, 205, 324^7, 401, 402^{1n}, 448^4, 451^{1n}, 463, 470 (V, VI, VIII, XI), 483, 508, 520, 523^1, 540, 579, 605, 614, App^{23}, Gl s.vv. Assembly, *Lex Caecilia et Didia, Lex Licinia de sodaliciis*

wage, 301^7, 646^{29}
walls, civic, 641^2
construction *or* repair of, 513, 538^2, 606
war, In^{9,26}, 9, 19^{22}, 41^5, 42^6, 43, 44, 46, 47, 49 (II), 50^7, 67, 105^{11} 107^{11}, 122^{9,11}, 127^7, 159, 225^{13}, 272^{10}, 308, 324, 341^2, 364, 400, 434^6, 442, 457, 479^6, 483, 484, 486, 487, 527, 614^{7,10}, 616^5, 617, 639, 642, 644^6, 646^{1,25}, App 10 (d), Gl s.vv. Mithras, slave (public). *See also* barbarians; invasion
Social, Gl s.v. as
Trojan, 614^{10}
ward, 31^4, 65^6, 149, 150, 516, 619, 621^{1n,8}, Gl s.v. guardian. *See also* child; guardianship *or* guardian; infant; minor
warranty, 515
water. *See* food *or* drink; phenomena, natural
weapon, 42, 44, 67, 94^3, 123, 159^{27}, 214^5, 400, 413, 417^8, 457, 476^{39}, 484, 496, 527^{10}, 562, 590, 617, 639, App 10 (f), Gl s.v. praetor
weekday, 52^3, 586
Monday, 17^3
Wednesday, 586^{1n}
Friday, 586^{1n,4}
Saturday, 23^4
weights and measures, Gl s.v. aedile
Whitsunday. *See* Pentecost
widow, 92, 117^7, 149, 150, 187^{1n}, 225, 227, 435^3, 442^1, 488, 496, 635^2, 638, Gl s.vv. *Lex Furia*, Novatians. *See also* widower
proposal of marriage to, 126
rape of, 92, 126, 638
widower, 187^{1n}, Gl s.v. Novatians. *See also* widow
wife, 31, 121, 122^4, 187, 214, 215, 225^{13}, 319^4, 329, 398, 435^3, 463^{1n}, 484, 485^{1n}, 487^{1n}, 525, 575, 596^2, 600, 620, 629, 641^8, 652, App 10 (f)^{36}. *See also* bride; husband; matron
of clergyman, 32, 102, 150^2, 372, 421, 613^4, 620
will, divine, In^{21}, 52, 53, 59, 61 (II), 85, 164, 167, 350, 469
will *or* testament, 26^1, 28^1, 35, 36, 117, 149^4, 150, 175, 176, 185, 187^{1n}, 189, 190, 204^5, 218, 219, 225, 230, 246, 249, 252, 259, 277, 289, 298, 321 (I), 337, 343, 391, 392, 395, 421, 480, 488, 489, 496^{12}, 499^{1n}, 507, 510, 514, 525, 565, 570, 572, 574, 575, 579, 583, 585^3, 595, 599, 607, 608, 612^2, 615, 622, 623^3, 624, 626, 628, 642^{12}, 652, Gl s.vv. guardian, *Lex Fufia et Caninia, Lex Leoniana, Lex Voconia*, master of the census. *See also* codicil; disherison; fideicommissary; intestacy; testation, right of; testator; trust
will *or* testament:
invalid, 150, 175, 218^4, 219, 225, 298, 391, 392, 496^{12}, 570, 623^3, 624^4, Gl s.v. *damnatio memoriae*

SUBJECTS

unduteous, 624⁴
wind. *See* phenomena, natural
wine. *See* food *or* drink
wineskin, Gl s.v. Ascodrogitans
witchcraft, 334²⁵. *See also* incantation; sorcery *or* sorcerer
witness *or* testimony, 26 35, 37¹, 44⁹, 47, 50, 67, 95, 164, 178, 204, 206⁶, 218⁴, 230, 285², 324⁷, 331, 354, 402, 403, 454⁴, 456, 479, 523¹, 537¹², 555, 559, 561, 577¹³, 614, 622, 626³, 627, 632, 639, 646⁹, 651, App 2
woman, childless, 31
   consecrated to God, 31¹ⁿ, 92, 126⁶, 247, 372, 485, 488, 496, 638. *See also* nun; virginity *or* virgin
   debarment from church for shorn hair, 215; from pleading lawsuit, 619⁵
   episcopal instruction to, 41¹
   extraneous, 372
   tutorship of, 621³
   as municipal senator, 157¹ⁿ
   as proprietor. *See* property, ownership of, by deaconess, by remarried widow, by widow
   as tenant farmer, 497
   as weaver, 80
womb, 546
wood, 301⁷, 439³. *See also* lumber; tree
   transporter of, Gl s.v. guild
   worker in, 133¹
wool, 520⁶, 551¹⁴
work, new, announcement of, 641³⁰
workman, 585. *See also* artisan
worship. *See* ceremony, religious; rite
   Catholic, 292, 299, 310. *See also* religion
   Christian, 1², 3, 4, 6–8, 14, 16, 18–20, 24, 29, 34⁴,⁵, 38¹ⁿ, 44, 46, 47, 52, 53, 59, 63, 67, 67³⁵, 75⁴², 86, 109, 124, 142, 159, 174, 193, 206⁷, 212¹, 214⁶, 224, 233, 236³, 243, 263³, 307, 310, 315, 323⁵, 324, 327, 333, 339, 355–8, 385, 386, 397¹ⁿ, 400, 411 (III), 429, 449, 455, 475, 480, 496, 512, 527, 554, 560, 567, 579, 600, 628, 633², App 10 (f), Gl s.vv. Caelicolans, chanter, lector, Tascodrogitans. *See also* cult, Christian; observance, Christian; religion; services, divine
   Jewish, 91, 190, 199, 214⁶, 303, 315¹, 332, 346¹ⁿ, Gl s.v. Caelicolans
   pagan, In²⁶, 1⁴, 3, 5–9, 12, 14, 34⁴, 41², 43 (II), 44, 45¹, 63, 95³⁴, 98¹⁵, 111, 117, 119, 124, 127⁷, 159¹⁶, 189, 190, 208, 220¹⁰,¹¹, 223², 231, 242, 259, 301, 340, 386³, 400, 424, 429, 489, 583, 598¹³, 602⁵, 641¹ⁿ, 651⁸,¹³, App 7, 8 (a), 10 (f)⁴¹, Gl s.vv. guild, Mithras, pontifex maximus, quindecimvir, virgin (Vestal). *See also* cult, foreign, imperial; deity *or* divinity, pagan; idolatry *or* idol; polytheism; rites, pagan
   freedom of, 3, 4, 7, 8, 12, 12², 13, 14, 44, 117, 123, 124 (III), 142, 159¹⁶, 166¹, 167¹¹, 215, 303, 333, 559
   regulation of In⁴⁴, 12, 24, 52, 166, 382¹ⁿ, 560, 579

Zealots, 159³⁴
Zoroastrians, Gl s.v. Manichaean

BIBLICAL QUOTATIONS AND ALLUSIONS

OLD TESTAMENT

Genesis
2. 2–3, **34⁵**; 2. 15–17, 3. 1–6, **350²⁶**; 4. 1–8, **159³⁴**; 13. 18, 14. 13, **63³**; 14. 14, **53¹²**; 17. 9–14, **76⁴**; 17. 23, **53¹²**; 18. 1–19, **63⁸**; 18. 1–22, **63⁴**; 20. 3, **223²**; 28. 22, **644⁶**; 29. 34, **399³**; 31. 24, **223²**

Exodus
3. 16, 18, **23²**; 7—12, App¹; 8. 1–15, Gl s.v. Batrachitans; 13. 19, **206⁶**; 15. 1–19, **651²⁰**; 19. 6, **16⁴**; 20. 8–11, **34⁵**; 22. 22, **516¹**; 28. 41, 29. 7, 21, 29, 30. 30, **651¹⁶**; 31. 12–17, 32. 1, 23, **34⁵**; 34. 16, **214²**; 35. 1–3, **34⁵**; 40. 13, 15, **651¹⁶**

Leviticus
4. 3, 6. 20, 22, 8. 12, 10. 7, 16. 32, **651¹⁶**; 19. 30, **34⁵**; 21. 10, **651¹⁶**; 23. 1–3, 26. 2, **34⁵**

Numbers
1. 47–54, **399³**; 3. 3, **651¹⁶**; 5. 9–10, **537¹⁶**; 11. 16, 24, 25, **23²**; 12. 6, **223²**; 13. 9–34, **241²**; 18. 8–19, **537¹⁶**; 18. 21, **644⁶**; 19. 11–22, **206⁶**; 35. 6, 9–34, **241²**; 35. 6, 11–15, 25–9, 32, **400⁹**; 35. 25, **651¹⁶**

Deuteronomy
5. 12–15, **34⁵**; 7. 3–4, **214²**; 14. 22–6, 14. 28–9, **644⁶**; 17. 6, **65¹³**; 18. 1–8, **537¹⁶**; 19. 12, **23²**; 19. 15, **65¹³**; 24. 16, **328³**; 32. 1–43, **651²⁰**; 21. 10–13, **225¹³**

Joshua
20. **241²**; 24. 32, **206⁶**

Judges
3. 5–7, **214²**; 5, **651²⁰**; 8. 19, **543¹⁰**; 17. 7–13, 18. 3–6, 14–22, **399³**

Ruth
3. 13, **543¹⁰**

1 Samuel
2. 1–10, **651²⁰**; 10. 24, **472⁴**; 14. 39, **543¹⁰**

1 Kings
1. 34, 39, **472⁴**; 2. 27, 2. 35, In⁴⁴; 3. 5, **223²**; 5—6, In⁴; 11. 1–8, 11. 2, 16. 31, **214²**

2 Kings
1. 34, 39, **472⁴**; 2. 27, 2. 35, In⁴⁴; 3. 5, **223²**; 5—6, In⁴⁴; 11. 1–8, 11. 2, 16. 31, **214²** 12. 4–16, In⁴⁴; 13. 21, **206⁶**; 14. 6, **328³**; 16. 10–16, In⁴⁴; 18. 5, In²³; 22. 3–6, In⁴⁴

1 Chronicles
16. 4–6, 37–41, 23. 24—26. 12, 28. 11—29.5, In⁴⁴; 29. 14, **644⁶**

2 Chronicles
2. 1—5. 1, 8. 14–15, In⁴⁴; 19. 5–7, **605¹³**; 24. 20–2, **159³⁴**; 25. 4, **328³**; 26. 16–21, **95³⁴**; 36. 23, In²³

Ezra
1. 2, In²³; 6. 14, **159³⁴**; 9. 12, **214²**; 10. 8, **173¹⁰**

Nehemiah
10. 29–30, 13. 23–9, **214²**

Esther 303⁴
Esther
3. 1–6, **95³⁴**; 3. 7, 13, **303¹**; 4. 14, In²²; 7. 10, **303³**; 8. 9, 12, 9. 17–32, **303¹**

Job
3. 17, **475⁸**; 21. 14, **645³²**

Psalms 651²⁰
Psalms
1. 1, **651¹³**; 2. 10–11, In²³; 22. 10, **546¹¹**; 25. 6–12, **67⁸⁵**; 28. 3, **645³⁷**; 41. 1, **520⁷**; 45. 7, **95⁶²**; 82. 1, 6, **49³,⁸**; 91. 10, **543¹¹**; 91. 11–12, **543⁷**; 95, **651²⁰**; 96. 11, 98. 8, **645²⁷**; 110. 4, In³¹; 115. 5, **69⁵**; 116. 15, **206⁵**; 135. 16, **69⁵**

Proverbs
7. 2, **645²⁹**; 8. 15, **645⁴**; 8. 22ff., **47²⁵**; 10. 19, **465³**; 16. 10, **645⁵**; 19. 17, **520⁷**; 20. 8, **645⁷**; 21. 1, **645⁶**

Ecclesiastes
3. 1–8, **385¹⁰**; 3. 7, **545¹**; 7. 26, **315¹²**; 8. 8, Gl s.v. Mithras

Song of Solomon 651²⁰

1344

BIBLICAL QUOTATIONS AND ALLUSIONS

Isaiah
9. 2, **475**[2]; 12, **651**[20]; 23. 8, **9**[7]; 26. 1–19, **651**[20]; 28. 12, **475**[3]; 28. 15, **645**[31]; 30. 15, **645**[40]; 32. 4, **645**[37]; 40. 3, In[52]; 44. 23, 45. 8, **645**[27]; 50. 11, **645**[38]; 55. 7, **645**[40]; 55. 12, **645**[27]

Jeremiah
1. 10, In[31]; 4. 22, **67**[3]; 5. 21, **69**[5]; 6. 1, 13. 20, **468**[7]; 22. 1–9, **483**[15]

Ezekiel
12. 2, **69**[5]; 18. 19–20, **328**[3]; 18. 23, 33. 11, **645**[40]; 38—9, **67**[28]

Daniel
2. 34–6; 2. 37, In[23]; 3. 1–18, **95**[34]; 3. 52–6, 51–90, **651**; 5. 18, In[23]; 6. 4–17, **95**[34]; 6. 8, 12, 15, **95**[43]; 3. 52–6, 57–90, **651**[29]; 11. 43. **67**[28]

Joel
2. 11, **603**[2]; 2. 12–13, **645**[40]; 2. 28, **223**[2]; 2. 31, **603**[2]

Jonah
2. 2–9, **651**[20]

Habakkuk
3. 2–16, **651**[20]

Zechariah
1. 1, **159**[34]

Malachi
4.2, **220**[10]

APOCRYPHA

Tobit
3. 8, 17, **159**[37]; 4. 7–9, **520**[7]; 4. 12–13, **214**[2]

Judith
16. 2–17, **651**[20]

Wisdom
3. 1–4, **443**[9]; 6. 1–3, In[23]; 15. 4, **645**[33]

Ecclesiasticus
26.29, **478**[23]; 44. 9, **479**[7]; 48, 13–14, **206**[6]

Song of the Three Holy Children
29–34, 35–68, **651**[20]

2 Maccabees
7, **95**[34]

NEW TESTAMENT

Matthew
Matthew **114**
2. 12, 22, 2. 13, 2. 19, **223**[2]; 3. 3, In[52]; 4. 1–2, **169**[3]; 4. 6, **543**[7]; 4. 16, **475**[2]; 5. 15, **543**[8]; 5. 16, **520**[7]; 5. 33–6, 5. 34–7, **255**[3]; 5. 35, **159**[5]; 6. 12, **49**[15]; 6. 14, **49**[7]; 7. 1–2, **605**[11]; 7. 1–5, **614**[13]; 7. 5, **7**[13]; 7. 14, **482**[7]; 7. 15, **382**[1]; 7. 21–2, **67**[4]; 8. 5–13, In[14]; 8. 28–34, **148**[4]; 9. 21, **206**[6]; 10. 22, **12**[33]; 10. 24, **484**[12]; 10. 32, **7**[22]; **457**[8]; 11. 19, **457**[13]; 11. 27, **67**[18]; 12. 30, **315**[6]; 12. 35, **59**[5]; 13. 11, **75**[42]; 13. 24–30, 36–40, **524**[24]; 14. 36, **206**[6]; 15. 22–8, **457**[15]; 16. 16, **475**[6]; 16. 17, **7**[2]; 16. 18, In[21,25,43]; **167**[5]; **545**[3]; 16. 19, **173**[11]; 18. 15–17, **17**[3]; 18. 15–18, **173**[11]; 18. 15–35, **49**[5]; 18. 16, **65**[13]; 19. 16–26, **127**[5]; 19. 21, **123**[8]; **411**[3]; 19. 23–4, **123**[9]; 21. 1–11, **543**[14]; 21. 9, **472**[4]; 21. 11, **112**[4]; 21. 31, **457**[14]; 22. 15–22, In[23]; 22. 21, In[32]; **62**[11]; **159**[12]; 23. 35, **159**[34]; 24. 5, **7**[14]; 24. 9, **12**[33]; 24. 11, 24, **7**[14]; **382**[1]; 25. 11, **67**[4]; 25. 36, **370**[1]; 26. 17–19, **75**[42]; 26. 24, **457**[11]; 26. 29, **23**[2]; 27. 11–25, **159**[32]; 27. 19, **159**[27]; 27. 24, **67**[35]; **99**[2]; **159**[27,32]; 27. 38–44, **457**[12]; 27. 54, In[14]; 28. 18–20, In[31]; 28. 19, In[36]; **158**[4], In[36]

Mark
1. 3, **62**[48]; 1. 12–13, **169**[3]; 1. 24, **75**[23]; 3. 17, **577**[10]; 4. 10, **645**[39]; 4. 11, **75**[42]; 4. 24, **605**[11]; 5. 1–17, **148**[4]; 7. 25–30, **457**[15]; 8. 18, **69**[5]; 9. 40, **315**[6]; 10. 17–27, **127**[5]; 11. 1–11, **543**[14]; 11. 10, **472**[4]; 11. 24–6, **49**[11]; 12. 13–17, In[23]; 12. 17, In[33]; **62**[11]; **159**[12]; 13. 6, **7**[13]; 13. 13, **12**[33]; 13. 22, **7**[13]; **382**[1]; 14. 12–25, **75**[42]; 14. 21, **457**[11]; 14. 70, **112**[4]; 15. 1–15, **159**[32]; 15. 27, 32, **457**[12]; 16. 15[36], In[36]

Luke
Luke **114**
1. 5–25, 39–45, 57–66, **159**[34]; 1. 26–38, **546**[3]; 1. 46–55, **651**[20]; 1. 48, **497**[3]; 1. 68–79, 2. 29–32, **651**[20]; 3. 4, In[52]; 4. 1–2, **169**[3]; 4. 10–11, **543**[7]; 4. 34, **75**[23]; 6. 22, **173**[10]; 6. 37, **49**[7]; 6. 37–8, **605**[11]; 6. 45, **59**[5]; 6. 46, **67**[4]; 7. 2–10, In[14]; 7. 27–9, 7. 34, **457**[13]; 8. 10, **75**[42]; 8. 26–37, **148**[4]; 9. 50, **315**[6]; 10. 22, **67**[18]; 11. 4, **49**[15]; 11. 23, **315**[6]; 11. 49, 11. 51, **159**[34]; 12. 8, **7**[20]; 12. 48, In[43]; 13. 25, **67**[4]; 15. 11–32, **645**[40]; 17. 3–4, **49**[5]; 17. 5, **103**[13]; 18. 18–27, **127**[5]; 19. 8, **520**[7]; 19. 28–40, **543**[14]; 19. 37–8, **472**[4]; 20. 20–6, In[23]; 20. 25, In[32]; **62**[11]; **159**[12]; 21. 8, **7**[13]; 21. 12, 17, **12**[33]; 22. 7–20, **75**[42]; 22. 28, In[31]; 22. 32, **167**[1n]; 22. 53,

44²⁶; 22. 59, 112⁴; 23. 1-7, 12-25, 159³²; 23. 46, 443⁹; 23. 47, In¹⁴; 24. 47, In³⁶; 27. 39-43, 447¹²

John
John 577⁸
1. 1-2, 167⁶; 1. 14, 159⁵⁰; 484¹⁶, 1. 23, In⁵²; 1. 40-41, 181⁵; 3. 19-21, 443¹⁴; 4. 7-30, 457¹⁴; 5. 18, 167⁶; 5. 23, 36, 37, 6. 44, 57, 542³³; 7. 41, 52, 112⁴; 8. 16, 18, 542³³; 9. 22, 34, 173¹⁰; 10. 11-16, 167¹ⁿ; 10. 16, In⁴³, 52³⁷, 645³⁶; 10. 26-7, 645³⁹; 10. 33, 167⁶; 10. 36, 542³³; 11. 25-6, 443⁹; 11. 41, 42, 542³³; 12. 12-13, 472⁴; 12. 12-19, 543¹⁴; 12. 42, 173¹⁰; 12. 48, 49¹²; 12. 49, 542³³; 13. 23, 574⁶,⁷; 13. 34, 159¹⁵; 14. 6, 95⁴³; 14. 16-17, 26, 156¹; 14. 24, 542³³; 14. 27, 546²¹; 15. 12, 15, 17, 159¹⁵; 15. 26, 156¹; 16. 2, 173¹⁰; 16. 7-11, 156¹; 17. 6-26, 167⁵; 17. 20-2, 167¹ⁿ; 17. 20-23, 52³⁷; 17. 21, 23, 25, 542³³; 18. 28—16, 159³²; 18. 36, In³¹; 19. 11, In²³; 19. 15, 52⁵¹; 19. 26, 577⁶,¹¹; 19. 37, 546¹²; 20. 2, 577⁶; 20. 21, 542³³; 21. 7, 577⁶; 21. 15-17, 167¹ⁿ; 561¹⁸; 21. 17, 645²; 21. 20, 577⁶,⁷

Acts
1. 8, In³⁶; 1. 15-26, 17³; 470⁶⁶; 579⁷; 1. 23-6, 543¹⁶; 1. 24, 651¹⁶; 1. 26, 614¹⁰; 2. 7, 112⁴; 3. 14-15, 546⁶; 4. 5-15, 23²; 4. 32-5, 515³; 5. 15, 206⁶; 5. 29, In³¹; 6. 1, 92¹; 6. 1-6, 17³; 515³; 6. 1-7, 470⁶⁶; 6. 4, 579⁴; 6. 5—7. 60, 566²; 6. 6, 651¹⁶; 7. 40, 34⁵; 8. 2, 577¹³; 8. 9-24, 422⁷; 8. 18-21, 519¹; 9. 1-2, 270²; 9. 15, 167²; 9. 39, 92¹; 10. 1-8, 17-48, In¹⁴; 11. 26, 103²; 112⁴; 13. 3, 651¹⁶; 13. 47, In³⁶; 15. 6-29, 17³; 470⁶⁶; 15. 20, 116¹³; 15. 22-31, 270²; 15. 23, 41⁴; 15. 29, 41⁴; 116¹³; 18. 3, 103⁷; 18. 12-17, In²⁷; 1⁴; 19. 12, 206⁸; 19. 19, 382²; 19. 23-41, 73⁷; 470⁵³; 20. 7, 34⁴; 20. 28, 167⁷; 20. 28-31, 382²; 20. 35, 520⁷; 21. 3, 9⁴; 21. 17-25, 470⁶⁶; 21. 19, 167²; 21. 31-3, App³⁴; 21. 39, 103⁷; 414⁶; 22. 5, 270³; 22. 21, 167²; 22. 28, 337⁶; 24. 5, 24. 14, 7¹³; 25. 9-12, 5¹; 25. 16, 1⁶; 26. 5, 7¹³; 28. 16-31, 167²; 28. 21, 270³

Romans
Romans 167²
1. 25, 44²⁰; 2. 1-3, 605¹¹; 2. 14, 44²⁰; 2. 16, 49¹⁸; 2. 17, 44¹⁹; 5. 12—6. 23, 350²⁹; 6. 3-4, 166⁴; 11. 13, 167²; 11. 21, 24, 44²⁰; 12. 1-5, In²⁰; 12. 4-5, 53¹⁷; 12. 5, In⁴³; 12. 18, 73⁶; 12. 19, 39⁷; 59⁹; 13. 1, In³¹; 13. 1-7, In²³; 159²¹; 13. 8, 159¹⁵; 14. 13, 49¹⁴; 15. 5, In⁴³; 15. 16, 167²; 16. 9, 181⁵; 16. 25, 75⁴²

1 Corinthians
1. 10, In⁴³; 2, 4. 1, 75⁴²; 4. 14, 620²; 5. 1-7, 173¹¹; 5. 5, 203¹; 5. 11, 382¹; 6. 1, 62¹¹; 6. 1-8, 17³; 6. 2-3, 614¹³; 6. 5, 53¹⁶; 7. 1, 2, 7-9, 34, 38, 496¹⁰; 7. 8, 9, 25, 34, 92¹; 7. 10, 27, 39, 372¹⁷; 7. 12, 16, 214²; 7. 14, 16, 372¹⁸; 7. 32-3, 579¹⁴; 7. 34, 496¹⁷; 8. 1, 8. 4, 41⁴; 8. 5, 148⁴; 8. 7-13, 8. 10, 41⁴; 9. 5, 372¹; 9. 7-14, 537¹⁶; 9. 13, 41⁴; 9. 13-14, 644⁶; 10. 20, 10. 20-1, 41⁴; 10. 21, 651¹³; 10. 25, 10. 25-7, 10. 28-33, 41⁴; 11. 3-15, 225¹²; 11. 19, 7¹³; 11. 20, 11. 23-9, 75⁴²; 12. 12-27, 53¹⁶; In⁴³; 12. 12, 20, 562¹⁸; 12. 13, In³⁷; 14. 10, 465³; 15, 75⁴²; 15. 12, 7¹³; 15. 22, 350²⁹; 15. 50, 7²⁰; 15. 53, 443⁹; 16. 2, 127⁵; 16. 22, 173¹¹

2 Corinthians
2. 5-11, 173¹¹; 3. 1, 270³; 3. 3, 645²⁸; 3. 6, In²¹; 5. 1, In²⁹; 6. 9, 193¹; 6. 14-18, 214²; 6. 15, 158⁴; 6. 16, 212¹; 9. 6-7, 127⁵; 520⁷; 11. 28, 450¹; 13. 11, In⁴³; 13. 14, 645⁴⁵

Galatians
Galatians 167²; 484; 486.
1. 7-9, 382¹; 1. 8-9, 173¹⁰; 1. 16, 7²¹; 1. 19, 487¹⁴; 2. 2, 167²; 2. 20, 159²⁸; 3. 28, In²⁸; 225¹³; 4. 4, 546¹⁰; 569³; 4. 8, 484¹³; 486¹³; 5. 20, 7¹³; 6. 6, 189²; 644⁶; 6. 10, 127⁵; 167¹ⁿ; 515³; 520⁷

Ephesians
Ephesians 167²
1. 4, 569⁴; 1. 10, In⁴³; 2. 2, 1³; 2. 19-22, 167⁵; 3. 8, 167²; 4. 3-6, In⁴³; 4. 14, 167¹ⁿ; 4. 25, 53¹⁶; 4. 27, 418⁵; 5. 16, 62²; 5. 25-7, 75⁵³; 5. 27, 645⁷; 5. 30, 53¹⁶; 562¹⁷; 5. 32, 75⁴²; 6. 11-18, 159¹⁸; 6. 12, In¹⁸; 1³; 7²¹

Philippians
Philippians 167²
1. 27, 2. 2, In⁴³; 2. 6, 167⁶; 2. 7-8, 546⁵; 2. 8, 457¹⁷; 546⁷; 4. 22, In¹³; App¹⁴

Colossians
Colossians 167²
1. 10, 103¹³; 1. 13, 44²⁶; 1. 17, 569⁴; 1. 26-7, 75⁴²; 2. 8, 382¹; 2. 9, 67²⁰; 2. 18, 7¹³; 3. 11, In²⁸; 3. 14-15, In⁴³; 4. 5, 62²

1 Thessalonians
4. 1-8, In²¹; 4. 9, 159¹⁵

2 Thessalonians
2. 2, 569³; 2. 3-12, 159³⁷; 3. 6, 382¹

BIBLICAL QUOTATIONS AND ALLUSIONS 1347

1 Timothy
1. 3, **523**¹; **577**¹⁵; 1. 4, **7**¹³; 1. 19–20, **173**¹¹; 2. 1–3, **1**⁴; 2. 7, **167**²; 3. 1–7, **61**¹²; **519**¹⁹; **579**²; 3. 2, **445**¹⁴; 3. 2–7, **361**³; 3. 2, 4, 5, **579**¹³; 3. 3, **571**¹²; 3. 4, **32**⁹; 4. 1, 4. 2, 4. 7, **7**¹³; 4. 14, **651**¹⁶; 5. 3–16, **92**¹; 5. 9, **225**²; 5. 14–15, **651**¹³; 6. 3–5, **476**²⁴; 6. 5, **7**¹³; 6. 15, In³¹; 6. 17–19, **520**⁷; 6. 20, **7**¹³; **382**¹

2 Timothy
2 Timothy **167**².
1. 6, **523**¹; **651**¹⁶; 1. 10, **443**⁹; 1. 11, **167**²; 1. 18, **577**¹⁵; 2. 15–17, **382**¹; 2. 16, **7**¹³; 2. 17–18, **173**¹¹; 2. 18, **7**¹³; 3. 6, **150**¹; 4. 12, **577**¹⁵

Titus
1 1, **359**⁸; 1. 4–5, **523**¹; 1. 6, **445**¹⁴; **579**¹³; 1. 6–9, **579**²; 1. 7, **579**¹²; 1. 7–9, **361**³; 1. 9, **382**¹; 3. 1, **159**²¹; 3. 5, **116**¹⁴; **527**⁵⁶; 3. 10, **173**¹¹; **645**¹⁰

Philemon **167**²

Hebrews
1. 1–5, **167**⁶; 1. 2, **546**¹⁰; **569**³; 1. 9, **95**⁶²; 2. 10, Gl s.v. Mithras; 2. 14, **7**²²; 4. 16, **206**⁶; 5. 6, 5. 10, 6. 20, 7. 1, 7. 11, 15, 7. 17, 21, In³¹; 10. 31, **603**²; 11. 4, **193**¹; 11. 10, 11. 16, In²⁹; 11. 38, 12. 4, **206**⁶; 12. 22, In²⁹; 13. 8, In²¹; 13. 16, **520**⁷; 13, 20–1, In²¹

James
1. 27, **516**¹; 2. 6, **605**¹⁰; 5. 12, **255**³

1 Peter
1. 20, **569**⁴; 2. 8, **543**⁸; 2. 9, **164**; 2. 13–17, In²³; 2. 13, 17, **159**²¹; 3. 18–20, **569**⁵; 4. 1, **561**⁷; **562**¹⁶; 5. 8, **651**¹³; 5. 13, **53**²

2 Peter
1. 16, 2. 1, **7**¹³

1 John
2. 15–17, In²¹; 2. 18, 2. 22, **7**¹³; 3. 11–24, **159**¹⁶; 3. 17, **127**⁸; **520**⁷; 3. 22, **481**¹⁴; 4. 1, 4. 3, **7**¹³; 4. 7–21, 5. 1–3, **159**¹⁵; 5. 4, **475**⁴; 5. 7, **569**²; **636**⁷

2 John
7, **7**¹³; 10–11, **173**¹¹

3 John
9–10, **173**¹¹

Jude
3, **47**³; **167**¹ⁿ; **195**⁴; **382**¹; **569**¹; 6, **49**⁶

Revelation
Revelation **159**²¹; **577**⁹
1. 6, **16**⁴; 1. 8, 11, **159**²⁵; 1. 9, **46**¹⁶; 1. 10, **34**⁵; 2. 1, 8, 12, 18, **551**¹; 2. 6, 15, **7**¹³; 3. 1, 7, 14, **551**¹; 3. 5, **7**²⁰; 4. 11, 5. 9–14, **472**⁴; 6. 9–11, **206**⁷; 7. 4, **7**²²; 7. 9–12, **472**⁴; 7. 9–17, **7**²²; 9. 11, **159**³⁷; 11. 15, In³¹; 11. 15–17, **472**⁴; 12. 3, App¹; 12. 3–17, **45**⁷; 13. 1, App¹; 14. 1, 3, **7**²²; 14. 13, **427**³; 15. 3–4, **472**⁴; 17–18, **159**²¹; 17. 3, 7, 12, 16, App¹; 18. 2, **651**¹³; 19. 1–4, 6–7, **472**⁴; 20. 2, **45**⁷; 21. 6, **159**²⁵; 21. 14, **167**⁵; 22. 13, **159**²⁵

CLASSICAL QUOTATIONS AND ALLUSIONS

AESCHYLUS: *Prom.* 1015, **67⁶**
AMMIANUS: *Res Gestae* 15.7.10, **637⁷**; 21.16.18, **95⁴¹**; 22.5.3-4, **112¹ⁿ**; 22.10.7, **116²**; 22.11.11, **111¹ⁿ**; 22.13.2, **119⁵**; 22.16.18, **347¹³**; 23.1.4, **111²⁴**; 25.4.20, **116²**; 27.3.12-13, **137¹**; 30.4.13, **619⁷**
APPIAN: *Bell. Civ.* 2.91, **116¹**; *Bell. Lib.* 1.1, 20.136, **646¹⁴**; *Bell. Syr.* 8.50, **67³⁷**
ARISTOPHANES: *Aves* 91, **225¹³**; *Eq.* 756, **117¹⁰**; *Thesm.* 838, **225¹³**
ARISTOTLE: *Metaph.* 1045B-51A, **159⁵⁴**; 1073A-4B, **313¹**; *Phys.* 195B-8A, **223²**; *Pol,* 1253A, **652⁴**; 1324A, 1325A, **147²**
ARRIAN: *Epict. Diat.* 4.1.14, **255³**
ASCONIUS: *In Cor.* 67, *In Pis.* 6, 8, **133¹**
AURELIUS: *Ad Se Ipsum,* **3⁴**

BOETHIUS: *De Consolatione Philosophiae,* **533¹**; *De Cons. Phil.* 5.1, **223²**

CAESAR: *De Bello Gallico,* **203⁴**
CATULLUS: *Carm.* 11.11-12, 29.429.12, **46⁹**
CICERO: *Acad.* 2.47.146, **619⁸**; *Ad Att.* 1.1.2, **220²**; 1.16.11, 2.19.3, **472⁴**; 3.15.4, **133¹**; 4.1.4, **220⁴**; 14.2.1, **472⁴**; *Ad Fam.* 3.8.5, **67³⁷**; 3.11.2, **382¹**; 7.1.3, **509⁵**; 15.2.1, **548³**; *Ad Q. Fr.* 2.3.5, **133¹**; *Cato Maior* 3.7, **59⁴**; *De Div.* 1.24.49, **223²**; 2.47.98, **220⁴**; 2.65.134, **223²**; *De Dom.* 16.41, **324⁷**; *De Fin.* 2.5.15, In⁵⁴; *De Inv.* 2.17.53, **382¹**; *De Leg.* 2.19.47-21.53, **623⁷**; *De Off.* 1.13.39-40, **619⁸**; 1.14.42-17.58, **515³**; 1.25.89, **152¹**; 2.18.62-3, **515³**; 2.18.63, **127⁵**; 3.26.97-32.115, 3.29.108, *De Or.* 2.64.260, **619⁸**; *De Rep.* 6.18.18-19, In⁵⁴; *In Cat.* 2.10.23, **593³**; 4.6.13, **646²⁶**; *In Pis.* 4.9, **133¹**; *In Verr.* 1.10.32, 2.1.4.9, **605³**; 2.1.9.25, **625¹²**; 2.1.42.108, **204⁵**; 2.5.8.19, **605³**; 2.5.9.23, **1⁵**; *Lael.* 7.23, **193¹**; *Orat.* 34.120, In¹; *Parad. Stoic.* 20-6, **330⁶**; *Phil.* 2.23.56, 3.14.35, 8.9.26, **593³**; 13.6.14, **1⁴**; *Pro Clu.* 10.29, **605³**; *Pro Planc.* 15.36, *Pro. Sest* 25.55, **133¹**; *Pro Sex. Rosc. Amer.* 3.8, **605³**; 19.55; **334³**; *Timaeus,* In⁵⁴; **648⁶**; *Tusc. Disp.* 1.37.89, **479⁶**; 2.11.27, **279⁹**
CLAUDIAN: *In Eut.* 1.8, **246¹**
CORPUS INSCRIPTIONUM LATINARUM 3.13734, **25¹,²**
CURTIUS RUFUS: *Hist. Alex. Mag. Maced.* 10.6.1-18, **614⁷**

DIO CASSIUS: *Hist. Rom.* 38.13.2, **133¹**; 43.20, **472⁴**; 44.6.1, **255³**; 44.35.2, **608⁴**; 55.10.1, **141³**; 55.11, **313¹**; 56.27.1, **382¹**; 57.8.3, **255³**; 57.15.7, 58.27.1-3, **313¹**; 62 [61].20.5, 62[63].20.5, **472⁴**
DIO CHRYSOSTOM: *Orat.* 34, *Tars. Alt.* 48, **577¹**
DIOGENES LAERTIUS: *Vitae* 1.5.3, **644⁶**

EURIPIDES: *Hipp.* 1162-1248, 1440-58, **397¹**; *Iph. Taur.* 1193, **214⁵**; *Med.* 278, **117¹⁰**; 384-5, 784-9, 1125-6, 1159-1221, **135⁵**

FLORUS: *Epit.* 1.31.7-18, **646¹⁴**
FRONTO: *Prin. Hist.* 17, **141³**

GELLIUS: *Noct. Att.* 4.20.3-5, **619⁷**; 10.15.8, 10, **399¹¹**

HERODOTUS: *Hist.* 2.121, **68⁴**; 8.98, **648⁶**
HESYCHIUS: *Patria Cplis.* 1.55, **220⁴**
HIPPOCRATES: *De Arte* 3, 14, **429⁵**
HOMER: *Il.* 1.63, 2.1-34, **223²**; 5.31, **67¹¹**; 5.484, **103⁸**; 9.63, **652⁴**; *Od.* 8.266-366, **67¹²**; 11.92-149, **150¹**; 12.73-126, 12.234-59, In⁵³; 17.218, **59⁴**; 22.334-6, **400⁹**
HORACE: *Carm.* 1.35.29-30, **46⁷**; 2.10.5, In³⁸; 3.3.57-72, **62²**; 3.30.1, **308¹⁵**; 4.9.25-8, **479³⁷**; 4.14.47-8, **46⁹**; *Ep.* 1.1.59-60, **614⁴**; *Serm.* 2.5, **150¹**

JOSEPHUS: *Ant. Iud.* 12.3.3.142, **23²**; 13.9.1.257-8, 13.11.3.318, **76⁴**; 14.7.2.117, 14.10.2.190-5, **17³**; 14.10.8.215, **133¹**; 14.12.2.304, 14.12.3.313, **341²**; 15.11.1.380-7.425, *Bell Iud.* 1.21.1.401, In⁴⁴; 4.5.4.334-44, **159³⁴**

IULIAN: *Ad Reg. Hel.* 150A, 154D, **122¹³**; *Ad Them.* 265C, **122¹²**; *Adversus Galilaeos,* **393¹**; *Adv. Galil.* 43A, 238B-D, 305D-6A, **122³**; 327B-C, 333B-D, **122¹⁴**; *Contra Christianos, Epistulae,* **119⁵**; *Ep.* 288A-305D, **208³**; 376A-C, **121**; 376C-D, **119**; 378C-80D, **111**; 380D-81A, **118**; 398C-9A, **115**; 404B-C, **112**; 411C-D, **113⁴**; 422A-4A, **116**; 424B-5A, **123**; 429C-32A, **208³**; 432C-D, **122**; 435D-8C, **117**; 450B-1D, **119¹**; 452A, **116¹⁶**; 452A-4B, **208³**; *Frag. Ep.,* **111¹**; *Orationes,* **119⁵**

CLASSICAL QUOTATIONS AND ALLUSIONS 1349

JUVENAL: *Sat.* 1.3.62, **167**[1n]; 4.10.81, **141**[4]; 5.14.97, **315**[1]
LIBANIUS: *Cont. Flor.* 46.22, **97**[1]
LIVY: *Ab Urbe Cond.* 5.21.2, **644**[6]; 10.47.3, **496**[5]; 21.22.6–9, **223**[2]; 22.51.4, In[51]; 22.53.10, 43.15.8, **619**[7]
LUCAN: *Phar.* 3.950–1001, **62**[2]
LUCIAN: *De Dea Syria* 28, **411**[3]
LUCRETIUS: *De Rer. Nat.* 2.79, **648**[7]

MACROBIUS: *Comm. in Somn. Scip.* 2.4.12, In[54]
MARTIAL: *Epig.* 2.4.3–8, 10.65.14–15, 12.20.1–2, **372**[1]
MATERNUS: *Mathesis* 1.10.14, **313**[1]
MELANTHIUS: *Frag.*, **111**

NAMATIAN: *De Red. Suo* 2.50, Tab[5]
NEPOS: *Att.* 13.2, **220**[4]
NICOLAUS DAMASCENUS: *Aug.* 20.68, **62**[2]
NOTITIA DIGNITATUM, **353**[6], Gl s.v. chief of the notaries

ORIENTIS GRAECI INSCRIPTIONES SELECTAE 2.678, **255**[3]
OVID, *Ep. ex Ponto* 1.2.13–22, *Trist.* 3.10.51–76, 4.1.75–84, 5.10.15–34, **523**[3]

PATERCULUS: *Hist. Rom.* 2.12.3, **523**[1]
PERSIUS: *Sat.* 2.69, **508**[6], **598**[13]
PHILOSTRATUS: *Vita Apol. Tyan.* 1.15, **1**[4]
PLATO: *Ep.* 7.344A, **397**[2]; *Leges* 666B, **117**[10]; 933B–E, **135**[4]; *Phaedo*, *Phaedrus* 245C ff, **443**[9]; *Pol.* 328A, **648**[7]; 608D, **443**[9]; 614B–21D, In[54]; *Protag.* 338A, **117**[10]; *Timaeus*, In[54], **648**[6]
PLAUTUS: *Aul.* 2–27, **223**[2]
PLINY THE ELDER: *Nat. Hist.* 2.5.18, **127**[7]; 8.7.21, **509**[6]; 11.70.184, **604**[3]
PLINY THE YOUNGER: *Ep.* 2.20, **150**[1]; 6.20.15, **3**[25]; 9.6, **236**[3]; 10.34, 10.93 **133**[1]; 10.96.2, **12**[33]; 10.96.3–8, **1**[2]; 10.96.6, **45**[1]; 10.96.7, **133**[1], App 3; 10.97, **1**, App 3
PLUTARCH: *Caes.* 50.2, **116**[1]; 57.5, **646**[14]; *Cato Maior* 27.1, **140**[1]; *Cato Minor* 19.4, **65**[13]; *C. Gracch.* 11.1, 13.1, **646**[14]; *Mor.* 453F, 551A, **111**[7]; *Numa* 10.3, **399**[11]; *Quaest. Rom.* 14D, **225**[5]; *Rom.* 12.1, **220**[4]
PROCOPIUS: *De Aedificiis*, **550**[1]; *De Aed.* 1.1.9, **575**[1]; 1.1.22–78, **505**[1]; 5.1.4–6, **568**[1]; *De Bellis*, **550**[1]; *De Bell.* 3.4.1., 3.5.8, **646**[14]; 3.8.4, **646**[9]; 3.8.20, **646**[8]; 3.20.7, **646**[14]; *Historia Arcana*, **550**[1]; *Hist. Arc.* 9.31, **630**[6]; 10.13–14, 11.40, 15.9–10, 17.27, **630**[8]

QUINTILIAN: *Inst. Orat.* 8.5.1., **622**[7]

RES GESTAE DIVI AUGUSTI or MONUMENTUM ANCYRANUM, **48**[9]; *Res Gestae* 3.15, **141**[3], **474**[2]; 3.17, **474**[2]
SALLUST: *Bell. Iug.* 5.4, **19**[22]
SCRIPTORES HISTORIAE AUGUSTAE: *Avid. Cass.* 13.1.5, *Claud.* 4.3–4, 18.1–3, *Gord.* 11.9–10, **472**[4]; *Had.* 14.2, **76**[3]; *Max. et Balb.* 2.9–12, *Maxim.* 16.3–7, 26.1–4, *Prob.* 11.6–9, 12.8, **472**[4]; *Sev.* 17.1, App. 5; *Sev. Alex.* 6.1., 6.3–5, 7, 8. 2–3, 9.1, 9.3, 9.5–6, 10.1, 10.3, 10.6–8, 11.2, 12.1, **472**[4]; 19.1, **508**[7]; 22.4, 29.2, **4**[2]; 33.2, **133**[1]; 43.6–7, 45.7, 49.6, 51.7, **4**[2]; 56.9–10, *Tac.* 4.1–4, 5.1–2, 7.1, 7.4, **472**[4]
SENECA, LUCIUS or MARCUS ANNAEUS: *Controv.* 10.pr.5, **382**[1]
SENECA, LUCIUS ANNAEUS: *De Ben.* 5.14.2, **168**[1]; *Hipp.* 611, **372**[1]; 997–1114, **397**[1]; *Med.* 570–7, 670–738, 740–842, **135**[5]; *Nat. Quaest.* 6.26.5, **9**[8]
SERVIUS: *Comm. in Verg. Aen.* 4.459, **646**[14]
STRABO: *Geog.* 12.4.7, **48**[12], **468**[7]; 17.15, **646**[14]
SUETONIUS: *Aug.* 7.2, In[30]; 32.1, **133**[1]; 55, **382**[1]; 56.2, **472**[4]; 89.1, **122**[12]; *Dom.* 7.1, **236**[3]; 23.1, App **2**; *Gaius* 15.3, **619**[7]; 27.3, **255**[3]; 55.2, **236**[3]; *Iul.* 37.2, **116**[1], 40.2, **220**[3]; 41.3, **141**[9]; 42.3, **133**[1]; 49.4, **472**[4]; 78.1, **641**[8]; 79.3, **62**[2]; 84.1, **641**[8]; *Nero* 2.1, **523**[1]; 8, **472**[4]; 16.2, **1**[1]; 20.3, **472**[4]; *Tib.* 14.4, **313**[1]; 26.1, **386**[8]; 37.3, **241**[1]; 62.3, **313**[1]; *Tit.* 8.1, **207**[8]; *Vesp.* 11, **631**[1]; *Vit.* 7.1, **236**[3]
SYMMACHUS: *Rel. de Ara Vict.* 3.15–17, **429**[81]

TACITUS: *Agr.* 1.1–2, **479**[5]; 46.4, **479**[5,7]; *Ann.* 1.1.6, **73**[19]; 1.72.3–4, **382**[1]; 1.73.5, **3**[15]; 2.56.1, **106**[6]; 3.24.2–3, **214**[4]; 3.36.1, **400**[9]; 3.38.1, **1**[4]; 3.54.2, In[9]; 3.60.2, **241**[1]; 4.11.5, In[22]; 4.67.6, **241**[1], **400**[9]; 6.20.3—21.5, **313**[1]; 12.53.1, **631**[1]; 15.44.4, **1**[1]; 16.4.4, **472**[4]; *Ger.* 19.1, **225**[13]; *Hist.* 1.4, In[45]
TERENCE *And.* 555, **47**[98]
THUCYDIDES: *Hist.* 4.46–8, **137**[1]
TIBULLUS: *Eleg.* 2.5.23, **140**[1]; 3.1.23–8, **372**[1]

VARRO: *De Ling. Lat.* 6.11, **604**[3]
VEGETIUS: *Epit. Rei Mil.* 2.5, **127**[8], **555**[4]
VERGIL: *Aen.* 1.12–14, **646**[14]; 1.278–9, In[25]; 2.201, **614**[10]; 3.57, **508**[5]; 3.303–5, **641**[17]; 4.64, **242**[10]; 5.483–4, **429**[30]; 6.304, **395**[15]; 6.581–3, In[31]; *Ecl.* 1.66, **46**[9]; 8.73–5, **579**[7], **646**[8]
XENOPHON: *Poroi*, **606**[2]
ZOSIMUS: *Hist.* 2.38, **97**[1]

LEGAL QUOTATIONS AND ALLUSIONS

ACTA PROCONSULARIA, $21^{1n,9}$; 328^9, App 8 (a)
AMBROSE: *Ep.* 18.3, 150^1; 21.4,5, 136^1
AMMIANUS: *Res Gestae* 15.7.10, 637^7; 22.10.7, 25.4.20, 116^2; 30.4.13, 619^{10}
ASCONIUS: *In Pis.* 6, 8, *In Cor.* 67, 133^1
AUGUSTINE: *Brev. Coll.* 3.25.43, 328^1 *Cont. Cresc.* 3.71.83, 27^3; *Ep.* 33.5, 28^1; 43.20, 24^1, 27^1; 133, 139, 152, 153, 370^1
BIBLE: Ex. 20. 3–5, 641^4; Num. 5.9–10, 18.8–9, 537^{16}; 35.6, 11–15, 25–9, 32, 400^9; Deut. 17.6, 65^{13}; 18.1–8, 537^{16}; 19.5, Matt. 18.16, 65^{13}; Acts 18.12–27, 1^4; 22.28, 337^6; 25.9–12,5^1; 25.16, 1^5; I Cor. 6.1–8, 17^3; 9.7–14, 537^{16}
BONIFACE I: *Epp.* 13–15, 375^3
BREVIARIUM ALARICIANUM, In^2, 34^5, Gl s.v. interpretation
BRUNS, C. G., *Fontes Iuris Romani Antiqui*, 268–70 (7th ed., Tübingen, 1909), 341^2

CA 2.37–56, 17^3; 8. 47.7, 628^3; 8.47.27, 613^4; 8.47.39, 8.47.39–40, 579^{16}; 8.47.43–4, 651^5; 8.47.81, 628^3
CSEL 26.26, 20^{10}; 26.27, 20^9; 26.197–204, 21^{1n}, 328^9; 26.202.5–7, 26.203.20–3, 21^9
CASSIODORUS: HE 6.1.32, 112^{1n}; 6.4.8–12, 6.7.2, 6.7.4, 6.13.1–3, 117^7; 7.1, 112^{1n}; 7.39.1–2, 30, 35, 147^4; 8.12, 159^{16}; 9.30.23–4, In^{49}
CICERO: *Acad.* 2.47.146, 619^8; *Ad Att.* 1.1.2, 220^2; 3.15.4, 133^1; *Ad Fam.* 3.11.2, 382^1; *Ad Q. Fr.* 2.3.5, 133^1; *De Dom.* 16.41, 324^7; *De Inv.* 2.17.53, 382^1; *De Leg.* 2.19.47—21.53, 623^7; *De Off.* 1.25.89, 152^1; 3.29.108, *De Or.* 2.64.260, 619^8; *In Pis.* 4.9, 133^7; *In Verr.* 1.10.32, 2.1.4.9, 605^3; 2.1.9.25, 625^{12}; 2.1.42.108, 204^5; 2.5.8.19, 605^3; 2.5.9.23, 1^5; *Phil.* 2.23.56, 593^3; 13.6.14, 1^4; *Pro Clu.* 10.29, 605^3; *Pro. Planc.* 15.36, *Pro Sest.* 25.55, 133^1; *Pro Sex. Rosc. Amer.* 3.8, 605^3; 19.55, 334^3
CODEX GREGORIANUS, 578^5, 590^6 CG 7, 156^1
CODEX HERMOGENIANUS, 578^5, 590^6
CODEX IURIS CANONICI, 607^6, Gl s.v. *ius canonicum*; 2.1.1.2.120, 62^{11}

CODEX IUSTINIANUS (CI), In 1, 34^5, 114^2, 167^{1n}, 375^{1n}, 436^{1n}, 517^{1n}, 530^{1n}, 531^{1n}, 539^{1n}, $578^{1n,2,5,7}$, $590^{1n,8}$, 639^8, 645^{1n}, 650^8, Gl s.v. *Novellae Iustiniani*; Const. *Cordi*, 578^2, 590^8; *Cordi* 1, 3, *Haec* 2, *Summa pr.*, 114^2; 1.3.9., 225^3; 1.3.24, 488^{16}; 1.5.2, 254^{1n}; 1.7.1.10, 375^7; 1.21.2, 168^1; 1.23.6, In^{15}; 1.34.1, 519^{12}; 1.38.1, 619^5; 2.58.1, 605^5; 3.1.13.1, 65^6; 3.2.4, 518^9; 3.13.2, 3.13.5, 3.19.3, 478^{16}; 3.43.1, 593^{1n}; 3.43.1.4, 651^6; 3.44.1, 641^{14}; 3.44.2, $641^{17,21,22,26}$; 3.44.4,6–8, 641^{17}; 3.44.9, 641^{26}; 3.44.12, 641^{14}; 3.44.13, $641^{17,24}$; 3.44.14, 641^{14}; 4.1.2, 255^3; 4.1.11, 4.1.12, 605^5; 4.5, 640^2; 4.10.14, 604^8; 4.20.9, 65^{13}; 4.20.16. pr., 611^{13}; 4.30.14, 582^{1n}; 4.66.2, 632^{10}; 5.1.5, 517^{1n}; 5.4.23, 649^8; 5.13.1. pr., In^8; 5.16.4, 31^4, 641^9; 5.26–7, 525^2; 5.27.10, 525^8; 5.35.2, 635^2; 6.5.1, 642^{12}; 6.23.4, 615^{13}; 6.43.1 604^9; 6.43.1.1, 640^6; 6.48.1, 36^1; 7.3, 392^3; 7.21.1–8, 190^8; 7.22.3, 65^6; 7.26–40, 641^{23}; 7.37.3.1d, 141^3; 7.39.2, 7.39.4, 7.39.6, 65^6; 7.39.7.1, 604^8; 7.40.1, 65^6; 7.42, 309^6; 7.65.1, 603^3; 8.1, 641^{29}; 8.10.7, 95^{41}; 8.11.6, 212^2; 8.11.10, 59^{10}; 8.37–43, 641^{25}; 8.48.5, 37^1; 8.50, 308^{14}; 9.4.1, 204^3; 9.9.5, 190^8; 9.9.29, 168^1; 9.9.29.4, 214^5; 9.18, 313^1; 9.18.2, 313^1; 9.18.8, 248^2; 9.19, 641^7; 9.19.1, 641^{26}; 9.19.1–6, 443^4; 9.19.5, 119^1, 168^1; 9.19.7, 443^4; 9.22–4, 204^5; 9.29.2, 9.29.3, 168^1; 9.36, 1^5; 9.47.20, In^{49}; 10.27.3, 534^{1n}; 10.32, Gl s.v. *curial*; 10.32.56, 10.32.57, 257^1; 10.35.4, 629^8; 10.39.5, Gl s.v. *curial*; 11.1.1, 97^1; 11.4.1, 431^4; 11.8.2, 11.8.9, 11.8.11, 11.8.12, 11.8.13, 11.8.15, 11.9.4, 11.9.5, 273^2; 11.16.1, 133^1; 11.22.1, $470^{39,43}$; 11.48.2, 11.48.7, 107^2; 11.48.13, 528^3; 11.48.15, 107^2; 11.48.21, 528^2; 11.48.23, 107^2; 11.48.24, 631^{1n}; 11.52, 443^{15}; 11.52.1, 528^5; 12.8.1, 12.17.1, 12.28.4, 168^1; 12.30.1, 624^2; 12.37.13, 168^1; 12.37.19, $535^{1n,2}$; 12.40.5, 168^1; 12.46.1, 124^1; 12.50.3, 12.50.4, 95^{41}; 12.63.1, 168^1
CODEX REPETITAE PRAELECTIONIS, In^3, 590^8
CODEX THEODOSIANUS (CT), In 1^9, 34^5, 114^2, 128^{1n}, 156^1, 157^{1n}, 176^8, 205^{1n},

1350

LEGAL QUOTATIONS AND ALLUSIONS

283^{1n}, 285^3, 293^4, 336^{1n}, 375^{1n}, 472^4, 478, 578^5, 590^{6,7}, Gl and s.v. interpretation
Const. *Quantum* 168^1
GESTA SENATUS ROMANI DE <CODICE> THEODOSIANO PUBLICANDO 4, 114^2; 5, 472^4; 1.1.2, 310^4; 1.1.3, 176^8; 1.1.5, 293^4; 1.1.5–6, 501^2; 1.4.3, 641^{13}; 1.6.4, 55^2; 1.6.7. 439^3; 1.6.9, 168^1; 1.12.1, 1.12.3, 65^6; 1.32.1, 273^2; 2.1.10, 341^5; 2.6.1, 2.6.2, 2.6.3, 2.7.2, 65^6; 2.8.18, 220^7; 2.8.26, 332^{1n}; 2.10.6, 501^2; 2.12.5, 619^5; 2.15.1, 2.16.2, 65^6; 2.19.5, 190^8; 2.33.4, 285^3; 3.5.6, 517^3; 3.5.11, 517^2; 3.5.13, 581^{14}; 3.16.1, 443^4; 3.17, 635^2; 3.32.1, 65^6; 4.6, 525^2; 4.6.1, 525^4; 4.6.3, 4.8.7, 4.11.1, 4.11.2, 65^6; 4.13.4, 106^2; 4.14.1, 4.22.1, 65^6; 5.2.1, 233^9, 421^1; 5.7., 308^{14}; 5.9.1, 331^5; 5.17.1, 421^4; 443^{15}, 528^5; 5.18.1, 478^{27}; 5.19.1, 337^6; 6.2.21, 330^{1n}; 6.5.2, 168^1; 6.18.1, 330^1; 6.24.4, 168^1; 6.27.3, 256^2, Gl s.v. magistrian; 6.29.9, 6.35.13, 168^1; 6.35.15, 6.36.1, 624^3; 6.38.1, 7.4.28, 7.4.30, 168^1; 7.5.1, 7.5.2, 133^1; 7.8.10, 168^1; 7.20.2, 124^1; 7.21.3, 497^6; 8.4.16, 383^6; 8.5.5–10, 12–15, 95^{41}; 8.8.3, 220^7; 8.8.8., 332in; 8.11.4, 168^1; 8.12.1, 3,5–7, 522^6; 9.1, 334^7; 9.1.3, 619^5; 9.7.2, 65^6, 214^3; 9.7.5, 214^{1n,6}; 9.16, 313^1; 9.16.8, 248^2; 9.17 443^4, 641^{17}; 9.17.5, 119^1, 168^1; 9.17.7, 641^{14}; 9.19.1, 204^3; 9.19.2, 65^6; 9.23.1, 168^1; 9.24.1, 92^2, 619^5, 638^{10,13}; 9.24.2, 92^2; 9.29.1, 164^7; 9.34, 1^5; 9.34.1, 27^3; 9.38.2, 171^1; 9.38.3, 9.38.7, 9.38.8, 443^4; 9.40.3, 5–7, 9, 133^1; 9. 40.13, In^{48}; 9.40.17, 246^1; 9.40.18, 328^3; 9.44.1, 400^9; 10.1.1, 10.1.4, 65^6; 10.1.8, 148^1; 10.3.1, 119^5; 10.7, App^{14}, 10.10, 372^{22}, 10.10.1, 10.10.2, 10.10.4, 10.10.10, 440^8; 10.10.16, 168^1; 10.18.1, 10.18.2, 223^3; 10.20.5, 10.20.12, 10.20.14, 10.20.15, 10.20.16, 10.20.17, 10.20.18, 10.21.3, 273^2; 11.7.13, 220^7; 11.16.15, 11.16.18, 133^1; 11.27.1–2, 474^2; 11.28.10, 11.29.5, 168^1; 11.30.1, 11.30.3, 65^6; 11.30.6, 168^1; 11.30.8, 65^6; 11.30.16, 309^6; 11.35.1, 65^6; 11.36.4, 168^1, 214^5; 11.36.15, 11.36.16, 146^3; 12.1, Gl s.v. curial; 12.1.7, 12.1.12, 233^7, Gl s.v. curial; 12.1.64, 441^6; 12.1.70, 497^6; 12.1.75, 208^3; 12.1.86, 233^7; 12.1.107, 233^5; 12.1.160, 285^3; 12.1.189, 12.1.190, 257^1; 13, Gl s.v. guild; 13.1.9, 273^2; 13.3.1, 186^6; 13.3.5, 13.3.6, 116^{1n}; 13.4.4, 168^1; 13.5.2, 133^1; 13.5.7, 62^2, 617^{10}; 13.7.2, 431^4; 13.10.3, 107^2; 13.10.4, 149^1; 14, Gl s.v. guild; 14.2.4, 330^1; 14.3.1–8, 10–17, 19–22, 14.4.9, 133^1; 14.13.1, 375^7; 14.17.3, 4, 6, 133^1; 14.27, 257^1; 14.27.1, 257^{1n,5}; 15.1.13, 641^{12}; 15.1.22, 212^2; 15.1.27, 168^1; 15.1.31, 59^{10}; 15.4, 526^4; 15.5.5, 220^5; 15.7.11, 247^2; 15.11.1, 243^2; 16.4.1, 205^{1n}, 16.5, 156^1; 16.5.1, 16.5.2, 16.5.38–66, 524^{19}; 16.5.24, 166^{1n}; 16.5.31, 260^2; 16.8.2, 188^2, 267^7; 16.8.3, 188^3; 16.8.4, 23^2, 267^7; 16.8.8, 16.8.11, 341^3; 16.8.14, 341^2; 16.8.15, 341^3; 16.8.17, 341^2; 16.8.20, 332^8; 16.8.27, 376^{1n}, 378^{1n}; 16.8.29, 341^2; 16.10, 242^{1n}; 16.10.3, 16.10.4, 424^3; 16.10.6, 301^8; 16.10.7, 168^1, 424^3; 16.10.8, 301^8, 424^3; 16.10.10, 253^6, 424^3; 16.10.11, 168^1, 253^6, 424^3; 16.10.13, 424^3; 16.10.14–19, 301^5; 16.10.15, 424^3; 16.10.16, 341^4, 424^3; 16.10.18, 16.10.19, 16.10.20, 424^3; 16.10.22, 16.10.23, 242^2; 16.10.24, 242^{1n}; 16.11.3, 324^9
CODEX VETUS In^3
COLL. 8.2, 204^5; 15.3, 156^1
COLLECTIO AVELLANA In 1, 645^{1n}
CONCORDIA DISCORDANTIUM CANONUM Gl s.v. *ius canonicum*
CONSTITUTIO ANTONINIANA Gl s.v. peregrine
CONSTITUTION OF THE UNITED STATES, AMENDMENT III, 83^5
CORPUS IURIS CANONICI Gl
CORPUS IURIS CIVILIS In^{2,3}, 308^{15}, 505^2, 578^{1n}, 590^{1n}, 617^{1n}, 639^{1n,8}, Gl and s.v. Digesta, Institutiones Iustiniani, Novellae Iustiniani
COUNCIL OF ROME (c. 368), *Epistola ad Gratianum et Valentinianum*, 164^{1n}
CYPRIAN: *Acta Proconsularia* App^{11}; *Acta Procons.* 1.3, App 8 (a); *Ep.* 43.3, App 7; 80.1, App 8 (b)

DIGESTA or *PANDECTAE* (D) In^{3,9}, 4^2, 308^{15}, 602^{1n}, 617^{1n,1,4}, 639^8, 642^{1n}, 643^{1n}, Gl and s.v. *Novellae Iustiniani*; Const. *Tanta* 616^4; 1.1.7, 65^{10}; 1.1.7.1, 150^3; 1.3.32. pr., 375^7; 1.4.1, In^9; 1.5.4.1, 631^4; 1.8.1. pr., 1.8.6.2, 641^5; 1.8.6.3, 641^{12,13}; 1.8.6.4, 641^{14,18,22}; 1.8.6.5, 1.8.7, 641^{17}; 1.8.9. pr., 1.8.9.1, 641^{12}; 1.8.9.3, 641^2; 1.8.9.5, 641^{27}; 1.16.7.1, 641^{12}; 1.18.13, 4^2; 1.18.13. pr., 168^1; 2.2.1. pr, 332^5; 2.4.2, 619^5; 3.4.1. pr, 133^1; 4.4.41, 625^{12}; 8.1.14.1, 641^{17}; 8.2.20.2, 429^{36}; 9.2.29.7, 413^8; 10.2, 641^{18}; 10.2.4.2, 168^1; 10.3, 641^{18}; 11.5.1. pr., 11.5.1.1, 11.5.1.4, 11.5.2.1, 11.5.4. pr., 593^3; 11.7.2.1, 641^{18}; 11.7.2.1–3, 641^{21}; 11.7.2.2, 5, 641^{17}; 11.7.2.4, 641^{18}; 11.7.2.6, 641^{17}; 11.7.2.7, 641^{20}; 11.7.2.9, 11.7.3, 11.7.4, 641^{14};

1352 LEGAL QUOTATIONS AND ALLUSIONS

11.7.6.1, **641**[17]; 11.7.7, **641**[21,24]; 11.7.8. pr., **641**[14]; 11.7.9, **641**[31]; 11.7.10, 11.7.12. pr.–1, 11.7.36, 11.7.37.1, **641**[17]; 11.7.39, 11.7.40, **641**[14]; 11.7.41, **641**[14,18]; 11.7.42, **641**[17]; 11.7.43, **641**[18,20,31]; 11.7.44, **641**[14]; 11.7.46. pr., **641**[20]; 11.8.1. pr.–4, **641**[31]; 11.8.1.5–10, **641**[17,31]; 11.8.3–5, **641**[17]; 11.8.4, **641**[24]; 12.2, **605**[2]; 12.2.13.6, **255**[3]; 12.6, **640**[2]; 18.1.4, 18.1.6. pr., **641**[5,26]; 18.1.62.1, **641**[28]; 18.1.73. pr., **641**[13]; 19.1.13.8, **641**[27]; 19.5, **598**[10]; 22.1.24. pr., 22.1.32. pr., **612**[9]; 22.5.3.2., **619**[8]; 22.5.12, **65**[13]; 22.6.9. pr., **310**[4]; 23.2.1, **214**[6]; 24.1.1., 24.1.3. pr., **31**[4]; 24.1.5.10–11, **641**[14]; 24.1.5.12, **641**[9]; 25.3.1.2, **242**[6]; 25.7, **525**[2]; 27.10.16. pr., **608**[4]; 30.39.9, **641**[5]; 33.1.4, **612**[16]; 34.5.20, **36**[1]; 35.2.1. pr., **392**[4]; 35.2.68. pr., **612**[19]; 36.2.10, **612**[16]; 39.1.1.1, 39.1.1.17, **641**[31]; 40.1.25, 40.5.13, **607**[4]; 40.12.1–3, **631**[5]; 40.15, **190**[8]; 41.1.3, **641**[5]; 41.2.30.1, **641**[5,24]; 41.3–10, 41.3.3, **641**[23]; 41.3.9, **641**[5,23]; 43, **641**[29]; 43.1.1. pr., 43.1.2.1, 43.1.2.1–2, 43.6.1.2, 43.6.1.2–3, 43.8.2.19, **641**[31]; 43.24.12, **627**[4]; 44.6.3, **641**[10]; 45–6.5, **641**[25]; 45.1.27, **168**[1]; 45.1.38.25, 45.1.83.5, 45.1.91.1, 45.1.137.6, **641**[25]; 47.10.3, **394**[5]; 47.12, **443**[4], **641**[17]; 47.12.2, **641**[31]; 47.12.3.4, 47.12.3.5, **641**[14]; 47.12.4, **641**[17]; 48.2.7, **334**[6]; 48.2.7.5, 48.4.1, **4**[2]; 48.4.1. pr., **168**[1]; 48.5, **638**[14]; 48.8.11. pr., **76**[4]; 48.9.9. pr., **214**[5]; 48.10, **204**[5]; 48.13.1, **641**[5]; 48.13.7, **168**[1]; 48.13.7(6), **4**[2]; 48.13.4.2, 48.13.11.1, 48.13.12.1, **168**[1]; 48.18, 48.18.3, 48.18.10.1, 12, 15, **204**[3]; 48.19.30, **3**[34]; 50.6.6.12–13, **133**[1]; 50.9.1, **347**[13]; 50.17.63, **612**[9]
DIO CASSIUS: *Hist. Rom.* 38.13.2, **133**[1]; 44.35.2, **608**[4]; 56.27.1, **382**[1]
DONATION OF CONSTANTINE In[46], **364**[12]

EDICTUM THEODORICI In[2]
EPISTOLA ECCLESIARUM VIENNENSIS ET LUGDUNENSIS App 4
EUSEBIUS: *De Mart. Pal. praef.* 1–2, App 10 (a); 2, App 10 (b); 2.2–3, App[36]; 2.4., App 10 (c); 3.1., App 10 (d); 4.8, App 10 (e); 6, App[36]; 8.1., App 10 (e); 9.2, **8**[5], App 10 (f); 9.4–13 *et seq.*, 13.2, 13.10, App. 10 (f); 13.14, App[49]; *HE* 3.20.5, App 2; 3.33.3, **1**[3]; 4.8.6, **2**[1n]; 4.12.1, **3**[8]; 4.26.10, App[6]; 5.1.44, 47, App 4; 5.5.1–6, In[46]; 6.3.1, App. 5; 6.28, App 6; 6.41.1, App 7; 7.30.18–19, **5**[1]; 7.30.21, App 9;

8.2.4–5, App 10 (a); 8.2.5, App 10 (b); 8.5.1, App 10 (a); 8.6.8, App 10 (b); 8.6.10, App 10 (c); 8.14.9, App 10 (f); 9.1.1, **13**[12]; 9.2.1, App 10 (f); 9.4.1, 9.5.1, App 10 (f); 9.7.1, App[53]; 9.10.8, 9.10.11, App 10 (a); 10.5.1, **12**[4]; 10.5.9–11, 16–17, App 10 (a); 10.8.10, 14–19, **42**[1]; *VC* 1.15, App[16]; 1.51, **47**[10]; 1.51–4, 56, **42**[1]; 1.58, App 10 (f); 2.1–2, 5, **42**[1]; 2.23, **46**[26]; 2.47, In[12]; 3.6, **48**[2]; 3.21, **49**[26]; 4.23, **34**[5]; 4.26, **31**[1n]; 4.37–9, **43**[1n]
EVAGRIUS: *HE* 1.13, **376**[1n]; 3.12, **523**[1]; 3.39, **97**[1]; 4.14, **646**[9]

FELIX III (II): *Ep.* 9, In[31]
FIRA 1.30, **59**[24]; 1.31, 1.33, **324**[7]; 1.37, **392**[4], **621**[3]; 1.37–40, **628**[3]; 1.39–40, **608**[12], **628**[2]; 1.43, **612**[14]; 1.44, **641**[23]; 1.52, **135**[4], **382**[1]; 1.55, **135**[4]; 1.64, **528**[7], **625**[14]; 1.66, **641**[14]; 1.69, **443**[4]; 1.154–6, In[9]; 1.169–75, **108**[1]; 1.205, **255**[3]; 1.211, **81**[5]; 1.244–5, **341**[2]; 1.291–4, **133**[1]; 1.331, **25**[9]; 1.331–2, **606**[20]; 1.335–89, **375**[7]; 1.337–89, Gl s.v. praetor; 1.339, **625**[9]; 1.353, **443**[4]; 1.375–86, **641**[29]; 1.376–7, **443**[3]; 1.408, **1**[4]; 1.420–2, **186**[6]; 1.437, 1.464, **65**[6]; 2.285, **615**[1]; 2.331, **602**[4]; 2.334, **641**[14]; 2.519–34, **601**[3]; 2.523, **23**[5]; 2.580–1, **156**[1]; 2.794, **32**[9], **503**[3], **509**[1]; 2.794–5, **515**[1n,10,18]; 3.91–121, **133**[1]; 3.223–4, **443**[4]; 3.574–6, **28**[1]
FRAGMENTA VATICANA 263, 264a, 310, **601**[3]

GAIUS (GI): *Institutiones*, **640**[1]; 1.5, **94**[1]; 1.18, **607**[1]; 1.42–6, **392**[3]; 1.84, 1.85, **631**[1]; 1.86, 91, 161, **631**[3]; 1.144, 1.154, 1.155, 1.185, **628**[2]; 1.188, **621**[2]; 1.199–200, **608**[6]; 2.3, 9, **598**[3], **641**[5]; 2.4, **641**[3]; 2.5, **641**[12]; 2.6, **641**[14]; 2.7a, **641**[12]; 2.8, **641**[2]; 2.40–61, **641**[23]; 2.91, 94, **602**[1]; 2.97–190, **488**[18]; 2.109, **626**[3]; 2.124, **496**[14]; 2.174–90, **488**[17]; 2.201, **640**[5]; 2.224, 2.225–6, **392**[4]; 3.92–127, **641**[25]; 3.164–5, **602**[1]; 4.2, **604**[6]; 4.3, **598**[8]; 4.5, **612**[13]; 4.18–19, **598**[9]; 4.30, Gl s.v. *legis actio*; 4.42, **641**[18]; 4.46, 183, **598**[10]; 4.130, 133, **65**[9]; 4.138–70, **641**[29]; 4.139, **641**[30]; 4.154–5, **478**[11]; 4.171, **605**[2], **640**[16]
GELLIUS: *Noct. Att.* 4.20.3–5, **619**[8]. 10.5.8, 10, **399**[11]
GREGORY NAZIANZEN: *Orat.* 4, **112**[4]

H 238, **18**[8]
HERMES 8 (1874) 167–72, **119**[1]

ICLV 1.5, **45**[1]; 1.14, **443**[4]; 1.808–51, 2.3823–83, **139**[2]

LEGAL QUOTATIONS AND ALLUSIONS 1353

INSCRIPTIONES LATINAE SELECTAE 1.705, **45**[1]
INSTITUTIONES IUSTINIANI (II) In[3], **639**[1n,9], **640**[1n,1], **641**[1n], Gl and s.v. *Novellae Iustiniani*; 1.2.6, **94**[1]; 1.13.3, 1.15. pr., **628**[2]; 1.20. pr., **621**[5], **628**[2]; 1.20.5, **621**[5,7,8]; 1.23. pr., **255**[2]; 1.23.1, **608**[4]; 1.23.3, **621**[5]; 1.24. pr., **608**[6]; 2.1.7, **608**[3]; 2.1.10, **641**[2]; 2.1.39, **223**[3]; 2.3.1, **606**[14]; 2.6, 2.6. pr., **641**[23]; 2.7.2, **581**[4]; 2.11. pr., **626**[3]; 2.11.6, 2.12. pr., **624**[3]; 2.18.1, **624**[4]; 2.18.6–7, **570**[1]; 2.20.6, **595**[6]; 2.22. pr., **392**[3]; 3.6.6., **572**[3]; 3.12.1, **631**[1n]; 3.15.20, **641**[25]; 3.24.3, **537**[6]; 3.27.4, **641**[18]; 3.28.1–2, **602**[1]; 3.37.3, **641**[18]; 4.4.8, **478**[11]; 4.6.1, **604**[6]; 4.6.1–2, **598**[8]; 4.6.12, **598**[10]; 4.6.15, **598**[9], **612**[13]; 4.6.19, **612**[14]; 4.6.20, **640**[7], **641**[18]; 4.6.33, **582**[5], 4.13.2, **585**[3]; 4.15, **641**[29]; 4.15. pr., **641**[30]; 4.15.6, **478**[11]; 4.16. pr., **605**[2]; 4.16.1, **491**[7]; **612**[14]; 4.16.3, **598**[10]; 4.17.4, 4.17.5, **641**[18]; 4.18.4, **214**[5]; 4.18.7, **204**[5]
INSTITUTUM NERONIANUM **1**[4], App[3,8]
ISIDORE OF SEVILLE: *Orig.* 15.4.2, **641**[2]

JEROME: *Ep.* 52.6, **150**[1]
JOSEPHUS: *Ant. Iud.* 14.7.2.117, 14.10.2.190–5, **17**[3]; 14.10.8.215, **133**[1]; *Bell. Iud.* 4.5.4.334–44, **159**[34]
JULIAN: *Ep.* 288A–305D, **208**[3]; 411C–D, **113**[4]; 429C–32A, **208**[3]; 450B–1D, **119**[1]; 452A–4B, **208**[3]

LNMaior. 9, 11, **499**[1n]
LNMarc. 4, **525**[2]; 4.1.4, **525**[4]
LNS 1, **496**[1n]
LNT 1.5, In[19]; 5.1, **207**[3]; 6, **497**[6]; 13, **309**[6]; 17.1, 18.1, **168**[1]; 22, **525**[2]
LNV 7.1, **168**[1]; 27, **168**[1], **478**[27]; 31, **478**[27]; 34.1, **133**[1]

LACTANTIUS: *De Mort. Pers.* 6.2, App 9; 10, App[36]; 11.8, 13.1, 13.2–3, App 10 (a); 14, App 10 (b); 14.3–5, App[36]; 15.4–5, App[27]; 15.6–7, App[16]; 21.7, App 10 (e); 36.3–7, App 10 (f); 48.1, **11**[4,12]; *Inst. Div.* 5.11.19, **4**[2]
LEO I: *Ep.* 15, **203**[1]
LEX AEBUTIA **65**[9], Gl; *Aelia et Sentia*, **607**[1], Gl; *alearia* **593**[3]; *Aquilia* **413**[6], **640**, (I, III), Gl; *Augusta* **195**[1n], Gl; *Caecilia et Didia* **324**[7], Gl; *Cincia de donis et muneribus* **31**[4], **601**[3], Gl; *Clodia de collegiis, Clodia de collegiis restituendis novisque instituendis* **133**[1], Gl; *Constantiniana* 76, **341**; *Cornelia de falsis* **204**[5]; *Cornelia de iniuriis* **478**[11]; *Cornelia testamentaria, Cornelia testamentaria nummaria* **204**[5]; *de imperio Vespasiani* In[9], Gl; *Falcidia* **392**[4], **623**, Gl; *Fufia et Caninia* **392**[3], Gl and s.v. *Lex Aelia et Sentia*; *Furia* **392**[4], Gl; *Iulia de adulteriis coercendis* **214**[4], **638**[14], Gl; *Iulia de maiestate* **1**[4], **382**[1], Gl; *Iulia de maritandis ordinibus* **31**[1], Gl and s.vv. *Lex Iulia de adulteriis coercendis*; *Lex Iulia et Papia Poppaea*; *Iulia et Papia Poppaea* **31**[1], **496**[6], Gl; *Iulia peculatus* Gl; *Leonina* **514**, **624**, Gl; *Licinia de sodaliciis* **133**[1], Gl; *Plaetoria* **608**[12], Gl; *Remmia* **334**[3]; Gl; *Romana Burgundionum, Romana Ostrogothorum, Romana Visigothorum* In[2], Gl s.v. *interpretation*; *Rubria de Gallia Cisalpina* **108**[1]; *Salpensana* 25, **255**[3]; *Voconia* **392**[4], Gl;
LIBELLUS PRECUM **195**[1n]
LIBER IURIS SYRO-ROMANUS 117, **32**[9]; 118, **503**[3], **509**[1], **515**[1n,10,18]
LIVY: *Ab Urbe Cond.* 22.53.10, 43.15.8, **619**[8]

M 6.584, 585, 589, **470**[3]; 7.173–6, **472**[20]; 7.219–28, **447**[3]; 7.221–8, **447**[4]; 7.273–6, **473**[1]; 7.523–30, 7.536–7, **495**[2]; 7.537–627, **495**[6]
MAMA 1, no. 416, 7, no. 304, **43**[12]
MARE no. 139, no. 141, **83**[5]; pp. 84–116, **16**[1]; p. 495, **43**[7]
MINUCIUS FELIX: *Oct.* 2.3, **220**[2]

NICEPHORUS: *HE* 10.4, **119**[5]; 10.5, **112**[1n], **117**[1n,7]; 10.10, 10.24, **119**[5]
NOMOCANON Gl s.v. *ius canonicum*
NOVELLAE IUSTINIANI (N) In[3], **578**[6], **633**[1], Gl; 7, **568**[2]; 7.8, **584**[1]; 81.3, **32**[9]; 111, **604**[1n]; 117.12, **629**[22]; 120.10, **641**[11]; 131.1, **470**[70], **476**[1n], **613**[2]; 134.11, **629**[22]
NOVELS, POST-THEODOSIAN Gl s.v. *interpretation*

OPTATUS: *De Schis. Donat.* 3.6, **203**[1]

PL 8.768, **120**[2]; 11.1231–1418, **328**[1]; 11.1257, **324**[2]; 33.806, **325**[9]
PALLADIUS: *Dial. de Vita Chrys.* 3, **284**[3], **285**[3,6]; 11, 20, **284**[3]
PANDECTAE: see *Digesta*
PAUL: *Sent.* 1.13a.2, **602**[4]; 1.21.1, 1.21.2, **641**[14]
PITRA 2.549, **529**[2]
PLATO: *Leges* 933B–E, **135**[4]
PLINY: *Ep.* 10.34, 10.93, **133**[1]; 10.96.2, **1**[3], **12**[33]; 10.96.3–8, **1**[2]; 10.96.7, **133**[1], App 3
PLUTARCH: *Cato Minor* 19.4, **65**[13]; *Numa* 10.3, **399**[11]
POSSIDIUS: *Aug. Vita* 19, **28**[1]

QUINTILIAN: *Inst. Orat.* 8.5.1, **619**[8]

RELIQUIAE IURIS ECCLESIASTICI: ANTIQUISSIMAE no. 3, pp. 18–20, **112**[4]

RUFINUS: *HE* 8.2.4, App 10 (a); 10.28, **112**[1n]

SCRIPTORES HISTORIAE AUGUSTAE: *Sev. Alex.* 33.2, **133**[1]; 49.6, **4**[2], **498**[2]

SENATUS CONSULTUM CLAUDIANUM **631**[1n]

SENATUS CONSULTUM PERSICIANUM **31**[1]

SENECA, LUCIUS or MARCUS ANNAEUS: *Controv.* 10 pr. 5, **382**[1]

SENECA, LUCIUS ANNAEUS: *De Ben.* 5.14.2, **168**[1]

SOCRATES: *HE* 3.1, **112**[1n]; 3.15, **119**[5]; 4.24, **147**[5]; 4.32, **159**[16]; 5.2, **166**[1]; 5.14, **370**[1]; 6.5, **246**[1]

SOZOMEN: *HE* 5.4, **119**[5]; 5.5, **112**[1n], **117**[7], **119**[5]; 5.11, **119**[5]; 6.19–20, **147**[5]; 6.36, **159**[16]; 7.1, **166**[1]; 7.16, **225**[1n]; 8.7, **246**[1]

SUETONIUS: *Aug.* 32.1, **133**[1]; 55, **382**[1]; *Dom.* 23.1, App 2; *Gaius* 15.3, **619**[6]; *Iul.* 42.3, **133**[1]; *Tib.* 37.3, **241**[1]; *Vesp.* 11, **631**[1]

SULPICIUS SEVERUS: *Chron.* 2.9.3, App 1; 2.47.6, **288**[9]; 2.48.5, **288**[14]; 2.50.5–6, **370**[1]

Σύνταγμα Τῶν Θείων Καὶ Ἱερῶν Κανόνων Gl s.v. *ius canonicum*

TT 2.1a, **592**[3]; 2.3, 3.5, **324**[7]; 5.1, **621**[3]; 5.1, 6, 7, **628**[3]; 5.3, **392**[4]; 5.6, **608**[12]; 5.6–7, **628**[2]; 6.2, **612**[14]; 6.5, **641**[23]; 8.1, **382**[1]; 8.1a–1b, 8.8a–8b, **135**[4]; 9.1–2, **528**[7]; 9.3, **625**[14]; 10.1, **641**[14]; 10.10, **443**[4]

TACITUS: *Ann.* 1.72.3–4, **382**[1]; 3.36.1, **400**[9]; 3.38.1, **1**[4]; 3.60.2, **241**[1]; 4.67.6, **400**[9]; 12.53.1, **631**[1]

TERTULLIAN: *Ad Nat.* 1.7, App[3]; *Ad Scap.* 4, App 5; *Apol.* 2.7, **1**[3]; 4.4, App[3]; 5.6, **In**[46]; 5.7, **2**[20]; 10.1, **1**[4]; 38.1–2, 39, App[7]

THEODORET: *HE* 3.4.1, **112**[1n]; 4.22.27, 35, **147**[5]

TITULI EX CORPORE ULPIANI 22.6, **615**[1]

PATRISTIC QUOTATIONS AND ALLUSIONS

ALBERTUS MAGNUS: *De Gen. et Cor.*
2.3.5, **313**[1]
ACTS OF OUR LORD JESUS CHRIST DONE IN THE TIME OF PONTIUS PILATE or *ACTS OF PILATE*, see *Gospel of Nicodemus*
ACTS OF THE MARTYRS **1**[3]
AMBROSE: *De Off.* 2.15.68–75, **515**[3]; 2.28.136–7, **598**[13]; *De Virg.* 3.3.11, **465**[9]; *Ep.* 18.13, **150**[1]; 18.16, **515**[3]; 21.4, 5, **136**[1]; 23.15, **52**[22]; *Serm. cont. Aux.* 36, In[21]
ARISTIDES: *Apologia*, **2**[20]
ARIUS: *Thalia*, **67**[8,24]
ARNOBIUS: *Adv. Gent.* 1.1–24, **9**[9]
ATHANASIUS OF ALEXANDRIA: *Apol. adv. Ar.* 5, **68**[4]; 8, **68**[4,5]; 11–13, **68**[7]; 11–14, **68**[5]; 12, **78**[2]; 14, **68**[4]; 17, **68**[4,5]; 27, **68**[4]; 28, **68**[5,7]; 38, 42, **68**[4]; 46, **68**[4,5,7]; **78**[2]; 60, **68**[5,7]; 63, **68**[4,7]; 63–5, **68**[5]; 65, **68**[7]; 65–7, **68**[4]; 68, **68**[7]; 69, **68**[4]; 72, **68**[4,5,7]; 74, 76, **68**[5,7]; 80, **74**[7]; 83, **68**[5,7]; 85, **68**[4,5,7], **78**[2,3]; 87, **68**[4,5]; *De Syn.* 16, **156**[1]; *Ep. ad Afros Espic.* 2, **53**[12]; *Epistolae Heortasticae*, **52**[4]; *Hist. Ar. adv. Mon.* 35, **124**[21]; 66, **53**[12]
ATHANASIUS OF SAMOSATA: *The Conflict of Severus, Patriarch of Antioch*, **543**[In]
AUGUSTINE: *Brev. Coll.* 1.2, **325**[9]; 3.25.43, **328**[1]; *Conf.* 8.5, **116**[1]; 13.5, 11, **75**[42]; *Cont. Faust. Man.* 13.4, **156**[1]; *Cont. Cresc.* 3.71.83, **27**[3]; *Cont. Ep. Par.* 1.12.19, **293**[3]; *De Civ. Dei* 2.3, **1**[3]; 18.36, **95**[34]; 18.52, **116**[1]; 22.10, **206**[7]; *De Fide Rer. Quae Non Vid.* 7, **422**[6]; *De Natura et Gratia, De Peccatorum Meritis et Remissione et de Baptismo Parvulorum, De Perfectione Iustitiae Hominis, De Spiritu et Littera*, **350**[1]; *De Trin.* 2.9.16, *Ench. de Fide* 12.38, **562**[17]; *Ep.* 33.5, **28**[1]; 43.20, **24**[1], **27**[1]; 44.13, **315**[1]; 88.2, **17**[11], **19**[11]; 133, 139, 152, 153, **370**[1]; *Serm.* 131.10, **350**[4]

BASIL: *Ep.* 198, **107**[7];
BEDE: *HE.* 3.25, **52**[2]
BONIFACE: *Epp.* 13–15, **375**[3]

CA 1.6, **382**[1]; 2.2, **445**[14]; 2.37–56, **17**[3]; 3.20, **579**[2]; 4.9, **264**[1], **127**[5], **308**[6], **515**[3]; 5.12,

491[7]; 6.17, **445**[14]; 6.18, **645**[10]; 8.3–5, 8.47, **579**[2]; 8.47.7, **628**[3]; 8.47.13–16, **270**[3]; 8.47.14, **61**[11]; 8.47.17, **445**[14]; 8.47.20, **491**[7]; 8.47.27, **613**[4]; 8.47.30, **579**[21]; 8.47.32–4, **270**[3]; 8.47.39, **579**[15]; 8.47.39–40, **579**[16]; 8.47.43–4, **651**[5]; 8.47.45, **167**[11]; 8.47.46, **158**[4], **167**[11]; 8.47.47, **158**[4]; 8.47.62, 8.47.64, **167**[11]; 8.47.81, **628**[3]
CSEL 18, **203**[1]; 26, **19**[1]; 26.16, **244**[4]; 26.26, **20**[10]; 26.27, **20**[9]; 26. 197–204, **21**[1n]; **328**[9]; 26.202.5–7, 26.203.20–3, **21**[9]; 26.206–8, **20**[8]; 35.2–4, **137**[1]; 35.66–7, **353**[6]; 35.74–6, **363**[2]; 35.565, **548**[1]; 35.561–2, **547**[2]; 35.586, **550**[7]; 35.591–2, **549**[4]; 35.605–7, **558**[5]; 35.607–10, **554**[3]; 35.624.2–7, **560**[10]; 35.652, **563**[3]; 35.658–9, **563**[7]; 35.703–7, 35.707–10, 35.715–16, **560**[18]; 35.716–22, **564**[1]; 39, **484**[25]
CAELESTIUS: *Libellus Fidei* **350**[6]
CASSIODORUS: *HE* 4.19.4, **482**[3]; 5.15.2, **93**[5]; 6.1.32, **112**[1n]; 6.4.8–12, **119**[5]; 6.7.1, **112**[1n]; 6.7.2, **117**[7]; 6.7.4, 6.10.1, 6.11.1–4, 6.12.7–13, 6.13.1–3, 6.17, 6.30.2, 6.30.15, 6.32.1–3, 6.32.1–4, **119**[5]; 7.39.1–2, 30, 35, **147**[5]; 8.12, **159**[16]; 9.30.3–29, In[49]; *Var.* 3.51, **236**[3]
CERTAMEN SANCTI MARTYRIS MERCURII or *ACTA SANCTI MERCURII* App[11]
CHRYSOSTOM: *see* John Chrysostom
CLEMENT OF ALEXANDRIA: *Strom.* 3.6.52–3, **613**[4]
CLEMENT OF ROME: 1 *Cor.* pr., **167**[1n]; 38.4, **75**[42]; 61, **1**[4]
COUNCIL OF ANTIOCH (ante 60): Canon 1, **112**[4]; Carthage (416): *Epistola contra Pelagii ac Coelestii Errores*, **350**[2]; Carthage (417): *Epistola contra Haeresim Pelagii et Coelestii*, **350**[9]; Carthage (418) Canons 1–9, **350**[11]; Chalcedon (451): Canon 3, 4, 5, **472**[20]; 7, **16**[1n], **495**[1]; 14–16, **613**[4]; 28, **375**[7], **470**[70], **475**[10,12], **482**[1n,5], **495**[5]; Constantinople (381): Canon 2, **375**[5], **577**[2]; 3, **375**[7], **442**[7], **470**[22,70], **475**[10], **495**[5], **526**[8]; 7, **205**[9]; Elvira (c. 300): Canon 33, **372**[4]; Milevis (416): *Epistola contra Eamdem Pelagii et Coelestii Haeresim*, **350**[2]; Nicaea (325): Canon 3, **372**[3], **613**[4]; 4, **470**[41,61,74], **523**[1]; 5, **169**[3]; 6, **375**[5], **442**[7], **470**[74], **577**[2]; 7, **470**[44]; 8, **57**[1]; 15, **61**[11]; Rome

1355

1356　　PATRISTIC QUOTATIONS AND ALLUSIONS

(c. 368): *Epistola ad Gratianum et Valentinianum,* **164**^{1}; Sardica (c. 343): Canon 7, **370**^{1}; Toledo (400): Canon 1, **372**^{4}
CYPRIAN: *Acta Proconsularia* App^{11}; *Acta Procons.* 1, 3, App 8 (a); *Ep.* 2, **154**^{2}; 43.3, App 7; 55.8, 68.2, **523**^{1}; 80.1, App 8 (b)
CYRIL OF ALEXANDRIA: *Contra Iulianum* **119**^{5}; *Cont. Iulian.* 6, **393**^{1}; *De Recta Fide ad Reginas I, II, De Recta Fide ad Theodosium* **398**^{3}; *Duodecim Capita* **411**$^{\text{in},1}$, **527, 542**
CYRIL OF JERUSALEM: *Cat.* 4.10, 4.14, 13.4, 16.4, **303**^{3}; 18.23, **167**^{9}

DECRETUM DAMASINUM **375**^{7}
DECRETUM GELASIANUM **375**^{7}
DESCENT OF MARY **159**^{34}
DIDACHE 14.2, 15.3, **17**^{3}

EPIPHANIUS: *Haer.* 2.2.69.4, **67**^{8}; 2.2.69.9, **67**^{1,2,11,12}; 3.1.70.11, **52**^{22}; 26.12, **159**^{34}
EPISTLE OF BARNABAS 9.7-9, **53**^{12}
EPISTOLA ECCLESIARUM VIENNENSIS ET LUGDUNENSIS App 4^{11}
EUSEBIUS: *De Martyribus Palaestinae* App^{11}; *De Mart. Pal. praef.* 1-2, App 10 (a); *praef.* 2, App 10 (b); 2.2-3, App ^{36}; 2.4, App 10 (c); 3.1, App 10 (d); 4.8, App 10 (e); 6, App^{36}; 8.1 App 10 (e) 9.2, **8**^{5}, App 10 (f); 9.4-13 *et seq.* App (10 (f); 9.8-11, 11.15-16, App^{53}; 13.2, 13.10, App 10 (f); 13.14, App^{49}; *Historia Ecclesiastica* **415**^{6}; *HE* 1.9.3, 1.11.9, App^{58}; 1.13.5, **42**^{9}; 1.13.6-10, 1.13.11-22, 2.1.6-7, **42**^{5}; 2.2.6, **4**^{2}; 2.15, 2.16, 2.24, **53**^{2} 3.4.5, **523**^{1}; 3.19-20.7, App 2; 3.30.1, **613**^{4}; 3.32.7-8, App^5; 3.33.3, **1**^{3}; 3.39.15, **53**^{2}; 4.3, **2**^{20}; 4.8.6, **2**^{in}; 4.10, App^6; 4.12.1, **3**^{8}; 4.14.10, **3**^{3}; 4.15.1-47, App^6; 4.15.6, **3**^{20}; 4.15.18, 21, **255**^{3}; 4.15.41, App^{53}; 4.18.2, **3**^{3}; 4.23.2, App^6; 4.26.2, **3**^{3}; 4.26.7-10, **4**^{2}; 4.26.7-11, In^5; 4.26.10, App^6; 5. *praef.* 1, **3**^{3}; 5.1.44, 47, App 4; 5.1.59, 61-3, App^{53}; 5.4.3 (5.5.1), **3**^{3}; 5.5.1-6, In^{14,46}; 5.6.4, App^6; 5 9.1, **3**^{3}; 5.23-5, **52**^{3}; 5.23.2-4, **470**^{66}; 5.24.9, **5**^{1}; 6.1.1, 6.3.1, App 5; 6.3.3., **189**^{2}; 6.5.5-6, **255**^{3}; 6.28, App 6; 6.41.1, App 7; 6.43.2, **645**^{40}; 7.7.4, **68**^{1}; 7.10.3, App^{14}; 7.30.18-21, **5**^{1}; 7.30.21, App 9; 8.1.4, App^{16}; 8.2.4-5, App 10 (a); 8.2.5, App 10 (b); 8.4, App^{16}; 8.5.1, App 10 (a); 8.6.8, App 10 (b); 8.6.10, App 10 (c); 8.7.6, App^{53}; 8.14.9 App 10 (f); 8.16.2, App^{16}; 9.1.1, **13**^{12}; 9.2, **9**^{1}; 9.2.1, 9.4.1, App 10 (f); 9.4.2,

9^1, App^{57}; 9.5.1, App 10 (f); 9.6.1, 4, App^{50}; 9.7.1, **9**^{1}, App^{55}; 9.9a.4-6, **9**^{1}; 9.10.8, 9.10.11, 10.5.9-11, 16-17, App 10 (a); 10.6.2, In^{14}; 10.8.8; **42**^{3}; 10.8.10, 14-19, **42**^{1}; 10.8.17, App^{53}; *VC* 1.15, App^{16}; 1.28, 1.29-31, **38**^{2}; 1.31, 44^{17}, **119**^{5}; 1.32, 42, In^{14}; 1.44, In^{29},48^{in}; 1.51, 47^{10}; 1.51-4, 56, **42**^{1}; 1.56-8, App^{16}; 1.58, App 10 (f); 2.1-2, 5, **42**^{1}; 2.5, 2.7, 2.12, 14, 2.16, **38**^{2}; 2.23, **46**^{26}; 2.47, In^{12}; 2.63, 73, In^{14}; 3.6, **48**^{2,19}; 3.7, **48**^{19}; 3.8, **53**^{12}; 3.13, **67**^{33}; 3.21, **49**^{26}; 3.26-7, **54**^{6}; 3.33-40, 54^{in}; 3.36, **54**^{39}; 4.14, 4.15, 4.17, **38**^{2}; 4.18, 4.19, 38^{in}; 4.21, 4.22, **38**^{2}; 4.23, **34**^{5}; 4.24, 48^{in}; 4.24, 49, In^{29}; 4.26, **31**^{in}; 4.32, **49**^{1}; 4.37-9, 43^{in}; 4.47, **48**^{19}; 4.57, 4 61-2, **38**^{2}
EVAGRIUS: *HE* 1.13, 376^{in}; 2.8, **495**^{2}; 3.12, **523**^{1}; 3.39-40, **97**^{1}; 4.14, **646**^{9}

FELIX III (II): *Ep.* 9, 11: *Tractatus*, In^{31}

GELASIUS I: *Ep.* 8, In^{31}
GOSPEL OF NICODEMUS or *ACTS OF OUR LORD JESUS CHRIST DONE IN THE TIME OF PONTIUS PILATE* or *ACTS OF PILATE* App^{58}; 9.4, **159**^{30}
GREGORY I: *Dialogi* **297**^{3}
GREGORY NAZIANZEN: *Orat.* 4, **112**^{4}

HIPPOLYTUS: *Apos. Trad.* 34, **97**^{4}

ILCV 1.5, **45**^{1}; 1.14, **443**^{4}; 1.709B, **618**^{13}; 1.808-51, **139**^{2}; 1.1752, 1753, **45**^{1}; 1.1761, **211**^{1}; 1.1857, **200**^{1}; 2.3458, **68**^{1}; 2.3823-83, **139**^{2}
IGNATIUS: *Ad Smyrn.* 7.1, **75**^{42}; 8.2, **167**^{9}
INNOCENT I: *Epistola Aurelio et Caeteris* **350**^{3}; *Epistola Quinque Episcopis* **350**^{8}; *Epistola Silvano et Caeteris* **350**^{3}
IRENAEUS OF LYON: *Adv. Haer.* 3.3.2, 167^{in}; 3.3.3, App^5
IRENAEUS OF TYRE: *Synodicon adversus Tragoediam Irenaei* **426**^{in}
ISIDORE OF SEVILLE: *Orig.* 9.3.4, **614**^{5}; 15.2.11, **43**^{2}; 15.4.2, **641**^{2}

JEROME: *Chron.* anno 363, **116**^{1}; *Comm. in Amos* 2.5.283, In^{54}, **648**^{6}; *De Vir. Illus.* 80, In^{14}; *Dialogus adversus Pelagianos* **350**^{1}; *Dial. cont. Lucif.* 19, **105**^{2}; *Ep.* 22.30, In^{54}; 30.5, In^{46}; 52.6, **150**^{1}; 58.3.5, **54**^{6}; 69.9, **629**^{6}; 146.1.7, **167**^{9}
JOHN CHRYSOSTOM: *Adversus Eos Qui apud Se Habent Virgines Subintroductas* **372**^{2}; *Homiliae Duae in Eutro-*

PATRISTIC QUOTATIONS AND ALLUSIONS

pium **246**[1]; *Quod Regulares Feminae Viris Cohabitare Non Debeant*, **372**[2]
JUSTIN MARTYR: *Apologies* In[46]; *Apol. pro Christ.* 1.67.3, **34**[5]; 2.2, App[6]

LACTANTIUS: *De Mortibus Persecutorum* **46**[8]; *De Mort. Pers.* 6.2, App[11]; 7–52, **44**[15]; 10, App[36]; 10.1–5, **44**[10]; 10.6—11.8, App[16]; 11.8, App 10 (a); 12, App[16]; 12.2–5, **212**[1]; 13.1, 13.2–3, App. 10 (a); 14, App. 10 (b); 14.3–5, 15.1, App[36]; 15.4–5, App[27]; 15.6–7, App[16]; 21.7, App 10 (e); 21.11, App[53]; 23, **67**[37]; 31.1, App[16]; 36.3, **9**[1]; 36.3–7, App 10†(f); 44.5, **119**[5]; 44.5–6, **38**[2]; 48.1, **12**[4,12]; *Inst. Div.* 5.2.2., **212**[1]; 5.11.19, **4**[2]; 5.19.11, **167**[11]
LEO I: *Ep.* 7, **440**[5]; 15, **203**[1]; 95.2, **459**[1]; 106, **482**[5]; 165, **561**[13]; *Serm.* 82[80].2, In[36]; *Tome* **470**[34], **471**[1n,1], **475**[6], **524**, **542**, **546**[18]

M 1.662, 1.669–70, **470**[66]; 3.236, **93**[8]; 4.888–92, 4.1068–84, **470**[21]; 4.1123–8, **406**[1]; 4.1183–96, **470**[21]; 4.1232, **402**[4]; 5.1265–90, **470**[23]; 6.563–6, **470**[4]; 6.584, 6.585, 6.589, **470**[3]; 7.5–8, **470**[4]; 7.47–50, **470**[30]; 7.49–50, **470**[31]; 7.51–60, **470**[31]; 7.107–10, **471**[2]; 7.117–18, **471**[3]; 7.169–72, **472**[14]; 7.171–4, **472**[16]; 7.173–4, **472**[19]; 7.173–6, **472**[20]; 7.211–12, **447**[2]; 7.219–28, **447**[3]; 7.221–8, **447**[4]; 7.273–6, **473**[1]; 7.309–10, 7.311–12, **470**[61]; 7.369–70, 7.427–8, **470**[70]; 7.520–1, **487**[1,2]; 7.523–30, 7.536–7, **495**[2]; 7.537–627, **495**[6]; 8.188–92, **560**[16]
MARCELLINE AND FAUSTINUS: *Libellus Precum* **195**[1n]
MARTYRIUM SANCTI POLYCARPI App[6,11]
MART. POL. 9.2, 10.1, **255**[5]; 12.2, **577**[13]; 18.2–3, **206**[7], **577**[13]
MEMOIRS OF PILATE AND OF OUR SAVIOUR App 10 (f)
MINUCIUS FELIX: *Oct.* 2.3, **220**[2]

NICEPHORUS: *HE* 10.4, **119**[5]; 10.5, **112**[1n], **117**[1n,7], **119**[5], **120**[5]; 10.7, 10.8, 10.9, 10.10, **119**[5]; 10.20, **120**[5]; 10.23, 10.24, 10.29, **119**[5]

OPTATUS: *De Schis. Donat.* 1.3, **24**[4]; 3.3, In[21]; 3.6, **203**[1]; App 4, **20**[8]
ORACULA SIBYLLINA 3.323–33, **67**[27]
ORIGEN: *Cont. Cels.* 8.29, **112**[4]
OROSIUS: *Adv. Pag.* 7.4.6–7, **4**[2]

P 40–41, **452**[1]
PG 47.495–732, **372**[2]; 65.855–74, **637**[18]; 84.739, **414**[1]; 120.757, **53**[3]

PL 8.768, **120**[2]; 11.1231–418, **328**[1]; 11.1257, **324**[2]; 11.1350, **326**[10]; 11.1417, **326**[8]; 11.1508, **326**[10]; 33.806, **325**[9]; 45.1679–792, **350**[14]; 54.951–60, **475**[1n]
PO. 18.634, 677, 679, **630**[8]
P. Lond. 1913–22, **68**[2]
PALLADIUS: *Dialogus de Vita Sancti Joannis Chrysostomi* **284**[1n]; *Dial. de Vita Chrys.* 2, **284**[4], **285**[6]; 3, **284**[3], **285**[3,6]; 5, **284**[4], **372**[2], **515**[3]; 8, **284**[4]; 10, **285**[2,3]; 11, **284**[3]; 17, **228**[1]; 20, **284**[3]; *Historia Lausiaca* **228**[1], **284**[2], **330**[4], **446**[10]; *Hist. Laus.* 18, **614**[7]; 36, In[54]
PASSIO MARTYRUM SCILLITANORUM App[11]
PASSIO SANCTARUM MARTYRUM PERPETUAE ET FELICITATIS App[11]; 4.3, **68**[1]
PELAGIUS: *Libellus Fidei* **350**[5]
PEREGRINATIO AD LOCA SANCTA **484**[25]
POSSIDIUS: *Aug. Vita* 19, **28**[1]; 23, **515**[3]; 24, **598**[13]
PROCLUS: *Tome* **427**[1n], **637**[18]

QUADRATUS: *Agologia* 2[20]

RUFINUS: *HE* 1.32, **116**[1]; 8.2.4, App 10 (a); 10.28, **112**[1n]; 10.33, **119**[5]

SIDONIUS: *Ep* 5.8.3, **519**[5]
SOCRATES: *HE* 1.7, In[14]; 2.13, **141**[3]; 2.17, **482**[3]; 2.36, **93**[5]; 2.38, **120**[5]; 3.1, **112**[1n]; 3.11, **120**[5]; 3.13, 3.15, **119**[5]; 3.16, **116**[1]; 4.24, **147**[5]; 4.32, **159**[16]; 5.2, **166**[1]; 5.14, **370**[1]; 6.5, **246**[1]; 6.18, **285**[3]; 7.21, **598**[13]
SOZOMEN: *HE* 2.3, **617**[10]; 3.10, **482**[3]; 3.15, **189**[2]; 4.9, **93**[5]; 5.3, **43**[5]; 5.4, **119**[5]; 5.5, **112**[1n], **117**[7], **119**[5], **120**[5]; 5.8, 5.9, 5.10, 5.11, **119**[5]; 5.15, **117**[14]; 5.17, **119**[5]; 5.18, **116**[1]; 6.6, **119**[5]; 6.19–20, **147**[5]; 6.36, **159**[16]; 7.1, **166**[1]; 7.16, **225**[1n]; 8.7, **246**[1]
SULPICIUS SEVERUS: *Chron.* 2.9.3, App 1; 2.28.1—33.3, App[1]; 2.46.5, **203**[1]; 2.47.6, **288**[9]; 2.48.5, **288**[14,15]; 2.49.1, 3, **288**[14]; 2.50.5–6, **370**[1]; *Dialogi* **297**[3]

TERTULLIAN: *Ad Nationes* App[8]; *Ad Nat.* 1.7 App[3]; 1.17, **255**[3]; *Ad Scap.* 2, **167**[11], **255**[2]; 4, App 5; *Ad Ux.* 2.2–8, **214**[2]; *Apol.* 2.7, **1**[3]; 3.6, **422**[11]; 4.4, App[3]; 5.2, **4**[2]; 5.6, In[46]; 5.7, **2**[19]; 6.3, **247**[2]; 10.1, **1**[4]; 21.1, **1**[4]; 21.24, **4**[2]; 28.3, **255**[2]; 30–33, **1**[4]; 32.2, 35.10, **255**[3]; 38.1–2, 39, App[7]; 39.1, 5, 11, **4**[4]; 40.2, **1**[3]; *De Bapt.* 17, In[43]; *De Carn. Chr.* 5, **75**[42]; *De Cor.* 3, **393**[1]; *De*

Exhort. Cast. 7, **16**⁴; De Orat. 23, **34**¹; De Praescriptione Haereticorum **569**¹; De Praes. Haer. 6, 8, **167**⁵; 20–2, **167**⁵, **569**¹; 25–8, 31, **569**¹; 32, **167**⁵, **569**¹; 35–7, **569**¹; 36, **167**⁵; 41, **189**²; De Pud. 1.6, In²⁶; 13, **68**¹; De Spectaculis **154**³, **236**³; De Spect. 5–13, **651**¹³; 9, **236**³; De Virg. Vel. 7, **225**¹³

THEODORE OF TRIMUTHUS **225**¹³; De Vita et Exsilio S. Joan. Chrys. 8, **295**³

THEODORET: HE 1.8.1, **53**¹²; 2.22, **159**⁴⁶; 3.4.1, **112**¹ⁿ; 3.7.1, 3, 3.7.6–10, **119**⁵; 3.8, **116**¹; 3.8.2, 3.12, 3.16.2–3, 3.17.8, **119**⁵; 4.22.27, 35, **147**⁵; 5.16.6–5.18.23, In⁴⁹

TITUS OF BOSTRA: Contra Manichaeos **117**¹³

VICTOR OF VITA: Historia Persecutionis Africanae Provinciae **646**⁷; 1.8.25, **598**¹³

VINCENT OF LÉRINS: Comm. Prim. 2, In⁵²

WISDOM OF GOD **159**³⁴

ZOSIMUS: Epistola Aurelio et Ceteris **350**¹⁰; Epistola contra Africanos Episcopos **350**⁷; Epistola Universis Episcopis per Africam, **350**⁸; Epistola Zosimi **350**¹²

www.ingramcontent.com/pod-product-compliance
Lightning Source LLC
Chambersburg PA
CBHW052046290426
44111CB00011B/1631